The Art of Editing

FOURTH EDITION

The Art of

FLOYD K. BASKETTE
UNIVERSITY OF COLORADO

JACK Z. SISSORS
MEDILL SCHOOL OF JOURNALISM, NORTHWESTERN UNIVERSITY

BRIAN S. BROOKS
UNIVERSITY OF MISSOURI SCHOOL OF JOURNALISM

Editing

MACMILLAN PUBLISHING COMPANY
NEW YORK

Collier Macmillan Publishers
LONDON

PRINTED IN THE UNITED STATES OF AMERICA

Macmillan Publishing Company
866 Third Avenue, New York, New York 10022

Collier Macmillan Canada, Inc.

LIBRARY OF CONGRESS CATALOGING IN PUBLICATION DATA

Baskette, Floyd K.
    The art of editing.

    Includes index.
    1. Journalism—Editing. 2. Copy-reading. I. Sissors,
Jack Z. II. Brooks, Brian S.
III. Title.
PN4778.B3   1986   070.4′1   85-13746
ISBN   0-02-306290-8

Printing: 6 7 8   Year: 9 0 1 2 3 4 5

ISBN   0-02-306290-8

Preface

It is with great pleasure that we present to you the Fourth Edition of *The Art of Editing,* a text that in its first three editions met with widespread acceptance and approval. We think there is good reason for that success: It is the most comprehensive and up-to-date text in its field.

In this edition, as in the earlier ones, we have attempted to explain how editors do their jobs. Because no two editors work alike, or edit in exactly the same way, writing an editing text is difficult and challenging. We have attempted to deal with the problem by using examples of how good editors have edited a story. It is important to recognize that these examples are but *one* way to edit a story. There may be many other ways. In editing, there is often no absolute, no *right* and *wrong.* We have sought the advice of many editors in constructing our examples. If editing is an art, as we believe, then we have gone to the artists to see how it is done.

The editors who have helped us with these examples are too numerous to mention. We have taken examples, both good and bad, from newspapers from coast to coast. Through these examples, we learn how to edit and how not to edit. We learn how to write headlines and how not to write headlines. We learn how to design pages and how not to design pages. But through it all, we learn. There is no end to the process of education in daily journalism.

Journalism is an interesting, exciting and stimulating profession. Editing is a vital and important part of journalism, both print and broadcast. Newspapers, magazines, radio and television wouldn't be nearly as good without editors as they are with editors;

they can be superb with top-flight editors. We hope this book inspires some to consider editing as a career.

Much of the text is intended as preparation for the prospective newspaper copy editor, the pathway into editing chosen by most students; but the basics of editing apply to magazine and broadcast editors as well. Most of the techniques are the same, and the excitement is universal.

Still, it is difficult for any book to capture the excitement of the copy desk because the beginner first must master the intricacies of the editor's art. Attention to detail is of primary importance at the copy desk, and we believe this book attends to that detail more thoroughly than any other. We hope we have done so as interestingly as possible.

This edition has one significant change in format compared to the earlier ones. It is written in wire-service style, which is used by most newspapers in the United States. Because students are expected to write and edit in this style, we believe it makes sense to use it in their text. Numerous other improvements have been made from cover to cover.

We are indebted to our colleagues, students and editors who read chapters and offered many helpful suggestions. Special gratitude is extended to Dale Spencer, an attorney and teacher whose advice was invaluable in updating the chapter on press law; Mackie Morris, a teacher and broadcaster who prepared most of the chapter on broadcast editing; and Barbara Luebke, who wrote the section on stereotyping in Chapter 7.

We hope this edition is prepared with the same high standards set by our colleague, Floyd K. Baskette, who died in 1979. His name remains on the title page of this edition because his work is of enduring quality, and much of it remains from the first two editions.

We have changed and updated, but one old axiom holds true: Editing is an art no matter where or by whom it is practiced. To those who will accept the challenge of careful editing, this volume is dedicated.

Columbia, Missouri   B.S.B.
Evanston, Illinois   J.Z.S.

Contents

Appendixes

Index

PART I

The Copy Editor in Perspective

1

The Editor

The State of Editing

Columnist James J. Kilpatrick, one of the great newspaper writers of our time, laments the demise of editing quality in newspapers. He writes:

> To read almost any American daily today is to conclude that copy editors have vanished as completely from our city rooms as the ivory-billed woodpecker has vanished from the southern woodlands. We appear to have reared a generation of young reporters whose mastery of spelling, to put the matter mildly, is something less than nil. . . . Once there was a white-haired geezer in an eye shade to intercept a reporter's copy, and to explain gently but firmly to the author that *phase* and *faze* are different words, and that *affect* and *effect* ought not to be confused. The old geezer has gone, and literacy with him.[1]

Kilpatrick's fond memories of the good old days probably are enhanced by the passage of time. The fact is that newspapers always have made errors, and the newspapers edited by crotchety old copy editors wearing green eye shades were no exception. Still, few would disagree with Kilpatrick that language skills in general have deteriorated. Newspapers, without a doubt, have been affected.

Too many reporters and editors at today's newspapers are products of an educational system with misguided priorities. There was a time not so long ago when it was fashionable to consider pho-

---

1. James J. Kilpatrick, "Doesn't Anyone Edit Copy Anymore?" *Washington Journalism Review,* October 1984, p. 44.

netic spelling adequate. Rote memorization of spelling words was a waste of time, educational trendsetters told us. Grammar was viewed as an exercise in nit-picking. The consequences of that abandonment of the basics is commonly acknowledged today as one of the great tragedies of modern education. Now, a back-to-basics movement has swept the country, and there is evidence that teachers in today's elementary and secondary schools—some of whom were victims of the errors of the past—are at least attempting to emphasize language skills. Unfortunately, that won't help those who failed to learn, including many reporters and editors now on the job.

Kilpatrick writes:

> Let us contend, in sweet charity and self-defense, that virtually all of [the mistakes in newspapers are] a consequence not of ignorance but of the carelessness that walks with a wandering mind. If that is the best we can say, what have we said? Not much. I know that newspapers operate under the terrible pressure of deadlines. That fact . . . may help to explain, but it provides a feeble excuse.[2]

Figure 1-1 Columnist James J. Kilpatrick is convinced that the copy editors of today are not as good as those of earlier generations.

Another feeble excuse for mistakes is offered by broadcasters who say, "Grammar isn't important in radio or television. Spoken English and written English are different." That may be true, but should it be? Clearly, the answer is no. The generations that have grown up with television unfortunately don't even blink when broadcasters read on the air, "The City Council voted today to raise *their* salaries to $15,000 a year." Such mistakes in the use of pronouns are so common that many people don't even notice. Nor do they notice when a newspaper advertisement reads, "This group of pearls *are* specially selected by our buyers." Nor when words are misspelled as in *occassions, accidently, wintery* and *accomodate.*

2. Ibid., p. 47.

Fortunately, many people *do* notice, so perhaps there is hope.

Journalism, whether print or broadcast, is a profession that demands a mastery of language skills. Words, not cameras or microphones or video display terminals, are the primary tools of the trade. As in any craft, mastering the use of those tools is essential to success. Good editors know that, and they value highly those who possess those skills. This book is designed to help.

The Editor's Duties

Every editor edits. That is, every editor determines to some extent what will and will not be published or broadcast. Usually, those decisions are based on that editor's perception of the mission and philosophy of the publication or broadcast station.

This book emphasizes the skills of editing, but learning those skills without a thorough understanding of the philosophy of editing would be like learning to hit a baseball without knowing why hitting is important. Why bother to hit if you don't know to run to first base? In editing, it is important to know not only *when* a change in copy should be made but also *why* that change should be made.

Good editing depends on the exercise of good judgment. For that reason it is an art, not a science. To be sure, in some aspects of editing—accuracy, grammar and spelling, for example—there are only right and wrong answers, as often is the case in science. But editing also involves discretion: knowing when to use which word, when to change a word or two for clarity and when to leave a passage as the writer has written it. Often, the best editing decisions are those in which no change is made. Making the right decisions in such cases is clearly an art.

The editing skills taught herein will be those used at newspapers in general and at newspaper copy desks in particular. Those same skills, however, apply directly to magazine and broadcast editing. Editing for those media differs slightly from newspaper editing because of special requirements, so separate chapters to highlight those differences are included in this book. Still, the skills required of all editors are much the same as those required of newspaper copy editors, the valuable members of a newspaper's staff who have the final crack at copy before it appears in print. Copy editors, it has been said, are the last line of defense before a newspaper goes to press. As such, they are considered indispensable by top editors but remain anonymous to the public. Unlike the names of reporters, who frequently receive bylines, copy editors' names seldom appear in print.

Some believe that absence of recognition accounts for the scarcity of journalism graduates who profess interest in copy desk work. Editing, it is said, isn't as glamorous or as exciting as reporting. But those who view desk work as boring clearly have never experienced it. To the desk come the major news stories of the day—the space walk, the eruption of a volcano, the election of a president, the rescue of a lost child. The desk is the heart of the newspaper, and it throbs with all the news from near and far. Someone must shape that news, size it, display it and send it to the reader.

The copy editor is a diamond cutter who refines and polishes, removes the flaws and shapes the stone into a gem. The editor searches for flaws and inaccuracies, and prunes the useless, the unnecessary qualifiers and the redundancies. The editor adds movement to the story by substituting active verbs for passive ones, specifics for generalities. The editor keeps sentences short so that readers can grasp one idea at a time and still not suffer from writing that reads like a first-grade text.

Editing is creative work, too. Editors at many newspapers have opportunities to do page layout, and few newspaper jobs require more creativity than that.

Ah, but editing isn't as much fun as writing, some say. Why learn editing skills if you want to write? Columnist Kilpatrick knows. Although considered one of the great writers of our time, he bemoans the demise of *editing* skills. Good writers know that good editing can make their prose even better. Good writers know that good editors can save them great embarrassment. They also know that editing skills complement writing skills. Editing the work of others helps you learn to avoid their mistakes when you write. Editing also helps you learn the importance of clarity. Often, what is clear to the writer isn't clear at all to the editor—or to the reader. There also is this reality: Almost everyone who enters newspaper, magazine or broadcast work eventually will do some editing.

So, there is general agreement among the enlightened that editing is important. But there is less agreement about just what an editor is supposed to do. Kenn Finkel of the *Dallas Times Herald* tried to outline the duties of an editor at a workshop on editing skills:

> The editor is the conscience of the writer and the newspaper. He does his job when he challenges. He should approach every story with a challenge to see if it meets the newspaper's standards. It is his duty to help every story he edits.
>
> The editor should, when time allows, read a story from top to bottom before making changes. It is important to understand all of what the writer is trying to say.
>
> Having read the story through, the editor can remove words, correct grammar, smooth sentence flow and do other things that make a story more pleasing to the reader.
>
> The editor must make sure that all questions are answered. If he has questions, then the reader will. The editor can attempt to find the answers and work them into the story. Or he can return the story to the writer (call the wire service if it's a wire story) to get the answers.

There is more to editing than making a story read smoothly. The editor must satisfy himself that the story is fair; that both sides of an issue are presented; that, if a person accuses another in a quote, the accused gets a chance to reply; that topics mentioned in the abstract are brought to specifics; and that there are no unanswered questions.

The editor need not be a great writer to work efficiently. But he should be able to recognize good writing when he sees it. He should know when an adjective is performing an important job and when it is clutter.

A good editor has a love for the language. He is tuned to subtle rhythms or the awesome power of combinations of words. He should edit by sound, *listen* for good writing.[3]

The *Bulletin* of the American Society of Newspaper Editors asked some of the nation's top editors what they look for when hiring copy editors. Replied David Lipman, managing editor of the *St. Louis Post-Dispatch:* "A commitment to accuracy. An inner ear for English that lives and breathes. The knack of grasping not only what a story says but also what it fails to say. The good sense to leave well enough alone. Finally, a sense of humor."[4]

Marjorie Paxson, publisher of the *Muskogee* (Okla.) *Phoenix & Times Democrat* offered this: "A person who knows grammar, spelling and pays attention to detail. A perfectionist. One who can handle routine without having a fidget fit; who will use creativity and imagination to offset the routine; who is well-informed on a variety of subjects. A quick thinker with initiative, alertness, intelligence and awareness."[5]

It's little wonder that editors have trouble finding people who meet all those criteria. Much is demanded of the copy editor.

The Value of the Copy Editor

No position on the newspaper offers greater opportunity for growth than that of copy editor. Work as a copy editor provides the chance to continue an education and an incentive to climb to the top of the newspaper's hierarchy. Copy editors must of necessity accumulate a warehouse full of facts they have gleaned from the thousands of stories they have been compelled to read and edit or from the references they have had to consult to verify information.

Copy editors are super detectives who incessantly search stories for clues about how to transform mediocre articles into epics. The legendary Carr Van Anda of *The New York Times* studied ocean charts and astronomical formulas to find missing links in a story. Few editors today would correct an Einstein formula, as Van Anda

3. Kenn Finkel, speech to Penney-Missouri Newspaper Workshop, Columbia, Mo., March 8, 1983.
4. "10 Editors Tell What They Look for in a Copy Editor," *ASNE Bulletin,* February 1984, p. 30.
5. Ibid., p. 31.

did, but if they are willing they can probe, question, authenticate and exercise their powers of deduction.

Historically, a stint on the copy desk has been considered important to professional advancement at newspapers. The desk serves as an important spawning ground for administrative editors because those who serve there have a more complete picture of how the newspaper operates than those who do not. The reporter has little feel for copy flow and production requirements; copy editors develop that in the normal course of their duties. Thus, if two equally talented individuals are contending for promotion, the one with copy desk experience probably will have the inside track.

There are encouraging signs that the lot of the copy editor is improving. Many newspapers pay copy editors more than reporters as an incentive for the best and brightest to work at the desk. Journalism schools and departments have awakened to the reality that copy editors are more difficult to find than reporters and have responded by improving course offerings in editing. This, in turn, encourages more good students to pursue careers in editing. No longer do editors require that newcomers work as reporters before becoming copy editors; many now realize that hiring people who *want* to be copy editors is more important than reporting experience. Many of the best newspapers in the United States and Canada now have editors who never worked as reporters.

Furthermore, the artificial barriers that once prevented women from becoming copy editors have been torn down. No longer is the copy desk a man's domain. Women with editing skills have risen to important positions at many newspapers, large and small.

All of this indicates that new life may yet be breathed into the profession of copy editing. If, as Kilpatrick and others suggest, there is a serious problem with the quality of editing, many journalists have hope that things will improve. They have hope that the art of editing is not a lost art.

2

The Editor and the Reader

Editors have a choice: They can edit their newspapers by the seat-of-the-pants method or they can approach the process more intelligently by reading the best available research on the public's reading habits. Increasingly, they choose the latter as the more logical approach.

Few editors, if any, approach the day-to-day editing of newspapers with statistical analyses of their audiences in hand as guides to making decisions. There is no time for that in the hectic world of newspapers. But, increasingly, editors study the latest research when making changes in the content of their newspapers. Audience research gained new respect in the industry in the 1970s as editors tried to determine ways to counter some alarming realities:

1. Real circulation of U.S. daily newspapers dropped sharply in 1974 and again in 1975. That appears to have been an aberration because real circulation has continued to increase slightly since then. The somber warning of that figure, however, convinced industry leaders that something was wrong with what newspapers were doing.[1]
2. Market penetration of newspapers (total circulation of daily newspapers divided by the number of households in a market) continues to decline. Although circulation continues to grow, the population is growing more rapidly than newspaper read-

1. "Facts About Newspapers," an annual statistical survey of the American newspaper business published by the American Newspaper Publishers Association.

ership, and fewer families are subscribing to more than one newspaper.

3. The length of time the average reader spends with the newspaper each day is declining. The average reader spent 28 minutes a day reading newspapers in 1965–66, but that figure had declined to 21 minutes by 1975–76 (see Figure 2-1).[2]

Age	1965–66 Minutes/day	1975–76 Minutes/day	Differences Minutes/day
18–24	15	10	-5
25–34	23	16	-7
35–44	27	22	-5
45–54	33	22	-11
55–65	40	26	-14
TOTAL	28	21	-7

Figure 2-1 Differences in time spent reading newspapers in 1965–66 vs. 1975–76. (Source: Daily News Habits of the American Public, ANPA Research Report No. 15, September 22, 1978.)

4. Newspapers to a great extent had become a medium of the middle-aged and elderly. Young people weren't reading, and there are indications they still aren't.[3]
5. Some leading newspapers, including such important ones as the *Chicago Daily News,* failed.

These factors and others convinced editors and publishers of the 1970s that they needed better information about readership patterns, the impact of television on newspapers and hundreds of other issues. The result was a flurry of readership research unparalleled in U.S. newspaper history. Clearly, editors of the 1980s know more about the reading public than the editors of any other era. That gives them a better chance of succeeding in the marketplace.

The Newspaper as a Commodity

There was a time not so long ago when newspaper editors had the luxury of working almost independently of the other managers of their newspapers. Newsrooms were sacred, and no one in advertising or circulation departments presumed to tell editors how to edit their newspapers.

Now, editors meet regularly with top management executives and the heads of other departments to develop marketing strategies. There is a realization that news departments must work with other departments to develop marketing plans for their products. Sometimes that results in decisions to change the content of newspapers. Usually the final decisions about such changes are left to

2. John P. Robinson, "Daily News Habits of the American Public," ANPA Research Report No. 15, September 22, 1978.

3. Ernest F. Larkin, Gerald L. Grotta and Philip Stout, "The 21-34-Year-Old Market and the Daily Newspaper," ANPA Research Report No. 1, April 8, 1977.

editors, but today the heads of other departments are more likely to make suggestions. Most editors are inclined to listen. Advertising and circulation people have extensive contact with the public, and often they hear compliments and complaints about their newspapers that editors never hear. Good editors appreciate hearing those things.

The danger, of course, is that the editor may go too far in an attempt to accommodate others. A newspaper full of nothing but what the public *wants* to read would be a poor one in most editors' judgment. Editors must balance what the public *wants* to read with what it *needs* to read. Only then will the newspaper fulfill its role as guardian of the public's welfare. Today's editors know that the key to a newspaper's integrity—not to mention its existence—lies in its ability to remain financially sound. A marginally solvent newspaper may be more susceptible to advertiser influence on editorial decisions. So attention to the demands of the marketplace is important. But it also is important to remember that the press is the only private institution mentioned in the U.S. Constitution. That is tacit recognition of the fact that newspapers, while competing in the marketplace, also have a special mission in our society.

The fact that editors are now active participants in marketing the newspaper should not be viewed negatively. The fact is that a newspaper is a manufactured product, a commodity, and like other products it must be marketed aggressively. A newspaper's marketing strategy probably will work best if all departments—including the news department—are working to accomplish the same goals.

Editors of the 1980s know that successful market strategies are a plus: Their newspapers will be stronger and more people will read the work of their staffs. Only then will the full potential of a free press be unleashed.

Some Generalizations About U.S. Audiences

Each newspaper should conduct its own market research to determine what readers like and dislike about the product. What works in New York City may not work at all in Fort Scott, Kan. Extensive research has been conducted at the national level, however, and these studies give us some important clues about how newspapers are perceived.

Probably the most important study of this type was conducted in 1984 by Ruth Clark, president of Clark, Martire & Bartolomeo Inc., a market research firm, for the American Society of Newspaper Editors.[4] The study, funded by United Press International as a service to the industry, revealed these major findings:

1. Readers expect *news* in their newspapers, whether it's national,

4. Ruth Clark, Clark, Martire & Bartolomeo Inc., "Relating to Readers in the '80s," American Society of Newspaper Editors, May 1984.

state, regional or local. What editors call *hard news,* or late-breaking developments, is most important.

2. Readers want information about health, science, technology, diet, nutrition and similar subjects but will figure out for themselves how to cope with all that. Newspapers don't need to tell them.

3. Overall, readers like their newspapers. Most think they are indispensable, although younger readers aren't so sure about that. Most agree that newspapers are here to stay, regardless of the potential that television and computer screens may have for disseminating information.

4. On the negative side, readers sometimes feel manipulated by editors and question whether they are fair and unbiased in covering and allocating space to various constituencies.[5]

These are the major themes that emerged from Clark's study, "Relating to Readers in the '80s." They are strikingly different from the results of a similar study conducted by Clark in 1978, "Changing Needs of Changing Readers." The earlier study concluded that:

1. Readers were more interested in local news than in regional, state, national and international news.

2. There was a major gulf separating readers and editors. Readers felt alienated from newspapers.

3. Readers demanded attention to their needs and wanted articles that helped them cope in a complex world.

4. There was a perceived failure of newspapers to respond to the readers' search for self-fulfillment. This was seen as part of the focus on self that had become a prevailing social value of the 1970s.[6]

Can it be that such far-reaching changes occurred in readers' expectations of newspapers in just six years? Clark concludes that such dramatic changes are not only possible but easily explained. During the period 1978 to 1984, newspapers introduced a bevy of special sections, added lifestyle features, tossed in more service and advice columns and produced sections catering to "me" or "you." There was an explosion in the use of color, technology improved the quality of newsprint, inks and reproduction, and two new national newspapers, *USA Today* and the national editions of *The New York Times,* were introduced.

As quickly as newspapers changed, so did the world, the country and the lives of individual readers, Clark says. During the period

5. Ibid., p. 9.

6. Ruth Clark, "Changing Needs of Changing Readers," American Society of Newspaper Editors, 1978.

1978 to 1984, the United States underwent inflation, recession, unemployment, international crises and developing concern about its prestige abroad and its ability to compete in world markets. "In the late '70s," Clark writes, "key words used to describe the preoccupations of the public were *self* and *self-fulfillment;* today, the buzzwords are *hi tech* and *making it.*"[7]

It is only reasonable to expect that such dramatic changes have an impact on the readership of newspapers and the reading public. So, while we can learn much about our readers from the wealth of research data available to us, it is important to remember that ours is a dynamic society in a constant state of change. What works this year may not work next year. With that word of caution, let's examine the findings of Clark's 1984 study in more detail.

Trends in Readership Patterns

People believe their own newspaper tends to be better than most, and that should be encouraging to editors. A minority of readers, although a substantial one at 39 percent, believes the local newspaper is biased. Most (57 percent) believe that newspaper stories in general are not usually fair. More than half (53 percent) believe that newspaper stories are usually accurate, but 84 percent describe their own paper as accurate.[8]

Editors need to deal with the issue of bias, whether real or perceived, because it has enormous implications. They need to find ways to make their newspapers more believable. The problem is greater at the national level, however, While most people believe that newspapers are unfair, 88 percent believe their local paper really cares about the community. Translating that feeling of concern to the national level would lead to major improvement in the perception of newspapers.

Clark's study found that readers want complete newspapers, even in small communities. Readers of smaller newspapers (under 75,000 circulation) place more emphasis on local and regional news, while readers of larger newspapers tilt toward national and international news. But when it comes to performance, readers of smaller papers give them poorer marks on national and international news, while readers of larger papers are not satisfied with the local coverage they receive.

Young readers continue to be difficult to lure. One encouraging sign for newspapers, however, is that those 18 to 24 are more concerned about keeping up with the news than the "baby boomers," those 25 to 34. Among the "baby boomers," 44 percent say that keeping up with the news is important, but 51 percent of the 18-to-24 group feels that way.[9]

7. Clark, 1984, pp. 7–8.
8. Ibid., p. 10.
9. Ibid., p. 10.

The Improving Climate for Newspapers

Clark concludes that four findings of her 1984 study show a favorable climate for newspapers:

1. *Readers want hard news.* Most (60 percent) agree that a newspaper's main job is to see that the public is well-informed about the issues of the day (see Figure 2.2). Even better, 73 percent say that "What I like most about newspapers is keeping up with the news." Readers also want complete newspapers with detailed news. Most editors see the newspaper's role exactly that way.

One interesting change from the 1978 study is that readers are no longer so insistent on their right to skip the important news of the day. They now feel a social commitment to keep up with the news. About 77 percent agree with the statement that "I find a greater need to keep up with things and to be better informed than I did in the past."

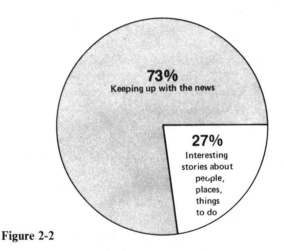

Figure 2-2

A major criticism of television news, once viewed as a major stumbling block to increased newspaper readership, is that it is too sketchy. Probably for that reason, 80 percent indicate that after they see something on television they look forward to getting the details in the daily paper. This finding supports the findings of other studies, which show that newspaper reading and television news viewing tend to be complementary, not competitive. The cities in which television news ratings are the highest also tend to be those in which newspaper readership is strong.

Important issues of the day are business, consumerism, health and health care, the environment, family, children and education. Less important are personal-advice columns, club news, weddings and engagement reports. Clark also discovered that the gender gap is closing: Women today are interested in the same topics as men, and they express a desire to see more sports and business coverage, once thought to be the provinces of male readers.

Editors must remember, however, that providing hard news is not enough. Fully 40 percent of readers believe that a newspaper's main job is to provide the information they need for their daily lives. Coupons, advertisements, listings, television logs and similar material are expected in the daily newspaper.

2. *Ties to readers are strong.* In the world of the '80s, Clark writes, the relationship of readers and editors is essentially positive. The gap between readers and editors found in the 1978 study has eroded. In 1984, 67 percent of respondents disagreed with this statement: "Newspaper editors are more interested in the opinions of other editors than they are in satisfying the needs of their readers." If there is any gap between readers and editors at present, it revolves around the fairness issue; 42 percent of readers believe that even their own newspaper attempts to manipulate them.

Freedom of the press wins resounding support from the public. A 1979 study by the Public Agenda Foundation discovered that 49 percent of the public agreed that "the president has a right to stop a newspaper from publishing a story he feels is biased or inaccurate." Clark found in 1984 that only 25 percent agreed. Readers were quite critical of President Ronald Reagan's attempts to limit newspaper coverage of the invasion of Grenada in 1984. Seventy-four percent agreed that it is "important to have the press present when military forces of any considerable size are sent into another country."

3. *Newspapers are here to stay.* Nine of 10 people interviewed in Clark's study said they had read a daily newspaper in the past week, and most (78 percent) had read a daily newspaper three or four times during that period (see Figure 2.3). Clearly, newspaper reading is still a staple of American life. Besides being ubiquitous, newspapers are generally regarded as indispensable; 64 percent agree that "there really is no substitute for a newspaper every day." Newspapers also get high marks for affordability. About 85 percent consider newspapers one of the biggest bargains of the 1980s.

4. *The public's evaluation of newspapers.* Readers believe newspapers are delivering on most of the terms of what Clark calls the "new social contract." That is, readers find newspapers satisfactory in most major areas of interest—hard news, human-interest items, sports and entertainment coverage. Newspapers also get high marks for appearance (69 percent believe newspapers are more attractive than they used to be), which undoubtedly is a reflection of the increased emphasis editors have placed on the

Figure 2-3

THE NEWSPAPER MARKETPLACE
(Base: Total Sample)

	%
Total Weekday Newspaper Readers (Read in the last week)	90
Time of Day	
Read a A.M. paper	36
Read a P.M. paper	36
Read both A.M. and P.M.	9
Read all all-day paper	7
Read a national daily paper	7
Number of Papers Read	
One paper	68
More than one paper	22
Frequency of Reading	
Regularly (3 or more times a week)	78
Occasionally (1–2 times a week or less)	22
Home delivered	68
Total Sunday Newspaper Readers (Read in the last month)	83
Sunday papers read every week	77
Only read a Sunday paper	5
No Daily Paper Read in Last Week	10
No Daily or Sunday Paper Read	5

Source: Relating to Readers in the '80s, Clark, Martire & Bartolomeo Inc.

design of newspapers in recent years. A measure of the increased respect for newspapers is the greater willingness of readers to listen to the views of editors; 75 percent want their newspapers to devote more space to editorials. And, while still regarded by some as too sensational, newspapers are seen as less sensational than television—and as less sketchy. Newspapers are the generally preferred news source for most people, except for readers of smaller papers, who depend on television more for national news.[10]

The Challenge of Today's Readers   Close to half (43 percent) of readers admit that despite their good intentions, they often are too busy to keep up with the news. Yet

10. Ibid., pp. 11–14.

Clark suggests that there are ways for newspapers to win the battle for the reader's time. She lists these suggestions from readers:

1. Give us a complete, balanced paper with solid reporting of national and international news but equal quality in coverage of local news.
2. Strike a balance between bad news and other important news we need to know. Don't sensationalize or attempt to manipulate public opinion.
3. Give us the important details we don't get from television news, but remember we're short of time.
4. Do a better job of covering the new subjects of major interest—business news, health, consumerism, science, technology, schools and education, family, children and religion.
5. Realize that women today are interested in the sports and business pages you used to put out for your male readers. Of course, women are still interested in food, fashion and other traditional subjects, and you should keep those features going. But recognize they are not the attractions they once were.
6. Make us feel we belong. You need to widen your focus if you are to win more regular readers among young people, working women and members of minority groups. We look at your newspaper to see if we belong, and too often we feel we do not. It's a sore point and a source of grievance.
7. Tell us more about yourselves—your editors and reporters.
8. Count us in on the fight to preserve the First Amendment. We're ready to support *our* right to know.
9. Get to know us better. We are a far more serious, concerned, interested and demanding audience than you have served in the past[11] (see Figure 2.4).

The editor who pays attention to those findings and edits a newspaper accordingly should have little trouble achieving acceptance of the product in the marketplace.

The Lesson of *USA Today*

One of the more interesting newspaper developments of recent years has been the emergence of *USA Today* as a national newspaper. From nowhere, in a matter of two years it became the third most widely circulated newspaper in the United States. Despite efforts of *The New York Times* to become a national newspaper and the rousing success of *The Wall Street Journal,* a business-oriented publication, *USA Today* is the country's first successful general-interest newspaper (see Figure 2.5).

The Gannett Co., which publishes *USA Today,* took a huge gamble in attempting to create such a newspaper, which employs the latest satellite technology to distribute completed pages to printing plants around the country. *USA Today*'s editors seem to have found the right combination to strike the public's fancy: abundant

11. Ibid., p. 17.

use of color, including four-color photos in all four sections; short stories; and colorful, informative graphics, including charts and graphs. Interestingly, while *USA Today* is a hit with the public, it has been received less enthusiastically by advertisers, who say it must compete with slick magazines for their dollars. And, while *USA Today* may be the flashiest newspaper ever published, it still may not be as appealing as magazines with coated paper and even better color reproduction. The result is that despite the newspaper's impressive circulation successes, its future remains in doubt.

Figure 2-4

PROFILE OF REGULAR NEWSPAPER READERS

	%
Total Regular Readers	69
Age	
18–24 years of age	60
25–34 years of age	63
35–49 years of age	75
50 years of age and over	75
Education	
Less than high school	59
High school graduate	71
Some college	71
College graduate	75
Family Income	
Under $15,000	61
$15,000–$24,999	70
$25,000–$34,999	70
$35,000 and over	78
Race	
White	71
Non-white	61
Sex	
Men	69
Women	69

Source: Relating to Readers in the '80s, Clark Martine & Bartolomeo Inc.

Figure 2-5   *USA Today* has been a success with the public.

It will take both circulation and advertising revenue to make such an ambitious project a financial success.

The lessons of *USA Today*'s success with the public aren't lost on the nation's most progressive editors, despite some snide remarks leveled at the paper by those who consider splashy color and short stories an appeal to the lowest common denominator. Clearly, *USA Today* has set new standards for using color in newspapers and for innovative uses of charts and graphs. Its colorful weather map has been copied by many of the nation's large dailies, and *informational graphics* are the latest rage.

Editors who pay attention to such trends and developments are able to respond more quickly to changes in the marketplace than those who don't. That is not meant to suggest that editors should rush out and change their papers to emulate *USA Today*. For many that would be a serious mistake. But Gannett's editors were innovative in their approach to this newspaper, and to ignore the lessons of their success would be tragic.

Other Assistance for Editors

Ruth Clark's study and the lessons of innovative newspapers such as *USA Today* help local editors make decisions about the future of their newspapers. Some supplement those sources with their own readership studies. Other studies have been conducted that also deserve the editor's attention.

Sources of those studies include the *News Research Report* series of the American Newspaper Publishers Association; *Journalism Quarterly,* the traditional publication outlet for those conducting media research; and *Newspaper Research Journal,* a publication of the Newspaper Division of the Association for Education in Journalism. Other sources are the *Newspaper Readership Report* of The Newspaper Readership Council, also published by ANPA, and *The Editors' Exchange,* a series of newsletters published by the American Society of Newspaper Editors. These newsletters outline approaches to solving specific readership problems.

Most of the research that editors will find most useful has been conducted since the mid-1970s. Some earlier research, however, merits examination. One notable series titled *News Research for Better Newspapers* was issued by ANPA from 1965 to 1975. In that series, edited by the late Prof. Chilton Bush of Stanford University, editors can find such useful information as:

1. Stories written in the conventional inverted pyramid format suffer a readership decline of 11.3 percent in the first five paragraphs, 3.46 in the second five, 1.74 percent in the third five and .54 percent in the fourth five (Bush, Volume III, Page 15).
2. The practice of jumping stories from one page to another results in a significant loss of readers. About half never follow the story to the jump page (Bush, III, 9).[12]

Much of that type of research, still useful to editors, is not being duplicated today because of the need to tackle more complex subjects. Presumably, the validity of data Bush produced on such subjects will have changed little.

Credibility and the Media

A major factor in the newspaper–reader relationship is credibility. If readers believe that newspapers are biased and unfair, as Ruth Clark found, it is only reasonable to assume that they will read what is written in newspapers with skepticism.

Newspapers reinforce such doubts about their credibility when they obstinately refuse to admit their errors, when the names of people and places are consistently misspelled or inaccurate, and when hoaxes of one sort or another are uncovered. One such event that shocked newspaper editors occurred in 1981 when the Janet Cooke affair was revealed. Cooke, a reporter for the *Washington Post,* won a Pulitzer Prize for a story about a child named Jimmy who became a heroin addict. Subsequently, it was learned that

12. Chilton Bush, "News Research for Better Newspapers." Seven volumes were published between 1965 and 1975.

Jimmy didn't exist and that Cooke had invented the fictional youngster as a composite of situations involving children she had learned about while doing research for her story. The resulting publicity damaged the credibility of the press nationwide.

The *Washington Post* also was involved in another of the most celebrated scandals in American history, the Watergate affair that eventually led to the resignation of President Richard Nixon. Through a series of stories featuring anonymous sources, the *Post* and reporters Carl Bernstein and Bob Woodward unraveled the involvement of Nixon and his aides in the burglary of the Democratic Party headquarters in the Watergate apartment complex in Washington, D.C. The service the newspaper performed in that investigation probably is unparalleled in U.S. newspaper history, but along the way the many stories with anonymous sources raised serious questions about the credibility of the media. Editors today are reluctant to use anonymous sources without compelling reasons to do so.

Editors concerned about their credibility have tried to find ways to convince the public that newspapers are in fact reliable. These range from simple steps such as working to reduce annoying typographical errors to elaborate schemes designed to check the accuracy of reporters' work.

To enhance the newspaper's image, today's editors readily admit errors. Some papers run a daily notice, prominently displayed, inviting and encouraging readers to call attention to errors in the paper. Another editor regularly conducts an accuracy check of his newspaper's locally written news stories. A clipping of the story is mailed to the source along with a brief query on the accuracy of facts in the story and headline. Another editor invites persons involved in controversy to present amplifying statements when they feel their positions have not been fully or fairly represented.

More corrections are being printed, even though this practice is distasteful to editors. When the old *Minneapolis Star* had to print four corrections on one day, the editor warned the staff, "Let's hope it is a record that is never equaled—or something besides the sky will fall." The *Boca Raton* (Fla.) *News* candidly tells its readers of its corrections under the heading, "Dumb Things We Did."

More balance in opinion is evident in the use of syndicated columnists whose opinions differ from those of the newspaper and in expanded letters-to-the-editor columns.

Some newspapers are using ombudsmen to hear readers' complaints and a few belong to local, regional or national press councils. More are providing reader service columns to identify newspapers with readers' personal concerns. More attention is being given to internal criticism in employee publications or at staff conferences.

A newspaper's credibility depends essentially on its accuracy and balance. In the endeavor to assure accuracy both in fact and in language, the copy editor's role is paramount.

Readability Measurements

Readership measures the extent to which an item is read. Readability measures the ease with which an item can be read, or, more accurately, it tries to measure some of the things that make reading difficult.

A readability measurement is no formula for writing, nor was it ever intended to be. Rather, it is a tool that may be used in rewriting or editing to improve the writing or to check the writing style from various departments of a paper or from the wire services.

Most readability formulas are based on concepts long familiar to newspaper editors. Short sentences generally are easier to read than long ones, and short words generally are more likely to be comprehended than long ones. Two of the better-known formulas developed by readability experts use sentence and word lengths as key ingredients. The Flesch formula, devised by Rudolph Flesch, uses 100-word samples to measure average sentence length and number of syllables. The formula multiplies the average number of words in the sentence by 1.015 and the total syllable count by .846. The two factors are added, then subtracted from 206.835 to arrive at a readability score.[13] Some newspapers periodically use computers to test the readability of news stories.

Robert Gunning uses a similar procedure to determine the *fog index.* He adds the average sentence length in words and the number of words of three syllables or more (omitting capitalized words; combinations of short, easy words like *butterfly;* and verb forms made into three syllables by adding -ed, -es, or -ing). The sum is multiplied by .4 to get the *fog index.*[14]

Suppose the sample contains an average of 16 words to the sentence and a total of 150 syllables. By the Flesch formula the sample would have a readability score of 64, which Flesch rates as standard or fitting the style of the *Reader's Digest.* In the same sample and assuming the hard words at 10 percent, the *fog index* of the Gunning scale would be 10, or at the reading level of high school sophomores and fitting *Time* magazine style.

The wire services thought enough of both formulas to get an evaluation of their news reports. Gunning conducted the evaluation for United Press (now United Press International) and Flesch did two measurements for the Associated Press.

Neither Flesch nor Gunning tests content or word familiarity. All they suggest is that if passages from a story or the whole story average more than 20 words to the sentence and the number of hard words in a sample of 100 words exceeds 10 percent, a majority of readers will find the passages difficult to understand.

13. Rudolph Flesch, *The Art of Readable Writing* (New York: Harper & Row, 1949), p. 197.
14. Robert Gunning, *The Technique of Clear Writing* (New York: McGraw-Hill, 1952), pp. 36–37.

The formula designers would not recommend that copy editors pare all long sentences to 20 words or less and all long words to monosyllables. Long sentences, if they are graceful and meaningful, should be kept intact. Mixed with shorter sentences, they give variety to style and provide the pacing necessary in good writing. A long word may still be a plain word.

An editorial executive of *The New York Times* preferred to measure density of ideas in sentences rather than sentence length itself and came up with a pattern of "one idea, one sentence." A special issue of the newsroom publication *Winners & Sinners* was devoted to this pattern and reports of reading tests on two versions of the same articles. One tested the comprehension of the articles as they were written originally. Another tested the articles when rewritten to lower the density of ideas in the sentence. The "one-idea, one-sentence" dictum is not taken literally even at the *Times,* but, the editors insist, "Generally it speeds reading if there is only one idea to a sentence."

The number of unfamiliar words in passages also has been found to be an element in readability. Edgar Dale and Jeanne S. Chall at Ohio State University prepared a list of 3,000 words known to 80 percent of fourth-graders. The word-load factor in the Dale-Chall formula consists of a count of words outside the list. Only 4 percent of the words on the Dale-Chall list are words of three or more syllables.[15]

Editing stories to reduce the number of words outside the word-familiarity list would be time-consuming and impractical. The lists would have to be revised periodically to take out words that no longer are familiar and to add new words that have become part of everyday language—even to fourth-graders.

Most readability formulas use a few fundamental elements but neglect context or story structure. Thus, a passage in gibberish could rate as highly readable on the Flesch, Gunning and Dale-Chall scales. This was demonstrated by Wilson L. Taylor at the University of Illinois Institute of Communications Research. Taylor developed the *cloze* procedure (from "close" or "closure" in Gestalt psychology) to test context. In this procedure he omitted certain words—usually every fifth word—and asked respondents to fill in the missing words. He then graded them on the number of correct words they could fill in. Of passages from eight writers, the Taylor method ranked samples of Gertrude Stein's semi-intelligible prose as next to the most difficult. The most difficult was a passage from James Joyce.[16] Both the Dale-Chall and the Flesch scales rated the Stein passage as the easiest to read and the Joyce

15. Edgar Dale and Jeanne S. Chall, "A Formula for Predicting Readability," *Education Research Bulletin,* **27**:45–55 (February 18, 1948).
16. Wilson L. Taylor, "Cloze Procedure: A New Tool for Measuring Readability," *Journalism Quarterly,* **30**:415–33 (Fall 1953).

passage in a tie for fourth with a passage from Erskine Caldwell. To test for human interest, Flesch measures personal words and sentences. Sentences that mention persons and have them saying and doing things increase readability.

The *cloze* procedure suggests the unfamiliar words may be used and understood if they are placed in a context in which the reader can guess the word's meaning.

News Judgment

Once editors have learned as much as they can about their audiences through readership research, and once they have learned as much as they can about readability from Flesch, Gunning and others, they must apply their knowledge the best way they can. They have no time to conduct research to determine whether a story will be well-read, nor do they have time to apply readability formulas. Typically, they apply the same criteria used for decades to determine whether a story is to be used at all, whether it is to be used in full or in part, and where it is to be placed within the newspaper. These criteria are:

1. *Audience.* No two audiences are alike, so it is reasonable to assume that readers' tastes differ from city to city. Audiences may differ even within a city. Readers of *The New York Times,* for example, may have tastes that differ significantly from those of readers of the *New York Daily News.* Good editors have a feel for the interests of their audiences, and in many cases readership research has helped to clarify those interests.
2. *Impact.* The number of people affected by an event is often critical in determining how extensively an account of it will be read. If garbage rates are to increase throughout the city, the story has more impact than it would if the garbage rates of only 15 families were affected.
3. *Proximity.* If the event happened nearby, it may be more interesting to a newspaper's readers than it would be if it happened in another country.
4. *Timeliness.* News is important when it happens, and old news is of little value to readers.
5. *Prominence.* Prominent people are of more interest than those who are not. If the president changes his hairstyle, that may be news. If the local butcher does so, chances are that few people care.
6. *Oddity.* A 30-pound tomato may be interesting, and therefore newsworthy, because such a tomato is unusual. Events that are firsts or lasts, and therefore historic, also may be unusual enough to merit attention in the news.
7. *Conflict.* Sports events, crime, political races and disputes often are newsworthy because conflict, unfortunately, plays such an important role in modern society.

Seldom does a news event qualify for inclusion in the newspaper on all of these counts. The editor weighs each story to determine if it has one or more of these values. If the story does, there is a good chance it will be printed. If it includes most or all of these criteria, it may well be worthy of Page One. Judging the news, then, is at best an inexact science, despite the wealth of readership research available.

3

The Tools and How to Use Them

Staff Organization

The size of a newspaper more than any other factor determines the extent of an editor's duties. Editors of some weekly newspapers take and process pictures, write stories, edit those stories, lay out pages, write headlines, set type and paste up pages. A few may even operate the printing press. Most dailies, on the other hand, have specialists for each of those duties.

Large dailies, known as metros, sometimes have beat reporters who write only about government, sports, entertainment or other types of news, photographers who take only certain types of pictures and copy editors who handle only certain types of stories. The *Louisville Courier-Journal,* for example, once had a copy editor-lawyer who specialized in crime and court stories and other items with legal implications. That same newspaper had another copy editor who was completing his work on a doctoral degree in education. Predictably, he handled all the newspaper's education stories.

The size of a newspaper also determines how the copy desk is organized. Many small newspapers have universal desks (Figure 3-1) charged with processing copy from all departments.

Most metros have departmentalized copy desks (Figure 3-2). In this system separate desks handle local, national, international, sports, business, lifestyle and possibly other categories of news. Editors of those desks supervise the reporters who gather the news as well as the copy editors who process the reporters' work. Wire and local news are grouped by category and each desk edits and

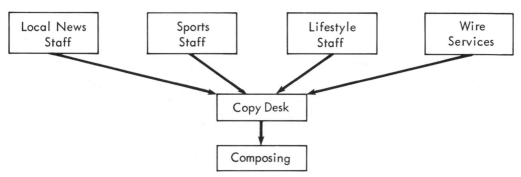

Figure 3-1 Universal copy desk system.

designs its own pages. The news editor or an assistant managing editor coordinates the activities of those desks. That editor decides which stories are to be held for the front page and other key pages, where major stories contributed by the various desks are mixed. A separate staff, supervised by the coordinating editor, edits those pages.

Many newspapers use a semidepartmentalized system (Figure 3-3) in which one desk handles all but sports, lifestyle and Sunday magazine copy. Staffs of those desks do their own editing and page layout.

There are, of course, almost as many variations of these organizational forms as there are newspapers in the United States. It is possible, however, to make some generalizations about the titles and job descriptions of those who write and edit newspapers (Figure 3-4).

At the top of the organizational ladder is the editor, or editor-in-chief, who is responsible for the editorial content of the newspaper. This includes everything from local to international news in categories ranging from sports to business to entertainment. The editor's responsibilities even include the comics and the editorial page.

The editor's top assistants are the editorial page editor and the managing editor. Both report directly to the editor, so the news and opinion functions of the newspaper are distinctly separate. The editorial page editor deals with opinion; the managing editor, who may have one or more assistant managing editors, is responsible for all news gathering operations.

Typically, the city editor, news editor and photo editor report directly to the managing editor, but at larger newspapers that may not be the case. The city editor supervises local news gathering, the news editor directs the copy desk, and the photo editor, as the title implies, supervises the photography department and helps to determine how pictures are used.

The sports, lifestyle and financial editors, and editors of other

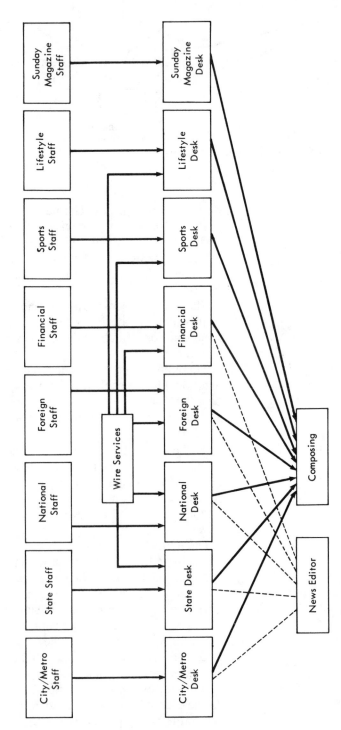

Figure 3-2 Departmentalized copy desk system.

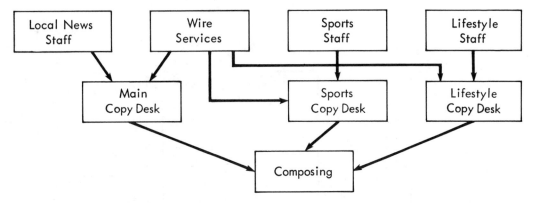

Figure 3-3   Semidepartmentalized copy desk system.

specialized desks, may report directly to the managing editor, or, particularly at large newspapers, to an assistant managing editor.

Reporters, copy editors and photographers report to the desk editors to whom they are assigned, regardless of the system. Editorial assistants known as copy clerks run errands for the editors. Modern electronic newsrooms have technicians who keep electronic terminals and other equipment operating properly.

Internal organization of the copy desk is structured according to the needs of the newspaper. Typically, a universal or semidepartmentalized desk is headed by the news editor, who may double as copy desk chief or slot editor. The "slot editor," a term derived from the structure of the traditional U- or H-shaped copy desk (Figure 3-5), sits in the middle of the U or H—the slot—and is charged with layout of the newspaper. The term "slot" persists, although most newspapers have abandoned the traditional copy desk in favor of a series of clustered office desks to accommodate electronic editing terminals more easily (Figure 3-6).

Copy editors, once known as "rim men" or "rim women" because they sat on the outside, or rim, of the U- or H-shaped desk, also may be assigned specific duties and perhaps other titles. The wire editor sifts through the thousands of words of material sent to the newspaper from one or more wire services. The state editor processes a page or two of news from throughout the state, and yet another editor may be assigned nothing but the front page. This system allows one individual to concentrate on the content and appearance of that key page.

Although the range of duties tends to increase as the size of the newspaper decreases, the goal of the editor—to produce the best possible newspaper—remains the same.

Copy Flow Patterns

Just as the size of the newspaper determines the extent of an editor's duties, the production system in use determines the tools with which he or she works.

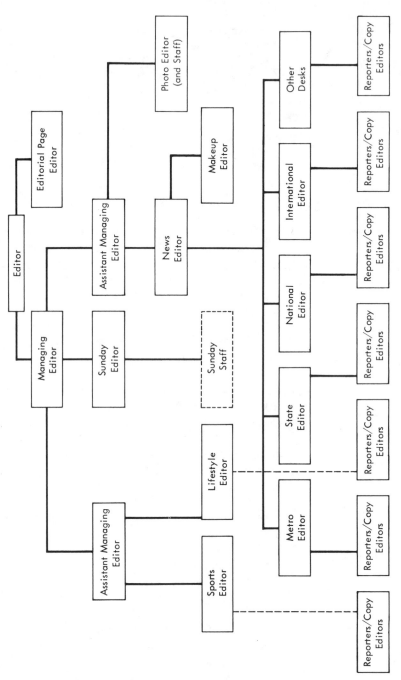

Figure 3-4 Typical staff organization of the metropolitan daily newspaper.

Figure 3-5 Traditional copy desk. This H-shaped desk, which served both the *Louisville* (Ky.) *Courier-Journal* and the *Louisville Times,* provided working space for more than 20 copy editors. The center arm of the H was occupied by the news or slot editor, assistant news editor, managing editor and assistant managing editor. The newsroom has since been redesigned to accommodate the hardware of the new technology. [*Photo courtesy of the* Courier-Journal *and the Louisville* Times.]

Figure 3-6 Computerized newsroom. All news stories are written and edited on video display terminals at the *Huntington* (W.Va.) *Advertiser.* [*Photo courtesy of Huntington Publishing Co.*]

As recently as 1970 almost every newspaper in the United States employed the traditional copy processing system. Reporters wrote their stories on typewriters and editors penciled in corrections until finally the paper copy was sent to the composing room to be converted into type. The emergence of electronic editing in the early 1970s changed that pattern radically. Most newspapers now use video display terminals (VDTs), keyboards with attached television-like screens similar to those used for years by airline reservations agents.

VDT technology in less than 10 years transformed the typical newsroom from a bastion of 19th-century methods into a showcase of contemporary computer technique. Nothing quite like it had occurred in the newspaper industry since the introduction of Ottmar Mergenthaler's Linotype machine in the 1880s.

The technology used affects the way reporters and editors go about their jobs, but copy flow patterns are similar in all systems. When VDTs were introduced, manufacturers tried to duplicate existing copy flow patterns to minimize changes in entrenched newsroom procedures.

The process begins with the reporter, who writes the story and submits it to the editor who assigned it, usually the city editor or metro editor. That editor reads the story, makes the corrections in the process, and either approves the story for publication or returns it to the reporter for revision. When the story is ready, it is sent to the news editor or copy desk chief. That editor determines the length of the story, decides where it should be placed in the newspaper and assigns a headline based upon its position on the page layout.

The editor then passes the story to a copy editor, who carries out the editor's instructions. The copy editor trims the story to fit the space reserved, does the final editing and writes the headline. The story then is returned to the news editor, who approves the headline and scans the copy before sending both to the composing room for typesetting.

That, in simplified form, is the basic copy flow pattern. The exact procedure, however, is determined by staff organization and the technology in use at the newspaper. Because VDT and traditional technologies are distinctly different, it is necessary to describe both systems.

Traditional Process

Reporters working at newspapers using traditional copy processing techniques write their stories on manual or electric typewriters. An original and two or three copies, constituting a "book," are prepared. Inexpensive paper, often newsprint cut to 8½- by 11-inch size, is used. Stories are double- or triple-spaced, depending on the newspaper's custom, to allow for the reporter and editors to make handwritten corrections using established copy-editing symbols (see Figure 3-7). A perfect manuscript is not expected, nor is it

Take out word and ~~and~~ close up space

Add word   stet

Retain ~~crossed-out~~ portion

Transpose letters/(words) or

capitalize word: /lower-case letter

Indent for paragraph

No ¶ Don't indent

Insert period: ...John said⊙

Insert comma: John‸who...

Insert apostrophe: Johns other wife

Insert quotation marks: John said, I'll go.

Insert hyphens: Jack and Jill School

Insert parentheses:(John is his last name.)

Use a circle to indicate:

    Abbreviation: (Colonel) Smith

    No abbreviation: the (col.) said

    Use figure: (six hundred)

    Spell out figure: He had (5) boys

    Directions to compositors:

    (bf)   Set boldface. Wavy line also denotes boldface: At the Alladin

    (lf)   Set lightface

    (bc)   Set boldface capitals

    (bfclc)   Set boldface capital and lower-case

    (sc)   Set small capitals. Two lines under letters denote small
               capitals: Macky

    (sh)   Subhead. Write the subhead between lines of copy

    (ital.)   Set in italic type. Underscore denotes italic: fog index

    (Rom.)   Set in Roman type

    (dc)
    (15-pica) Set type in double-column measure or in measure indicated

Figure 3-7

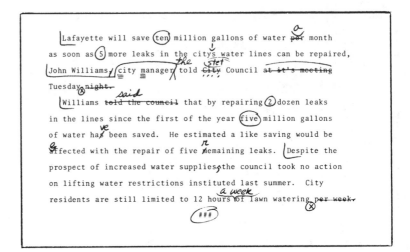

Figure 3-8   An example of edited copy.

necessary, but relatively "clean" copy helps to minimize errors of misinterpretation later in the production process.

The reporter saves one carbon copy of the story for future reference and submits the original and other carbons to the city editor. The original is used for copy processing and the carbons are filed for future reference or used as substitutes for misplaced originals. Editors use the same copy editing symbols as the reporter to make changes as the story makes its way through the editing process (Figure 3-8).

Either the slot editor or the copy editor marks typesetting instructions on the copy. When the story reaches the composing room, the compositor must know which typeface to use, what size of type is needed, the width (or measure) of the column, and whether special handling is desired. Special settings are required for inset pictures (called half-column cuts or thumbnails), initial letters (large capital letters at the beginning of the text) and other special treatments for typographical impact.

Headlines are written either at the top of the story, the method often used for headlining brief articles, or on separate half sheets of standard-size copy paper. They, too, must be marked for typesetting.

Finally, the story and headline are sent to the composing room, where compositors set the type. After the type is set, proofs are made and a proofreader compares the typeset version with the edited copy. The proofreader uses proofreading symbols (see Appendix II) to mark corrections, which are set and placed in position in the typeset copy. Editors also use proofreading symbols, which differ slightly from copy editing symbols, when reading proofs of typeset copy or when making changes in text from one edition to the next.

The whole process of editing and typesetting with traditional methods is riddled with redundancy. Editors consider redundancy in the newsroom a desirable trait because the more times a story is read, the more errors are detected and deleted. They object, however, to redundant keyboarding in the composing room, where errors easily can be introduced.

The VDT Process Most daily newspapers in the United States and Canada have video display terminals, and VDTs are rapidly gaining acceptance in the weekly newspaper market. Editors consider VDTs the best tools available for writing and editing copy (Figure 3-9).

Video terminals place in the hands of editors final control over what is set in type, and, consequently, what appears in the newspaper. Compositors are not necessary because the work of reporters and editors is stored in computer memory and subsequently is used to drive high-speed phototypesetting machines. Proofreaders also are unnecessary because phototypesetters are extremely accurate; machine errors, common with old, hot-metal linecasters, are almost nonexistent. This means that at most newspapers an editor is the last to read a story before it appears in the newspaper. Control of the newspaper's content is placed where it belongs—in the hands of the editors.

Figure 3-9   Reporters and editors at most newspapers now use video display terminals on which to write and edit. [*Photo by Joe Edens*]

As a result, editors place a premium on talented copy editors who refuse to accept what is merely adequate and instead strive for perfection. No longer can editors tolerate the copy editor who believes, "That's good enough. The composing room will straighten it out." Unfortunately, too many of those people were tolerated in the past.

Editors who employ talented copy editors like the VDT process. Their papers are more accurate and contain fewer typographical errors than in the past. No longer is there a danger of a compositor misinterpreting an editor's hand-scrawled instructions.

Reporters and editors using VDTs write and edit on the keyboards attached to their video terminals. More than 20 manufacturers sell VDTs for newspaper use, so there is little standardization. Almost all use a standard typewriter keyboard layout for alphanumeric functions, but there the similarity ends. Most terminals have keys for text editing and manipulation, but the manufacturer decides where those keys are placed. This proves to be a disadvantage for the newcomer to a newspaper, who may have learned to use editing keys placed to the left of the alphanumeric portion of the keyboard rather than to the right.

A lighted rectangle, called a cursor, indicates the position in the text where the next character typed will be placed. A bank of cursor control keys allows the user to move the cursor forward, backward, up or down. Errors are corrected by inserting characters, overstriking, or moving blocks of text from one position to another until perfect copy is produced. Another bank of keys permits text manipulation. With these keys, stories are filed in computer memory, recalled for editing, and routed from editor to editor and finally to the phototypesetter through a series of queues, the electronic equivalents of in-baskets.

At some point, an editor must place a computer-coded instruction, called a format, at the top of the story to instruct the phototypesetter to set the type as the editor wants. Other codes may be inserted to produce initial letters, insets for half-column pictures or other special treatments.

When VDTs were first introduced, some argued that editors had become compositors because they had taken on duties formerly handled in the composing room. Newsroom employees with union representation made this contention in labor negotiations and in some cases the issue was taken to arbitration. Almost without exception, arbitrators ruled that the technology employed had not substantially changed the duties and functions of copy editors.[1]

---

1. Significant decisions in this area were made in arbitrations between the Newspaper Guild of Pittsburgh, Local 61, and Post-Gazette Publishing Co., and between the Vancouver-New Westminster Newspaper Guild, Local 115, and Pacific Press Limited, publisher of the *Vancouver* (B.C.) *Province* and *Sun.* In the Vancouver decision, the arbitrator found that duties of some key personnel and some clerks had been changed as a result of the introduction of VDTs, but no substantial change was found in the duties and functions of copy editors.

Their reasoning was that editors had been required to mark copy for typesetting, insets and other special handling even when traditional copy processing procedures were employed. Formats used in the best VDT systems allow markup similar to that always used; there is no need for the editor to learn complicated typesetting codes.

Similarly, contentions that editors now have more responsibility because of the absence of compositors and proofreaders fell on deaf ears. Editors always had been responsible for the content of the newspaper; now they had been given tools to do that job more effectively.

Such disputes tend to distort the fact that VDTs have won widespread acceptance. In one nationwide survey of copy editors, 89 percent said they preferred working with VDTs over working with pencil and paper.[2] That same survey showed that editors believe VDT editing allows them to be more accurate and that using VDTs they are more likely to make the extensive revisions necessary to produce a truly exceptional newspaper. An impressive 46 percent indicated that VDTs had helped them to become more accurate editors. Only 10 percent thought that VDTs had affected editorial accuracy adversely.

Emerging Technologies

Some newspapers have started designing pages on computer terminals as a means of eliminating the labor-intensive composing room makeup process. With this system, known as pagination, completed pages are produced by full-page phototypesetters, or laser technology is used to create printing plates and the composing process is eliminated altogether. Pagination creates additional work for the copy desk, which must make precise decisions about where stories are to be trimmed and how to avoid widows (short lines at the tops of columns), and similar decisions that once were made by printers. Most newspapers that have switched to pagination have been able to eliminate jobs in the composing room but have found it necessary to add to the copy desk staff.

A few newspapers also have started programming for cable television, videotex and teletext, all of which are forms of electronic home delivery of news in text format (see Chapter 19). Often, the copy desk is responsible for such programming and copy editors take turns in preparing text for such cablecasts. A couple of newspapers, including Long Island's *Newsday*, have tried to market television-like newscasts produced by newsroom personnel. Like pagination, such operations take time and often require the newspaper to hire more employees.

2. Linda J. Shipley, James K. Gentry and John W. Clarke, *VDT vs. Pencil: A Comparison of Speed and Accuracy,* University of Missouri School of Journalism (1979).

Many of the new technologies introduced in U.S. and Canadian newsrooms have had their greatest impact on copy desks. As such systems continue to evolve, there is every likelihood that the demand for talented copy editors will continue to grow.

Technology in Perspective

Video display terminals changed the face of American newsrooms during the 1970s. Most editors are convinced the changes were for the better. Technology streamlined the production of American newspapers at a time when positive change was desperately needed. Spiraling costs of newsprint were partially offset by savings realized in composing room work force reductions. Newer phototypesetting procedures married well with microwave and satellite transmission of fully composed pages to remote printing plants, reducing for some publishers the difficulty of distributing newspapers through traffic-clogged streets.

Tribute should be paid to the American Newspaper Publishers Association, and particularly its ANPA Research Institute, which encouraged and helped to develop and promote those technological advances. Through technology that allowed reporters and editors to realize their role in the critical newspaper production process, old barriers to communication within newspaper plants came tumbling down. No longer can reporters and editors assume the attitude that production is the province of another department. That always was a shortsighted attitude, and in the modern newspaper plant reporters and editors know it.

PART II

Copy Editing Skills

4

The Editing Process

The Copy Editor's Responsibilities

Of all the copy editor's duties, editing for accuracy is probably the most important. A newspaper that is inaccurate soon loses its credibility, and, ultimately, its readers.

Good reporting, of course, is the key ingredient in ensuring accuracy. But all who edit the story share that responsibility. Editors ensure accuracy by questioning the reporter about the information obtained and the means of obtaining it, and by checking verifiable facts. Usually it is the city editor who questions the reporter and the copy editor who checks verifiable facts. The spelling of names and the accuracy of addresses can be checked in telephone books, city directories and similar source materials. The newspaper's library, almanacs, stylebooks, dictionaries and other references are used to check other facts. The good newspaper provides its staff with these source materials, and the good copy editor uses them frequently.

Ensuring accuracy is important, but the copy editor's job entails much more than that. This chapter and those that follow outline what is expected of the copy editor. In general, though, those responsibilities include:

1. Ensuring accuracy.
2. Trimming unnecessary words.
3. Protecting and polishing the language.
4. Correcting inconsistencies.
5. Making the story conform to style.

6. Eliminating libelous statements.
7. Eliminating passages in poor taste.
8. Making certain the story is readable and complete.
9. Ensuring fairness.

The copy editor who does each of these things in every story will be a valuable addition to the newspaper's staff. The importance of accuracy already has been emphasized, but a brief review of the other responsibilities may be useful.

When trimming unnecessary words, adjectives and adverbs often are suspect. If an event is *very interesting,* it is sufficient to say it is *interesting. Very* is an overworked word that has become almost meaningless. Similarly, *totally destroyed* is worse, not better, than *destroyed.* Meaningless phrases also should be eliminated. *At the corner of Ninth and Elm streets* is no better than *at Ninth and Elm streets.*

The copy editor must polish the language, and to do so must know the difference between a conjunction and a preposition and be aware of the perils of misplacing modifiers. The copy editor also must be able to spell and to use words properly. Copy editors, and certainly students in an editing course, would benefit by getting into the habit of using a dictionary and learning to use words properly. Chapter 5 shows how the copy editor deals with the language.

The top-flight copy editor also will recognize inconsistencies within a story. Here is a good example:

> Mrs. John E. Simpson, 81, of 914 E. Texas Ave., died Saturday at Boone County Hospital after an illness of several months.
>
> Mrs. Simpson was born in Audrain County Dec. 21, 1900, to the late John and Mary Simpson. . . .

The inconsistency is that Mrs. Simpson likely did not have the same maiden and married names. Therefore, her parents' surname must be checked. The alert copy editor would have detected that possible error and questioned the city desk about it. And, depending upon the year in which the story is written, the age and date of birth may not agree.

Annoying inconsistencies also result from failure to conform to the newspaper's style. The word "style," as used here, refers to the consistency provided by rules of usage and in no way limits a reporter's individual writing style. Style, for example, dictates that the correct spelling is *employee,* not *employe,* which can be found in some dictionaries. It may be annoying to the reader to find the word spelled one way in one story and another way in the next. The importance of style is emphasized in Chapter 6.

The copy editor faces other problems, many of which cannot be solved by consulting dictionaries and stylebooks. One of those problems is recognizing and eliminating libelous statements. Libel laws vary from state to state, so one of the first duties of a copy editor after taking a job is to check the laws of the state. A thorough discussion of legal limitations on the press can be found in Chapter 8. The law and interpretations of it usually can answer questions about whether a statement is libelous.

More difficult to resolve are questions of good taste. Some newspapers have policies banning profanity of any type; others permit the use of some words but not others. Most editors would object to a story detailing what occurred during a rape; some would not. These are matters of judgment. When in doubt, the wise copy editor will consult a top-ranking editor for a ruling.

The copy editor makes certain the story is fair and readable. Writing that is good, and therefore readable, has five characteristics:

1. It is precise.
2. It is clear.
3. It has a pace appropriate to the content.
4. It uses transitional devices that lead the reader from one thought to the next.
5. It appeals to the reader's senses.

Writing is precise when words are used in the way they should be used, and it is clear when simple sentences and correct grammar are employed. Pacing is a matter of using varied sentence length. The use of short, choppy sentences conveys action, tension or movement. Conversely, long sentences slow the reader. Transitions help the reader tackle the story, and sharp, descriptive words appeal to the reader's senses to bring him or her close to the action.

Good writing employs all of these principles. There is no reason why they should be used in novels but not in newspaper stories. The argument that reporters don't have time to produce quality writing is a poor excuse, understandable as it may be, for mediocrity. It can be done, and the best newspapers in this country are proving it. The quality of writing depends upon the reporter, but the copy editor can do much to help. Good editing invariably complements good writing. Occasionally good editing can save mediocre writing. Poor editing can make it worse or destroy it.

Newspaper Writing

Newspaper journalism always has attracted good writers. The best today rank with the stars of the past, including such legendary figures as Stephen Crane, Mark Twain and Ernest Hemingway, all of whom began their writing careers as newspaper reporters. As a class, however, reporters are mediocre as writers. Much of this mediocrity can be attributed to the deadline pressure under which reporters write, the lack of enthusiasm for the subjects about which they write and the straightjacket of the traditional inverted pyramid style.

The deadline pressure will always exist because newspaper production necessitates the setting of deadlines. That's why the pro who can pound out a readable story in a matter of minutes is a valued member of the newsroom staff. Those other excuses for mediocrity, however, fail to stand up under close examination. A wise editor once said: "There are no dull stories, only dull reporters." The message is clear: a good reporter can find a good story in almost any situation. Blaming the event or situation for a mediocre story is inexcusable. Finally, reporters no longer should feel shackled by the inverted pyramid approach to newspaper writing. Other writing styles have gained acceptance nationwide, and the newspaper that ignores them misses the opportunity to keep its readers interested.

The copy editor must have a thorough understanding of newspaper writing styles, or story forms, so that he or she can recognize them quickly. It would be a serious mistake to assume that every story should be written in the inverted pyramid style. Editing to achieve that effect without grasping what the writer is trying to accomplish can destroy a good story. The most popular forms:

The Inverted Pyramid Approach

This classic style, with its crammed leads and recitation of facts in descending order of importance, should not be dismissed. It still is the staple of newspaper writing. Fast-breaking news stories lend themselves to this treatment. Indeed, the form was developed by newspaper writers, who found it worked well in meeting the needs of their fast-paced business.

The inverted pyramid story has three main parts:

1. The lead.
2. Support and development of the lead.
3. Details in descending order of importance.

Typically, stories written in this form have the traditional lead that tells the reader who, what, when, where, why and perhaps how. Here is an example of an inverted pyramid story:

SPRINGFIELD, Mass (UPI)—A man screaming "I'm the king" slashed his way through a crowded hospital emergency room with a long-bladed paring knife Monday, killed a 6-year-old boy and injured five other people.

Willie Robinson, 42, infuriated when he and his young granddaughter were burned with cleaning fluid during a domestic quarrel at his apartment, stabbed his wife and ran amok at Bay State Medical Center's Springfield Unit a short time later, police said.

"He had a really wild look in his eyes," said Sgt. George Bishop, a hospital security guard.

"There was an awful lot of blood."

Robinson had been taken to the hospital by his nephew for treatment of burns, then "went berserk." He wounded five persons in the emergency room and killed Anthony Lombardi, 6, of Agawam, police said.

Police said Robinson stabbed several women and a guard and then pinned the boy down at an ambulance entrance, stabbed him repeatedly and screamed, "I'm the king, I'm the king. Now I've done it. I'm done."

The boy died about two hours later of wounds in the neck, throat and arms.

The boy's mother, Rose Lombardi, 30, was listed in serious condition with multiple stab wounds.

Police said Robinson would be charged with murder and seven counts of assault and battery.

The Narrative Approach

Some newspaper editors believe there is an increasing need to use the narrative, magazine style in newspaper stories. In the narrative, there may be no breaking news at all, but rather a wealth of new and interesting information that will make it news nevertheless.

Some of these concepts already have been tried successfully. Some news events heavily covered by television have been presented in the narrative rather than in the traditional news style. Here is an example of the narrative approach:

MADRID (UPI)—"You will write about me and my photo will be published on every front page," boasted 16-year-old Mariano Garcia. "I will be a great bull fighter one day."

This was his dream and the theme he returned to time and again during our 200-mile drive from Saragossa to Madrid.

It was on Feb. 23 in the outskirts of Saragossa that Mariano had asked me for a ride.

"I want to go to Madrid and start a career as a bull fighter," the boy said in the accents of his native Mancha.

Mariano's was a classic story of Spain: The eager youth deserting the misery of his sun-baked village with its white-washed walls for the danger and glory of the bull ring.

When he learned that I was a newsman, Mariano pulled a pencil stub and sort of calling card out of his pocket. The card bore an amateurish sketch of the Virgin Mary and Jesus. Across it he scrawled his name in bold letters.

"The Virgin and the Christ are my protectors," he said.

Then he talked with wide-eyed dreaminess of how the bull paws the ground with his left forefoot when excited, of his sudden charges, of the secrets of the matador's capework and of the "pata, rabo y orejas"—the hoofs, tail and ears of the bull—the highest honors the fickle Spanish crowd can pay a matador.

For two years, Mariano tried to get a start on the road to fame and fortune. It came not in Madrid, but at San Martin de Lavega.

The bull he met Thursday was six years old, fat, limping, and the sharp tips of his horns had been clipped. But the old bull could be dangerous. He had survived the ring once and remembered well how the matador evaded his charges and the hooking of his horns.

Mariano made three or four passes with his cape. But the bull was old and the boy was young and the fickle crowd was bored.

"Just a meletilla," some shouted, "just a beginner."

Another matador stepped in to divert the bull. But the animal had his eyes fixed on Mariano. Suddenly, he charged the boy and knocked him down.

Then the old bull drove his blunted left horn into Mariano's skull.

It was a quick kill, as the good matador's sword should be quick.

Mariano Garcia's mother and father carried his body in a bloodstained sheet to the local cemetery. And today I wrote the story Mariano promised I would write.

This type of storytelling has the quality once described by Earl J. Johnson of UPI: "to hold the reader's interest and stimulate some imagination to see, feel and understand the news."

The Personalized Approach

Business and financial news may not be the most glamorous of subjects for most readers, but *The Wall Street Journal* knows how to make such stories compelling. Here's an example of the Journal's personalized approach:

Home on the Range Is a Part-Time Deal for Many Cowboys

They Keep Cows Just for Fun, Helping Keep Prices Low; Job After Banker's Hours

By Marj Charlier
Staff Reporter of The Wall Street Journal

HUNTLEY, Mont.—C.T. Ripley has a redwood ranch house, with cowhides adorning the walls and floors. He also has a red pickup truck, with a color-matched stock trailer, and six cowboy hats, for whatever the occasion demands.

"I am a cowboy," he says. "That's all I've ever wanted to be."

In truth, he is an oil-refinery employee. But on the side for the past couple of years, he has been putting together his 200-acre "Almosta Ranch." Now he is ready to buy some cattle. He will probably lose money on them, but there is the income from the job sustaining him and the romance of the open range spurring him. He will do it anyway.

Such part-time ranchers are a big problem for full-time cattlemen, many of whom are losing their shirts. The would-be cowboys add up to too many cows, standing the law of supply and demand on its head.

Demand for red meat has tumbled the past decade, depressed by health concerns and recession-induced penny-pinching. As a result, the price ranchers command for cattle has fallen 25%, adjusted for inflation. Cattle-herd liquidations would seem to be in order, to bring supply in line with demand and strengthen prices. Some cows have been culled, but analysts suggest the herds must be cut much more to ensure long-term profits.

Small herds compound the price problem. More than 80% of the nation's herds have fewer than 100 head of cattle, kept mostly by part-time farmers and those who make their living raising grain. Many of these maintain their livestock, despite the low prices, because cattle aren't their main source of income. Some cattle also are kept at a loss because they provide a tax shelter against other income.

The bottom line: Cow-calf operators (the cowboys who keep beef cows that produce calves for sale to feed lots) have sustained losses eight out of the last 10 years. . . .

The *Journal's* personalized approach is part of a well-designed formula that newspaper has popularized. It is a four-step process:

1. Focus on the individual.
2. Transition to the larger issue.
3. Report on the larger issue.
4. Return to the opening character for the close.

To tell the part-time ranchers' story in the inverted pyramid formula probably would have been less effective.

The Chronological Approach

American newspapers of the Colonial period often used the chronological approach in their news accounts. This approach should be used sparingly, but occasionally it can be effective. A detailed account of a gunman's siege may lend itself to this treatment. So may a reconstruction of a pilot's frantic final moments before an airplane crash or a step-by-step account of how a legislative bill was altered to appease lobbyists.

When the chronological approach is used, the formula works this way:

1. A summary lead.
2. Transition to the chronological account.
3. The chronological account.

4. A closing summary or reversion to the inverted pyramid.

One good time to use the chronological approach is when the subject of an interview relates a complicated series of events. There's nothing wrong with allowing the subject to tell the story with a minimum of interference from the writer. Here's an excellent example from United Press International:

COLUMBIA, S.C. (UPI)—The 5-foot waves sloshed over her face, the chilly water of Lake Marion numbed her body and for a moment Lynne Heath thought about giving up and drowning. But her stubborn temper took over and she kept struggling toward shore.

"I fussed at God. I didn't want to die that way," Ms. Heath, 20, said in an interview Sunday.

"My father is dead, and I talked to him. I told him, 'Hey Dad, put in a good word for me with God. I'm too young to die.' I was stubborn."

The interview was the first time Ms. Heath has talked with the news media about the boating accident March 14 in which her fiance and two other people died. Ms. Heath managed to survive by swimming 90 minutes in the 52-degree water of Lake Marion until she reached shore.

Ms. Heath, her fiance, Kevin Brown, 22, Kevin Morris, 20, and assistant county solicitor Harrison Heller III, 29, were on a fishing trip on the huge lake about a mile from shore when the wind picked up and the water became rough.

The gas tank in the 16-foot fiberglass boat shifted, Ms. Heath said, and the boat took on water and quickly sank.

Heller—who could not swim—was the only one wearing a life preserver. The other preservers went down with the boat.

Ms. Heath said they looked around for something—flotsam or a stump or anything to hold onto—but there was nothing but high waves whipping across the 20-foot-deep water.

"I didn't realize how much danger we were in," she recalled. "Kevin (Brown) looked back at Kevin Morris. He couldn't have lived with himself if he had not gone back to help. Please tell everyone that he went back to help the others.

"I looked at him and I said, 'It's all right. I love you.' The look on his face is one I'll never forget.

"I started swimming toward some houses I had seen on shore. I would swim a little way and the waves would push me back. Waves would come over my head and you would have to hold your breath and then just keep going.

"I have never been a strong swimmer, but I was determined to make it. I swam with the back stroke awhile, the breast stroke, the side stroke. I saw white birds flying over and it made me mad because I wondered why I couldn't just fly out there.

"The sun was shining and it made me feel better. I knew I had to get out of my clothes and shoes. I took off my tennis shoes and my jeans were waterlogged and heavy. I had trouble getting them off.

"I had Girl Scout training and so I tried to make my jeans into a life preserver, but the zipper wouldn't work.

"Soon I had stripped down to my purple tube top and panties. I am 5-foot-2½ and I weighed 122 then. I weigh 112 now. Maybe the baby fat helped with hypothermia."

"At one point I was fixing to give up and I said no, 'My mom will have a nervous breakdown.'

"I'm very stubborn and I have a very hot temper. I think it was my temper. I was mad.

"Finally, after 90 minutes, I got to this beach," she said. "I sat there for about 10 seconds and got my legs to stop shaking so badly. Then I started half crawling and running to the houses about a mile down the beach.

"Briars ripped at my legs but I didn't care. When I got to the house I found these six steep steps. I ran up and just fell in through a screen door."

Mr. and Mrs. Gilbert Minor, a retired couple, wrapped her in a blanket and gave her hot black coffee with lots of sugar while she blurted out the story and asked that authorities be called to help the others.

"We all know it was a miracle," said her mother, Rebecca.

Heller's body has been recovered, and Brown and Morris are presumed drowned.

The writer provides a strong introduction for three paragraphs and then uses the fourth as a transition. The chronological account, much of it direct quotes, begins with the fifth paragraph. Finally, the author provides a summary paragraph. The success of this story is striking evidence that the chronological approach should not be dismissed as unworkable.

The First-Person Approach

The first-person approach also should be used sparingly, but on the right occasion it is quite effective to have the writer become a part of the story. The first person can be used when the reporter is an eyewitness to an event. It also can be used in participatory journalism, when reporters become ambulance attendants or police officers for a day.

The inverted pyramid was developed as a device to facilitate trimming of the story in the composing room as the deadline neared. Because facts were in descending order of importance, trimming from the bottom was simple. Traditional copy processing procedures made story length estimates imprecise, so trimming frequently was necessary. Computer technology used in modern newspaper plants permits copy editors to determine the exact length of a story before it is typeset, so page layouts can be more precise. This makes it more feasible for newspapers to use alternate writing styles, which, unlike the inverted pyramid, often employ formal closings. Technology has made it simple for newspapers to escape the traditional inverted pyramid writing style.

Copy editors have no business changing a writer's style. But copy editors have every obligation to insist that the story be correct in spelling, grammar and syntax: it is their duty to make copy compact and readable.

Most copy can be tightened. Even if only a few words in a paragraph are removed, the total saving in space will be considerable. Some stories, notably material from the wires and syndicates, can be trimmed sharply. But the copy editor should not overedit. If a story is so poorly organized it has to be rewritten, the story should be returned to the originating editor. Rewriting is not a copy editor's job. Nor should the copy editor make unnecessary minor changes. Indiscreet butchering of local copy is a sure way to damage morale in the newsroom.

Honing the Lead

The lead of a story is its most important element because the lead's quality may well determine whether the reader is hooked or skips the story in favor of another. Editors hesitate to impose formulas for writing by limiting sentence length, but on one point they are almost unanimous: the lead of a story must be short. How short? A Hearst editor demanded short leads and finally got one of only one word. The *Chicago Tribune* applauded this three-word lead:

"Money and race." An even better one read: "Are nudes prudes?"

Ralph McGill, late editor of the *Atlanta Constitution*, liked what he called a flawless lead in the Bible: "There was a man in the land of Uz whose name was Job." That all-time best-seller probably has another of the best leads ever written: "In the beginning God created the heaven and the earth."

Columnist Tom Fesperman uses short leads and short sentences to move his readers along:

> There was a quail whose name was Hercules.
>
> Don't ask me how he got that name. I have spotted a lot of quail in my time, and I wouldn't call any of them Hercules.
>
> Even so. Let us get on with the story.
>
> It is not exactly accurate to say that Hercules was born in Arizona. It's more exact to say he was hatched. . . .

The copy editor's eye brightens when he or she reads leads that rank with these classics:

> Only in Russia could Peter and the Wolf die on the same night (Stalin's death).

> Today the Japanese fleet submitted itself to the destinies of war—and lost.

> They're burying a generation today. (Texas school explosion.)

> The moon still shines on the moonshine stills in the hills of Pennsylvania.

> Fifty thousand Irishmen—by birth, by adoption and by profession—marched up Fifth Avenue today.

Most lead problems arise when reporters try to see how much they can pack into the lead. More often, they should try to see how much they can leave out:

Original

The former girlfriend of a man charged with killing a local bartender almost four years ago testified Monday that she has never seen another man who claims he killed the victim and that she was with him that night.

Edited

A man who says he actually committed the murder for which another man is on trial was contradicted in court Monday.

—Roy H. Copperud

Original

Columbia Gas Transmission Corp. has started discussions with its subsidiaries and major customers that could result in increasing the supply of natural gas to its Kentucky subsidiary—and thus to industrial users in the central and northeastern parts of the state who now face a total cutoff of supplies this winter.

Edited

Columbia Gas Transmission Corp. has started a search for ways to save industrial users in central and northeastern Kentucky from a threatened total cutoff of gas this winter.

—Wallace Carroll

One way to avoid long, cluttered leads is to substitute simple sentences for compound ones:

LONDON—Thirty years ago today, a 27-year-old princess was crowned Queen Elizabeth II, and Britain, in an outpouring of emotional fervor unmatched since, hailed her coronation as the beginning of a new Elizabethan era of splendor and achievement.	LONDON—Thirty years ago today, a 27-year-old princess was crowned Queen Elizabeth II. Britain, in an outpouring of emotional fervor unmatched since, hailed her coronation as the beginning of a new Elizabethan era of splendor and achievement.

The lead should be pruned of minor details that could come later in the story if they are needed:

Donald E. Brodie, son of William Brodie, for more than three decades a member of the display advertising department of the News, and Mrs. Brodie, 106 W. 41st St., was graduated from Jefferson Medical College last week.	Donald E. Brodie, son of Mr. and Mrs. William Brodie, 106 W. 41st St., was graduated from Jefferson Medical College last week. For more than three decades, William Brodie was a member of the display advertising department of the News.

The lead need not be long to be cluttered and unreadable:

First National is one of four American banks, and the American Express which issues travelers checks throughout the nation.	First National, three other American banks, and the American Express Co. issue travelers checks throughout the nation.

Leads that Mislead   A good lead contains qualities other than brevity. It must inform and summarize. It must be straightforward; it cannot back into the action. It sets the mood, the pace and the flavor of the story. It accomplishes what the term implies: it guides, directs, points to and induces. If it is a suspended-interest lead, it must be so tantalizing and intriguing that the reader cannot help but continue.

In an effort to get the maximum punch in the lead, the overzealous reporter may overstate. When this happens, the lead is not supported by the story or ignores facts contained in it. It stretches and therefore distorts. It is the type of lead that reads, "All hell broke loose in city hall last night." Then the final sentence reads, "When the dispute subsided, the councilmen shook hands and the mayor adjourned the session."

No matter how appealingly you wrap up the lead, it is no good if it gives a wrong impression or tells a lie. The "souped up" lead invites a sensational headline. If the copy editor lets the overextended lead stand, then tries to top the lead with a calm headline, the editor is likely to have the headline tossed back with the suggestion that more punch be put into it. Some copy editors have been known to "doctor" the lead to justify a sensational headline.

Akin to the sensationalized lead is the opinion lead. This type of lead offers a judgment rather than fact. Often it fails to distinguish between mere puffery and news: "Construction features described as newer in concept than space travel will be part of the easy-to-shop-in Almart store to open soon on the Kirkwood Highway."

Don't Back into It   John Smith returns home from a meeting and his roommate asks, "What happened at the meeting?"

"Well," replies John, "Jim Jones opened the meeting at 8 and Bill Prentice read the minutes of the previous meeting, and—"

"Good night, John."

Too many news leads read like secretarial reports, and that is especially true of leads on speech stories. Few care that a nursing consultant spoke at a group's "regular monthly meeting," or care to know the title of the talk. Readers want to know *what* that person said. That's the news. They won't wade through three paragraphs to learn in the fourth paragraph that "the epileptic child should be treated as a normal person." The lead should get to the point of the story immediately. Like this:

Original
Dean F. Snodgrass of the University of California's Hastings College of Law says the American Bar Association's longtime ban on news photographs in courtrooms is archaic and unrealistic.

Edited
The rule against news photographs in courtrooms is archaic and unrealistic, a law school dean says.
—AP Writing Committee

Original
The Brookside Club will consider a subcommittee proposal that calls for changes in representation on the Community Council at its meeting at noon Wednesday in the Community Center.

Edited
Changes in representation on the Community Council will be considered Wednesday by the Brookside Club.
—Roy H. Copperud

Indirect
An Atlanta businessman who joined two anti-black, anti-Jewish groups and turned over information to the FBI today associated a man on trial for dynamiting the Jewish temple with race-hating John Kasper.

Direct
A man on trial for dynamiting the Jewish temple was linked today with race-hating John Kasper by an FBI undercover agent.

Inactive
A top-ranking rocket AFD space weapons expert coupled a disclosure of his resignation from the Air Force today with a blast at the senior scientists upon whom the services rely for technological advice.

Active, Tight
A top-level Air Force space weapons expert blasted civilian scientists today and said he has resigned.

Cliché Leads

Clichés, because of their familiarity, often produce leads that sound like so many the reader has read before. The result is a "so-what?" attitude:

> Quick action by two alert policemen was credited with saving the life of. . . .

> Police and volunteers staged a massive manhunt today for a man who. . . .

Say-nothing Leads

If a say-nothing lead causes the copy editor to ask, "So what else is new?" the chances are the readers will have the same reaction.

> DETROIT—Somber was the word for the memorial services to American dead of the War of 1812 Sunday.

> Fire so hot it burned the mud guards off and melted a small section of an aluminum trailer damaged the trailer. . . .

This is almost like writing, "Fire so hot that it burned the roof and walls and destroyed all the furnishings damaged the house of John Doe. . . . "

Illogical Leads

Frequently, illogical leads occur when the writer presents the idea backward or uses a non sequitur, a phrase that is nonsensical or defies logic.

> State police attributed an auto collision and the alertness of witnesses to the rapid apprehension of Benjamin Petrucci. . . .

Either the apprehension was attributed to the collision and the alert witnesses or the collision and the witnesses were credited with the apprehension. Other examples:

> Hoping to encourage transient parking at its facilities, the city parking authority yesterday voted to increase rates at two lots.

Charging more for parking hardly seems to be the way to encourage more of it.

> Three small brothers died last night in a fire that burned out two rooms of their home while their father was at work and their mother was visiting a neighbor.

Note how much clearer the revision is: "Left unattended, three small brothers perished in a fire last night that destroyed two rooms of their home. Their father was at work and their mother was visiting a neighbor."

Extensive Identification

Another problem is extensive identification, sometimes even preceding the name:

> Former Assistant Secretary of State for Latin American Affairs Lincoln Gordon said today. . . .

This results in unnecessary clutter in the lead. Long titles should follow names.

Too Many Statistics Burdensome statistics or numbers also may clutter the lead. Including those statistics later in the story may help alleviate problems such as these:

> At 7 p.m. yesterday 60 persons fled a three-story apartment building at 2523 E. 38th St. when a carelessly discarded cigarette sent smoke billowing through the building.
>
> Louis Ezzo, 29, of Plainville, a school bus driver, was charged by state police with speeding and violation of a statute limiting school bus speeds to 40 miles an hour at 3:30 p.m. yesterday on I-95 Groton.
>
> A 14-year-old boy fired three shots into a third-floor apartment at 91 Monmouth St. yesterday to climax an argument with a 39-year-old mother who had defended her 9-year-old daughter against an attack by the boy.

Overattribution Sometimes attribution isn't needed in the lead. Including it there merely creates clutter:

> Mimi La Belle, Blanktown exotic dancer, was arrested on a charge of indecent exposure last night, officers George Smith and Henry Brown said Monday.

Underattribution On other occasions the attribution must be included in the lead. An Associated Press reference book comments, "Don't be afraid to begin a story by naming the source. It is awkward sometimes, but also sometimes is the best and most direct way to put the story in proper perspective and balance when the source must be established clearly in the reader's mind if he is properly to understand the story." An example:

> All Delawareans over 45 should be vaccinated now against Asian flu.

The attribution should have been in the lead because this is opinion, the consensus of a number of health officials.

Second-Day Lead on a First-Day Story Every veteran wire editor knows that frequently a wire story's first lead is better than its second, third or fourth. A lead telling the reader an airliner crashed today, killing 50 passengers, is better than a later lead reporting that an investigation is under way to determine the cause of an airline crash that killed 50 passengers. If the first lead tells the story adequately, why replace it with a second and often weaker lead?

The first lead:

> HOLYOKE, Mass—At least six persons—four of them children—perished early today when a fire, reportedly set by an arsonist, swept a five-story tenement.

The second lead (with a second-day angle):

> HOLYOKE, Mass—The body of a little boy about two years old was recovered today, raising the death toll in a tenement house fire to seven.

And the third lead (back on the beam):

> HOLYOKE, Mass—Seven persons—five of them children—perished when a general alarm midnight blaze, believed set, destroyed a five-story tenement.

Conversely, a first-day lead sounds like old news when placed on a second-day story. Copy editors allow such mistakes to appear in print when they fail to keep up with the news. It is important that copy editors read the newspaper each day. Those who don't fail to recognize whether the story is the first on the subject or a followup. That may make a big difference in the way the lead and headline are written.

Editing the Story Most experienced editors suggest that the editing process be divided into three distinct steps:

1. Read the story.
2. Edit it thoroughly.
3. Reread the story.

Copy editors frequently skip the first step or abbreviate it by scanning the story for the gist of the news. To do so may be a mistake because intelligent editing decisions cannot be made unless the copy editor understands the purpose of the story and the style in which it is written. That understanding is developed with a quick but thorough reading.

Some editors try to skip the third step, too. They do so at the risk of missing errors that should have been detected the first time or missing errors they introduced during the editing process. Few sins are greater on the copy desk than to introduce an error during the editing process. The more times a story is read, the more likely errors will be detected.

Unfortunately, deadline pressures sometimes dictate that step one or three, or both, be skipped. When this is done, it becomes increasingly important for the copy editor to do a thorough job the first time through the story.

To illustrate the editing process, let's see how one copy editor edited this story on the defeat of a bill in the Missouri General Assembly:

(BLUE LAW)

(BFC)] State capital bureau [

~~Missouri's city streets and stores will continue to be deserted on Sundays, at least for another year.~~

JEFFERSON CITY —

The House Tuesday afternoon rejected a bill that would have sub~~mitted the~~ mitted the repeal of the state's blue laws to the voters in November.

The measure was ~~soundly~~ defeated 97-53, ~~with two members present but not voting.~~

~~The~~ state's blue laws, or Sunday closing laws, prohibit ~~the~~ Sunday sales of nonessential ~~chosen merchandise~~ goods, including automobiles, clothing, jewelry and hardware items.

During a ~~lengthy~~ four-hour debate ~~that lasted four hours~~, the original bill was amended twice. ~~several times~~ One amendment would have placed ~~to place~~ the issue on this November ballot, and another would have required ~~The bill also was amended to require~~ that counties and cities decide whether to ~~exercise local option to approve~~ repeal ~~of blue~~ the blue laws ~~locally if the~~ within their jurisdictions. ~~measure was approved by voters in Nov.~~

Several amendments were defeated. One ~~that~~ would have required employers to ~~pay as much as twice the wages per hour~~ increase wages for employees ~~working~~ employed ~~who~~ on Sundays. Another would have set a

~~Rep. James Russell, a Florissant Democrat, included in one amendment the proviso that employers be fined~~ fine $1,000 for each violation of the wage requirements. ~~His amendment lost.~~

(MORE)

(BLUE LAWS -- first add)

Another ~~amendment, introduced~~ defeated amendment, would ~~by Rep. Jerry McBride, St. Louis, would~~ have levied a ~~1¢~~ one-cent excise tax on retail businesses open on Sunday. Proceeds ~~ceeds~~ from this were to have gone to city and county treasuries.

~~The McBride amendment also was defeated.~~

~~During debate~~ much of the support for blue law repeal came from urban representatives whose ~~constituents~~ districts include large retail chain stores and businesses that supported repeal ~~of the existing law~~ during committee hearings.

~~In the end, the majority of the house agreed with Rep. Walter Meyer,~~

~~D-Bellefontaine Neighbors, that "this bill is all screwed up."~~

Area

~~Local~~ Democrat̶i̶c̶ ~~Reps.~~ Ray Hamlett of Ladonia, Joe Holt of Fulton and

John Rollins, of Columbia, and Republican Reps/ Larry Mead and Harold

Reisch all voted in favor of putting repeal on the ballot.

This alert copy editor recognized immediately that, while the lead was well-written, it also was inaccurate. The state's streets and stores are not deserted on Sundays. The reporter, reaching for a bright lead, overstated the case.

Because the story is from the newspaper's state capital bureau, it needs a dateline, which the copy editor inserted. The second paragraph became the lead and the third paragraph was tightened and combined with the second. Note that the editor struck the phrase "with two members present but not voting." In many states there is a difference between present but not voting and abstaining. An abstention allows the legislator to change his or her vote later; present but not voting does not. The copy editor decided that in this case it wasn't important, so the phrase was deleted.

The story is confusing as written, probably because the reporter was too close to the subject to realize that readers would have difficulty following its meaning. As the editor edited the story, fuzzy passages were clarified and the story was tightened. Distinction was made between the amendments that were adopted and defeated before the bill itself was defeated.

The editor deleted the next-to-last paragraph because the legislator quoted used a colloquialism that may have been offensive to some readers. Because it added nothing to the story, it was deleted.

The last paragraph illustrates how important it is to use common sense when editing. Conformity to the stylebook would have called for the identification of each legislator by party affiliation and district number. Because there are five of them, the paragraph would have been difficult to read. The editor decided that the legislators' hometowns gave more information to the reader than the district number, and grouping by party affiliation made the paragraph less awkward than it would have been if the editor had followed stylebook practice.

Such editing helps the reader make sense of the story. As a result, it is good editing.

5

Protecting the Language

Abusing English   Newspapers, because of their mass appeal, have a significant impact on the development—and deterioration—of English usage in the United States. If the quality of English usage is deteriorating, as many experts have charged, then newspapers must share the blame.

The copy editor plays a major role in protecting the language against abuse. One who knows how to spell, makes certain a story is written in proper English, recognizes and clarifies fuzzy passages, and protects the meaning of words is a valuable member of the staff. The copy editor who neglects those chores contributes to the erosion of the language, and, ultimately, to the detriment of communication. Clear writing, and correct spelling and grammar contribute to the ready communication of ideas.

Edwin Newman, television commentator and author of *Strictly Speaking* and *A Civil Tongue,* deplores the degradation of the language and asks, "Will America be the death of English?" He argues that it may be too much to hope for the stilted and pompous phrase, the slogan and the cliché to be banished, but he argues that they should not dominate the language.

The message was even more forcibly put by Wallace Carroll, former editor and publisher of the *Winston-Salem Journal & Sentinel:*

> The bastardization of our mother tongue is really a disaster for all of us in the news business. The English language is our bread and

butter, but when ground glass is mixed with flour and grit with the butter, our customers are likely to lose their appetite for what we serve them.

Our job is to interpret—to translate. Yet our translators—that is our reporters and copy editors—find it more and more difficult to do this basic job of translation. To begin with, they reach us from universities that are tending to become glorified jargon factories, and for four years or more they have been immured in a little cosmos where jargon is too often mistaken for knowledge or wisdom.[1]

Carroll is correct in his assessment, but it is important to remember that language is always changing. As columnist James J. Kilpatrick writes:

Ours is a constantly changing language. In speech, as in anything else, the acceptability of change is a matter of personal taste. [Some object] to "host" as a verb—"Johnny Carson hosted the show." I, too, would object. Neither have I yielded to "chair," as in "He chaired the committee." Yet my ear is no longer offended by "to service," "to intern," "to model," "to vacation."[2]

Despite this, it is not the job of the copy editor to initiate change in the language. That role is better left to others. Copy editors serve their readers best by ensuring that copy conforms to accepted standards. With that in mind, let's review some of the common problems of spelling, grammar and usage.

Spelling

One reason so many misspelled words escape the attention of the copy desk is that copy editors are unable to recognize incorrect spelling, even of simple words. Here is a list of the most frequently misspelled words:

accede	asinine	buses (vehicles)
accommodate	ax*	busses (kisses)
accumulate		
adherence	balloon	Canada geese
admissible	battalion	caress
advertent	bellwether	cave-in
advertise	berserk	chaperon
adviser*	blond (adj., noun	cigarette
all right	for male)	commitment
alleged	blonde (noun for	consensus
allotted, allotment	female)	consistent
appall	boyfriend	consul

*Preferred spelling. Words in parentheses also indicate common newspaper usage.

1. *The Bulletin of the American Society of Newspaper Editors,* May 1970, p. 2.

2. James J. Kilpatrick, syndicated column for the Washington *Star* Syndicate, August 1969.

controversy
council
counsel

demagogue
descendant
dietitian
disastrous
dissension
drunkenness

embarrass
emphysema
employee*
exhilarating

feud
firefighter
fraudulent
fulfill

gaiety
goodbye*
grammar
greyhound
grisly
guerrilla

hangar (aircraft
shelter)
hanger (hanging
device)
harass
hemorrhage
hitchhiker

impostor
incredible
indestructible
indispensable
irresistible

judgment*

kidnapped*

lambastes
largess
liaison
likable
liquefy

mantel (shelf)
mantle (covering)
marijuana
marshal

nerve-racking

occasion
occurred

papier-mache
parallel
paraphernalia
pastime
penicillin
percent*
percentage
permissible
personnel
picnicking
pinscher
playwright
politicking
pompon
preceding
principal (main)
principle (concept)
privilege
procedure
prostate
publicly

quandary
questionnaire
queue

rarefy
reconnaissance
restaurateur
rock 'n' roll (rock-
and-roll)

sacrilegious
seize
separate
siege
sizable
skillful
stationary (not
movable)
stationery (writing
material)
strait-laced
strong-arm
subpoena
summonses
supersede

teen-age (adj.)
teen-ager (noun)
theater*
tumultuous

vacuum
vice versa
vilify

weird
whiskey* (whisky
for Scotch)
wield
wondrous

x-ray (noun, verb
and adj.)

Good editors learn to check all words about which they have doubts. The best have more doubts than the worst.

*Preferred spelling. Words in parentheses also indicate common newspaper usage.

Grammar

Grammatical problems help to destroy a newspaper's credibility among its well-educated readers. Grammatical errors can destroy otherwise clear writing or distort the meaning of a sentence. Let's review the parts of speech:

The Parts of Speech

To understand the English language and how it works, one first must know the eight parts of speech. They are *verbs, nouns, pronouns, adjectives* (including the articles), *adverbs, prepositions, conjunctions* and *interjections.* Let's review the uses of each.

Verbs

A verb is a word or group of words that expresses action or state of being. There are two kinds of verbs, finite and non-finite (or verbal). The finite verb works with the subject of the sentence to give a sense of completeness. A non-finite verb works as a nominal, much as a noun, or as a modifier. Compare the two:

Finite	Non-finite
The police *charged* him with robbery.	The police, *having charged* him with robbery . . .

Let's discuss finite verbs now and take up the verbals later.

Person and Number   Finite verbs can be distinguished by *person* (first, second and third) and *number* (singular and plural). Most verbs have a different form only in the third person singular of the present tense:

	Singular	Plural
First Person	I drink	we drink
Second Person	you drink	you drink
Third Person	he (she, it) *drinks*	they drink

An exception is the verb *to be:*

	Singular	Plural
First Person	I am	we are
Second Person	you are	you are
Third Person	he (she, it) *is*	they are

Verbs also frequently have *auxiliary,* or helping, verbs. These can be:

1. Modal auxiliaries. Examples of these auxiliaries, which are added to the main verb, are *will, would, can* and *must:* He *will go* to the store.
2. Perfect auxiliaries. These consist of a form of the verb *have* fol-

lowed by a verb with an *-en* or *-ed* ending: He *has walked* to the store.
3. Progressive auxiliaries. These are a part of the verb *be* plus an *-ing* ending: He *was going* to the store.
4. Passive auxiliaries. These are a part of the verb *be* plus an *-en* or *-ed* ending: He *had walked* to the store.

Moods, Voices and Tenses   Other properties of verbs, in addition to person and number, are *moods, voices* and *tenses.* The three moods, *indicative, imperative* and *subjunctive,* indicate differences in the intention of the writer or speaker. The indicative mood is used to make an assertion or to ask a question:

- The man *drove* to the store.
- Where *is* he *going?*

The imperative mood is used for commands, directions or requests:

- Command: *Drive to the store.*
- Direction: *Take* the next right turn.
- Request: Please *drive* me to the store.

The subjunctive mood expresses a condition contrary to fact: "If I *were* wealthy, I would quit work." In this case, the speaker indicates an absence of wealth, so the expression is contrary to fact. The present tense forms of the subjunctive are *(if) I be, (if) you be, (if) he, she* or *it be, (if) we be, (if) you be* and *(if) they be.* The past tense forms are *(if) I were, (if) you were, (if) he, she* or *it were, (if) we were, (if) you were* and *(if) they were.* Unlike other verbs, which differ in the third person singular of the present tense, the subjunctive remains the same: *(if) he drive,* not *if he drives.*

Journalists prefer the *active voice* of verbs rather than the *passive voice* because in the active voice the subject of the sentence does the acting:

The *president fired* the secretary of state.

In the passive voice, the subject of the sentence is acted upon:

The *secretary of state was fired* by the president.

The passive voice therefore diverts attention from the person doing the acting to the person or thing being acted upon. In some cases, the writer or editor may find that preferable:

The *president was shot* today by a man who dislikes his foreign policy.

Clearly, in such a case the person acted upon is more important than the person doing the acting. But in most cases the active voice is better. It is more direct and less wordy.

The most common tenses in English are the *present tense,* the *past tense* and the *future tense.* These three tenses indicate the time *now,* the time *past* and the time *to come.* The action of the verb also can be shown to have occurred at some definite time in the present, past or future. This state is indicated by the three *perfect* tenses, which denote perfected, or finished, action or state of being. Finally there are the *progressive tenses,* which are used to indicate action that is continuing or progressing in the present, past or future. Thus, various first-person forms of the verb *to see:*

* Present: *I see*
* Past: *I saw*
* Future: *I shall see*
* Present Perfect: *I have seen*
* Past Perfect: *I had seen*
* Future Perfect: *I shall have seen*
* Present Progressive: *I am seeing*
* Past Progressive: *I was seeing*
* Future Progressive: *I shall be seeing*
* Present Perfect Progressive: *I have been seeing*
* Past Perfect Progressive: *I had been seeing*
* Future Perfect Progressive: *I shall have been seeing*

The progressives are wordy and awkward, and therefore are seldom used. On occasion, however, they are useful tenses to indicate degrees of past or ongoing action. A verb that in its own meaning already expresses continuity does not need a progressive form. Thus, it is unnecessary to write, "I am living in Utah." In this case, "I live in Utah" is adequate. But compare these sentences:

> She *drove* to the store.
> She *was driving* to the store.

The second accurately stresses the continuity of the action.

Here are the principal parts of the verb *to be* and its conjugation:

* Infinitive: *to be*
* Perfect infinitive: *to have been*
* Present participle: *being*
* Present perfect participle: *having been*
* Past participle: *been*

Indicative Mood

	Singular	Plural
	Present Tense	
First Person	I am	we are
Second Person	you are	you are
Third Person	he (she, it) is	they are

	Singular	Plural
	Past Tense	
First Person	I was	we were
Second Person	you were	you were
Third Person	he (she, it) was	they were
	Future Tense	
First Person	I shall be	we shall be
Second Person	you will be	you will be
Third Person	he (she, it) will be	They will be
	Present Perfect Tense	
First Person	I have been	we have been
Second Person	you have been	you have been
Third Person	he (she, it) has been	they have been
	Past Perfect Tense	
First Person	I had been	we had been
Second Person	you had been	you had been
Third Person	he (she, it) had been	they had been
	Future Perfect Tense	
First Person	I shall have been	we shall have been
Second Person	you will have been	you will have been
Third Person	he (she, it) will have been	they will have been

Imperative Mood

• be

Subjunctive Mood

• Present Tense: *if I (you, he, she, it, we, they) be*
• Past Tense: *if I (you, he, she, it, we, they) were*

Now let's conjugate a *regular verb,* one in which the past tense and past participle are formed by adding *-ed (destroyed)* or *-d (removed):*

Active Voice	Passive Voice
Infinitive: *to walk, walk*	*to be walked, be walked*
Perfect Infinitive: *to have walked*	*to have been walked*
Present Participle: *walking*	*being walked*
Perfect Participle: *having walked*	*having been walked*
Past Participle: *walked*	*been walked*

Indicative Mood

Singular	Plural	Singular	Plural
	Present Tense		
1. I walk	we walk	I am walked	we are walked
2. you walk	you walk	you are walked	you are walked

Singular	Plural	Singular	Plural
3. he (she, it) walks	they walk	he (she, it) is walked	they are walked

Past Tense

Singular	Plural	Singular	Plural
1. I walked	we walked	I was walked	we were walked
2. you walked	you walked	you were walked	you were walked
3. he (she, it) walked	they walked	he (she, it) was walked	they were walked

Future Tense

Singular	Plural	Singular	Plural
1. I shall walk	we shall walk	I shall be walked	we shall be walked
2. you will walk	you will walk	you will be walked	we shall be walked
3. he (she, it) will walk	they will walk	he (she, it) will be walked	they will be walked

Present Perfect Tense

Singular	Plural	Singular	Plural
1. I have walked	we have walked	I have been walked	we have been walked
2. you have walked	you have walked	you have been walked	you have been walked
3. he (she, it) has walked	they have walked	he (she, it) has been walked	they have been walked

Past Perfect Tense

Singular	Plural	Singular	Plural
1. I had walked	we had walked	I had been walked	we had been walked
2. you had walked	you had walked	you had been walked	you had been walked
3. he (she, it) had walked	they had walked	he (she, it) had been walked	they had been walked

Future Perfect Tense

Singular	Plural	Singular	Plural
1. I shall have walked	we shall have walked	I shall have been walked	we shall have been walked
2. you will have walked	you will have walked	you will have been walked	you will have been walked
3. he (she, it) will have walked	they will have walked	he (she, it) will have been walked	they will have been walked

Imperative Mood

• walk

Subjunctive Mood
Present Tense

if I (you, he, she, it, we, they)   if I (you, he she, it, we, they)
  walk   be walked

Past Tense

if I (you, he, she, it, we) walked   if I (you, he, she, it, we) were
                                        walked

Irregular verbs are those that do not follow the principle of adding *-ed* or *-d* to form the past tense and past participle. Some examples:

Infinitive and Present Tense	Past Tense	Past Participle
begin	began	begun
break	broke	broken
come	came	come
eat	ate	eaten
do	did	done
fly	flew	flown
have (has)	had	had
leave	left	left
lie	lay	lain
sit	sat	sat
tear	tore	torn
win	won	won

Verbs also are classified as *transitive* and *intransitive,* terms that describe their use in a sentence. Transitive verbs require objects to complete their meaning:

> The president *fired* the *secretary of state.*

Without the object, secretary of state, the sentence would be incomplete.

Intransitive verbs make assertions without requiring objects:

> The moon *shines.*
> The cowboy *is* on his horse.

Many verbs are both intransitive and transitive. An example:

> Intransitive: She *breathes.*
> Transitive: She *breathes* foul air.

Used in the intransitive manner, the verb indicates that the woman is alive. Used transitively, it refers to an experience she is having.

Verbals   Verbals are verbs that have lost their subjects, their ability to indicate definite time, and their ability to express such ideas as necessity, obligation and possibility. There are three kinds of verbals, *infinitives, present participles* and *past participles.*

Infinitives begin with the word *to.* Here are examples of infinitives in context:

> *To forgive* is divine. (present, active form)
> *To be forgiving* is divine. (present progressive, active form)
> She was happy *to have been forgiving.* (perfect passive form)
> *To have been forgiving* would have pleased her. (perfect passive form used as the subjunctive form of the infinitive)

In the active voice, a verb has two participles, present and past. The present participle, such as *milking,* expresses action in progress. The past participle, *milked,* expresses finished action. *Having milked* is a modified form of the past participle known as the perfect participle. The passive forms are *being milked* for the present, *milked* for the past, and *having been milked* for the perfect participle.

Participles are not considered parts of speech because they are used as adjectives and nouns, and in some cases stand alone. Here are some examples:

> Freedom *Enlightening* the Nation is the name of the statue on the campus. (*Enlightening* is a participle used as an adjective to modify Freedom.)
> *Acting* like a gentleman is *acting* properly. (The first *acting* is a participle used as the subject of a sentence. The second is used as a predicate noun.)
> *Granting* that, we still need to call the doctor. (The present participle *granting* is used independently.)

A present participle that functions as a noun is called a *gerund.* Some examples:

> *Swimming* is my favorite activity in the summer.
> *Drinking* too much is bad for your health.

Nouns

A noun is a person, place or thing. There are two kinds of nouns: *proper nouns* are used as titles for specific persons or places, and sometimes things; *common nouns* are used in the absence of a proper title. Proper nouns are capitalized; common nouns are not. An example:

> New York *City* is the nation's largest city.
> The *city* was built beside the river.

In the first sentence, *city* is a part of a title and therefore must be capitalized. In the second sentence, *city* is used as a common noun.

Nouns can be either singular or plural. Usually, the plural is formed by adding -*s* or -*es* to the end of the word: *jeep, jeeps; box, boxes.* But words ending in *y* and *f* sometimes change before a plural ending: *hoof, hooves; sky, skies.* Unfortunately, that's not always true: *roof, roofs.* Check a dictionary if you are in doubt. A complicating factor is that some nouns have irregular plural forms: *sheep, sheep; goose, geese.* And some nouns normally occur in the singular only: *dust,* not *dusts: courage,* not *courages.*

Nouns also can take the possessive case, and newspapers observe these rules:

1. Plural nouns not ending in *s:* Add *'s: the alumni's contributions, women's rights.*
2. Plural nouns ending in *s:* Add only an apostrophe: *the girls' pony, the ships' wake.*
3. Nouns plural in form but singular in meaning: Add only an apostrophe: *measles' effects, mathematics' rules.*
4. Singular nouns not ending in *s:* Add *'s: the church's needs, the girl's toys, Marx's theories.*
5. Singular common nouns ending in *s:* Add *'s* unless the next word begins with *s: the hostess's invitation, the hostess' seat.*
6. Singular proper nouns ending in *s:* Add only an apostrophe: *Ceres' rites, Socrates' life.*

For other rules that pertain to possessives, consult the wire service stylebooks.

Nouns have several possible uses in sentences. They can be used as:

1. The subject, object, or complement of a finite verb or verbal.
2. The object of a preposition.
3. A modifier following another noun, or an *appositive,* as it is called: my brother *Wesley.*
4. A modifier before another noun: a *noun* clause.
5. The modifier of an adjective or verb:
   They were *battle* weary. (modifies the adjective *weary*)
   They left *Monday.* (modifies the verb *left*)

Pronouns

A pronoun takes the place of a noun in a sentence. When pronouns replace other words, they take the meaning of those replaced words. The replaced words are known as the *antecedent* of the pronoun. The antecedent usually is a noun and its modifiers, but it can be a complete sentence. Some examples:

The man hit *his* head on the door. (*His* replaces *the man.*)
I have suggested to my brother, *who* lives in Phoenix, that we consider a joint vacation. (*Who* replaces *my brother.*)
The Atlanta Braves have a good team this year. *That* means the

Braves could win the pennant. (*That* replaces the full sentence establishing that the Braves have a good team.)

There are several types of pronouns: *personal, relative, interrogative, demonstrative, indefinite* and *intensive.*

Personal pronouns have *cases*, either *nominative, possessive* or *objective; person*, either *first, second* or *third;* and *number*, either *singular* or *plural:*

First Person

Case	Singular	Plural
Nominative	I	we
Possessive	my, mine	our, ours
Objective	me	us

Second Person

Case	Singular	Plural
Nominative	you	you
Possessive	your, yours	your, yours
Objective	you	you

Third Person

Case	Singular			Plural
	Masculine	*Feminine*	*Neuter*	
Nominative	he	she	it	they
Possessive	his	her, hers	its	their, theirs
Objective	him	her	it	them

Relative pronouns are those imbedded inside sentences to help the writer avoid the repetition of nouns:

The butter—the butter he bought yesterday—is already gone.
The butter, *which* he bought yesterday, is already gone.

The relative pronouns are *who, whom, whose, that* and *which*. Sometimes the relative pronoun can be omitted:

The butter he bought yesterday is already gone.

Interrogative pronouns are used to introduce questions. They are *who, whom, whose, which* and *what:*

Who will win the marathon?
Whose shirt is that in the washing machine?

The demonstrative pronouns, *this, these, that* and *those*, indicate nearness to or distance from the speaker:

This is my best chance to succeed.
Those shirts in the washing machine are mine.

Indefinite pronouns have vague or unknown antecedents. They include words such as *somebody, everyone, whoever, all, each* and *either:*

> *Somebody* stole my laundry basket.
> *Each* of the girls in the class is smart.

Intensive pronouns, which end with *self* or *selves,* repeat and intensify the noun antecedent:

> I shot *myself* in the leg.
> Jim *himself* will pitch the ninth inning.

Myself should not be used in place of *me:*

> Professor Barrett gave A's to Sandra and *me* (not *myself*).

The *nominative, objective* and *possessive* cases mentioned earlier have various uses. The nominative pronouns, *I, we, you, he, she, it, they, who* and *whoever,* are to serve as the subject, to serve as the subject repeated, to express the subject when the verb is deleted and to follow the verb *be:*

> Marilyn and *I* are close friends. (subject)
> Marilyn and I, *who* are close friends, will go to the party together. (subject repeated)
> She is a better mathematician than *he.* (implied verb *is* deleted)
> It is *I.* (following a form of the verb *be*)

The pronouns used in the objective case, also known as the *accusative,* are *me, us, her, him, them, who* and *whomever.* The objective case is used to express the object of a verb, verbal or preposition; to express the object repeated; to express the object when the verb is deleted; and to express the nominal before the infinitive:

> She forced *me* to take the Fifth Amendment. (direct object of verb)
> Give the ticket to *whomever* the police found illegally parked. (object of preposition)
> Many of *us* coal miners have black lung disease. (object repeated)
> She did not rank him as highly as *me.* (verb deleted; read it *she did me*)
> The Tigers wanted *him* to be traded to the Red Sox. (nominal before infinitive)

Possessive pronouns, as the name implies, show possession of things. But the possessive case, also known as the *genitive,* can be used to show independent possession:

Regular Possessives	Independent Possessives
my	mine
our	ours
your	yours
her	hers
his	his
its	its
their	theirs
whose	whose

Some examples of usage:

> I think *my husband* will mow the grass today. (regular)
> I like *mine* better. (independent)

Possessives are determinants used before nouns, but a possessive also may function in a gerund phrase as the introductory word:

> *Her* dropping the course was ridiculous, the professor said.

Adjectives

Adjectives are words that add to the meaning of nouns or pronouns. In this sense an adjective describes, limits or modifies the noun or pronoun to make it clearer. The two major kinds of adjectives are *descriptive* and *limiting.* An adjective that answers the question *what kind?* is a descriptive adjective:

> The *handsome* man stepped out of the coach.

Handsome in the sentence above is a *common adjective,* which is one of three kinds of descriptive adjectives. Others are *participial adjectives* (the *dried* fruit) and *proper adjectives* (the *Indian* princess). A descriptive adjective sometimes is used to complete the meaning of the verb *to be* or any of its forms. When used that way, the adjective is known as a *predicate adjective.* Other verbs, including *seem, look, feel* and *taste,* also may be followed by predicate adjectives:

> The milkshake tastes *sweet.*

Descriptive adjective sometimes can be used as the subject of a sentence when the article *the* is placed in front of them:

> The *loneliest* call the hot line regularly.

The other major form of adjective, the limiting adjective, tells how many, how often, what number or what amount:

> The *five* generals paid homage to George VI.

The articles—*a, an,* and *the*—form a special group of limiting adjectives.

All adjectives except the four *demonstrative* ones, *this, that, these* and *those,* change form to show difference in amount or degree. There are three degrees of comparison, *positive, comparative,* and *superlative.* Most adjectives of more than one syllable form the comparative by using *more* or *less* in front of the adjective. The superlative is formed the same way by using *most* and *least:*

Positive	Comparative	Superlative
thorough	more thorough	most thorough
willing	more willing	least willing

The endings *-er* or *-est* are added to most adjectives of one syllable to form the comparative and superlative:

Positive	Comparative	Superlative
clear	clearer	clearest
strong	stronger	strongest

Some words, however, have irregular comparisons: *good, well; many, much; better, best.*

Adverbs

Adverbs change or add to the meaning of verbs. They are words that help verbs, just as adjectives help nouns. Adverbs are classified three ways by use. The first is *simple* adverbs, which are used to modify:

She looked *happily* at her elder son.

The second use is as *conjunctive* adverbs:

He took the bottle home; *however,* he did not drink.

The conjunctive adverbs include *therefore, consequently, moreover, nevertheless, accordingly, otherwise,* and *wherefore.* The third classification of adverbs by use is *interrogative:*

When did he take the big step?

Adverbs also are classified by time, place, degree, manner and assertion. For details of those usages, consult a grammar book.

Like adjectives, some adverbs have comparative and superlative forms:

Positive	Comparative	Superlative
fast	faster	fastest
soon	sooner	soonest
little	less	least
well	better	best

Prepositions

A preposition is a connecting word that shows a relationship between its object and some other word in the sentence. Common prepositions include *in, on, at, by, against, above, upon, from, of, without, under, over, through* and *during.* There are many others.

The object of the preposition must be in the objective case, except when the object is a double possessive:

> The museum has several hats *of Washington's.*

The object may be a noun, an adjective or adverb used as a noun, an infinitive, a participle or a clause. All, however, must be used as nouns.

Conjunctions

Another connecting word is the conjunction, which is used to connect words, phrases, clauses and sentences. *Coordinating conjunctions* connect two words, phrases, clauses or sentences that are grammatically equal. Two independent clauses connected by a coordinating conjunction form a *compound sentence:*

> John will attend Harvard, *and* Mary plans to go to Yale.

Note that a coordinating conjunction must be preceded by a comma.

The coordinating conjunctions include *and, also, both, as well as, moreover, further, likewise, either, or, neither, nor, else, whether, otherwise, but, yet, still, only, nevertheless, whereas, therefore, hence, consequently, so, so that* and *thus.* Some conjunctions, such as *either* and *or* and *neither* and *nor,* come in pairs and are known as *correlative conjunctions.*

Subordinating conjunctions join a subordinate clause to the principal clause of a sentence. Such sentences are known as *complex sentences.* In this construction, the two elements are not grammatically equal:

> She can ride horses better *than* I can.

In this case, *than* connects the main clause, *She can ride horses better,* to the subordinate clause, *than I can.* (*ride horses* is understood).

Common subordinating conjunctions include *when, as, since, before, after, until, where, because, if, unless, although, though, even if, that, so that* and *in order that.*

Interjections

An interjection is a word used as an exclamation to express surprise, pain or some other intense emotion. It has no grammatical relation to other words and can be used alone. Some examples: *Ouch!, Whew!, Darn!, Help!* and *Oh!*

Usage

Knowing the parts of speech is essential to understanding the English language, but that alone is not enough. The real difficulty lies in trying to make words and sentences work together to convey meaning. Often, what *sounds* correct may not *be* correct because of common misuse. Let's examine some of the common misuses of the language.

Subject-Predicate Disagreement

The editors of *After the Fact,* internal publication of the *Louisville Courier-Journal,* lamented, "Everybody knows that subjects and verbs should come in matched pairs: singulars together and plurals together. But, sadly, we let too many unmarriageables slip into the paper." Some examples:

There are two things that either Sloane or Hollenbach have. . . .

The thought is: " . . . things that Sloane has or that Hollenbach has." Remember, when nouns are connected by either . . . or, neither . . . nor, ONLY the noun closest to the verb should be considered in deciding whether a singular or plural verb is required. If the second half of the noun is singular, use a singular verb, and vice versa.

. . . the continuing lag in industrial production and the rise in unemployment is a result of inflation.

Lag and rise *are* . . .

An American Bar Association accreditation team, in addition to a citizens' panel, have both recommended this.

"Team" is the subject; the verb must be "has." Parenthetical matter should be ignored in selecting the number of the verb.

It's moved to a point where the anxiety and the concern is unrealistic.

Anxiety and concern *are* . . .

The monotony of the concrete walls painted in dull green and blue are broken only . . .

Monotony *is* . . .

A two-thirds vote by both houses of Congress and ratification by three-quarters of the states is necessary.

Vote and ratification *are* . . .

Non Sequiturs

A non sequitur is an error in logic; the phrase means "it does not follow":

A guard at the Allied Kid Co., he died at 7:10 a.m., about five minutes after one of the youths implicated in the attack was taken into custody.

This implies that guards die at 7:10 a.m. Can we infer that workers die at 8:10 and executives at 9:10?

Worn on a chain with swivel and button, this model retails at $39.95.

How much does it cost if I just carry it loose in my pocket?

"Because breath is so vital to life," Burmeister explained, "the field of inhalation therapy and the development of breathing equipment have become increasingly important in medical science today."

It may be true that these things are increasingly important, but not because breath is vital to life. Breath was just as important to life 3,000 years ago as it is today.

Stored in an air-conditioned room in lower Manhattan, the tapes contain information on the reading habits of one million Americans.

The nature of the information on these tapes is not in any way related to the place of their storage, or the condition of the air there. An easy way to edit this sentence is to start with the subject: "The tapes, stored in an air-conditioned room in lower Manhattan, contain information. . . ."

Planned by Jones, Blake and Droza, Detroit architects, the new school has 18 classrooms in addition to such standard facilities as cafeteria and library.

This implies that it's a natural thing to expect a school planned by that particular firm to have 18 classrooms and the other features.

Completed three years ago, the plant is 301 feet by 339 feet and is a one-story structure containing. . . .

A plant of exactly that size could have been completed 50 years ago or yesterday.

This particular error crops up most frequently in obituaries:

Unmarried, Jones is survived by his mother, Mrs . . .

Born in Iowa, he worked on two newspapers in Illinois before coming to St. Louis.

Dangling Modifiers   The dangling modifier is one of the most common errors committed by beginning writers and by all who write in a hurry. The writer knows what is intended but doesn't say it, forcing the reader to rearrange the sentence to grasp its meaning. Some examples:

> If convicted of the assault and battery charge, a judge may impose any sentence he sees fit on the defendants.

"If convicted" applies to the defendants, not to the judge.

> Besides being cut on the left cheek and bloodied in the nose, Zeck's purse was attached for $825.

> Already hospitalized a month, doctors estimate it will be three or four months before he is out again.

> An E-shaped building, the fire started in the southwest wing.

> A "natural" fertilizer, he predicted that it would solve many problems.

> After blowing out the candles atop his birthday cake in three puffs, a movie camera flashed old fight films on the screen near the bar.

> The fluoroscopic system makes moving pictures and tape recordings of the mouth and throat while speaking, chewing and swallowing.

> Short and readable, I finished it off in about 45 minutes.

Relative Pronoun

No one can say what the most common grammatical errors in news writing are, but near the top must be the misuse of the relative pronoun.

Leon Stolz of the *Chicago Tribune* advised reporters and copy editors, "If you have trouble deciding whether the relative pronoun should be who or whom, you can usually find the right answer by remembering that *who* is nominative, like the personal pronouns *he, she* and *they. Whom* is objective, like *him, her* and *them.* Turn the clause into an independent sentence and substitute a personal pronoun for the relative pronoun."

Applying the Stolz formula:

> After his decision to cancel the trip, he sent most of the officials who he had invited to attend.

He invited *they* to attend?

> The repeal gives property owners absolute freedom in deciding who they will rent or sell to.

They will rent to *they*?

> Miss Barbara Warren, who he met while they were medical students at Passavant Hospital. . . .

He met *she*?

> In his last eight games, covering 13⅔ innings, the skinny Texan, who teammates call "Twiggy," has held opponents scoreless.

They call *he* Twiggy?

> The paper said two residents of the housing project were known to have been a young man whom they said looked like the description of the sniper.

They said *him* looked like the description of the sniper?

Reporters and copy editors frequently have trouble distinguishing between *that* and *which*. *That* is preferred when introducing restrictive (essential) clauses that refer to inanimate objects, places, ideas and animals, *which* introduces nonrestrictive (nonessential) clauses which are nondefining and parenthetical. Two examples:

> The river that flows northward through Egypt is the Nile.

> The Missouri River, which flows into the Mississippi at St. Louis, is cleaner than it was 10 years ago.

Note that nonrestrictive clauses are set off with commas.

Word Clutter

Clutter words dirty a newspaper, waste space and get in the reader's way. Every day, stories die because strings of clutter words didn't die at the typewriter or on the copy desk.

Reporters should be whacked when they write:

> She was on the operating table from 8 p.m. *last night* until 5 a.m. *this morning.*

Last night and *this morning* are *redundant.*

> For mankind, *the biologists who study genetics* seem to offer . . .

Try *geneticists.*

> He was a Democratic nominee for *U.S.* Congress from the 7th *Congressional* District but lost in the *final* election to *incumbent* Rep. Donald W. Riegle Jr.

Not everyone can get four redundancies into one sentence.

> He said the USDA is *currently* spending . . .
> Justice said Double Spring had been *in the process of* phasing out its operation . . .
> Hayley has some 30 *different* (fish) tanks in his home.
> Retired Adm. Jackson R. Tate slipped away to a secret retreat yesterday for his *first meeting* with the daughter *he has never met* . . .

Compression, shortcuts to ideas, is one of the cardinal virtues of good writing. "The field is 50 feet in length" should be "The field is 50 feet long." "He is said to be resentful" means simply, "He is said to resent."

Pacing is gained by substituting short words for long words and single words for phrases: "big" for "enormous," "find" for "discover," "approving" for "applying its stamp of approval,"

"Smith's failure" for "the fact that Smith had not succeeded," "field work" for "work in the field."

Compression eliminates the superfluous: "pledged *to secrecy* not to disclose," "wrote a formal letter of resignation" ("resigned"), "read from a *prepared* statement," "go into details" ("elaborate"). A few words may say a lot; a lot of words may say little.

Most experienced copy editors can add to this list of circumlocutions:

A bolt of lightning (lightning)

A great number of times
   (often, frequently)

A large number of (many)

A period of several weeks
   (several weeks)

A small number of (few)

A sufficient number of
   (enough)

Absolute guarantee
   (guarantee)

Accidentally stumbled
   (stumbled)

Advance planning (planning)

Advance reservations
   (reservations)

All of a sudden (suddenly)

As a general rule (usually)

Assessed a fine (fined)

At a later date (later)

At the hour of noon (at noon)

At the present time (now)

At 12 noon (at noon)

At 12 midnight (at midnight)

At the conclusion of (after)

At the corner of 16th and Elm
   (at 16th and Elm)

Bald-headed (bald)

Called attention to the fact
   (reminded)

Climb up (climb)

Commute back and forth
   (commute)

Completely decapitated
   (decapitated)

Completely destroyed
   (destroyed)

Completely surrounded
   (surrounded)

Consensus of opinion
   (consensus)

Cost the sum of $5 (cost $5)

Despite the fact that
   (although)

Disclosed for the first time
   (disclosed)

Draw to a close (end)

Due to the fact that (because)

During the winter months
   (during the winter)

End result (result)

Entered a bid of (bid)

Exact replica (replica)

Exchanged wedding vows
   (married)

Few in number (few)

Filled to capacity (filled)

First priority (priority)

First prototype (prototype)

For a period of 10 days (for 10
   days)

Foreign imports (imports)

Free gift (gift)

Free pass (pass)

General public (public)

Grand total (total)

Heat up (heat)

Hostile antagonist (antagonist)

Incumbent governor
   (governor)

In addition to (and, besides, also)
In back of (behind)
In case of (if, concerning)
In order to balance (to balance)
In the absence of (without)
In the event that (if)
In the immediate vicinity of (near)
In the near future (soon)
In the not too distant future (eventually)
Introduced a new (introduced)
Is going to (will)
Is in the process of making application (is applying)
Is of the opinion that (believes)

Jewish rabbi (rabbi)

Kept an eye on (watched)

Large-sized man (large man)
Lift up (lift)

Made good his escape (escaped)
Major portion of (most of)
Married his wife (married)
Merged together (merged)
Midway between (between)

New bride (bride)
New construction (construction)
New innovation (innovation)
New record (record)

Off of (off)
Old adage (adage)
Old cliché (cliché)
On account of (because)
On two different occasions (twice)
Once in a great while (seldom, rarely)

Partially damaged (damaged)
Partially destroyed (damaged)
Past history (history)
Period of time (period)
Placed its seal of approval on (approved)
Possibly might (might)
Postponed until later (postponed)
Prior to (before)
Promoted to the rank of (promoted to)

Qualified expert (expert)

Receded back (receded)
Recur again (recur)
Reduce down (reduce)
Refer back (refer)
Remand back (remand)
Revise downward (lower)
Rise up (rise)
Rose to the defense of (defended)

Self-confessed (confessed)
Short space of time (short time)
Since the time when (since)
Sprung a surprise (surprised)
Started off with (started with)
Strangled to death (strangled)
Summer season (summer)
Sworn affidavits (affidavits)

Tendered his resignation (resigned)
There is no doubt that (doubtless)
Total operating costs (operating costs)
True facts (facts)

Underground subway (subway)
United in holy matrimony (married)
Upward adjustment (increase)

Voiced objections (objected) Widow of the late (widow)

             With the exception of (except)

Went up in flames (burned)

Whether or not (whether)   Young juveniles (juveniles)

Wrong Words Good reporters are meticulous in presenting the facts for a story. Others are not so precise in their choice of words. By habit, they write "compose" when they mean "comprise," "affect" when they want "effect," "credible" for "creditable." They use "include," then list all the elements.

Each time a word is misused it loses some of its value as a precision tool. AP reported that "U.S. officials connived with ITT." There was no connivance, which means closing one's eyes to wrongdoing. The precise word would have been "conspired," if, indeed, that is the charge.

Note these examples that got by the copy desk:

> He has been an "intricate part of the general community".... (The writer meant "integral," meaning essential.)

> The two officers are charged with dispersing corporate funds.... (The word is "disburse"—to pay out, to expend. Disperse means to scatter in various directions; distribute widely.)

> A story indicating that a man might not be qualified for his job says: "Miller refutes all that," and then he says why he is capable. ("Denies" would have been much better.)

> A football pass pattern was referred to as a "flair out." ("Flair" means a natural talent or aptitude. The word is "flare" or expanding outward in shape or configuration.)

> Mrs. Reece, a spritely woman . . . (She may be a sprite—an elf or pixie—but what the writer probably meant was "sprightly"— full of life.)

> His testimony about the night preceding the crime was collaborated, in part, by his mother.... ("corroborated," perhaps?)

> The MSD could be the biggest benefactor in Kentucky under a ... reimbursement program. (It should be "beneficiary," one who receives; "benefactor" is the giver.)

Other terms frequently misused:

- Adopted, passed—resolutions are adopted or approved; bills are passed. In legislative jargon, *passed* also can mean passed by for the day or for that meeting.
- Aggravate, irritate—the first means to make worse. The second means to incite or provoke.
- Amateur, novice—an *amateur* is a nonprofessional. A *novice* is a beginner.
- Amount, number—*amount* indicates the general quantity. *Number* indicates an enumerable quantity.

* And, but—**State treasurer is Democrat but also servant of people,** the headline said. The implication here is that the official is a servant of the people despite being Democrat.
* Avenge, revenge—*avenge* for another. *Revenge* for self.
* Bale, bail—a farmer's hay is *baled;* water is *bailed* out of a boat; a prisoner is released on *bail.* (*Bond* is cash or property given as a security for an appearance or for some performance.)
* Biannual, biennial—the first means twice a year. The second means every two years. The copy editor could help the reader by substituting "every six months" for *biannual* and "every other year" for *biennial.*
* Bills, legislation—"The president announced he will send Congress legislation aimed at liberalizing trade with Eastern Europe." *Legislation* is the laws enacted by a legislative power. The president, of course, is not such a power. What he sends to Congress is proposed legislation or bills.
* Canvas, canvass—the first is a cloth. The second means to solicit.
* Celebrant, celebrator—a *celebrant* presides over a religious rite. A *celebrator* celebrates.
* Center around—something can be centered in, centered at or centered on, but it cannot be centered around.
* Collision—"Cars driven by Robert F. Clagett and Mrs. Lois Trant were damaged yesterday when they collided on Denison Avenue. Stonington police reported that Mrs. Trant stopped her car before making a turn into Isham Street and it was hit in the rear by the other vehicle." Two objects can *collide* only when both are in motion and going—usually but not always—in opposite directions. It is not a *collision* when one car is standing still.
* Compared with, compared—the first uses specific similarities or differences: "He *compared* Johnson with Wilson." The second notes general or metaphysical resemblance: "You might *compare* him to a weasel."
* Comprise, compose—*comprise* is not synonymous with *compose,* but actually almost its opposite. "The secretaries of State, Defense, Interior and other departments compose the cabinet." That is, they constitute it. "The cabinet comprises the secretaries of the state, Defense, Interior and other departments." That is, it includes, embraces, contains them.
* Concert, recital—two or more performers give a *concert.* One performer gives a recital.
* Continuous, continual—if it rains steadily every day for a week it rains *continuously.* If it rains only part of every day for a week it rains *continually* or intermittently.
* Damage, damages—the first means loss or harm; the second is a legal word meaning money paid or ordered to be paid as compensation for loss or injury. The plural has no other meaning.
* Ecology, environmental—ecology is concerned with the interre-

lationship of organisms and their environment. Environmental refers to conditions or forces that influence or modify surroundings.

- Farther, further—the distinction is between extension of space and expansion of thought.
- Flaunt, flout—the first means to wave or flutter showily. The second means to mock or treat with contempt. "The students *flouted* the authority of the school board."
- Flounder, founder—horses *flounder*—struggle, thrash about—in the mud. Ships *founder* or sink. Of course, horses can founder when they become disabled from overeating.
- Grant, subsidy—a *grant* is money given to public companies. A *subsidy* is help to a private enterprise.
- Grizzly, grisly—"Miss Karmel begins her work in a valley of shadows that deepen and darken as she heaps one grizzly happening upon the next." One *grizzly* heaped upon the next produces only two angry bears. The word the writer wants is *grisly.*
- Half-mast, half-staff—masts are on ships. Flagstaffs are mounted on buildings or in the ground.
- Hardy, hearty—a story of four visiting policemen from Africa said they expressed appreciation for their hardy welcome. If that's what they said, they meant *hearty.*
- Hopeful, hopefully—incorrect for "it is hoped" or "I hope." Literally, "in a hopeful manner."
- Impassable, impassible—the first is that which cannot be passed. The second is that which can't suffer or be made to show signs of emotion.
- Imply, infer—the speaker does the *implying,* and the listener the *inferring.*
- Mean, median—*mean* is the average. If the high is 80 and the low is 50, the mean is 65. *Median* means that half are above a certain point, half below.
- Oral, verbal—all language is *verbal*—"of words." But only *oral* language is spoken. Verbal refers to the written form.
- People, persons—*person* is the human being. *People* are the body of persons—"American people." There is no rule saying a large number can't be referred to as *people*—"61 million people."
- Retire, resign, replace—*replace* for *retire* is a cold, curt and cruel word with which to publicly acknowledge years of faithful and interested service. Subtle differences in words can be important. To say that someone has quit a job when he resigned to accept another suggests that he left in a huff.
- Sewage, sewerage—*sewage* is human waste, sometimes called municipal or sanitary waste. *Sewerage* is the system to carry away sewage. They are sewerage (not sewage) plants. Industrial waste is the waste from factories. Some cities have storm sewers to carry away rain water and sanitary sewers for sewage.
- Sustenance, subsistence—"The two survived despite little

besides melted snow for subsistence." No wonder they almost
starved. The word is *sustenance.*

- Tall, high—properly, a building, tree or man is *tall.* A plane, bird
or cloud is *high.*

Reader-stoppers   An ear for language is as important as an eye for grammar. "This
doesn't sound right," the copy editor protests after spotting fuzzy
passages. Careful reading of copy and careful editing will enable
the copy editor to ferret out unclear or nonsensical expressions.

As explained by one engineer to Reed, one of the reasons for the
high cost of repairing the streets is that the space between the concrete and the ground presents problems of pumping liquid concrete between.

We can only hope that Reed understands.

Gangs of white rowdies roamed the area last night attacking cars
bearing blacks with baseball bats, bricks and stones.

Who had the bats?

Three counties, Meigs, Pike and Vinton, get more than 85 percent
from the state. Morgan gets 90.3 percent.

How many counties?

Many of the 800 executives and clerical people will be transferred,
and some probably will be eliminated.

That's rough on people.

In Bedford Hospital with a bullet wound in his left chest is Sal-
vatore Carcione.

A person has but one chest.

Victims in the other cars were not hurt.

Then why were they victims?

Monday will be the first day of a new way of delivering an
expanded hot-meal program to senior citizens in Genesse County.

Would the "program" or the "meals" be delivered?

The delegation ... was welcomed by 20,000 mostly black
supporters.

What color was the other part of each supporter?

Many of the players hovered around 5 feet 2.

They must have looked funny up in the air like that.

> Indignant at being arrested after waiving extradition, Graham lashed out . . .

Was he indignant because of the facts leading to his extradition, or to his arrest?

A misplaced time element leads to awkward construction.

> Parents protesting the closing of Briensburg School yesterday tried to. . . .

Did they protest yesterday only? Was the school closed yesterday? Or did they "try to" yesterday?
Another:

> Phillips, acting chairman yesterday of a parent steering committee, said, "All or none."

Was he acting chairman yesterday only? If so, when did he deliver the quote?

Omission

> Dodson told police he had awakened and found his wife missing.

He didn't wake up and find her missing. He woke and found that his wife was missing.

> Robert Lowell, Pulitzer Prize-winning American poet who refused a White House invitation to express his disapproval of American policies, has been nominated. . . .

The writer meant to say Lowell refused the invitation because of his disapproval.

Wrong Word Order

> An insufficient water supply problem for firefighting at Fitch Senior School will be discussed next Thursday.

Try this: "The problem of insufficient water supply for firefighting at Fitch. . . "

> White segregationists waving Confederate flags and black integrationists marched past each other yesterday

Or did white segregationists waving flags march past black integrationists yesterday?

> Joseph H. Hughes Jr. of Los Angeles wrote to many of his late son's, Coast Guard Ensign Joseph H. Hughes III, friends.

Translation: "wrote to many friends of his late son. . . ."

Confusing Antecedent

> The accidental ruling by the coroner last month removed the possibility of suicide in Miss McDonald's death.

The coroner did not make an accidental ruling. He made an accidental-death ruling.

> Donald Vann, 22, was fined $25 yesterday on two charges after being accused of hitting a waitress during an argument with a crutch.

Who won the argument, Donald or the crutch?

> His head shaved and drugged with sleeping pills, the youngster was dropped off on a residential street.

Does this mean the victim's head was shaved with sleeping pills?

> Miss Adele Hudlin agreed to give the dog a home, even though she already had two of her own.

Does she have two homes or two dogs?

> They (the Smiths) have been married 24 years and have two children. Both are 53.

Misuse of Adjectives Effective adjectives strengthen nouns if they are informative rather than descriptive: "7-foot Steve Stipanovich" rather than "towering Steve Stipanovich."

Many adjectives are redundant, "loaded," incorrect or misplaced.

- Redundant—armed gunmen, chilly 30 degrees below zero, exact replica, foreign imports.
- Editorial adjectives—blistering reply, cocky labor leader, so-called liberal, strong words.
- Incorrect adjectives—"Whirring or grinding television cameras": television cameras are electronic devices and do not whir or grind. "A Pole with an unpronounceable name": every name is pronounceable by somebody. "An unnamed man": every man has a name; the adjective should be *unidentified.*
- Improperly placed adjectives—"Unfair labor practices strike": the practices, not the strike, are unfair. "The treacherous 26-mile Arkansas down-river race": the river, not the race, is treacherous.

Searching for the right word takes time. Editors urge copy editors to omit an adjective rather than to rely on a shoddy term.

Clichés A good writer uses a fresh and appropriate figure of speech to enhance the story. The copy editor should distinguish between the fresh and the stale. This isn't always easy because some words and phrases are used repeatedly in the news report.

The Associated Press ran nearly 400,000 words of its copy through a computer to determine which of the tired words and phrases were used most frequently. The result: hailed, backlash, in the wake of, informed, violence flared, kickoff, death and destruction, riot-torn, tinder dry, racially troubled, voters marched to the polls, jam-packed, grinding crash, confrontation, oil-rich nation, no immediate comment, cautious (or guarded) optimism, limped into port.

Copy editors can add to the list of tired expressions:

Acid test
Area girl
Average (reader, voter, etc.)

Banquet (never a dinner)
Belt tightening
Bitter (dispute)
Blistering (accusation)
Bloody riot
Bombshell (announcement, etc.)
Boost
Briefing
Brutal (murder, slaying)

Cardinal sin
Caught the eye of ·
Controversial issue
Coveted trophy
Crack (troops, train, etc.)
Cutback

Daring (holdup, etc.)
Deficit-ridden
Devastating (flood, fire)
Devout (Catholic, etc.)
Do your own thing
Dumped

-ees (trainees, escapees)
Experts
Eye (to see)
Eyeball to eyeball

Fiery holocaust
Fire broke out, swept
Fire of undetermined origin
Foot the bill
Freak accident

Gap (generation, credibility, etc.)

Hammer out
Hard-core, hard-nosed
Hike
Historical document
Hobbled by injury
Hosted
Hurled

Identity crisis
Initial (for first)
In terms of
-ize (finalize, formalize)

Junket

Keeled over

Led to safety
Luxurious (apartment, love nest, etc.)

Made off with
Miraculous (cure, escape, etc.)
Momentous occasion

Name of the game

Opt for
Overwhelming majority

Passing motorist
Plush (hotel, apartment, etc.)
Police were summoned
Pressure (as a verb)
Probe

Relocate (for move)
Reportedly, reputedly

Seasoned (observers, etc.)   Top-level meeting
Senseless murder   Tragic accident
Shot in the arm   Turn thumbs down
Staged a riot (or protest)
Standing ovation   Uneasy truce
Stems from   Unveiled
Stinging rebuke   Upcoming
Sweeping changes
Swing into high gear   Vast expanse
                                    Verbalize
Task force   Violence erupted
Tense (or uneasy) calm   Violent explosion
Terminate (for end)
Thorough (or all-out)   Whirlwind (tour, junket)
   investigation
Timely hit   Young boys

Know the Idiom   Careless use of the idiom (the grammatical structure peculiar to our language) occurs frequently in the news report. Usually the fault lies in the prepositions or conjunctions.

Three times as many Americans were killed than [as] in any similar period.

It remains uncertain as to when the deadline for the first payment will be. (Omit *as to.*)

She had always been able to get through the performance on [of] this taxing role.

The economist accused him with [of] failing to make a decision. (You charge somebody with blundering, but you accuse him of it.)

He said the guns are against the law except under [in] certain specified situations. (But, under conditions or circumstances.)

Dressen is no different than [from] other experts. (*Different* may be followed by *than* when introducing a clause: "The patient is no different than he was yesterday.")

Five men were pelted by [with] stones.

The reason for the new name is because the college's mission has been changed. (*Is that* the college's mission has been changed.)

He said he would not call on [for] assistance from police except as a last resort. (Call the police or call on the police for assistance.)

In other idiomatic expressions, the phrase should be correct.

These men and women could care less about Reagan's legislative magic. (The correct phrase is "couldn't care less.")

Gerunds, but not past participles, require the possessive:

It was the first instance of a city [city's] losing its funds.

He said he didn't know anything about Hollenbach [Hollenbach's] interceding in his behalf.

Jargon   A university press release announcing a significant engineering meeting on the campus reported that one of the major papers would be on "the aerodynamic heating of blunt, axisymmetric, re-entry bodies with laminar boundary layer at zero and at large angles of yaw in supersonic and hypersonic air streams." To the consumer of news, that title is *gobbledygook.* Translated, the topic suggested, "How hot does a space ship get when it swings back into the air around the earth?"

Doctors, lawyers, educators, engineers, government officials, scientists, sociologists, economists and others have their professional jargon or shoptalk peculiar to the profession. Sometimes this jargon is used to impress the uninitiated; sometimes it is a cover-up.

Here is how Daniel Melcher, president of the R. R. Bowker Co., translated three examples of gobbledygook:

A mnemonic code of three, four or five characters was assigned to each primary source.
"Producers' and distributors' names are abbreviated."

Sources were provided with an effort-saving structured response form.
"Questionnaires were sent to producers and distributors."

The editorial work is paralleled by a machine processing effort that translates the worksheets into decks of punched cards.
"The entries are typed on cards, which are then punched for ease of sorting."

A judge's ruling on a case involving an actress contained this sentence: "Such vanity doubtless is due to the adulation which the public showers on the denizens of the entertainment world in a profusion wholly disproportionate to the intrinsic contribution which they make to the scheme of things." That's pretentious verbosity. So, too, is this from an educator:

The educator will hold a practicum for disadvantaged children who are under-achieving in reading.

Try "Slow learners who can't read."

Translation is needed when a story on education contains "professional terms" such as *paraprofessionals, academically talented, disadvantaged* (culturally deprived, impoverished students) and *ungraded* and *nongraded classrooms.*

In a special study of state wire reporting, The Associated Press found that unintelligible jargon appeared in legislature stories ("resolves," "engrossment," "tucked in committee"), in alphabet soup references to agencies and organizations (SGA, the UCA, CRS, LTA and MMA), in Weather Service forecasts and in market reports. AP then noted, "Neither weather reports nor markets are sacrosanct to editorial pencils."

The copy editor can help the reader by substituting laymen's words for technical terms and by killing on sight words like *implement* and the *-ize* words.

Here are translations of some technical terms that frequently appear in the news report:

Term	*Translation*
Motivated or motivationed	Moved
Object	Aim
Mentality	Mind
Percentage	Part
Assignment	Task or job
Astronomical	Big

Some common euphemisms:

Term	*Translation*
Container	Can
Continental breakfast	Juice, roll and coffee
Dialogue, conversation	Talk, discussion
Planned parenthood	Birth control
Revised upward	Raised
Withdrawal	Retreat

Slang

Many editors will agree with this advice from The Associated Press: "Use of slang should be a rarity in the news report." Some editors might even dream that use of slang can be reduced in sports stories, in the signed columns, in comic strips and in ads.

Slang in direct quotations helps reveal the speaker's personality. The reader expects the gangster to use terms of the underworld. He does not expect the reporter to resort to slang such as "The Brinton household is a go-go preparing . . . for guests."

Some slang words should be avoided because they are offensive ("cops" for *policemen*, "gobs" for *sailors,* "wops" for *Italians*): others are avoided because they reveal a writer's carelessness ("got clobbered" for *was defeated*).

A few examples from a wire service show how a copy editor can overcome the slang:

> "The Supreme Court ruled today that a lower court goofed." What's wrong with the proper word *erred?*

> A Los Angeles story spoke of a couple getting "a few belts in one of the local bars." What's wrong with *drinks* if that's what they got?

> A Washington reporter wrote that "well-heeled admirers of the senator have shelled out $7,000." We suppose that *well-heeled* means wealthy and that *shelled out* means contributed.

Parallelism

Good usage insists that similar ideas or elements in a sentence be phrased in a similar structural or grammatical from. You would say, "I like gardening, fishing and hunting," not "I like gardening, fishing and to hunt." In the following, the word *requiring* makes a nonparallel construction: "Instead of requiring expensive cobalt drill bits, disposable brass pins are used."

Comparisons should compare similar things. Here is a sentence that compares an apple (the increase) with a pumpkin (the sales): "Consolidated sales of Cottontex Corp. for the first six months of this year were $490 million, an increase of $27 million compared with the first half of last year." Use "an increase of $27 million over the previous year's first half." "The solider was ragged, unshaven, yet walked with a proud step." Make it read, "The soldier was ragged and unshaven, yet walked with a proud step."

Omission of *and* produces a nonparallel construction: "He worked on newspapers in Washington, New Jersey, New York, and on the Paris *Herald Tribune.*" Use "He worked on newspapers in Washington, New Jersey and New York, and on. . . . "

But *and* should not be used superfluously: "He was identified as John Delanor Smith, three times convicted on narcotic charges and who reportedly serves as an enforcer for Mafia drug bosses on the east coast."

Mixed Metaphors

Legislative Hall here was swarming with lobbyists as the second session of the 121st General Assembly got under way yesterday.

With lawmakers treading water while awaiting Gov. Elbert N. Carvel's state and budget messages, due tomorrow, lobbyists had a field day.

In two paragraphs the story pictured Legislative Hall as a beehive, a swimming pool and an athletic field.

Breaking domestic ties with gold would make the nation's gold stock a real barometer of international fever for gold.

Do you shove that barometer under your tongue or what?

They hope to unravel a sticky turn of events that was further complicated recently.

Did you ever try to unravel glue, molasses, maple syrup or other similar strings or yarns?

Mock Ruralisms

Here is some advice from Leon Stolz of the *Chicago Tribune:* "If you hold your quota to one mock ruralism a century, your readers will not feel deprived." Expressions such as "seeing as how" or "allowed as how" are supposed to give a folksy touch. They don't. They merely make the writer sound stupid.

Foreign Words   When copy editors come across foreign expressions in the news
report they should be sure of the spelling, the use and the translation. Unless it is a commonly known expression, the copy editor
provides the translation if the reporter has not done so. The headline writer who tried to add a flavor of French with "C'est La
Killy" needed advice on proper usage of French articles. The number in Latin words can cause trouble. For instance, *data* is plural
and *datum* is singular. But *datum* is rarely used and *data* can be
either singular (as a synonym for information) or plural (as a synonym for facts). *Trivia* is always plural; *bona fides* is always singular. *Media, criteria, insignia* and *phenomena* are plural.

A foreign expression has its place in the report if it supplies a
real need or flavor or has no precise native substitute *(blasé, chic,
simpatico)*.

Copy editors frequently are confronted with problems of translation, not as a rule directly from a foreign language but from a
foreign correspondent's translation. Translations made abroad are
often hurried; many are the work of men and women more at
home in another language than in English. The translations may
be accurate but not idiomatic. Some examples:

An AP dispatch telling of a factory explosion in Germany read,
"Most of the victims were buried when the roof of a large factory
hall came down following the explosion. . . . The blast . . . damaged five other halls. . . . " What is factory hall? The copy editor
would have saved readers a puzzled moment if the dispatch had
been changed to read, "Most of the victims were buried when the
factory roof fell on them. The blast . . . damaged five other sections
of the plant."

Newspapers display an affectation when they use foreign terms
not readily understood by their readers. Examples:

> Some (restaurants) have retained an authentic belle-epoque
> ambience. (What does it mean?)

> When 13-year-old Pascale Le Tourze returns to her "lycee" in
> France . . . (What reader will use a dictionary to find out that Pas-
> cale will attend a French public secondary school?)

6

Style Notes

Newspapers adhere to rules of style to avoid inconsistencies that would annoy the reader. The writing in newspapers, like the writing in good books, must be clear, concise and free of irritating inconsistencies. Adherence to style rules gives the newspaper a sense of consistency that would be absent if *goodbye* were used in one story and *goodby* in the next. Stylebooks provide guidance in spelling, word usage, punctuation, titles and many other areas.

Most newspapers follow style rules developed jointly by The Associated Press and United Press International (see Appendix I). Each agency issues its own stylebook, but almost all rules are consistent as a service to those who subscribe to both. Newspapers have embraced these rules as their own, although most have exceptions. A few papers, primarily small dailies and weeklies, follow no stylebook at all.

Style rules should not be confused with individual writing styles; the two in no way conflict. Individual writing styles can and should be developed within the constraints of style rules.

The AP and UPI stylebooks are voluminous and few have the ability to memorize their content. But it helps to learn as much of their content as possible to minimize time spent in referring to them. Let's take a look at some of the key rules of style and how newspapers apply those rules.

Identifications Shakespeare knew the value of a name. In *Othello* he had Iago say, "But he that filches from me my good name / Robs me of that which not enriches him / And makes me poor indeed." A name misspelled is a person misidentified. Of all the errors a newspaper is capable of making, one of the most serious is a misspelled or a misused name. In radio and television it is the mispronounced name.

One of the important roles of the copy editor is to make sure that all names in the copy are double-checked. The proper form is the form the person uses. It may be Alex rather than Alexander, Jim rather than James, Carin rather than Karen. The individual may or may not have a middle initial, with or without a period. Former President Harry S. Truman had no middle name. Some newspapers once used his middle initial without a period, but most now include it. Truman expressed indifference to the issue. Men's first names are seldom used alone, except in sports copy. The same should be true for first names of women.

Anyone resents an attempt at cleverness when a name is involved. Such "cuteness" should be felled on sight:

> Orange County will have a lemon as district attorney. Jack Lemon was elected to the job yesterday.

> Of the five patrolmen on the staff, two are crooks.

The last name was Crook.

A title generally precedes a name unless it is a long title. It is Harley F. Taylor, principal of Philip C. Showell School, rather than Philip C. Showell School Principal Harley F. Taylor.

Nor should the story make the reader guess at the identification. Here is an example:

> Albert A. Ballew took issue with Mayor Locher today for announcing in advance that the post of administrative assistant in the Safety Department will be filled by a black.
> The president of the Collinwood Improvement Council commended the mayor for creating the post, but added. . . .

Now then, who is the president of the Collinwood Improvement Council? Will readers assume it is Ballew? The solution is simple: "Ballew, president of the Collinwood Improvement Council, commended the mayor. . . ."

In recent years newspaper editors have grappled with the difficult problem of whether to abandon use of the courtesy titles traditionally given to women. Most newspapers use the last name only to refer to men on second reference but use the courtesy titles *Miss, Mrs.* or *Ms.* on second reference to women. Feminists and others argue that men and women should be treated equally in news columns and insist that newspapers abandon this practice. For editors caught in the middle of this debate, it is a no-win situation. If they continue to use courtesy titles, feminists and others protest. If they drop courtesy titles, older people, in particular, are offended. Many elderly women prefer to be called *Miss* or *Mrs.* followed by a family name. They consider it demeaning to be called by the last name only. The number of people who object to this practice is not large, however, so many editors have decided to drop courtesy titles altogether. A few newspapers, including the *Kansas City Star* and *Times,* have done the opposite by choosing to start using courtesy titles for men as well as women.

Wire service style has had a strong impact in influencing many editors to retain courtesy titles. Now, however, United Press International has abandoned the practice and The Associated Press shows signs of doing the same.

It is unlikely that courtesy titles will disappear altogether. In a story about a married couple, it is useful to distinguish between the two on second and subsequent references by using, for example, *Mr. Rodriquez* and *Mrs. Rodriquez.* Using first or given names instead would be cumbersome and in some cases may give the reader the impression that the reporter is "talking down" to the couple. Some newspapers also use courtesy titles in obituaries and in editorials.

Newspaper style may dictate that certain positions be neuterized (chairperson for chairman) but even this rule could lead to the absurd (*personkind* for *mankind*). The joint stylebook disallows these forms unless they are formal titles.

Editors can be fair to both sexes by eliminating purely sexist adjectives, by using plural forms when possible and by substituting the relative pronouns *they* or *them* for *he* or *him.*

Newspaper style calls for females to be called girls until they are 18 and women thereafter. Males are boys until they are 18 and men thereafter.

Appropriateness should determine whether males and females 18 and older or even those under 18 should be referred to by the familiar given name.

A married woman's original name can cause trouble: "He married the former Constance Coleman in 1931." This is incorrect; Constance Coleman was Constance Coleman when he married her. He married Constance Coleman. His wife is the former Constance Coleman.

Woman is used as a general descriptive possessive—woman's rights. *Women's* is used as a specific—women's club (but Woman's Christian Temperance Union). It is women fliers, Young Women's Christian Association, women workers, but woman suffrage. It is never *the Smith woman.*

Foreign names are tricky. In Spanish-speaking countries, individuals usually have two last names, the father's and the mother's—Adolfo Lopez Mateos. On second reference, Lopez Mateos should be used. In headlines, Lopez Mateos is preferred, but Lopez will do.

Newspapers have adopted the official Chinese spelling known as

Pinyin. Thus, *Foochow* becomes *Fuzhou.* Familiar names of places and people, including Peking and Mao Tse-tung, still take the familiar American spelling.

In Arabic names, *al* generally is hyphenated—al-Sabah, al-Azhar. Some Arabs drop the article—Mamoun Kuzbari, not al-Kuzbari, but it should be used if the individual prefers. Compound names should be left intact—Abdullah, Abdel, Abdur. Pasha and Bey titles have been abolished. Royal titles are used with first names—Emir Faisel, Sheik Abdullah. *Haj* is used with the first name in both first and subsequent references—Haj Amin al-Hussein, Haj Amin.

The *U* in Burmese names means uncle, our equivalent of *Mr.,* or master. *Daw* means *Mrs.* or *Miss.* Many Burmese have only one name—*U Thant.* If a Burmese has two names, both should be used—*U Tin Maung, Tin Maung.*

Some Koreans put the family name first—*Park Chung Hee.* The second reference should be *Park,* not *Chung Hee,* the given name.

Many Indonesians have only one name—*Sukarno,* not *Achmed Sukarno.*

Swedish surnames usually end in *-son,* and Danish names usually end in *-sen.*

Trade Names

Few editors have escaped letters that begin something like this: "Dear Sir: The attached clipping from your paper of July 14th contains a mention of our product and we very much appreciate this unsolicited publicity. However, the name of our product was used with a lowercase "c." As you know. . . . "

Makers of trade-name products want to protect their rights under the Lanham Trademark Act of 1947 and insist that in any reference to the product name the manufacturer's spelling and capitalization be used. This is to protect the trade name from becoming generic, as happened to aspirin, cellophane, escalator, milk of magnesia, zipper, linoleum and shredded wheat.

Much of the confusion and protest can be eliminated simply by using a generic term rather than the specific trade name—*petroleum jelly* for *Vaseline, freezer* for *Deepfreeze, fiber glass* for *Fiberglas, artificial grass* for *Astroturf.*

When the product is trade-named and there is no substitute, the trade name should be used, especially if it is pertinent to the story. The withholding of such information on the ground of free publicity is a disservice to readers.

Institutions should be labeled correctly—Lloyd's, not Lloyd's of London; J.C. Penney Co. (Penneys in ads, Penney's in other usages); American Geographical Society; National Geographic Society.

Religion
Jewish congregations should be identified in news stories as Orthodox, Conservative or Reform, and the terminology of the congregation concerned should be followed in naming the place of worship as a temple or a synagogue. When grouping, the generic term is "Jewish houses of worship."

To help readers, the copy editor should insert "branch of Judaism" or whatever other phrase might be necessary to convey the proper meaning.

Most Orthodox congregations use *synagogue*. Reform groups use *temple* and Conservative congregations use one word or the other, but *synagogue* is preferred. It is never *church*, which applies to Christian bodies.

Sect has a derogatory connotation. Generally it means a church group espousing Christianity without the traditional liturgical forms. *Religion* is an all-inclusive word for Judaism, Islam, Christianity and others. *Faith* generally is associated with Protestants. *Denomination* should be used only when referring to the church bodies within the Protestant community.

Religious labels can be misleading. *Jews* and *Judaism* are general terms. *Israelis* refer to nationals of the state of Israel and *Jews* to those who profess Judaism. The state of Israel is not the center of or the spokesman for Judaism. Some Jews are Zionists; some are not.

Not all denominations use *Church* in the organization's title. It is the First Baptist Church but the American Baptist Convention. It is the Church of Jesus Christ of Latter-day Saints (but Mormon Church is acceptable); its units are missions, stakes and wards. It is the Episcopal Church, not the Episcopalian Church. Its members are Episcopalians, but the adjective is *Episcopal*: Episcopal clergymen.

Mass may be *celebrated, said* or *sung.* The rosary is *recited* or *said.* The copy editor can avoid confusion by making the statement read something like this: "The mass (or rosary) will be at 7 p.m." The Benediction of the Blessed Sacrament is neither "held" nor "given"; services close with it.

The order of the Ten Commandments varies depending on the version of the Bible used. Confusion can be spared if the commandment number is omitted. Also to be deleted are references to the burning of a church mortgage unless there actually is a burning ceremony. It is an elegant but ridiculous way of saying the mortgage has been paid off.

The usual style in identifying ministers is *the Rev.,* followed by the individual's full name on first reference and only the surname on second reference. If the minister has a doctorate, the style is *the Rev. Dr.,* or simply *Dr.* on subsequent references. *Reverend* should not be used standing alone, nor should plural forms be used, such as the Revs. John Jones and Richard Smith. Churches of Christ do not use the term *reverend* in reference to ministers. They are called *brothers.*

Rabbis take *Rabbi* for a title.

Priests who are rectors, heads of religious houses or presidents of institutions and provinces of religious orders take *Very Rev.* and are addressed as *Father.* Priests who have doctorates in divinity or philosophy are identified as *the Rev. Dr.* and are addressed either as *Dr.* or *Father.* For further guidance, consult the stylebook, which contains rules pertinent to usages in all religions.

The words *Catholic* and *parochial* are not synonymous. There are parochial schools other than Catholic schools. The writer should not assume that a person is a Roman Catholic simply because he is a priest or a bishop. Other religions also have priests and bishops.

Not all old churches merit the designation of *shrine.* Some are just old churches. *Shrine* denotes some special distinction, historic or ecclesiastical. Usually, shrines are structures or places that have religious connections or that are hallowed by their associations with events or persons of historic significance, such as Mt. Vernon.

Use *nun* when appropriate for women in religious orders. The word *sister* is confusing except with the person's name (Sister Mary Edward).

Death Stories

People die of heart *illness,* not "failure"; after a *long* illness, not an "extended" illness; *unexpectedly,* not "suddenly"; *outright,* not "instantly"; *following* or *after* an operation, not "as a result of" an operation; *apparently of a heart attack,* not of an "apparent heart attack." A person dies *of* a disease, not "from" a disease.

The age of the person who died is important to the reader. The copy editor should check the age given with the year of birth. Generally, the person's profession or occupation, the extent of the illness and the cause of death are recorded, but without details. The length of the story is dictated by the fame of the person. Winston Churchill's obit ran 18 pages in *The New York Times.*

A person *leaves* an estate; that person is *survived* by a family. A man is survived by his *wife,* not his widow. A woman is survived by her *husband,* not her widower. A man or woman is survived by children if they are children and by sons and daughters if they are adults.

If the family requests that the story include the statement that memorial donations may be made to a particular organization, the statement should be used. Whether such a statement should contain the phrase "in lieu of flowers" is a matter of policy. A few papers, in deference to florists, do not carry the phrase, but that practice is widely discredited as currying favor with advertisers.

A straightforward account of a death is better than one told euphemistically. The plain terms are *died,* not "passed away" or "succumbed"; *body,* not "remains" or "corpse"; *coffin,* not "casket"; *funeral* or *services,* not "obsequies"; *burial,* not "interment," unless interred in a tomb above the ground. Flowery expressions such as "two of whom reside in St. Louis" and "became associated with the company shortly after college" show no more respect for the dead than do the plain expressions "live in St. Louis" or "went to work for the company."

Few stories in a newspaper are more likely to be written by formula than the obituary. There isn't much the desk can do about the conventional style except to contrast it with those that take a fresh approach. Here is a lead from an Associated Press story:

NEW YORK (AP)—If you are a movie fan, you will remember Mary Boland as the fluttery matron, the foolishly fond mother, the ladylike scatterbrain. The character actress who died yesterday at 80 was none of these in real life.

The copy editor should be on guard for the correct spelling of all names used in the death story and for slips such as "cemetary" for *cemetery* and "creamation" for *cremation.* Errors are inexcusable:

> A postmorten failed to disclose the cause of death because the girl's body was too badly decomposed.

The correct spelling is *postmortem,* or, preferably, use *autopsy.*

> Thousands followed the cortege.

The thousands must have been *in,* not "following," the cortege (the funeral procession). Even after death, a medal won by a serviceman is awarded to him. It may be *presented* to his widow, but it is not *awarded* to his widow.

If the service is at a mortuary, the name of the mortuary should be included for the convenience of mourners. A funeral service is *at* a place, not *from* it. A funeral mass usually is *offered;* a funeral service is *held.* Even so, "held" often is redundant: "The service will be at 2 p.m. Thursday . . . "

The passage should leave no doubt for whom the service was held. This one did: "Services for 7-year-old Michael L—, son of a Genoa Intermediate School District official who was struck and killed by a car Monday in Bay City, will be held. . . . "

People are *people,* not "assaults" or "traffic deaths" or "fatals" or "dead on arrivals":

> A youth stabbed at a downtown intersection and a woman pedestrian run down by a car were among assaults on six persons reported to police during the night.

> **Hugo man among nine traffic deaths**

> Dead on arrival at Hurley after the crash was Oscar W . . .

The events in a person's life that should be included in the obituary pose a problem for the desk. One story told of the death of a former school administrator who died at 87. It said he had been the first principal of a high school and had served in that capacity for 17 years. Then the story noted that he resigned two months before he was found guilty of taking $150 from the school yearbook fund and was fined $500. Should an account of a minor crime committed a quarter of a century ago be included in the obituary? To those who knew the former principal intimately, the old theft was not news. Those who didn't know him personally probably would not care about the single flaw in an otherwise distinguished career. Sometimes, however, it is necessary to include unsavory details in obituaries. Good editors do not hesitate to do so.

Medical News

Reporters and copy editors have no business playing doctor. If a child is injured in an accident, the seriousness of the injury should be determined by medical authorities. To say that a person who was not even admitted to the hospital was "seriously injured" is editorializing.

Hospitals may report that a patient is in a "guarded condition," but the term has no meaning for the reader and should be deleted. The same goes for "he is resting comfortably."

One may not sustain a "fractured leg," which seldom causes death, but one may sustain a heart attack. A person may suffer a *fracture of the leg* or a *leg fracture* or, better still, simply a *broken leg*. Injuries are *suffered* or *sustained*, not *received*.

A story described a murder suspect as "a diabetic of the worst type who must have 15 units of insulin daily." The quotes were attributed to the FBI. An editor commented, "In my book, that is a mild diabetic, unless the story means that the suspect is a diabetic who requires 15 units of regular insulin before each meal. A wire service should not rely on the FBI for diagnosis of diabetes and the severity of the case."

Doctor and *scientist* are vague words to many readers. *Doctor* may be a medical doctor, a dentist, a veterinarian, an osteopath, a minister or a professor. The story would be clearer if it named the doctor's specialty or the scientist's specific activity, whether biology, physics, electronics or astronautics.

Medical doctors diagnose the illness, not the patient. The proper term to use in determining the remedy or in forecasting the probable course and termination of a disease is *prognosis*.

Mothers are *delivered;* babies are *born*.

Everyone has a temperature. *Fever* describes above-normal temperature.

Everyone has a heart condition. It is news only if someone's heart is in bad condition.

"The wife of the governor underwent major surgery and physicians reported she apparently had been cured of a malignant tumor." It is unlikely that any doctor said she was *cured* of a malignant tumor. They avoid that word with malignant growths.

"A team of five surgeons performed a hysterectomy, appendectomy and complete abdominal exploration." Why the unnecessary details? It would have been enough to say, "Five surgeons performed the abdominal operation."

Unless they are essential to the story, trade names of narcotics or poisons should be avoided. If a person dies of an overdose of sleeping pills, the story should not specify the number of pills taken.

Also, use *Caesarean section* or *Caesarean operation.*

Usually, no sane person has his leg broken. Use the passive tense: "His leg was broken."

Use the expression *physicians and dentists,* not *doctors and dentists.* The second suggests that dentists are not doctors.

A doctor who specializes in anesthesia is an anesthesiologist, not an anesthetist.

A person may wear a sling on his or her right arm. That person doesn't wear his or her right arm in a sling.

"He suffered a severed tendon in his right Achilles' heel last winter." It was the Achilles' tendon in his right heel or his right Achilles' tendon.

"A jaundice epidemic also was spreading in Gaya, Indian health officials said. The disease claimed 30 lives." Jaundice is not a disease but a sign of the existence of one or another of a great many diseases.

Technical terms should be translated:

Term	Translation	Term	Translation
Abrasion	Scrape	Suturing	Sewing
Contusion	Bruise	Hemorrhaging	Bleeding
Lacerations	Cuts	Obese	Fat
Fracture	Break	Respire	Breathe

Weather

An editor said, "Ever since the National Weather Service started naming hurricanes after females, reporters can't resist the temptation to be cute." He then cited as an example the lead, "Hilda—never a lady and now no longer a hurricane—spent the weekend in Louisiana, leaving behind death, destruction and misery." That, the editor said, is giddy treatment for a disaster causing 35 deaths and millions of dollars in property damage. The potential for passages in poor taste is not lessened by the fact that men's names are now used for hurricanes, too.

Another editor noted that a story referred to "the turbulent eye of the giant storm." Later in the story the reporter wrote that the eye of the hurricane is the dead-calm center.

A story predicted that a hurricane was headed for Farmington and was expected to cause millions of dollars in damage. So the Farmington merchants boarded their windows, the tourists canceled their reservations, and the hurricane went around Farmington. This is the trouble when an editor lets a reporter expand a prediction into a warning.

The headline **Freeze tonight expected to make driving hazardous** was based on this lead: "Freezing temperatures forecast for tonight may lead to a continuation of hazardous driving conditions as a result of last night's snow and freezing rain." The story made no mention of anyone's saying there would still be dampness on the ground when freezing temperatures arrived. There wasn't, and driving was unimpeded.

A lead said, "One word, 'miserable,' was the U.S. weatherman's description today of the first day of spring." The head was **Snow predicted; it's spring, miserable.** It was the weatherman's prediction, not his description. The sun stayed out all day, the clouds stayed away, and readers of the paper must have wondered where this U.S. weatherman was located.

Temperatures can become *higher* or *lower*, not "cooler" or "warmer."

In flood stories, the copy should tell where the flood water came from and where it will run off. The expression *flash flood* is either a special term for a rush of water let down a weir to permit passage of a boat or a sudden destructive rush of water down a narrow gully or over a sloping surface in desert regions, caused by heavy rains in the mountains or foothills. It is often used loosely for any sudden gush of water.

Weather stories, more than most others, have an affinity for the cliché, the fuzzy image, overwriting, mixed metaphors, contrived similes and other absurdities.

"A Houdini snow did some tricks yesterday that left most of the state shivering from a spine-tingling storm." Houdini gained fame as an escape artist, not as an ordinary magician. Did the snow escape, or was it just a tricky snow? After the lead, the 22-inch story never mentioned the angle again. *Spine-tingling* means full of suspense or uncertainty or even terror. Sports writers are fond of using it to describe a close game, called a *heart stopper* by more ecstatic writers, often in conjunction with a *gutsy performance.* If a cliché must be used, a very cold storm is *spine-chilling,* not "spine-tingling."

"Old Man Winter yesterday stretched his icy fingers and dumped a blanket of snow on the state." How would reporters ever write about the weather without Old Man Winter, Jack Frost, Icy Fingers and Old Sol? Why do rain and snow never *fall?* They are always "dumped."

"At least two persons were killed in yesterday's snowstorm, marked at times by blizzard-like gales of wind." By Weather Service standards, this is an exaggeration and a contradiction. By any standard, it is a redundancy. A blizzard is one thing. Gales are something else. Gales of wind? What else, unless maybe it was gales of laughter from discerning readers.

An editor's moral: Good colorful writing is to be encouraged. But a simply written story with no gimmicks is better than circus writing that goes awry. To quote a champion image-maker, Shakespeare, in *Sonnet 94,* "Lilies that fester smell far worse than weeds."

Blizzards are hard to define because wind and temperatures may vary. The safe way is to avoid calling a snowstorm a *blizzard* unless the Weather Service describes it as such. Generally, a blizzard occurs when there are winds of 35 mph or more that whip falling snow or snow already on the ground and when temperatures are 20 degrees above zero Fahrenheit, or lower.

A severe blizzard has winds that are 45 mph or more, temperatures 10 degrees above zero or lower and great density of snow either falling or whipped from the ground.

The Weather Service insists that ice storms are not sleet. Sleet is frozen raindrops. The service uses the terms *ice storm, freezing rain* and *freezing drizzle* to warn the public when a coating of ice is expected on the ground.

A cyclone is a storm with heavy rain and winds rotating about a moving center of low atmospheric pressure.

A *hurricane* has winds above 74 mph.

A *typhoon* is a violent cyclonic storm or hurricane occurring in the China Seas and adjacent regions, chiefly from July to October.

Here is a handy table for referring to wind conditions:

Light	up to 7 mph	Strong	25 to 38 mph
Gentle	8 to 12 mph	Gale	39 to 54 mph
Moderate	13 to 18 mph	Whole gale	55 to 75 mph
Fresh	19 to 24 mph		

The word *chinook* should not be used unless so designated by the Weather Service.

Temperatures are measured by various scales. Zero degree Celsius is freezing, and 100 degrees Celsius is boiling. Celsius is preferred over the older term centigrade. On the Fahrenheit scale, 32 degrees is freezing, and 212 degrees (at sea level) is boiling. On the Kelvin scale, 273 degrees is freezing, and 373 degrees is boiling. To convert degrees Celsius to Fahrenheit, multiply the Celsius measurement by nine-fifths and add 32. To convert degrees Fahrenheit to Celsius, subtract 32 from the Fahrenheit measurement and multiply by five-ninths. Thus, 10 degrees Celsius is 50 degrees Fahrenheit. To convert degrees Kelvin to Celsius degrees, subtract 273 from the Kelvin reading.

Avoid these weather clichés:

Fog rolled (crept or crawled) in	Mercury dropped (dipped,
Fog-shrouded city	zoomed, plummeted)
Winds aloft	Rain failed to dampen
Biting (bitter) cold	Hurricane howled
Hail-splattered	Storm-tossed

Disaster

Conjecturing about possible damage to settlements from forest fires is as needless as conjectures on weather damage. The story should concentrate on the definite loss. Stories of forest fires should define the specific area burned, the area threatened and the type of timber. Be wary of death estimates because officials tend to overstate during the initial shock of the event.

Most stories of earthquakes attempt to describe the magnitude of the tremor. One measurement is the Richter scale, which shows relative magnitude. It starts with magnitude 1 and progresses in units with each unit 10 times stronger than the previous one. Thus, magnitude 3 is 10 times stronger than magnitude 2, which, in turn is 10 times stronger than magnitude 1. On this scale the strongest earthquakes recorded were the South American earthquake of 1906 and the Japanese earthquake of 1933, both at a magnitude of 8.9. Intensity generally refers to the duration or to the damage caused by the shock.

In train and plane crashes the story should include train or flight number, the place of departure, the destination and times of departure and expected arrival. Airplanes may collide on the ground or in the air (not "midair"). Let investigators *search* the wreckage, not "comb" or "sift" it.

In fire stories, the truth is that in 9 of 10 cases when people are "led to safety," they're not. Except for an occasional child or infirm adult, they simply have the common sense to leave the building without waiting for a firefighter to "lead them to safety."

In both fire and flood stories the residents of the area are rarely taken from their homes or asked to leave. Instead, they're always told to "evacuate" or they're "evacuated." What's wrong with *vacate?*

Eliminate terms such as *three-alarm fire* and *second-degree burns* unless they are explained.

"An estimated $40,000 worth of damage was done Jan. 29. . . . " Damage isn't worth anything. Quite the contrary.

"The full tragedy of Hurricane Betsy unfolded today as the death toll rose past 50, and damages soared into many millions." *Damage* was the correct word here. You collect *damages* in court.

Avoid these disaster clichés:

Rampaging rivers   Tinder-dry forest
Weary firefighters   Raging brush fire
Fiery holocaust   Traffic fatals or triple fatals
Flames licked (leaped, swept)   (police station jargon)
Searing heat

Labor Disputes Stories of labor controversies should give the reasons for the dispute, how long the strike has been in progress and the claims by both the union and the company.

Copy editors should be on guard against wrong or loaded terms. Examples: In a closed shop the employer may hire only those who are members of the union. In a union shop, the employer may select employees but the workers are required to join the union within a specified time after starting work. A conciliator or mediator in a labor dispute merely recommends terms of a settlement. The decision of an arbitrator usually is binding. There is a tendency in labor stories to refer to management proposals as "offers" and to labor proposals as "demands." The correct word should be used for the correct connotation.

Strikebreaker and *scab,* which are loaded terms, have no place in the news if used to describe men or women who act as individuals in accepting positions vacated by strikers. The expression "honored the picket line" frequently appears in the news even though a more accurage expression is "refused (or declined) to cross a picket line."

Union leader is usually preferred to *labor leader.* A longshoreman is a waterfront leader. A stevedore usually is considered an employee.

On estimates of wages or production lost, the story should have authoritative sources, not street-corner guesses. An individual, however voluble, does not speak for the majority unless that person has been authorized to do so. Statements by workers or by minor officials should be downplayed until they are documented.

If a worker gets a 10-cent-an-hour increase effective immediately, an additional 10 cents a year hence and another 10 cents the third year, that worker does not receive a 30-cent-an-hour increase. The increase at the time of settlement is still 10 cents an hour. It also is common to read, "The company has been on strike for the last 25 days." No. The employees are on strike. The company has been struck.

Criminal court terms should not be applied to labor findings unless the dispute has been taken to a criminal court. The National Labor Relations Board is not a court, and its findings or recommendations should not be expressed in criminal court terminology. In most settlements, neither side is "found guilty" or "fined." A finding or a determination may be made or a penalty may be assessed.

Financial News   A news release from a bank included the following: "The book value of each share outstanding will approximate $21.87 on Dec. 31, and if the current yield of 4.27 percent continues to bear the same relationship to the market price it should rise to $32 or $33, according to . . . " The copy editor changed the ambiguous *it* to *the book value*. Actually, the release intended *it* to refer to the market price, which shows what can happen when copy editors change copy without knowing what they are doing.

Another story quoted an oil company official as saying that "the refinery would produce $7 million in additional real estate taxes." It should have been obvious that this was a wholly unrealistic figure, but for good measure there was an ad in the same paper that placed the total tax figure at about $200,000 and read, "The initial installation will add about $7 million a year to the economy of the state, not including taxes."

A story and headline said the interest on the state debt accounted for 21 percent of the state government's spending. An accompanying graph showed, however, that the figure was for debt service, which includes both interest and amortization, or payments on principal.

All who edit copy for financial pages should have at least elementary knowledge of business terms. If they can't distinguish between a balance sheet and a profit-and-loss statement, between earnings and gross operating income, and between a net profit and net cash income, they have some homework to do.

This reality was emphasized by a syndicated financial columnist who cautioned business news desks against using misleading headlines such as **Stocks plummet—Dow Jones average off 12 points.** It may be a loss, the columnist noted, but hardly a calamity. The Dow Jones Industrial Average may indicate that the market is up, but in reality it may be sinking. Freak gains by a few of the 30 stocks used in compiling the Dow average may have pushed up that particular indicator. Nor does a slight market drop call for a headline such as **Investors lose millions in market value of stocks.** They lost nothing of the sort. On that day, countless investors the nation over had substantial paper profits on their stocks. If they sold, they were gainers on the buying price in real terms; if they held, they had neither gains nor losses.

The Dow Jones average is one of several indexes used to gauge the stock market. Each uses its own statistical technique to show market changes. The Dow Jones bases its index on 30 stocks. It is an index-number change, not a percentage change.

Reporters of dividends should use the designation given by the firm (regular, special, extra, increases, interim) and show what was paid previously if there is no specified designation such as regular or quarterly.

The story should say if there is a special, or extra, dividend paid with the regular dividend and include the amount of previous added payments. When the usual dividend is not paid, or reduced, some firms issue an explanatory statement, the gist of which should be included in the story.

Newswire stylebooks recommend that news of corporate activities and business and financial news be stripped of technical terms. There should be some explanation of the firm's business (plastics, rubber, electronics) if there is no indication of the nature of the business in the firm's name. The location of the company's home office should be included.

Savings and loan firms object to being called banks. Some commercial banks likewise object when savings and loan firms are called banks. There need be no confusion if the institution is identified by its proper name. In subsequent references the words *company* or *institution* are used. Some newspapers permit **S&L firm** in tight headlines. Actually a *firm* is a partnership or unincorporated group. It should not be used for an incorporated company. *Concern* is a better word for the latter.

Jargon has no place in the business story. "Near-term question marks in the national economy—either of which could put a damper on the business expansion—are residential housing and foreign trade, the Northern Trust Co. said in its December issue of *Business Comments.*" Are near-term question marks economy question marks? If so, can they put a damper on anything? Isn't all housing residential?

> Major producers scrambled today to adjust steel prices to newly emerging industry-wide patterns. . . . The welter of price changes was in marked contrast with the old-time industry practice of posting across-the-board hikes.
>
> This approach apparently breathed its last in April when it ran into an administration buzzsaw, and a general price boost initiated then by United States Steel Corp., the industry giant, collapsed under White House fire.

Readers of financial pages read for information. False color is not needed to retain these readers. This story should have been edited heavily on the desk:

> Stock of the Communications Satellite Corp. went into an assigned orbit yesterday on three major stock exchanges, rocketing to an apogee of $46 a share and a perigee of $42 and closing at $42.37, unchanged.
>
> It was the first day of listed trading on the exchanges. The stock previously was traded over-the-counter.
>
> The countdown on the first transaction on the New York stock exchange was delayed 12 minutes by an initial jam of buy and sell orders. . . .

Percentages and Numbers

Two types of errors appear frequently in stories dealing with percentages. One is the failure to distinguish between percentage and percentage points; the other lies in comparing the change with a new figure rather than the original one. For example, when a tax rate is increased from $5 per $100 of assessed valuation to $5.50, the increase is 10 percent. New figure less old figure, divided by old figure:

$$\$5.50 - \$5 = .50; \frac{.50}{\$5} = .10 \text{ or 10 percent.}$$

"Jones pointed out that the retail markup for most other brands is approximately 33 percent, whereas the markup on Brand J is 50 percent, or 17 percent higher." No. It is 17 percentage points higher but 51.5 percent higher. Divide 17 by 33.

"Dover's metropolitan population jumped from 16,000 just 10 years ago to more than 23,000 last year, an increase of better than 70 percent." Wrong again. It's a little less than 44 percent.

Is the figure misleading or inaccurate? The story said, "A total of $6,274 was raised at each of the four downtown stations." This adds up to $25,096. The writer intended the sentence to mean, "A total of $6,274 was raised at four stations." A not-so-sharp copy editor let this one get by: "Almost 500,000 slaves were shipped in this interstate trade. When one considers the average price of $800, the trade accounted for almost $20 million."

Are terms representing figures vague? In inheritance stories, it is better to name the amount and let the reader decide whether the amount is a "fortune." One of the wire service editors noted, "Fifteen thousand might be a fortune to a bootblack, but $200,000 would not be a fortune to a Rockefeller."

For some reason, many stories contain gambling odds, chances and probabilities. When a princess gave birth to a son, reporters quickly latched on to the odds on his name. Anthony was 1-2, George was even money, and Albert was 3-1. One headline played up the third in the betting. The name chosen was William. All of this shows the foolishness of editors who play into the hands of gamblers. If odds must be included in the story, they should be accurate. The story said that because weather records showed that in the last 86 years it had rained only 19 times on May 27, the odds were 8-1 against rain for the big relay event. The odds mean nothing to readers except to those who like to point out that in the story just mentioned the odds actually were 3½-1.

"Dr. Frank Rubovits said the children came from a single egg. He said the chance of this occurring 'probably is about 3 million to 1.'" He meant the odds against this occurring. The chance of this occurring is 1 in 3 million.

"The Tarapur plant will be the world's second largest atomic generator of electricity. The largest will be the 500-ton megawatt plant at Hinkley Point in Britain." A 500-ton megawatt plant makes no sense. What the writer meant was a 500-megawatt plant.

Some readers may rely on the idiom and insist that "five times as much as" means the same as "five times higher than" or "five times more than." If so, five times as much as $50 is $250 and five times higher than $50 is still $250. Others contend that the second should be $300. If earnings this year are 3½ times as large as last year's, they are actually 2½ times larger than last year's.

Insist on this style: 40,000 to 50,000 miles, not 40 to 50,000 miles; $3 million to $5 million, not $3 to $5 million.

"The committee recommended that a bid of $26,386.60 be accepted. After recommending the higher bid, the committee also had to recommend that an additional $326.60 be appropriated for the fire truck, because only $26,000 was included in the budget." The sum is still $60 short of the bid.

Equivalents should be included in stories that contain large sums. Most readers cannot visualize $20 billion, but they can understand it if there is an indication as to how much the amount would mean to each individual.

Here is one editor's advice to the staff:

> We can do a service for those important people out there if we use terms they are most acquainted with. For example, to most of our readers a ton of corn is more easily visualized if it is reported as bushels, about 36 in this case. We normally report yields and prices in bushels and that is the measurement most readers know. The same goes for petroleum; barrels is probably more recognizable than tons. When the opportunity presents itself, translate the figures into the best-known measurement.

Nothing is duller or more unreadable than a numbers story. If figures are the important part of the story, they should be related to something—or at least presented as comparisons.

Two of the most common mathematical errors in news copy are the use of millions for billions and vice versa and a construction such as "Five were injured . . . " when only four names are listed.

Ships and Boats

Do not use nautical terms unless they're used properly. "Capt. Albert S. Kelly, 75, the pilot who manned the Delta Queen's tiller yesterday . . . " What he manned was the *helm* or *wheel.* Few vessels except sailboats are guided with a tiller.

A story referred to a 27-foot ship. Nothing as small as 27 feet is a *ship. Ship* refers to big seagoing vessels such as tankers, freighters and ocean liners. Sailors insist that if it can be hoisted onto another craft it is a boat, and if it is too large for that it is a ship. Specific terms such as *cabin cruiser, sloop, schooner, barge* and *dredge* are appropriate.

"A rescue fleet ranging from primitive bayou pirogues to helicopters prowled through the night." That should send the copy editor to a dictionary so the editor can explain to readers that a pirogue is a canoe or a dugout. Better yet, simply use the more common term.

"The youths got to the pier just before the gangplank was lowered." When a ship sails, the gangplank is *raised.*

Commercial ships are measured by volume, the measurement of all enclosed space on the ship expressed in units of 100 cubic feet to the ton. Fuller description gives passenger capacity, length and age. The size of vessels is expressed in tonnage, the weight in long tons of a ship and all its contents (called displacement). A long ton is 2,240 pounds. All this is confusing to many readers. Copy editors should translate into terms recognized by readers, who can visualize length, age and firing power more readily than tonnage: "The 615-foot Bradley, longer than two football fields, . . ."

A knot is a measure of speed, not distance (nautical miles an hour). A nautical mile is about 1¼ land miles. "Knots per hour" is redundant.

Some readers may understand when the story says, "The limestone carrier was en route home in ballast." All will understand if the story says simply that the ship was going home empty.

Sports

Some of the best writing in American newspapers appears in the sports pages. So does some of the worst.

Sports pages should be, and are, the liveliest in the paper. They have action photos, a melange of spectator and participant sports and an array of personalities. Sports writers have more latitude than do other reporters. The good ones are among the best in the business; the undisciplined ones are among the worst.

Attractive pages and free expression mean little if the sports section is unintelligible to half the paper's readers. Too often, the editing reflects the attitude that if readers don't understand the lingo they should look elsewhere in the paper for information and entertainment.

The potential for readers of the sports section is greater than ever because of the growing number of participants in golf, bowling, fishing, boating and tennis. The spectator sports, especially automobile racing, football, golf, basketball, baseball and hockey, attract great audiences, thanks to the vast number of television viewers. Thus the sports pages, if edited intelligently, can become the most appealing section in the paper. But first, writers and copy editors must improve their manners.

A report of a contest or struggle should appeal to readers if it is composed in straightforward, clear English. The style can be vigorous without being forced, honest without being awesome. Sports fans do not need the sensational to keep their interest whetted. Those who are only mildly interested won't become sports page regulars if the stories are confusing.

Know the Game

One of the elementary rules in sports writing is to tell the reader the name of the game. Yet many stories talk about the Cubs and Pirates but never say specifically that the contest is a baseball game. Some writers assume that if the story refers to the contest as a "dribble derby" all sports page readers must understand that the story concerns a basketball game.

The story may contain references to parts of the game yet never mention the specific game. Here is an example:

Three Teams Tied in Sliceroo

Three teams tied for low at 59 in the sweepstakes division as the 11th annual Sliceroo got under way Thursday at Lakewood Country Club.

Deadlocked at 59 were the teams of . . .

In the driving contest, it was . . .

In the putting and chipping contest . . .

A best ball is set for Friday and a low net for Saturday, final day of the Sliceroo. A $5,000 hole-in-one competition on the 124-yard 11th hole is set for both final days.

Golfers will understand the story. But nongolfers, even many who enjoy watching golf matches on television, should be told outright that the story concerns a golf tournament. The added information would not offend the golfers. It might encourage a nongolfer to read on.

Some stories fail to state categorically who played whom. The writer assumes that if the opponents' managers are named, all hard-core sports readers will recognize the contestants. Perhaps so, but the casual reader might like to know, too. The caption under a two-column picture read, "They can't believe their eyes. Coach Andy S—, left, and Manager May S—, right, showed disbelief and disgruntlement as the Braves belt Pitcher Don C—for five runs in the eighth inning of their exhibition baseball game Wednesday at Clearwater, Fla. The Braves won, 10-2." Now, whom did the Braves play?

Not all readers understand the technical terms used to describe a sports contest. It might be necessary to explain that a seeded team gets a favored placement in the first round, and that if Smith beats Jones 2-1 in match play it means that golfer Smith is two holes ahead of golfer Jones with only one hole left to play and is, therefore, the winner. The name of the sport should be used in reference to the various cups. The Davis Cup is an international trophy for men tennis players. The Heisman Trophy is an award presented annually to the outstanding college football player in the nation. America's Cup refers to yachting, and America Cup to golfing.

Unanswered Questions

Answering more questions is one way to win more readers for the sports department. The key questions frequently overlooked are how and why. Why did the coach decide to punt on fourth down instead of trying to make one foot for a first down? How do tournament organizers get the funds to award $200,000 in prizes?

"The shadow of tragedy drew a black edge around a golden day at Sportsman's Park yesterday, bringing home the danger of horse racing with an impact that cut through the $68,950 Illinois Derby like a spotlight in darkness." So, what happened?

The best training for copy editors on the sports desk is a stint on the news copy desk. But before they go on the sports desk they should become familiar with the intricacies of all sports so they can catch the technical errors in sports copy. Here are examples:

"Center fielder Tony Cafar, whose fine relay after chasing the ball 'a country mile' held Ripley to a triple . . . " Unless Tony also made a throw of "a country mile," another player, a shortstop or second baseman, made the relay throw after taking a good throw from Tony.

When a writer covering a basketball game refers to a "foul shot," the reference should be deleted on the sports desk rim. The fouled player gets a free throw from the free-throw line, not the foul line or the charity lane.

The copy editor also has to be alert for some of the wild flights of imagination used by sports writers. "The Tar Heels hurdled their last major obstacle on the way to an unbeaten season but still had a long row to hoe." Is this a track meet or a county fair?

The following passage is a sure way to discourage sports page readers:

> His trouble in yesterday's 27-6 victory over the Dallas Cowboys before 72,062, largest crowd ever to see the Chiefs, was the reason Moore was in the trenches to receive a shattering kick with 6:24 left in the game.

This example suggests another tendency in sports copy—turning the story into a numbers game. Box scores, league standings and records have a place in the sports story, but generally they should have a subordinate rather than a dominant role.

Abbreviated Sports

The addiction for abbreviation is strong in both sports copy and headlines. **Broncos get first AFC win over NFC** announces a headline. It means that Denver's professional football team scored the first victory of the season by an American Football Conference team over a National Football Conference team.

The seventh paragraph of a story referred to the NASL. The reader, if interested, had to reread the lead to know that the initials stand for North American Soccer League.

"Color" in Sports   An editor told his colleagues, "There is nothing more exciting than a good contest. There is nothing duller than reading about it the next day." Yet many spectators who watch a Saturday contest can't wait to read about it the next morning. What were the coaches' and players' reactions to the game? What was the turning point? How long was the pass that won the game? What's the reporter's comment on the crowd's behavior?

So, if there is an audience for the report of a contest, the story needs no special flourishes. Loaded terms such as "wily mentor," "genial bossman," "vaunted running game," "dazzling run" and "astute field general" add little or nothing to the story. Adjectives lend false color. The Associated Press reported a "vise-tight race," "the red-hot Cardinals" and the "torrid 13-4 pace" as if these modifiers were needed to lure readers.

If all copy editors were permitted to aim their pencils at copy submitted by the prima donnas of the sports world, there would be no sentence structures like the following ones: "Benny (Kid) Paret showed 'very slight improvement' in his battle for life today while his embittered manager branded the New York State Athletic Commission's report absolving Referee Ruby Goldstein of blame for the boxer's condition as a whitewash."

"Jones, who has been bothered by a sore rib this spring, played eight innings yesterday, collected two singles and drove in a run." He didn't collect them; he hit them.

"Ortiz threw his first bomb in the second round when he nailed Laguna with a left and right to the jaw." How can you nail something with a bomb?

"Left-hander Carlton, who started on the mound for Philadelphia, recovered from a shaky start and pitched six-hit ball for eight innings before a walk and a botched-up double play caused the manager to protect a 4-1 lead, as a result of a three-run homer by Mike Schmidt in the seventh." The sentence is hard to understand because it is overstuffed and because the facts are not told in chronological order. Revised: "Left-hander Carlton started on the mound for Philadelphia. He recovered from a shaky start and pitched six-hit ball for eight innings. Then a walk and a missed double play caused the manager to bring in a new pitcher. Philadelphia was leading, 4-1, as a result of a three-run homer by Mike Schmidt in the seventh."

Here is how to tell a story upside down: "Waldrop's 17-yard explosion for his eighth touchdown of the season punctuated a 65-yard march from Army's reception of the kickoff by a courageous Falcon team, which had gone ahead for the second time in the game, 10-7, in the ninth minute of the final period."

An overstuffed sentence of any sort will be just as damaging, and harder to repair, than compound sentence leads. Note this one: "The heaviest betting non-holiday Monday crowd in the Balmoral Jockey club's eight years at Washington Park poured $1,066,919 into the machines yesterday on a nine-race program headed by the

$7,500 Harvey purse, a six-furlong dash which drew six starters and was won by Mighty Fennec, piloted by Bill Hartack." Revised: "Horse-race fans put $1,066,919 into the Washington Park machines yesterday on a nine-race program. It was the heaviest betting non-holiday Monday crowd in the Balmoral Jockey club's eight years at the park. The $7,500 Harvey purse for the six-furlong race drew six starters. It was won by Mighty Fennec, ridden by Bill Hartack."

"'Statistics don't tell the story,' he explained, looking many straight in the eye." If he looked more than one person straight in the eyes while he said that, he must have been a long time between words.

Synonym Sickness

It takes good editing to convert some sports writers into Homers and Hemingways. At least, though, copy editors can try to help writers improve their ways of telling a story.

Copy editors can excise clichés such as "paydirt," "turned the tables," "hammered (or slammed) a homerun," "Big Eight hardwoods," "circuit clout," "gridder," "hoopster," "thinclads," "tanksters," "sweet revenge," "rocky road," "free loads" (free throws), "droughts" (losing streaks), "standing-room-only crowds," "put a cap on the basket," "as the seconds ticked off the clock," "unblemished records," "paced the team," "outclassed but game," "roared from behind," "sea of mud," "vaunted defense," "coveted trophy" and "last-ditch effort."

They can insist on the correct word. Boxers may have *altercations* (oral) with their managers. They have *fights* with other boxers.

They can tone down exaggerated expressions like "mighty atom of the ring," "destiny's distance man" or "Northwestern comes off tremendous effort Monday" (Northwestern tried hard). They can cut out redundancy in phrases such as "with 30,000 spectators looking on."

They can resist the temptation to use synonyms for verbs *wins, beats* and *defeats:* annihilates, atomizes, batters, belts, bests, blanks, blasts, boots home, clips, clobbers, cops, crushes, downs, drops, dumps, edges, ekes out, gallops over, gangs up on, gouges, gets past, H-bombs, halts, humiliates, impales, laces, lashes, lassoes, licks, murders, outslugs, outscraps, orbits, overcomes, paces, pastes, pins, racks up, rallies, rolls over, romps over, routs, scores, sets back, shades, shaves, sinks, slows, snares, spanks, squeaks by, squeezes by, stampedes, stomps, stops, subdues, surges, sweeps, tops, topples, triggers, trips, trounces, tumbles, turns back, vanquishes, wallops, whips, whomps and wrecks.

They will let the ball be *hit,* not always banged, bashed, belted, blooped, bombed, boomed, bumped, chopped, clunked, clouted, conked, cracked, dribbled, drilled, dropped, driven, hacked, knifed, lashed, lined, plastered, plunked, poked, pooped, pumped, punched, pummeled, pushed, rapped, ripped, rocked, slapped, sliced, slugged, smashed, spilled, spanked, stubbed, swatted, tagged, tapped, tipped, topped, trickled, whipped, whistled, whomped and whooped.

They will let a ball be *thrown* and only occasionally tossed, twirled, fired and hurled.

They will let a ball be *kicked,* occasionally punted and never toed or booted.

They will resist the shopworn puns: Birds (Eagles, Orioles, Cardinals) soar or claw; Lions (Tigers, Bears, Cubs) roar, claw or lick; Braves (Tribesmen, Indians) scalp or tomahawk; Mustangs (Colts, Broncos) buck, gallop, throw or kick.

They will insist on neutrality in all sports copy and avoid slanting the story in favor of the home team.

They will not string modifiers endlessly: "The Pistons won 29 and lost 40 under the guidance of the then only 24 years old DuBusschere."

Lifestyle

One of the brighter changes in newspapers in recent years has been the transformation of the society pages, with their emphasis on club and cupid items, to the family or lifestyle section, which has a broader-based appeal.

Such sections still carry engagement announcements and wedding stories, but their added fare is foods, fashions, finance, health, education, books and other cultural affairs. They are edited for active men and women in all ranks, not solely for those in the top rank of society.

The better editors regard readers of lifestyle sections as alert individuals who are concerned with social problems such as prostitution, racism, civil disorders, prisons, alcoholism and educational reforms. Such editors strive to make their pages informative as well as entertaining.

Some papers now handle engagements, weddings and births as record items. And a few charge for engagement and wedding stories and pictures unless the event is obviously news, such as the wedding of Prince Charles. Most, however, recognize the value of these items and continue to publish them as news.

To add some spice to its pages devoted to wedding accounts, the Gannett Rochester Newspapers started a "Wedding Scrapbook" page in its Saturday section, "Brides Book for Greater Rochester." Included were features on how the couple met, amusing incidents of the participants on the way to the ceremony and pictures of the couple in faraway places.

Wedding and engagement stories are with us to stay, but some customs, such as not giving the bridegroom much recognition, may change. This point was delightfully argued by Paul Brookshire in his column in the *South Dade* (Homestead, Fla.) *New Leader.*

Here are some excerpts:

> In these days when the world is quaking in its boots and news of great significance is daily swept into newspaper trash cans for lack of space, it is sickening to read paragraph after paragraph about some little girl changing HER name to HIS.
>
> The groom? He apparently wasn't dressed at all ... if he was even there. But Mother and Mother-in-Law? Yes. They were fashion plates in beige ensembles and matching accessories or something.
>
> I ask you. Is it a wedding or a fashion show?
>
> If it is a fashion show, why isn't it held in a hotel ballroom and why isn't the groom given a tiny bit of credit for showing up with his clothes on?
>
> The blackout of the bridegroom in wedding accounts is an unpardonable sin. If the groom is mentioned at all he is afforded as much space as an atheist gets on the church page.
>
> And pictures. Did you ever see a photograph of a bridegroom? Maybe in the Post Office but not in the newspaper.
>
> I'm going on record right now in favor of wedding announcements being run as legal notices—payable in advance by the father of the bride.
>
> Better still, if the bride insists on giving a minute, detailed description of every inch of clothing she happens to have on her person, I suggest she take out a paid display advertisement.
>
> In this manner, trade names may be used and shops that sold the girl all her glorious gear could get equal space on the same page.
>
> Newspapers would reap untold profits from this arrangement and readers might be able to get some world news for a change instead of bouffant skirts highlighted with tiers of lace and aqua frocks with aqua tipped orchids and maize silk linen ensembles with ... whatever you wear with maize silk linen ensembles.

Even though many newspapers have changed the society section to a lifestyle section, some retain a static style, especially on engagement and wedding stories. Wedding story leads too often read like these:

> First Methodist Church in Littleton was the setting for the double-ring wedding rites of ...

> Miss Cynthia Jones has become the bride of Joe Smith, it was announced by her parents ...

> After a wedding trip to Las Vegas, Nev., Mr. and Mrs. Jones will live in ...

> All Saints Roman Catholic Church was the setting for the single-ring rites ...

Newspapers continue to use the following:

• Stock words and phrases—holy matrimony, high noon, benedicts, exchanged nuptial vows.

- Descriptive adjectives—attractive, pretty, beautiful, charming, lovely.
- Non sequiturs—"Given in marriage by her parents, the bride wore a white silk organza gown with a sabrina neckline and short sleeves." "Wearing a gown of white lace cotton over taffeta with empire waistline, square neckline and short sleeves, the bride was given in marriage by her father."
- Confusing collectives—"The couple is on a trip to northern Wisconsin and will live at 300 Fairmount Ave., Whitefish Bay, when they return." Generally, a collective noun takes a singular verb when the noun indicates a group acting as a unit and a plural verb when it means individuals performing individual actions: "The Board of Park Commissioners gave its blessings . . . " "The platoon fought its way up the hill. . . . " "Their headquarters is in the Bennett building. . . . " "The crew have returned to their homes." Therefore, make it couple *are,* not *is.*
- Details—gown and flower descriptions and social affiliations that reflect status.
- Euphemistic headlines—**Betrothal told, Holy vows exchanged, Wedding ceremonies solemnized.**

Excerpts from an error-filled account of a wedding reveal the unbelievable triteness of such stories:

> A petite white United Methodist Church nestled below the towering Rocky Mountains in Lyons, Colo., was the setting for the marriage of Shirley Ann M— and Wesley William B— on Aug. 4. A happy sun brought warmth and color through the old-fashioned peaked stained glass windows at precisely 3 p.m. when Gloria L . . . played The Wedding March, and guests stood from hand-carved oak seats, curved into an intimate half-circle to witness the double-ring ceremony. . . .
>
> The Rev. D. L. N— officiated at the afternoon ceremony amid arrangements of mint-green carnations, white gladiolas, and white daisies with giant white satin bows which adorned the altar. Pews were delightfully enhanced with waterfall baskets of fresh greenery and wild mountain flowers plucked early that morning from beside the St. Vrain River and tied with lime and powder blue satin ribbons. . . .
>
> The bride tossed her bouquet from the stairway and "went away" all dressed in white and yellow.

Talented copy editors will not allow writers to single out women's achievements with sexist terms such as housewife (rather than homemaker) and woman doctor (simply use doctor). They will delete phrases like "is affiliated with," "refreshments will be served," "featured speaker," "special guests," "noon luncheon," "dinner meeting." They will refuse to let a person "host (or hostess) a party," "gavel a meeting" or "chair a committee."

They will not let reporters go out of their way to use *female, feminine* and *ladies* in all manner of sentences where the word *women* would be proper and more appropriate, if, indeed, even that word is necessary.

They will catch slips such as "Mrs. Richard Roe, nee Jane Doe." *Nee* means "born" and people are born only with their surnames. The first (not Christian) name is given later.

They will remain on guard for awkward sentences:

> Do you keep track of your weight and lose the first 5 or 10 pounds too much?

> Seniors realize the importance of proper dress more than younger students, but after a while they catch on.

All copy for lifestyle sections, as well as for the other sections of the paper, should be edited for its news value. This should apply to the syndicated features as well as to the locally produced copy. Similarly, the headlines should reflect as much care and thought as do those on Page One.

7

The Copy Editor on Guard

Perils of the Superlative

Writing that something is the "first," "only," "biggest," "best" or "a record" seldom adds to a story. Often it backfires.

When President Lyndon Johnson rode in a Canadian government plane, one wire service said he was the first American president to travel aboard an airplane of a foreign government. He wasn't. President Dwight Eisenhower flew in a Royal Air Force Comet from London to Scotland in 1959 to visit Queen Elizabeth.

Another wire service characterized Gouverneur Morris as "the penman of the Constitution" and Lewis Morris as the "only New York signer of the Declaration of Independence." The man who penned the Constitution was Jacob Shallus, and there were four New York signers of the Declaration of Independence.

When President Johnson ordered the American flag to be flown at half-staff in mourning for Winston Churchill, the stories said, "This is the first time such an honor had been accorded to a foreigner." This is not so. President John Kennedy ordered half-staffing after the death of Dag Hammarskjöld, former secretary-general of the United Nations.

A California obituary identified a woman as the "first postmistress" in the nation. A Missouri story reported the closing of America's "shortest commercial railroad." Both statements were disproved.

The Associated Press described Herbert Lehman of New York as the "first person of the Jewish faith ever to hold a Senate seat." The AP had to acknowledge that it was wrong by at least six men and more than 100 years. Jewish senators who preceded Lehman were David Levy Yulee of Florida, Judah P. Benjamin of Louisiana, Benjamin F. Jonas of Louisiana, Joseph Simon of Oregon, Isidore Raynor of Maryland and Simon Guggenheim of Colorado.

When United Press International described the Flying Scotsman, a famous British locomotive, as the first steam locomotive to exceed 100 mph, railroad buffs hurried to set the record straight. Records show that on May 10, 1893, the New York Central No. 999 was timed unofficially at 112.5 mph on a one-mile stretch between Batavia and Buffalo. On March 1, 1901, the Savannah, Florida and Western (later part of Atlantic Coast Line, later Seaboard Coast Line) No. 1901 was timed at 120 mph. On June 12, 1905, the Pennsylvania Special traveled three miles near Elida, Ohio, in 85 seconds for an average of 127 mph.

A story described New York's former 15-cent municipal transit fare as the lowest in the nation. San Francisco's also was 15 cents at that time. Another story said Disneyland's 306-foot painting of the Grand Canyon would be "the longest painting in the world." The Battle of Atlanta painting in Atlanta's Cyclorama building is 400 feet long.

A story from Louisville described a conviction as the first under a new law barring interstate shipment of gambling material. Two months earlier two men had been convicted under the same law. A Billy Graham rally was described as having the largest audience for a single meeting. But a Rosary Crusade in San Francisco had been attended by 500,000, a bigger crowd than Graham's.

The story said, without attribution, that Mary Martin had been "seen by an astonishing 100 million persons in her two performances of Peter Pan." No one knows exactly how many persons watched the performances. At best, it was an estimate based on a projection of percentages of TV sets in use turned to a certain program.

All these are examples of abused statistics that invade the news report. One story indicated that New York City has 8 million rats. Another quoted the American Medical Association as saying that only 5 percent of Americans dream in color. How can anyone know such exact figures? Highway deaths may increase from one year to the next, but one possible explanation may be that there are more vehicles on streets and highways. Highway deaths on holiday weekends are higher than normal because such weekends often are longer. "The toll has dropped so that last year there were only 81 traffic deaths here, an all-time low." Since when? 1942? 1776? 1900? "The ships were built in record time." What was the previous record?

All superlatives should be checked. If they cannot be verified, at least they can be softened: "One of the most despicable crimes in the world ..."; "One of the hardest-working actresses in Germany. . . ."

Most historical references also should be checked. A story said that Helga Kraft, who was born in 1893, had been a former singer on the Chautauqua circuit and had appeared with Mme. Schumann-Heink and Jenny Lind. Jenny Lind died in 1887, six years before Kraft was born.

An AP story referred to the "turnover of jumbo C130 cargo planes." The C130 is not classified as a jumbo plane.

Beware of the Hoax

Old stories have a way of appearing on the copy desk disguised as news. These hoaxes are likely to show up occasionally:

—The story of a 16-year-old baby sitter who adhered to a freshly painted toilet seat for hours. A doctor administered to her, tripped and knocked himself out. Both were carried off in an ambulance for repairs and both sued the family who engaged the sitter.

—A driver flagged by a stalled motorist who asked her for a push. Told she would have to get up to 35 mph to get the stalled car started, she backed off, gunned the motor and rammed his car at 35 mph.

—The sheriff who was called to a farm to investigate the theft of 2,025 pigs discovered that only two sows and 25 pigs were missing. The farmer who reported the loss lisped.

—A farmer armed with a shotgun went to a chicken house to rout a suspected thief. The farmer stumbled, and the gun went off, killing all his hens.

—The story, usually from some obscure hill hamlet in the east of Europe or in Asia, of an eagle carrying off a 3-year-old child.

—A Sunday driver who called police to report that someone stole the steering wheel and all the pedals from his car. A squad car was sent to the scene, but before police arrived the man called back and said, "Everything is all right. I was looking in the back seat."

—Someone reports he has found a copy, in near perfect condition, of the Jan. 4, 1800, issue of the Ulster County *Gazette*. The paper is prized not only for its age but because it contains a statement made by the U.S. Senate to President John Adams following the death of George Washington 21 days earlier. It refers to Washington as "Father of our country." Few copies of the original exist, but there are many reproductions.

—A story from Harrisburg, Pa., told about six students permanently blinded by looking at the sun after taking LSD. It was not until after the story had received wide play and had been the subject of editorials and columns that the hoax was discovered.

—A group of young stockbrokers got credit for plotting a hoax against New York newspapers during the depression days of the 1930s. They created a fictitious football team at a fictitious college and every Saturday during the fall they phoned in the results of the fictitious football game. The hoax was uncovered near the end of the football season when the ficititious college team began appearing in the ranks of the untied and undefeated teams.

—The bricklayer story makes the rounds periodically, usually with a change in locale. The story may have been reworked from a vaudeville gag of earlier days. It is recorded by a British accent comedian as a monologue under the title of "Hoffnung at the Oxford Club." Fred Allen used it as a skit on one of his radio shows in the 1930s. In 1945 the story was retold in an anthology of humor edited by H. Allen Smith. Three versions had their setting in Korea, Barbados and Vietnam. In World War II the "bricklayer" was a sailor on the USS Saratoga requesting a five-day leave extension. Here is the Barbados version, courtesy of UPI:

LONDON (UPI)—The Manchester Guardian today quoted as "an example of stoicism" the following unsigned letter—ostensibly from a bricklayer in the Barbados to his contracting firm:

"Respected Sir,

"When I got to the building, I found that the hurricane had knocked some bricks off the top. So I rigged up a beam with a pulley at the top of the building and hoisted up a couple of barrels full of bricks. When I had fixed up the building, there was a lot of bricks left over.

"I hoisted the barrel back up again and secured the line at the bottom, and then went up and filled the barrel with the extra bricks. Then I went to the bottom and cast off the line.

"Unfortunately, the barrel of bricks was heavier than I was, and before I knew what was happening the barrel started down, jerking me off the ground. I decided to hang on and halfway up I met the barrel coming down and received a severe blow on the shoulder.

"I then continued to the top, banging my head against the beam and getting my fingers jammed in the pulley. When the barrel hit the ground it bursted its bottom, allowing all the bricks to spill out.

"I was now heavier than the barrel and so started down again at high speed. Halfway down, I met the barrel coming up and received severe injuries to my shins. When I hit the ground I landed on the bricks, got several painful cuts from the sharp edges.

"At this point I must have lost my presence of mind, because I let go the line. The barrel then came down, giving me another heavy blow on the head and putting me in the hospital.

"I respectfully request sick leave."

Perhaps, as one editor has suggested, the original version dealt with the building of the Cheops pyramid or the Parthenon. The story seems to have magic appeal for reporters and copy editors.

Some others, though not hoaxes, are impossible or misleading:

—A man received a series of summonses to pay a tax bill. The notices said he owed $0.00 in taxes and $0.00 in penalties. He was warned that his personal belongings would be attached if he didn't pay. He sent the tax office a check for $0.00 and got a receipt for that amount. Sometimes the yarn is applied to the non payment of a non charge from an electric company and a threat to cut off service unless the bill is paid—or to a tuition demand on a student studying at a college on a tax-free scholarship.

—A fake story may be hard to detect. This fraud got by the desk of a New York newspaper: "The thallus or ruling monarch of the principality of Marchantia will arrive here today on a two-day visit as part of a State Department tour."

—Newspapers have worn out the gag about the man who

answered "twice a week" opposite "sex" on a census question-naire. Others that newspapers could do without include:

> Undercover investigators yesterday said they ended a suburban sex ring where housewives worked as call girls to supplement the family income.

> Smith will help to direct a volunteer effort embracing several thousand housewives, who will be calling on their neighbors for contributions.

> In Germany yesterday, Mrs. R— issued a statement to the German press agency in which she denied ever having improper relations with men other than her husband while in Washington.

Misquotations

A careful copy editor would be wise to keep a quotation reference at hand while handling copy containing references to often-repeated quotations or attribution of such quotations.

Such a reference will stop reporters from attributing "Go west, young man" to Horace Greeley. The advice was given by John Babson Lane in 1851. Greeley used the expression in an editorial in the *New York Tribune* but amplified it: "Go west, young man, and grow up with the country."

Charles Dudley Warner, not Mark Twain, should get credit for "Everybody talks about the weather, but nobody does anything about it." Bill Nye, the humorist, originated the saying, "There are just two people entitled to refer to themselves as 'we'—one is the editor, and the other is the fellow with a tapeworm." Mark Twain later revised the statement: "Only presidents, editors, and people with tapeworms have the right to use the editorial 'we.'"

Voltaire is wrongly credited with the quotation. "I may not agree with what you say, but I will defend to the death your right to say it." Most likely it is a paraphrase of Voltaire's "Think for yourselves, and let others enjoy the privilege to do so too." Gen. John J. Pershing did not exclaim, "Lafayette, we are here!" It was uttered by Charles E. Stanton, chief disbursing officer of the American Expeditionary Forces.

Careless writers attribute the "gilded lily" business to Shakespeare. But what Shakespeare wrote was, "To gild refined gold, to paint the lily." Similarly, the Bible does not say that money is the root of all evil. It says, "Love of money is the root of all evil." Music doesn't have charms to soothe the savage beast. Congreve said, "Music hath charms to soothe the savage breast." And Thomas Hardy did not refer to "the maddening crowd" but to "the madding crowd."

Up to the time of his death, a South African dentist, Philip Blaiberg, had survived with an implanted heart. In an account of Blaiberg's death, a UPI reporter wrote that Blaiberg's last act was to scribble a quote from the Persian poet Omar Khayyám: " . . . for I shall not pass this way again." A Connecticut editor questioned the attribution, causing UPI to send out a correction. The probable author is Stephen Grellet and the usually accepted full quotation is, "I shall pass through this world but once. If, therefore, there by any kindness I can show or any good thing I can do, let me do it now. Let me not defer or neglect it, for I shall not pass this way again."

A sports column tribute concluded, "In the words of the late Grantland Rice: 'When the great scorer comes to write beside your name,/It's not whether you won or lost but how you played the game.'" What Rice really said was, "When the One Great Scorer comes to write against your name—/He marks—not that you won or lost—but how you played the game." Reporters should never quote poetry from memory. When poetry shows up in a piece of copy, the copy editor should assume it's wrong and look it up.

The cutlines began, "Like Topsy, Baptist Hospital and Bowman Gray School of Medicine apparently just grew." The literary allusion is to Topsy's reply to Miss Ophelia's question, "Do you know who made you?" in *Uncle Tom's Cabin:* "Nobody, as I knows on,' said the child with a short laugh . . . 'I 'spect I growed. Don't think nobody made me.'" It is a fine point, but it can be presumed that those familiar enough with the book to recognize the simile would wince at Topsy's newly acquired polish. For others, it would be meaningless anyway.

The story quoted a structural linguist's feelings about people who object to ending sentences with prepositions: "You remember what Winston Churchill said when an aide corrected a line in one of Churchill's speeches because it ended in a preposition? Churchill told the aide: 'This is an outrage up with which I will not put.'" Churchill was misquoted. What he said (and even this may be apocryphal) was, "This is the type of arrant pedantry up with which I shall not put."

A column criticizing the overuse of the word *gourmet* said, "I am reminded of the line of poetry which told of the moth flitting its wings signifying nothing." Was it perchance not a poem but a Shakespeare play, and not a moth flitting its wings but "a tale told by an idiot, full of sound and fury, signifying nothing"?

"We've come a long way since Commodore Vanderbilt said, 'The public be damned.'" But the commodore never said it. It was William H. Vanderbilt, son of Cornelius, the so-called commodore, who made the remark.

"Robert Burns, the old Scotchman, said: 'Oh that we would see ourselves as others see us.'" Burns was a distinguished poet, hardly the "old Scotchman." Careful writers prefer *Scot* or *Scotsman* to *Scotchman,* as do the Scots themselves. The actual quotation: "Oh wad some power the giftie gie us/To see oursels as others see us!"

Changing Quotes   Copy editors often have to decide whether to make corrections in direct quotations. Should they correct the syntax of the speaker? If the goof is within quote marks, should it remain? Did the speaker use poor English or did the reporter write poor English? Do the persons quoted get a friendly or an unfriendly pencil on the desk? Perhaps it was the writer rather than the speaker who used poor grammar. Usually the language is corrected in direct quotes unless, as one editor commented, it is done with malice aforethought when "we want to show someone ain't no good at talking," or the speaker is expected to abuse the language or a speaker, such as the president, makes a slip of the tongue. Some editors, however, insist that the quotation marks be deleted, even when the quotation is changed only slightly.

Attributions   Copy editors will save reporters from attribution logjams if they remember this question: Is it clear who is talking? If the reporter shifts to a second speaker, the story should identify the new speaker immediately, not at the end of the quotation. The reader assumes the first speaker is still talking.

Sometimes the source cannot be named, yet the statement is newsworthy. The editor assumes readers understand this when a story contains phrases like "a spokesman," "a usually reliable source," "a government official" and "it was learned." Many editors prefer not to use quotes around either fact or opinion ascribed to an unnamed source. Some editors understandably deplore the faceless source protection. These editors say, in effect, that if a government official with a special interest in Latin American affairs terms a resolution "worse than useless," why can't the fearless official be named? By withholding identity, papers shamelessly do other people's bidding.

Nonattribution denies the reader a very essential fact—often *the* essential fact—the source of the information, of the idea, of the speculation, of the proposal, of the supposition—even, sometimes, of the accusation. "Republican State Headquarters issued a statement today blasting. . . ." This is a statement of faceless political critics. Such statements should be attributed either to individuals or to official party organizations that are willing to stand behind them. There's no such organization as Republican State Headquarters.

Synonyms of Attribution. Is the synonym for *said* apt? Do "added," "pointed out," "offered," "admitted," "disclosed," "noted," "revealed," "indicated," "conceded," "explained" or "cited the fact that" give the quotation an editorial tone?

Do the synonyms for *said* convey a hint of doubt as to the veracity of the credited source ("according to," "said he believes")?

"According to" actually refers to the content, not to the speaker: "According to the mayor's letter . . .," not "According to the mayor. . . ."

Does the writer use gestures for words?

> "We're gonna put on a show, too," grinned Wags.
> "Now I can invite my friends to play on the grass," Donna beamed.
> "The bill will be paid," the official smiled.
> "I heard something pop in my shoulder," he winced on his way to the dressing room.

No matter how good a grinner or wincer, how bright a beamer or how broad a smiler, you just can't grin, wince, beam or smile a quote. If it's a quip, that should be obvious from the context. If it isn't, saying so won't make it so. An exclamation mark may be used after a brief expletive, but it looks silly after a long sentence.

Said is a simple verb that usually is preferable to others used in an effort to convey determination, skepticism and wit. Usually the quoted matter can speak for itself. Many of the best writers use *said* almost exclusively. *Said* used repeatedly can give emphasis; it is not weakened by repetition.

Does the quoted word invite the reader to disbelieve the statement?

"Father Divine's blond wife was at his bedside, along with his 18 'secretaries.'" By placing quotes around secretaries, the writer expressed an opinion, not a fact.

Do scattergun quotations bewilder the reader?

"The actress said she would wed Wilding 'at the end of the week.'"

"The blood-covered body of a 'brilliant' 19-year-old Williams College sophomore was found today—a rifle nearby—in a fraternity house room. Police Chief George A. Royal said it was 'apparently murder.'"

Is the source given immediately in a controversial quotation?

When the information is disputable, the source should come at the beginning; it should not be appended to the statement. "The administration budget has imposed a tremendous burden on consumers, Sen. Jane Doe contended in calling for revisions." Change it to read, "Sen. Jane Doe called for revisions and contended that the administration budget has imposed a tremendous burden on consumers."

Does the quotation reveal precisely what the speaker said? "Stewart still maintains 'he called it as he saw it.'" You can't quote someone in the third person.

Does an awkwardly split quote interrupt the speaker? "'He,' said Jones, 'needs a wig.'"

Are the circumstances of the statement clear? Was the statement made in an interview, a report, a letter, a public speech? Was it in

English or a translation? Was it prepared or extemporaneous? Was it made over a network or a single station? What network? What station?

Is that attribution overworked? In some crime or accident stories, phrases such as "police said" or "Patrolman Jones reported" are used in almost every sentence. A blanket attribution such as "police gave this account of the accident" would ease the monotony for the readers.

Tell Them, Don't Tease Them

News is regarded one way in the newspaper officer and another way by its readers. In the newsroom the reporter is constantly admonished to "keep 'em short." "How much do you have on that hotel death?" the city editor asks. "Enough for about 14 inches," answers the reporter. "Hold it to 7," orders the superior. "We're short on space today."

So the reporter prunes the story to 7 inches. The story reaches the copy desk and an editor goes to work to make it even tighter.

All this, of course, is unknown to the reader who sits down to enjoy the newspaper. A headline catches the eye: **80-foot fall at hotel ends actor's grim joke.** The reader begins the story: " 'Watch me do a trick,' said the 26-year-old actor to his companion, and he stepped out the eight-floor window of their downtown hotel early Sunday." Muses the reader, "I was downtown early Sunday morning. I wonder what hotel it was and what time?" The story doesn't answer his questions. It did identify the victim. Also his companion. Near the end of the story was a brief description of the companion, Paul Lynde: "Lynde is a widely known actor, investigators said." "Funny I never heard of him," the reader again muses. "Wonder what he appeared in?" This was the story as sent by The Associated Press. For the morning papers the story failed to identify the hotel, did not give the time of the fall and identified Lynde only as a widely known actor. Readers of afternoon papers got some of the missing details. The hotel was the Sir Francis Drake, the time was "the wee hours Sunday morning" and Lynde was identified as a comedian who appeared in the Broadway and film versions of "Bye Bye Birdie" with Dick Van Dyke and in the movie "Under the Yum Yum Tree" as Imogene Coca's henpecked husband.

The ability to give details is the newspaper's great advantage over its competitors. Readers relate to the news. The more involved they become in the events, the more avid readers they become. In short, they demand the whole story down to the last detail. If the story said, 'Hastings Banda, the leader of Nyasaland, received his education in Ohio," the reader wants to know, "Where in Ohio?" "At what university?" "When?" The reader relates to the news. "I wonder if that's the same Banda I knew when I was at Ohio State in the 1950s.

A wire story about a plane crash in New York City said the 79 passengers included "two young opera singers en route to a South Carolina concert, prominent Southern businessmen, a former Virginia college beauty queen." The story as sent drew this protest from a client's managing editor: "Who the people are who die in these crashes is a point of equal or more interest than the circumstances of the crash. We all identify with them—where they are going, where they are coming from. I want to know what opera those opera singers were going to sing in." The details were in a sidebar, but the sidebar was not sent on the circuit to which the newspaper subscribed.

A newspaper had a three-column photo and a 6-inch story on the announcement that the Speakman Co. would move its general offices to new quarters. And what does the Speakman Co. do? The story didn't say.

A story related that a man had gone to court to fight for a seat in the legislature, but it did not tell to which party he belonged. Another told of a woman mugged while waiting for a bus at Delaware and Woodlawn avenues, but did not give the time of the incident, which would be of interest to those who ride the bus.

When handling a story about an airplane crash, the cost of the plane is an important part of the piece and should be included.

In a wire story about a fighting policeman, the gist of the story was that the outcome of the bout would determine whether the policeman would try for the jackpot in the ring or give it up for his pay as a patrolman. Everything seemed to be in the story except the weight division, an important item to boxing fans.

A story was about a drunk chimpanzee that supposedly escaped and created havoc around the countryside by trying to break into homes. But the story failed to tell who owned the chimp, what he was doing in the county, how he got anything to drink and what finally happened after a game warden arrived on the scene. These were basic questions the reporter forgot to answer. The copy editor should have checked.

A paper had a three-column picture and story about consecration ceremonies at the Cherry Hill Methodist Church's new "Harlan House." The story told that Harlan House was named for "Miss Mollie" Harlan, that the Rev. Dr. Darcy Littleton took part in the ceremonies, that "Miss Mollie" is not buried in the Cherry Hill Cemetery, that Littleton is now with Goodwill Industries in Wilmington, that G. Harlan Wells spoke and that the Rev. R. Jerris Cooke conducted the service. But when all this was said and the picture was examined, readers were still left to guess what Harlan House is or who Mollie Harlan was that the house should be named for her. Was she related to G. Harlan Wells?

A paper reported in detail the arrest of a minister on charges of operating a motor vehicle without a license, failure to carry a car registration card, disorderly conduct and disobeying a police officer. When three of the four charges were dismissed, the story failed to tell why. Answer: It is standard procedure to dismiss the license and registration charges when a driver has simply forgotten to carry the documents.

A Page One story told the fascinating details of a divorce decree upheld by the state Supreme Court but failed to mention the names of the parties in the case.

Another story gave an account of the Senate's 78–8 approval of the president's trade bill but failed to tell who the eight opponents were and, even worse, how the senators from the paper's state voted on the measure. This was a revolutionary trade measure that had been in the news for months and was finally opposed by only eight senators. Wasn't anyone who handled the story curious about their names?

A story in March said, "The Bahais will celebrate New Year's eve at the Bahai center. There will be readings and music." The story read, "New Year's Day tomorrow is known as Naw-Ruz." Couldn't the music and the refreshments be dropped and tell instead who Bahais are and what the heck New Year's Day is doing in the middle of March?

A skindiver stayed under water for 31 hours and spent much of his time reading a paperback book. There was no word to explain what kept the pages from disintegrating. (The paper was a glossy stock.)

A housewife won a fat prize in a magazine advertising contest. There was no hint what she did to win, a point made more important by the statement that the woman could neither read nor write.

Another story concerned a judge who reversed his own conviction of a union leader for breach of the peace. The reversal, said the story, was based on "new evidence" but failed to tell readers the nature of the new evidence.

The story said the black students, 105 of the 120 blacks enrolled at Northwestern, marched out of the building singing. It failed to mention the songs they sang, a detail that might have shed more light on their behavior.

If any part of the story is confusing, the copy editor should supply explanations to make the story understandable. Obviously, the explanation should not be as hard to understand as the phrase itself. For instance:

> Congress in 1946 waived government immunity to suits in tort (a civil wrong in which a legal action may lie) and permitted suits on tort claims against the United States.

The parenthetical explanation hardly aids most readers. If an explanation is required it should be one that really helps.

> As a rule, sovereign government may not be sued by its citizens unless the government consents. In 1946 Congress gave blanket permission to citizens to sue the U.S. government if they thought it was responsible for injuries to them or their property.

The story told of a boy who died, apparently of suffocation after he choked on a hot dog in his home. Police said the boy left the table after dinner and was found choking in his bathroom. His mother slapped him on the back in a vain attempt to dislodge the obstruction. Firefighters took him to a hospital where he was pronounced dead. A few lines of first-aid instruction at the end of the story might have served to save other lives.

A woman who was hospitalized twice in a short time asked to be transferred from one hospital to another to be near her husband. What ailed hubby? It wasn't explained.

The Royal Navy dropped the unit *fathom* and started measuring depths in meters. The story told all about it. All, that is, except how deep a fathom is.

A story contained the statement "where family income is below federal poverty levels" but neglected to tell the readers what the poverty level is by federal standards.

"A bell captain in a midtown hotel was arrested for scalping World Series tickets." Why the reluctance to name the hotel? A directive reminded editors, "In these days, when GIs, businessmen, students, school teachers et al. are traveling throughout the world, such identification is often of interest to many readers. The part of town where a news event occurs is sometimes pertinent too in stories from the big cities that are frequented by travelers."

Here is a complete story as one newspaper printed it:

TALLAHASSEE—The simmering feud between Republican Gov. Claude Kirk of Florida and his Democratic cabinet erupted into a full scale shouting battle today, and Kirk ordered an end to weekly cabinet meetings for the first time in state history.

Cabinet members immediately declared they would go on meeting anyway.

The stormy session began with the cabinet refusing to spend $35,000 on a federal liaison office that Kirk wants to open in Washington.

Some readers must have wondered how a Republican governor came to have a Democratic cabinet, what officials belong to the cabinet, what can be accomplished by cabinet meetings not attended by the governor and whether the weekly meeting is required by law.

The first rule in writing or editing a story is to ask yourself: Who will read the item and what will they most want to know about the subject? Both the writer and the copy editor should pare the story for word economy. They should not pare it for fact economy.

Extraneous Facts News presents the pertinent facts. That is, every story should answer all the questions the reader expects answered. If a big story returns after having been out of the news, it should contain a short background or reminder. Readers don't carry clips to check background.

Robert J. Casey, an author and former reporter for the defunct

Chicago Daily News, once observed, "Too many facts can louse up a good story." If a fact isn't vital in telling the news, it should be omitted. It is an example of string saving. Stray bits have a way of bringing trouble. A buried reference to a 30-year-old hanging "from an apple tree on Joe Smith's farm" brought a libel suit. Joe Smith was still living; the hanging wasn't on his farm. The reference added nothing to the story but taught the editor a lesson.

This could be held to a paragraph or two; it is not worth five column inches of type:

Robert F. Kelley today was named chairman of this year's Democratic Jefferson-Jackson Day dinner.

The appointment was announced jointly by Democratic State Chairman John M.C— and National Committeeman William S. P—.

Kelley, administrative assistant for 12 years to ex-Sen. J. Allen F— Jr. in Washington, said he will name a dinner committee, site, date and speaker in a "few days."

The Jefferson-Jackson Day dinner, traditionally held in late April or early May, is the largest meeting of its kind held by the Democrats each year.

Kelley said he already is trying to line up a "nationally known" speaker for the occasion.

Kelley, now associated with the legal department of the D—Co., has been a member of the dinner committee for several years. This is his first assignment as chairman of the affair.

Kelley was a vice chairman of last year's Community Fund drive and has a wide background in party and civic affairs.

He is a past president of the Delaware State Society and the Administrative Assistants and Secretaries Club in the nation's capital.

More Precision

A school board (or board of education) is a group of individuals elected by the citizens to direct the operation of the school system. It is not a place, not an office, not a building, not the school system.

"He studied French under E. B. DeSauze, the retired supervisor of the school board's language department." DeSauze was supervisor of foreign languages for the public schools. The school board has no language department.

It is the American Museum of Natural History, not the Museum of Natural History in New York City, and the Smithsonian Institution, not the Smithsonian Institute.

The U.S. Supreme Court did not ban prayers in school. The court banned the requirement that children pray any particular prayer, or the writing by public authorities of a required prayer. The decision had to do with public schools. It did not interfere with required prayers in church-operated schools.

Gas and *gasoline* are not synonymous. Gas is either natural or manufactured. Some explosions are caused by gas, some by gasoline. The story and headline should contain the precise term. Similarly, in stories of food poisoning, the copy should specify whether the story is referring to canned or bottled foodstuffs.

Reporters and headline writers are fond of writing that taxes will "eat up" a will or a fortune or an estate. Taxes may deplete the bank account, but they can't eat up anything.

"A defective 20 mm cannon ... suddenly fired and the shell killed one airman and injured another." The writer should have said *unexpectedly* rather than "suddenly," *a shell* rather than "the shell," and *bullet, slug* or *projectile* rather than "shell."

Pistol is a general term for a small firearm. It can be single-loading, or a revolver or an automatic. Clip-loading pistols are sometimes called automatics, but they usually are semiautomatics or self-loaders. The barrel diameter of rifles and pistols is expressed in calibers (.22). A shotgun bore is expressed by its gauge (12-gauge) except for the .410.

"A 20-year-old robber was dead as the result of a gun battle in which 14 shots were fired at point-blank range." "Point-blank range" is an archaic expression based on the firing of cannon. Because the expression is meaningless to today's readers, why use it?

Ethnic Groups

"It is perhaps the most cosmopolitan area in the city, stronghold of the Poles and densely populated with other ethnic groups including Czechs, Bohemians, Slovaks and some Italians," one story reported. But Czechs and Bohemians are one and the same people. The Czech lands include Bohemia and Moravia. Some Bohemians prefer to be called Czechs. Slovaks are a separate people, although there is a strong language affinity. There is a difference between a Slovak and a Slovenian, as any editor would soon realize should the two be confused.

Wire service copy sometimes fails to explain terms common in one section of the nation but not in another. For instance, readers may deduce that *bracero* is a Mexican laborer. If the word can't be explained, it should be eliminated so as not to puzzle readers who don't know Spanish.

An executive city editor gave the copy chief trouble for failure to catch the idiocy of an "anti-Soviet" play written in the czarist days. Even though *Soviet* technically refers to an organizational system within the Communist structure, it is now generally accepted as a reference to the U.S.S.R. Russia, of course, is only one of the republics in the Soviet Union but is used as the equivalent of the U.S.S.R. In headlines, *Russia* or *Soviet* means Soviet Union.

Britain or *Great Britain* refers to the largest of the British Isles and consists of England, Scotland and Wales. *United Kingdom* should be used when England, Scotland, Wales and Northern Ireland are meant. A Briton is a native or subject of Britain. Despite the fact that other nationals of the United Kingdom may be annoyed when *England* is used as the equivalent of *Britain* or the *United Kingdom,* the use of *England* in the wider sense is acceptable.

Stereotypes

It is imperative that the copy editor be on guard against unnecessary stereotyping in copy. People have become increasingly sensitive to demeaning and derogatory labels, and the editor has been forced to confront them in copy. The copy editor on guard frees copy from conscious and unconscious semantic bias. To do that, an awareness of stereotypes is necessary.

People live in two worlds: the one they experience directly and the one they know about from other sources. There is no doubt that the first world is smaller, and that the second is created largely by the mass media. Thus, what Walter Lippmann called "the pictures in our heads"—our view of reality—are formed largely by information channeled to us through the media. For that reason alone, the process of stereotyping is insidious because it tends to distort our view of reality.

A stereotype is a standardized mental picture representing an oversimplified opinion, emotion, attitude or uncritical judgment of a person, group, race, issue or event. It often results in demeaning or ridiculing the subject.

We stereotype out of necessity; stereotypes provide us with a shorthand way of looking at the world. For example, we might form a stereotype based on personal experience: Whenever certain weather conditions have appeared, it has rained. So, when we feel high humidity and see dark clouds, we carry umbrellas. This oversimplified reaction to an event makes our lives easier. We can react to the situation without thinking. In this example, what we believe to be true is grounded in fact, or at least in personal experience; it usually has rained on us under these conditions. So, not all stereotypes are without fact. Nor are they all dangerous. In this example, we might be inconvenienced if it did not rain and we had to carry umbrellas all day, but that is all. Nor are all stereotypes negative: Blondes have more fun.

Most stereotypes, however, are not this innocuous.

Language, the words with which we communicate about our world, reflects the prejudices of society. Because English, through most of its history, evolved in a white, Angle-Saxon, patriarchial society, its vocabulary and grammar frequently reflect attitudes that exclude or demean minorities and women.[1]

Words are so much more than they appear to be. As semanticists tell us, words represent attitudes and beliefs. The words chosen by an individual say as much about the individual as anything else.

When we stereotype, we label (people especially), and once we do that, the label tends to attract more attributes than it should.

---

[1] Casey Miller and Kate Swift, *The Handbook of Nonsexist Writing* (New York: Lippincott & Crowell, 1980), p. 3.

Like a snowball rolling down a hill, the label becomes all-encompassing. The words and images that are caught up in it classify people indiscriminately:

Women . . . are fragile. Mexicans . . . are lazy. Blacks . . . are on welfare. Indians . . . are drunks. Professors . . . are absent-minded. Old people . . . are senile.

When people are presented in a stereotyped manner according to race, that is racism. In the last decade or so, the general public has begun to be aware that language also stereotypes according to sex, which is sexism. Even newer than sexism is ageism, stereotyping according to age.

While there is no excuse for reporters whose stereotypes spill over into their writing, there is less excuse for copy editors who pass copy with racist, sexist or ageist assumptions and statements. For the copy editor, these "isms" ought to be added to the list of "red flags"—those things in copy, headlines, cutlines, even the premise of a story itself—that cause the editor to step back, to wonder why.

As Miller and Swift write, "The need today . . . is to be in command of language, not used by it, and so the challenge is to find clear, convincing, graceful ways to say accurately what we want to say."[2]

Racism

There was a time when racism in newspapers was blatant; racial identifications were mandatory. Certain stories were not written because of the race of the participants; others were written for the same reason. Generally, that no longer is the case. Racism in the media, as in much of society, has become subtle.

That is not to say that it is impossible to find examples of blatant racism.

A story about a bomb threat to a northern Wisconsin high school included this: "According to the complaint filed at the Minocqua Police Department, (the secretary) reported that the threat came from a male Indian's voice." Just how does a male Indian sound?

The *Chicago Tribune,* not too many years ago, described the subject of one of its stories as "the well-dressed, articulate black man." The implication was that it was out of the ordinary for a black man to be well-dressed and articulate.

Subtle racism is more difficult to identify.

A story from *The New York Times* News Service about an explosion at a day-care center in a black section of Atlanta included this:

"'I heard a real loud boom and I ran out the door and saw the smoke and dust and ran down here,' said Eugene Drewery, 30, an unemployed construction worker. . . . " It might be suggested that it was necessary to describe the man as unemployed to explain

[2] Miller and Swift, p. 8.

why he was home in the middle of the day. It is, however, sexist to assume a young man should not be home during the day and irrelevant to the story to include his job status. Instead, the reader is helped to jump to the conclusion that the witness was just another unemployed black man.

A writer in the *Minneapolis Tribune* used the following anecdote to begin his story about a high school celebrating its state basketball championship:

"One of the posters done up Sunday for the celebration honoring North High School's boys' basketball team was misspelled.

"The one that said 'Team Minneapolis' was all right and so were the ones that said 'State Champs!' and 'Polar Power,' but over on the front wall of the gymnasium, right underneath the big polar bear, was a banner proclaiming *'Congradulations.'*

"One of the women helping with the decorations spotted the error. 'Oh, no,' she said, 'that's what they'll show on TV.'

"Before long a new poster, with the blue tempera paint that spelled 'Congratulations' still dripping, was taped up over the old one.

"Image is important to the people of North High School, because this school in the heart of one of the city's poorest neighborhoods has had such a bad image for so long. But on this afternoon of celebration after an evening of achievement, the people of North High were talking of pride in their community, their school and, of course, their basketball team. . . . "

A copy editor headlined the story: **North High spirit triumphs over spelling.**

A week later, the paper's reader representative explained in his column what an eye-opener the story proved to be for the *Tribune,* which received numerous complaints about the headline and the story from members of the North High community, teachers and students. The Minneapolis Urban League requested and received a meeting with *Tribune* staff members involved in the story. As the *Tribune* ombudsman explained to his readers:

"The meeting . . . forced some of us to decide that the headline and, by extension, the story did indeed display an insensitivity both to the feelings of the North High community and to the danger of reinforcing stereotypes.

"(The) assistant managing editor of the *Tribune* reflected after the meeting that (the reporter) 'wrote in good faith a story in which he made choices of material that he thought told the story of a school with image problems trying to cope with those problems on a day of pride and triumph. But he produced a story that did almost precisely the opposite in the eyes of lots and lots of readers. The headline exacerbated the problem. . . .'

"But the *Tribune's* real failure was not so much in the writing of the story as in not taking a second step, said (the assistant managing editor). Some editor should have looked at the story with an awareness of the stereotypes and the danger of reinforcing them. That editor should have anticipated the effect of the story and ordered changes."

Sexism

Like racism, sexism is prevalent in copy in both blatant and subtle forms. Unlike racism, however, blatant sexism is common in most American newspapers.

It has been and remains common to describe women in news stories in ways that men making news seldom have been described, even though, for example, the stylebooks of The Associated Press and United Press International clearly state that "women should receive the same treatment as men in all areas of coverage."

Irrelevant descriptions of women's appearances remain. Note the incongruity of these two consecutive paragraphs:

"At 8:58 p.m. Nancy Reagan—wearing a red dress and large gold earrings—was greeted by an ovation as she entered the gallery.

"Two minutes later, Reagan entered the chamber to an explosion of applause." (Apparently it was unnecessary to describe the president's attire.)

UPI carried the practice to extremes when Joan Kennedy received her master's degree. Wrote UPI, "Mrs. Kennedy, dressed in a black cap and gown, marched under the sunny skies with some 400 other graduates. . . . "

Copy editors must recognize slanted adjectives and descriptive phrases that serve only to reinforce sexual stereotypes:

—"Patricia Brennan, an auburn-haired 24-year-old with the look of a mischievous tomboy, claims she never stood in front of the Post Office and yelled, 'Nah, nah! Anything you can do we can do better.'"

—"Alcott shared the opening day lead with Barbara Moxness. . . . The personable 24-year-old brunette from Santa Monica, Calif., started the day four strokes ahead. . . . "

—"Nancy Freitas, 32, a blonde with green eyes and a preference for strictly feminine, tailored attire, is the new general manager of the San Diego Breakers of the International Volleyball Association."

One of the most common problems faced by newspapers is that of how to refer to women in stories. Many newspapers have dropped the traditional practice of using courtesy titles for women, but the use of such titles remains common. One exception is on sports pages, where it is more common to treat men and women similarly—without courtesy titles. Whatever a newspaper's policy, the copy editor should assure consistent treatment.

It is incorrect to write Mrs. Mary Smith, since she is not married to Mary; she is either Mary Smith or Mrs. John Smith. It is unacceptable to treat men and women of equal position differently, as in the story that made these identifications: "Ms. Long, 29, is a physician. . . . " and "Dr. Stanley Mohler. . . . " Equivalent terms should be applied to men and women in a story or headline: lady/gentleman; woman/man; girl/boy. This headline, then, should have been unacceptable:

**Lady doctors
and male nurses**

**Male nurse walks tightrope
of compassion and tradition**

These headlines also should not have been written:

**Brattleboro Man Found Dead
Montpelier Girl Found Dead**

He was 18; she was 26.

There are times when a copy editor might even question the entire approach a reporter has taken in a story on the basis that it only reinforces sexual stereotypes, much as the Minneapolis reporter was cited for reinforcing racial stereotypes.

For example, a reporter began her story this way: "Mothers aren't the only ones who can tell us how to eat properly. A computer can, too." And so could a father. But this reporter reinforces the prevailing stereotype that it is the mother's role to look out for the needs of children. Further, there is a more subtle implication that a computer can replace a mother. The story easily could have been made more acceptable; the copy editor could have changed the lead to read, "Parents aren't the only ones. . . . "

A similar sexist role is prescribed by the writer whose lead read: "The women were not the only ones who enjoyed themselves at the . . . Homemakers School last night. . . . The men and children had a good time, too, sampling the good food. . . . "

How many stereotyped images can you identify in this lead, which shows that men also can be victims of reportorial sexism?

> "It's your weekly trip to the hairdresser. Your hair has been shampooed, cut, colored and curled, and you're ready to bake under the dryer. As you sit there, reading your latest issue of Vogue magazine, you turn to your neighbor to discuss the newest trends in skirt length.
>
> "Suddenly, you realize you're face to face with a man—and he's in curlers.
>
> "You can react three ways.
>
> "You can blush and wish you were dead.
>
> "You can quickly end the conversation and wish you'd worn makeup.
>
> "You can keep talking and wonder if he's dating anyone."

Ageism

Ageist stereotypes have been around as long as those based on race and sex. One that comes immediately to mind is the "Confucius say . . ." variety—the wiseness of old age. Only now, however, are people beginning to explore the implications of stereotypes about aging and the aged, and the complex set of problems they have helped to create.

Common stereotypes portray the old as poor, isolated, sick, unhappy, rigid, reactionary, unproductive, and grandparently.

The Gray Panthers, activists who serve as advocates for the old, designed their Media Watch Project to allow viewers to identify and publicize ageist stereotypes in television programming and commercials. They urge alertness for several stereotypes:

—Physical appearance: face always blank or expressionless; body always bent over and infirm.

—Clothing: men's baggy and unpressed; women's frumpy and ill-fitting.

—Speech: halting and high-pitched; stubborn, rigid, forgetful.

The Gray Panthers also warn of distortions, in which old age is depicted either as an idyllic or a moribund stage of life, and omissions, in which the concerns and positive aspects of aging are omitted.

The sensitive copy editor will be alert for ageism in copy and headlines.

In this example, from a story about a visit to central Missouri by Clare Booth Luce, both ageist and sexist stereotypes are evident. An alert copy editor deleted the paragraph from the story (See Figure 7.1).

"She remained standing during the reception, even though she is frail since cataract surgery a few years ago. Her eyes are still bright blue, and her beauty shines despite her years. The attitude of the young college men attested to her attractiveness—they all wanted to kiss her."

Figure 7-1 An account of the visit of Clare Booth Luce prompted ageist and sexist stereotypes that were deleted by the copy editor. (Columbia Missourian)

Apparently, age alone sometimes is enough to qualify one as grandmotherly or grandfatherly. A headline on a sports page announced: Local Grandmother Wins Bowling Tourney. In the story, no mention was made of grandchildren. The woman was, however, identified as being 58. Another reporter wrote that "Cora is a grandmotherly sort. . . . " without elaborating on just what that was to say about Cora. And the copy editor who asked in a head-line, "Can one live happily ever after retirement?" by implication stated that retirement generally is not a time of happiness.

Edit to the Final Stop	"Tanglewood Barn Theater ended its regular season with a bang in its production of 'Wonderful Town' Wednesday night." Last paragraph: "The show will be repeated at 8:15 p.m. through Sunday."

"His companion said Fennell dived from the boat, swam away, went under and never came up." Last paragraph: "Interment will be in Mt. Zion Cemetery." What was to be buried in lieu of the body that never came up?

"The largest single cost of the trial was jury expenses, which total $3,807." Later: "Another cost was $20,015 paid to extra guards and bailiffs."

A story concerned a robber. Part of it went like this: "The suspect apparently hid in the store when it closed at 9 p.m. About 11 p.m. he confronted a security guard, Paul H. Hogue, 57, of 5625 Lowell Blvd., as he was turning off the lights in the budget store of the basement." Last paragraph: "According to parole officials, Hogue's parole was suspended June 6 for failure to report and he was being sought as a parole violator." A correction sufficed in this case, but a correction does no credit to the reporter or to the copy editor.

Negated Negatives	The House voted 63-94 against overriding the committee's disapproval of a bill by Rep. Charles L. Hughes to repeal the women's eight-hour law.

The reader can't be sure at first or even on the third reading whether the vote favored or opposed the eight-hour law for women. Instead, the reader is obliged to take the time to spell it all out. The eight-hour day for women is on the books. Hughes introduced a bill to repeat it (negative 1). The committee disapproved (negative 2) the proposal, thus sustaining the existing law. If the House had voted to override (negative 3) the committee, it would have favored repealing the law. But the House voted against (negative 4) overriding, thus upholding the law as it stands. This is what the story should have said in the first place:

The House voted 94-63 to keep the women's eight-hour law.

How to put five negative ideas in one sentence: "Earlier the Senate refused to override its executive committee's disapproval of a bill to eliminate the non-communist oath required for state employees." The reader would have had less trouble understanding the sentence if it had been edited to read, "The Senate agreed with its executive committee that state employees should be required, as at present, to take a non-communist oath."

"There weren't many in the Turkey Day crowd of 11,554 who could doubt that Central lacked leadership in its 13-7 victory over Northern." Revised: "Few in the crowd of 11,554 could doubt that Central was well led in its 13-7 victory over Northern."

Taste

An editor of a morning newspaper said his newspaper likes to protect those who read during breakfast against the incursions of unpalatable news. How then, he asked, did this sentence get to the breakfast table: "Plans to take still another sample were canceled when Hutchinson become ill and threw up." Actually, he *vomited.* Had the story said he became nauseated, anyone who is familiar with 10½ beers—Hutchinson's load in less than 2½ hours—would have gotten the point.

The *Los Angeles Times* and other metropolitan newspapers have adopted a screen code to control and avoid lewd advertising in entertainment copy. One of the advertising executives of the *Times* said, "It is not our intention to be either picayunish or prudish in our evaluation, but we are convinced that moral and social values have not decayed as frequently as portrayed, and we trust that together we can find a better standard of values in the area of good taste." Among subjects banned are bust measurements, compromising positions, double meaning, nude figures or silhouettes, nymphomania, perversion, and suggestive use of narcotics, instruments or alcohol. Words avoided include cuties, girlie, lust, nymph, party girls, play girls, scanty panties, sexpot, strippers and third sex.

The caution should apply equally to amusement promotion copy and to all other copy. Both wire services direct their editors to downplay anatomy. Copy editors should apply heavy pencils to stories about the "10 best undressed women" and about an actress hired because of her uncommonly ample bosom. Better yet, those stories should not be used.

There is no necessity to run everything turned in as news by the staff, the wire services or the syndicates. There is an obligation to print the news. There also is an obligation to edit it.

Some vulgarisms get into the report, usually when they are said by a public figure at a public gathering and in a justifiable news context. Most member papers used the following lead from London even though the AP headed the dispatch with a cautionary note: " 'Gentlemen,' said Prince Philip, 'I think it is time we pulled our fingers out.'"

But the editor of a Dayton, Ohio, newspaper was forced to resign when management panicked because 50 callers protested after the editor had approved the inclusion of dialog, including words connoting sexual intercourse, in a Page One murder story. The fact that the dialog was from a direct transcript of testimony during the hearing had no effect on management's decision. Nor did the fact that 110,000 or so other readers didn't complain.

Is *s.o.b.* milder than the full expression? If the president of the United States refers to a syndicated columnist as an "s.o.b.," that's news. The columnist in question passed off the slur by saying the president obviously meant "sons of brotherhood." Another president used the phrase "sons of business."

When Jack Ruby shot Lee Harvey Oswald, accused of assassinating President John F. Kennedy, Ruby is purported to have exclaimed, "I hope I killed the son of a bitch." The quote appeared in the news dispatches from Dallas. There was a day when editors would have substituted dashes or asterisks for the words. Some bannered the quote, but with initials: **Jack Ruby—"I hope I killed the s.o.b."**

Frankness used in good taste is preferable to yesterday's euphemisms, such as "social disease" for *syphilis,* "intimate relationship" for *sexual intercourse,* "assault" for *rape.* Why refer to washrooms and toilets in public buildings, such as schools, as "bathrooms?" Ever try to take a bath in one?

This story was published in a daily under a two-column headline:

Coed Reports Rape

An 18-year-old university student claimed she was raped early Sunday morning by a man she met in a local nightclub, sheriff's officers said.

The woman said she was drinking and dancing with the man at the Sweet Lass lounge before accepting a ride to the man's apartment. The man invited her to his apartment for some drugs, she told officers.

When the couple arrived at the apartment, the man invited the woman into the bedroom and the woman accepted. The man then partially undressed the woman (she completed the undressing) and attempted to have sexual relations with her, she said.

The woman told police she said no to the man but did not resist his advances.

After a brief period, the woman said the man "gave up, rolled over and went to sleep."

While the man slept, the student said she got dressed and went to her dormitory. Because of her intoxicated condition, the woman said she was unsure whether the sexual act was completed.

The reporter should never have submitted this nonstory. The story should never have passed the city desk and certainly should have been challenged on the copy desk. No one was arrested or charged, so there was no news value. It is, at best, but idle chatter and has no place in a family newspaper.

8

Legal Limitations on the Press

The editor who lives in constant fear of a damage suit, the copy editor who sniffs libel in every story and thereby tries to make the safe safer and the reporter who thinks it is cute to refer to an inept council member as a simian have no place on a newspaper. The first procrastinates and vacillates, the second makes the copy vapid, and the third lands the publisher in court.

Neither the reporter nor the copy editor need be a lawyer, but both should know enough about the legal aspects of journalism to know when to consult a lawyer. Some of these trouble spots are discussed in this chapter.

The press can use its immense freedom vigorously. Only when it abuses its freedom does it face punishment.

We need no license to establish a press and start publishing. Nor must we submit copy to any censor before or after publication. We can criticize the government and its officials severely and have no fear that the doors to the newspaper will be padlocked. In our system, no government—federal, state, county or municipal—can be libeled. The newspaper is not a public utility. It can reject or accept any story, advertisement, picture or letter it wishes.

We do not have to beg or bribe officials to get a quota of newsprint. The newspaper is not dependent on the government for government advertising (except for the possible exception of legal advertising). We do not face the threat of withdrawal of the government's privileges should we disagree with its policies.

Courts generally cannot exercise prior restraint to prevent publication of information, although one lower court did in the *Pen-*

tagon Papers case. Punishment, if any, comes after publication. Long ago we rejected the notion that the greater the truth, the greater the libel. We can report, portray or comment on anyone who becomes newsworthy. Even the president is not immune from press coverage. Criminal libel still is possible, but most libel is considered a civil wrong.

References to a half–dozen U.S. Supreme Court decisions will indicate the scope of the freedom the press enjoys. Some early cases helped to establish the principles that truth is a defense in libel, and that the jury may determine both the law and the fact. The court has prohibited a discriminatory tax on the press. The court has told judges that neither inherent nor reasonable tendency is sufficient to justify restriction of free expression and that contempt of court is to be used only when there is a clear and present danger of interfering with the orderly administration of justice. The court has held that comment on or about public officials is privileged, even if false, provided there is no "actual malice." The court defined actual malice as publication with knowledge that the information is false or with reckless disregard of whether it is false. This privilege now covers public figures—those in the public limelight—as well as public officials.

This brief review is intended to remind editors of the unusual liberties we enjoy. It should not deter editors and publishers from maintaining a constant vigil to preserve and extend these freedoms. We still have the problems of news management at all levels of government. We still have some judges and attorneys who would dry up most news of crime until after the trial. In many jurisdictions we still cannot use cameras in the courtroom. We still have judges who prohibit publication of the names of trial jurors. We still have those who would like to censor what we read, hear or view. We still wrestle with the problem of what constitutes obscenity and who is to decide what is obscene. Worst of all, we have many in our society who care little about press freedom. If these people could have their way they would return to 16th-century England and the Court of Star Chamber where any criticism of the realm was promptly punished. What some people don't realize is that the freedom to read, to listen and to view is their right, not the special privilege of any commercial enterprise.

The Libel Hazard Publishers and broadcasters face risks far greater than do most other professional or business executives. More than a century ago a London editor, John T. Delane of the *Times,* said, "The Press lives by disclosures." All disclosures are hazardous. If errors occur, they are public and may subject the error maker to liability.

The day is rare when any publisher or broadcaster doesn't commit errors—wrong facts, wrong names and identifications, wrong addresses, wrong dates, wrong spelling or pronunciation, wrong grammar or wrong headlines. Fortunately, only a handful of such errors are serious enough to prompt lawsuits.

Few libels are deliberate. Almost all result from erroneous reporting, misunderstanding of the law or careless editing.

Misunderstanding the Law

In an attempt to foster understanding of the law, here is a review of some common situations:

1. There is a common assumption that if a statement originated from an outside source, it is safe. That is wrong because a newspaper or broadcast station is responsible for whatever it publishes or broadcasts from whatever source—advertisements, letters, feature stories.
2. There is a feeling that if a person is not named, he or she may not sue. That is not true because a plaintiff sometimes can be identified by means other than name.
3. There is a feeling that if the harmful statement concerns a group, individual members cannot sue. That is wrong because some groups are small enough (juries, team members, council members) so that each can be identified and therefore each may have a case.
4. Another common error is misjudging the extent of privilege in an arrest. Statements by the police as to the guilt of the prisoner or that the prisoner "has a record a mile long" are not privileged. All persons are presumed innocent until they are proved guilty.

Carelessness in Reporting and Editing

These situations may prove to be dangerous:

1. Mistaken identity. Similarity of names doesn't necessarily mean similarity of identity. People in trouble often give fictitious names. Identification should be qualified by phrases explaining the situation such as "who gave his name as . . .," "listed by police as . . ." or "identified by a card in her purse as. . . ." In listing addresses in crime and court stories, some papers use the block instead of a specific number. Several families might live at the same address.
2. Clothing the damaging statement with *alleged* or *allegedly.* Qualification with these words carries no protection.
3. "Needled" headlines. Qualifications are difficult in a headline because of the limited character count. The assumption is wrong that as long as the story is safe the head can take liberties. Many readers read only the headline. A picture caption also may be libelous. Within the story itself, statements usually cannot be taken out of context to create a libel. The story usually must be considered in its entirety.
4. The assumption that a person with an unsavory reputation

can't be libeled. A man may be a notorious drunk but that doesn't necessarily make him a thief.

5. Confession stories pose dangers until the confession has been admitted as evidence in court. In pretrial stages, it is better professionally to say merely that the prisoner has made a statement.

6. The assumption that any statement made by one person to another about another is protected if the reporter can prove that the first person actually made the statement about the second. That is not true in most states. If A tells a group that B is a liar, the reporter must be prepared to prove not that A made the statement, but that B is, in fact, a liar.

| **Libelous Statements** | The legal definition of libel is damage to a person's reputation caused by bringing that person into hatred, contempt or ridicule in the eyes of a substantial and respectable group. Anything in a newspaper is libelous if it damages a living person's reputation or has an adverse effect on that person's means of earning a living. The same applies to businesses and to institutions. |

A story is defamatory if it accuses a living person of a crime or immorality or imputes a crime or immorality; if it states or insinuates that a person is insane or has a loathsome or contagious disease; if it tends in any way to subject the victim to public hatred, contempt or ridicule or causes others to shun that person or refuse to do business; or if it asserts a want of capacity to conduct one's business, occupation or profession.

Wrong assumptions sometimes can make a statement defamatory. A person who sets fire to a dwelling is not necessarily an arsonist. A person who kills another is not necessarily a murderer. Some items in a newspaper are false but not necessarily defamatory. A false report that a man has died usually is not libelous.

A statement may cause someone pain and anguish, but mere vituperation does not make a libel; it must be substantial. It is not enough that the statement may disturb that person. It must damage that person in the estimation of those in the community or of those with whom the person does business.

Libel can be avoided if the staff exercises responsibility in accuracy, exactness and judgment. But even when libel does occur it need not terrify the staff. Some cases are not serious enough to entice a lawyer to take the case to court.

Only the person libeled has cause for action. Relatives, even though they may have suffered because of the false and defamatory statements, have no recourse in libel. The offended person must bring suit within the statutory period (ranging from one to six years depending on the jurisdiction). If the person should die before or during the trial, there may be no continuation of the case by survivors.

If a person has been libeled, that individual may ask the publication to print a correction. This could satisfy because it tends to set the record straight. In states having retraction laws, the plaintiff can collect only actual damages—and no punitive damages—if the retraction is made on request and within a certain time limit.

Sometimes newspapers may offer to run a correction, possibly offer a nominal payment, and then obtain a release from further liability. This procedure saves the time and cost of a trial and may eliminate the possibility of major judgments against the newspaper.

Suppose the plaintiff insists on taking the rascal editor into court. The plaintiff must hire a lawyer and pay the filing fee. The person should be advised of the defenses available to the newspaper—constitutional defense, truth, privilege, fair comment and right of reply. Because libel concerns reputation, the plaintiff's reputation, good name and esteem can be put at issue. If there is a skeleton in the closet, that person may hesitate to have the past revealed in court. If the person is a public figure or public official the plaintiff will have the burden of proving the material was published with actual malice.

Suppose the plaintiff should win in lower court. That person may get damages of hundreds of thousands of dollars—or only a few cents. If the defending publisher loses, an appeal is likely, even to the U.S. Supreme Court if the question involves a constitutional issue. Is the plaintiff able to pay appeal court costs if the case is lost? As a final protection, most publishers buy libel insurance.

Most of the larger dailies have their own lawyers to advise them on sensitive stories. Some lawyers urge, "When in doubt leave it out." But the publisher's attitude is, "This is something that should be published. How can it be published safely?" On extra-sensitive stories in which the precise wording has been dictated by an attorney, the desk should make no changes. The headline must be as carefully phrased.

Libel may involve business corporations as well as individuals. A corporation, partnership or trust or other business may be damaged if untrue statements tend to prejudice the entity in the conduct of its trade or business or deter others from dealing with it. Non-profit organizations likewise may collect damages resulting from a publication that tends to prejudice them in the public estimation and thereby interferes with the conduct of their activites.

Libel Defenses

Constitutional

In a landmark decision in 1964, the U.S. Supreme Court ruled that the constitutional provisions of the First and Fourteenth amendments could be used as a defense against libel if the defamatory words were used to describe the public acts of public officials and were published without actual malice (New York Times Co. v. Sullivan, 376 U.S. 254, 1964).

The court argued that debate on public issues should be uninhibited, robust and wide–open, and that the debate could well include vehement, caustic and sometimes unpleasantly sharp attacks on government and public officials.

The *Times* decision defined malice specifically and placed the burden of proving actual malice on the plaintiff. The court defined actual malice as knowledge that a statement is false or reckless disregard of whether it is false.

The ruling was later extended to include public figures, those in the public eye but not in public office, who thrust themselves into the vortex of public debate (AP v. Walker, 383 U.S. 130, 1967) or pervasive public figures (Curtis Publishing Co. v. Butts, 388 U.S. 130, 1967).

It was used to permit robust discussion in criminal libel cases (Garrison v. Louisiana, 379 U.S. 64, 1964) and in privacy cases where the issue is in the public interest (Hill v. Time, 385 U.S. 374, 1967).

Finally, the *Times* rule was extended to include private persons involved in public interest issues (Rosenbloom v. Metromedia, 403 U.S. 29, 1971).

In 1974 the court clarified the Rosenbloom plurality decision and ruled that the Constitution does not require that private persons involved in public issues prove actual malice in suits seeking actual damages for defamation (Gertz v. Welch, 418 U.S. 323, 1974).

One effect of the Gertz decision was to permit the states to make their own interpretation of libel defense standards for private individuals seeking actual damages. Since the ruling, 22 jurisdictions have given private individuals more protection against damaging statements than accorded to public officials or public figures. Those jurisdictions are Arizona, Arkansas, the District of Columbia, Florida, Hawaii, Illinois, Kansas, Kentucky, Louisiana, Maryland, Massachusetts, New Hampshire, New Mexico, Ohio, Oklahoma, South Carolina, Tennessee, Texas, Utah, Washington, West Virginia and Wisconsin. In these jurisdictions the negligence test is applied. It requires reporters to use the same care in reporting and writing as any reasonable reporter would use under the same or similar circumstances.

Four states—Alaska, Colorado, Indiana and Michigan—use the same standards for private citizens as for public figures and public officials. New York requires private citizens to prove that the reporter exercised "grossly irresponsible conduct." Standards have not yet been set in other states.[1]

---

[1] The Missouri Group, *News Reporting and Writing* (New York: St. Martin's Press, 1985).

Truth

Truth is an absolute defense to libel. The truth must be as broad and as complete as the publication upon which the charge was made. Truth offered in evidence need not mean the literal accuracy of the published charge but rather the substance or gist of the charge.

If the defending publisher relies on a document as evidence to show truth, he or she must be sure the document can be produced at the trial and be admitted in evidence. If the publisher relies on a witness to give testimony as to truth, the publisher must be assured the witness is qualified to testify. To take an extreme example, a publisher could not rely on the testimony of a doctor who is prohibited from violating doctor–patient relationships.

Privilege

Reports of judicial, legislative and executive proceedings—federal, state or municipal—may be published and successfully defended as qualified privilege. The qualifications are that the report be fair and substantially accurate and complete.

For example, a food inspector may make an official report to a board of health describing conditions found at a certain establishment. The information, even though false, may be reported safely as long as the newspaper's account is full, fair and accurate. If truth is required in the newspaper account, then privilege would be worthless as a defense. What a food inspector may say about Sunday school teachers at a meeting of a service club is not privileged. Only the official acting in an official capacity can be defended as privileged.

Statements of attorneys or civic organization officials usually are not privileged, nor are press releases from government bureaus.

In many states the mere filing of a complaint, petition, affidavit or other document is not privileged. Anyone can go to the court clerk and file a complaint containing false, scandalous and damaging statements about another merely upon payment of a filing fee. Proof of the fact that libelous statements are contained in the document is not a basis for privilege.

Fair Comment and Criticism

Newspapers are free to discuss public affairs and to comment on the conduct of all public officials, even a low–ranking park board member. This defense has three qualifications: (1) The comment is founded on facts or what the publisher had reasonable grounds to believe are facts. (2) The comment is not made with intent to damage. Here, the burden of proof is on the plaintiff. (3) The comment does not involve the private life or moral character of a person except when it has a direct bearing on qualifications or work.

Those who put themselves or their work before the public are subject to public assessment of their performance, however strong the terms of censure may be. Decisions of the U.S. Supreme Court suggest that, short of malice and reckless disregard of their truths, all debates on public issues should be uninhibited, robust and wide-open, and that such debates may well include vehement, caustic and sometimes unpleasantly sharp attacks on government and public officials. The same freedom could very well apply to comments on anyone in the public eye. The only limitation on the press is that the comments cannot be based on misstatements.

This should not be construed as license. Character and public reputation are priceless possessions and are not good hunting grounds simply because a person holds public office, aspires to public office or in any manner offers talents to the public. There is a difference between assessing the fitness of a candidate or commenting on the products of a public performer and a reckless attack on character and reputation.

Corrections

The publication of a correction technically admits the libel and therefore negates truth as a defense. But when the defense of truth is not clearly evident, the publisher should make the decision to correct.

When made, the correction should be full and frank and used as conspicuously as the article complained of.

A reporter obtained her story over the phone from the judge's secretary. She took her notes in shorthand. When she transcribed her notes, she mistook DWS (driving while under suspension) for DWI (driving while intoxicated) and thus wrote falsely that a certain person had pleaded guilty to driving while intoxicated. Even if this story had been edited by another, it is unlikely the copy editor would have caught the error. The paper should have printed a correction to indicate lack of malice and to escape punitive damages should the injured person sue for libel.

But the second story was not a clear correction and this should have been caught by a copy editor. The headline read **Ex-sheriff's patrolman admits count.** The lead: "A man who five months ago was suspended from the Franklin County Sheriff's Patrol was arraigned in Municipal Court here yesterday, pleading guilty to driving for the past nine years on a suspended license." Later, the story said that the patrolman had been dropped from the force for "misuse of authority" and then qualified that statement with another to the effect the patrolman had to resign on order of the Office of Strategic Information, Fort Ethan Allen, Vt.

The patrolman sued for libel. The defense tried to argue that the crime of driving while the license was suspended was as serious as the crime of driving while intoxicated and therefore the newspaper should not be held accountable for a minor error. The jury disagreed and returned a judgment of $3,500 for the former patrolman.

Right of Privacy A libel action is brought to protect a person's reputation against defamation. Privacy is an action to protect a person's right to be left alone. The distinction between the two is not as clear as it once was because privacy is now being used as an alternative to libel or in conjunction with libel.

Privacy is an expanding legal doctrine with so much vagueness and ill-defined limits that the press has difficulty in knowing where it stands legally.

Privacy encompasses four torts:

1. Intrusion on the plaintiff's seclusion or solitude, or into private affairs.
2. Public disclosure of embarrassing private facts about the plaintiff.
3. Publicity that places the plaintiff in a false light in the public eye.
4. Appropriation, for the defendant's advantage, of the plaintiff's name or likeness.

Newspaper accounts generally concern newsworthy subjects who have forfeited, voluntarily or involuntarily, their rights of privacy. Privacy does not protect a person or that person's actions if they are a matter of legitimate public interest. Newsworthiness is based on three basic components: public interest, public figures and public records.

Generally, a person who voluntarily participates in a public event abandons the right of privacy. Thus, a newspaper may legitimately display the types of persons who join the Easter parade. But a newspaper in Alabama had to pay damages to a woman photographed while her skirts were blown above her head by an air jet in a fun house at a county fair. She was recognizable because her children were with her.

Some risk is involved in printing photographs taken of people without their consent in their homes or in hospital beds. Pictures showing ways to beat the summer heat may be humorous to readers but not to the hefty lady fanning herself under a tree in her own backyard.

Truth usually is not accepted as a defense in a privacy invasion case, but truth, combined with publishing information released to the public in official court records, is a defense. In other words, the defense is adequate if the information is truthful, comes from an open, public trial or comes from court documents that are open for public inspection.

The increasing number of damage suits claiming invasion of privacy suggest that privacy should concern editors as much as libel actions.

Seven states recognize the right to privacy in statutes. Utah gives corporations a right of privacy. And both Utah and Virginia permit surviving relatives to bring privacy actions against the exploitation of the names or likenesses of deceased relatives. The federal courts recognize an action for an invasion of privacy.

Juvenile Delinquents

It is not illegal for a newspaper to publish the name of a juvenile. But some states do not allow officials to release news or pictures of juveniles, defined in most states as anyone under the age of 18. Many officials insist that names of juvenile offenders be withheld on the theory that there is greater opportunity for rehabilitation if the youth is not stigmatized by publicity that may affect him or her for years.

In some states the children's code gives exclusive jurisdiction to the juvenile court over offenders under 14, regardless of the acts committed, and gives concurrent jurisdiction to the district court over youngsters between 16 and 18, unless the crime involved is punishable by either death or life imprisonment if committed by an adult. In murder cases involving youths 14 and over, the district court has original jurisdiction.

Coverage of juvenile matters may be allowed under the following circumstances:

1. Public hearings. A U.S. Supreme Court decision extends to juveniles the same due process of law guarantees provided adults in criminal proceedings. The juvenile has the same rights against self-incrimination, to representation and even to a jury trial. Even in juvenile court, the youngster has a right to a public trial if requested. But after the finding of the jury at a public trial, the juvenile could still be placed before a juvenile court for disposition, out of sight of the press and the public.
2. Permission of the court. If the code permits it, the judge may, at his or her discretion, allow coverage concerning the hearing of a juvenile. Frequently, the judge of a juvenile court allows reporters to attend juvenile court sessions but does not permit identification of the youthful offender. There may be publication of news of such cases that may serve as a warning to violators of laws for the protection of children, provided that any reference to any child involved be so disguised as to prevent identification.
3. Traffic cases. Names of persons of any age may be used in traffic cases.

Copy editors should be alert to the distinction between a juvenile and a minor. In most states a minor is defined as anyone under the age of 21, although some states have reduced the age of majority to 18.

Plagiarism and Copyright Infringement

Plagiarism and copyright infringement are still other areas of concern to the copy editor. Only news stories, not the news itself, can be copyrighted. Even if a newspaper does not protect itself by copyrighting the entire paper or individual stories, it still has a property right in its news and can prevent others from "lifting" the material.

It is assumed that copy editors will be so thoroughly familiar with the contents of opposition papers that they will be able to spot material that copies or paraphrases too closely the work of others.

If a wire service sends out a story based on the story of another member or client, copy editors should not delete the wire service credit to the originator of the story. Nor should they delete any credit on stories or pictures. They may, if directed, compile stories from various sources into one comprehensive story, adding the sources from which the story was compiled.

If their own paper publishes a story to be copyrighted, copy editors should ensure that the notice is complete—the notice of copyright, the date and by whom.

In editing book review copy, copy editors should have some notion of the limits of fair use of the author's quotes. The problem is relatively minor because few copyright owners would object to the publishing of extracts in a review, especially if the review were favorable. If the review has to be trimmed, the trimming probably would come in the quoted extracts.

Lotteries

A lottery is any scheme containing three elements—consideration paid, a prize or award and determination of the winner by chance. This includes all drawings for prizes and raffles, and games such as bingo and keno. It is immaterial who sponsors the scheme. Pictures and advertising matter referring to lotteries and similar gift enterprises are barred from the mail.

Newspapers may not be permitted to announce them or to announce results. Federal law now exempts newspapers in states with legal lotteries as long as they confine themselves to reporting state lotteries. Stories also may be used in cases in which something of news value happened as a result of the lottery. An example would be a story concerning a laborer who became wealthy overnight by having a winning ticket on the Irish Sweepstakes. This would probably be considered a legitimate human interest story rather than a promotion for horse races and lotteries.

Crime and Courts

No longer do American editors play crime by the standards of past generations. They print crime news, but they do not rely on crime stories, even a sex-triangle murder, to boost street sales. Topics such as space and ocean exploration compete with crime for the attention and interest of today's more sophisticated readers.

Crime is a part of the news record, however, and will be carried if newspapers are to fulfill their obligations to readers. Minor crimes, unless they have unusual angles, generally are merely listed. When it is presented in detail, the crime story should be written with the same thoroughness and sensitivity that experts give other subjects. Some observers argue that newspapers should offer more news of criminal court activities—but with the constructive purpose of showing the community the origins and anatomy of crime.

Copy editors who handle crime stories should make sure that their reports contain no prejudicial statements that could deprive the defendants of fair trials. Their headlines should avoid labels.

One editor admonished his staff, "We should be sensitive about assumption of guilt, not only to avoid libel but to avoid criticism and a bad impression on readers." The caution was occasioned by this lead: "With the dealer who sold a .32-caliber pistol to Mrs. Marian C—apparently located, Shaker Heights police today were using handwriting expert Joseph Tholl to link the accused slayer of Cremer Y—, 8, to the weapon purchase." The whole tone of this lead is an assumption of guilt and the effort of police to pin the crime on somebody. It should have said the police were trying to determine whether Mrs. C—was linked to the gun purchase—not trying to link her.

Here is a conviction lead:

FAYETTEVILLE, N.C. (AP)—Two Marines are being held without bond after terrorizing a family, stealing a car, and trading shots with officers.

They were identified as . . .

They told officers after their Saturday capture they were members of the National Abolitionist Forces, which they described as a militant black group.

In reference to this story, the general news editor said in part, "We do not have a formal set of guidelines for handling crime news, but this story certainly does not conform to regular AP practice. It makes us authority for that statement that the two men held had terrorized a family, stolen a car and traded shots with officers. All we should have said was that they were charged with doing all those things, and who had made the charge."

Correct Terminology

Newsworthy crimes and trials are covered in detail so that essential information may be conveyed to the public.

Copy editors have to have some knowledge of legal terms and the legal process if they are to make the story and headline technically correct yet meaningful to the layman. *Arrested* is a simple verb understood by all readers. It is better than *apprehended* or *taken into custody.* It is equal to *captured.* A person who is cited, summoned or given a ticket is not arrested.

An *arraignment* is a formal proceeding at which a defendant steps forward to give the court a plea of guilty or not guilty. It should not be used interchangeably with *preliminary hearing,* which is held in a magistrate's court and is a device to show probable cause that a crime has been committed and that there is a likely suspect.

Bail is the security given for the release of a prisoner. The reporter reveals ignorance when writing, "The woman is now in jail under $5,000 bail." She can't be in jail under bail. She can be free on bail or she can be held in lieu of bail.

A *parole* is a conditional release of a prisoner with an indeterminate or unexpired sentence. *Probation* allows a person convicted of some offense to go free, under suspension of sentence during good behavior, and generally under the supervision of a probation officer.

The word *alleged* is a trap. Used in reference to a specific person (Jones, the alleged gambler), it offers no immunity from libel. Jones may be charged with gambling or indicted for gambling. In both instances, *alleged* is redundant. The charge is an allegation or an assertion without proof but carries an indication of an ability to produce proof.

A jail sentence does not mean, necessarily, that a person has been jailed. The individual may be free on bail or free pending an appeal.

Listing the wrong name in a crime story is the surest route to libel action. Thorough verification of first, middle and last names, of addresses and of relationships is a necessity in editing the crime story.

Names of women or children in rape cases or attempted rape cases generally should not be used. Nor should the story give any clue to their addresses in a way by which they can be identified. An exception is when the rape victim is murdered.

Sentences may be consecutive or concurrent. If a man is sentenced to consecutive three-year terms, he faces six years of imprisonment. If his sentences are concurrent, he faces three years. But why use these terms? The total sentence is what counts with the readers and the prisoner.

If a man has been sentenced to five years but the sentence is suspended, he is given a suspended five-year sentence, not a five-year suspended sentence.

Juries are of two kinds—investigative (grand) and trial (petit). If a grand jury finds evidence sufficient to warrant a trial, it issues a *true bill* or indictment. If sufficient evidence is lacking, the return is a *no-bill* or *not-true bill.* "Jones indicted" means as much as "the grand jury indicted Jones." To say "the grand jury failed to indict Jones" implies it shirked its duty.

A *verdict* is the finding of a jury. A judge renders decisions, judgments, rulings and opinions, but seldom verdicts, unless the right to a jury trial is waived. Although verdicts are returned in both criminal and civil actions by juries, a guilty verdict is found only in criminal actions. Judges declare, not order, mistrials. Attorneys general or similar officials give opinions, not rulings.

Corpus delicti refers to the evidence necessary to establish that a crime has been committed. It is not restricted to the body of a murder victim; it can apply as well to the charred remains of a burned house.

Nolo contendere is a legalistic way of saying that a defendant, although not admitting guilt, will not fight a criminal prosecution. *Nolle prosequi* means the prosecutor or plaintiff will proceed no further in the action or suit. Most readers will understand the translation more readily than the Latin expression.

The Fifth Amendment guarantees the due process of law protection for all citizens. The report should not suggest that the use of this protection is a cover-up for guilt. Phrases such as "hiding behind the Fifth" should be eliminated.

The story should distinguish between an act itself and an action. *Replevin,* for example, is an action to recover property wrongfully taken or detained. Trouble will arise if the copy editor lets the reporter translate the action too freely: "Mrs. Marsh filed the replevin action to recover furniture stolen from her home by her estranged husband." So, too, with the tort of *conversion.* "Wrongful conversion" may imply theft, but neither the copy nor the head should convey such implication.

Keeping track of the plaintiff and the defendant should pose no problem except in appellate proceedings in which the original defendant may become the appellant. The confusion is not lessened by substituting *appellee* and *appellant.* The best way is to repeat the names of the principals.

In some civil suits the main news peg is the enormous sum sought by the plaintiff. Whether the same angle should be included in the headline is questionable. In some damage claims the relief sought is far greater than the plaintiff expects to collect. The judgment actually awarded is the news and the headline.

Misused Terms

Copy editors can "tidy up" the crime and court report by watching for the following:

All narcotics are drugs, but many drugs are not narcotics.

A defendant may plead guilty or not guilty to a charge or a crime. There is no such plea as innocent. A defendant may be judged not guilty by reason of insanity. He is not innocent by reason of insanity. An acquittal means the defendant has been found not guilty. The danger of dropping the *not* has caused some editors to insist on using *innocent* rather than *not guilty.*

All lawsuits are tried in courts. *Court litigation,* therefore, is redundant.

Statements are either written or oral (not verbal).

"Would-be robber" has no more validity than a "would-be ballplayer."

The word *lawman* has no place in the report. It can mean too many things—a village constable, a sheriff's deputy or the sheriff, a prosecutor, a bailiff, a judge, an FBI agent, a revenue agent and so on. *Lawman* in contemporary America is a "hillbilly" word. Its merit is that it suggests a social setting. Almost always a more precise word will be found more suitable in a newspaper.

Use *sheriff's deputies* rather than *deputy sheriffs.*

Divorces are granted or obtained. Medals are won or awarded.

"Hit-and-run," "ax-murder," "torture-murder" and the like are newspaper clichés. They should be changed to "hit by an automobile that failed to stop," "killed with an ax," "tortured and murdered."

There's no such thing as an *attempted holdup.* A holdup is a robbery even if the bad guy got nothing from the victim.

Misplacement of words makes the reporter and the copy editor look ridiculous:

"An 80-year-old man . . . pleaded guilty yesterday to reduced charges of attempted indecent and immoral practices in Jefferson Criminal Court."

"Seven persons have been fined . . . for impaired driving in Fenton District Court."

Legal Jargon

Legal jargon also should be avoided:

"The case was continued for disposition because the attorney requested no probation report be made on the boy before adjudication."

W.J. Brier and J.B. Rollins of Montana State University studied some Missoula, Mont., adults and their understanding of legal terms. Here are the terms incorrectly defined by more than half the respondents, followed by the correct explanation:

- *Accessories before the fact*—those charged with helping another who committed the felony.
- *Extradition*—surrendered the prisoner to officials of another state.
- *Arraigned*—brought to court to answer to a criminal charge.
- *Bound over*—held on bail for trial.
- *Indicted*—accused or charged by a grand jury.
- *Civil action*—pertaining to private rights of individuals and to legal proceedings against these individuals.
- *Extortion*—oppressive or illegal obtaining of money or other things of value.

- *Remanded*—sent the case back to a lower court for review.
- *Continuance*—adjournment of the case.
- *Felony*—a crime of a graver nature than a misdemeanor, usually an offense punishable by imprisonment or death.
- *Writ of habeas corpus*—an order to bring the prisoner to court so the court may determine if he has been denied his legal rights.
- *Administratrix*—administrator: always female.
- *Stay order*—stop the action or suspend the legal proceeding.
- *An information*—an accusation or a charge filed by a prosecutor.
- *Venire*—those summoned to serve as jurors.
- *Demurrer*—a pleading admitting the facts in a complaint or answer but contending they are legally insufficient.

Other misunderstood terms include:

- "Released on her personal recognizance"—released on her word of honor to do a particular act.
- " . . . make a determination on the voluntariness of a confession"—decide whether a confession is voluntary.
- " . . . the plaintiff is . . ."—" . . . the suit was filed by . . ."

Terms that should be translated include: *ambulatory* (movable), *bequest* (gift), *debenture* (obligation), *domicile* (home), *in camera* (in the judge's office), *liquidate* (settle), *litigant* (participant), *paralegals* (legal assistants), *plat* (map), *res judicata* (matter already decided).

If a prison loses the right to vote, that person is *disfranchised*, not disenfranchised.

Lawyers are fond of word-doubling: *last will and testament, null and void, on or about, written instrument.* Another is *and/or.* "The maximum sentence . . . is a $20,000 fine and-or 15 years' imprisonment." The maximum would be the fine and 15 years.

Few readers understand the meaning of the word *writ* (a judge's order or a court order). "In a petition for a writ of mandamus, the new bank's incorporators asked the court. . . ." The copy editor should have changed that to "The new bank's incorporators asked the court to. . . ." or if the term mandamus was essential, it should have been explained (a court order telling a public official to do something).

Euphemisms

Euphemisms include "attorney" for *lawyer,* "sexually assaulted" or "sexually attacked" for *raped.* Not all jurists, who profess to be or are versed in the law, are judges, and certainly not all judges are jurists.

Threadbare Phrases

Here are some threadbare phrases that too often appear in newspapers: stern warning, brilliant defense, shattered body, police speculated, on the lam, soberly pronounced sentence, robed justices, curfew clamped.

Be Exact   A *robber* steals by force. A *thief* steals without resorting to force. Theft suggests stealth. A *burglar* makes an unauthorized entry into a building. If a burglar is caught in the act, pulls a gun on the homeowner and makes off with the family silverware, that person is a robber. It is redundant to use the phrase armed robber.

Theft and *larceny* both mean the taking of what belongs to another. *Larceny* is the more specific term and can be proved only when the thief has the stolen property. Pickpockets and shoplifters are thieves.

"Statutory grounds for divorce" is redundant. All grounds for divorce are statutory in the state where the divorce is granted.

Charge has many shades of meaning and is often misused. "The psychologist charged last night that black high school students generally do not think of the university as a friendly place." The statement was more an observation than a charge.

Members of the Supreme Court are justices, but not judges or supreme judges. The title of the U.S. Supreme Court's chief justice is Chief Justice of the United States.

Words such as *looted, robbed* and *swindled* should be used properly: "Two men were fined and given suspended sentences yesterday in Municipal Court for stealing newsracks and looting money from them." "Thieves broke into 26 automobiles parked near the plant and looted some small items." Money is not looted. That from which it is taken is looted. Nor is money robbed. A bank is robbed; the money is stolen. "A man in uniform swindled $1,759 from a woman." No, the person is swindled, not the money.

Some papers object to saying that fines and sentences are *given,* on the ground that they are not gifts.

9

Handling the Wire

Wire Service Technology

Perhaps no area of journalism has been affected more by technological development than the wire services. The major services in the United States, the Associated Press and United Press International, both have invested heavily in computerized equipment that has vastly improved their ability to deliver the news. Most newspaper offices no longer have Teletype machines clattering away to deliver the news at speeds of 50 to 70 words a minute. In their place are computer data links over which AP and UPI transmit stories directly into the newspaper's computer at speeds of 1,200 words a minute. Many broadcast stations have high-speed printers to receive copy at that rate, too.

Even the means of transmission has changed. For many years, wire news was transmitted over leased telephone lines in a complicated network that stretched around the world. Today, most of those lines have been replaced by satellite links. The process begins when the wire service beams news material to a satellite orbiting above the earth. The signal bounces off the satellite and is received by receiving dishes atop newspaper and broadcast station offices. Despite the cost of this sophisticated technology, the wire services have saved millions of dollars in reduced telephone line charges.

Newspapers and broadcast stations have been helped by such developments, too. They get the news faster, cost increases are minimized and reliability is improved. Satellite delivery generally is less subject to interference, and the resulting garbled copy, than telephone transmission.

All this is possible because of the remarkable developments in data transmission that have occurred in the past 20 years. Business and industry, spurred by the need for instant communication with far-flung plants and workers, and the need for the latest information on prices, stock market trends and similar information, led the demand for improved communication. Emergence of the personal computer, improved satellite technology and the shrinking cost of mass data storage have made it possible to do things that once were merely dreams. A traveling salesperson is as close to the office computer as the nearest telephone. With a portable personal computer (some of which fit into a briefcase and weigh less than 10 pounds) and a telephone, that salesperson can report expenses, check for messages from the boss and call up for the latest price of the company's stock. And that's just the beginning. There are literally thousands of data bases available to those with the proper security codes.

Some of those data bases also provide the user with access to the wire services. News from The Associated Press is offered to subscribers to Dow Jones News Retrieval and CompuServe. UPI news is available on The Source and NewsNet. News provided that way, however, is not available for broadcast or reprinting; it is intended solely for the individual consumer. Nor is that news indexed by importance, properly sorted or headlined. And it is expensive; those connected to such services pay for access by the minute. For all those reasons, there is ample reason to suspect that consumption of the news by home computer will never replace the services provided by print and broadcast editors—sorting, editing, indexing and headlining the news.

How the System Works

Stories delivered by the wire services originate from several sources:

1. Copy developed by the agencies' own large staffs of reporters, feature writers, analysts, columnists and photographers.
2. Rewrites of stories developed by subscribers. Newspapers or broadcast stations contracting with a wire service agree to make their own news files available to the service, either by providing proofs or computer printouts of stories. Other wire service staffers rewrite from any source available—smaller papers, research reports and other publications.
3. Stringers or correspondents in communities where there is no bureau. Such stringers frequently are newspaper reporters and are called stringers because of the old practice of paying a correspondent by his string of stories represented in column inches.
4. Exchanges with other news agencies, such as foreign agencies.

A reporter telephones a story to the state bureau of UPI. If the story has statewide interest, UPI files the story on its state wire. If the story has regional interest, the state bureau offers it to a regional bureau, or, in some cases, the state office may offer the story directly to the national desk.

The national desk thus becomes the nerve center for the entire operation of the news agency. That desk collects news from all the state, regional and foreign bureaus, culls the material, then returns it to the regional and state bureaus or to subscribers directly.

The operation sometimes is referred to as a gatekeeping system. A Dutch story, for example, would have to get by the Amsterdam office before it could be disseminated in Holland. The same story would have to clear the London bureau before being relayed to New York and the national desk. That desk then would decide whether the story should be distributed nationally. The desk could send the story directly to newspapers or route it through regional and state bureaus. In the latter cases, the regional bureau would judge whether to transmit the story to a state bureau and a state bureau would have the option of relaying the story to subscribers. A wire editor then would accept or reject the story. Finally, the reader would become the ultimate gatekeeper by deciding which stories to read and which to ignore.

Small- and medium-sized dailies usually subscribe to only one wire service. Because both agencies cover approximately the same news, the choice for smaller dailies usually rests with the service offering the better state report. But because enough difference exists between the two agencies, larger papers are compelled to subscribe to both services.

Traditionally, the wire service has opened the news cycle with a news budget or summary that indicates to editors the dozen or more top national and international stories that were in hand or were developing.

Today's wire editors may get a four- or five-line abstract of the complete offering—foreign, national, regional and state—transmitted directly to the newspaper's computer. From these abstracts or from VDT directories wire editors select the stories in which they think their readers are interested. Then they retrieve those stories directly from the newspaper's computer.

With high-speed service, the AP and UPI can deliver up-to-the-minute stories that are better written and better edited than those in the past. Wire editors are spared the task of plowing through scores of stories they don't want; they have more time to consolidate the offerings of both major wire services and other news syndicates.

AP and UPI gather news from around the world to serve subscribers both at home and abroad. Both offer—in addition to general news—features, special interest news (sports, business, religion), analyses or interpretives and pictures.[1]

[1] AP and UPI provide similar services, but they are organized differently. AP is a cooperative owned by its member newspapers and broadcast stations. UPI is a privately owned company.

The primary wire ("A" wire) originates in New York City or Washington and carries top national and international news. The AP devotes a secondary national wire, or "B" wire, to national and international news. UPI does the same, but "splits" once an hour allow for transmission of state and regional news.

Separate national wires deliver sports, markets and pictures. Smaller dailies rely primarily on the state wire, a combination of the main news wires, sports, markets—and state or regional news. The state bureau also delivers pictures, both by facsimile transmission and by mail. Both services provide subscribers with individually requested stories. Broadcast stations have access to special radio wires but may also have, if they desire, any of the other wires.

Types of Circuits

Not all newspapers have converted to high-speed service; many small papers have continued to use slow-speed wires because of lower cost. For similar reasons, many broadcast stations still use slow-speed wires. So, it is important to learn about both.

Slow-Speed

Slow-speed copy may be delivered to a newspaper by Teletype, typically at 66 words a minute, in one of several forms. If it is in all-capital letters, which is increasingly rare, the copy editor assumes the letters are all in lowercase and marks the letters to be capitalized with a single underline (Figure 9-1). If the copy is in caps and lowercase or full caps and small caps, the editor handles it the same as local copy (Figure 9-2). Most newspapers using traditional copy processing procedures use neither of those forms, but instead edit Teletypesetter (or TTS) monitor copy, which accompanies the perforated TTS tape used to drive typesetters.

The key to TTS handling is the book number or code number visible on the tape (see Figure 9-3). The tapes are strung on pegs corresponding to the book or computer number (peg 1 for tapes 1, 11, 21, etc.). The monitor copy is edited and sent to the composing room where an operator selects the proper tape and feeds it directly into a phototypesetter. Sluglines, headlines and editing changes are manually punched on other tapes. Because of the time used, and the chances for errors in perforating the tape, heavy editing of TTS wire copy is discouraged.

High-Speed

The wire services' high-speed circuits are referred to variously as dataspeed, DataStream, DataNews or DataFeature. The circuits permit the agencies to hold back stories until they can be wrapped up or be self-contained.

Dataspeed circuits originally were used to transmit tabular matter such as the stock market and sports boxscores. Today the services deliver the national wires, as well as feature syndicated and supplemental copy, on such circuits. To illustrate the advantage of

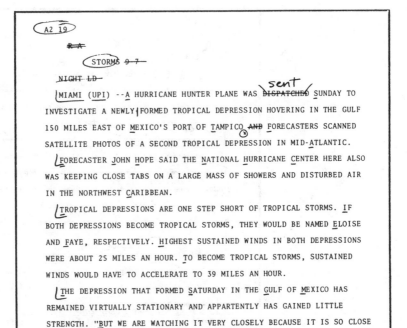

Figure 9-1 Editing all-cap wire copy. The copy editor assumes the story is in lowercase, then marks the appropriate capital letters.

the faster transmission (1,200 words a minute), AP was able to release for wire movement the president's State of Union message and the new Wholesale Price Index in the same time it took to move the initial bulletin on the slow-speed A wire.

Newspapers receiving high-speed transmissions usually capture all the wire services transmit directly in a computer. One circuit is used for almost all the services available, and selector devices are installed at the newspaper to filter out services to which the paper does not subscribe. If a newspaper purchases the A wire, B wire and sports wire, but not the financial wire, the selector blocks reception of financial items. The others are allowed to pass into the newspaper's computer system for storage and later retrieval.

United Press International uses its DataNews circuit for most of its own services and all syndicate copy. Thus, a newspaper client can select which UPI services it wants and on the same circuit it can receive copy from *The New York Times* News Service, the *Washington Post-Los Angeles Times* Syndicate or many other supplemental services. This "piggyback" feature makes UPI service less expensive than AP service because AP uses two circuits—DataStream for news and DataFeature for supplementals—to transmit the same amount of information. UPI also uses individ-

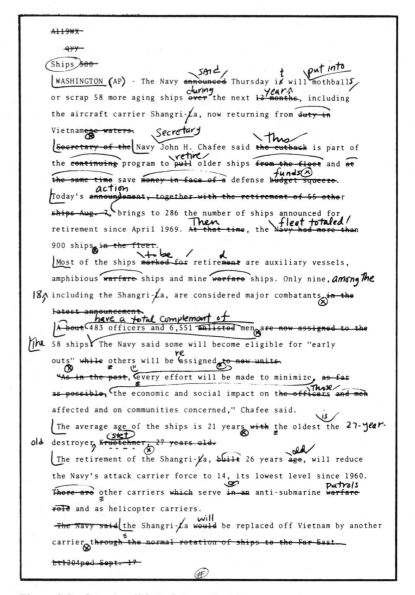

Figure 9-2 Sample editing of a caps and lowercase wire story.

ual selector codes for each client. With this system, when a client asks for an item to be repeated, it can be sent directly to that client without clogging the computer storage facilities of other newspapers with multiple copies of the same story. Both services use separate circuits for high-speed transmission of stock market tables.

Almost all newspapers that subscribe to high-speed services edit those stories on VDTs, but high-speed printers are available for backup in case the newspaper's computer fails.

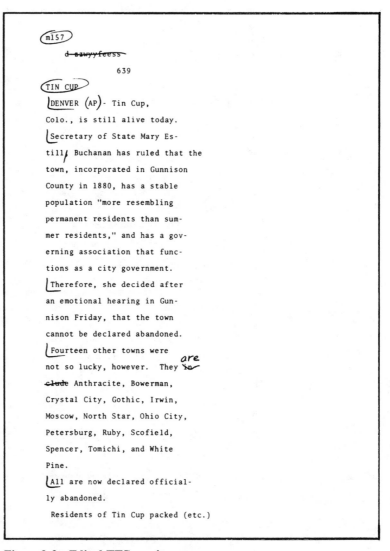

Figure 9-3 Edited TTS monitor copy.

Budgets and Priorities

The wire services operate on 12-hour time cycles—PMs for afternoon papers, AMs for morning papers. The cycles often overlap so that stories breaking near the cycle change are offered to both cycles or stories early in one cycle are picked up on stories late in the other cycle. In each cycle slow-speed Teletypes deliver approximately 200 items, but this includes advisories (messages to editors) and separate book or file numbers delivered in takes or segments. The cycle also includes new leads, inserts and adds. High-speed wires carry many more items during a cycle.

```
         d lbylczzcczzc
Starting AMs Report, a201 Next
1202pED 03-07


    a201
        r lbylczzcv
AP NEWS DIGEST
Saturday AMS
  Here are the top news stories in sight for AMs at this hour. The
General Desk supervisor is Ed Dennehy. He may be reached at 212
262-6093 if you have urgent questions about the spot news report.
ECONOMIC-ENERGY
  WASHINGTON - The unemployment rate remained stable at 8.2 per cent
last month, largely because 580,000 persons stopped looking for work,
the labor department reports. New material. With Wirephoto chart
NY15.
  WASHINGTON - The Social Security System is plunging into deficit, an
advisory panel tells Congress, and should be strengthened with
general tax revenues. New material. Wirephoto upcoming.
  DETROIT - With six plants closed this week, Ford soon may step up
production next week to keep pace with General Motors, Chrysler and
American Motors, all of which will have every plant in operation.
Developing, to be announced officially late in afternoon.
  UNDATED - Millions of Americans with visions of ripe red tomatoes
and leafy green lettuce at home-grown costs are planning vegetable
plots this summer. But there are plenty of pitfalls between garden and
table. New, Consumer Scorecard, by Louise Cook.
```

Figure 9-4   Wire service budget.

For a morning paper, the wire news day begins about noon with
the following:

> a200
> d lbylczzcczzc
> Starting AMs Report, a 201 Next
> 1202pED 03-07

Then follows the news digest (or budget), notifying editors of the
dozen or more top news stories in sight (Figure 9-4). An addition
to the first budget may come a short time later. The budget is used
to give wire editors a glimpse of the major stories forthcoming and
aids them in planning space allocations.

Major stories breaking after the budget has been delivered are
designated:

FLASH—a two- or three-word statement alerting editors to a

story of unusual importance: President shot. On the old teleprinter machines a warning bell signifying a flash brought editors running to the machine. Today a flash is seldom used because a bulletin serves the same purpose and is almost as fast.

BULLETIN (BUN)—a short summary, usually no more than a lead, of a major story. Again, it is used primarily to alert editors and is not intended for publication unless the bulletin arrives at deadline. A bulletin also may be used to signal corrections such as a mandatory "kill" on a portion of a story that could be libelous.

BULLETIN MATTER—expands the bulletin with more, but brief, details. Unless the deadline is a factor, the wire editor holds up the story for a more detailed account.

URGENT—calls editors' attention to new material or to corrections on stories sent previously.

Sorting the Pieces Wire editors have two considerations in selecting wire copy for publication—the significance of the stories and the space allotted for wire copy. If space is tight, fewer wire stories are used and heavier trims may be made on those that are used.

Budget stories usually, but not necessarily, get top priority. When stories listed on the budget arrive they are so indicated by BUDGET, BJT or SKED, together with the length in words. If such stories are developing or are likely to have additional or new material, the editor places each story in a folder or VDT holding queue and concentrates on stories that will stand.

Eventually the stories in the folder or holding queue have to be typeset. This is done by working backward—taking the latest book number and latest time indicator. The fifth and last lead may eliminate the fourth lead but pick up on the third lead and so forth until the story is compact and in order.

The Associated Press has added a feature called DataRecaps to aid wire editors in handling a breaking story. Previously, editors had to assemble the pieces from multiple leads, inserts, subs and adds or wait until space was cleared on the wire for a no-pickup lead. Now, the service notifies wire editors a recap is coming, then delivers a complete story at 1,200 words a minute. UPI does much the same with frequent "writethrus."

Starts and stops occur even on copy apparently wrapped up. A story arriving early in the morning describes a congressional appropriation of $5.9 *billion* to provide jobs for the unemployed. Fifty items later editors are informed that the figure should be changed to $6.4 *million*. Still later, New York sends the message that the original $5.9 *million* should stand. Eventually the service again corrects the figure to the original $5.9 *billion*. Such changes pose few problems for the editor if the story has not yet been typeset. The editor simply changes the copy on paper or on the VDT.

Editing the Wire

On each news cycle, even the wire editors of large newspapers have more stories than they can use.

At newspapers with traditional wire desks, editing starts with stripping the machines. That means that on any circuit someone clears all copy from the Teletype and sorts the stories for the various departments—sports, family living, entertainment, business and the like.

The wire editor then rips apart the individual stories and arranges them for Page One (usually the top budget stories), some for inside pages and still others for future use. Stories for the inside pages usually are handled first because such stories seldom change. The final selection of stories for Page One depends on local copy, pictures and the design of the page. At papers using VDT systems, the same process takes place, but stories are sorted into various holding queues until processing begins.

On larger dailies using all the wires from the two major national news agencies, the flow of copy is monumental, even though the wire editor does not have to confront some of the special wires such as sports and markets.

One way to handle this spate of copy is to categorize the news— one folder or queue for stories from Washington, D.C., another for New York and international, another for national, another for regional, another for area copy and the like. VDTs do that automatically.

An advantage of the paper receiving more than one news service is that the editor can use the story from one service to check facts against the same story from another service, such as casualty figures, proper names and spellings. If there is a serious discrepancy in facts, the editor asks the state or regional bureau for verification.

Wires Make Mistakes

Two points should be kept in mind as you edit wire copy. The first is that neither wire service tailors copy for a particular newspaper. Abundant details are included but most stories are constructed so that papers may trim sharply and still have the gist of the report, or they can use the full account.

The second point is that the wire isn't sacred. Both AP and UPI have a deserved reputation for accuracy, impartiality and speed of delivery. They also make errors, sometimes colossal ones.

A source who turned out to be unreliable caused United Press to release a premature armistice story during World War I. A confused signal from a New Jersey courthouse caused AP to give the wrong penalty for Bruno Richard Hauptmann, convicted in the kidnapping and slaying of the Lindbergh child. The state wire, more often than not, is poorly written and poorly edited. Even the wire executives admit they still have bonehead editing and some stories that don't make sense. In both agencies, the stories abound with partial quotes, despite repeated protests from subscribers.

Both services have advisory committees, usually composed of managing editors, who monitor writing performance. Here is one example from the APME (Associated Press Managing Editors) writing committee:

DETROIT (AP)—Two Detroit factory workers were killed Wednesday evening on their jobs, Detroit police said today. *(Clearly an industrial accident.)*

The two men, employees of the Hercules Forging Co., were identified as James H—, 51, the father of nine children, and M.C. Mc—, 37, both of Detroit. Mc— may have been struck accidentally, police reported. *(Oh, somebody struck him accidentally, but hit the other fellow on purpose.)*

Police said they had a man in custody and added he would probably be charged in connection with the deaths. *(Let's see, both of them were killed by the same man, but one death may* have been an accident, but the suspect is charged with two murders?)*

Police say they interviewed 15 workers at the plant who could give no reason for the shootings. *(Now gunplay gets into this story.)*

Witnesses told police the man confronted H—with a carbine and shot him when he tried to run. He fired a second shot after H—fell, they said.

The third shot, apparently aimed at another workman, hit Mc—, police said. *(Now we are beginning to understand that what started out sounding like an industrial accident has become double murder.)*

Peculiarities of Wire Copy

At most newspapers, wire copy is edited the same way as local copy, but a few peculiarities apply to the editing of wire news. First, wire news, unlike local news, usually carries a *dateline,* which indicates the city of the story's origin. Despite the name of the device, most newspapers no longer include in the dateline the date the story was written:

Old Dateline

OVERLAND PARK, Kan., Jan. 12 (AP)—An apparent good Samaritan who helped start a woman's car talked about how dangerous it was to be out at night then pulled a gun and took her purse, police said. . . .

Modern Dateline

OVERLAND PARK, Kan. (AP)—An apparent good Samaritan who helped start a woman's car talked about how dangerous it was to be out at night then pulled a gun and took her purse, police said. . . .

Note that the city of origin is in capital letters and the state or nation is in uppercase and lowercase letters. At most newspapers, style calls for the dateline to be followed by the wire service logotype in parentheses and a dash. The paragraph indentation comes before the dateline, not at the start of the first paragraph.

Stories that contain material from more than one location are called *undated* stories. They carry no dateline but a credit line for the wire service:

By The Associated Press

Arab extremists said today they would blow up American installations throughout the Middle East unless all Americans leave Beirut immediately. . . .

Stories compiled from accounts supplied by more than one wire service carry similar credit lines:

From our wire services

LA PAZ, Bolivia—Mountain climbers experienced in winter climbing tried today to reach the wreckage of an Eastern Airlines Boeing 727, which crashed Monday while approaching La Paz in a snowstorm.

When editors combine stories, they must be sensitive to the fact that wire stories are copyrighted. If material in the story was supplied exclusively by one service, that service should be credited within the text. Combining the stories this way often provides a newspaper's readers with a better story than could be obtained from either of the major services alone. Good newspapers make a habit of doing this frequently.

Wire stories often use the word *here* to refer to the city included in the dateline. If the editor has removed the dateline during the editing process, the city must be inserted in the text. Otherwise, *here* is understood to be the city in which the newspaper is published.

Both major wire services use Eastern time in their stories. Some newspapers outside the Eastern time zone prefer to convert those times by subtracting one hour for Central time, two for Mountain or three for Pacific. When this is done, if the dateline remains on the story, it will be necessry to use phrases such as *3 p.m. St. Louis time* or *3 p.m. PDT* in the text. The newspaper's local style will specify which form is to be used.

Localizing Wire Stories

Wire stories often become ideas for local stories. If Congress has reduced the amount of money it will provide for loans to college students, a newspaper in a college town may want to contact the college's financial aid officer to determine what effect the measure will have locally.

When the Soviet Union shot down a Korean Airlines plane, the *Columbia Missourian* learned that two people were aboard who had just completed their doctoral degrees at the University of Missouri. Their daughter was with them aboard the jet. Because members of the family had lived in Columbia for several years, many people knew them. As a result, a major international story became a good local story:

Recent University graduates Somchai Pakaranodom and his wife, Wantanee, were on their way back to Thailand after living in Columbia for four years. They never made it.

The couple, along with their 7-year-old daughter Pom, were among the 269 killed when a Soviet jet shot down Korean Air Lines Flight 007 north of Japan.

"We had laughed about the flight schedule," education Professor Dorothy Watson recalled Friday, sitting in her living room where a week earlier she had thrown a going-away party for the Pakaranodoms.

The couple left Columbia Saturday. They were traveling first to Chicago then on to New York to catch the flight to Seoul and eventually on to Bangkok, Thailand.

With the sound of news reports about the crash coming over the television from the next room, Mrs. Watson fought back the tears. "I kept thinking they couldn't possibly be on the plane," she said. "It is just such a waste, so stupid."

At first she didn't connect the crash with her friends.

On Friday, another faculty member called to break the news to her. She said even then she refused to believe it, until Korean Air Lines confirmed the family was on the flight.

Both Fulbright scholars, the Pakaranodoms received their doctoral degrees from the University Aug. 5. Somchai's degree was in agricultural engineering, Wantanee's in reading education. . . .

Localizing wire stories can be done in several ways. The story can be rewritten to emphasize the local angle, a separate local sidebar to the wire story can be written, or a simple insert in the wire story may be sufficient.

New Leads, Inserts, Takes

After copy has left the copy desk, changes sometimes have to be made because of new developments, corrections or additional information.

Under the traditional system, the routine for new leads and inserts works this way:

Obtain a proof of the story from the composing room. This proof has several designations, including "marker," "Cx" or "fix." Draw a block around the portion of the lead to be deleted and write in the margin: "Kill for new lead." On the remaining portion, write in the margin: "Pickup" (Figure 9-5).

The new copy will be marked "New lede FARM." At the end of the new lead, write "pickup" and indicate the paragraph where the story resumes: "The trend . . ." (2nd graf).

Assume two insertions are to be made, one between the fourth and fifth paragraphs, the other between the seventh and eighth paragraphs. Use the proof to show where the inserts are to go, marking one "insert A" in the margin, the other "insert B."

The copy would be marked "insert A fourth graph FARM" and "insert B seventh graph FARM," and each would close with "end insert."

Return both the copy and the proof to the composing room.

If more information is to be added to the end of the story, the copy editor simply uses the notation "Add FARM" on the copy. No proof or marker is necessary.

On VDT editing terminals, new leads and inserts, whether from the wires or local generation, are handled at first as separate stories

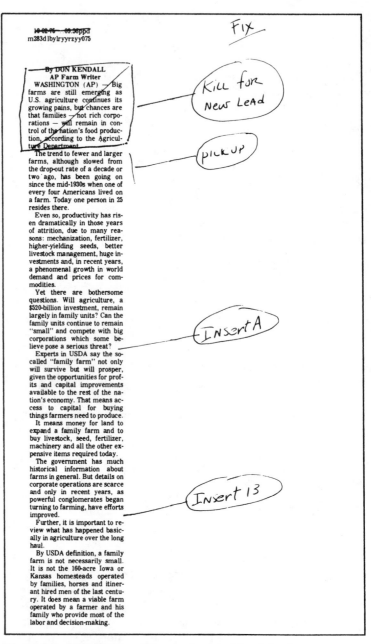

Figure 9-5 Marking proof for new lead and two insertions.

under their own file number if the earlier version has already been typeset. Copy editors set these in the same measure as the earlier story, retain the pickup line so those in the pasteup department can see it, and typeset the later revision—whether add, insert or lead. If the new lead comes in before the story has been typeset, the copy editor can call the lead to the screen, insert the old story

```
    m290

    FARM 2nd lead 110

       WASHINGTON (AP)--Urban sprawl, highways, parks, airports....
    The trend: 2nd graf m283

    m295

    FARM Insert 70

       WASHINGTON FARM m283, updating, insert after 4th graf:
    threat?

       Meanwhile, the total land area in farms also has been....
    Experts in USDA, etc. 5th graf.

    m299

    FARM  Insert 40

       WASHINGTON FARM m283, further updating, insert after 7th graf:
    improved.

       Economic recovery and further industrialization during....
    Further, etc. 8th graf.
```

Figure 9-6   Copy for new leads and inserts. m290 is the book number on the new lead (110 words) of the original story (book number m283). The story picks up at the second paragraph of the original, beginning "The trend . . ." Copy for the two inserts (70 and 40 words long) indicates the position of the inserts.

into that file, delete what should come out and typeset the story as a unit.

If the story has been sent to the typesetter but a copy of the story is in the storage file, the story can be recalled and corrected on a VDT. The original story is then put on the screen and merging is accomplished by using the VDT paragraph insert feature. Finally, a copy of the typeset strip can be obtained and indications for new leads and inserts can be made on that proof. Because modern phototypesetters are so fast, some newspapers choose to set the entire story a second time.

A story breaking near deadline may have to be handled in small segments or "takes" to minimize the time needed for typesetting. The first take usually is no more than the lead. It would carry the slug word, for example, MAYOR. If the head size has not been determined, the slug would indicate that the head will come later—HTC or HTK.

The first take ends with "more." The second take is slugged "1st add MAYOR" and similarly is kept open with "more." The process is repeated until the final take, usually so indicated, as "sixth and last add MAYOR." This segment closes with an endmark.

The copy editor keeps notes as the story moves so that the headline can be written as soon as the final take is in.

With the new technology this procedure is no longer as important as it once was because of the speed with which copy can now be written, edited and set into type.

Other News Syndicates

Syndication of news by major metropolitan newspapers, a combination of such papers or a newspaper chain have made it possible for dailies to give readers a variety and depth of news coverage. Among such news syndicates are *The New York Times* News Service, *Washington Post-Los Angeles Times* Syndicate, and the Copley and Gannett news services. By syndicating their news, the publishers participating in the supplemental services are able to recoup some of the costs of news gathering and, in fact, have been able to expand news coverage.

The wire services similarly offer their own feature syndicates that include news and features from other newspapers (London Express) or from parent corporations (Scripps-Howard News Service).

The services mentioned are among the more than 200 syndicates offering publishers news, features, pictures, and special services. In addition to giving spot and secondary news, these services provide sports, foods, fashions, bylined columns and features ranging from amateur photography to zoo animals.

Picture Services

Both major wire services offer picture service to their subscribers. The Associated Press service, called Laserphoto, uses laser beam technology to scan the photo at the transmission point, convert it to digital language for telephone or satellite transmission, and, using another laser beam, convert it back to picture form at the newspaper. UPI's service, Unifax II, operates similarly but with a wet-process chemical system similar to those found in some office copiers.

Both services plan to offer computer-to-computer digital transmission of photos when newspapers have computer systems able to store and process them.

PART III

Headline Writing Skills

10

Creating the Headline

**Headline
Functions**

A copy editor's first task is to correct and refine copy. This means, as outlined in earlier chapters, checking copy for accuracy, clarity, conciseness, tone and consistency of style.

A second task is to write a headline that:

1. Attracts the reader's attention.
2. Summarizes the story.
3. Helps the reader index the contents of the page.
4. Depicts the mood of the story.
5. Helps set the tone of the newspaper.
6. Provides adequate typographic relief.

Those are the major functions of headlines. Not every headline can accomplish each of those tasks, but editors who write headlines with these goals in mind will write better headlines than those who ignore them.

Good headlines attract the reader's attention to stories that otherwise may be ignored. The day's best story may have little or no impact if the headline fails to *sell* it, or attract the reader's attention. Headlines sell stories in many ways, but often they do so by focusing on how the reader's life will be affected. For example, if the City Council has approved a city budget of $30 million for the coming year, one approach is to headline the story:

Council approves $30 million budget

Another approach, one that does a better job of selling the story, might be this:

City tax rate to remain unchanged

That approach answers the questions the reader is most likely to ask about the council's action: How will it affect me? Some headlines attract attention because of the magnitude of the event they address:

Earthquake in Algeria kills 20,000

Others attract attention because the headline is clever or unusual:

Hunger pangs
Thief finds sandwich goodies,
wine provide appetizing loot

Each story requires a different approach, and the headline writer who is able to find the correct one to attract the reader's attention is a valued member of the newspaper's staff.

Most headlines appear over new stories that are designed to inform, not entertain, so the headline that simply summarizes the story as concisely and accurately as possible is the bread and butter of the headline writer:

U.S., China to sign major grain deal

Such headlines seldom win prizes for originality or prompt readers to write letter of praise. But a newspaper full of headlines that get right to the point is a newspaper that is easy to read. The reader knows what the story is about and can make an intelligent decision about whether to read more. The headlines serve to summarize the news, much as five-minute radio newscasts do.

If the headlines on a page do a good job of summarizing the stories, the editors have created for their readers a form of index to the page. This also helps the reader determine what will be read and what will be bypassed. In one sense, good headlines help readers determine what *not* to read. And, while that may seem counterproductive to the newspaper's objectives, it is realistic to recognize that a reader will partake of only a small percentage of the newspaper's offerings. Newspapers help make those choices easier by providing a choice of fare, much as supermarket managers offer their customers various brands of green beans. That may not be an appealing comparison to those who view newspapers as entitites above that sort of thing, but it *is* realistic. To ignore that reality is a mistake.

The headline also serves to set the mood for the story. The straightforward news headline indicates to the reader that the story it accompanies is a serious one. Similarly, a headline above a how-to-do-it story should reflect the story's content:

It's easy to save by changing your car's oil

Setting the mood is even more important when writing headlines for humorous stories. One newspaper hurt readership of a bright story during the streaking craze of the early 1970s by using a straight headline:

Judge lectures streaker

The story was a humorous account of the court appearance of a group of college students who had run across a softball diamond in the nude. In the second edition, the headline writer did a much better job:

**Streaker gets the pitch
It's a whole nude ball game**

The mood was set for the reader to enjoy the story.

Headlines probably reveal as much about the tone, or character, of a newspaper as anything it contains. If the top story on the front page is headlined **Cops seek lover in ax murder** and the second story carries the headline **Jackie O. flips over new beau,** there can be little doubt about the nature of the publication. Serious tones, as well as sensational ones, can be set with headlines.

Finally, headlines serve the purpose of providing typographic relief. They separate stories on the page and relieve the tedium that would exist with masses of text-sized type. This function will be discussed in detail in Chapters 13–16.

Headline Styles

Styles of headlines, like fashions, change constantly, even though their functions remain the same. Because the headline style is an important factor in determining what can and cannot be included in a headline, it may be useful to review the development of those styles from an historical perspective.

Newspapers' first news display lines were short and slender, usually a single crossline giving little more than a topical label: *Latest From Europe.* By adding more lines or by varying the length of the lines, designers created the hanging indention, the inverted pyramid and the pyramid:

```
XXXXXXXXXXX     XXXXXXXXXXXX        XXXXXX
 XXXXXXXXX       XXXXXXXXX        XXXXXXXXX
 XXXXXXXXX        XXXXXX        XXXXXXXXXXXX
```

Later, by centering the second line and making the third flush with the right-hand margin, they developed the stepline. It became one of the most popular styles of headlines and still is in use at a few newspapers:

Heavy Rain
Shuts Down
All Beaches

The next move was to combine these elements—a stepline, an inverted pyramid, a crossline, then another inverted pyramid. The units under the introductory head became known as *banks* or *decks*. An article in *The Quill* cited one found in a western newspaper describing a reporter's interview with Gen. Phil Sheridan in 1883:

FRISKY PHIL

Gazette Reporter Holds
Interesting Interview
With Hero of Winchester

The Great Warrior Receives the
Newspaperman with Open Arms;
He is More or Less Broken up on
the craft anyway

HE TRAVELS IN A SPECIAL
MILITARY COACH AND LIVES
ON THE FAT OF THE LAND

Sheridan is Many Miles Away,
but the Champagne We Drank
with him Lingers with Us Still

We Feel a Little Puffed
Up Over Our Success At-
tending Our Reception by
Little Phil, But Man Is
Mortal

May He Who Watches Over the
Sparrows of the Field Never
Remove His Field Glasses from
the Diminutive Form and Great
Soul of Phil Sheridan

Throughout most of America's history newspaper headlines have tended to depict the mood of the times as well as the tone of the paper. **Jerked to Jesus** shouted the *Chicago Times* on Nov. 27, 1875, in headlining the account of a hanging. Some other classics:

AWFUL EVENT

**President Lincoln
Shot by an Assassin.**

The Deed Done at Ford's
Theatre Last Night

The Act of a Desperate Rebel

**The President Still Alive at
Last Accounts**

No Hopes Entertained of His
Recovery

---

*Attempted Assassination of
Secretary Seward*

Details of the Dreadful Tragedy

The New York Times

**AMERICA IS
MISTRESS
OF AIR**

**Wright's Machine Is
Perfect; Uncle
Sam Buys**

**Overland Trip With
Passenger Succeeds**

**"We Flew Eighty Miles an Hour
Coming Back," Says
Lieutenant.**

The Denver Post

**PEARY WIRES HE HAS NAILED STARS AND STRIPES
TO THE NORTH POLE AND IS ON HIS WAY HOME**

**OFFICIAL MESSAGE
SENT ARCTIC CLUB**

**Backers Were Momen-
tarily Expecting Veteran**

**Explorer to Report Suc-
cessful Quest of Goal
Reached by his Rival**

**Latter Sends His Instru-
ments and Records to the
United States for Examin-
ation and Will Prove His
Claims Before a Jury of
Scientists of Two Conti-
nents-Dispells All Doubt.**

The Denver Post

Big type and clamoring messages still weren't enough for some newspapers in the late 1800s. According to Gene Fowler, an executive told the owners of the *Denver Post,* "You've got to make this paper look different. Get some bigger headline type. Put red ink on Page One. You've got to turn Denver's eyes to the *Post* every day, and away from the other papers." So the *Post* ran its headlines in red to catch the readers' attention. The message had to be gripping. According to Fowler's version, Harry Tammen, co-owner of the *Post,* was so incensed over a lifeless banner that he grabbed a piece of copy paper and composed one of his own: **Jealous Gun-Gal Plugs Her Lover Low.** When the copy desk protested the headline wouldn't fit, Tammen snapped, "Then use any old type you can find. Tear up somebody's ad if necessary." Still the desk wasn't satisfied. "It isn't good grammar," the desk chief argued. But Tammen wouldn't budge. "That's the trouble with this paper," he is quoted as saying. "Too damned much grammar. Let's can the grammar and get out a live sheet."

The battle for circulation was hot. So were the headlines. Many also were colorful:

Demon of the Belfry Sent Through the Trap

Dons Planned to Skedaddle in the Night

Does It Hurt to Be Born?

**Conductors Robbing Little Girls
of Their Half-Fare Tickets**

Do You Believe in God?

During and after the Spanish-American War some newspapers used as many as 16 decks, or headline units, to describe the story. Frequently the head was longer than the story.

With improved presses and a greater variety of type available, designers were able to expand the headline. Eventually the main

Page One head stretched across the page and became known as the *banner, streamer* or *ribbon*. On some papers it was called, simply, the *line*. This headline sometimes called for the largest type available in the shop. When metal type wasn't adequate for the occasion, printers fashioned letters from wood (called *furniture*). A 12-liner meant that the line was 12 picas, or 144 points (two inches).

During this period, the names of headline forms were derived from their use or position on the page. A story placed above the nameplate and banner headline is called a *skyline,* and the accompanying headline is known as a *skyline head.* Sometimes the skyline head stands alone but carries a notation about where the story can be found.

A headline may have several parts—the main headline and auxiliary headlines known as *decks, dropouts* or *banks.* These are not to be confused with *subheads* or lines of type (usually in boldface) sometimes placed between paragraphs in the story.

A *kicker* headline is a short line of display type, usually no larger than half the point size of the main headline and placed over the main part of the headline. On some papers the kicker is termed the *eyebrow* or *tagline.*

A *stet head* is a standing headline such as **Today in history.**

A *reverse plate* headline is one that reverses the color values so that the letters are in white on a black background. A *reverse kicker,* in which one line in larger type is above the deck, is called a *hammer* or a *barker.*

As the tone of the newspaper was moderated after the turn of the century, so were the headlines. Banner headlines still shout the news, occasionally in red ink, but gloom and doom headlines have virtually disappeared. Understating is more likely to be found in headlines today than overstating. Extra editions have been out of date for a long time. And no longer do circulation managers hurry into the city room to demand a banner headline that will increase the newspaper's street sales.

Between World Wars I and II the cult of simplification, known as streamlining, brought changes in the newspaper headline. Designers put more air or white space into the head by having each line flush left, with a zigzagged, or ragged, right margin:

```
XXXXXXX    XXXXX      XXXXXXXX
XXXXXXX    XXXXXXX    XXXXXXX
XXXXX      XXXXXXXX   XXXXXXXX
```

Urged by this spirit of simplification, they abolished the decorative *gingerbread* such as fancy boxes and reduced the number of banks or eliminated them altogether except for the deck reading out from a major head—called a *readout* or *dropout.* They argued that the *flush left* head was easier to read than the traditional head and that it was easier to write because the count was less demanding.

Another part of the streamlining process was the introduction of modern sans serif typefaces to challenge the traditional roman typefaces such as Century, Caslon, Goudy and Garamond (see Chapter 13). Advocates of the new design contended that sans serif faces such as Helvetica and Univers were less ornate than the roman ones, gave more display in the smaller sizes, contained more thin letters (thus extending the count) and afforded greater mixture of faces because of their relative uniformity.

Headlines in all-capital letters gradually gave way to capital and lower case letters, which are easier to read. In modern headline design, only the first word of the headline and proper names are capitalized. This form of headline capitalization is known as *downstyle.*

The wider columns in contemporary newspaper design give headline writers a better chance to make meaningful statements because of a better count in one-column heads. The trend away from vertical makeup and toward horizontal makeup provides more multicolumn headlines on the page. Such *spread heads* can be written effectively in one line.

Traditionally, the headline has headed the column and hence its name. But the headline need not necessarily go at the top of the news column (see Figures 14-23, 14-24 and 14-25).

Increased emphasis on news display in recent years has prompted designers to discard established rules in favor of headline styles that complement the story. Design concepts borrowed from magazines are used increasingly. Thus, newspapers now contain flush-right headlines, hammer heads are proliferating and decks, or dropouts, are returning (Figure 10-1). Through it all, the flush-left headline remains dominant.

The Headline Writing Process

Readers read the headline first, then the story. Copy editors work in reverse; they first read the story, then write the headline. This often leads to confusing heads because copy editors mistakenly assume that if readers will only read the story they will understand what the headline is trying to convey. But except in rare cases, when the headline deliberately is designed to tease the reader, the headline must be instantly clear. In most cases, the reader will not read a story simply to find out what the headline means.

Headline writing, then, involves two critical steps:

1. Selecting which details to use.
2. Phrasing them properly within the space available.

The copy editor exercises editorial judgment in completing the first step in the process. Most use the *key-word method* in which the copy editor asks: "Which words must be included in the headline to convey to the reader the meaning of the story?" In its sim-

GAME 2: *Rockets don't want a rhinoceros on their backs, so Bird rates special attention from rising star...*

To Weigh 5 Days of Testimony

Zimmerman Case Goes to the Jury

HDC Buys Seven Old Homes on W. Vine, Will Renew Them

To Convert Them to 18 Apartments Under U.S. Rent-Subsidy Plan

Tilt!

EM to bar pinball halls to youths

Police Expand Task Force

Missing Persons Bureau Placed Under Redding's Command

Suicide and euthanasia

Christiaan Barnard tackles controversial subject

Japan's time for expansive ceremony is passing

Hirohito's reign may end era

The summer place

Feeling at home in a second home

Joe Swisher's story

Look into his eyes, listen to his account and then decide for yourself: Is this man a child molester?

TICKS

The Best Defense? A Good, Strong Dose of Prevention

Pressure to phase out local rent control laws

Senate bill ties housing funds to city regulations, but it wouldn't affect L.A.

ROBOTS:
GE Moves Into Automation

Boston has a T*(itle)* party

76ers blow 3-1 lead, Celtics win East

Animal magnetism

'Be Kind Week' or not, volunteers care for dumped pets

Figure 10-1 Sample headline styles.

plest form, this involves answering the question: "Who does what?" Thus, most good headlines, like all good sentences, have a subject and predicate, and usually a direct object:

Tornado strikes Jonesboro

That done, the copy editor tries to make the headline fit. Synonyms may be necessary to shorten the phrase and more concise verbs may help:

Twister rips Jonesboro

That in simplified form, is the essence of headline writing. But it is seldom that easy. All newspapers have rules to define the limits of what is acceptable, and such factors as the width of the column and the width of the characters in the typeface to be used must be considered. In the sections that follow, the complexity of headline writing will become apparent. Through it all, however, it may be useful to keep in mind the two critical steps outlined above.

The Headline Order

Typically, the copy editor receives a headline order when assigned to edit a story. The editor responsible for layout will have determined the headline size and style based upon the length and significance of the story and its placement on the page. (In some cases, the copy may be marked *HTK,* or "hed to kum," indicating that a layout decision has not been made and therefore no headline size has been determined. When this occurs, the copy editor merely edits the story; the headline will be written later.)

Each newspaper has its own schedule showing headline designations and line count, the maximum number of units that will fit on a line in the specified typeface and size (see Figure 10-2). Practice varies as to how headlines are designated. Here are four methods:

1. *Number designation.* Headlines of one or two columns are assigned a number. A 2 head, for example, might call for a one-column, two-line head in 24-point Bodoni, capitals and lower case. A 22 head would be the same as a 2 head but in two columns. Sometimes the number corresponds with the type size and style. A 24 head would be in 24 points, and a 25 would be in 24 points italic.

2. *Letter designation.* Here letters are used to show the type family and size. If C calls for 30-point Vogue extrabold, the head might be indicated as follows: 2C=. This means two columns, two lines of 30-point Vogue extrabold. The letter may also indicate the headline style. If D, for instance, means a one-column head

Headline Schedule

This headline schedule lists the unit count (maximum count) per line of headlines of the indicated column width and type size. It does not list each headline by number of lines since, for example, the count per line for a 1-24-2 would be the same as that for a 1-24-3.

Bodoni Bold and Bodoni Bold Italic

Headline	Maximum	Headline	Maximum	Headline	Maximum
1-14	21	4-36	39	4-60	23 1/2
1-18	18	2-48	14	5-60	30
1-24	13	3-48	21	6-60	36
2-24	26 1/2	4-48	29	2-72	7
1-30	10 1/2	5-48	37	3-72	14 1/2
2-30	23	6-48	44	4-72	20
1-36	9	2-60	11 1/2	5-72	24 1/2
2-36	19	3-60	17 1/2	6-72	30
3-36	29				

Avoid using headlines not listed above. For example, 14BB would not be used across two columns.

Bodoni Light and Bodoni Light Italic

Headline	Maximum	Headline	Maximum	Headline	Maximum
1-14	22	4-36	42	4-60	25 1/2
1-18	19	1-48	7	5-60	32
1-24	14	2-48	15	6-60	38 1/2
2-24	29	3-48	23 1/2	2-72	7 1/2
1-30	11	4-48	31 1/2	3-72	15 1/2
2-30	24	5-48	40	4-72	21 1/2
1-36	9 1/2	6-48	48	5-72	26 1/2
2-36	20 1/2	2-60	12 1/2	6-72	32
3-36	31	3-60	19		

Poster Bodoni

Headline	Maximum	Headline	Maximum	Headline	Maximum
1-14	16	1-30	8	1-60	4
1-18	13	1-36	6 1/2	1-72	3
1-24	10 1/2	1-48	5		

Note: To figure the maximum count for Poster Bodoni headlines of more than one column, multiply the maximum for one column by the number of columns.

Italic and Roman versions of the same headline type size should count the same.

In all cases, count spaces between words as one-half. Count numerals (except 1), the dollar sign ($), the percentage symbol (%) and devices of similar width as one and one-half (1 1/2).

Figure 10-2 Sample headline schedule.

in three lines of type, ½D would be one column in two lines. Or if D is a headline with a deck, the ½D would be the same head but without the deck.

3. *Designation by numbers and type family.* A designation such as 1-24-3 Bod. means one column, 24 points, three lines of Bodoni; 3-36-1 (or 3361) TBCI means three columns of 36 point, one line of Tempo bold condensed italic. At some papers, the first number designates the column width, the second number the number of lines and the third number the size of type (2/3/36).

4. *Computer code designations.* The code F (for font) 406, could well mean the 400 series (Gothic) and 6 could indicate the size of type (48 point). The code numbers thus identify size and family of type, line width, number of lines and whether the head is to be roman or italic.

Here are some of the common abbreviations used in headline designations:

- *X* for extra (VXBI means Vogue extrabold italics).
- *x* for italics (2302) SP *x* means two columns, two lines of 30-point Spartan italics).
- *It., I.* or *ital.* for italics.
- *K* for kicker line or eyebrow (2302K).
- *H* for hammer and inverted kicker (3361H); also called barker head.
- *J* for jump or runover head.
- *RO* for readout, or *DO* for dropout, under a main multicolumn headline.
- *W* for wicket head.
- *Sh* for subhead.
- *R* for roman (VXBR is Vogue extrabold roman)

Counting the Headline

Most newspapers now have computer systems that allow the copy editor to press a button and determine almost instantly whether a headline will fit. This is possible when computers are programmed with the width value of each character available in the typeface (See Figure 10-3). At split-second speed the computer can add the width values of the characters the copy editor has assembled on the VDT screen and determine whether that total exceeds the maximum width value of the line in the specified typeface, size and column width (See Figure 10-4). The availability of this feature simplifies the copy editor's work. If it is not available, the copy editor turns to time-tested manual methods of calculation.

The easiest way to count a headline manually is with the typewriter system—one letter for all letters, figures, punctuation and space between words. If a line has a maximum of 18 units as spec-

```
UNISETTER FILMSTRIP FONT WIDTH TABLES
(Note  fonts listed in same order as on filmstrip)

Load  UNI Font No & Name        CQ Font No & Sequence            STRIP C
    STRIP A                                                 :  Font 1 News #2  (same as strip A)   032  Sec#1011
01  Font 1 News #2                032  Sec#1011             :  Font 3 News #2 Bold  ( " )          033  Sec#1011
02  Font 3 News #2 Bold           033  Sec#1011             :  Font 4 Sans #1  ( " )              049  Sec#1011
03  Font 2 News #2 Italic         313  Sec#1011             09 Font 90 Sans #1 Hvy  SPECIAL USE   050  Sec#1011
04  Font 4 Sans #1                049  Sec#1011
    STRIP B
05  Font 5 English Times          705  Sec#1011
06  Font 6 Times Italic           705  Sec#1011
07  Font 7 Times Bold             707  Sec#1011
08  Font 9 Franklin Wide          415  Sec#1000
```

```
UNISETTER STRIP 'A1'  Sequence # 1011
<F01 T>, Unisetter Font #032
     News #2 (Std TTS Widths)
000 000 .        NULL TF
164 021 5,        1 t
157 030 45,       2 o
150 033 35,       3 h
156 033 34,       4 n
155 054 345,      5 a
154 018 25,       6 l
162 027 24,       7 r
147 033 245,      8 g
151 018 23,       9 i
160 033 235,     10 p
143 030 234,     11 c
166 033 2345,    12 v
145 030 1,       13 e
172 027 15,      14 z
144 033 14,      15 d
142 033 145,     16 b
163 027 13,      17 s
171 033 135,     18 y
146 021 134,     19 f
170 033 1345,    20 x
141 033 12,      21 a
167 045 125,     22 w
152 021 124,     23 j
165 033 123,     24 u
161 033 1235,    25 q
153 033 1234,    26 k
124 039 95,      27 T
117 042 545,     28 O
110 045 535,     29 H
116 045 534,     30 N
115 054 5345,    31 M
114 039 525,     32 L
122 045 524,     33 R
107 045 5245,    34 G
111 024 523,     35 I
120 042 5235,    36 P
103 039 5234,    37 C
126 042 52345,   38 V
105 045 51,      39 E
132 036 515,     40 Z
104 045 514,     41 D
102 042 5145,    42 B
123 033 513,     43 S
131 045 5135,    44 Y
106 042 5134,    45 F
130 045 51345,   46 X
101 042 512,     47 A
127 054 5125,    48 W
112 033 5124,    49 J
125 045 5123,    50 U
121 045 51235,   51 Q
113 045 51234,   52 K
134 054 P2,      53 BLR
056 018 0345,    54 period
054 018 034,     55 comma
060 027 0235,    56 zero
061 027 01345,   57 1
062 027 0125,    58 2
063 027 01,      59 3
064 027 024,     60 4
065 027 05,      61 5
066 027 0135,    62 6
067 027 0123,    63 7
070 027 023,     64 8
071 027 045,     65 9
073 018 0245,    66 Semicolon
072 018 80245,   67 Colon
044 027 012,     68 Dollar
033 027 S01235,  69 EM leader
032 054 SS025,   70 EM space
034 054 035,     71 EM leader
176 054 PS05,    72 Copyright
052 027 4,       73 Asterik
077 033 80235,   74 Question Mark
001 027 S01345,  75 1/8
002 027 S0125,   76 1/4
003 027 S01,     77 3/8
004 027 S024,    78 1/2
005 054 805,     79 5/8
006 054 S0135,   80 3/4
007 054 S0123,   81 7/8
037 054 S023,    82 EM Dash
046 042 S045,    83 Ampersand
034 054 S035,    84 EM leader
051 027 015,     85 Closed paren
050 027 S015,    86 Open paren
041 021 S012,    87 Exclamation mark
175 054 P024,    88 Register mark
055 018 014,     89 Hyphen
053 054 S014,    90 Plus sign
033 027 01235,   91 EN leader
177 054 PS0125,  92 Check
137 018 P0134,   93 Close bracket
136 018 PS0134,  94 Open bracket
010 054 PS03,    95 1/3
```

```
174 054 PS01345,  96 Solid Star
042 018 S04,      97 Unquote
047 018 04,       98 Quote
011 054 PS0124,   99 2/3
057 027 P0124,   100 Slash
043 054 P03,     101 Number sign
032 054 P025,    102 EM space
174 054 P01345,  103 Open Star
133 027 P0125,   104 Open Brace
173 027 P01,     105 Closed Brace
100 054 P05,     107 At sign
222 054 P0135,   108 Times sign
075 054 P0123,   109 Equals sign
252 054 PS023,   110 Division sign
140 027 P045,    111 Foot mark
230 027 P0235,   112 Inch mark
074 027 PS2,     113 Cents
049 054 PS4,     114 Percent sign
076 027 PS01,    115 Degree mark
233 027 PS012345,116 EN dash
135 027 P012345, 117 EN bullet
200 054 PS0135,  118 Open box
030 018 0,         thin space
031 027 0234,      EM space
032 054 013,       EM space
040 000 3,         space bar
356 050 0,HALF SIZE PS
357 050 0,HALF SIZE PW
360 050 0,SUP PS
361 050 0,SUP PW
362 050 0,SUP VB
363 050 0,INF PS
364 050 0,INF PW
365 030 0,INF VA
371 014 0,MIN
372 000 0,NOM
373 060 0,MAX
376 000 0,DEVCR
377 000 0,DEV0
END
UNISETTER STRIP 'A3'  Sequence # 1011
<F02 T-F01>, Unisetter Font #313
          News #2 Ital (Std TTS Widths)
377 000 0,DEV0
END
UNISETTER STRIP 'A2'  Sequence # 1011
<F03 T-F01>, Unisetter Font #032
          News #2 BOLD (TTS Widths)
377 000 0,DEV0
END

UNISETTER STRIP 'A4'  Sequence # 1011
<F04 T-F01>, Unisetter Font #049
          Sans #1 (Std TTS Widths)
377 000 0,DEV0
END

UNISETTER STRIP 'B1'  Sequence # 1011
<F05 T-F01>, Unisetter Font #0705
          English Times
000 000 :        NULL TF
164 018 5,        1 t
157 030 45,       2 o
150 030 35,       3 h
156 030 34,       4 n
155 045 345,      5 a
154 015 25,       6 l
162 021 24,       7 r
147 030 245,      8 g
151 015 23,       9 i
160 030 235,     10 p
143 024 234,     11 c
166 027 2345,    12 v
145 024 1,       13 e
172 024 15,      14 z
144 030 14,      14 d
```

```
...027 P0125,    104 Open Brace
173 027 P01,     105 Closed Brace
100 054 P05,     107 At sign
222 054 P0135,   108 Times sign
075 054 P0123,   109 Equals sign
252 054 PS023,   110 Division sign
140 027 P045,    111 Foot mark
230 027 P0235,   112 Inch mark
074 027 PS2,     113 Cents
045 054 PS4,     114 Percent sign
076 027 PS01,    115 Degree mark
233 027 PS012345,116 EN dash
135 027 P012345, 117 EN bullet
200 054 PS0135,  118 Open box
030 018 0,         thin space
031 027 0234,      EM space
032 054 013,       EM space
040 000 3,         space bar
377 000 0,DEV0
END
```

```
UNISETTER STRIP 'B2'  Sequence # 1011
<F06 T-F05>, Unisetter Font #706
               English Times ITALIC
377 000 0,DEV0
END

UNISETTER STRIP 'B3'  Sequence # 1011
<F07 T-F05>, Unisetter Font #707
               English Times BOLD
377 000 0,DEV0
END

UNISETTER STRIP 'B4'  Sequence # 1000 NC
<F09 T-F01>, Unisetter Font #415
          Franklin Wide
000 000 , NULL TF
164 026 5,        1 t
157 038 45,       2 o
150 039 35,       3 h
156 039 34,       4 n
155 060 345,      5 a
154 018 25,       6 l
162 027 24,       7 r
147 040 245,      8 g
151 018 23,       9 i
160 039 235,     10 p
143 035 234,     11 c
166 036 2345,    12 v
145 037 1,       13 e
172 034 15,      14 z
144 041 14,      15 d
142 041 145,     16 b
163 034 13,      17 s
171 037 135,     18 y
146 025 134,     19 f
170 038 1345,    20 x
141 037 12,      21 a
167 051 125,     22 w
152 021 124,     23 j
165 039 123,     24 u
161 039 1235,    25 q
153 040 1234,    26 k
124 039 95,      27 T
117 050 545,     28 O
110 050 535,     29 H
116 049 534,     30 N
115 060 5345,    31 M
114 040 525,     32 L
122 048 524,     33 R
107 050 5245,    34 G
111 022 523,     35 I
120 048 5235,    36 P
103 047 5234,    37 C
126 046 52345,   38 V
105 042 51,      39 E
132 046 515,     40 Z
104 050 514,     41 D
102 049 5145,    42 B
123 044 513,     43 S
131 046 5135,    44 Y
106 041 5134,    45 F
130 047 51345,   46 X
101 047 812,     47 A
127 063 5125,    48 W
112 028 5124,    49 J
125 049 5123,    50 U
121 050 51235,   51 Q
113 048 51234,   52 K
077 036 035,     71 Question mark
046 039 9035,    84 Ampersand
041 021 5012,    87 Exclamation mark
137 021 P0134,   93 Closed brackets
136 021 PS0134,  94 Open brackets
042 018 04,      97 Unquote
047 018 S04,     98 Quote
030 019 0,         Thin space
031 028 0234,      EN space
032 055 013,       EM space
040 000 3,         Space bar
361 070 00,SUP PW
362 030 00,SUP VB
364 070 00,INF PW
365 030 00,INF VA
371 017 00,MIN
372 000 00,NOM
373 060 00,MAX
377 000 00,DEV 0
END

UNISETTER STRIP 'C1'   Same as F01
UNISETTER STRIP 'C2'   Same as F03
UNISETTER STRIP 'C3'   Same as F04

UNISETTER STRIP 'C4'   SPECIAL USE ONLY
<F90 T-F01>, Unisetter Font #050
          SANS #1 HVY
113 048 S1234,   52 K
130 047 S1345,   46 X
377 000 0,DEV0
END
```

Figure 10-3 Width values are progammed into computerized editing systems so they can determine the escapement (width) value of each character in a font. This allows the computer to add width values of all the characters in a line for hyphenation and justification routes. [*Courtesy of Hastech Inc.*]

Figure 10-4 Width values programmed into a computerized editing system allow the copy editor to determine whether a headline fits the space available. Here, the editor has composed a headline and dropout and learns that the headline is 10 picas short and the dropout is eight picas short. This is indicated by the right-hand column of numbers preceding the lines. [*Photo by Joe Edens*]

ified by the newspaper's headline schedule (See Figure 10-2) and the head has 15 counts, it will fit, unless it contains several fat letters (such as M and W). In that case, the headline writer recounts the line using the popular Standard Method:

Lowercase letters	1 unit
Uppercase letters	1½ units
Exceptions	
Lowercase f, l, i, t and j	½ unit
Lowercase m and w	1½ units
Uppercase M and W	2 units
Spaces	½ unit
Punctuation	½ unit
Uppercase 1 and numeral 1	½ unit

Because of the variation in the widths of letters in different families of type or even within the same family, the Standard Method is not always correct. The letter *i*, for example, usually is thinner than the lowercase *t*. And in some faces *r* is thinner than *d* or *g* and a string of zeroes will likely make the line too long.

That reality led journalism professors at the University of Missouri to develop a more accurate method of counting that has been adopted by many newspapers. If it is used, no headline will be too long, regardless of the type family used. The counts:

Lowercase letters	1 unit
Uppercase letters	1½ units
Exceptions	
Lowercase i, 1	½ unit
Lowercase m, w	1½
Uppercase I and numeral 1	½ unit
Uppercase M and W	2 units
Spaces	½ unit
Numerals (except 1)	1½ units
Period, Comma, Quotation mark	½ unit
Dollar sign, percentage symbol, dash and question mark	1½ units

All headline writers are expected to keep within the maximum count allowable. It is costly and time-consuming to have heads reset. If it appears that the desired head slightly exceeds the maximum count, the writer may provide an optional word as a substitute for a long word. The compositor then can try to fit the head as originally written. If it won't fit, the optional word can be used.

Some desk editors insist that each line of the head, even in a flush left head, take nearly the full count. Others argue there is merit in a ragged right edge. In a stepped head the lines cannot vary more than two or three units or the head will not step properly. Unless a special effect is desired, each line should fill at least two-thirds of the maximum type-line width.

The copy editor should not write several heads for the same story and invite the editor to choose. The copy editor should submit only the best head possible within the available count.

Forming the Headline

Occasionally the desk editor or some other executive will suggest an angle that should go into the head or call attention to an angle that should be avoided. Usually, however, headline writers are on their own. They know that within a matter of minutes they must edit the copy and create a headline that will epitomize the story and that will make a statement in an easy-to-digest capsule.

By the time copy editors have edited the copy they should have an idea brewing for the head. They begin by noting key words or phrases. These are their building blocks.

With these blocks copy editors try to make an accurate and coherent statement. First they try to phrase the statement in the active voice. If that fails, they use the passive. If possible, they try to get key words and a verb in the top line.

Take a routine accident story:

Three Atlantans were killed Friday when their car collided with a garbage truck on Highway 85 at Thames Road in Clayton County.
The victims were: . . .

Patrolman C. F. Thornton said the truck was driven north on Highway 85 by . . .
The auto pulled into the highway from Thames Road and was hit by the truck, Thornton said.

The headline order calls for a one-column, three-line head with a maximum of nine units. In this story the lead almost writes the head. The obvious statement is "Three Atlantans killed as car and truck collide." **3 Atlantans** won't fit, so the writer settles for **3 killed.** For the second line the writer tries **in truck,** and for the third line **car collision.** The headline writer discards **car collision** because it is too long; **car crash** will fit. By changing the second line from **in truck** to **as truck** the writer gains another verb in the third line. The head now reads **3 killed as truck, car crash.**

Key headline words are like signposts. They attract the reader's attention and provide information. Such words, meaningfully phrased, produce effective headlines.

Note how quickly the key words *(Dutch, prince, born)* emerge in the lead of a wire story: "Crown Princess Beatrix gave birth to a son last night and Dutchmen went wild with joy at the arrival of a king-to-be in a realm where queens have reigned since 1890." One copy editor used the key words this way:

Dutch treat
A prince is born,
first in century

Many dull heads can be improved if the writer will make the extra effort. Sometimes the first idea for the head is the best; often it is not. If the editor rejects the lifeless heads and insists on better ones, that editor inspires everyone on the rim to try harder. Furthermore, a good performance on news heads is likely to generate better headlines in all departments of the paper.

The job of the copy editor is to create effective headlines for all copy. The big story often is easier to handle than the routine one because the banner story has more action and thus more headline building blocks.

The usual death and wedding stories offer little opportunity for bright, original headlines. There are only so many ways to announce a wedding or a death in a head, and the writer dare not try to be clever in handling these topics. The standing gag on the copy desk is, "Let's put some life in these obit heads." If Jonathan Doe dies, that is all the headline can say, except to include his age: **Jonathan Doe dies at 65** or **Jonathan Doe dead at 65.** If he were a former mayor, that fact would be used: **Jonathan Doe, ex-mayor, dies.** Get the story interest in the head: **Lillian Roe, former postmaster, dies** is less newsworthy than **Lillian Roe, mother of selectman, dies.**

The Title Lesson

Beginning headline writers might start with what Carl Riblet Jr., an expert on the subject, calls the title lesson. Learners start by listing the titles of all the books they have read. This is to demonstrate that readers can recall titles even if they have forgotten the contents. It also demonstrates the effectiveness of an apt title. A good title helps sell the product, as illustrated by those revised by alert publishers: "Old Time Legends Together with Sketches, Experimental and Ideal" *(The Scarlet Letter)*, "Pencil Sketches of English Society" *(Vanity Fair),* "The Life and Adventures of a Smalltown Doctor" *(Main Street),* "Alice's Adventures Underground" *(Alice in Wonderland).*

Limiting the learner to a one-line head with a maximum of 15 or 20 units forces the beginner to pack action in a few words, to merge as many elements as possible from the story, to indicate the tone or mood of the story and, finally, to compose an interesting statement. Riblet gives this example:

A young man said he and a middle-aged business agent had been drinking in a saloon. They went to the older man's apartment. There they quarreled over a gambling debt. The younger man told police he was threatened with a .30-caliber rifle. In self-defense, he picked up a bow and arrow and shot the older man in the stomach. The younger man tried to pull out the arrow but it broke and the wounded man died.

The copy editor got the story with instructions to write a one-line, 20-count head. He knew the paper's rule that every headline must contain a verb. He wrote: **Business agent slain.** In this instance it would seem wiser to bend the rule and get the key words in the headline: **Bow and arrow killing.** This lesson has practical value in writing the one-line head, such as the banner **Mayor censured** or **Steelers No.1,** the kicker **Smelly problem** or **Circus magic,** the column heading **The goldkeepers,** the filler head **Postal auction,** or the magazine feature **Acrobat on skis.**

Headline Rules

Practices vary, but on some desks no headline writer is permitted to hang conjunctions, parts of verbs, prepositions or modifiers on the end of any line of a headline. Like many newspaper rules, this one can be waived, but only if an exceptionally better headline can be created.

Rigid rules can bring grief to copy desks. One newspaper chain has two ironclad rules: No head may contain a contraction. Every head must contain a verb. This leads to some dull and tortured heads, especially on offbeat feature stories.

The *Los Angeles Times* evidently has no policy against splitting ideas in heads. It may be argued that in the one-column headline readers see the headline as a unit and do not have to read each line separately as they would in a multicolumn head. Eventually experiments may be designed to test whether readers can comprehend a split head as easily as they can one that breaks on sense. Until the results of such tests are available, headline writers should phrase headlines by sense. The practice can't hurt them if they join a desk that tolerates splits. A talented copy editor will take no longer on a phrased headline than on a split headline.

Good phrasing in a headline helps the reader grasp its meaning quickly. Each line should be a unit in itself. If one line depends on another to convey an idea, the headline loses its rhythm. It may cause the reader to grope for the meaning. Note the differences in the original and the revised heads:

Original	*Revised*
Thousands join Easter parade in Philadelphia	**Thousands join Easter parade in Philadelphia**
Men need to sleep longer, report shows	**Men require more sleep, study reveals**
Stay calm, Browns, you'll soon know your title foe	**Just stay calm Browns; you'll know foe soon**
Football ticket exchange to be revised next fall	**Ticket exchange for football to be revised**
Jones loses new bid for freedom	**Jones again loses bid for freedom**
Four Russian women tour Denver area	**Four women from Russia tour Denver**
Ordnance station to welcome commander	**Naval ordnance station to welcome commander**
U.S. eyeing New Mexico site for nuclear wastes	**U.S. favors New Mexico for nuclear waste burial**

Expanded California doctors'
malpractice strike threatened

Doctors' malpractice
strike in California
may expand

Police work draws
in Japanese women

Police work lures
Japanese women

What follows is a list of headline rules one editor distributed to his staff. He did so with the warning: "Rule No. 1 is that any other rule can be broken if you have a valid reason for doing so." That's good advice, even though many of these rules are common in news-rooms around the country. His list:

- Draw your headline from information near the top of the story. If the story has a punch ending, don't give it away in the headline.
- Build your headline around key words—those that must be included.
- Build on words in the story, paraphrasing if necessary, but it's best to avoid parroting the lead.
- Emphasize the positive unless the story demands the negative.
- Include a subject and predicate (expressed or implied).
- Try to use a verb in the top line.
- Maintain neutrality.
- Remember the rules of grammar and observe them.
- Eliminate articles and most adjectives and adverbs—except in feature headlines.
- Try to arouse the reader's interest. Remember that one function of the headline is to attract the reader to the story.
- Try to capture the flavor of the story.
- Make certain your headline is easy to read.
- Abbreviate sparingly.
- Verify the accuracy of your headline and be certain it has no double meaning.
- Verify that you've written the headline required.
- Verify the count of each line.
- Use short, simple words, but avoid such overworked and mis-used words as *flay, rap, eye* (as a verb) and *probe*. The use of such words is known as *headlinese*.
- Make the headline definite. Tell specifically what happened.
- If the main element is a characterization, the subsidiary element (dropout or kicker) should support that characterization.
- Never exaggerate. Build the headline on facts in the story. If a statement is qualified in the story, it must be qualified in the headline as well.
- Make the headline complete in itself. Each headline must have

a subject and a predicate. The implied verb *is* may be used. (**Note:** In feature headlines, this rule is sometimes violated. You may want to use a headline that is similar in construction to a book or magazine title, suggestive of the story rather than a synopsis of it.)

- Never write a headline that begins with a verb and has no subject, such as *Vote against compensation bill.* The result is a headline that commands the reader to do something, a meaning entirely different than the one intended.
- Phrase your headline in the present tense if possible, even though the event has been completed. This form is known as the historical present. Do not, however, link the present tense with a past date, such as *Jon Doe dies yesterday.* If a past date is so important that it must be used, the verb should be in the past tense. In most cases, the date can be omitted: *John Doe dies of pneumonia.*
- Do not use the present tense to indicate future events unless some word is included to clarify the meaning, as *City Council meets tonight.*
- Don't write a headline after a single reading of the story.
- Don't be afraid to ask questions if you fail to understand the story.
- Don't just fill a line. Say something.
- Don't violate the rules of headline writing just to make a line fit.
- Don't use common last names (*Smith, Jones,* etc.) or other names that are not easily recognized.
- Don't use the speaker's name in the top line. What he or she said is more important.
- Don't use *is* and *are* in headlines.
- Don't mislead the reader.
- Don't split nouns and their modifiers, verb forms and prepositional phrases over two lines.
- Don't use *said* when you mean *said to be.*
- Don't use *feel* or *believes* or *thinks.*
- Don't pad headlines with unnecessary words.
- Don't use double quotation marks in headlines or in other devices using headline type (kickers or dropouts).
- Don't use slang.
- Don't write question heads.

Some of these rules, and a few this editor missed, merit further explanation.

Use the Present Tense

Unless the story is about a current or future event, most news is concerned with past events. But the headline, to give the effect of immediacy, uses the present tense for past events: **British doctors vouch for birth control bill; City has bumper crop of junk cars; Jonathan Doe dies at 65.**

Suppose the headline announces a future event in the present tense. The reader won't know whether the event has occurred or will occur. **Powell's wife tells everything** means that the wife has testified. But if the reader learns from the story that the testimony will not be given until the following day, the reader knows the head was misleading. The head should have read **Powell's wife to tell everything.** The present tense can never be used if the date is included on a past event: **Jonathan Doe dies Wednesday.**

On future events the headline may use the future, *will be;* the infinitive, *to be;* or the present: **Traffic parley opens Monday.** *Scheduled* is a seldom-used headline word because of its length. Convenient substitutes are *set* and *slated* and consequently are worked to death in heads over stories of future events. It happens like this: **Two speakers set** and the reader wonders, "On eggs?"

Headline Punctuation

The period is never used in headlines except after abbreviations. Use single quotes instead of full quotes because the single quote takes less space and may be more appealing typographically in large, headline-size type. The comma may replace *and* and a semi-colon may even indicate a complete break: **Tumbling spacecraft tangles chute; cosmonaut plummets to death.** The semicolon also indicates a full stop. Unless it is a last resort, neither the dash nor the colon should be used as a substitute for *says.* When used, the colon comes after the speaker, and the dash after what was said: **McCoy: Dual role too big; Dual role too big—McCoy.**

Use Abbreviations Sparingly

Few beginning headline writers have escaped the abbreviation addiction. It occurs when the writer tries to cram too much into the head. The story said a woman under hypnosis had imagined herself as a reincarnation of an 18th-century Bridey Murphy in Ireland. The theory was discounted by a professor of psychology at a state university. This is how a student headlined the story: **CU psych. prof. doubts B.M. story.** A simple head such as **Professor doubts 'Bridey' claims** would have given readers enough information to lead them into the story.

Abbreviations clutter the headline: **Mo. village U.S. choice for Pan-Am.** It could have been written as **Missouri favored as Pan-Am site.**

An abbreviation that has more than one meaning leads to confusion, especially when the headline writer also is guilty of poor phrasing: **Ten girls are added to St. Vincent Candy Striper unit** or **Ill. man asks Pa. to join Miss. in Mass. protest,** or **Nebron New L.A. Muni Asst. P.J.** (He was elected assistant presiding judge of the Los Angeles Municipal Court.)

Headline writers frequently overestimate the ability of readers to understand the initials used in headlines. Some are easily recognized, such as FBI, YWCA, DAR. Others aren't, such as AAUW, NAACP, ICBM. On many newspapers the style calls for abbreviations and acronyms without periods in headlines. Other newspapers use periods for two-letter abbreviations, including U.S. and U.N., but TV frequently is an exception.

Some contractions are acceptable in heads; others aren't. *Won't, don't* and *shouldn't* give no trouble, but *she'll, he'll, who're,* and the "s" and "d" contractions do: **Triplets 'fine'; so's the mother of 22** or **Mother'd rather switch than fight.** Try to read this aloud: **Anymore service, the town hall'll collapse.**

Grammar in Headlines

Although headline writers must constantly compress statements, they have no license to abuse the language. A grammatical error emblazoned in 48-point type may be more embarrassing than a half-dozen language errors buried in body type. The writer normally would say **Russian girls urged to stop copying Paris.** But the second line was too long so the writer settled for **Russian girls urged 'stop copying Paris.'** A comma should have been used to introduce the quoted clause. Transposing the lines would have produced a better head. A headline read **Jones best of 2 choices, senator says.** He can't be the best if there are only two choices.

One headline read: **Woman reports she is robbed by man posing as inspector.** The present tense "reports" is correct. However, the second verb should be "was" to show that she is reporting a previous event.

A standing rule on use of proper names in headlines is that the names should be instantly recognizable to most readers. **Union under investigation gave to Tiernan campaign.** Unless this headline is for a Rhode Island paper, most readers won't recognize the name of a former Rhode Island congressman.

Copy editors who can't catch spelling errors have no place on the copy desk. They are a menace if they repeat the errors in the headline, as in these: **Rodeo parade has governor as marshall; Kidnap victim trys to identify captors.**

Headlining Sports

Sports pages report on contests involving action and drama, and headlines over such stories should be the easiest in the paper to write. Yet, because of the jargon used by sports writers and the numerous synonyms signaling a victory of one team over another, the sports story headline has become a jumble.

A reader says to his companion, "I see that the Jayhawks crunched the Cornhuskers." "Yeah?" asks a University of Nebraska basketball fan. "By how much?" "Ninety-eight to 94," replies the reader. If that's a crunching, what verb describes a 98-38 victory?

The struggle for substitutes for *wins, beats,* and *defeats* produces verbs such as *bests, downs, smears* and *swamps.* Presumably, the reader reads a sports page to find out who wins in what races. What does it matter, then, if simple words like *wins* or *defeats* are used over and over? Certainly they are better than editorialized counterparts such as *clobbers, wallops, flattens* and *trounces.*

Avoid Slang

A straight head that tells the reader precisely what happened is always better than one in which the writer resorts to slang. Slang in heads, as well as in copy, lowers the tone of the paper and consequently lowers the readers' estimation of the paper. The headline, no less than the copy, should speak to the general reader, not to reporters and other specialists.

Here is an object lesson from a San Diego newspaper. The second edition carried a six-column head in the lifestyle section: **Kids going to pot are aided.** Under the head was a three-column cut showing a girl sitting on a bed in a holding room at Juvenile Hall. The picture also revealed a toilet stool in one corner of the room. To the relief of the embarrassed editor, the top line in the third edition was revised to **Teen narcotic users aided.**

Don't Repeat Words

Another restriction on headline writing is that major words in the headline cannot be repeated unless done so for effect in a feature head. The rule has little logic except to prevent obvious padding, such as **Campus to launch campus chest drive** and **Wind-lashed blizzard lashes plains states.**

If the main head contains a word like *fire,* the readout or drop-out could easily include a synonym. *Blaze* would be an acceptable one; *inferno* would not.

Repetition is sometimes used deliberately to heighten a feature: **Thinkers failures, professor thinks; New look? never! old look's better; Pokey driving sends three back to pokey.**

Down with Headlinese

Faced with the problem of making a statement in a nine-unit line, headline writers have to grab the shortest nouns and verbs possible. They are tempted to use overworked words such as *hits, nabs, chief* or *set* because such words help to make the headline fit. Or, they may reach for words with symbolic meanings, such as *flays, slaps, grills, hop* or *probe.* Nothing is "approved"; it is "OK'd" or "given nod." All are headline clichés and have no place in today's paper. Yet even the trade papers continue to use them: **Miami Herald grills Sinatra in libel probe.**

The headline should not falsify the story. Many of the headlinese words do, at least by implication. If the story tells about the mayor mildly rebuking the council, the headline writer lies when he or she uses verbs like *hits, slaps, scores, raps, rips* or *flays.* An *investigation* or a *questioning* is not necessarily a "grilling"; a *dispute* is not always a "row" or a "clash." *Cops* went out with prohibition. Today's word is *police.*

Others that should be shunned are "quiz" for *question,* "hop" for *voyage,* "talks" for *conference,* "aide" for *assistant,* "chief" for *president* or *chairman,* "solon" for *legislator* or *congressman,* "probe" for *inquiry,* "nabs" for *arrests,* "meet" for *meeting,* "bests" for *defeats,* "guts" for *destroys,* "snag" for *problem,* "stirs" for *incites* and "hike" for *increase.*

During America's involvement in Vietnam, millions of readers must have wondered what headlines were trying to say with the incessant use of "Viet" and its variations. The word was used indiscriminately to refer to North Vietnam, South Vietnam, the Viet Cong, the North Vietnamese army, the South Vietnamese army and the Vietnamese people.

Don't Invite Libel or Contempt

Because of the strong impression a headline may make on a reader, courts have ruled that a headline may be actionable even though the story under the head is free of libel. Here are a few examples:

> **Shuberts gouge $1,000 from Klein brothers**
> **'You were right,' father tells cop who shot his son**
> **McLane bares Old Hickory fraud charges**
> **Doctor kills child**
> **Gone to her drummer**
> **A missing hotel maid being pursued by an irate parent**
> **John R. Brinkley—quack**

A wrong name in a headline over a crime story is one way to involve the paper in a libel action.

The headline writer, no less than the reporter, must understand that under our system a person is presumed innocent of any crime charged until proved guilty by a jury. Heads that proclaim **Kidnaper caught, Blackmailers exposed, Robber arrested,** or **Spy caught** have the effect of convicting the suspects (even the innocent) before they have been tried.

If unnamed masked gunmen hold up a liquor store owner and escape with $1,000 in cash, the head may refer to them as "robbers" or "gunmen." Later, if two men are arrested in connection with the robbery as suspects or are actually charged with the crime, the head cannot refer to them as "robbers" but must use a qualifier: **Police question robbery suspects.** For the story on the arrest the headline should say **Two arrested in robbery,** not **Two arrested for robbery.** The first is a shortened form of "in connection with"; the second makes them guilty. Even "in" may cause trouble. **Three women arrested in prostitution** should be changed to **Three women charged with prostitution.**

The lesson should be elementary to anyone in the publishing business, but even on the more carefully edited papers heads are sometimes guilty of jumping to conclusions. This was illustrated in the stories concerning the assassination of President John F. Kennedy. Lee Harvey Oswald was branded the assassin even though, technically, he was merely arrested on a charge of murder. In a statement of apology, the managing editor of *The New York Times* said his paper should not have labeled Oswald an assassin.

In their worst days, newspapers encouraged headline words that defiled: **Fanged fiend, Sex maniac, Mad-dog killer.** Even today some newspapers permit both reporter and copy editor to use a label that will forever brand the victim. When a 17-year-old boy was convicted of rape and sentenced to 25 to 40 years in the state penitentiary, one newspaper immediately branded him *Denver's daylight rapist.* Another paper glorified him as *The phantom rapist.* Suppose an appeal reverses the conviction? What erases the stigma put on the youth by a newspaper?

The copy editor who put quotes around **Honest count** in an election story learned to his sorrow that he had commited a libel for his paper. The implication of the quotes, of course, is that the newspaper doesn't believe what is being said.

Miscellaneous Rules

Emphasis in the headline should be on the positive rather than the negative when possible. If the rodeo parade fails to come off as scheduled because of rain, the head makes a positive statement: **Rain cancels rodeo parade,** not **No rodeo parade because of rain.** The news value is lacking in the headline that says **No one hurt as plane crashes.** The positive statement would be **90 passengers escape injury as plane crashes into mountain.** Here are three negating words in a headline: **Tax writers veto lids on oil write-off.** Better: **Tax writers leave oil tax as it stands.**

The negative is illustrated in this headline from an English paper: **Only small earthquake; but not many killed.**

This admonition does not apply to feature heads in which the negative helps make the feature: **No laws against drowning, but it's unhealthy; Not-so-gay nineties** (on weather story); **Laundry gives no quarter until suit is pressed.**

The question head, except on features, is suspect for two reasons: It tends to editorialize, and newspaper heads are supposed to supply answers, not ask questions. If the headline asks the reader a question, the answer, obviously, should be in the story. If the answer is buried deep in the story, the question headline should be shunned. A five-column head asked, **Did Anastasia murder help kill barber shaves?** The lead repeated the same question, but the reader was compelled to look through a dozen paragraphs only to learn that the question referred to a frivolous remark that should have been used only to color the story.

Enjoy the Game

It's fun to write headlines because headline writing is a creative activity. Copy editors have the satisfaction of knowing that their headlines will be read. They would like to think that the head is intriguing enough to invite the reader to read the story. When they write a head that capsules the story, they get a smile from the executive in the slot and, sometimes, some praise.

Somerset Maugham said you cannot write well unless you write much. Similarly, you can't write good heads until you have written many. After they have been on the desk for a while, copy editors begin to think in headline phrases. When they read a story they automatically reconstruct the headline the way they would have written it. A good headline inspires them to write good ones, too.

They may dash off a head in less time than it took them to edit the copy. Then on a small story they may get stuck. They may write a dozen versions, read and reread the story, and then try again. As a last resort, they may ask the desk chief for an angle. The longer they are on the desk the more adept they become at shifting gears for headline ideas. They try not to admit that any head is impossible to write. If a synonym eludes them they search the dictionary or a thesaurus until they find the right one.

If they have a flair for rhyme, they apply it to a brightener: **Nudes in a pool play it cool as onlookers drool.**

Every story is a challenge. After the writer has refined the story it almost becomes the copy editor's story. The enthusiasm of copy editors is reflected in a newspaper's headlines. Good copy editors seek to put all the drama, the pathos or the humor of the story into the headline. The clever ones, or the "heady heads," as one columnist calls them, may show up later in office critiques or in trade journals:

> **Council makes short work of long agenda**
> **Hen's whopper now a whooper**
> **Stop the clock, daylight time is getting off**
> **Lake carriers clear decks for battle with railroads**
> **'Dolly' says 'Golly' after helloful year**
> **Tickets cricket, legislators told**
> **Quints have a happy, happy, happy, happy, happy birthday** (First birthday party for quintuplets of Catonsville, Md.)

11

Avoiding Headline Problems

The headline must be as accurate as the story itself. Like inaccurate stories, inaccurate headlines invite libel suits and destroy one of the newspaper's most valuable commodities—its credibility. Inaccuracy, though, is merely one of many pitfalls in headline writing. Others include overstating, missing the point of the story, taking statements out of context, confusing the reader, attempting poor or inappropriate puns, writing headlines that are in poor taste, using words with double meanings and giving away the punchline of a suspended-interest story. Numerous examples in this chapter point out the danger of careless handling on the copy desk.

Making It Accurate

The key to ensuring accuracy is close and careful reading of the story. Erroneous headlines result when the copy editor doesn't understand the story, infers something that is not in the story, fails to portray the full dimension of the story, or fails to shift gears before moving from one story to the next. Some examples:

Family Weekly tied to Arab oil interests. The lead said the magazine had become a member of a corporate family that has close ties with the oil tycoons of Iran and Venezuela. Neither is an Arab nation. Iran is a Moslem country.

Proxmire in Qatar. But the story was about former Sen. William Fulbright of Arkansas, not Sen. William Proxmire of Wisconsin.

Cowboys nip Jayhawks 68-66 on buzzer shot. The lead said that

Kansas (the Jayhawks) beat Oklahoma State (the Cowboys) by two points in a Big Eight conference basketball game.

Player shuns rain, wind and the course. If golfer Gary Player had shunned them, he wouldn't have played. He conquered rain and wind to lick the course.

Paducah's bonding law said hazy. The details weren't hazy; the subject of the story was hazy about the details.

3 in family face charges of fraud. They were arrested in a fraud investigation, but the charges were perjury.

United Brands chairman falls to his death. The story said the man jumped.

Black child's adopted mother fights on. The child didn't select the mother; it was the other way around. Make it "adoptive."

Do-nothing Congress irks U.S. energy chief. The spokesman criticized Democrats, not Congress as a whole, and the "do-nothing" charge was limited to oil imports.

Four held in robbery of piggy bank. The bank was the loot; the robbery was at a girls' home.

White House hints at ceiling on oil spending. The subject of the story was oil imports.

Greek plebiscite set Dec. 8. The vote was set for Dec. 8. The setting didn't come on that date.

Patricia Neal well after three strokes. The story said she wore a leg brace and heavy shoes and had a patch over one eye.

If that pooch bites you can collect $200. The story said the animal had to have rabies for you to collect up to $200.

Didn't like her face, shoots TV announcer. A man fired a gun at her but missed.

Graham backs sterilization view. Although he backed one viewpoint, he criticized the program generally.

Bishop says segregation is justified. The lead quoted the bishop as saying that Christians are not morally justified in aiding segregation.

Schools help pay expenses for Forsyth County's dogs. The story said the dog-tax money helps support the schools.

Civic ballet auditions scheduled Saturday. One listens to auditions; one looks at tryouts or trials.

Youth, 19, breaks parole, subject to whipping post. The story correctly said he had been on probation.

Circus clown's daughter dies from high wire fall. Second paragraph of story: "The 19-year-old aerialist was reported in good condition at Paterson General Hospital with fractures of the pelvis, both wrists and collarbone."

India-China relations worsen. The story was datelined Jakarta and had nothing to do with India.

Chicago to see outstanding moon eclipse. The story wasn't about a moon eclipse; it was about an eclipse of the sun. And "outstanding" is hardly an appropriate way to describe an eclipse.

Brilliant modern study of Holy Roman emperor. The story was a review of a book on Emperor Hadrian who was born A.D. 76 and died in 138. The Holy Roman Empire lasted from A.D. 800 to 1806.

Big Three September sales up 22,147 over year ago. The lead mentioned Chrysler, General Motors and American Motors. The latter is not one of the Big Three, but Ford is.

Israelis release Arabs to regain heroes' bodies. Nowhere does the story call them heroes. The two were executed during World War II for assassinating a British official.

Overstating

Akin to the inaccurate headline is one that goes beyond the story, fails to give the qualifications contained in the story, or confuses facts with speculations. Examples:

West Louisville students at UL to get more aid. The lead said they may get it.

Integration may improve learning, study indicates. But the lead was two-sided, indicating an improvement in one area and a loss in another. The headline should reflect divided results or views, especially in highly emotional news subjects.

Pakistan, U.S. discuss lifting of embargo on lethal weapons. The story said, correctly, that the embargo may be eased. And aren't all weapons lethal?

Arabs vote to support PLO claim to West Bank. The story said that Arab foreign ministers voted to recommend such action to their heads of state. The head implies final action.

Schools get 60% of local property tax. This reflects fairly what the lead said but fails to reveal an explanation, later in the story, that the schools get a proportion of the contributions of various levels of government—federal, state and local. Although the local property tax contributes 60 percent, the amount is far less than 60 percent of the total local property tax.

Here's what happens when a copy editor gets carried away: **Bacon enlivens buttermilk muffins.** (The genius who thought of enlivening buttermilk muffins must be assumed to have done so with his tongue in his cheek and a piece of paper in his mouth.) **County heavens to explode with color.** (Perhaps a booster head for a fireworks display, but slightly exaggerated.)

Commanding

Headlines that begin with verbs can be read as commands to the reader and should be avoided. A New York City newspaper splashed a 144-point headline over the story of the shooting of Medgar Evers, a civil rights advocate. The head: **Slay NAACP leader!** Another head may have given the impression that a murder was being planned: **Slaying of girl in home considered.** In reality, police were trying to determine if the murder took place in the girl's house or in a nearby field.

Here are some other examples of heads that command:

**Save eight
from fire**

**Buy another
school site**

Arrest 50 pickets   **Find 2 bodies,**
in rubber strike   **nab suspect**

Assassinate U.S. envoy

Editorializing

The reporter has ample space to attribute, qualify and provide full description. The copy editor, however, has a limited amount of space in the headline to convey the meaning of the story. As a result, there is a tendency to eliminate necessary attribution or qualification and to use loaded terms such as *thugs, cops, pinkos, yippies* and *deadbeats* to describe the participants. The result is an editorialized headline.

If an opponent of the Equal Rights Amendment states that passage of an amendment would subject women to the draft, it is editorializing to headline the story: **ERA would subject women to draft.** Attribution is essential: **ERA would subject women to draft, Schlafly says.**

Every word in a headline should be justified by a specific statement within the story. Was the sergeant who led a Marine platoon into a creek, drowning six recruits, drunk? Most headlines said he was, but the story carried the qualification "under the influence of alcohol to an unknown degree." Similarly, did Sen. Joseph McCarthy actually call Gen. George Marshall a traitor? The headlines said he did, but the quotation proves that the statements may be open to more than one interpretation.

Consider this common construction: **Author scores federal misuse of strip studies.** The head states as a fact that the federal government is misusing studies on strip mining. The story credited that view only to the author. In other words, the headline states an opinion as a fact.

Even though the headline reports in essence what the story says, one loaded term in the headline will distort the story. If Israel, for reasons it can justify, turns down a compromise plan offered by the United States concerning the West Bank problem, the head creates a negative attitude among readers when it proclaims **Israel spurns U.S. compromise.**

It often is difficult to put qualification in heads because of count limitations. But if the lack of qualifications distorts the head, trouble arises. A story explained that a company that was expected to bid on a project to build a fair exhibit was bowing out of the project because the exhibit's design was not structurally sound. The headline, without qualification, went too far and brought a sharp protest from the construction firm's president: **Builder quits, calls state world's fair exhibit 'unsound'.**

Sensationalizing

Another temptation of the headline writer is to spot a minor, sensational element in the story and use that element in the head. A story had to do with the policy of banks in honoring outdated checks. It quoted a bank president as saying, "The bank will take the checks." In intervening paragraphs several persons were quoted as having had no trouble cashing their checks. Then in the 11th paragraph was the statement: "A Claymont teacher, who refused to give her name, said she had tried to cash her check last night and it had been refused." She was the only person mentioned in the story as having had any difficulty. Yet the headline writer grabbed this element and produced a head that did not reflect the story:

> **State paychecks dated 1980**
> **Can't cash it,**
> **teacher says**

Missing the Point

The headline-writing process starts as soon as a copy editor starts reading the story. If the lead can't suggest a headline, chances are the lead is weak. If a stronger element appears later in the story, it should be moved closer to the lead. The point is so elementary that every reporter should be required to take a turn on the copy desk if for no other reason than to teach that person how to visualize the headline before beginning the story.

Although the headline ideally emerges from the lead, and generally occupies the top line (with succeeding lines offering qualifications or other dimensions of the story), it frequently has to go beyond the lead to portray the full dimensions of the story. When that occurs, the qualifying paragraphs should be moved to a higher position in the story. Example: **U.S. firm to design spying system for Israel.** The lead was qualified. Not until the 15th paragraph was the truth of the head supported. That paragraph should have been moved far up in the story.

The head usually avoids the exact words of the lead. Once is enough for most readers. Lead: "Despite record prices, Americans today are burning more gasoline than ever before and that casts some doubt on the administration's policy of using higher prices to deter use." Headline: **Despite record gasoline prices, Americans are burning more fuel.** A paraphrase would avoid the repetition: **Drivers won't let record gas prices stop them from burning up fuel.** Since the story tended to be interpretive, the head could reflect the mood: **Hang the high price of gasoline, just fill 'er up and let 'er roar.** Most copy editors try to avoid duplicating the lead, but if doing so provides the best possible head, it is a mistake to obfuscate.

Boring the Reader

A headline that gives no more information than the label on a vegetable can is aptly known as a label head. Generally these are the standing heads for columns that appear day by day or week by week, like **Social Notes** or **Niwot News.** They tell the reader nothing. They defy the purpose of a display line, which is to lure the reader.

Almost as bad are the yawny, ho-hum heads that make the reader ask, "So what else is new?" The writer who grabs a generality rather than a specific for the head is more than likely to produce a say-nothing head. Such writers prefer **Many persons killed** to **1,000 persons killed.** "Factors" is about the dullest headline word imaginable. **Factors slow car input.** Something is responsible for either output or input. In this case, a parts shortage was the main cause.

Notice how little information is provided in the following samples:

Financial program explained

Development plans described

Class night to be today

Pan Am jet lands safely

**Wadsworth derailment
puts 13 cars off rails**

**Rotarians hear
Korean bishop**

Meeting to be held

**Newark
Rotary told
of planning**

**Coroner seeks cause
of why driver died**

**Autopsy scheduled
for dead Akronite**

**Broyhill speaks
at big picnic**

**Committee will study 2
problems**

**Cars collide
at intersection**

Stating the Obvious

Readers read newspapers to get the news. If the headline tells them the obvious, they have been short-changed. Here are examples of the obvious statement:

Fall shirts offer new innovations (Not to be confused with those old innovations.)

**Corn field selected
as place for annual
county husking bee**

**Warm house best
in cold climate**

**Turkish ship
sinks in water
near Cyprus**

**Californian, 20,
drowns in water
of Lake Mohave**

Rehashing Old News

Some stories, like announcements, offer little or no news to invite fresh headlines. Yet even if the second-day story offers nothing new, the headlines cannot be a repetition of the first-day story lead.

Suppose on Monday the story says that Coach Ralston will speak at the high school awards dinner. If Ralston is prominent, his name can be in the head: **Ralston to speak at awards dinner.** On Thursday comes a follow-up story, again saying that Coach Ralston will be the awards dinner speaker. If the headline writer repeats the Monday headline readers will wonder if they are reading today's paper. The desk editor will wonder why copy editors won't keep up with the news. The problem is to find a new element, even a minor one, like this: **Tickets available for awards dinner.** So the dinner comes off on Friday, as scheduled. If the Saturday headline says **Ralston speaks at awards dinner,** readers learn nothing new. The action is what he said: **Ralston denounces 'cry baby' athletes.** Or, if the story lacks newsworthy quotes, another facet of the affair goes into the head: **30 athletes get awards.**

Missing a Dimension

The headline must portray the story in context. That is, the headline should not repeat what was said yesterday or the day before that or a week ago. It may be a second-day story with a fresh angle. To judge the news fairly and accurately, the copy editor must keep up with the news through daily reading of a newspaper. The headline writer must also know how the opposition displayed the story so that a different wording can be used.

There is no trick in writing a vague, generalized headline statement. The real art of headline writing comes in analyzing the story for the how, the why or the consequences. If the story has more than one dimension, the head should reflect the full story, not part of it. Take this horrible example: **D.J. company union (IAPE) withdraws COLA provision.** That's three too many abbreviations. Worse, the head fails to capture the real meaning of the story, which was that the union (Independent Association of Publisher's Employes Inc.) reached an agreement with Dow Jones & Co. providing for across-the-board pay increases. In return, the union agreed to withdraw its demand for a cost-of-living adjustment (COLA). And IAPE is an independent union, not a company union.

Other examples?

> **Report says school 'integration' still not achieved.** The report was already several days old. This was a columnist's view of the matter, and it called for something more than a straight news head.
>
> **Carroll to use funds for coal-road repair.** This was not the news. The governor had said previously that he might use general fund money. The head should have reflected the fact that the governor NOW plans to use road fund money.

Documents link royal family to sex scandal. Somehow the head should have told readers the story did not describe scandals in Britain's present royal family but concerned an unlordly lord in Queen Victoria's court almost a century ago.

Coroner says teeth aid in identifying dead. That was news decades ago. The news, as explained in the story, was about the number of methods used in medical detective work.

Police chase, capture 2 Alabama van thieves. Unless the item is for an Alabama paper, who cares about a run-of-the-mill crime? It turns out the thieves were 12 years old, a fact that should have been in the headline to justify the story.

If only one element emerges in the headline, the head fails to do justice to the story. This headline is weak: **Man injured in accident.** At least one person in a community is injured in an accident nearly every day. The word *man* is a faraway word. *Driver* is closer. "Injured in accident" can be shortened to "injured" if the word *driver* replaces *man*. Now the top line can read: **Driver injured.** A second element in the story shows that he was wearing a seat belt. Marrying the two ideas produces a head like this: **Injured driver wore seat belt.** The original head is passable but weak. The revised head gives more information and is an attention-getter.

Notice how a good copy editor can make a pedestrian head come alive and have more meaning:

Original	*Revised*
6 priests lose duties after rap of bishop	**Priests fired after calling bishop callous**
Man says robber returned to house a second time	**Intruder hits, robs man in home, returns later for lost jacket**
Gardening idea from Mexico helps increase tomato output	**Texan doubles tomato crop with Mexican water tip**
Four-car accident Friday	**6 injured as 4 cars collide**
Gary project funded by U.S. closes down	**South Inc. runs out of money, closes in Gary**
Motorist, 59, dies of apparent coronary	**Motorist dies at wheel; car hits telephone pole**
Vandals leave $4,000 loss in N. side school	**Vandals visit school for 3d time in week**

N.U. trustees O.K. new hearing system	N.U. students get bigger judicial role
Postman dies in fall while washing walls	Wall washer killed in fall through window
Children to host fete for parents	Children to honor parents on 25th
Senate amends bill to cut pay increase for top judges	Senate amends bill to give top judges 15% pay boost
Statistics released on test	Here's that test; can you pass it?
Heart of glacier Tunnel town inaugurated	*Drama in Arctic* 25 imperiled by blizzard
State approves housing plan	State approves another dorm
10¢ fare is urged for the elderly	10¢ fare is urged for those over 65
Two persons killed, 6 wounded in attacks by Ulster terrorists	2 killed, 6 wounded by Ulster terrorists; 6-year toll at 1,238

Muddling the Head

Because many words can be either verbs or nouns, the headline writer should make sure that such words can't be taken either way. The reader will likely ascribe the wrong meaning:

Population growth: doom writers' field day. Cue: "doom" is intended as a noun. **Doom writers capitalize on population growth.**

Study heralds cop selectivity profile. Cue: "heralds" is a verb, "cop" a noun. Better: **Study draws profile of an ideal cop.**

Flourish floors drabness. Cue: The second word is the verb.

Resort wear showing cues orchestra women's benefit. It's anyone's guess what this means with so many words that double as nouns or verbs.

Flexible can not dangerous. Can is a noun here, not a verb.

Project job needs with new method. "Project" is intended as a verb. Perhaps "foresee" would do the trick.

The lack of a verb may force the reader to reread the head:

4 children die in fire while mother away; If the count won't permit "mother is away," the head should be recast: **Mother away; 4 children die in home fire.**

Physician says president well. But "president" is the objective case and the head literally says the physician is a capable elocutionist. By transposing the lines, president is in the nominative case and the verb is understood: **President well, physician says.**

Some desk chiefs have an aversion to using "to be" forms of the verb in heads. Others insist that if the verb is needed to make the head clear it should be used or the head should be recast. Often the lack of a vital auxiliary verb produces gibberish: **Rookie admits prisoners struck. Thai pleas said less important than U.S. lives. East-west rail service said unfeasible.**

Ex-convict fatally shot fleeing cop. Here is the copy editor's thought: "Ex-convict (is) fatally shot (while) fleeing (from) cop." But many readers will follow the normal order of subject, then predicate, so they read "(An) ex-convict fatally shot (a) fleeing cop." Not good, but perhaps passable: **Ex-convict killed while fleeing police.**

Trooper kills man who had slain wife. Does this mean the trooper killed the man who had slain his (the trooper's) wife? Or that the trooper killed a wife slayer? Or that he killed a man whose wife had been slain by someone else?

Official says CIA, FBI may have 'destroyed' files. To most readers this means the two agencies possibly destroyed some secret files. The quotes around "destroyed" suggest that perhaps they didn't destroy the files. The story, though, said that files previously reported as having been destroyed may still be in the hands of the CIA and FBI. A clearer head: **Official says CIA, FBI may hold 'destroyed' files.**

An easy way to get tortured prose in headlines is to clothe nouns in human garb. Like these:

Fear drives guardsmen to panic.

Tornadoes slice through Iowa.

Span crashes hurt four, none serious. (Some writers apparently think a headline provides a license for changing an adverb to an adjective.)

Smoke brings firefighters to Galt house. (If smoke can impel action, it would "send" the firefighters.)

Rains force roads to close; few families to evacuate. (Rains can't force roads; they can force somebody to close the roads.)

Again, a cardinal rule in headline-writing is that the headline, standing alone, must be instantly clear to readers. If the headline puzzles them, they assume the story will also be puzzling and will turn to something they can understand. Examples:

Bob Walker in town: Steer wrestler 'ads' to take. This is gibberish to readers. If they had taken time to read the story they would have learned that Bob Walker, a Marlboro Country man, had participated in the steer-wrestling contest at a stock show rodeo.

Scarcity sandwiches Jim between signs of the times. This makes sense only if readers know that during an inauguration ceremony a student named Jim paraded through the audience wearing a sandwich board sign reading "I need a job."

Next surge in food costs to be mild. If it's mild, how can it be a surge?

Doctor urges sex, abortion rules shifts. What the good doctor said was that sex taboos are out of date.

Out-of-town Busch strike is felt here. Busch refers to a beer.

Water falls; calls build to Niagara. Want to know what idea this head is trying to convey? The water pressure in Penns Grove had fallen and the water company had received many complaints.

5 from Mt. Pleasant win handicapped essay prizes. What's a handicapped essay? Or was it the prizes that were handicapped?

Suit curbing shed, fence sites loses. If readers take long enough, eventually they will understand that someone lost a lawsuit that would have restricted sites for sheds and fences.

Parked car collides with church. A church on wheels, perhaps?

Elm disease is thriving throughout Longmont. Somehow one doesn't normally think of a disease as thriving. Make it "spreading."

Writing Bad Puns The rule is that a pun in a head must be a good one or the impulse to commit it to print should be suppressed. When they're bad they're awful:

**Unbreakable window
solves a big pane**

**Rod isn't Lavering
for WCT 'big apple'**

Battle of Buicks Saturday
**You buffs 'auto' be told;
'Little Indy' revving up**

This story illustrates the danger of trying to be too cute:

The president of the American Foundrymen's Society told UPI in an interview that small, specialized foundries are shrinking in number because of problems concerned with scrap shortages, high material costs and the high price of conforming to anti-pollution laws and other requirements. Although the number of such small foundries is not great, the shrinkage is causing problems for the Defense Department, designers, manufacturers and investors. Overall, the statement said, the foundry business is flourishing as the nation's sixth largest industry in terms of value added.

Some headline writers could not resist the foundry-foundering pun and thus distorted the story's meaning:

America's foundry business is foundering

Foundry business flounders

(This proves that the writer couldn't distinguish between founder and flounder.)

Other headline writers stressed only one dimension of the story:

Foundries dwindling

**Foundry industry
in big trouble**

**Foundry failures are   Foundry industry
accelerating   suffering shrinkage**

A spot survey of papers using the story showed that slightly more than half (58 percent) of the headlines were reasonably fair and accurate:

Small foundries are disappearing

Small foundries having big financial woes

Foundry firms hurt by material scarcity

A few headlines got both dimensions:

Industry, military hurt by foundry ills

A few were incredibly inept:

Foundry institute shrinkage eyed

Amateur boat builders face problems

Industry needs help, ferret out foundry

Avoiding Bad Taste

Newspapers must, of necessity, reveal human sorrows as well as joys, afflictions as well as strengths. No story or headline should mock those who have misfortunes. The newspaper belongs in the parlor where good taste is observed.

A story related that a Johannesburg motorist, whose car stalled on railroad tracks, died under the wheels of a train when he was unable to release his jammed seat belt. The victim may have been unknown to readers in an American community, but death is a common tragedy and should be treated with respect, something the copy editor forgot: **Belted to death.**

A minor story told about a man digging his own grave, starving while lying in it for 21 days and dying two hours after being found. The headline: **Down . . . and then out.**

Another story related how a woman survived a 200-foot leap from a bridge, suffering only minor injuries. Investigators said the woman landed in about four feet of water near shore. The item was insensitively headed: **Higher bridge needed.**

Avoiding Double Meanings

A headline is unclear if it can imply more than one meaning. Some readers may grasp the meaning intended; others won't. An ad writer for a coffee company created a double meaning in this slogan: "The reason so many people buy Red & White Coffee is that 'They Know No Better.'"

Boy struck by auto in better condition. Than if he had been hit by a truck?

Rector sees sex as gourmet meal. He said people would be healthier if they looked on sex as a gourmet meal rather than something distasteful.

U.S. to close one Air Force base in Spain: Moron facility will shut in December. The facility is in Moron, Spain.

Rape classes planned. Rape will be the subject of the classes.

YWCA opens public series with abortion. Abortions will be discussed at the first class meeting.

Catlett takes credit for Cincinnati's loss. Then who took the blame?

Flint mother-in-law wounded in argument. That's better than being shot in the head.

Place names like Virgin, Utah; Fertile, Minn., and Bloomer, Wis., inevitably invite a two-faced headline if the town is used:

**Virgin woman
gives birth
to twins**

**Man loses hand
in Bloomer**

Other geographical terms:

**Book in pocket
saves man shot
in South End**

**Three Boston
waitresses shot
in North End**

Unusual family names of officials—Love, Fortune, Dies, Church, Oyster—also invite two-faced headlines:

**Oyster probes
unknown jam**

**Picks Fortune
for Indiana
revenue chief**

**Wallace attacks
U.S. grant**

**Fink heads bridge
charity unit**

**Billy Hooks
patient in Durham**

**Slaughter re-creates
Constantine's Rome**

**Winchell defies
Hoffman and Dies**

Presidents and presidential candidates have been victims of two-faced heads:

Ike to get girls' calf

**Goose given
to Eisenhower**

**LBJ giving bull
to Mexican people**

**Johnson putting rusty
on White House green**

Robert Kennedy stoned	**Ford, Reagan neck in presidential primary**

Case and *chest* produce these headlines:

Ord Phillips gets two years in cigarette case	**Chest pleas issued for mother's milk bank**

The worst possible headline verb is eyes:

Frear resting, eyes return	**Green eyes major title**
Sidewalks to be eyed in Elsmere	**Alleged Rhodes perjury said eyed**

More double-takes in headlines:

Five nudes pinched at stag show	**Patients feel doctors' pinch**
Suspect's counsel says: Winsett quizzed in nude	**Governors' seats held key to South**
Swine housing to be aired	**Flies to attend wedding of son**
Top swine prize to county youth	**Boy chasing fox found rabid**
Publisher says bar endangers press freedom	**Franklin pair is improved after shooting**
N.J. Assembly passes drunk driving test	**Wife charges husband killed her for money**
Club to serve world culture	**Andalusia girl improved after drinking poison**
Relatives served at family dinner	**W. Side woman dies of burns; mate critical**
Proud Optimists fathers have sons at banquet	**Expectant mother, 23, is anxious for facts**

Man with two
broken legs saves
one from drowning

Sex educator says
kindergarten's the
time

Bed aflame, jumps
from fourth floor

Lawmen from Mexico
barbecue guests

Colonel's wife found
by body holding knife
in hand

President says women
responding adequately

Wiley tours sewage
plant, gathers
ammunition for fight
against diversion move

New restrooms
big assets
for shoppers

Police slay suspect
bound over for trial

Oklahoman hit by auto
riding on motorcycle

Burned-out pupils
use old high school

Telluride women
donate pots
for airplanes

Local option fast time
offered to skirt problem

Engineers to hear
ground water talk

U.S. to fire Europe
into stationary orbit

Illegitimacy talks

No water—
so firemen improvised

Dupont hits Talbot
on billboards

Two accused
of kidnaping
slain man

State dinner featured
cat, American food

Admiral likes
to make waves

Pennsauken's safety chief
quits blaming politics

Bradley school
getting new head

Youth hangs self in cell
after uncle tries to help

Man on way to Italy
to see family killed

Heroin busts up

Glacier Lake still
up in the air

Handicapped
hearing set

Chef says U.S.
courts ulcers

Man who shot himself
accidentally dies

U.S. capital does well
in booming Venezuela

Stores on 4th
between Walnut and
Chestnut to dress up rears

Turnpike bonds may bar state aid for Sound span	**State hunts teeth in swimming ban**
Pentagon requests cuts by committee	**Rev. Branford funeral fixed**

Even the lifestyle pages contain two-faced headlines:

Italian cookies easy to make	**Guide, don't push child**
Fresh dates are great	**Nurses awarded for poster art**
O'Brien peas in squash	**Strong attire right for bill's death**
Male underwear will reveal new colorful sights	**Carries on for husband**
	Designer's death blow to theater

Giving Away the Punchline

Some features are constructed so that the punch line comes at the end, rather than at the beginning, of the story, Obviously, if the point of the story is revealed in the headline, the story loses its effectiveness. The following story calls for a teaser head or even a title:

> One Saturday afternoon not long ago a night watchman named Stan Mikalowsky was window-shopping with his 5-year-old daughter, Wanda, and as they passed a toy shop the child pointed excitedly to a doll nearly as big as she was.
>
> The price tag was only $1 less than the watchman's weekly pay check, and his first impulse was to walk away, but when the youngster refused to budge he shrugged and led her into the store.
>
> When Stan got home and unwrapped the doll, his wife was furious.
>
> "We owe the butcher for three weeks, and we're $10 short on the room rent," she said. "So you got to blow in a week's pay for a toy."
>
> "What's the difference?" said the night watchman. "Doll or no doll, we're always behind. For once let the kid have something she wants."
>
> One word led to many others and finally Stan put on his hat and stomped out of the house.
>
> Mrs. Mikalowsky fed the child and put her to bed with the doll next to her and then, worried about Stan, decided to go looking for him at the corner bar and make up with him. To keep his supper warm, she left the gas stove on, and in her haste threw her apron over the back of a chair in such a way that one of the strings landed close to a burner.

Fifteen minutes later when the Mikalowskys came rushing out of the bar, their frame house was in flames and firemen had to restrain the father from rushing in to save his daughter.

"You wouldn't be any use in there," a cop told him. "Don't worry, they'll get her out."

Fireman Joe Miller, himself a father, climbed a ladder to the bedroom window, and the crowd hushed as he disappeared into the smoke. A few minutes later, coughing and blinking, he climbed down, a blanket-wrapped bundle in his arms. . . .

The local newspaper headlined its story with the line that should have been saved for the finish:

Fireman rescues life-size doll
as child dies in flames

PART IV

Pictures, Graphics and Design

12

Picture Editing

Rewriting often can turn a poorly written news story into an acceptable one. Little can be done to change the subject matter of a cliché photo, such as tree plantings, ribbon cuttings, proclamation signings and the passing of checks, certificates or awards from one person to another. Yet newspapers use many photographs of these situations simply because of the tradition that "chicken-dinner" stuff must be photographed. It is a tradition that should be scrapped, and most good newspapers already have done so.

Only on a rare occasion would a city editor permit reporters to share their time with sports, Sunday supplements or the advertising department. Yet, that is what happens on papers with a small staff of photographers.

One consequence is that too often good local news and feature stories are less effective than they could be because the additional information that accompanying pictures could provide is missing. Another is that too often mediocre, space-wasting pictures from the wire services or syndicates are given more attention than they deserve.

A picture editor is almost as essential to a newspaper as a city editor. Some executive—preferably one with a background in photography—should be responsible for assigning photographers to news and feature events. Someone in authority should insist that all pictures, including those from news agencies, be edited and that cutlines, or captions, be intelligently written.

If it is a good picture, it should get a good play, just as a top story gets a big headline. If pictures are a vital part of the story, editors should be willing to cut back on words, if necessary, to provide space for pictures. Some events can be told better in words than in pictures. Conversely, other events are essentially graphic, and editors need little or no text to get the message across.

Pictures can "dress up" a page. But if their only purpose is to break up the type, they are poorly used. The large number of pictures used—even on front pages—without an accompanying story suggests that the pictures are being used for their graphic value rather than for their storytelling value. Ideally, pictures and stories should work together.

Still pictures, even action shots, may not be able to compete with television in some ways, but still photography—the print media's tool—can add color to words and can capture moods. Originality starts with the picture. Its values are interest, composition and quality of reproduction.

A small, poor-quality picture should be rejected because the flaws will be magnified in the enlargement. Facsimile prints may be retouched, but the quality is seldom as good as pictures made from glossy prints. Generally, pictures reproduce better if they are reduced rather than enlarged, but content, not technical quality, should be the factor that determines the play a picture is given.

Photographer-Editor Relationships

An encouraging development in recent years has been the trend toward making photographers full partners in the newspaper editorial process. Historically, photographers have been second-class citizens in the newspaper hierarchy. They have not enjoyed the prestige of the reporter or the copy editor, and with rare exception their opinions have been ignored or have not been solicited.

Many insightful editors have now realized that photographers possess an intangible quality known as visual literacy, a trait sometimes lacking even in the best of wordsmiths. Photographers should have a voice in how their pictures are displayed, and editors who have attempted to give them a voice invariably have been pleased with the results. The number of newspapers using pictures well is increasing each year, although leading picture editors agree that there is ample room for improvement. For every newspaper using pictures well, it is easy to find three still using the line-'em-up-and-shoot-'em approach.

A key to improvement in the quality of a newspaper's pictures is allowing the photographer to become involved in the story from the outset. If possible, the photographer should accompany the reporter as information for the story is gathered. If that is impossible, allowing the photographer to read the story—or to take time to talk with the reporter about the thrust of it—will help ensure a picture that complements the story. Newspapers throughout the country each day are filled with pictures that fail to convey a message because the reporter, photographer and editor failed to communicate.

An important part of this communications process involves writing the photo order, the document given to the photographer when an assignment is made. A photographer for the *Columbia Missourian* once received an order that called for a picture of an elementary school principal. The order instructed the photographer to meet the principal in his office at 3:15 p.m. and to take a picture of him at his desk. It mentioned that the principal would be unavailable until that time. The story focused on how the principal went out of his way to help frightened first-graders find the right bus during the first few weeks of school. Because the reporter failed to mention that when he wrote the photo order, the photographer followed his instructions exactly. He arrived at 3:15 and took the picture. Only after returning to the office did he learn of the thrust of the story and discover that the principal was "unavailable" 15 minutes earlier because he had been helping students find their buses. The best picture situation had been missed.

Words and pictures are most effective when they work together. For that to happen, reporters, photographers and editors must work together. Often the best approach is to let the photographer read the story and determine how to illustrate it. The photographer, after all, should be the expert in visual communication.

Editing Decisions

Most pictures, like most news stories, can be improved with editing. The picture editor, like the copy editor, must make decisions that affect the quality of the finished product. The picture editor must determine:

1. Which photo or photos complement the written story or tell a story of their own.
2. Whether cropping enhances the image.
3. What size a photo must be to communicate effectively.
4. Whether retouching is necessary.

Selection

Picture selection is critical because valuable space is wasted if the picture does nothing more than depict a scene that could be described more efficiently with words. The old adage that a picture is worth a thousand words is not necessarily true. If the picture adds nothing to the reader's understanding of a story, it should be rejected.

Conversely, some pictures capture the emotion or flavor of a situation more vividly than words. In other situations, words and pictures provide perfect complements.

A talented picture editor, experienced in visual communication, can provide the guidance necessary for successful use of pictures. Smaller papers without the luxury of full-time picture editors can turn to their photographers for advice, but often the news editor or copy editor must make such decisions. When that is necessary, an appreciation for the importance of visual communication is essential for good results.

Internal procedures reflect a newspaper's picture selection philosophy. Some allow the photographer to make the decision; the pictures he or she submits to the desk are the only ones considered for publication. This procedure may assure selection of the picture best in technical quality, but that picture may not be the best to complement the story. A picture editor, working closely with the photographer, the city editor and copy editors, should have a better understanding of the story and be able to make the best selection. Contact prints, miniature proofs of the photographer's negatives, allow the photographer, reporter and editors to review all frames available so the best selection can be made (Figure 12-1).

Cropping

A photograph is a composition. The composition should help the reader grasp the picture's message clearly and immediately. If the picture is too cluttered, the reader's eyes scan the picture looking for a place to rest. But if the picture contains a strong focal point, the reader at least has a place to start. A prime job of a picture editor, therefore, is to help the photographer take out some unnecessary details to strengthen the overall view.

It could be that some elements within the picture are stronger than the full picture. Some picture editors try to find these interest points and patterns by moving two L-shaped pieces of cardboard over the picture. This helps to guide the editor in cropping. The picture editor looks for a focal point, or chief spot of interest. If other points of interest are present, the picture editor tries to retain them. The editor searches for patterns that can be strengthened by cropping. The pattern helps give the picture harmonious and balanced composition. Among these patterns are various letter shapes—L, U, S, Z, T, O—and geometric patterns such as a star, circle, a cross or a combination of these.

Because most news and feature pictures contain people, the picture editor strives to help the photographer depict them as dramatically as possible. The editor must decide how many persons to include in the picture, how much of a person to include and what background is essential.

Historically, newspapers have opted for the tightest possible cropping to conserve valuable space. Severe cropping, however, may damage a picture to the point that not printing it would have been preferable. Those who win awards for picture editing appreciate the fact that background is essential to some photographs. As a result, they tend to crop tightly less often than do editors with more traditional approaches to picture editing. In Figures 12-2a and 12-2b, tight cropping allows the reader to see interesting detail.

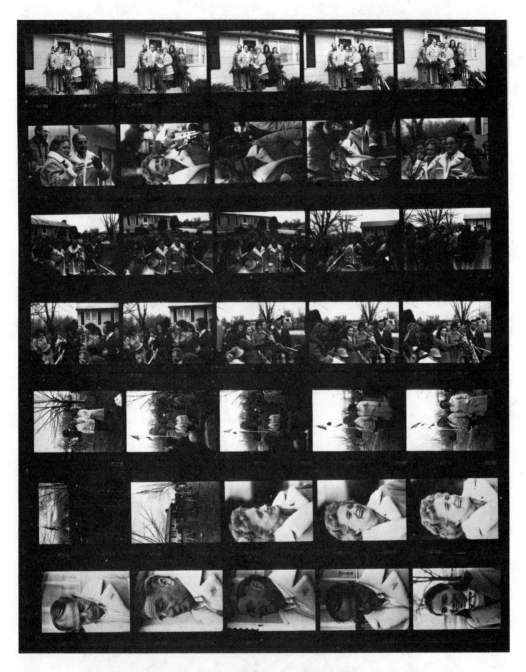

Figure 12-1 Contact print sheet. Photographers and editors often choose pictures from contact prints of the available negatives.

Figures 12-2a and 12-2b   Footprint on the lunar soil. An example of how cropping (b) can bring out an interesting detail in a photograph (a). The close-up view was photographed with a lunar surface camera during the Apollo II lunar surface extravehicular activity. [*Photographs courtesy of the National Aeronautics and Space Administration.*]

Sizing

But in Figures 12-3a and 12-3b, tight cropping eliminates the environment and damages the meaning of the picture. Those who can distinguish between these approaches are valuable members of newspaper staffs. They possess visual literacy.

The reproduction size of a photograph should be determined by the value of the picture, not the amount of space available. Too often, newspaper editors try to reduce a photograph to fit a space and destroy the impact of the photo in the process. Common sense should dictate that a picture of 15 individuals will be ineffective if it appears as a two-column photo. More likely, such a photo will require three or even four columns of space.

Talented picture editors know that, when sizing pictures, the greatest danger is making them too small. If the choice is between a two-column picture and a three-column picture, the wise picture editor opts for the larger size. Pictures can be too large, but more often they are damaged by making them too small. Another alternative may be available. Modern production techniques make it easy for the editor to publish a 2½-column photo. Text to the side of it is simply set in a wider measure to fill the space.

Sizing of any photograph is an important decision, but sizing of pictures in multi-photograph packages is particularly important. In such packages, one photograph should be dominant. The use of multiple pictures allows the editor flexibility that may not exist in single-picture situations. If a picture editor selects a photo of a harried liquor store clerk who has just been robbed and a photo of the outside of the store where the robbery occurred, the editor has three choices:

1. Devote equal space to the two pictures. This is the least desirable choice since neither picture would be dominant and, consequently, neither would have eye-catching impact.
2. Make the outside shot dominant and the closeup of the clerk secondary. This would work, but the dominant picture, which merely serves as a locater, would have little impact. The impact of human emotion, evident in the clerk's face, would be diminished.
3. Make the facial expression dominant with good sizing and make the outside shot as small as 1½ columns. The outside shot, standing alone, would look ridiculous if used in that size. But used in conjunction with another, larger photo, it would work well.

Dramatic size contrast is an effective device to use in multi-picture packages (Figures 12-4a and 12-4b). An editor with an eye trained in visual communication understands the usefulness of reversing normal sizing patterns for added impact.

Retouching

Some pictures can be improved by retouching, the process of toning down or eliminating extraneous distractions within the frame.

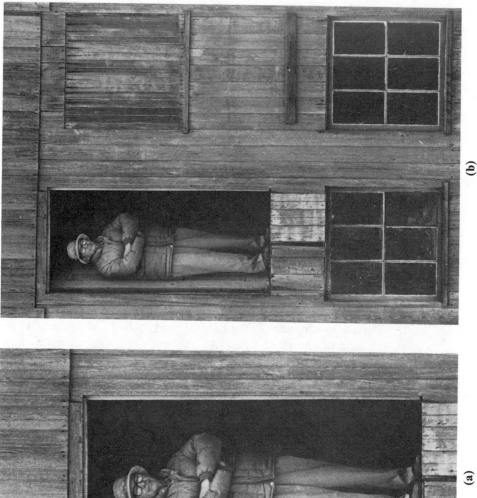

(a)

(b)

Figures 12-3a and 12-3b Tight cropping occasionally can destroy the impact of a picture (a). Here, tight cropping takes the farmer out of his environment by making it difficult or impossible for the reader to determine that the setting is a barn (b). [Columbia Missourian *photos by Manny Crisostomo*]

(a)

(b)

Figures 12-4a and 12-4b Many editors would run the overall flooding shot larger than the picture of the farmer laying sandbags in place. The pairing, however, has more impact if the close shot of the farmer is run larger than the scene-setting overall picture. [Columbia Missourian *photos by Lee Meyer and Mike Asher.*]

Retouching

Retouching can be accomplished with an airbrush, an instrument that applies a liquid pigment to a surface by means of compressed air (Figures 12-5a and 12-5b). Retouching also can be done by brushing on a retouching liquid or paste (Figures 12-6a and 12-6b) or by using retouching pencils of varying colors.

Care must be exercised, however, to ensure that the meaning and content of the picture are not changed. Retouching a photograph to alter its meaning is as unethical as changing a direct quotation to alter a speaker's meaning.

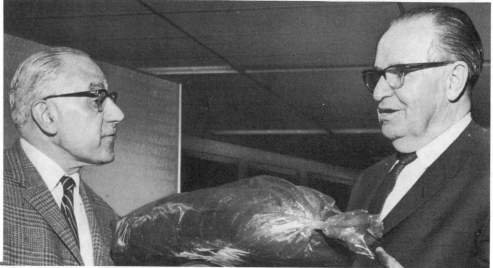

Figures 12-5a and 12-5b   Editing a picture. The original picture (upper) was retouched slightly with an air brush to highlight the faces, thus preparing the lower picture for publication. [*Photograph courtesy of the* Denver Post.]

Figure 12-6a   The weekly *Range Leader* of Cheyenne Wells, Colo., teased its readers with this shot of three mule deer caught in a fog. A cutline is necessary to tell readers why their eyes deceive them. [*Photo by Bob Scales, courtesy of the* Range Leader.]

Figure 12-6b   A photographer can get a silhouette effect by brushing on white retouching liquid, but care must be exercised. Here, the fluid is clearly visible in the finished photo. When reproduced, it may appear to be amateurishly handled.

Pictures As Copy   When the picture has been processed, someone—reporter or photographer—supplies the information for the cutline. The picture
and cutline information then go to the appropriate department
where the editor decides whether to use the picture and, if so, how
to display it.

Before submitting a picture to the engraving or camera department, the editor supplies enough information to get the correct
picture in the correct place with the correct cutline. A picture, like
a story, generally carries an identifying slug. To ensure that the
picture will match the screened mechanical reproduction, the cutline, and, if need be, the story, the editor uses a slugline.

A slip of paper clipped on the picture or taped to the back normally contains information such as:

1. The slug, or picture identification.
2. The size of the desired screened reproduction.
3. Special handling instructions.
4. The department, edition and page.
5. The date the photo is to appear.
6. The date and time the picture was sent to the production
   department.
7. Whether the picture stands alone or accompanies a story.

The picture is then routed directly to the camera room or indi-
rectly through the art department. The cutline goes to the composing room. Cutline copy contains, in addition to the cutlines,
essential directions to match cutline and picture.

Some photo editors use a style similar to one shown in Figure
12-7.

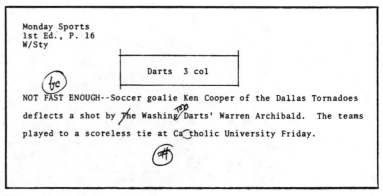

Figure 12-7   Photo cutline style.

If the picture is to go with a story, the information is carried on both the cutline and the story copy. The reason is obvious. Unless properly slugged, the story may appear on Page 3 and the photo on Page 16.

Sometimes the photo may be separated from the story deliberately. A teaser picture may be used on Page One to entice readers to read the story on another page. If a long story has two illustrations, one illustration often is used on the page where the story begins and the other on the jump page. On major events such as the death of a president, pictures may be scattered on several pages. In that event, readers are directed to these pages with a guideline such as "More pictures on pages 5, 7 and 16."

Sometimes the mechanical reproduction of the photo is made in reverse. The result can be ludicrous, particularly if the picture shows a sign or if the principals are wearing uniforms containing letters or numerals.

The person responsible for checking page proofs makes sure the correct headline is over the correct story and that the cutlines under pictures of a local politician and a jackass are not reversed.

The Enlarging, Reducing Formula

At most newspapers, photographers make 8-by-10-inch prints. Photos then are enlarged or reduced as necessary during the screening process. Photos are enlarged or reduced in proportion to their width and depth. A simple method of determining this proportion is to draw a diagonal line from the upper-left to the lower-right corner of the photograph as cropped. It is best to draw this line on the back of the picture to make sure the line is not accidentally reproduced in the newspaper. Then measure the reproduction width along the top of the picture and draw a vertical line at that point. The point where the vertical line intersects the diagonal line indicates the reproduction depth of the picture.

A more common procedure is to measure in picas or inches the width and depth of the photograph as cropped. Because the editor knows the width he or she wants the picture to be when it is reproduced, a proportion wheel (Figure 12-8) allows that editor to determine the reproduction depth quickly. The percentage of enlargement or reproduction is known as the SOR, or size of reproduction. If a photograph is being enlarged, the SOR will be greater than 100 percent. If the photograph is being reduced, the SOR will be less than 100 percent. Knowing this allows the editor to make a quick check to determine if reproduction instructions to the engraver or camera room are correct.

If the picture margins are uneven, the editor may place a sheet of tissue paper over the picture and draw the diagonal and connecting lines on the tissue to determine reproduction depth. Or,

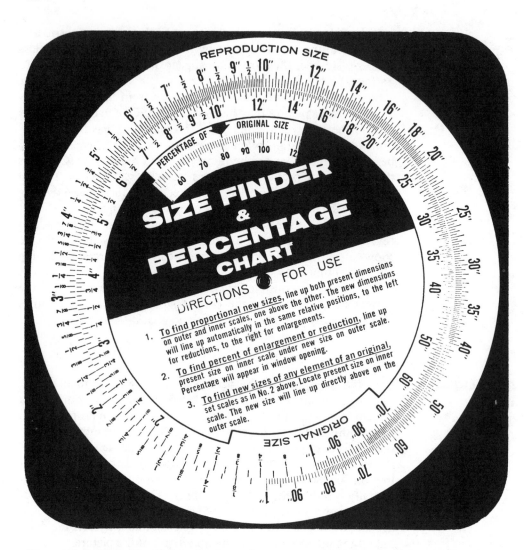

Figure 12-8 Example of disc showing enlargement and reduction ratios. The finder is set at dimensions in Figure 12-8 with 4⅛″ on the inner circle matching 3⅜″ on the outer circle. The figure 6⁵⁄₁₆″ is opposite the inner figure of 7¾″ and the SOR, or size of reproduction, is 81 percent. The numerals on the wheel, while marked as inches, also can represent picas if the newspaper uses that unit of measurement in sizing photographs.

the editor may measure the picture area and use a mathematical proportion to determine reproduction depth. Suppose the picture is 48 picas wide and 60 picas deep and the reproduction width is 34 picas. Simple cross-multiplication is used to determine the unknown dimension: 48:34::60:X. The answer is 42½ picas in depth.

If the editor decides to make the picture 34 picas wide and 45 picas deep, then X will be substituted for one of the picture measurements to determine the extent of the crop to produce the 34 by 45 proportion. If X is substituted for the width of the picture, then X:34::60:45. 45X equals 2040, and X equals 45.3. Subtracting 45.3 from 48 shows a crop of 2.7 picas on the width of the picture.

Some picture editors place a plastic sheet over the picture. Column widths and inches are drawn on the sheet and a string is attached to the sheet in the upper-left corner. By positioning the string from the upper-left to the lower-right corners of the picture, the editor can determine the depth of the enlargement or reduction (Figure 12-9).

Pictures may be reduced in any proportion, but some newspapers adhere fairly closely to standard reductions such as one-fifth, one-third and one-half.

Figure 12-9   A clear plastic sheet placed over a photograph enables a picture editor to size a picture quickly. A string attached to the plastic sheet is extended from the upper-left to the lower-right corner of the picture to show the depth of the picture in five columns or less.

Pictures Can Lie   The picture editor makes the same kind of editorial judgment about a picture that the city editor and the wire editor make about a local story and a wire story. Does the picture tell the whole story or only part of it? Does it distort, editorialize, mislead? Does it omit important details or include details that create an erroneous impression? In other words, is the picture loaded?

The point was raised by James Russell Wiggins, former editor of the *Washington Post,* during a lecture at the University of North Dakota. "The camera," he said, "can be a notorious, compulsive, unashamed and mischievous liar."

To illustrate, he said he once declined to print a photograph of President Harry Truman walking across the platform of Union Station before a backdrop formed by a row of caskets just shipped in from the Korean war. "What that camera said was that the Korean war was 'Truman's war,' just what thousands of the president's critics were saying."

He also commented on the distorted portrait of police officers during civil disorders. The pictures may have been representative of the action, but they failed to tell what really happened in perspective and why.

"The camera does not tell the truth," said Wiggins, "and because what it tells is not the whole truth, skepticism about the media rises in the minds of readers who know that policemen, whatever their undoubted faults, are not always wrong."

A picture may be striking and it may be narrative. But if it conveys a false or distorted impression it would be better left unpublished.

Picture editors often can show subjective judgment in the selection of pictures. Suppose an editor has four or five pictures of a public figure. Some editors will select the picture showing the figure more favorably; others will pick one depicting him less favorably. Many of the pictures used of former President Nixon, even before his resignation, were editorialized. Pictures of former President Jimmy Carter were similarly criticized.

Taste in Picture Editing   It was a tragic fire in a metropolitan area. A woman and a child took refuge from the fire on an ironwork balcony. As firefighters tried to rescue the woman and the child, the balcony collapsed, plunging the woman to her death and the child to a miraculous survival. Photographers took sequence shots of the action

(Figures 12-10a and 12-10b). Should a picture editor use the pictures?

Some readers will be incensed, accusing the papers of sensationalism, poor taste, invasion of privacy, insensitivity and a tasteless display of human tragedy to sell newspapers.

Picture editors could reply that their duty is to present the news, whether of good things or bad, of the pleasant or the unpleasant. Defending the judgment to use the pictures on Page One, Watson Sims, editor of the *Battle Creek* (Mich.) *Enquirer and News,* said, "The essential purpose of journalism is to help the reader understand what is happening in this world and thereby help him to appreciate those things he finds good and to try to correct those things he finds bad."

On the flood of pictures depicting the war in Vietnam, surely among the most memorable were the Saigon chief of police executing a prisoner, terrified children fleeing a napalm attack, and the flaming suicide of a Buddhist monk. Such scenes were part of the war record and deserved to be shown.

Photos of fire deaths may tell more than the tragedy depicted in the burned and mangled bodies. Implicit could be the lessons of inadequate inspection, faulty construction, carelessness with matches, arson, antiquated fire-fighting equipment or the like.

Picture editors have few criteria to guide them. Their news judgment and their own conscience tell them whether to order a picture for Page One showing a man in Australia mauled to death by polar bears after he fell or dived into a pool in the bears' enclosure in a zoo. Of the hundreds of pictures available that day, surely a better one could have been found for Page One. If the scene is such as to cause an editor to turn away and say, "Here I don't belong," chances are the readers will have the same reaction. Not all of life's tragedies have to be depicted. The gauge is importance and newsworthiness.

Picture Pages   Some newspapers devote an entire page to pictures with a minimum of text. Some use part of the page for pictures, the rest for text matter. Some pages are made up of unrelated photos; some are devoted to related pictures. Some use part of the page for sequence pictures and leave the remainder for unrelated pictures or text matter. Increasingly, photo pages on a single subject are used to tell a story more forcefully than words can tell it (see Figure 12-11).

Figure 12-10a Two of the controversial sequence shots of a fire tragedy in a Boston apartment. Scores of readers protested the use of these widely distributed photos. Most editors defended the use of the pictures. [*Photos by Stanley Forman of the* Boston Herald-American, *distributed by UPI.*]

Figure 12-10b

PEOPLE

Columbia Missourian
Sunday, Jan. 27, 1985—Page 1

Handicapped farmer keeps a dream alive

Above, Landhuis gives some tips to a hired hand before handing over the controls. At left, lifts are too expensive for the farmer, so he depends on the use of his arms.

Landhuis says a sure way to check his cows for sickness and stress is to feed them mineral salts from a dish.

Tenacity helps Landhuis farm, raise cattle

By Mitchell B. Chamberlain
Missourian staff writer

As a child, when his friends wanted to become policemen, firefighters, doctors or lawyers, Marion Landhuis dreamed of becoming a farmer.

Ten years ago, after a successful career in a management position for Montgomery Ward and Co. and then at Texaco Inc., Landhuis, then 37, finally exercised his stock options and used his savings to buy a farm with his brother. He raised corn, wheat and soybeans at the 212-acre farm east of Columbia and started a cow-calf operation.

Then his dream of farming was nearly shattered.

On Sept. 4, 1980, Landhuis was shot in the back during a robbery in Callaway County. The bullet, which is still lodged in his spine, paralyzed him from the waist down.

For 109 days, Landhuis was hospitalized in Columbia Regional Hospital. "It's difficult to keep your positive disposition when you're utilizing all of your energies just to live," he said.

To get through each day, he takes medication to control the pain. Even with the medication, it requires an enormous amount of tenacity to cope, he says.

Nevertheless, Landhuis is still trying to do some farming on a limited basis. He has a heard of cattle that he tends, and he farms a plot of land north of town. Most of the 212-acre farm has been rented to his neighbor.

Although Landhuis says there is equipment available to aid the handicapped farmer, it is often quite expensive. There are lifts available to help the handicapped farmer onto his machinery and hand controls for locomotion, but most of the equipment is not under warranty, he says.

"Farmers represent about 3 percent of the population," Landhuis says. "Handicapped farmers represent only a very small percentage of this."

"There are so few of us, it is not economically feasible for manufacturers to cheaply produce farm equipment for such a small population."

In general, the handicapped person must be innovative, he says. Many cities are not built with the handicapped in mind.

"Columbia is pretty good to its handicapped citizens," Landhuis says. Many buildings have automatic doors and ramps to aid those in wheelchairs.

But these features represent costly additions that many businesses or communities are not willing to spend, he says, and often the handicapped are overlooked.

Today his smile carefully conceals his pain. Landhuis says he constantly works at keeping a positive attitude.

"Since there is snow on the ground, I can't even feed the cows," he said. "My wife has to do it, and that really hurts me."

The psychological effects of becoming paraplegic can be devastating.

But Landhuis' optimistic outlook on life is his mainstay, he says.

He says he has received a great deal of support from his family. His wife, Pauline, was at his side daily during of his long hospital stay, he says.

Friends have helped support him morally, as well as, financially.

As he recuperated in the hospital, about 20 area farmers used their own equipment to harvest his soybean crop.

Medical bills from Columbia Regional Hospital added up to more than $15,000; a fund was created to pay the expenses because Landhuis did not have any medical insurance.

People from all over the country contributed money, he says.

But even with the support of family and friends, Landhuis' recuperation has been difficult.

There was no apparent progress for the first six months after his injury, he says. Now, progress is slow.

"I'm a realist," he says. "I know I'll probably never be able to walk again, but there are other things to do in life than complain about my situation."

Above, Landhuis stuffs wood for the furnace in a bag as his wife, Pauline, piles it up for him. At right, Marion talks with another bidder at the Columbia sale barn — always trying to keep up with what's new.

Photos by Chris Fennewald

Figure 12-11 Consistent internal spacing is important in producing a strong picture page. White space should bleed to the outside margins.

Here are a few pointers on picture pages:

1. Three or four large pictures make a more appealing picture page than eight or 10 smaller ones.

2. Let one picture, the best available, dominate the page.

3. Emphasize the upper-left portion of the page either with a dominant picture or a large headline.

4. If the content allows, crop some of the pictures severely to achieve either wide, shallow, horizontal ones or narrow, long, vertical ones.

5. In a picture series or sequence, place a big picture in the bottom right corner of the page. It is the logical stopping point.

6. Let the page breathe. White space makes both the pictures and the text stand out. But while doing so, keep interior spacing standard and allow white space to bleed to the outside. Trapped interior white space is distracting.

7. Don't align pictures with a T square. An off-alignment often provides extra white space or leaves room for a cutline.

8. If a picture page has to be made up in a hurry, pick the best picture, rough-sketch it on a dummy, slug and schedule the picture and get it to the engraver or camera department. Then edit the other pictures. The cutlines can be written while the editor looks at photocopies of the pictures.

9. Vary picture page patterns. Don't make today's picture page look like last Saturday's.

10. Cutlines need not appear below the pictures. In fact, a narrow cutline beside the picture may be easier to read than a wider one below it.

11. In a sequence or series of pictures, don't repeat in one cutline what was said in another.

12. If all the pictures were taken by one photograper or provided by one wire service, a single credit line on the page will suffice. Too many credits give the page a bulletin board effect.

13. In a photo-essay page, keep the cutlines as brief as possible. Usually, the pictures tell most of the story, especially if the headline has established the theme.

14. Headlines generally are more effective at the left or right of the page or under the main pictures. Occasionally the head may be overprinted on the main picture if the type does not rob the picture of important details.

**Cutline
Guidelines**

Picture texts are known by many names—cutlines, captions, underlines (or overlines), legends. A caption suggests a heading over a picture, but many editors use the term to refer to the lines under the picture. *Legend* may refer either to the text or to the heading. If a heading or catchline is used, it should be under, not over, the picture.

The copy editor "sells" the reporter's story by means of a compelling headline. By the same token, the picture editor can help control the photographic image with a cutline message. The primary purpose of the cutline message is to get the reader to respond to the photo in the manner intended by the photographer and the picture editor.

Readers first concentrate on the focal point of the picture, then glance at the other parts. Then, presumably, most turn to the cutline to confirm what they have seen in the picture. The cutline provides the answers to questions of who, what, where, when, why and how, unless some of these are apparent in the picture.

The cutline interprets and expands upon what the picture says to the reader. It may point out the inconspicuous but significant. It may comment on the revealing or amusing parts of the picture if these are not self-evident. The cutline helps explain ambiguities, comments on what is not made clear in the picture and mentions what the picture fails to show if that is necessary.

The ideal cutline is direct, brief and sometimes bright. It is a concise statement, not a news story. It gets to the point immediately and avoids the "go back to the beginning" of the background situation.

If the picture accompanies a story, the cutline doesn't duplicate the details readers can find in the story. It should, however, contain enough information to satisfy the readers who will not read the story. Ideally, the picture and the cutline will induce readers to read the story. Normally the cutline of a picture with story is limited to two or three lines.

Even when the picture relates to the story, the cutline should not go beyond what the picture reveals. Nor should the facts in the cutline differ from those in the story.

Cutlines stand out in the newspaper's sea of words and strike the reader with peculiar force. Every word should be weighed, especially for impact, emotional tone, impartiality and adherence to rules of grammar and the accepted language.

Anyone who tries to write or rewrite a cutline without seeing the picture risks errors. The writer should examine the cropped picture, not the original one. The cutline has to confine itself to the portion of the picture the reader will see. If the cutline says a woman is waving a handkerchief, the handkerchief must be in the picture. In a layout containing two or more pictures with a single cutline, the cutline writer should study the layout to make sure that left or right or top or bottom directions are correct.

Although no one should try to write a cutline without first looking at the picture, it frequently happens that pictures have to move to the production department quickly. The editor removes the cutlines (from wire service and syndicated pictures) and jots down the slug and size of the pictures and any revealing elements in the pictures that might be added to the cutlines. A photocopy of the picture may be made. Time permitting, a proofsheet showing pictures and their cutlines should be given to the picture editor.

When the cutline has been composed, the writer should compare the message with the picture. The number of people in the picture should be checked against the number of names in the cutline. Everyone appearing prominently in the picture should be identified. If a person is so obscured in the crowd that the person is not easily identifiable, that fact need not be brought to the reader's attention.

Writing the Cutline

Here are some tips on cutline writing:

1. *Don't tell the obvious.* If the person in the picture is pretty or attractive, that fact will be obvious from the picture. The picture will tell whether a man is smiling. It may be necessary, however, to tell why he is smiling. An explanation need not go as far as it did in the following: "Two women and a man stroll down the newly completed section of Rehoboth's boardwalk. They are, from left, Nancy Jackson, Dianne Johnson and Richard Bramble, all of West Chester." An editor remarked, "Even if some of the slower readers couldn't have figured out the sexes from the picture, the names are a dead giveaway."

2. *Don't editorialize.* A writer doesn't know whether someone is happy, glum or troubled. The cutline that described the judge as "weary but ready" when he arrived at court on the opening day of trial must have made readers wonder how the writer knew the judge was weary.

3. *Use specifics rather than generalities.* "A 10-pound book" is better than "a huge book." "A man, 70," is more descriptive than "an old man."

4. *Omit the obvious.* Because the readers know you are referring to the photograph, omit phrases such as "is pictured," "is shown" and "the picture above shows."

5. *Use "from left" rather than "from left to right."* The first means as much as the second and is shorter. Neither *left* nor *right* should be overworked. If one of two boys in a picture is wearing a white jersey, use that fact to identify him. If the president is in a golf cart with a professional golfer, readers shouldn't have to be told which one is the president.

6. *Avoid "looking on."* One of the worst things you can say about a person in a photo is that he or she is "looking on." If that is all the person is doing, the photo is superfluous. Perhaps something like this will help: "William McGoo, background, is campaign treasurer."

7. *Don't kid the readers.* They will know whether this is a "recent photo." Give the date the photo was taken if it is an old photo. Also, let readers know where the picture was taken—but not how. Most readers don't care about all the sleet and snow the photographer had to go through to get the picture. Also, readers aren't stupid. If the cutline says three persons in a Girl Scout picture are looking over a drawing of a new camp, readers aren't fooled if the picture shows two of the girls behind the drawing; they obviously can't be looking it over. If a special lens was used, resulting in a distortion of distance or size, the reader should be told what happened.

8. *Write cutlines in the present tense.* This enhances the immediacy of the pictures they accompany. The past tense is used if the sentence contains the date or if it gives additional facts not described in the action in the picture. The cutline may use both present and past tenses, but the past time-element should not be used in the same sentence with a present-tense verb describing the action.

9. *Make sure the cutline is accurate.* Double-check the spelling of names. The paper, not the photographer, gets the blame for inaccuracies. Cutline errors occur because someone, the photographer or the reporter accompanying the photographer, failed to give the picture desk enough, or accurate, information from which to construct a cutline. Apparently assuming that any big horn is a tuba, a cutline writer wrote about a horn player with half his tuba missing. His editor was quick to reprimand, "Umpteen million high school kids, ex-bandsmen and musicians in general know better."

10. *Double-check the photo with the cutline identification.* The

wrong person pictured as "the most-wanted fugitive" is a sure way to invite libel.

11. *Be careful.* Writing a cutline requires as much care and skill as writing a story or a headline. The reader should not have to puzzle out the meaning of the description. Notice these jarring examples:

"Fearing new outbreaks of violence, the results of Sunday's election have been withheld."

"Also killed in the accident was the father of five children driving the other vehicle."

"Yum! Yum! A corn dog satisfies that ravishing fair appetite." The word, obviously, was *ravenous,* not *ravishing.*

Don't hit the reader over the head with the obvious. If the photo shows a firefighter dousing hot timbers after a warehouse fire and a firefighter already has been mentioned in the text, it is ridiculous to add that "firefighters were called" in the cutline.

12. *Avoid last-line widows or hangers.* The cutline should be written so that the final line is a full line, or nearly so. If the writer knows the number of characters per pica in the type used for the cutline, the writer can set the typewriter stops so that each typewritten line corresponds with the type line. Cutlines written on VDTs can be composed to check line endings. When the lines are doubled (two 2-columns for a four-column picture), the writer should write an even number of lines.

13. *Cutlines should be bright if warranted by the picture.* Biting humor and sarcasm have no place in cutlines.

14. *The cutline should describe the event as shown in the picture, not the event itself.* Viewers will be puzzled if the cutline describes action they do not see. Sometimes, however, an explanation of what is not shown is justified. If the picture shows a football player leaping high to catch a pass for a touchdown, viewers might like to know who threw the pass.

A wire service delivered a combination of three pictures showing the vice president as he played in a celebrity golf tournament. He missed a putt, then buried his head in his hands. But golfers looking closely saw the third picture obviously was not taken on the green, and that while the man had a putter in two pictures he held a wood in the third. The cutline should have explained that after he missed the putt he grabbed another club, walked off the green and then showed his displeasure with the miss.

15. *Update the information.* Because a lapse occurs between the time a picture of an event is taken and the time a viewer sees the picture in the newspaper, care should be taken to update the information in the cutline. If the first report was that three bodies were found in the wreckage, but subsequently two more bodies were found, the cutline should contain the latest figure.

Or, for a picture taken in one season but presented in another, the cutline should reflect the time difference. An example: "Big band singer Helen O'Connor, left, reminisces with Pat and Art Modell backstage at Blossom Music Center this summer. . . ." Reading that on Dec. 1, it is difficult to decide when it happened, especially with a present-tense verb and frost in the air.

16. *Be exact.* In local pictures, the addresses of the persons shown may be helpful. If youngsters appear in the picture they should be identified by names, ages, names of parents and addresses.

17. *Credit the photographer.* If the picture is exceptional, credit may be given to the photographer in the cutline, perhaps with a brief description of how he or she achieved the creation. On picture pages containing text matter, the photographer's credit should be displayed as prominently as the writer's. Photo credit lines seldom are used on one-column or half-column portraits.

18. *Pictures without cutlines.* Although pictures normally carry cutlines, mood or special occasion pictures sometimes appear without cutlines if the message is obvious from the picture itself. Not all who look at pictures will also read the cutlines. In fact, the decline is severe enough to suggest that many readers satisfy their curiosity merely by looking at the picture.

19. *Creating slugs.* In writing a series of cutlines for related shots, use only one picture slug, followed by a number—moon 1, moon 2 and so on.

20. *Know your style.* Some papers use one style for cutlines with a story and another style for cutlines on pictures without a story (called *stand-alones* or *no-story*). A picture with a story might call for one, two or three words in boldface caps to start the cutline. In stand-alones a small head or *catchline* might be placed over the cutline (Figure 12-12).

21. *Give the location.* If the dateline is knocked out in the cutline, make sure that somewhere in the cutline the location is included. Example: "GUARDING GOATS—Joe Fair, a 70-year-old pensioner, looks over his goats Rosebud and Tagalong, the subject of much furor in this northeastern Missouri

Potential pies

Although it's more than a month until jack-o'-lanterns will be needed for the festivities of Allhallows eve, the seasonal harvest of pumpkins has begun in the fields of Valley View Farms in Adams County.

Onion harvest

Onions previously dug from the ground were being topped and boxed by a six-man crew working at the Yosh Nigo farm on U.S. 50, near Uranium Downs this morning. Onions are among the last of the season's crops which farmers are hastening to gather while the weather is still good.

Sentinel photo by Dennis Hogan

HIGH-RISE EXCITEMENT—Fans on balconies watch first lap of qualifying race for the Long Beach Grand Prix. Brian Redman won main event in a Lola before an estimated 75,000 spectators.
DETAILS IN SPORTS SECTION

Times photo by Joe Kennedy

The way it was, then...

No, this wasn't taken from last night's bout in Manila when champion Muhammad Ali faced Joe Frazier for the third time. This shot was taken during the 15th round of their first meeting in March, 1971, when and the heavyweight title. During their second encounter, in January 1974, there were no knockdowns and very little else. Ali was a 2-1 favorite around the world to win, but in Manila the odds dropped to 6-5 for Ali. (Defender photo)

Sargent Shriver

All weld and good

Sparks fly as Larry Page welds a latch on the door of a boxcar. He was working yesterday in the Penn-Central Railroad yards outside of Jeffersonville, Ind.

Staff Photo
by Bud Komenish

Figure 12-12   Cutline styles. Edmund Arnold, an authority on typography, argues that when display is added to the cutline, readership increases as much as 25 percent.

community, boyhood home of Mark Twain. . . ." The Missouri community was Hannibal, but the cutline didn't say so.

22. *Rewrite wire service cutlines.* The same pictures from news agencies and syndicates appear in smaller dailies as well as in metropolitan dailies. Some papers merely reset the cutline supplied with the pictures. Most, if not all, such cutlines should be rewritten to add to the story told in the picture and to indicate some originality on the paper's part.

23. *Watch the mood.* The mood of the cutline should match the mood of the picture. The cutline for a feature photo may stress light writing. Restraint is observed for pictures showing tragedy or dealing with a serious subject.

13

What an Editor Should Know About Typography

Typography is the art of using type to facilitate communication. Type itself does not communicate very much. But if the type selected for printing is correct, it helps the communication process by enabling the audience to read easier and faster. Therefore, the choice of type and its arrangement on a page is critical to maximizing reading. Type is simply a facilitating process that every editor should know.

Using type correctly starts with the ability to differentiate from among the many nuances found in the design of letters. This ability is developed over time as one begins to know what to look for in comparing one typeface with another. Beginners should pay attention to the slight ways in which type differ, as a means of better understanding how to use type. For example, the three capital A's shown in Figure 13-1 each have a different characteristic that make them distinct. The New Caslon A has a heavier right-side element than the other two, and it has an overhang at the very top. It is also a slightly larger letter than the other two. The Century Schoolbook A has a heavier left-side element than the New Caslon. The Cooper Oldstyle right-side element is curved as are the bottom serifs. These differences, albeit slight, give a typeface its "character." That's why so many different typefaces exist. Each meets a somewhat different need. Failure to recognize these differences may result in failure to fully appreciate typography. Shown in Figure 13-1 are some of the details of type differences.

The examples shown in Figure 13-1 are not the only ways that type differs. Five others that are more obvious, and that an editor

WHAT TO LOOK FOR
WHEN STUDYING TYPEFACES

Beginners should pay attention to the slight ways in which letters differ. Shown below are a few examples of three typefaces.

Each Type is 36 pt.:	New Caslon	Century Schoolbook	Cooper Oldstyle
Capitals:			
A	A	A	A
M	M	M	M
Q	Q	Q	Q
T	T	T	T
Lower case:			
a	a	a	a
e	e	e	e
f	f	f	f
g	g	g	g

Other letters that should be examined:
E   O   R   S   W   Y
i   k   r   s   t   y

Figure 13-1   What to look for when studying typefaces.

should know are listed and explained afterwards. The five differences must be specified by the editor when requesting headlines or body type for a special story.

Five Ways in Which Typefaces Differ and Sample Specifications

How these could be specified:	*(1) By Point Size*	*(2) By Type Family*	*(3) By Weight*	*(4) By Width*	*(5) By Styles*
Example 1	24 pt.	Bodoni	Lightface	Regular	Italic
Example 2	60 pt.	Century	Boldface	Condensed	Roman

The material presented in the table is helpful in understanding typography. Furthermore, knowing these five ways in which type can be differentiated may help editors choose from the many typefaces that are available for a newspaper's page layout. The person who created the original newspaper design usually specified the range of type faces that can be used in the newspaper. Therefore editors are not completely free to choose any typeface they wish. Nevertheless editors sometimes have options to choose type, and it is important to know how they differ.

In some newspaper plants, computers have been programmed to help editors make type selections. For example, if an editor opts for a three-column story, then a particular type family, size, width, weight and style may automatically be recommended by the computer.

Details of the Five Ways in Which Type Differ

Type Sizes Differences

Most typefaces are measured in units called *points*. A point is a unit of printer's measurement of about ½₂ inch. Twelve points equal 1 pica, and 6 picas equal 1 inch. Although type could be classified by picas or inches (for example, 72-point type could be called 6-pica type or 1-inch type), it is common practice to limit classification to point-size identification.

Types come in a limited range of sizes in most print shops or newspapers, and within this range are carefully spaced intervals. For example, metal type usually is manufactured from 4 point (the smallest-sized type) to 96 point. Larger sizes of type may be in the form of wood (for letterpress printing) or photographs (for offset printing). There are some exceptions to this range; but not many in common use. The sizes of type most often available in newspapers and print shops, and considered to be standard sizes are as follows:

6, 8, 10, 12, 14, 18, 24, 30, 36, 42, 48, 60 and 72 point

At the lower end of the range, the intervals vary by only 1 or 2 points, whereas at the upper end, the intervals vary by 12 points.

SIZE IN
POINTS

6	abcdefghijklmnopqrstuvwxyzabcdefghijklmnopqrstuvwxyzabcdefghijklmnopqrstuvwx
7	abcdefghijklmnopqrstuvwxyzabcdefghijklmnopqrstuvwxyzabcdefghijklmnopqr
8	abcdefghijklmnopqrstuvwxyzabcdefghijklmnopqrstuvwxyzabcdefghijkl
9	abcdefghijklmnopqrstuvwxyzabcdefghijklmnopqrstuvwxyzabcdefg
10	abcdefghijklmnopqrstuvwxyzabcdefghijklmnopqrstuvwxyzabcd
11	abcdefghijklmnopqrstuvwxyzabcdefghijklmnopqrstuvwxyza
12	abcdefghijklmnopqrstuvwxyzabcdefghijklmnopqrstuvw
14	abcdefghijklmnopqrstuvwxyzabcdefghijklmnopqr
18	abcdefghijklmnopqrstuvwxyzabcdefg
24	abcdefghijklmnopqrstuvwxyz
30	abcdefghijklmnopqrstu
36	abcdefghijklmnopqr
42	abcdefghijklmno
48	abcdefghijklmn
60	abcdefghijkl
72	abcdefghij

Figure 13-2   Most frequently used type sizes. [*From* A Typographical Quest, *Number Three, Westvaco, N.Y., p. 4*]

The reason for this variance is that smaller sizes are used to fill a given amount of space and small variances are needed, but larger sizes are used mostly for headlines and small differences would be unnoticeable.

In newspapers that use phototypesetting machines, type may be set in almost any size that one desires. However, because of tradition, and the lack of time in producing a newspaper to meet deadlines, most editors use standard sized types rather than odd sizes.

In Figure 13-2 are examples of the standard sizes of typefaces found in most newspaper plants.

Type Differences by Families

Just as members of the same human family tend to have similar facial characteristics, so do members of a type family. A type family includes all variations of a given type having common characteristics. Some type families have many variations; others have few. Figure 13-3 shows one of the large families of typefaces.

Helvetica Hairline

Helvetica Light

Helvetica Regular

Helvetica Medium

Helvetica Demi-Bold

Helvetica Bold

Helvetica X-Bold

Helvetica Bold Condensed

Helvetica X-Bold Condensed

Helvetica Bold Condensed

Helvetica X-Bold Condensed

Helvetica Medium

Helvetica Bold

Figure 13-3 Some members of the Helvetica family.

Type Differences by Weights

Type may be differentiated by the weight of the letter. Most type-faces are manufactured in lightface and boldface. Some faces are manufactured in medium, demibold heavy, and ultrabold as well. The terminology here tends to be confusing. One manufacturer titles its medium-weight type *demibold,* whereas another calls its, *medium.* The terms *heavy, bold* or *black* also may mean the same thing. Figure 13-4 shows common examples of type weights.

Bauer Beton Light

Bauer Beton Medium

Futura Demibold

Bauer Beton Bold

BERNHARD GOTHIC HEAVY

Bernhard Gothic Extra Heavy

Bauer Beton Extra Bold

Futura Ultrabold

Figure 13-4   Various weights of typefaces.

Type May Be Differentiated by Letter Widths

Most typefaces are manufactured in normal (or regular) widths. Regular widths comprise the greatest amount of reading matter. But wide and narrow type also is available. Type manufacturers have created extracondensed, condensed, expanded and extended typefaces in addition to regular. These extra widths, however, are not manufactured in all type sizes or families. Therefore, it is necessary to check your newspaper's headline schedule to see if a desired width is available (see Figure 13-5).

Figure 13-5   Variations in letter widths.

Type Differentiated by Style

There are a number of ways to differentiate type by style. Each of them helps the editor find some unique quality which most typefaces have. Here are a number of style differentiations and classifications:

Six general styles:	Roman
	Italic
	Sans Serif
	Text
	Script
	Cursive
Two very broad styles:	Oldstyle
	Modern (Sometimes called Transitional)
Two more broad styles:	Traditional
	Contemporary
Company of production:	Each manufacturing company may make the same type family

The six general styles. A discriminating classification divides type into broad classifications termed roman, italic, text, sans serif, script and cursive. This method of classification has sometimes been called the *race* of a type. Thus roman types might have been created in Rome and italic types created in Italy. But it is better to think of these classifications as simply style characteristics that help in differentiating and identifying typefaces. Square serif is sometimes added to make a seventh style.

Roman Type

Roman type is best identified by other characteristics than its name. It has a vertical shape; it has serifs; it usually has combinations of thick and thin elements in each letter (called stem and hairlines, respectively) (see Figure 13-6). Some type experts con-

A B C D E F G H I J
Q R S T U V W X Y

Figure 13-6   A roman typeface. It is vertical.

sider all vertically shaped letters to be roman, even those without serifs or with no variations in the widths of letter elements (stem and hairline). This form of classification, therefore, may be confusing to the beginner because a roman type will have two purposes: one to distinguish it from sans serifs and the other to distinguish it from italics. For simplicity's sake, it is best to use the classification as first described.

Italic Type

Italic types are characterized by their slanted letter shapes. Although italic types were originally designed to make it possible to print many letters in relatively little space, their use today is limited to citations or words that must be emphasized. They also are used in headlines and body types. Today, italic types are designed to accompany roman types, so that there is consistency in the family of design. Figure 13-7 shows an italic type of the same family.

ABCDEFGHIJKLMNO pqrstu

Figure 13-7   Italic face of the Bodoni Bold family.

Sans Serifs (or Gothic) Types

In America, printers use two terms to identify typefaces having no serifs. One is *sans serif:* the other is *Gothic.* The term *sans serif* comes from the French word *sans,* meaning "without," or *without* serifs. The other term, *Gothic,* is a misnomer. Originally Gothic type meant the churchy-looking types Americans often called "Old English." But today printers use the term *Gothic* also to refer to serifless type (see Figure 13-8).

24 point Microgramma Bold (Foundry)

ABCDEFGHIJKLM

24 point Futura Bold (Foundry)

ABCDEFGHIJKLMNOPQR

Figure 13-8   Two different style san-serifs. Note the differences in their heights. Some type manufacturers vary type designs for competitive reasons.

Text Type

Text type is often incorrectly called Gothic because it looks like Gothic architecture of the middle ages. But printers call it text because it appears to have a texture, like cloth, when printed in large masses. These letters were originally drawn with a broad-nibbed pen and were created to show a minimum of curves. Today the type is used for church printing or where a conservative headline is needed. Students should never have text set in all-capital letters for two reasons: (1) It was never drawn that way originally, having always utilized capital and lower case letters; (2) it is difficult to read when set in all-capital letters (see Figures 13-9 and 13-10).

HARD TO READ

Figure 13-9   Cloister text set in all-capital letters.

Easier to read

Figure 13-10   Cloister text set in caps and lower case. It is much easier to read than all capitals.

Script Type

Script-style letters resemble handwriting. Although the type designers have tried to make it appear as if all the letters are joined, small spaces can be seen between the letters. Some script letters appear to have been written with a brush, whereas others look as if they were drawn with a calligraphic pen. Script type, too, should never be prepared in all-capital letters because it is hard to read in that form (see Figures 13-11 and 13-12).

HARD TO READ

Figure 13-11   Brush script set in all caps.

Easier to read

Figure 13-12   Brush script set in caps and lower case.

Cursive Types

Cursive type styles are characterized by their ornateness. Although they look much like script typefaces, they are easily differentiated from script because they are more ornate. Cursives are used mostly in advertising but occasionally are used for compartmentalized headlines on the Lifestyle page (see Figure 13-13).

ABCDEFGHIJKLMNOPST
abcdefghijklmnopqrstuvwxyzabcdefg 12345

Figure 13-13   A cursive type face.

Oldstyle versus Modern Typefaces

Editors may note that some typefaces are labeled "oldstyle" or "modern." The term "oldstyle" may be interpreted literally, because it is a style designation. But the term "modern" may be misleading. Modern type does not refer to contemporary times, but to style, and both styles are being designed today. Figure 13-14 shows some differences.

Some Other Important Facts About Type

Decisions about Line Widths

The width of newspaper columns has been standardized somewhat through the cooperative efforts of the American Association of Advertising Agencies and the American Newspaper Publishers Association. These two groups have created what is known as Standard Advertising Units (SAUs). The purpose of standardizing widths was to make it relatively easy to create advertising which at one time had many different size column widths. Now that most newspapers have the same column widths, it is relatively easy to create ads.

To some extent, these advertising column widths affect news story column widths, especially where news and advertising appear on the same page. Even where advertising does not appear, such as on the front page, many American newspapers have adopted the SAU column widths. The column width sizes for a six-column paper are shown below:

Column Widths for Six-Column Newspapers
(Also Called "Broadsheets")

1-column	$2\frac{1}{16}$ inches
2-column	$4\frac{1}{4}$ inches*
3-column	$6\frac{7}{16}$ inches*
4-column	$8\frac{5}{8}$ inches*
5-column	$10\frac{13}{16}$ inches*
6-column	13 inches*

* includes space between columns

	Oldstyle	Modern
Transitions between thick and thin elements: 　　Oldstyle: gradual and gentle 　　Modern: more abrupt	 e	 e
Serif elements: 　　Oldstyle: a combination of 　　　　thick and thin 　　Modern: Usually thin	 h	 h
Serif brackets: 　　Oldstyle: may have them 　　Modern: usually doesn't	 I	 I
Serif angles on b, d, h, i, j, k, l, m, n, p, r 　　Oldstyle: usually slants down 　　Modern: usually is horizontal	 p	 p
Distribution of letter weights 　　Oldstyle: on a diagonal axis 　　Modern: on a vertical axis	 c	 c
General appearance in large quantities: 　　Oldstyle: friendly, warm, readable 　　　　typeface 　　Modern: color, business–like, chic	EDUCATION: T Education: To p on which educati on is properly to communication	EDUCATION: T Education: To p on which educati on is properly to communication
Uses: 　　Oldstyle: Headlines and body type 　　Modern: Headlines, and occasionally 　　　　for body type		

Figure 13-14 Some major differences between oldstyle (Caslon) and modern (Bodoni) typefaces. Other oldstyle and modern typeface differences are not as pronounced.

Therefore, editors simply mark copy by the column, and the typesetter knows how wide each column should be. But at times, an editor is asked to mark up copy for a column width that does not conform to the SAU measures. Then the decision about how wide a column should be depends on how a story or page was designed. The layout person specifies the column widths.

How to Measure Type from a Printed Page

There is no problem in measuring a piece of metal type, but because metal type is a thing of the past, editors must be able to measure it from a printed page, such as a type specimen book, or from another newspaper. Specimen books usually indicate the size of most typefaces, but occasionally they do not.

Type Shoulders. Printed type is difficult to measure because one has to account for the space underneath the lower case letters (See Figure 13-15). This space is called a "shoulder" and it is there to allow for descenders of letters such as g, p, q and y. But shoulders vary from typeface to typeface. Some have large shoulders, others have small ones. How can the shoulder space be determined?

PROFITS

Figure 13-15   It is difficult to measure this line of type because ascenders' depth is not shown.

To dramatize the problem Figure 13-16 shows imaginary lines by which letters are created on a piece of metal type. These lines are called (1) base line, on which all letters other than g, p, q and y rest; (2) cap line, to which most capital letters and tall letters rise; (3) lower case line, where small letters align (called the "x" height of letters); and (4) descender line. Each line helps in aligning letters.

Figure 13-16   Drawing of a piece of metal type and imaginary lines that define ascenders, descenders, and x-height.

In measuring the letter "h" it is necessary to allow room for the shoulder underneath the letter. The ascender rises above the lower case line but there is no descender below the base line. Thus, when one wants to measure type from a printed page, one must allow space for the descenders. To accurately determine ascender space one simply looks for a capital letter or one with an ascender. If it were necessary to measure the point size of a line of capital letters it would be necessary to take the space normally used for descenders into consideration in order to have an accurate measurement (see Figures 13-17 and 13-18).

equipped   Measure this distance

Figure 13-17   This word can be measured accurately by drawing a line across the ascenders and descenders and measuring the distance between.

E E E E E E E

Figure 13-18   Why printed type is so difficult to measure. Each of these letter "E's" is 48 points high, but the shoulders of each varies.

An Introduction to Leading

How much space should be placed between lines of body type? This spacing is called "leading" (pronounced ledding). Remember that leading for body type usually has been determined at the time that a newspaper creates its basic design. Therefore, computer typesetters may be preset to control the amount of line spacing that the designer recommended. The machine automatically provides the leading desired.

However, one should not assume that because the leading has been preset, that it never can or should vary. In most newspaper operations, provisions have been made for changing the leading occasionally to meet certain needs, most often in feature stories and/or special kinds of stories. When a story has been written of a momentous nature, and editors want to feature it, then additional leading should be used. Leading usually makes lines of type easier to read, because it gives readers more and easier opportunities to focus their eyes on the type.

Also, when setting long lines of type (20 picas or longer) and the shoulders of typefaces are very short, some leading should be used.

What then are the leading options? If a newspaper uses no leading at all, that practice is called setting type "solid." (Actually there is a tiny bit of space between lines of type when it is set solid, caused by white space at the bottom, or shoulder, of each letter.)

Options range from one-half-point to six-point leading for body type, and the range is extended from three to about 12 points of leading for headlines. The only way to know how type will look after it is leaded is to set a sample paragraph or two and study its readability. See Figure 13-19 for samples of alternative leading.

LINE SPACING

The principle of making each line of type an easy eyeful can be aided by the generous (but not too generous) use of space between the lines. This provides a "right-of-way" for the eye along the top and bottom of each line. Types with short ascenders and descenders and large lower case letters need more space between lines than faces with long ascenders and descenders and small lower case letters. A fairly safe rule is to let the spacing between the lines approximately equal the space between the words.

The above paragraph is set with generous spacing (3-point leads) between lines, while *this* paragraph is set with no leads and is consequently tougher ploughing for the eye. The type is the same size but looks smaller. Educated instinct will in time tell you the difference between jamming and scattering type lines.

Figure 13-19   The top paragraph has been leaded three points. The bottom has been set solid. Leading usually makes lines of type easier to read.

Also see discussion in Spacing in Newspaper Typography that follows.[1]

Spacing in Newspaper Typography

Good typography depends so much on the manner in which words and lines are spaced that a separate discussion is in order here. There are a number of different places in newspaper makeup where type spacing is very important. These places are:

1. between lines of a headline
2. between headline and the story below it
3. between headline and different story above it
4. between body type and illustrations or ads
5. between paragraphs
6. between subheads and body type above and below
7. between words
8. between letters

Each of these will be discussed separately.

Headline Spacing. The research on line spacing is indeterminate. Yet there is a feeling that lines with generous space between

[1] Don Herold, *ATA Handbook,* Advertising Typographers Association of America, Inc., p. 24

them are easier to read than those tightly spaced. Obviously, there is a point where too much space between lines becomes unsightly. Figures 13-20 and 13-21 show examples of various kinds of line spacing. Therefore, too much space between lines of a headline is undesirable. One must judge whether there is too much space by deciding whether all lines can be read as a single entity (desirable) or as a collection of individual lines (undesirable). Care should be taken to avoid having too much space between lines of a headline. The objective is to make all the lines of a head appear as a single entity. When there is too much space, each line receives too much emphasis.

The responsibility for maintaining good headline spacing lies not only with the printer, typesetter or pasteup person, but with the editor as well.

Heat Wave
Hits Cities
Near Coast

Figure 13-20   It is obvious that more space is needed between these lines.

Heat Wave

Hits Cities

Near Coast

Figure 13-21   Words are easier to read with more spacing between them. However, too much space between lines could make reading difficult.

Spacing between headlines and story underneath. One of the most *unattractive* ways of placing headlines on top of stories is to have little or no space underneath the head. The objective is to position the headline so that it gets attention, and does not crowd the first line of the body copy underneath. The amount of space underneath a head, then, depends on the depth of shoulder that accompanies the headline typeface. If the shoulder is large, then little extra space is necessary. If it is small, additional space is required. Essentially, there ought to be about 12 points of space between the baseline of the type and the top of the first line underneath for typefaces from 14 points to about 36. Typefaces larger than 36 points may need two to four extra points of space plus the 12 points mentioned above. Smaller size headlines may need only eight to 10 points of space between the baseline and the top of the line underneath (See Figure 13-22).

This same principle of spacing applies to standing heads. Such heads also need adequate space above and below them.

Bob Mann stages rally
to take Pensacola lead

PENSACOLA, Fla. (UPI) — Bob Mann fired seven birdies and one eagle for a 9-under-par 63 Saturday to take a come-from-behind

Mann, who shared the 1978 National Team Play title with Wayne Levi but has never won an individual title in his three years on

Figure 13-22   Headline is too close to body type.

Spacing between headlines and a story above. A general rule of thumb about the spacing of headlines is that there should be at least 1½ times as much space above as below. The purpose of more space above than below is to make it clear to the reader that a story above is not part of the headline below. In bygone days, stories ended with a "30" dash. Today, white space is substituted for the dash. But the reader must never be confused by spacing. Therefore, a generous amount of space should be placed above headlines. For larger sized headlines, from 36 point type and larger, this space may be as much as two picas. For smaller sizes (14 to 36 point type) the space above the head may be anywhere from 18 points to two picas (see Figure 13-23).

The size, timing and details of the tax cut envisioned by Senate Democrats would be set by the Finance Committee.

O'Neill's view

WASHINGTON (AP) — House Speaker Thomas P. O'Neill said today he sees no possibility that a tax cut could be enacted by Congress before the November election.

Criticizing Republican senators for trying to push through a tax cut in the Senate on Thursday, the Massachusetts Democrat said it was "very unstable"

Figure 13-23   Improper spacing above and below a headline. There should be more space above than below to make it clear that the headline belongs to the story below.

Spacing between body type and illustrations or ads. An area of typography that is overlooked many times in the contemporary newspaper is the spacing of type on top of illustrations and ads (and sometimes below illustrations). The problem usually is that the type is positioned too close to these elements (see Figure 13-24). As a result, the reader's attention is diverted from news copy to either an illustration or an ad. Again, as a rule of thumb, there ought to be no less than one pica space separating elements, and more, if possible. The one pica of space therefore allows both the story and/or the illustration below to get the attention each deserves. Furthermore, space between body type and illustrations of more than one pica simply looks much more attractive than with less than one pica of space between elements.

Spacing between paragraphs. It has been the practice in setting type not to place any space between paragraphs of a story. However, when a particular story is a bit short for the column space allotted (in pasting the news on a page), it is a common practice to place an extra amount of space between each paragraph to lengthen the story.

It is recommended, however, that one or two points of space be deliberately placed between paragraphs in order to make the story easier to read, especially if it is long. Paragraph spacing tends to bring more light into a story and give the reader short pauses while reading paragraphs. There is no research to prove the value of this extra space between paragraphs, but there is usually a more attractive appearance to a long story with spacing than there is without. It is a matter of artistic judgment for the most part.

Spacing above and below subheads. When subheads are used between paragraphs of a long story, there should be more space above the subhead than below. Generally, about four points are placed above and two points below. The purpose of this spacing is to allow the subhead to be seen and perform the function for which it is used. Subheads are used to break up the large masses of type in a long story. Without subheads, this type has a gray, boring appearance that tends to discourage the reader. With subheads, the gray area is now broken up somewhat, and the type looks more interesting. Furthermore, a subhead allows the reader a half-second breather before continuing on. If a story is interesting, perhaps, subheads are not needed. But all stories cannot be equally interesting to all readers, and there is logic in adding them. The space above and below a subhead should help rather than hinder

Figure 13-24   **Body type is too close to the advertisement. This makes the story above somewhat difficult to read.**

reading. Generally, a subhead is added to a story about every fourth or fifth paragraph (see Figure 13-25).

Dets. Joseph McSorley, Bernard Joseph and Howard Baynard.

The three teachers were arraigned before Municipal Judge Ralph Dennis.

Police said they presented a search and seizure warrant to Miss Pincus at 6:30 P. M. Monday at her second floor apartment. They said they found a package wrapped in foil allegedly containing hashish lying on a table.

WAITED FOR SECOND

Miss Pincus attended the University of Wisconsin.

The officers said they then spent several hours in Stetzer's

It was estimated that as much as 20 acres might be needed for such facilities.

OPPOSITION VOICED

Any use of park land for school purposes, however, would have to be approved by the park commission, which has demonstrated strong opposition to the plan.

The only site among the four suggested which the Board of Education could purchase through condemnation is the Five Points tract.

Tate opposes use of this land, however, because its private use could mean attrac-

Figure 13-25 Space is needed above and below each subhead. Subhead at right needs a bit more space above it.

Word Spacing. Spacing between words should be narrow rather than wide. When narrow word spacing is used, it often helps the reader see more words at one sighting, and therefore speed up the reading process. However, there ought to be enough space between words for the reader to recognize where one word ends and another begins. Phototypesetting sometimes increases the space between words too much (see Figure 13-26). Of course, the other extreme of long words in narrow line widths also is undesirable. These gaps of white space slow down the reading because each word has to be read individually, instead of in groups. Generally, the space between words should be about one-third the size of type used. Nine-point type would have three-point-word spacing.

The Pittsburgh Steelers will have to do without All-Pro linebacker Jack Ham in the playoffs due to a dislocated ankle that   may   need surgery. . . . Heavyweight Marvis Fraier, whose father, Joe, once was the world heavyweight champ, was one of five Americans who won gold medals in

Figure 13-26 Poor word-spacing in line four. Reading is slowed because of it.

Letterspacing. Letterspacing usually is done for headlines that are too short. As a result of adding spacing between letters, the line is made to appear longer. Letterspacing usually is not programmed for body type on the phototypesetting machine, but is possible. It can easily be done when type is set on a Linotype. If letterspacing needs to be done, no more than one point should be added between the letters in headlines under 14 points. Two points of space may be added between type that is over 14 points high, and even more for large type. Generally, letterspacing should be avoided, if possible, because it tends to call attention to the words that receive the extra space. The reader may stop and notice that a word has been spaced out. Any time the reader is made to stop the flow of reading, typography is relatively poor.

How to Use Type Effectively

If editors want to use type effectively, they must be able to differentiate type. That isn't all that is required, but it certainly is the first step along the way. What follows then are some basic principles on making intelligent type selections, and then arranging the type in the most readable manner.

Type Selection Principles

Legibility. Any typefaces selected for printing must be legible. A legible type is one that is easy to read, because every letter is easily deciphered. When a typeface is not legible, then readers may read a lowercase "c" for an "e," or perhaps, be confused by any group of letters that look like some other letters. Illegible type may require readers to spend extra time trying to figure out the meaning of words. If the news is fascinating, readers probably will read a story regardless of its type's legibility.

Most newspaper editors use legible type for their main news. The place where illegible type could appear would be for feature story headlines and/or body types, and where an editor is looking for some unique typeface. Presumably that type would be selected to call the reader's attention to the story, or perhaps to make the bodytype fit the unique nature of the story.

When legible types are selected, and reading becomes easier, then readers may be able to read more of what has been written in the amount of time normally allocated for reading newspapers. Whether they will read more depends on factors other than typography.

Almost all typefaces in common printing use today are *somewhat* legible. It isn't necessary to consult research to learn which are legible types, because legibility isn't an "either/or" evaluation. It is a matter of choosing the better alternative available. Shown below are two typefaces: Caslon and Galia. Readers might well say both are legible, but there is no question that Caslon is much more legible than Galia. Perhaps a short headline of Galia may cause no reading difficulties, but Caslon could be used in short or long headlines and still be readable.

Education

EDUCATION

Figure 13-27   Legible versus less legible typeface.

Select attractive typefaces. Of the thousands of typefaces that are available for printing, some are much more attractive than others. The problem here isn't one of legibility, but degrees of attractiveness. In order to decide which typeface is most attractive, editors should have a sense of artistic appreciation and good taste. Editors will sometimes select a typeface which is cleverly designed, but not the most attractive. Cleverness is often associated with attractiveness. On the other hand, when artists are asked which typefaces are most attractive, they tend to select very simple, plain typefaces rather than clever or ornate types.

Choosing the best type size and weights. There is a problem in selecting typefaces without also considering their point size and weight at the same time.

To determine which size and weight is needed for type, one must relate those qualities to the column width in which type is to be set. A 36-point headline, set in a one-column width, rarely looks readable. The problem is that only one short word could be set in a one-column space. That's hardly a headline worth having, unless it is a "hammerhead." (A hammerhead is a one-word headline, used in conjuction with other, longer headlines underneath to tell a striking fact about a piece of news.)

The editor should therefore decide how many words of any size type are necessary to have within a given column width. This is easy to determine when using a computer. When no computer is available, the editor has to count the number of characters that any typeface can be set within a desired column width. It is a matter of editorial judgment about how many words of a headline should appear on one line.

A second consideration, however, is to select a type weight that is appropriate for the type size. Headlines may be too small, and insignificant in lightface type, but look very nice in boldface of the same size. Therefore, the editor has to balance type size and weight at the same time, in order fully to answer this question. Sometimes, an editor can achieve the effect of more weight by using larger typefaces even though they are set in lightface letters. More often, however, a larger and bolder typeface is needed to get the readers' attention. Readers skim headlines looking for an interesting story. Editors should help readers find interesting stories.

Obviously headlines that are too small, but bold, will also not get the attention they need. So editors must learn to perceive size and weight at the same time, when making type selection decisions.

Problems in Selecting Headline Types

Condensed type makes poor headlines. Much, though not all, of condensed types makes a poor selection for headlines. This is especially true of *extra* condensed typefaces. The problem is that extreme condensation of letters in a headline distorts the letters too much, and they become difficult to read. On the other hand, some condensed type that does not squeeze letters very much can be suitable. It depends on the degree of condensation (see Figure 13-28).

Fitzgerald students top state and region scores

Figure 13-28   **Some condensed type headlines may be a bit difficult to read.**

But even then, when roman typefaces are used for most of a headline schedule and it is mixed with condensed type, the mixture of the two can be difficult to read.

Unusual typefaces. Any typeface that calls attention to itself usually is undesirable. The only exception would be one- or two-word headlines that sometimes appear on feature stories and which are surrounded by generous amounts of white space. They can be suitable. The extra white space seems to allow readers a little more time to decipher the words than is needed for ordinary letters.

But, occasionally, letters are selected for their novelty rather than their suitability, and seem amateurish rather than professional.

All capital headlines. Type set in all capitals usually is more difficult to read than when set in caps and lower case, or in "downstyle" (only the first letter is set in caps). Most readers read by recognizing word shapes of caps and lower-case letters with their ascenders and descenders. All-capital letters have none of these differences, and readers must put the letters together to form words:

a slower process. See Figure 13-29 below that graphically shows the problem. Also see Figure 13-30.

Figure 13-29 Caps and lower case letters can more easily be recognized than all cap letters.

CAPS VS. LOWER CASE

There is little doubt that lower case letters are more easily read than caps. Some typographers like to avoid capitals, even in headlines.

In fact, the recognizability of words seems to lie chiefly in the upper half of the lower case letters as illustrated below:

11. Frank had been expecting a letter from his brother for several days;
so as soon as he found it on the kitchen
table he ate it as quickly as possible

11. Frank had been expecting a letter from his brother for several days,
so as soon as he found it on the kitchen
table he ate it as quickly as possible.

Figure 13-30 The legibility of type seems to lie in the upper half of lower case letters.

Selecting type families. Which type family is best for a headline on a particular kind of story? There usually isn't much choice available in most newspaper offices. One selects from whatever is available, suggesting that there is no problem here. But even with a limited number of choices, there may be good or bad options from which an editor may choose. So the answer is that the type selected ought to match the nature of the story, if possible.

Matching a typeface to the nature of a story is based on the connotation that each type family has. Type families differ just as humans do. Therefore, it is necessary to know the connotations of each typeface that a newspaper owns. It is not a difficult task to evaluate most of these connotations (see Figure 13-31).

Elegance
Clearcut Initial—French Script

MODERNISM
Kabel Light

DIGNITY
Forum

UNUSUALNESS
Newfangle

Antiquity
Satanick

NATURE
Sylvan

Sincerity
Baskerville

STRENGTH
John Hancock

Distinctiveness
Civilité

CHEAPNESS
Mid-Gothic

Figure 13-31 Connotations of various typefaces. [*Courtesy of International Typographical Union*] Also see Figure 13-32.

The Problem of Type that Causes Fatigue. Despite the fact that editors may select a legible type for a story, that type may cause a great deal of reader fatigue. In other words, some typefaces tend to cause readers' eyes to tire.

As American readers grow older, they may have more trouble reading their newspapers. Some of them have written to their local editors asking that the bodytype faces be set in larger sizes. Some editors have begun to use larger types, like 10-, 11- or 12-point types.

But there is one kind of type in particular that is considered to be fatiguing: sans serif body types. Sans serif typefaces in headlines seem to cause no fatigue problems because letters are fairly large, and there is a generous amount of space around headlines. But sans serif typefaces, especially in the light-weight versions, tend to be so monotonous in color that they are boring.

Another kind of type falls into the same category: condensed body type. Letters that look "squeezed" tend to be harder to read en mass and tend to be fatiguing.

The solution to reader fatigue, of course, is to avoid those type-

Shown below are samples of common headline typefaces and the connotations that many graphic designers agree upon:

Cheltentam Bold:

a homey, down-to-earth face that is often used for human interest stories. Not very attractive, but has a warmth and power that an editor needs occasionally.

ABCDEFGHIJKLMNOPQRSTUVWXYZ
abcdefghijklmnopqrstuvwxyz

Bookman:

a very readable type, that is not a bit pretentious. This type is even more down-to-earth than Cheltenham. Excellent for headlines, and cutlines, but not body type, because its letters are too wide.

ABCDEFGHIJKLMNOPQRSTUVWXYZ
abcdefghijklmnopqrstuvwxyz

Garamond Bold:

an elegant, charming, readable type. It isn't very bold—but it is readable and has wide applications.

ABCDEFGHIJKLMNOPQRSTUVWXYZ
abcdefghijklmnopqrstuvwxyz

Times Roman Bold:

a type for today. It is frequently used in body type and heavier versions are used for headlines. It appears to be quite readable, and versatile.

ABCDEFGHIJKLMNOPQRSTUVWXYZ
abcdefghijklmnopqrstuvwxyz

Century Bold:

a schoolbookish type. In fact, there is a special version called Century Schoolbook. But both have the same common, everyday, readable look. Not elegant. Just plain readable.

ABCDEFGHIJKLMNOPQRSTUVWXYZ
abcdefghijklmnopqrstuvwxyz

Figure 13-32   Connotations of common headline typefaces.

faces. However, for certain purposes, these typefaces look attractive and some editors might want to use them anyway. If a sans serif or condensed face must be used in large quantities, then the solution to making them more readable is to add more space between the lines. This will give the reader the opportunity to see the words in more contrasting ambiance.

Some Other Important Considerations in Using Type

1. It isn't wise to mix more than two letter styles in one paragraph. For example, it is acceptable to mix roman and italic, or roman and boldface in one paragraph. But it would not look attractive to mix roman, italic, and boldface in one paragraph. The reason: there would be too much contrast, and the mixture would call too much attention to the type and not its message.

2. Type should not be set in very short or long measures. Both are difficult to read. Some experts recommend that the maximum line width be about one-and-a-half lower-case alphabets. To implement this idea, the user must first have a particular typeface set in its lower-case alphabet, or find a sample in a type sample book and then measure the width. Slight variations in this measured width will not matter.

   A line of type should rarely be set less than four picas wide because it is difficult to fit many words in such a small space. Even a four-pica width should be limited to very small type such as 6- or no more than 7-point type. On the other hand, type should rarely be set longer than 30 picas wide. Exceptions to this rule are situations where the type being set is 18 points or larger in height.

3. For headlines, too many different sizes or faces on the same page should be avoided. The best technique is to use monotypographic harmony, meaning harmony based on the use of a single type family. But, when many different sizes or variations of the same family are used, the effect is unharmonious. However, if an editor requires more than one type family on a single page, then the number should be limited to two, with one being used predominately and the other sparingly.

4. Agate (5½- point) type is used exclusively for box scores of athletic games and long lists of names (such as in a graduating class). But this type size should never be used for the main text of a story. Because of its size, it is compact and saves space, but it is always a supplement to the main body of reading matter.

5. The beginner should watch for unusual and unsightly spacing between letters of a word set in large type. This usually occurs when setting combinations of any of the following capital letters: A, L, P, T, V and W. For example, A and V have more

white space between them (AV) than do N and I (NI), or other similar combinations. When any of the above letters are used in combination in large headline, the printer should be asked to cut the type in such a way as to eliminate the unsightly space. The printer may be willing to do so if time is available. However, in phototypesetting, it is easy and therefore advisable to overlap capital letters to avoid unsightly spacing.

6. A change of pace in typefaces for headlines is attractive if it is not overdone. This means that an italic or an ultraboldface headline may be used on a page that has predominantly roman typeface headlines. When more than one such variation is used, the contrasting effect is lost.

7. Contrast is a key to beautiful typography. But the contrast should be relatively strong. When headline typefaces are used that are different, but not radically so, the mixture on a page will appear to be "a wrong font," rather than a contrasting headline.

8. Narrow word-spacing is easier to read than wide word-spacing. "Cold" typesetting machines often produce wide word-spacing. If not controlled, wide word-spacing calls attention to itself and not the meaning of the words.

The best way to understand type is to be able to differentiate the many kinds of existing typefaces. Unless the slight variations in letters shapes are known, one typeface may appear as good as another. Once the differences in typefaces have been learned, however, the editor can develop an aesthetic sense, or taste, of what looks attractive in print, based on some elementary artistic principles.

Developing Artistic Judgment

Developing a sense of artistic judgment in type is best done by studying type in print, no matter where it appears. For example, beautifully set type often appears in a magazine, a book, or a financial report. If one works at developing a sensitivity to what looks good in print, one will be alert to such printing. Then it is advisable to make a mental note of the way type was set or why it looks so good. An editor may use this idea, by adjusting it to the newspaper environment, if it is at all possible. In this manner an editor uses type to aid communication. However, the editor should know and keep up with typographic research. Almost every year, there are new studies that can add to one's knowledge of how to use type. While research cannot answer whether one typeface is more appropriate than another for a headline, there are many helpful things to be learned from research. In fact, as more studies are conducted, some of the older ideas on using type will be rejected or replaced.

How Type Is Composed

Type is composed (or set) today primarily by phototypesetting methods, a technique that may be characterized as "cold type" because the print is cold and hot lead is not involved in the process. "Hot type," on the other hand, consists of letters that have been molded with hot lead. It is almost a thing of the past. Some hot type machines still exist, but it is only a matter of time until they are replaced with cold type machines. A discussion of how these machines work follows.

All phototypesetting machines expose photosensitive paper or film to a light image of each character to be set, either electromechanically or by CRT (cathode ray tube) technology.

In the electromechanical method, a character matrix made of film or glass is prepared in which all the characters of a particular typeface (font) are etched into the surface. The matrix is then mechanically rotated until the desired character is in the proper position, a xenon lamp is flashed, and a light image of the character is projected through a lens which magnifies it to the desired size. The image is reflected by mirror onto the photosensitive paper. Thus, one character has been "set."

Characters are set next to each other to form words and lines by movement of the mirror. For each new line, the paper is moved vertically the proper distance. For each new character size, a different fixed lens or a zoom lens is rotated into the light path (see Figures 13-33 and 13-34).

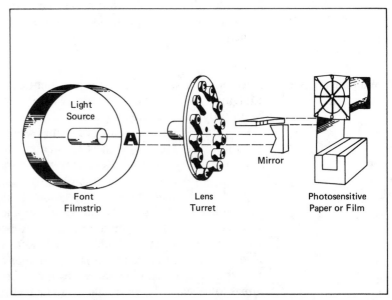

Figure 13-33 Diagram of how an electromechanical phototypesetter works.

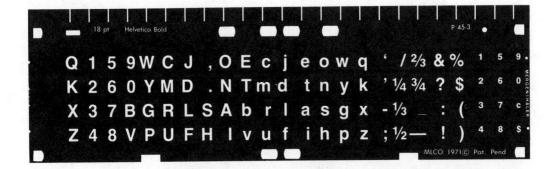

Figure 13-34   Film strip used on the V-I-P Phototypesetter, and the strip on a drum. [*Courtesy of Merganthaler Company.*]

Cathode ray tube phototypesetting is divided into two categories.

In the first instance, light images of *all* characters in a particular typeface are projected onto a "reading CRT," similar to a television camera tube in that light images are converted into electronic impulses. These impulses are stored in a computer and each character is magnified to the desired size and assembled by the computer and sent to a "printout CRT." This tube reconverts the impulses to light images which are beamed onto photographic paper, similar to the way photographic contact prints are made (see Figure 13-35).

In the second instance—digitization—character shapes do not physically exist on film or a grid. They are simply digital information that exists only in computer memory. Each character is produced by "painting" this information on paper, using a cathode ray tube and tiny fiber optics with a bonded face plate to project a matrix of thousands of overlapping strokes which form the character. The more strokes, the sharper the character (see Figure 13-36).

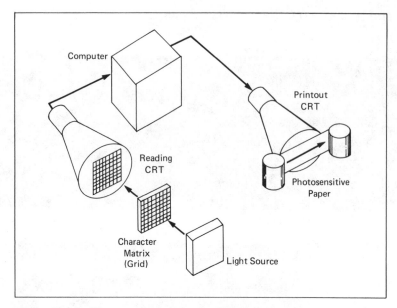

Figure 13-35   How a cathode ray tube (CRT) phototypesetter works.

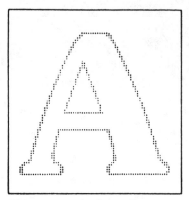

Characters exist in outline within magnetic memory.

CRT "paints" character within outline

Final character appears sharp and solid.

Figure 13-36   How a digitized CRT phototypesetter works.

The most recent development in cold type machines is one whose most distinguishing feature is that it uses a laser beam to set type instead of the photographic process. The laser beam will generate (or create) letters from a memory unit and can be called forth by pressing appropriate buttons. The machine will then create letter characters, somewhat like the digital CRT phototypesetter, through a series of strokes.

However, the most innovative function of this machine is that it will enable the user to generate line art (like normal printing) and even halftones. Users then can layout each page on a screen and convert it directly from the screen to an offset printing plate, thereby saving a great deal of time and effort in getting newspapers to the printing press (see Figure 13-37).

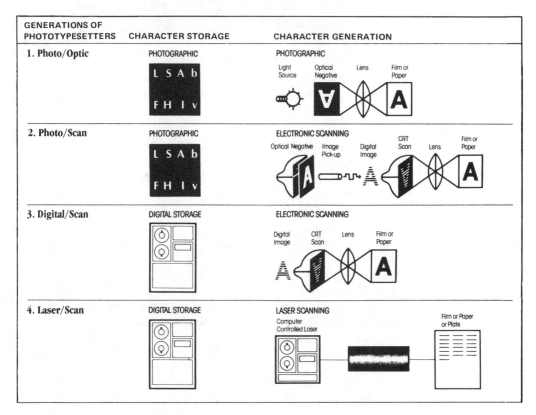

Figure 13-37   A graph showing four generations of phototypesetters. [*Courtesy of U & LC International Typeface Corp.*]

The laser typesetting machine has not had wide distribution as of this writing, but it is expected to be the machine of the future.

Pagination Machines

One of the ideas similar to laser technology of typesetting is a machine that can—with the aid of a computer, a video display ter-

Figure 13-38   The Hastech NewsPro. Shows an operator using keyboard to review page layout on right side and a news story on the left. [*Courtesy of Hastech Inc.*]

minal and a phototypesetter—produce a complete page of type and pictures, properly positioned as an editor desires, ready to be converted into a plate. In fact, the idea has been conceived of even going one step further: producing a plate ready for offset printing directly from the video display terminal. At present it is possible to type stories, edit and proofread them, and in the case of advertisements, position elements of an ad. However, the page must still be dummied on a sheet of paper or on a video display terminal. Halftone pictures cannot be handled very well on present machines, and technology has not advanced to the point where an entire page can be converted directly into a printed plate. On those machines where advertisements can be made up, using a VDT, the pictures in the ad can be positioned only in outline form. The pictures will have to be converted to screened prints and later pasted into position on the phototypeset ad. There is a great deal of optimism in the industry that a pagination machine will be developed, although it may be a number of years before it is ready for mass production.

One such pagination machine is now in use at the Westchester-Rockland Newspaper Group in New York state. The machine is named *Page Pro,* and it was developed by Hastech, a subsidiary of Hendrix Electronics Inc.

The Page Pro has two video display screens side by side, but one (the smaller) is used for VDT editing, and the other (larger) for positioning stories on a page (see Figure 13-39).

The operator can set a story and see it on the editor screen. Then the operator can move this story to the larger screen and position

Figure 13-39   An editor's layout terminal, which allows for quick creation of page dummies through the use of microcomputer *mouse* and pad. The *mouse* allows an editor to move stories around on the screen. [*Courtesy of Hastech Inc.*]

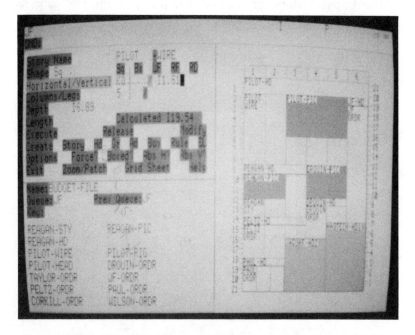

Figure 13-40   This scene shows a closeup of computer screen with three windows: page layout, command menu and text directory. [*Courtesy of Hastech Inc.*]

it on a page outline. The words of the body copy do not appear on the larger screen; only headlines do. Body copy is represented by what appear to be straight pencil lines (see Figure 13-40). However, the operator may choose to enlarge a story on the positioning screen and see the typeface in which the story was set, with its accompanying headline (see Figure 13-40). Normally, however, stories are positioned on the large screen with only headlines and straight lines. If a story is too long, the operator can transfer it to the smaller screen and cut some lines from it. If the story does not fit the space on the larger screen, the operator can call up fillers from the computer, or write more copy. The ability to move stories from the pagination screen to the editing screen and back again is called the *interactive* capability of the machine.

After each story has been positioned on the larger screen, and the entire page is completely filled with stories, the operator simply presses a button that starts the transfer of the page from a collection of stories set in type to camera-ready copy of a page. From the copy will come a printing plate. Halftones cannot be handled on most pagination units yet, but it is expected that they will be soon. Ads can be placed in position on a page in some pagination units now.

Pasteup of Newspaper Pages

After the type of a newspaper page has been set, it is usually pasted onto a specially prepared sheet of paper called a "pasteup grid."

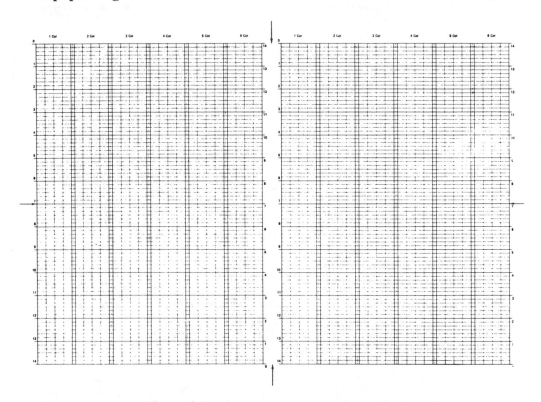

Figure 13-41 A newspaper pasteup sheet with grid outlines.

Grid sheets are printed in light blue ink so that the lines will serve as pasteup guides but will not photograph (Figure 13-41). (The camera film will not pick up blue ink unless a special filter is used.) Figure 13-42 shows the pasteup process.

Figure 13-42 Pasting up a newspaper page. [*Courtesy of Quad City* (Iowa) *Times*]

From this point on the pasted newspaper is photographed and converted into a film negative. The negative is used to make a zinc offset printing plate and the page is printed.

14

Theory and Practice of Newspaper Layout

When newspaper editors arrange news, pictures and other stories on a page they are, in effect, packaging their product. In fact, there is great similarity between editors' and manufacturers' packages. Both use the package as a convenient means of shipping contents to consumers and both use the package as a means of helping consumers use the product.

Packaging the News

An editor aids the reader by arranging news content in an orderly and easy-to-read manner. Occasionally, news stories are so unusual or interesting that readers will disregard poor design and suffer their way through the newspaper. But that doesn't occur every day. More often most readers drop off after the front page until they encounter the next interesting section. An editor's goal in packaging is to help the reader read faster and read more of what has been written on all pages.

The package has another, less obvious, function than making the contents easy to read. A manufacturer plans his package front by placing information about the contents in the form of a pattern that communicates through the appearance of the entire design as well as the words. This kind of communication may be thought of as the connotation of the news. Editors also may arrange the news so that the design resulting from an arrangement connotes something beyond the meaning of the words. Such connotations may range from a design telling the reader that a story is significant and serious to another design emphasizing a light-hearted, tongue-in-cheek approach. Connotations of the newspaper's whole design may give readers the feeling they are reading a conservative paper or one that is liberal or old-fashioned or progressive. The editor therefore is concerned with the orderly arrangement of the news as well as with creating appropriate connotations.

Changing Terminology: Makeup to Layout, or Design

For many years, the practice of arranging news on a page was called "makeup." As always, when makeup was finished, the result was called a "page design" (a noun). But at times the term design was used as a verb: to design a page.

In recent years, a newer term has been used frequently to describe what makeup persons do in arranging the news: it is called "layout" or "laying out a page." In the next three chapters we will use the latter two terms: to lay out or to design a page whenever we discuss page arranging.

The Objectives of Newspaper Layout and Design

Design exists primarily to facilitate readership. A newspaper is a collection of many stories, pictures, features and advertisements. When they are haphazardly placed within the newspaper or on any given page, they become a deterrent to reading because the effect is confusing. Foremost in planning a page is the goal of making every page easy to read. Newspaper pages should be designed so that as a result of being easy to read more people will read faster than they have before and read more of what has been written.

Newspapers are in competition with dynamic media such as television and radio. But even print media such as magazines and books are much easier to read than newspapers because they are more attractively designed. Obviously, it is easier to design magazines because more time is available for the arrangement of stories. But readers are not likely to be sympathetic with the problems of newspaper makeup editors. Readers know which media are the easiest and most pleasant to read. Therefore every effort should be made to overcome any inertia readers may have when they read a newspaper page. With this general objective in mind, it is then possible to state the specific objectives as follows:

Objective No. 1: Facilitate Reading

First, the editor should arrange the news in an orderly and convenient-to-read manner. When news is so arranged, the reader will be faced with a minimum of obstacles to overcome. Readers should know where every story starts and, if it is necessary to carry the story into another column, where the story ends. It should be easy to find any special news or feature of interest with a minimum of effort and confusion. Orderly arrangement is a significant criterion of good design.

Objective No. 2: Represent the Contemporary Scene

Second, news should be packaged in a format whose design is consistent with the nature of contemporary design found outside the newspaper. Furniture, automobiles and the architecture of buildings all reflect contemporary design. The format of a newspaper is the frame of reference in which the news is read. Contemporary news should therefore be packaged in a contemporary format. Modern design is symbolic and tells the reader that the newspaper is attuned to the times and is perceptive of what is going on in today's world. The design may communicate nonverbal symbols such as liberalism, conservatism, strength of character or even concern for social welfare. These qualities represent the image of the newspaper. Images are only feelings, attitudes and opinions, but they are important in making the newspaper's efforts appreciated. In the field of consumer product categories, Cadillacs, for example, convey an image of high social status and affluence, whereas Volkswagens convey an image of economy and convenience. The design of every product is carefully planned so that all consumers will perceive the product just as the manufacturer wants.

Objective No. 3: Make the Design Exciting

Third, and perhaps the most important, the design should be more exciting to the reader than ever before, because the newspaper is competing in a milieu of very dramatic and attractive media. The public can and does get its news and features from other sources such as magazines, television and radio. A broadcast medium obviously is exciting because it uses voice, music and other sounds to communicate. Magazines have used dramatic page makeup in full color to attract attention and to communicate. What can a newspaper editor do to compete? The answer: create an attractive, interesting design that dramatizes the news so that the newspaper will compare favorably with the other mass media.

In recent years, the newspaper industry has made special efforts to attract younger readers, but with only modest success. One way that this can be done is through attractive page designs, because younger people tend to be more appreciative than older people of new and contemporary page designs.

Objective No. 4: Make the Newspaper Attractive

Finally, the newspaper is a visual arts medium and is often evaluated in the same light as other visual arts. A newspaper should be attractive both as a visual arts medium and as a modern package because beauty for its own sake is one of the more important values in an affluent society. Newspaper design should reflect this value when presenting the news.

Graphic Responsibilities of Layout Editors

Although the objectives of layout and design are quite clear, they may not provide enough details about the specific objectives that editors face when laying out a page. (See the panel below for an overview of the editor's specific responsibilities.)

---

10 RESPONSIBILITIES OF LAYOUT EDITORS

A layout editor is responsible for the following:

1. for telling readers which stories are most important
2. for helping readers follow stories from column to column
3. for helping readers know on which page a story is continued and for helping readers find the continuation on that page
4. for helping readers know which other stories are related to the one being read
5. for helping readers know which pictures are related to which stories
6. for helping readers know where stories end and new ones begin
7. for keeping readers from losing interest in long stories
8. for setting type large enough, in the best typeface, in an optimum line width, and with optimum line spacing to maximize readability
9. for making the entire page interesting—not just the top
10. for helping readers with limited time available, to find just the stories they want

---

Principles of Artistic Design Applied to Newspapers

Achievement of the objectives of design and the responsibilities of layout editors are related to the application of artistic principles of design. The newspaper is a graphic art form, using words, pictures, color, lines and masses subject to the same principles of artistic design as other graphic art forms. Some graphic design principles suggest underlying bases for news page designs. The principles most applicable to newspapers are known as balance, contrast, proportion and unity.

Balance: A Means of Making the Page Appear Restful

Balance means equilibrium. It means that a page should not be overwhelmingly heavy in one section or extremely light in another. The consequence of designing an unbalanced page is that readers may have a vague feeling of uneasiness because of the concentration of weight in only one or two sections of the page. Most readers do not know whether a page is balanced or unbalanced. They are not artists and do not care about the principles of artistic design. Yet they often know that a certain page "feels" better to read than do other pages. One artistic goal of good designing is to bring about a feeling of equilibrium on each page. In newspaper design, the most frequent means of bringing about imbalance is to make a page top-heavy by placing large and bold headlines at the top while using almost insignificantly light headlines at the bottom. Another cause of imbalance is the practice of placing a large, dark picture at the top without having one of similar size or weight at the bottom. As a result of imbalance readers' eyes tend to gravitate toward the bolder sections of the page and away from the lighter portions. Assuming that every element on a page has value, an unbalanced page, theoretically, is more difficult to read than a balanced page.

Balance in newspaper design is achieved by visually weighing one element on a page with another on the opposite side of the page, using the optical center as a fulcrum. The optical center is a point where most persons think the true mathematical center is located. It is a little above and to the left of the mathematical center (see Figure 14-1). The practice of visually weighing one element on a page against another does not lead to precise balancing, but

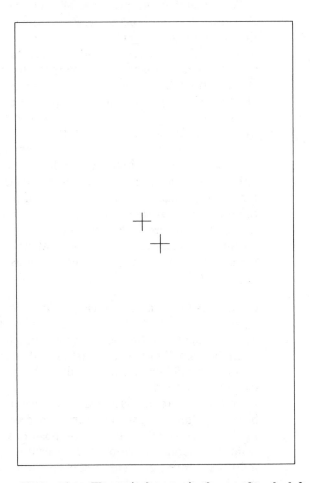

Figure 14-1   The optical center is above and to the left of the mathematical center. Balance takes place around the optical center.

there is no need for that degree of precision. All that is required is a feeling of equilibrium on a page, not precise mathematical weighing.

Which elements need balancing? Any element on a page that has visual weight should be balanced. To determine which elements have visual weight one need only squint at a page and notice that much of the printed material disappears. What remains are pictures, headlines and black type rules of any kind. Although it is true that even body type has some weight, it isn't significant enough for consideration in visual weighing. The goal is to distribute prominently weighted objects pleasantly on the page.

Balance is most often done by weighing elements at the top of a page with those at the bottom, rather than doing so from side to side. The principle of balance is the same as that of balancing a heavy person with a light person on a seesaw. The heavy person must move close to the fulcrum, whereas the lighter person must move farther away on the opposite side of the fulcrum.

To implement the principle of balance, the most outstanding elements, such as bold or large headlines at the top of a page, should be weighed against similar headlines at the bottom. If the bottom of the page has no bold or large headline, the page is likely to be top-heavy. Plans should be made to include such headlines at the bottom. The same procedure should be followed in placing pictures on a page. A headline or picture at the bottom need not be as large or as bold as one at the top because it is farther away from the fulcrum (see Figure 14-2).

Page balance may be formal or informal. Formal balance is achieved by placing headlines and pictures of the same size on either side of a page. It is sometimes called symmetrical rather than formal balance because one side of the page tends to mirror the other. In that sense there is balance. But symmetrical design may be unbalanced from top to bottom. Most newspapers employ an informal balance from top to bottom. The feeling of equilibrium is there even though it is not obvious.

Contrast

Contrast is the principle of using at least two or more elements on a page each of which is dramatically different from the other. One may be a light headline contrasting with a bold headline. Another might be a small picture contrasting with a larger one. Because one element is different from the other, the page is made to appear lively and interesting.

Contrast, therefore, is a means of preventing artistic pieces from becoming dull. Almost all art forms are created with some contrast in them—especially musical compositions, theatrical plays and printed material. A symphony, for example, contrasts a fast and loud first movement with a soft and slow second movement. A play has a relatively quiet scene contrasting with a lively scene. A book or magazine may have most pages printed in black and white

Figure 14-2 A balanced page. [*Courtesy of the* Chicago Tribune]

contrasting with full-color illustrations.

In page layout and design, contrast prevents a page from appearing too gray, a problem that occurs when there is too much body copy and too many light headlines. Gray pages appear uninviting and forbidding (see Figure 14-3).

Sometimes when a page has been deliberately designed to feature balance, it may lack contrast and appear rather dull and boring. The editor therefore may have to brighten that page by adding another picture and/or large, bolder headlines to bring about better contrast.

Indiscriminate use of contrast, however, is undesirable. If a page

Figure 14-3   A page that lacks contrast. It can be read without difficulty, but would be easier to read if it had more contrast. [*Courtesy of* Vincennes Sun-Commercial]

has too much contrast it may overpower the reader because the contrasting elements call attention to themselves and not to the page as a whole. The goal is to provide pleasant, not overpowering, contrast. To achieve this goal the layout person will have to develop a sense of good taste.

Contrast may be achieved in four general ways: by shape, size, weight and direction. Shape contrast may consist of a story set flush on both sides in opposition to another story set flush left, ragged right. Or an outline picture may be used with a rectangular-shaped picture.

Size contrast may be shown by using a large illustration on the same page with a smaller one, or large type contrasted with smaller type.

Weight contrast may employ a picture that appears very black with a lighter picture, or a story set in boldface type contrasted with one set in lighter typefaces.

Direction contrast could show vertically shaped stories contrasted with horizontally shaped stories.

These contrast alternatives are but a few of many that are possible on any given page. An objective of designing a page, however, is to achieve pleasant, rather than harsh or extreme, contrast. Too many contrasting elements on a single page may be artistically unsound and unattractive.

Proportion

Proportion is the principle of comparative relationships. In newspaper design the length of one line may be compared with the length of another, the shape of one story with shapes of others or the width of a photograph with its depth. The goal of designers is to create pages in which the proportions of elements are pleasing to the eye. Certain proportions in this culture tend to look more pleasing than others. The Greeks worked out the proportions of many of their temples in classical dimensions. Artists and designers try to use pleasing proportions in their works because the public has come to appreciate such relationships. For example, artists rarely use a square shape in preparing their work because a square appears dull and uninteresting. More pleasing is a rectangle because one dimension is greater than the other. Unequal proportions usually are more attractive than equal proportions. For that reason, newspapers, magazines and books have pages that are designed with the width being less than the depth.

In newspaper design, pleasing proportions should be considered in planning the sizes of pictures, headlines and even divisions of pages. Unfortunately, the design of newspaper pages often does not reflect the principle of good·proportions even though the size of paper pages does. The problem is that layout persons tend to think in terms of fitting news into columns, each of which is poorly proportioned. They can't be sure that the shape of the main story on a page is pleasantly related to other story shapes on that page. Persons using the total design concept are better able to control relationships and proportions than are makeup persons.

The beginner with little or no artistic training will have to develop a sense of proportion by following certain basic principles:

1. The best proportions are unequal and thereby not obvious. Therefore, an element on a given page should not have square dimensions, whether it is a picture, story shape, box or division of a page.
2. There are many pleasing proportions that can be used, but one of the easiest and most pleasing is a 3:5 relationship. It is easy to remember and easy to use. To determine the shape of a story, for example, the layout person needs only to decide arbitrarily

one dimension (either the width or the length). Then by multiplying (or dividing) that dimension by 1.62,[1] the other dimension may be found using the 3:5 proportion.

3. While it is easy to calculate the unknown dimensions to arrive
   at 3:5 proportions, beginners may find it more convenient to
   guess at these proportions. Of course, one should not guess
   without first learning what the proportions look like. Once that
   is learned, however, a guess may be made knowing that slight
   errors will not distort the story or picture shape. However, it is
   impractical for picture editors to size every story or picture by
   mathematical calculations. In fact, mathematical precision is
   not even a desirable goal in deciding on proportions because it
   limits artistic imagination.

   Also, most persons are not perceptive of precise mathematical proportions. But it should be obvious that a single-column
   story 11 picas wide and 64 picas long is not proportionately
   pleasing (Figure 14-4). For that reason, the page designer might
   divide that column into two equal-depth columns where the
   new dimensions would be 22.5 by 32 picas. If these dimensions
   were checked by the formula above, it would be found that the
   32-pica dimension should really be 36.450 picas (22.5 × 1.62).
   But few persons will object or complain about the difference.

4. In dividing a page, some unequal proportions should be used
   for determining the relationship of one area to another. For
   convenience a 3:5 relationship might again be used. But any
   proportion that is obvious should be avoided. Therefore, it
   would not do to divide a page in half either vertically or horizontally. The areas employed in the total design concept are

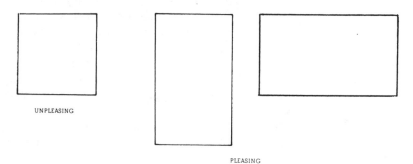

UNPLEASING

PLEASING

**Figure 14-4 Unpleasing and pleasing proportions. Story shapes look bet-
ter in the latter two shapes.**

1. 1.62 is a factor of a 3 to 4:85 relationship (most often called 3:5 for the sake
of convenience). The 3 to 4:85 relationship is also sometimes called a golden oblong
shape.

those whose proportions are critical to the aesthetic appearance of the entire page in pleasing proportions.

In determining the relationships of parts to wholes, the goal is to avoid exaggerated proportions as well. As attempts are made to have unequal dimensions there is the danger that they will become exaggerated. That is why the 3:5 proportion is suitable for most page design problems. When pleasing proportions are used on a page, the result is not only interesting but attractive.

Unity

The principle of unity concerns the effect of a page design that creates a single impression rather than multiple impressions. Stories on a unified page appear as if each contributes a significant share to the total page design. A page that does not have unity appears as a collection of stories, each of which may be fighting for the reader's attention to the detriment of a unified page appearance.

Lack of unity often results when stories are laid out from the top of the page downward. The layout editor is building a page piece by piece and cannot be sure how each story will contribute to the total page design until the layout is complete. At that point, however, the layout person may find that there is not enough time to shift stories around to achieve unity. The result is that readers may find it difficult to concentrate on any one part of a page because of too many centers of interest. A unified page, on the other hand, appears as if everything is in its correct position, and the page is therefore interesting.

How does one plan for a unified page? Through keeping the design of the entire page in mind at all times while working on any part of it. Each story, therefore, must be visually weighed against all other stories in terms of the probable appearance of the entire page. In page layouts, the editor may have to shift some stories around on the dummy until a satisfactory arrangement has been found. As with the other principles of artistic design, an appreciation of this one will have to be developed by layout editors through a sensitivity to good design.

Visualizing Total Page Structure

Although the objectives of newspaper design may be clear enough, beginners may have difficulty implementing them because they cannot visualize the structure of a page before it has been completely dummied. Sometimes, even after a page has appeared in print, beginners may not be able to see the design easily. To overcome this difficulty, they should resort to the process of drawing heavy black lines around each story on a printed page. Now the design will emerge and the editor can critically examine the total page design (see Figures 14-5, 14-6, and 14-7).

If a page is studied in the above manner occasionally, beginners

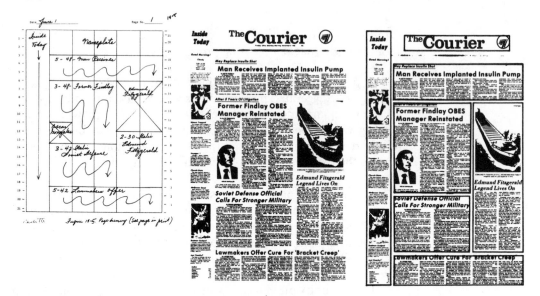

Figure 14-5   Page dummied.   Figure 14-6   Same page printed.   Figure 14-7   The design of page.
[*Courtesy of* Finlay *(Ohio)* Courier]

may be able to develop a feeling for page structure that should improve their abilities to create effective page designs.

How the Number of Pages in an Issue Is Determined

A preliminary step to page layout is the decision about how many pages an issue will have. An executive may start by considering the ratio of news to advertising. In the past a popular ratio was 40 percent news to 60 percent advertising. Today the ratio of news to advertising may be much smaller for many newspapers (30 percent news, 70 percent advertising). Although the smaller percentage of news may be used, it does not necessarily mean that less news than before is appearing in the newspaper. Because volume of advertising may be greater than before, a larger amount of news may be used in a 30:70 ratio than in a 40:60 one.

Press capacity, however, is another consideration in determining the number of pages in an issue. Some presses will print only in multiples of eight. None will print an odd number of pages without wasting space. Even for those presses that will print even numbers, there may be some objection by executives for printing an issue of, for example, 14 pages because a single loose sheet containing two pages must be inserted into a paper where three sheets are folded to print 12 pages. It is easier to increase the number of pages to 16, where four sheets of paper are folded.

When press capacity, or any other reason, requires that the volume of news or advertising be decreased, news is usually cut. Occasionally, however, an advertisement may be moved to another day in order to make the columns fit the number of pages required.

Where Page Layout Begins

Page layout is started at about the same time and place in the production of most newspapers: namely, after stories have been edited. But there are big differences from paper to paper on how layout is done, especially if computers are available. If editing is done with word-processing equipment, the editor will have a list of stories that are available for the next edition and the list can be seen on a video display screen.

On this list is the slug line for each story as an identification device. Also shown may be the headlines, the length of the stories in inches (or picas) and, perhaps, the kind of headline that it will carry (such as a two- or three-line). At times, with sophisticated computing equipment, the editor may even have sized each story with a code indicating whether it is one, two or more columns in width, rather than simply indicating its length.

The editors may use this list when they meet to decide which story to feature. Other stories are then available for filling the spaces after the main stories are positioned on a page.

If computers are not used, then someone has to keep track of all stories and then prepare a list similar to the one discussed above. However, this list like the one above eventually becomes the source of stories that are to be positioned on some page (see Figure 14-8). Usually there are stories left over that are not used on any one day.

But the list of stories becomes the source from which layout editors make their layouts.

Once a schedule of stories has been prepared, the editor is ready to lay out each page that has space remaining on it. In essence, an editor will position stories on each page dummy until most of the space has been filled. Some editors dummy only the most important stories and allow the printer (or paste-up person) to fill the remainder of the page. Others dummy the entire page. A better-looking page can be achieved if 90 percent or more of a page has been dummied because there is better control over the entire page design than in partial-page dummying.

The Mechanics of Preparing a Layout Dummy

A page dummy serves the same purpose as a blueprint—to tell the printer where to place each story, how long it will be and how it should be shaped. A goal of the layout editor should be to make the dummy as clear, accurate and concise as possible. Many dummies turn out to be a mass of scribbling rather than a neatly prepared blueprint that enables the printer to assemble type for a page with a minimum of confusion. The pressure of time is often

Slug [zone] Status		Description [Source]	5 Star/5* Final				GS	MW1 MW3
			C	D	N	S		
(Nation)			Su 9				Nu	✓
Workers pk mw3	12	Union decries parttime fed worker policy. DC, wires	K·11				✓	✓ / K·11
Clark pk mw3	22½	Outlook on Clark's successor at Interior. D^L, Maclean	K·11				✓	K·11
(Congress)	25	New Congress sworn in. DC, wires/Collin	✓				Nu	✓ / Sub 22
Growth pk mw3	7½	Nu technique helps kids grow. Boston, upi	K·11				✓	✓ / K·11
Price pk mw3	13	Will Mel Price stay as head of Armed Services? DC, Don'sky	K·11				✓	K·11
Abort pk mw3	12	Reagan statement; 2 more arrested in abortion bombings. DE, wires	✓				Nu	Su ? / Sub 13
(Clime)	13½	Snow snarls the Sunbelt wires	✓				Nu	Nu / Sub 14
Snekies pk mw3	5	Most "glass" was sugar. Ky, upi	K·11				✓	✓ / K·11
Notes	18½	About Washington column. Elsasser, Donosky	✓				Nu	✓ / ✓
Mass	12	40% of Catholics would like return of Latin. DC, ap	K·11				Nu	✓ / K·11
Seat	7	With Congress: No decision on Indiana house seat. DC, ap	To Congress					Nu / To Senate
Deaf	3	With Congress: Iowa senator asks handsign interpreter. up	✓				Nu	✓
Nuke pk mw1	10	PU REGIONAL STORY	off				✓	off / off
Heart	8	Upgrade condition to satisfactory. Ky, wires	✓				Nu	✓
JAMA	13	Study of "don't resuscitate" orders of doctors. Van	✓				Nu	✓
Westy	9	General almost ready to rest his case. NY, ap	✓				Nu	✓ / Sub 12
Scope	8	Disclose plans for world's biggest telescope. Cal, upi	✓				Nu	Sub 13
Deaver	12	Reagan aide to resign. DC, wires	✓				Nu	✓ / Sub 18

Figure 14-8 A schedule sheet used by the *Chicago Tribune*. Stories, length in inches, descriptions, and information about in which issue they will appear.

blamed for hard-to-read dummies. But the consequence of poor preparation may mean that time is wasted in the composing room when the printer tries to decipher the dummy. Therefore, every effort should be taken to make the dummy neat, accurate and concise.

Some guidelines for preparing a dummy are as follows:

1. A front page dummy is started by indicating the amount of space that the nameplate will take. (*Note:* a nameplate is the name of the newspaper that appears somewhere at the top of the front page. It is sometimes called the masthead, but that is incorrect. It is also called "the flag" by others.) Some newspapers have specially prepared dummies with space already allocated for the nameplate. Where this is not available a line should be drawn across the dummy indicating that the nameplate will occupy a certain depth.

2. Because most headlines have been assigned a number or some other designation in a headline schedule, this number and the slug for the story should be written wherever the story is to be placed on the dummy.

3. When a story with a one-column headline is noted on the dummy, the headline and slug word are indicated at the top of the story and a horizontal line is drawn across the column at the end. No arrows are needed to indicate that the story is to read in a downward direction. But when a story is continued to an adjacent column, then arrows should be used to show where the story is continued. The arrows warn the printer that the story has not been completed in the column where the headline appeared. Whenever there is some doubt about where a story is continued arrows should be used. But if they can be avoided they should be, because they tend to clutter the dummy.

4. Two-column lead paragraphs, cutlines and odd-measured stories (such as a 1½-column width) should be indicated on the layout by drawing wavy lines the width of the type. Straight lines should not be drawn as they may be confused with finish or "30" lines.

5. Pictures or cartoons should be labeled appropriately with the slug word and an indication that it is either a picture or cartoon. Some newspapers use a large X drawn to the corners of the picture to make it clear that the space is to be used for a picture and not a story.

6. Boxes are indicated by drawing a rectangle to the dimensions required and labeling the drawing with the word *box*.

7. Jumps should be indicated by the word *jump* (or RO for runover) and the page number to which the story is to be continued.

8. If a story of two or more columns reads into a single column, then a cutoff rule may be used to separate the material that appears under the headline from nonrelated material. Also, an arrow should be drawn from the headline into the appropriate column where the story is to be continued. If a banner headline reads out into a deck, this too should be indicated by an arrow.

9. Any layout arrangement that is radically different from what has been used before should be indicated with notations if there is doubt that it will be clear to the printer. Sometimes only an arrow is needed; sometimes a few words will explain the situation.

While dummying a page is important, and every editor should know how to do it, there are more important layout concepts and practices that should be known. The following material discusses some of the concepts and practices that affect the implementation of objectives for good page design.

Step by Step Instructions for Laying Out a Page

Before starting, it is assumed that a layout editor would have a good understanding of what it is that makes pages easy to read and look attractive.

Here then are steps in laying out a page.

Preliminary Step **1.** A list of stories that are available for today's edition should be studied. Presumably the editor will discuss the selection of most important stories with other editors or those who are responsible for making such decisions. The result will be that a limited number of stories will be designated for featured treatment. These stories are placed on the dummy first.

Preliminary Step **2.** Now the editor must decide precisely how these important stories will be given prominence and on which pages.

Here are some options for featuring these stories:

1. Placing the first and second most important stories in either the top left or right hand corners.
2. Boxing one large story on the front page, then placing it at either the top or bottom of the page. Or perhaps placing it above the nameplate.
3. Using a large picture with a story and positioning it all across the page horizontally (either at the top or bottom).
4. There are many other options that could be used.

Preliminary Step **3.** Decide which photos (or other kinds of art) are to be used and whether each is to be featured alone or with a story. Should the picture be boxed? Should it run in color? What kind of cutline and/or overline should it have?

Step 1. Place the art first on the page by drawing its position on the page dummy. If there are other "standing columns" place them at the same time (see Figure 14-9).

Step 2. Now place the most important stories in positions discussed above (see Figures 14-10 and 14-11).

Step 3. Stop at this point and survey the stories and art that have already been placed. Answer this question: "How can I build an attractive page design *around* the art and stories already placed?" Answer the question by dividing the remainder of the page into attractive sections, and then find stories to fill in these spaces (see Figure 14-12).

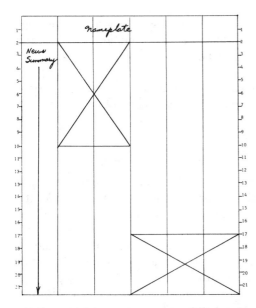

Figure 14-9 Step 1—place the art. Two photographs are positioned on the page. This practice will affect the shape of the number one story.

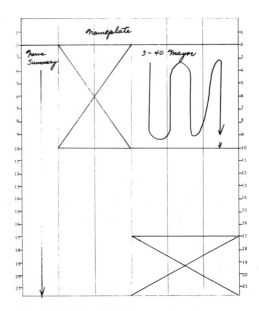

Figure 14-10 Step 2—position the most important story.

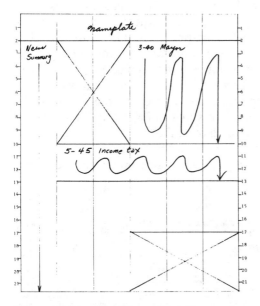

Figure 14-11 Step 3—position the number two story. At this point the layout person must visual the remainder of the page. There are alternative designs that could be used at this point.

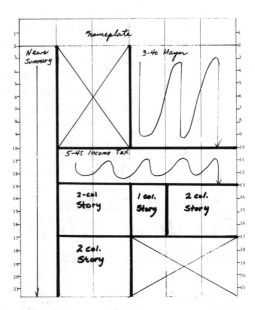

Figure 14-12 Step 4—draw lines to indicate the nature of the page design. Fill in with stories. A number of alternative designs could have been used.

Step 4. The result of No. 3 above will be a tentative page arrangement that may need to be revised a bit through trial and error until the right combination of stories and art end in an attractive and readable page.

Now the layout person can be assured that the most important stories are properly featured, and the remainder of the page is attractive.

Important Considerations in Page Layout

The following pages cover some important considerations that affect the layout of a page. They are very specific and fall under the heading of the mechanics of page layout.

Vertical and Horizontal Designs

A major consideration in layouts is the appearance of story shapes. In past years, story shapes have not been a major consideration of layout editors. But within recent years, when editors sought ways of making pages more attractive, story shapes have become important. The selection of the most appropriate shapes involves a number of considerations. The first one has to do with preventing a page from becoming one-directional. If there are too many vertically shaped stories all leading the reader's eyes downward, then the page looks old-fashioned and unattractive. Newspapers circa 1850 were all vertical in shape, and vertical makeup is distinctly old-fashioned. To avoid verticalness, an attempt should be made to achieve horizontal layout. Horizontal layout is distinguished by the fact that stories are continued into three or more adjacent columns and the shape of such stories is horizontal. Although a story may be continued into the next adjacent column, this does not necessarily produce horizontal layout because the shape of the story may be vertical. Another distinguishing feature of horizontal layout is that stories are squared off at the bottom. This means that the depth of each column where the story is continued is the same (Figure 14-13). However, a page using horizontally shaped stories

'Famous' on Way, Says Adams

Fabulous Beltline Development Seen

By ART THOMASON
Telegraph Staff Writer
A gigantic Christmas package was opened Wednesday at a Pride, Inc., meeting and it contained millions of dollars in future development along the Beltline Highway, including a Famous-Barr store in an enclosed mall shopping center.

Alton developer Homer Adams told the Pride board "unequivocally" that Famous-Barr will build a department store and mall containing 600,000 square feet under roof.

The announcement by Adams was the first official confirmation that Famous-Barr would build on the site located on the southeast corner of the Beltline and Seminary Road.

Famous-Barr, the parent store of the May Co., is one of the nation's largest retailers.

The May Co. is currently building one of its Venture Department discount stores on the northwest corner of Seminary and the beltline. Adams, too, developed the Venture project.

Adams said a separate development from Seminary west to Washington Avenue along the Beltline also is planned. The tract includes 14 sites designed for small businesses and not connected with the shopping center.

The shopping center will be the largest in the Alton area with enough parking for 5,000 cars, he said.

Adams also forecast that Beltline development should boost the immediate Alton area population to 100,000 by the 1970's.

The developer outlined other future development for the Beltline, some of it already under construction, including the Belscot Shopping Center, an amalgamation of the Bell Scott department stores; a Tri-City Grocery Co. store in the same shopping center complex which is under construction on the south side of the beltline near Buckmaster Lane. They were:

(1) A gigantic motor city — an elaborately designed outlay of businesses that sell anything with a motor;

(2) A 10-acre recreational center that will hopefully feature the Cinerama design, with inside recreational facilities and a large civic center;

(3) Conversion of the old brickyard at Alby Street Road into a 200-acre light industrial park, called the North Port Industrial Park;

(4) The Veterans of Foreign Wars Legion Post home, just north of the Beltline on Alby Street Road;

(5) A MacDonald's hamburger restaurant, now nearing completion near Washington Ave.;

(6) A Taco's restaurant that will feature Mexican dishes;

(7) A new Christian Science edifice near the Temple Israel, between Pierce and Levis lanes.

Adams promised that the development connected with his firm would use sophisticated landscaping techniques to protect residential areas and enhance the natural beauty.

For example, the developer pointed out that the Central Hardware Store, Bettendorfs and the Venture Store will be virtually screened from the view of residential areas behind it by using a landscaping plan that will beautify the area.

Figure 14-13   Horizontally shaped story. [*Courtesy of* Alton *(Ill.)* Evening Telegraph]

exclusively may be as monotonous as one where all stories are vertically shaped. The best looking pages have a mixture of shapes (Figure 14-14).

Figure 14-14 A page that shows both vertical and horizontal design. [*Courtesy of the* Boston *(Mass.)* Globe]

Avoiding Odd-Shaped Stories

A second consideration in layout should be that of avoiding odd-shaped stories. In traditional layout many stories are not squared off and take odd shapes. One such shape looks like an "inverted L" (Figure 14-15). It is caused by using a two- or three-column headline over a one-column story. The effect is like an upside-down "L." It may also be called an "uneven wrap" (see section on

Negro Clergyman Defeated

Council of Churches Picks Woman Leader

From Our Wire Services

DETROIT, Dec. 4. — Dr. Cynthia Wedel, an Episcopalian and ardent advocate of women's rights, won overwhelmingly over a Negro clergyman Thursday to become the first woman president of the National Council of Churches.

Mrs. Wedel, of Washington, defeated the Rev. Albert B. Cleage Jr. of Detroit 387-93 in secret balloting at the NCC's triennial general assembly.

When the vote was announced, Mr. Cleage, the first Negro candidate for the presi-

Profile and Picture
On Page 3

dency, went to a microphone on the assembly floor and castigated what he called the "White racist establishment of the NCC."

"This organization is anti-Christ and until young people or oppressed people take over, you'll remain anti-Christ" Mr. Cleage declared. "Time is

Korean Report Raps Operation of Center By Buck Foundation

By EDWARD N. EISEN
Of The Inquirer Staff

The State Commission on Charitable Organizations made the Pearl S. Buck Foundation produce a letter Thursday from Korea's embassy highly critical of the foundation's work in that country.

The letter, by Sung Kwoo Kim, counsel and consul general at the embassy in Washington, said a 10-day inspection in August at the foundation's Sosa Opportunities Center, west of Seoul, showed unsanitary conditions, overcrowding, misuse of funds and other shortcomings.

REASONS DIVULGED

The letter was produced at a commission hearing on the foundation's appeal for a license to solicit funds in Pennsylvania. The foundation was to have presented new evidence, as demanded by Joseph J. Kelley Jr., Secretary of the Commonwealth.

Figure 14-15   These are uneven wraps that are typical of traditional layouts.

wraps that follows). When more than one uneven wrap is used on a page, it tends to destroy the simplicity of the design. When an uneven wrap is used at the upper right-hand side and another one in the upper left side, the design becomes complex. Other stories and pictures must fit around these shapes and it is not an easy task. For example, the space underneath an uneven wrapped story in the right-hand column usually requires a picture to fill the space underneath the headline. If another headline is placed underneath the upper headline, the result may be unattractive. To avoid uneven wrapped stories, the layout editor should either use a single-column headline over a one-column story or wrap a story to the number of columns that the headline covers. A three-column headline then would have a story wrapped underneath for three columns, presumably, and squared off.

Another kind of odd shape is one in which a story is continued to adjacent columns but each column depth containing the story is a different length (Figure 14-16). Such shapes also tend to make the page look unattractive.

Wraps

A major consideration in layout is the problem of what to do with stories that must be continued into adjacent columns. Should they be jumped or wrapped into the next right-hand column? Jumps are undesirable for reasons given earlier. The best procedure is to wrap (or turn[2]) a story underneath a headline or a two-column lead paragraph. If the wrap is under a headline as shown in Figure 14-17, it should be very clear to the reader where the second column has been continued. Some editors, however, prefer to start a story with a two-column lead paragraph and wrap the second column under

[2] A *turn* is another name for a *wrap*.

SAIGON (AP) — Gen. William C. Westmoreland, departing after four years in command of U.S. forces in Vietnam, said today American strength was greater than ever "but it is unrealistic to expect a quick and easy defeat of the Hanoi-led enemy."

"If he feels time is on his side, he can go on a long time," Westmoreland said of the enemy in a farewell news conference on the eve of his departure to become Army chief of staff in Washington.

He added that he could not predict what would happen at the peace talks in Paris, but from his view the enemy still appeared to be in search of major military victory.

"Price Can Be Raised"

Westmoreland said he felt that a classical military victory was not possible in South Vietnam in view of U.S. policy decisions not to escalate the war or to enlarge its geographic boundaries.

He added: "But the enemy can be attrited, the price can be raised. It is being raised to the point that it could be intolerable for the enemy. It may reach the point of the question of the destruction of his country, and jeopardizing the future of his country, if he continues to pay

the price he is now paying and destined to pay in the future."

Westmoreland said the enemy had lost 113,000 men since the first of the year and added "he doesn't have the manpower or resources to take these losses in stride."

Sees Net Reduction

Westmoreland said that although infiltration continued at a serious pace down the Ho Chi Minh trail through Laos, the Hanoi government was not able to make up its manpower losses in the South and that since midsummer last year enemy strength had shown a net reduction.

He said Hanoi's strategy appeared to be to continue pressure against Saigon and its political structure and to seek some major victory on the battlefield.

Westmoreland departs tomorrow and will turn over the Saigon command to his deputy for the past year, Gen. Creighton Abrams Jr.

"At this time our military posture is at its height since our commitment," he said. "We are now capable of bringing major military pressure on the enemy.

"This we are doing, and the enemy is beginning to show the effect. The Vietnamese armed forces are growing stronger in size and effectiveness."

Headquarters Farewell

Earlier today, Westmoreland said goodbye with a "good luck and bless you all" to the officers and men of his headquarters.

"Please accept my very best wishes for continued success," Westmoreland told his staff,

"and my fervent hope that peace and security for the long suffering and freedom loving people of Vietnam will soon reward your efforts."

In his swing north yesterday, Westmoreland visited the headquarters of the South Vietnamese Army's 1st Military Corps in Da Nang, took a helicopter to Provisional Corps headquarters at Phu Bai 35 miles away, and visited the headquarters of the 3rd U.S. Marine Amphibious Force.

He wound up his tour with a flight to the nuclear carrier Enterprise in the Gulf of Tonkin to bid farewell to the U.S. 7th Fleet.

Figure 14-16   An odd-shaped story created to allow two one-column heads to be placed on each side of the protruding bottom leg without butting. This is an example of poor layout.

Bethlehem directors OK drydock work

The Bethlehem Steel Corp. board of directors officially plunged the company into the Pleasure Island drydock project by stamping its approval on the months of work by company officials.

Richard E. Blackinton, general manager of operations and facilities for Bethlehem Steel, said the operating agreement between Bethlehem and the Port of Port Arthur "still contains some details that have to be worked out, but things are proceeding on schedule."

He anticipates the drydock will be working by the end of March.

Plans call for transporting the drydock from Pearl Harbor, assembling it on Pleasure Island, and relocating and rebuilding about a mile of Texas 82.

Blackinton said the Army Corps of Engineers received

four objections to the drydock project but that he didn't expect them to delay corps approval of the dredging and operating permits.

Blackinton said one response came from the Environmental Protection Agency — which had questions not objections — and that Bethlehem was preparing an answer.

Karen Brown, a public information assistant with the Environmental Protection Agency in Dallas, said the agency questioned a private firm using a designated corps spoils area for disposing of dredge materials. Other questions by EPA involve whether Bethlehem considered other ways to dispose the dredge material, if a sediment analysis of the dredge material was conducted and if the drydock would cause adverse impact on area water quality.

Figure 14-17   Squaring off stories brings about a module.

Lorelei McDonald bride
of Jeffrey Earl Hammer

The wedding of Lorelei Shavonne McDonald, daughter of Mr. and Mrs. Lewis S. McDonald, 4313 Defiance Pike, Wayne, and Jeffrey Earl Hammer, son of Mr. and Mrs. Raymond Hammer, Gibsonburg, was solemnized Friday in St. Michael's Church. The Rev. Ray C. Przybyla officiated. The bride was given away by her father.

Altar decorations were two vases of yellow gladioli, ice blue carnations and white pompons with brown fall leaves.

With her lace-trimmed white wedding gown she wore a veil gathered to a lace bandeau and carried an old fashioned round bouquet of stephanotis, yellow silk rosebuds with baby's breath and ivy.

Her attendants were Mrs. Darlene Lentz of Bradner, matron of honor; and bridesmaids Mrs. Gary (Elaine) Lentz, Mrs. Alan (Patty) Adams and Ann Lentz, all of Bradner, and the bride's cousin, Mrs. Fred (Pam) Berno of Arcadia. Their colonial bouquets were light blue cosmos, white pompons and yellow silk rosebuds with baby's breath and ivy. The flower girl was the bride's niece, Michelle Cron of Portage.

The couple are at home at 110 County Road 26, Gibsonburg.

The bride, an Elmwood High School graduate, is employed at Fremont Memorial Hospital. The groom, who graduated from Gibsonburg High School, is employed by G.M. Sader Construction Co. of Bowling Green.

Figure 14-18   A wrap under a two-column lead paragraph. No cut-off rule is used at the top of the short leg. But some editors prefer such a rule.

the lead. In such situations, there are two variations in common use: (1) wrapping the second column with a cut-off rule to separate the wrap from the lead or (2) wrapping the second column without a cut-off rule as shown in Figure 14-18. The first technique is preferred. It is unfortunate that many editors have abandoned both of these techniques in the interest of saving production time. However, the benefits in graphic design outweigh the benefits in production time, and the practice of using two-column leads is a good one.

When a story is wrapped underneath a picture there is little danger of confusing the reader, so a cut-off rule is usually unnecessary (see Figure 14-19).

When a story is wrapped into an adjacent column at the top of a page without a covering headline it is called a raw wrap. In many instances raw wraps are undesirable and are forbidden at all times by some newspapers. The makeup editor faced with a raw wrap should ask that a headline be written to cover the wrap and make it clear that the wrap belongs to the headline above it. But occa-

Killer storm cuffs Rockies, Midwest

Associated Press

A winter storm already blamed for 11 deaths stretched from the southern Rockies to the upper Midwest today after burying parts of Arizona and Colorado under 20 inches of snow, unleashing tornadoes in Texas and downing ice-laden power lines in Kansas.

Six inches of new snow were already on the ground today in Kansas and Nebraska, and forecasters said more was on the way.

Raging thunderstorms spun off at least two tornadoes that damaged more than 100 homes and businesses in Texas yesterday and motorists in the western part of the state were warned that snow and freezing rain today would make driving hazardous.

In the Pacific Northwest, meanwhile, travelers' advisories were posted for the Cascade Mountains of Washington and Oregon as a new storm gathered strength in the Gulf of Alaska.

The mercury tumbled to 15 degrees below zero overnight in West Yellowstone, Mont., but in the East more than a dozen cities reported record high temperatures yesterday.

The storm that dumped up to 20 inches of snow over the southern Rockies yesterday, closing schools in parts of Colorado and Arizona and surprising residents as far south as Tucson, brought more snow but lesser accumulations to New Mexico and northeast Arizona.

"It's all going to slowly push east, but its hard to say how quickly," Steve Corfidi of the National Severe Storms Forecast Center in Kansas City, Mo., said today. "It's a more pronounced pattern than you normally

Associated Press

A tornado yesterday in Mesquite, Texas, damaged more than a dozen houses and business-es. It first touched down in Ferris, a community 25 miles southeast of Dallas.

expect . . . an interesting pattern. It keeps us busy."

Since Tuesday, the weather has been blamed for the deaths of seven motorists in Colorado, two in a 23-car pileup during a blinding dust storm yesterday about 70 miles southeast of Los Angeles, two in Oklahoma on slick roads and three in a fog bank in southeast Georgia.

Up to a foot of snow fell last night at Hawley Lake in Arizona's White Mountains, and 10 inches fell at Flagstaff in northern Arizona.

Thunderstorms raked north-central Texas yesterday, spawning tornadoes that damaged more than 100 homes Crow.

In Kansas, Wichita authorities said 15,000 homes and businesses temporarily lost electricity last night, as freezing rain snapped power lines. Service was restored within a few hours to about 12,000 residences, but Kansas Gas and Electric Co. officials said the rest were expected to go

Figure 14-19   A wrap underneath a photograph.

sionally it is permissible to use a raw wrap at the top of an advertisement where there is no doubt in the reader's mind that the wrap belongs to the headline on the left (Figure 14-20).

When there is not enough time to reset a headline to a wider column measure, another layout procedure is to avoid having to make wraps by filling the remaining space with stories of shorter length. Or, perhaps, a longer story can be shortened by cutting off some of the longer stories and combining them with fillers.

In dummying a page care should be taken to avoid the kind of wrap shown in Figure 14-21 where the reader is asked to jump from the bottom of a page to the very top above the ad. The size of the ad makes it appear as if the story has ended at the bottom. The makeup person should either cut the story and end it at the

Diabetes and
blood pressure

About a year and a half ago my doctor said I had high blood pressure and put me on medicine. In a short time my tests showed I was low on potassium, and he put me on potassium medicine and gradually increased it because my level was so low.

Then he did a glucose test and said I'm a borderline diabetic. If I understand what I read, sometimes when there is no diabetes in the family and it shows up, it can be caused by high blood pressure medicine. Is this so?

If my blood pressure is causing the problem why can't they just give me other medicines? I know there are

The doctor says
by Lawrence E. Lamb, M.D.

other medicines they can use.

Also, I'm 52 and going through the menopause. I'm somewhat overweight and trying to lose, as I need surgery for a bladder repair. I have a fibroid

tumor, so the doctor won't give me hormones for my hot flashes. He says it will cause me to bleed badly. Is it true that fibroid tumors sometimes dry up after the change in life? I have been to two doctors, and one says surgery now, the other to wait until I get my weight down.

I see you are really having a time. First, please make every effort to lose weight as it may help relieve your blood pressure and high blood sugar problems. Why don't you try my weight losing diet? It has helped a lot of people to lose weight. Send 90 cents for The Health Letter number 4-7, Weight Losing Diet. Address your letter to me in care of Paddock Publications, Radio City Station, New York, N. Y. 10019.

You are right, some high blood pressure medicines will cause the blood sugar to be high. It is often stated, though, that they merely unmask an underlying diabetic, but you are beginning to get on theoretical ground there. The same types of

medicine can and will cause the loss of potassium. And I would tend to agree that there are other medicines that could be used. The medicine used to eliminate salt and water that causes these problems, though, is very useful in combination with other medicines. The combination usually makes it possible to handle a patient's problem without so much risk of complications from the medicines.

Another problem with glucose tolerance tests is that they will give a result similar to that in diabetic if the person has not been eating any carbohydrates recently. Unless the patient is properly prepared for the test, it is of limited usefulness.

Estrogen hormones do enable fibroids to grow. If they are just under the lining of the uterus, hormones may cause you to bleed. And, some fibroids do shrink after the menopause. In general people do better

during and after surgery if they have no weight problems. Nevertheless when it needs to be done surgery can be done in really quite heavy people. I suspect your surgeon thinks he will get a better result if he is able to operate after you have lost weight.

Meanwhile I would suggest making every effort you can to lose weight to try to get out of this combined mess you are confronted with.

(Newspaper Enterprise Assn.)

Figure 14-20   A naked wrap at the top of a page. A headline should cover such wraps.

Weekend garden show attracts 500 visitors

Figure 14-21   A wrap from the bottom to the top of a page column four. This should be avoided.

bottom (placing a new story above the ad) or find a shorter story to place at the left of the ad.

Filling Remaining Space

When most of the page has been dummied, the makeup procedure is complete. Small spaces may remain because all stories did not fit precisely. The page dummy is sent to the composing room where a printer begins to assemble type and pictures into a page form. The remaining space may be filled in two ways: (1) If the space is large enough, fillers may be used. Editors assign someone the responsibility for seeing that there are a sufficient number of fillers available each day. (2) If the space is relatively small, then it is filled by leading. Leading is added between paragraphs until the column is filled.

Flexibility in Layout In planning the layout of large newspapers, some attention should be given to flexibility of design to accommodate late-breaking news. There are two considerations in planning for a flexible design. The first one is a mechanical consideration. Can one or two stories be replaced without too much effort? Remaking a page is a task that should be accomplished in the shortest amount of time to meet a press deadline. It may be necessary to rejustify as many as six columns of news in order to accommodate a late story. When the story to be replaced is odd-shaped, involving complex wraps, it will take more time to remake than it might if it were simply shaped. The new story may not be as long as the one it replaces, or it may be longer. Therefore, planning must be geared to making the design simple and flexible enough for any contingency.

A second consideration is the effect that a major story change will have on total page design. Although it is impossible to know how a late-breaking story will be shaped, it may be possible to anticipate how various-shaped stories will affect the design. If the original design is simple, chances are that any changes can be adapted easily to the old design without destroying the original appearance.

Additional Layout Considerations

Positioning of Nameplates The nameplate of a newspaper (often incorrectly called the masthead) is the name usually appearing at the top of Page One. Editors sometimes want to move the nameplate to other positions on the page because they assume that readers know the name of the newspaper they are reading and the space occupied by the nameplate might be better used for other purposes. Once a decision has been made to move the nameplate, then a question arises: Where on the page would the nameplate be most appropriate? Editors sometimes want to move it indiscriminately, considering the significance of news the most important criterion for positioning stories. Such editors feel that the nameplate is much less significant and therefore may be moved anywhere at almost any time. At other times, the nameplate seems to be moved around on Page One without any apparent reason.

On one hand, the logic of moving it from day to day seems reasonable. After all, most readers know the name of the newspaper without looking at the nameplate. But on the other hand, there are a number of reasons for keeping it in the top position most of the time. In debating the reasonableness of moving it around on the front page, one must consider all the purposes a nameplate serves.

Other than for simple identification purposes, a nameplate communicates the philosophical position of the publisher. The typefaces chosen for nameplates usually are distinguished looking and have strong connotations. The best position for communicating these connotations is at the top of the page because the top position itself communicates a feeling of authority. Any object standing foremost among other objects is judged to be more significant. When an object is buried, its importance is diminished.

But another consideration has to do with the importance of top position in serving as a device that provides readers with a feeling of stability as they read the paper. The nameplate usually represents the starting point for examining the contents of Page One. If it is not in its traditional position, readers may sometimes have a sense of uneasiness and a slight loss of familiarity with the paper. Whereas they know the news may change, the nameplate position will not, and the result is a page whose stability tends to make reading comfortable.

Furthermore, postal regulations require that a newspaper indicate that it is second-class material somewhere within the first five pages of the paper. In the past, this material might be placed in the editorial page masthead, or it might be buried in a box on Page 2. But it is also placed in small type near the nameplate, perhaps within the dateline rules that appear underneath it. If the nameplate serves this purpose, then it should remain at the top.

A final reason for keeping the nameplate at the top relates to its function in the total page design. A nameplate floated down in the page becomes a component of the page's design and thereby complicates the process of makeup and design. It is usually easier to make up a front page when the nameplate is at the top, with some exceptions of course.

Yet there is some logic to defend the decision to move it if the move is not radical and if it is not done often. There are times when a six-column, horizontally arranged story might well be placed above the nameplate. This story may be of such significance that the editors want to be sure that everyone sees it. The very top position should provide such assurance. But if this practice becomes regular, the importance of the nameplate is thereby diminished (Figure 14-22).

There is also some logic to support the idea that a nameplate may be moved from side to side, but always at the top of the page. One of the most unsightly makeup devices of newspapers are the

Figure 14-22 News stories above a nameplate.

ears. The editor may eliminate them, by moving the nameplate to either side of the page and moving a one- or two-column story to the top. Another reason for moving the nameplate to the side may be to make room for more news than would be possible otherwise. Perhaps the editors who are most likely to experiment with moving the nameplate are those involved with publishing college newspapers. Their decisions to move it sometimes is based on the need to be creative. What is creative, however, may not be easy to read.

There are other uses for nameplates throughout the newspaper, but these do not involve moving the front page nameplate. For example, some newspapers have identical nameplates on pages one and three. The effect of this arrangement is to present a second front page to readers so that different kinds of news may be featured on each front page. Although national news might be used exclusively on Page One, local news might be featured on Page Three.

Finally, there are modified nameplates that may be used in various sections of the newspaper. Family, sports or financial pages also might have special nameplates. In reality, however, these are standing headlines rather than nameplates, and although they are designed to resemble the front page nameplate, their function is to introduce special sections of the newspaper.

Contemporary Headline Placement

The traditional-minded layout editor thinks of headlines in terms of large display typefaces placed at the top of stories. This treatment is logical for pages designed to be strongly vertical in appearance. But when makeup is conceived of as being horizontal through the use of rectangularly shaped stories, headlines may be set in many different ways. These ways not only serve the purpose of summarizing the news but of making the page appear modern.

When horizontally shaped stories are used on a page, the headline may be placed in at least three places, and possibly a fourth. It may be placed at the left- or right-hand side, the center, or the bottom of the story. The last-named position is not as desirable as the others, but all are different from the traditional top position (Figures 14-23, 14-24 and 14-25).

Pachyderms perform as the GOP does Dallas

DALLAS (AP) — Elephants wearing red-white-and-blue dresses.

Elephants playing the harmonica.

Elephants waving American flags with their trunks.

A 700-pound elephant sculpted from Buick and Mercury bumpers.

The Republican National Convention, to get under way Aug. 20 here, is creating a virtual run on pachyderms.

Take 6-year-old "Kenya" of Africa, for instance. She's all booked up from Aug. 16 to Aug. 24.

Kenya will appear under the patriotic stage name of Betsy at the trendy Galleria shopping center wearing red, white and blue.

"She plays a harmonica," animal talent agency owner Chere Hickock told the Dallas Times Herald.

Unfortunately, the national anthem isn't in Kenya's er, Betsy's repertoire, Hickock said.

"She doesn't do any songs," Hickock explained.

Kenya/Betsy is also planning on a few parties, Hickock said: "We'll go to a party for a couple of hours and charge $400."

Fashionable Neiman-Marcus is not about to be outdone. Neiman spokeswoman Carolyn Cobb said there will be an elephant at a party at the downtown store on Aug. 19, the day before the convention begins.

After the party, the elephant will grace the store's display windows, Cobb added.

"Abu" is another Dallas-area elephant who will be donning his party duds next month.

Abu who stands 7 feet tall, weighs 7,000 pounds and needs an 18-wheel rig to get around town — has the Dallas Welcoming Committee reception downtown in Thanksgiving Square tentatively penciled in on his social calendar.

Even Republican delegates who eschew the parties, shopping extravaganzas and receptions will be seeing elephants before it's all over.

Oscar Pumpin, a self-described "heavy-metal" sculptor, has fashioned 80 scrap Buick and Mercury bumpers into a welded elephant that will stand outside the Dallas Convention Center.

Sen. John Tower, the Texas Republican who'll retire soon, will accept the statue on behalf of the GOP at a champagne-and-peanuts ceremony on Aug. 12.

The bumper beast, which was commissioned by a Dallas developer, is the largest Pumpin has ever made. Pumpin said he plans move it from his New York studio to Dallas — a 1,660-mile drive — this weekend.

Pumpin apparently has yet to meet Kenya, Dallas' harmonica-playing pachyderm. Pumpin said he gave his elephant a "normal elephant expression. Bland and bored."

Figure 14-23 Headline at left of a story.

China-watchers see shift from Mao revolution

By Tillman Durdin

HONG KONG—China-watchers are inclined to believe the Mao Tse-Tung-inspired Great Proletarian Cultural Revolution on the Communist mainland is at long last becoming a spent force.

Recent developments represent a decided gain for right-wing forces and a sharp setback for the radical aims and the most ardent partisans of the revolution as it was originally conceived.

FOREIGN REPORT

Directives from Peking in the last two months widen still further the authority and the latitude of the military of conservative, bureaucratic elements allied to the military in a common desire to bring order and stability out of the chaos generated by the revolution.

The Red Guards and other "rebel" revolutionaries have been the instrument and power base of the so-called Cultural Revolution group in Peking, a directorate headed by Chen Po-Tan, an intimate of Communist party Chairman Mao Tse-Tung, with Mao's wife, Chiang Ching, its deputy director.

In late 1966 and early 1967 the Red Guards and other radicals were on effective force.

They rampaged about the country spreading and mercilessly enforcing the tenets of the new Maoism, disrupting the old power structure at all levels, 'dragging out" the old power-holders for detnunciation and dismissal, staging massive demonstrations and fomenting a profound revolutionary climate.

Early in the game, however, these vanguard elements revealed what eventually became their greatest weakness and the cause of their downfall. They developed factions that began to fight each other in struggles and disputes over what was and who genuinely represented the Cultural Revolution and the Maoist philosophy.

In many cases officials threatened by the Cultural Revolution formed protective Red Guards of their own. These were set against guard groups seeking their ouster.

Since all groups, as well as the officals backing them, professed boundless loyalty to the revolution and Mao, it became difficult, indeed, often impossible, for officials and army men not directly involved to tell if any one Red Guard group was more genuinely Maoist than another and which to favor.

The faction fighting added chaos to turmoil.

Last fall the Peking leadership, under pressure from the army and moderates, authorized the military to move in and restore order. There was relative stability over the winter, but the Cultural Revolution's left-wing reasserted itself again this summer and the predictable faction-fighting flared up again on a national scale.

The regime now has authorized another crackdown, once more presumably because of arguments from military leaders and the Maoist right wing that to let the mounting strife go on would risk national disintegration.

This time the measures taken to subordinate the Red Guards and other revolutionaries of the left may mean the coup de grace for this sector of the Cultural Revolution.

Even Mao-Tse-Tung, whose concept of the revolution is "leftist and radical," has had to admit disillusionment with the Red Guards. Reliable Peking sources report here that he broke down and wept in a session with five Red Guard leaders in Peking in late July during which he bitterly condemned them for their disunity and failure to carry through effectively revolutionary objectives.

Mao has, reluctantly, it can be assumed, given his signature to directives which have authorized military units to suppress faction-fighting with arms, if necessary, normalize railway traffic, particularly along the Vietnam supply route through Kwangsi, and push through the formation of new power organs, or revolutionary committees, in provinces where they had not been organized at the end of July.

Closely related to these measures was a directive from Mao which proclaimed workers and peasants, backed by the army, as the leading force in the Cultural Revolution. Student Red Guards along with older intellectuals have been told they must integrate with the workers and peasants in a subordinate status.

Figure 14-24 Headline in the center-top of a story.

by dennis wheeler

With Thanksgiving approaching, it is that time again to pause and consider the historical background for one of our most beloved holidays.

The Thanksgiving story, known to most of us from our earliest grade school days, is one of bravery in the face of giant adversity; one of achievement in the hour of supreme testing. It inspires reverence and hope in all of us. It is one of the true roots of our well-known American stick-to-itness.

You all remember, of course, how it happened back there in 1621. The Pilgrims had arrived at Plymouth Rock and had established their tiny foothold on the wild North American continent. Their lives beset by disease and tribulation, they managed to survive for some months. And then came winter, and near starvation. And the first Thanksgiving, at which the noble Pilgrims raised their eyes heavenward to thank the Almighty for providing them with enough food to make it through the long night of winter.

THOSE, OF COURSE, are the bare facts of the Thanksgiving tale. But people sometimes lose sight of how the Plymouth Rock adventure fit into the larger fabric of history. They overlook what was going on in the rest of the world: they forget against what historical backdrop the Pilgrim landscape was painted.

Well, I can help. A history buff of sorts, I can supply some of this additional information, the better to illuminate our heritage.

First of all, remember that the Pilgrims landed in North America at about the same time that old Will Shakespeare was writing his stuff back in England. In fact, some historians surmise that when Shakespeare wrote the famous line "Out, out, brief candle!" in MacBeth, he was referring to Candle Mather, the famous Bible-thumping leader of the Pilgrims, who was expelled from England by the King for complicity in burning Joan of Arc at the stake.

IT IS ALSO noteworthy that the landing of the Pilgrims took place shortly after the English defeated the Spanish in the famous sea battle of 1588. that's the one in which Sir Francis Tarkenton defeated the Spanish Armadillo mainly because the captains of the Armadillo's ships lost the toss and had to fight into the wind.

That's important because if the Armadillo had won, we might all be speaking Spanish today instead of English. But then on the other hand it is questionable whether the Spanish could have colonized North America as successfully as the English did. The Spanish are, after all, warm weather people, so they probably would have taken one look at cold Plymouth Rock and said, "No way, senors."

Besides, everybody knows you can't raise tacos in New England.

And don't forget the French.

AT THIS TIME, the French, led by Father University of Marquette and Louis XVI Joliet were selling booze to the Indians and canoeing down the Cal-Sag canal. One wonders what would have happened if communications in those days had been what they are today. If they were, the French would have heard on the 6 o'clock news that the Pilgrims had landed in Massachusetts, and (knowing them) they would have built the Erie canal across the Appalachian mountains and invaded Massachusetts from the west. Who knows? The battle of Bunker Hill could have happened 150 years early. I ask you: if that had occurred, where would Boston be today? In Montreal, that's where.

Not only that, we'd be speaking French today instead of English. Which means the entertainment center of New Orleans would be called be the German Quarter.

Why the German Quarter? Well, it's obvious. Because at about the same time the Pilgrims landed, the 73rd battle for Alsace-Lorraine was being waged between the French and the Germans in the Black Forest. The Germans won that one, and in the subsequent Peace of Westphalia, Adolph Hitler was able to wrest huge territorial concessions from the losing Frenchmen. And among these would have been a piece of New Orleans, which had just been explored by University of Marquette and Louis XIV Joliet and claimed for France.

AND IT would have stuck, because you can grow saurkraut in a bayou.

But let's not jump so lightly over the Indians in this analysis. Remember, the Indians were here first, before any of these other guys, unless you want to count the Vikings, who under the leadership of Eric the Weird invaded the continent in the 11th Century, tried unsuccessfully to turn New York harbor into a fiord, and left in disgust two days later.

Most historians agree the Indians could have easily held on to North America against all European intruders if they had done just three things:

Dumped the tea into Boston harbor themselves instead of letting revolutionaires dressed up as Indians do it. Every-Everybody knows the economy of the colonies would have buckled under without tea.

— LISTENED, WHEN Sitting Bull solemnly warned, "You can't trust no white men" instead of retorting, "Sitting, that's a lot of Bull."

— Let Custer go instead of massacring him. Custer was such a lousy general he would have lost the West without any help from anybody.

But no. The Indians chose instead to attack trains and observe treaties. It was the latter act, of course, that spelled their downfall.

But what does all this have to do with Thanksgiving?

Well, it's simple. It all shows how differently the loose end of the sweater of history might have unraveled. It shows that almost any combination of events, had they occurred even a little differently, could have resulted in there being no Thanksgiving at all.

AND THAT would have been a terrible shame.

Because one thing is crystal clear: you can readily grow thankfulness for our many blessings anywhere in the North American continent.

. . . Thanksgiving's Place in History?

Figure 14-25 Headline at the bottom of a story.

If the headline is placed at the side of a story, it looks best if it aligns with the top line of body type. But the headline may be set flush left or flush right, both being contemporary treatments. The best position is at the left side of stories because readers proceed from the left to the right. Occasionally, the headline may look attractive when placed at the right.

When a story is given horizontal treatment and it is long, the headline may be embedded in the center with type on all sides. There is some danger that readers could be confused by this arrangement if they start reading directly underneath the headline instead of starting at the top of the left-hand column. To avoid that, the layout person must not start a sentence directly underneath the headline. This arrangement also requires the typesetter to plan typesetting around the headline. Because such treatment takes extra time, it is used primarily for feature stories.

Finally, a headline may be placed at the bottom of a story when the story is clearly set off from the remainder of the page, such as in a large box. When the headline is at the bottom of the box, it will be apparent that it belongs to the story above. If not set inside a box, there is a possibility the readers may assume it belongs to some other story. (See Figure 14-25).

Treatment of Lead Paragraphs

Lead paragraphs of most stories consist of placing the first paragraph at the top of a story set in type sizes that are larger than body type and, sometimes, leaded. The widths of most lead paragraphs are the same as body type, although occasionally they are set one or even two columns wider than the body type. Lead paragraphs are often made to stand out not only from the headlines above them but from the body type below.

In contemporary newspaper design, however, some lead paragraphs are often given more prominence than they would receive in traditional design. The feeling is that because lead paragraphs have replaced the old headline decks, they deserve more prominence. Decks were formerly used to summarize a story, each deck featuring one outstanding aspect of that story. The lead paragraph, by employing more words set in smaller-sized type than decks, did a better job of summarizing the essential details. But as lead paragraphs came into common use, they were often accorded no better type treatment than body type. In contemporary design, some have been made more dramatic in appearance and placed in more obvious positions relative to the remainder of the story.

When headlines are moved to the sides, center or bottom of a story, the lead paragraphs may be placed underneath the headline. However, in such cases, they should be set in a typeface and size that clearly contrasts with the remainder of the body type. Because the goal is to give them display treatment, the difference between lead paragraph appearance should be marked (Figure 14-26). The typeface should be one or two points larger than body type, set in

Earthwatch

Looking for something a little different to do on your vacation this year? Earthwatch can find you some work to do, helping scientists with menial — but worthwhile — tasks all over the world. How about counting ants? Or recording the habits of the spotted hyena?

By Daniel Q. Haney

BELMONT, Mass. (AP) — For $1,000 or so, people buy the opportunity to lie on their bellies in 150-degree heat and count ants. Or, if it seems more attractive, they find out whether they can fool wild llamas by lugging their dung heaps back and forth.

his wife, Eleanor, consider themselves to be conservationists, so they picked a bird banding trip to Panama last year.

"We wanted something where we could actually participate actively ourselves," says Karl. "It was the most unpleasant one we could find, because it was in the

wet season in the jungles of Panama with no housing or toilet facilities. But if we are really as ardent as we think we are, this would be the proof."

Before sunup each morning, Karl and his companions groped into the jungle ravines by flashlight to hang

up 15-foot-long mesh nets. Then, once an hour, they ventured back out into the torrential rains to identify, weigh, band and then free the captured birds.

"IT WAS very hard, but

(See Earthwatch, Page 2C)

Figure 14-26   A display paragraph underneath a headline. This style is very dramatic.

sans serif, boldface or italic. Leading is necessary to make the lead stand out and yet be readable. One final treatment may be to set the lead paragraph flush left with ragged right, a distinctly contemporary appearance.

New Approaches to Cutlines, Overlines and Underlines

The traditional way of identifying photographs is to place cutlines underneath them. Overlines and underlines may be used alone or with cutlines. If the photograph is less than three columns wide, the cutlines are set full width, but if the photograph is wider, the cutlines may be wrapped in two or more columns underneath. When overlines and underlines are used they are usually centered.

In contemporary layout, cutlines may be set flush left with ragged right or flush right with ragged left (Figure 14-27). When it is necessary to wrap cutlines into two adjacent columns, the flush left or flush right approach does not look pleasing. If, however, two pictures of the same size are placed next to each other (because they are related), it may be possible to set the cutlines flush left and the right cutlines flush right.

A particularly modern style of cutline treatment, borrowed from magazine design, is to place them at the lower side of photographs. In such positions, they may be set in very narrow measures (from 6 to 9 picas in width), flush on both sides. But they also may be given the flush left or flush right treatment. In the latter instance the cutlines are set differently, depending on which side of the photograph they are to be placed. When placed on the right side they should be flush left, and when placed on the left side they should be set flush right (Figures 14-28 and 14-29) because the type nearest the photograph is aligned and looks more attractive.

Overlines may be repositioned above cutlines placed at the sides of cuts. They, too, may receive the same flush left or flush right treatment as the cutlines. When positioned that way, there prob-

Boat delivery

in Britian

Policemen deliver a bottle of milk to Arthur Philpott, 70, by rubber raft yesterday in Yalding, England. Philpott has refused to leave his house since Sunday when torrential rains caused flooding throughout much of southeast England. Having submerged the basement of the Philpott's home, the raging flood waters began to seep into the upper story of the house, but Philpott refused to leave. See story page 16. (UPI Telephoto).

Figure 14-27   Cutlines set flush right, ragged left.

Getting ready

for inaugural

Although the next president has not yet been elected, work has already begun on erecting a presidential inaugural platform and a television tower on the east front of the Capitol. Here Ignatius A. Jones of Waldorf, Md. unloads lumber. (UPI Telephoto)

Figure 14-28   Cutlines flush on both sides.

ably will be a large amount of white space above the overline (or above the cutlines when there is no overline). But this white space will enhance the appearance of the treatment and should not be considered wasted space.

Oil spire plumbs ocean

Soaring 340 feet into the air like a spire, this crane is part of a new derrick for a pipe-laying vessel used to service offshore oil and gas fields. Owned by Standard Oil Co. (Ind.) and DeGroot Offshore Ltd., the vessel, Ocean Builder I, has the capacity to lift 2,000 tons.

Figure 14-29   Cutlines set flush right ragged left.

Inserts and Their Effects on Page Design

In traditional layout practices, editors often inserted freaks, refers or other material into the main body of a story. A freak is any material placed in a story that is set differently than the main story. Refer literally means something that refers to a related story. Inserts are additions to the story sometimes placed within the story body type. The ostensible purpose of breaking into a story was to provide information that would help the reader better understand the news. But no matter what the purpose was, the effect of any break in the news was a break in the reader's continuity.

What are the most likely alternative actions readers may take when confronted by an insert? They may notice the insert, ignore it temporarily and, upon finishing the article, return and read it. Another alternative is that readers may ignore it entirely. Or, they may stop and read it and then try to pick up the thread of thought in the remainder. But no matter which is done, the insert may break the flow of reading, if only for an instant, and because it may impede readership, it is undesirable (see Figure 14-30).

Hanzlik starts for Sonics

BELOIT DAILY NEWS, Thursday, Dec. 4.   Page 17

SEATTLE — There's a two hour time difference between Beloit and Seattle, but for Bill Hanzlik, there's a world of difference between the two cities.

In Beloit, Hanzlik was an all-state prep star at Beloit Memorial. In Seattle, he's a starting guard with the Seattle SuperSonics.

He's taken a quantum leap in the world of basketball. He's only a rookie, but he is hovering in the stratosphere of the sport and nightly tests his talents against stars like David Thompson and George Gervin.

As the world of big time, big money professional sports whirls around him, Hanzlik has been able to keep his feet firmly anchored on the ground.

As an example, he still seems happy to answer the questions from the home-town reporter. Even when the reporter hasn't called at the best of times.

The sports desk at the BDN gets cranking at 6 a.m. each day. So when this reporter called him at 11 a.m. it seemed like late afternoon. Actually the call for this phone interview roused Hanzlik from bed — it's still early morning in Seattle.

Hanzlik has had a great deal of exposure with the press, answering questions from flocks of reporters while starting at Nortre Dame. More pressure was put on his verbal abilities when he was the No. 1 draft pick by Seattle and the media wanted to know why. With all the attention, it might seem that Hanzlik could brush off the BDN. Instead, he cleared the morning from his throat and entered the conversation.

This wasn't the first time he'd been rudely awakened. The day after the pro draft he was rustled from sleep at 7 a.m. in Colorado where he was training with the U.S. Olympic basketball team. Even then he was happy to answer questions.

These examples illustrate his down-to-earth nature about the fantasy land of pro basketball. He knows, although he doesn't like to admit it, that he's a hero to many in Beloit. He also realizes that his starting role with the Sonics comes from being in the right place at the right time.

"I've been starting for about five games with Vinnie Johnson, and that's because Paul's (Westphal) been hurt. Paul will be out for a while and first they tried Freddie Brown starting, but he's better coming off the bench.

"These are the kind of breaks the NBA has. I got mine kind of early. I thought I'd have to wait longer to get a shot. I'm just trying to get the most out of it now.

Getting into the NBA is tough, but getting to start is a torturous task. It doesn't happen for many players, especially rookies. The contract holdout of all-pro Gus Williams from the Sonics this season has also helped give Hanzlik his chance.

"At practice, the day before the Dallas game, I was working with the first team and Lenny told me I'd start," Hanzlik said. "It feels great to start, but you can't get too charged up. You have to keep an even mental attitude because there are so many ups and downs during the season. I just have to be ready to play every night, and it's physically

tough."

Hanzlik's physical attributes have been the key to success for the 6-7 swingman. Art Thiel, in his column for the Seattle Post-Intelligencer, credits Hanzlik's nose for his contributions to the Sonics.

"What he (Hanzlik) does have is a nose," Thiel said. "True, it is more prominent than standard, but it is not so much the size that is important as location — thrust maddeningly in the on-court business of a number of big NBA guards."

With stats averaging around nine points, four rebounds, four assists and

"It feels great to start, but you can't get too charged up. You have to keep an even mental attitude because there are so many ups and downs during the season."

Bill Hanzlik

three steals a night, it's easy to see that Hanzlik's kamikaze hustle still makes him a defensive specialist.

"Defense in the NBA starts right up front, but that doesn't mean I stop at the offensive end. I'm still running the plays and setting picks. Defense is a lot different with the 24 second clock and there are so many picks you just have to fight through.

"The pro style is to be more physical. I ate my size and weight to my advantage. I don't get pounded. I do the pounding most of the time. I think I'm doing good on defense, but on any given night a player will get hot and there's nothing you can do. You just have to try to keep him from getting the ball so much.

"You've got to use your head when you play, since there's so much going on

If you do you can stay in the league a long time.

The awe of playing in the NBA has worn off. The game of basketball has become a business and it's the job Hanzlik has to do.

Days to relax are few and far between for the Sonics. If you're not playing, you're practicing. There's also the constant life of being on the road.

"In college you'd get a day off a week, but if you get one a month in the NBA you're lucky," he said. "You're looking at a different attitude in the pros. I played against some good players in college, but everybody is good in the pros. But once you get on the court you realize that you can play with them."

Pressure isn't new to him after playing in all the big games with the Fighting Irish. But there's added pressure in the pros, both from the media and from the fans. Blocking out the pressure and concentrating on the game brings success and wins in the NBA.

It's that altitude adjustment that has Hanzlik leaping with the best basketball players in the world. Imagine, he calls Westphal and Wilkens by first name and plays ball with the likes of Julius Erving. He even roomed with Jack Sikma for a time. Amazing that a kid from Beloit can do all that, isn't it?

Not to Hanzlik.

"I'm doing all that I wanted to do as a rookie," he said. "It feels pretty good and I just want to make the most of it."

(AP telephoto)

Bill Hanzlik drives to the hoop for the Sonics

> Rory
> Gillespie
> Sports writer

Figure 14-30   Insert that breaks into a story. It may break up large amounts of gray reading matter, but it may encourage readers to stop at that point.

Inserts also may be undesirable because they interrupt the rhythm of reading. Even if readers stop to read the insert, they may not read much more of the story.

Editors often tend to make inserts a continuing practice, perhaps at least one in every edition. Too many inserts on one day make the page appear to be full of spots that are unattractive and uninviting. Even when one insert is used it stands out as a spot on the page. In such situations, the layout editor interrupts the reader with rules and even a small headline within the insert. That one spot, then, may hamper the efforts of the editor to design a pleasing page because inserts tend to call attention to themselves.

The question then arises about what to do with the material that may have been used in inserts. One answer might be to place that material at either the beginning, the end or the top center of a story (see Figures 14-31, 14-32, 14-33). Perhaps it can be incorporated into the body of the story and not be obtrusive. Finally, by careful analysis of the news the editor may treat additional editorial material as another story and place it adjacent to the story in question. If there is reference to a picture, then this may be incorporated into the story set in lightface italics.

Boxed Stories

The use of boxed stories in contemporary modular layout is radically different from that in traditional layout. In traditional layout, a short, human interest story or an insert might have been placed in a box. Rarely was a long story boxed.

In contemporary layout, there is a need to dramatize a story or there is a need to dramatize the design on a given page, and a large boxed story is used. There is, of course, a danger in using too many such stories on a page. If only one is used per page, it may liven that page considerably.

'Many who attend law school
will never hang out a shingle.
Legal training will be used in
another area — it will always
stand them in good stead.'

Good lawyers
are his goal

By Maureen Milford
Staff writer

J. Kirkland Grant admits there's a national glut of lawyers,
but that's not going to stop him from cranking out hundreds — maybe thousands — of attorneys from the Delaware
Law School of Widener University.

The new dean of Delaware's only law school believes qual-.
ity, not quantity, is the real issue.

"It all depends on what kind of lawyers you're training.
Lawyers who are morally and ethically upright, as well as
competent, will always have enough work. The competition will
be rough, but there's always room at the top," said Grant, who
took over as dean in July.

The lawyer-professor said he hopes to get the Delaware legal
community to rally around the law school. His figures show that
20 percent of the lawyers in the state are Delaware Law School
graduates.

"It behooves the lawyers in the state to be very interested in
the law school. After all, it is the only law school in a corporate
state," Grant said.

Grant, who at age 37 is one of the youngest law school deans in
the country, has his work cut out for him. Many people in
Delaware's legal community are shaking their heads at the
number of people coming out of law school every year.
As one lawyer put it, "People are going to law school the way
they used to go into real estate." Another attorney expressed
concern that lawyers will take cases that have little or no merit
on a contingency basis simply to have work.

The new dean is aware of these concerns, but he says the
Delaware Law School graduates have proven themselves top
notch in the First State. "The greatest strengths of the law
school are its students and graduates," Grant said.

Delaware Law School was a familiar face to Grant when he
was offered the job as dean. In 1978 he served on the American
Bar Association inspection team for accreditation of the school.

See **DEAN** — B2, col. 5

J. Kirkland Grant

Staff photo by Pat Crowe

Figure 14-31   An insert before the headline. A very attractive approach.
[*Courtesy of the* Wilmington *(Del.)* Evening Journal]

Galileo didn't recognize Neptune

By Warren E. Leary
Associated Press

WASHINGTON — The famous
astronomer Galileo apparently did
not recognize a major planet when
he saw it and thus missed out on
adding the discovery to his list of
credits.

The 17th century genius, using one
of his early telescopes, saw the
planet Neptune without knowing
what it was. This left actual discovery to scientists hundreds of years
later, an astronomer said yesterday.

Charles T. Kowal of the California
Institute of Technology said he re-
examined records of Galileo's
observations and calculated that
the Italian physicist saw the planet
at least two times while working in
Florence.

Galileo saw Neptune on Dec. 28,
1612, and Jan. 28, 1613, but erron-
eously thought it was a "fixed star,"

even though he noted that it moved
in relation to another star, Kowal
reported to the National Science
Foundation, which finances part of
his work. Galileo's observations
were 234 years before the distant
planet formally was discovered.

Galileo, the first to put the tele-
scope to practical use, discovered
that the moon was marked by val-
leys and mountains, and reflected
light instead of generating its own.
He also discovered the four major
moons of Jupiter and noted the

'When he saw Neptune, he was
looking for satellites of Jupiter.'

peculiar form of Saturn, which was
later recognized as being caused by
its rings.

"When he saw Neptune, he
actually was looking for satellites
of Jupiter," Kowal said in a telephone interview. "It's also somewhat surprising that there are only
two observations. Neptune should
have been seen for the entire month
of January."

Neptune, second only to Pluto as
the solar system's most distant discovered planet, is 15 times more

massive than the Earth. Very little
is known about this cold, gaseous
planet because of its distance from
the sun — 2.8 billion miles — and
the fact that no spacecraft has ever
visited it.

Neptune was discovered on Sept.
23, 1846, by a young German astronomer, Johann Galle. Other scientists, notably John Couch Adams of
Britain and Urbain Leverrier of
France, calculated that an unknown
planet had to be in a certain position
because something was disturbing
the motion of the planet Uranus.

Galle looked at that calculated
position and found Neptune with
ease.

Kowal said he is looking for early
observations of Neptune because its
orbit around the sun still is not well
defined. The planet takes 165 years
to circle the sun and has not yet
completed one full revolution since
its discovery in 1846, he noted.

Figure 14-32   An insert top center of a story.

Britain, Ireland vow to push Ulster effort

**Leaders cite political,
security considerations**

By Steven Erlanger
Globe Staff

LONDON - At the end of their summit meeting yesterday, the British and Irish prime ministers, Margaret Thatcher and Garret FitzGerald, said they would accelerate their governments' search for a new political and security framework in Northern Ireland to which both Protestants and Catholics could give allegiance.

But they would not reveal any specific proposals, which they said their bureaucracies would refine before another summit early next year.

Thatcher called it "the fullest, frankest and most realistic" meeting on Northern Ireland she had ever had with an Irish prime minister. •

While sticking to her long-held position that as long as a majority desires it, Northern Ireland will remain part of the United Kingdom, Thatcher spoke more frankly than ever of the need to create a political and security system in the province that would "recognize and respect" the identities and rights of minority Catholics there.

Asked if that were an admission that the current system of direct rule from London did not fully respect the rights and identities of Catholics, she said: "The fact is that they are respected, and we are trying to make sure that they do."

That is a theme - Catholic alienation - that FitzGerald and Catholic leaders in the province have been pushing for months, and in a separate press conference, FitzGerald praised Thatcher for "getting to grips with what is a very complex and difficult problem" in the talks that began over dinner Sunday night at Thatcher's tightly guarded country residence, Chequers, and continued until late yesterday afternoon.

FitzGerald stressed that the summit was wide-ranging and "extremely down to earth, and that major progress had been made by the two sides in reaching "a common analysis of the problem." He

highlighted the connection between "the twin problems of security and politics," saying that sectarian terrorism could only be beaten when all of the people in Northern Ireland have a recognized stake in their system of government and policing.

"I don't think any enduring solution can be found without changes in the political structure as well as the security structure," he said. Only in that way could governments "end the alienation of the minority and the reign of terror" aimed at the majority.

Both leaders, by prior agreement, declined to discuss any specific proposals they had discussed.

"The fact is that today we reached a very considerable measure of agreement about the problem," FitzGerald said, "and we have a shared commitment to try to resolve it . . . We now have the basis of very serious discussions indeed, and which I hope will lead, at our next meeting, to concrete proposals."

To the disappointment of Irish officials, she put great emphasis on another

round of talks her new secretary of state for Northern Ireland, Douglas Hurd, will hold with the leaders of the major political parties in the province – excluding, as usual, Provisional Sinn Fein, the political wing of the Provisional Irish Republican Army.

Thatcher repeated again and again that no solution could be "imposed" from London or Dublin, that all constitutional parties in Ulster must get together – including the moderate Catholic Social Democratic and Labor Party (SDLP), which is currently boycotting the powerless Northern Ireland Assembly.

"The question is now whether the majority and minority parties will agree," she said. "Without that, we cannot impose from London. If we did it, it would not work. Our task is to try to persuade them to agree, to try to get a discussion going with them, and hope that with the passage of time, they will see the purpose and advantage of agreeing."

Irish officials said privately last night that while they were pessimistic about the results of such talks, since the Prot-

estant Unionists had never been willing to share power with Catholics, they recognized Thatcher's need to ensure Unionists did not feel betrayed.

They said that she understood Dublin's insistence that the two sovereign governments involved had to create "the framework" within which those talks took place, and must be prepared to move if they were not fruitful. British officials said FitzGerald would try to convince the SDLP, which has been losing ground to Sinn Fein, to participate in the talks as the spokesman for Ulster's Catholics.

Irish officials were also unhappy, if not surprised, by Thatcher's categorical dismissal of the three main proposals of the New Ireland Forum. An attempt by the Forum last May recommended three models: a united Ireland ruled from Dublin, a federal or confederal state, and joint authority shared by London and Dublin.

Yesterday Thatcher dismissed even joint authority as a "derogation of sovereignty," but Irish officials stressed the Forum's model itself was not their major concern.

Realistically, FitzGerald hopes for what his officials call "a diluted form of joint authority" in a British Ulster, whereby a Dublin official would sit with Hurd and advise him on key decisions, before they're made, that affect Catholics. Irish officials have also discussed adding a judge from the republic to sit alongside an Ulster one for security trials and a joint, London-Dublin consultative commission on all security matters.

Though Irish officials said they expected criticism at home for "talks that were just about more talks" from opposition leader Charles Haughey, they said FitzGerald had at last succeeded in concentrating Thatcher's mind on Catholics" even during the long miners' strike.

"Put it this way," one ranking Irish official said. "She's admitted for the first time that the current system is the tensions, the police and the judiciary isn't working. She's agreed to try to do something about it. In a real way, there's everything still to play for."

Irish Prime Minister Garret FitzGerald stands with British Prime Minister Margaret Thatcher before their meeting at Chequers yesterday.   POOL PHOTO VIA AP

'We reached a very considerable measure of agreement about the problem and we have a shared commitment to try to resolve it. . . . We now have the basis of very serious discussions indeed, and which I hope will lead, at our next meeting, to concrete proposals.'   Garret FitzGerald

**Figure 14-33   An insert bottom center of a story. [*Courtesy of the* Boston
(Mass.) Globe]**

When boxing a story, the editor assumes it is significant. Perhaps it is not as significant as the top two stories on the page, but it is still of major importance. The procedure, then, is to place the entire story in a boxed rule. The story must, of course, be squared off so that it fits neatly into the box. A photograph may accompany the story. But the keys to making this box look attractive are the use of type rules and more than an ordinary amount of white space inside the box. The only function of the type rule is to set the story apart from all other stories on the page. It usually will not look good if very heavy-weight rules are used. If a fancy border of any kind is used it will call attention to itself and not to the contents of the box. The white spaces, especially between the rules and the body type, are the framing devices that, with the hairline rules, make the story stand out and easy to read. Headlines within a box also may be set smaller and in lighter-faced types than those normally used because the rules and white space framing the box make a larger-sized type unnecessary. There is little competition from headlines outside the box.

Boxes, therefore, should be no less than two columns wide, and preferably larger, so that they may have dramatic impact. Some editors place at least one such box on every page where possible as a means of adding dramatic impact to the page. The position of such boxes on a page depends on the sizes and weights of other elements. When other headlines on the page are large and bold, a boxed story should be placed at the opposite side to bring about page balance. Often they look well at the bottom of the page. In some cases, they might well be used in place of the number-one story (upper-right side). (See Figure 14-31).

Policy for Design of Jump Heads

There is enough evidence available through research studies to prove that stories that have been jumped or continued to other pages lose a great deal of readership (see Chapter 2). Nevertheless, the practice of jumping stories sometimes cannot be avoided. Consequently, there should be a policy regarding the design of such heads.

There are two related problems that arise in the design of jump heads: (1) how to make them easy to find on a page; and (2) how to keep their design consistent with both the page and overall newspaper design. The first problem may seem to be easily resolved by setting the headlines in larger and bolder typefaces than other headlines. But if the type is too large or too bold, then it will call attention to itself and tend to make the page look unattractive. If it is too light, readers may not be able to find the heads. Both problems may be resolved if the following guidelines are observed.

1. It is important to have a jump head consist of at least one word from the original head, for the purpose of making a transition of ideas more easily. (See Figure 14-34).
2. The typefaces and style of arrangement should be consistent with the headline schedule used for other headlines.
3. The number of lines and sizes of type used for jump heads should be the same as if the jumped portion were a separate story. In such a case, the story length and importance would be considered.
4. A contrasting typeface may be used to help the head stand out. If Tempo has been used for most other headlines, a Bodoni Bold italic may provide the necessary contrast.
5. Stars, bullets or asterisks, if they are not too obtrusive, may pre-

---

ISRAEL   LEBANON

From Page 1

before the council convenes in which "circumstances may change."

He said the intention to boycott was "not a matter of principle. I see it as a form of political warfare."

From Page 1

850 soldiers were involved in the operation.

Ambulances recovered 70 bodies and 90 wounded persons from several combat zones during the day, but scores of other

Figure 14-34   Tombstoning jumped heads.

cede the first letter of the jump head to serve as attention-getting devices.

6. Ben Day screens may be used in the background for such heads. This is done easily for a newspaper printed by the offset technique. Where letterpress is being used, perhaps the page number from which the story originally started may be placed in a screened background. If a number of such page numbers could be screened and kept in logo form, they could be inserted easily under jump heads.

Tombstoning in Contemporary Design

Almost every editor, from the largest metropolitan newspaper or from the smallest high school paper, knows that tombstoning should be avoided. Tombstoning (also called *butting heads*) is a practice of placing two headlines next to each other in adjacent columns, both of which are set in the same type size, weight and style. They also have the same number of lines. But tombstoning was considered a poor layout practice in an age where only 6-point hairline rules were used between columns. Because some newspapers have used hairline rules of even less than 6 points (2- and 3-point rules), there was more of a danger that a reader might read across the column into the adjacent headline and be confused (Figure 14-34).

But in contemporary design, where the space between columns is at least 9 points and as much as 2 picas, tombstoning may not be objectionable. There may be so much white space between the columns that the reader can't be confused into reading a headline in the adjacent column. Then the only objection to tombstoning may be that there is not enough variety shown when two headlines of the same size, weight and number of lines are placed next to each other. This is a design consideration and one of the heads may be changed to provide more type variety on the page.

Banner Headlines

The use of daily across-the-page *banners* has been abandoned by many modern newspapers and often replaced by *spread heads* without readouts. A banner is a large size type headline that runs the full width of a page. A spread headline is a smaller size head running more than two columns and less than full width. But when a story is assigned a banner headline, it is assumed that the body copy will be placed in the extreme right-hand column. Even though the first, or left-hand, column is the most important position on the page, the right-hand column is the one which enables the reader to continue reading the story without returning to the left side of the page. In contemporary design, a number of questions arise affecting the reader's ability to continue reading the story smoothly. The answers to these questions lead to principles of handling banner headlines and readouts.

Can the story be continued in any other column? The reason for wanting to place the story elsewhere is to provide a change of pace and variety in makeup. The answer to the question is that there are few occasions when the story can be continued elsewhere. Least effective is to continue the story to an inside column. The reason it should not be placed anywhere but in the extreme right-hand column (with exceptions that will be noted) is that the reader will have to search for it if it is placed elsewhere. Although one may argue that the reader will not have to search very long, any time—even a fraction of a second—is too long. That fraction of a second may be just the timing that is necessary for the reader to switch to some more interesting story. After all, the reader may already know the material in the banner headline and perhaps isn't interested enough to continue when there are any impediments to reading. This is the problem of all layout devices. None should slow the reader more than a fraction of a second. If they are considered individually, each layout device may seem to be effective. But when there are many such devices on a page, the even rhythm of reading may be broken and reading becomes a troublesome rather than a pleasant experience.

When stories are continued from a banner headline to any column other than the extreme right, a cutoff rule is used to separate the banner from nonrelated stories. The assumption is that the only column not carrying a cutoff rule must be the one where the story is continued, and it will be obvious at a glance. Indeed, it is obvious at the right-hand side, less obvious when placed at the left-hand side (first column) and almost obscure when placed inside. Cutoff rules help, but not much. It is difficult to find the column where the story is continued.

Another question arises when using a banner headline. Can more than one story relating to the banner headline be arranged so that the banner reads into each story successfully? Such an occasion might be when an election story breaks and one political party wins both gubernatorial and mayoral races. The banner headline may therefore refer to both stories. When the readout headlines are only one column wide, they are often hard to find. But when they are two or more columns wide, they are relatively easy to find.

A final question concerns whether a banner headline should lead into a multiple- or single-column headline? One of the older layout rules was that when a large sized type was used in a top headline, the reader's eyes would have difficulty in adjusting to smaller types in the decks or lead paragraphs. Therefore, the reduction in size was supposed to be at least 50 percent. If a 120-point headline was used for the banner, then it should read into a headline of no less than 60-point type. The 60-point type would then read into a 30-point deck, which in turn might read into an 18-point deck and from there into a 10-point lead paragraph. There was never any valid evidence that readers had difficulty in adjusting their eyes to the changes in type sizes. Therefore, the only reason for reading from a banner into a multiple-column headline is simply to provide more details in the headline than could have been included in the banner. The only trouble with multiple-column headlines is that they usually lead into a single-column story, leaving the space underneath to be filled in the best way possible. If a headline for a nonrelated story is placed underneath a multiple-column headline, the effect might be to confuse the reader. At times a picture is placed underneath. But neither of these solutions looks attractive.

In contemporary layout, banner headlines often lead into a single-column headline, a simple device. Or, if a banner is used, it may lead into a three-column headline and a story may be wrapped for three columns underneath through the process of squaring off the bottom. A final alternative is to limit the use of banner headlines to rare occasions. When it is used with a multiple-column readout it won't look awkward because the news is so sensational. Too many multiple-column headlines on a page, however, make the page spotty because these headlines appear dark (being set in bold typefaces and relatively large-sized types). They become centers of interest because of their weight and may be difficult to balance.

15

An Introduction to Contemporary Design

When editors apply the principles of layout discussed in Chapter 14, they will find them helpful. But they also need to place these principles in the framework of a design style. Design styles determine what the end product of layout will look like. Two styles most often used in this country are called "contemporary" and "traditional." The more popular of the two is contemporary. This chapter, therefore, is a discussion of both styles, with special emphasis on contemporary design.

USA Today, A Striking Example of Contemporary Design

One of the most unusual examples of contemporary newspaper design in America is *USA Today,* a national newspaper which made its debut in September, 1982. Although this paper's design may be contemporary, it is different from contemporary designs of most other American newspapers (see Figure 15-1).

What makes this paper different is its content as well as its design. The content, to a great extent, was influenced by the findings of research about what many Americans wanted to read: a quick overview of national news, sports, investments, personalities, and the weather. The research project was one of the largest ever conducted on the subject of newspaper readership.

The design, however, was created without the aid of much research. Richard Curtis, director of Graphics and Research for *USA Today* said that very little of the research project mentioned above concerned design. Most design decisions were made arbi-

Figure 15-1   Front Page of *USA Today*. The bottom two corners each have colored graphics, and the top two have colored photographs. [*Courtesy of USA Today*]

trarily to meet the requirement of creating a unique styled paper that could compete successfully with entrenched newspapers. Subsequent research by the Simmons Market Research Bureau confirmed the idea that *USA Today* readers found the design to be attractive and appealing.

Comparisons of *USA Today* and 10 other major American newspapers were made for the same day, March 1, 1983, and a summary is shown below:[1]

1. *The paper runs more color than most other newspapers.* For example, it ran 13 full-color halftone pictures on March 1, while 10 other newspapers each ran a total of only 6 colored photos. It also ran 11 colored graphics on the same day, while the 10 other newspapers ran a total of only 2 each.

2. *It runs more black-and-white pictures.* At the same time, *USA Today* ran 72 black-and-white pictures, while the largest of the others ran 63. The smallest newspaper ran only 26 black-and-white photos.

3. *The average length of its stories tends to be short.* Stories ran an average of 5 inches, where the other 10 ran stories an average length of from 6.8 to 13.5 inches.

   Other design features of *USA Today* are:

4. *It runs one of the largest weather maps in color in the country.* It also probably devotes more space to weather stories than most other newspapers. The weather maps have received a great deal of favorable comment from the journalism community.

5. *It runs many stories over a gray or colored tint background.* A gray tint background serves somewhat the same function as a box: it sets a story apart from other stories on the same page. A colored tint background does the same thing and more: it brightens the type and the pages as well.

6. *It tends to run more boxes than other newspapers.* In the Dec. 12, 1984, edition it ran 31 boxes. Some were very small, while others were quite large. Some had hairline type rules around them, while others had tone borders around them.

7. *It uses a unique form of insert for lead paragraphs.* Some of its headlines use a half-column insert in light-face type, a form much different than used by most other newspapers (see Figure 15-2).

8. *It uses a vertical grid design.* Most American newspapers have moved away from vertical makeup to more horizontal styling, but *USA Today* has moved back.[2]

1. The newspapers were: the *Chicago Tribune, Los Angeles Times, Madison Capitol Times, Miami Herald, Milwaukee Journal and Sentinel, Long Island Newsday, New York Times, Wall Street Journal,* and *Washington Post.*

2. Lucas G. Staudacher, "Comparing USA Today's News Content" and "What about its ample use of photos, color or graphics?" from *A Look at USA Today,* A Report of the Changing Newspaper Committee, AP Managing Editor's Association, Louisville, Ky., Nov. 1-4, 1983, pp. 3-5.

COVER STORY

The crooner's newest fans: The young

The voice may be gravelly, but his career is entering its golden age

By Mike Clark
USA TODAY

In 1940, his ethereal backup vocal made Tommy Dorsey's *I'll Never Smile Again* the first No. 1 single ever charted by *Billboard* magazine.

Thirty years ago, his recording of *Young at Heart* lingered on the charts for five months. And even now, his 1980 rendition of *New York, New York* blasts through the Yankee Stadium sound system after every home baseball game.

Francis Albert Sinatra, who turns 69 today, is only nine months away from celebrating a half-century in show business. He rose to fame crooning '40s bobby-soxers into delirium, provided hours of shot-glass music for lonely '50s males — and now finds himself on a pedestal previously reserved for the most sacred icons of rock.

"It's been 50 years now, and it's really quite amazing," says *New York Times'* music critic John Rockwell, whose *Sinatra: An American Romantic* (Rolling Stone Press/Random House, $29.95) is the fifth in a series of lavish coffeetable books that have celebrated the Beatles, Elvis, the Stones and Bob Dylan.

Rockwell says, "Pop music is supposed to be the bastion of trendiness — everyone getting his 15 minutes of fame — and here's a guy who's survived incredible upheavals in

Please see COVER STORY next page ▶

Figure 15-2 Innovative insert underneath headline in *USA Today*. [*Courtesy* USA Today]

The net effect of all this (and other design techniques not mentioned here) is to cause quite a stir among newspaper designers throughout the country. Many have copied something from *USA Today*. Perhaps the most often copied technique is the added use of color. Not only are newspapers using more color photos than ever before, but many are using more colored tint blocks as a means of adding color inexpensively to a page. On the other hand, few newspaper designers are copying the gray tint backgrounds.

An Evaluation of USA Today's Design

There are three basic criteria that may be used to evaluate *USA Today's* design: (1) how it meets the needs of its editor and publisher as it tries to develop acceptance by readers in different cities throughout the country; (2) whether it could meet the needs of other American publishers and editors; and (3) does it conform to the principles of good design? It is important to keep in mind that this design was created to solve a problem, and it is assumed to have fulfilled this purpose admirably. Here then are some comments:

1. The design is atypical when compared to newspapers throughout the country. This does not make it a bad design. In fact, many of its readers like it, so it can afford to be different. On the other hand, its readers also are not the same as most other American newspapers. Research has shown that *USA Today's* readership tends to be younger, better educated and more affluent than readers of typical American newspapers. *USA Today's* readers appreciate the newspaper's unique design. Editors who have copied design concepts, selectively, from *USA Today,* seem not to have had negative feedback from their readers.

2. Its profuse use of color makes it stand out from among its competitors. That is precisely what the editors wanted it to do. Most other American newspapers pale by comparison. After all, the profuse use of color costs publishers more money, and some of them simply don't think it is worth the extra cost even though they would like more color.

American editors and publishers have been increasingly interested in adding more color to their newspapers, and some had made great progress toward this goal even before *USA Today* came on the scene. The *Chicago Tribune* and the *Milwaukee Journal* are two publications, for example, that have in the past used a great deal of color. Others are cautious about adding extra color. These papers are not in the intense competitive business stage that *USA Today* was and still is, because it had to do something to attract attention away from strongly established newspapers. Therefore its use of color serves a different purpose.

Color doesn't necessarily make a paper easier to read, but it does help make it brighter and more noticeable. In fact, there is fine line between the use and overuse of color. Judges in the Inland Daily Press Association design contest have criticized some newspapers for the overuse of color, saying these papers are harder to read.

USA Today also used color to enhance its image. In fact, it is sometimes called an avant-garde paper. Such labels may help sell the newspaper because readers may believe that it represents something really new on the communications scene. In other words, a bright newspaper stands out among duller ones and this may help build circulation somewhat. The question is whether the addition of large amounts of color would build circulation or help other newspapers in some way. The answer is that it probably would help, but other things like good reporting and writing are more important.

3. *USA Today* uses a strong vertical design, when most American newspapers are using less of it (see Figure 15-1). The vertical design is achieved through the use of a grid that does not vary much from day to day. Vertical design usually gives a newspaper an old-fashioned image, with some notable exceptions. Neither *The New York Times* nor *The Wall Street Journal* seems to suffer from using a vertical design. But these newspapers have created their images without the use of design and are known primarily for their contents. *The New York Times'* inside page designs, however, are distinctly contemporary, and quite attractive. They are much different from its front page design.

So the answer about vertical design is that it may be too vertical. It helps *USA Today* get part of its image, and it helps its staff prepare layouts quickly. But it is questionable whether it would help other papers very much.

4. The design of this paper uses gray tints underneath certain story modules, a practice that also is used by some American newspapers. The reason? Those modules are used to set certain stories apart from others as a means of calling attention to them, and they also comprise part of the total design. However, there is a question about whether these tints help or hinder reading in *USA Today* and other newspapers that use them. When the gray background is too dark, it probably hinders reading. But when these tints are light colored, such as yellows, oranges, tans or pinks, then readability may be enhanced (see Figure 15-3).

5. The profuse use of photographs is an excellent idea. When these photographs run in color they make the picture appear more interesting and lifelike. Most of the colored photographs are on the front page or in the front sections. But even the use of black-and-white photographs is a good idea. On the other hand, many of these pictures are head shots, or they are so small that they may make it difficult for readers to see much of the action. Headshot photos also tend to clutter the page design. Furthermore, contemporary designed papers tend to feature larger photographs, which makes pages appear more dramatic. In summary then, the use of many photographs is a good design practice, but their small sizes are questionable.

6. In conclusion, the design of this paper meets the needs of management that wanted to compete effectively against well-established papers in large cities. But it is not evident that other American newspapers would benefit from copying *all* of its unique features. One must remember that design should be functional. It certainly is functional for *USA Today*. Some of its ideas, such as more use of color or photographs, would also be functional for other newspapers. But the editorial policy of very short stories, vertical design and so forth may not be beneficial.

Perhaps the following statement by Christina Bradford, of the

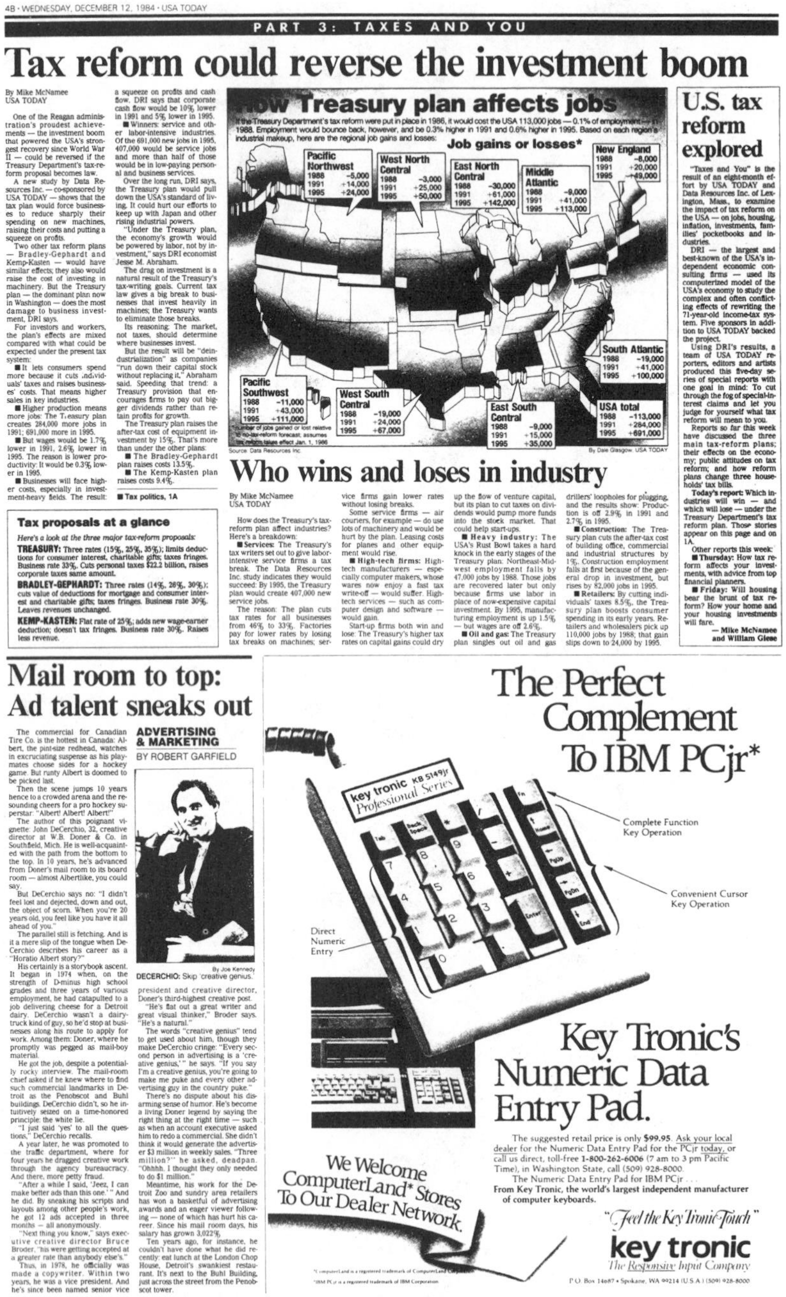

4B · WEDNESDAY, DECEMBER 12, 1984 · USA TODAY

PART 3: TAXES AND YOU

Tax reform could reverse the investment boom

By Mike McNamee
USA TODAY

One of the Reagan administration's proudest achievements — the investment boom that powered the USA's strongest recovery since World War II — could be reversed if the Treasury Department's tax-reform proposal becomes law.

A new study by Data Resources Inc. — co-sponsored by USA TODAY — shows that the tax plan would force businesses to reduce sharply their spending on new machines, raising their costs and putting a squeeze on profits.

Two other tax reform plans — Bradley-Gephardt and Kemp-Kasten — would have similar effects; they also would raise the cost of investing in machinery. But the Treasury plan — the dominant plan now in Washington — does the most damage to business investment, DRI says.

For investors and workers, the plan's effects are mixed compared with what could be expected under the present tax system:

■ It lets consumers spend more because it cuts individuals' taxes and raises businesses' costs. That means higher sales in key industries.

■ Higher production means more jobs: The Treasury plan creates 284,000 more jobs in 1991; 691,000 more in 1995.

■ But wages would be 1.7% lower in 1991, 2.6% lower in 1995. The reason is lower productivity: It would be 0.3% lower in 1995.

■ Businesses will face higher costs, especially in investment-heavy fields. The result: a squeeze on profits and cash flow. DRI says that corporate cash flow would be 10% lower in 1991 and 5% lower in 1995.

■ Winners: service and other labor-intensive industries. Of the 691,000 new jobs in 1995, 407,000 would be service jobs and more than half of those would be in low-paying personal and business services.

Over the long run, DRI says, the Treasury plan would pull down the USA's standard of living. It could hurt our efforts to keep up with Japan and other rising industrial powers.

"Under the Treasury plan, the economy's growth would be powered by labor, not by investment," says DRI economist Jesse M. Abraham.

The drag on investment is a natural result of the Treasury's tax-writing goals. Current tax law gives a big break to businesses that invest heavily in machines; the Treasury wants to eliminate those breaks.

Its reasoning: The market, not taxes, should determine where businesses invest.

But the result will be "deindustrialization" as companies "run down their capital stock without replacing it," Abraham said. Speeding that trend: a Treasury provision that encourages firms to pay out bigger dividends rather than retain profits for growth.

The Treasury plan raises the after-tax cost of equipment investment by 15%. That's more than under the other plans:

■ The Bradley-Gephardt plan raises costs 13.5%.

■ The Kemp-Kasten plan raises costs 9.4%.

■ Tax politics, 1A

Tax proposals at a glance

Here's a look at the three major tax-reform proposals:

TREASURY: Three rates (15%, 25%, 35%); limits deductions for consumer interest, charitable gifts; taxes fringes. Business rate 33%. Cuts personal taxes $22.2 billion, raises corporate taxes same amount.

BRADLEY-GEPHARDT: Three rates (14%, 26%, 30%); cuts value of deductions for mortgage and consumer interest and charitable gifts; taxes fringes. Business rate 30%. Leaves revenues unchanged.

KEMP-KASTEN: Flat rate of 25%; adds new wage-earner deduction; doesn't tax fringes. Business rate 30%. Raises less revenue.

How Treasury plan affects jobs

If the Treasury Department's tax reform were put in place in 1986, it would cost the USA 113,000 jobs — 0.1% of employment — in 1988. Employment would bounce back, however, and be 0.3% higher in 1991 and 0.6% higher in 1995. Based on each region's industrial makeup, here are the regional job gains and losses:

Job gains or losses*

Region	1988	1991	1995
Pacific Northwest	-5,000	+14,000	+24,000
West North Central	-3,000	+25,000	+50,000
East North Central	-30,000	+61,000	+142,000
Middle Atlantic	-9,000	+41,000	+113,000
New England	-8,000	+20,000	+49,000
South Atlantic	-19,000	+41,000	+100,000
Pacific Southwest	-11,000	+43,000	+111,000
West South Central	-19,000	+24,000	+67,000
East South Central	-9,000	+15,000	+35,000
USA total	-113,000	+284,000	+691,000

*number of jobs gained or lost relative to no-tax-reform forecast; assumes tax reform takes effect Jan. 1, 1986

Source: Data Resources Inc. By Dale Glasgow, USA TODAY

Who wins and loses in industry

By Mike McNamee
USA TODAY

How does the Treasury's tax-reform plan affect industries? Here's a breakdown:

■ **Services:** The Treasury's tax writers set out to give labor-intensive service firms a tax break. The Data Resources Inc. study indicates they would succeed: By 1995, the Treasury plan would create 407,000 new service jobs.

The reason: The plan cuts tax rates for all businesses from 46% to 33%. Factories pay for lower rates by losing tax breaks on machines; service firms gain lower rates without losing breaks.

Some service firms — air couriers, for example — do use lots of machinery and would be hurt by the plan. Leasing costs for planes and other equipment would rise.

■ **High-tech firms:** High-tech manufacturers — especially computer makers, whose wares now enjoy a fast tax write-off — would suffer. High-tech services — such as computer design and software — would gain.

Start-up firms both win and lose: The Treasury's higher tax rates on capital gains could dry up the flow of venture capital, but its plan to cut taxes on dividends would pump more funds into the stock market. That could help start-ups.

■ **Heavy industry:** The USA's Rust Bowl takes a hard knock in the early stages of the Treasury plan: Northeast-Midwest employment falls by 47,000 jobs by 1988. Those jobs are recovered later but only because firms use labor in place of now-expensive capital investment. By 1995, manufacturing employment is up 1.5% — but wages are off 2.6%.

■ **Oil and gas:** The Treasury plan singles out oil and gas drillers' loopholes for plugging, and the results show: Production is off 2.9% in 1991 and 2.7% in 1995.

■ **Construction:** The Treasury plan cuts the after-tax cost of building office, commercial and industrial structures by 1%. Construction employment falls at first because of the general drop in investment, but rises by 82,000 jobs in 1995.

■ **Retailers:** By cutting individuals' taxes 8.5%, the Treasury plan boosts consumer spending in its early years. Retailers and wholesalers pick up 110,000 jobs by 1988; that gain slips down to 24,000 by 1995.

U.S. tax reform explored

"Taxes and You" is the result of an eight-month effort by USA TODAY and Data Resources Inc. of Lexington, Mass., to examine the impact of tax reform on the USA — on jobs, housing, inflation, investments, families' pocketbooks and industries.

DRI — the largest and best-known of the USA's independent economic consulting firms — used its computerized model of the USA's economy to study the complex and often conflicting effects of rewriting the 71-year-old income-tax system. Five sponsors in addition to USA TODAY backed the project.

Using DRI's results, a team of USA TODAY reporters, editors and artists produced this five-day series of special reports with one goal in mind: To cut through the fog of special-interest claims and let you judge for yourself what tax reform will mean to you.

Reports so far this week have discussed the three main tax-reform plans; their effects on the economy; public attitudes on tax reform; and how reform plans change three households' tax bills.

Today's report: Which industries will win — and which will lose — under the Treasury Department's tax reform plan. Those stories appear on this page and on 1A.

Other reports this week:

■ **Thursday:** How tax reform affects your investments, with advice from top financial planners.

■ **Friday:** Will housing bear the brunt of tax reform? How your home and your housing investments will fare.

— Mike McNamee and William Giese

Mail room to top: Ad talent sneaks out

ADVERTISING & MARKETING
BY ROBERT GARFIELD

The commercial for Canadian Tire Co. is the hottest in Canada: Albert, the pint-size redhead, watches in excruciating suspense as his playmates choose sides for a hockey game. But runty Albert is doomed to be picked last.

Then the scene jumps 10 years hence to a crowded arena and the resounding cheers for a pro hockey superstar: "Albert! Albert! Albert!"

The author of this poignant vignette: John DeCerchio, 32, creative director at W.B. Doner & Co. in Southfield, Mich. He is well-acquainted with the path from the bottom to the top. In 10 years, he's advanced from Doner's mail room to its board room — almost Albertlike, you could say.

But DeCerchio says no: "I didn't feel lost and dejected, down and out, the object of scorn. When you're 20 years old, you feel like you have it all ahead of you."

The parallel still is fetching. And is it a mere slip of the tongue when DeCerchio describes his career as a "Horatio Albert story?"

His certainly is a storybook ascent. It began in 1974 when, on the strength of D-minus high school grades and three years of various employment, he had catapulted to a job delivering cheese for a Detroit dairy. DeCerchio wasn't a dairy-truck kind of guy, so he'd stop at businesses along his route to apply for work. Among them: Doner, where he promptly was pegged as mail-boy material.

He got the job, despite a potentially rocky interview. The mail-room chief asked if he knew where to find such commercial landmarks in Detroit as the Penobscot and Buhl buildings. DeCerchio didn't, so he intuitively seized on a time-honored principle: the white lie.

"I just said 'yes' to all the questions," DeCerchio recalls.

A year later, he was promoted to the traffic department, where for four years he dragged creative work through the agency bureaucracy. And there, more petty fraud.

"After a while I said, 'Jeez, I can make better ads than this one.'" And he did. By sneaking his scripts and layouts among other people's work, he got 12 ads accepted in three months — all anonymously.

"Next thing you know," says executive creative director Bruce Broder, "his were getting accepted at a greater rate than anybody else's."

Thus, in 1978, he officially was made a copywriter. Within two years, he was a vice president. And he's since been named senior vice president and creative director, Doner's third-highest creative post.

By Joe Kennedy
DECERCHIO: Skip 'creative genius.'

"He's flat out a great writer and great visual thinker," Broder says. "He's a natural."

The words "creative genius" tend to get used about him, though they make DeCerchio cringe: "Every second person in advertising is a 'creative genius,'" he says. "If you say I'm a creative genius, you're going to make me puke and every other advertising guy in the country puke."

There's no dispute about his disarming sense of humor. He's become a living Doner legend by saying the right thing at the right time — such as when an account executive asked him to redo a commercial. She didn't think it would generate the advertiser $3 million in weekly sales. "Three million?" he asked, deadpan. "Ohhhh. I thought they only needed to do $1 million."

Meantime, his work for the Detroit Zoo and sundry area retailers has won a basketful of advertising awards and an eager viewer following — none of which has hurt his career. Since his mail room days, his salary has grown 3,022%.

Ten years ago, for instance, he couldn't have done what he did recently: eat lunch at the London Chop House, Detroit's swankiest restaurant. It's next to the Buhl Building, just across the street from the Penobscot tower.

Figure 15-3 An inside page on *USA Today* showing two gray tint backgrounds. [*Courtesy of* USA Today]

Rochester Democrat & Chronicle, best epitomizes critics' attitudes towards *USA Today:* "Love it or hate it, you can't ignore it."[3]

Contemporary Layout Concepts

American editors began to make radical changes in newspaper design about 1970, when many switched from eight- to six-column papers. It was also about that time that publishers were changing from editing by hand to editing by computers and video display equipment. They were also changing from letterpress to offset printing equipment. It seemed to be the right time for newspaper design to have a new appearance.

Contemporary design consists of three new design ideas that helped achieve a new "look": modular, grid and total design. These three ideas are not independent but are part of what is called the contemporary design concept. They are, however, expressed in different manners from newspaper to newspaper throughout the country.

The Essence of Contemporary Design

What is contemporary layout or design? The following material summarizes the essence or main features that almost anyone can discern. Contemporary layouts are:

1. cleaner looking than traditional designs (which tended to be cluttered)
2. simpler in structure. One of the ways in which traditional design has been converted to contemporary is by squaring off all stories. In traditional layouts, a two-column story usually had one column longer than the other. When many such stories appeared on one page it tended to make the page appear complex
3. designed with the total page in mind. Therefore the entire page is interesting. In bygone days, only the top was interesting
4. noted for the use of larger photographs on the front and feature pages than have ever been used before
5. usually six columns to the page, whereas older papers had eight
6. using much more color than ever before
7. noted for using larger, more dramatic boxes
8. noted for using more graphics (charts, maps, tables, etc.)

Modular Layout

Contemporary layouts are often composed of modules. A *module* is one or more stories that have been grouped together, usually in a rectangular format. The columns in a module are squared-off. If there are two or more columns to a story, each column ends in the same place as the others. Therefore, one sees modules as rectangles rather than as odd-shaped stories that once were widely used in newspaper layout. These rectangles are either horizontal or verti-

3. Ibid.

cal in shape, and it is a mixture of these shapes that keeps a page from becoming boring. Modules also can be enclosed in boxes.

There are three major reasons for using modules in design. The first reason is that it enables the layout person clearly to separate one story from another. There is no intertwining with odd-shaped stories as there used to be. The consequence of separating stories is to make them easy to find and read. Story shapes are simple not complex.

The second reason for using modules is to make it easy to

Figure 15-4   Each story is a module. [*Courtesy of* Marietta *(Ga.)* Daily Journal]

accommodate late-breaking stories. One simply removes one module, which has a rectangular shape, and replaces it with another. Time and effort are saved: a worthwhile goal.

The third reason for using modules is perhaps the most important. It enables a layout person to create cleaner and simpler page structures, which are not only attractive but very readable.

It is relatively easy to implement the modular concept because it fits any type of layout style. It even can be used with traditional style layouts. It may be used without any rules around it (Figure 15-4) or inside boxed rules (Figure 15-5).

Figure 15-5   Four boxed modules. [*Courtesy of the* Mt. Prospect *(Ill.)* Daily Herald]

The most distinguishing feature of modules is that they are stories that are squared off. By squaring off, a story exists simply as a rectangle that is relatively easy to replace if necessary. When stories are squared off they need not be placed in boxes, and such stories can be positioned almost anywhere on a page. When they are not boxed, they can be set apart from other stories by generous amounts of white space above and below them.

When designing an entire page in modular form, either type rules or white space may be used to separate stories. Column rules, coupled with cut-off rules or boxed rules, can be the separating devices (Figure 15-6). If a newspaper does not use column rules,

Figure 15-6   An entire page made up of boxed modules.

then white space in columns and above and below stories may be used to separate stories.

The Grid Concept

The grid concept carries the modular idea one step further. Although the modular concept is flexible and can be used with almost any kind of layout, the grid concept has to stand alone as a single unit. A grid consists of an entire page of modules of varying sizes designed in a distinctly contemporary style. The concept gets its name from the meaning of the term *grid*. A *grid* may be defined as a pattern of intersecting lines forming rectangles of various sizes and shapes. From this definition one can understand why a football field is often called a gridiron. In newspaper design, the grid lines are usually column spaces and/or spaces separating stories.

The intersecting lines of grid layout are not accidentally designed; in fact, they are highly structured. They are carefully placed to divide a newspaper page into very clean-cut and simple-appearing modules whose whole total effect is contemporary. Stories are usually squared off and designed into either vertical or horizontal shapes. Furthermore, the division of space on a page is usually unequal—never mathematically equal (Figure 15-7). One can not conceive of a grid layout with three-column stories on the left and three-column stories on the right side of a page. A 3:3 division of space is not as attractive as an unequal division of space. It tends to call attention to itself and not the stories. Nevertheless, one sees 3:3 page divisions occasionally.

It is also important to realize that grid *as defined in this text is not the same term as some graphic designers use it. They tend to define a grid as a fixed layout format into which stories are placed. Here it should more properly be called "variable grid," meaning that there are different grids for different purposes. But most important, the grid is not created until after the photos and main stories have been positioned. Then a grid design is formed using the most important news of the day as a basis.*

Grid may feature either vertical or horizontal styling. In Figure 15-7 the grid design features a 4:2 division of space *vertically*. But in Figure 15-8 the grid is *horizontal*.

The objective of grid is to give a page a contemporary styling that is found in magazines, books and other reading materials. It makes a page look interesting. Furthermore, the layout personnel have complete control of page design. Pages don't look as if they had been designed accidentally. The top of the page is never top-heavy as may be found in traditional design. But story placement is still based on the importance of each story: more important stories still get featured treatment. The main difference, however, between grid and traditional layout is that all stories have an opportunity of being seen in grid, something that may or may not be true in traditional layout.

Figure 15-7   Modules in a grid design. Note the 4:2 page division and the grid column space that extends from the top to the bottom of the page. [*Courtesy of the* Beaumont *(Texas)* Enterprise]

Obviously the grid concept and contemporary layout have limitations in that readers could tire of stories shaped in rectangular form. Although there are many alternative grid designs that could be used, there may be a tendency to overuse a few designs.

The Total Design Concept

The total design concept is simply an extension of modular and grid concepts wherein the entire page is made interesting, not just the top. One can lay out a modular or grid design and have it

Braves sign Sutter to six-year deal for $10 million — Page 17

Metro Huntington FINAL

The Herald-Dispatch

26 Pages, 2 Sections — Huntington W.Va., SATURDAY Morning December 8, 1984 — 25 Cents

Artificial heart recipient hears wedding bells — Page 3

Still nothing sweeter than win over 'Eers, fans say

By JAMES McMILLER
Of The Herald-Dispatch staff

Indians arrest, later release Carbide chief

By TINA CHOU
Associated Press

$15 billion suit filed for victims

By ANDREW KATELL
Associated Press

Arab hijackers say they will kill more hostages

By ALEX EFTY,
Associated Press

Norris new chief for police force

By ELIZABETH SKEWES
Of The Herald-Dispatch staff

Donald L. Norris

Jay breaks his old record in $12.06 million campaign

From AP, staff dispatches

Florida law enforcement officers plan session to study Long case

By MICHAEL JOHNSON
Assistant city editor

Military likely to join budget-cutting drive

By MAUREEN SANTINI
AP White House correspondent

Rahall, Wise favor cuts, not methods .... Page 15

Figure 15-8 Modules in a grid design with three horizontal grid spaces that divide the page. The page has a horizontal look. [*Courtesy of* Huntington *(W.Va.)* Herald-Dispatch]

appear boring and even confusing. But a page that uses total design principles should be ultra simple and yet dramatic.

What makes a modular or grid design dramatic? The answer: Careful planning of a page to maximize dramatic possibilities. Large pictures, large boxes, the use of color and dramatic headlines will not of themselves make a page dramatic. But their positioning on a page may do so. That is what takes planning.

The following ideas are guidelines to total design:

1. Careful space division on a page is the one important key to this concept. No page should be divided into halves either vertically or horizontally. In other words, page balance will always be informal. This practice tends to create interesting pages.

2. In total design, the entire page is important—not just the top. The objective is to encourage readers to read everything on a page. Traditional page designers did not care much about the bottoms of pages.

3. As always, however, the most important stories must be positioned to achieve "maximum readership." Since this most likely will be at or near the top in many instances, the page will be laid out around the main stories and pictures. Then, once these key stories and photos have been placed the remainder of a page is dummied in a dramatic style.

4. Page layout persons should have in the back of their minds ideas on how to design the remainder of a page *around* the important stories/photos.

5. Total designed pages will have almost all stories squared off. Therefore a page will consist of various kinds of rectangles which look attractive relative to each other.

6. Usually there will be no less than five stories nor more than about 12 stories to a front page. Exceptions, of course, will occur. News summaries can take up the slack of the many stories that once appeared on the front page.

7. A generous amount of white space should appear between columns, such as no less than 1 pica of space. Also, the space between one story above and the next one below should have no less than 1 pica of space between them.

8. The test of whether the total design has been attained is when the entire page is not only interesting but inviting to readers.

Special Considerations in Contemporary Design

Top-Heavy Page Designs. The subject of top-heavy page designs was first presented in Chapter 14 under the subject of "balance." Top-heavy pages are created by layout personnel who place all important stories at the top. Since this chapter covers the practice of contemporary layout, it is important to discuss the subject again because it has both good and bad layout implications.

It is reasonable for layout editors to place all important stories at the top because it is a way to tell readers where to find them.

Specifics of Traditional versus Contemporary Design

Some newspaper editors in this country still lay out their newspapers in a traditional manner. The term "traditional" means that the layout has many of the characteristics that identify it with the past. Although there was no single traditional layout, it is important to know in what ways most traditional layouts differ from contemporary layouts. The table below shows the main differences:

Traditional Layout	Contemporary Layout
a. Nameplates were almost always at the top of a page.	a. Nameplates may be moved around near the top.
b. All important stories were placed at the top of a page.	b. Important stories may appear anywhere on the page, though many appear at the top.
c. Large headlines appeared at the top.	c. Large headlines may appear anywhere on a page.
d. Front page datelines had a rule above and below them.	d. Many datelines have only one rule, either above or below them.
e. Stories were wrapped unevenly from one column to the next.	e. Stories are squared-off at bottom in adjacent columns.
f. Many photographs were small and usually appeared at the top of a page.	f. Photographs tend to be larger and more dramatic. They may be placed anywhere on a page.
g. Almost all headlines had many decks.	g. Stories have only one deck, occasionally two.
h. Front pages usually had more than ten stories on them. Some had 20.	h. Front pages have longer and fewer stories. Some have only five or six stories.
i. Many type rules were used. There were cut-off rules, finish dashes, jim-dashes, etc.	i. Most type rules have been eliminated. Cut-off rules are used occasionally.
j. The entire bottom of pages tended to be gray and dull.	j. The bottoms of pages are often as interesting as the tops.
k. Pages looked dark and tight because columns were very close together, often only 3 points apart.	k. Pages look open and light because columns are at least a pica apart.

That is why the practice has been continued for so many years. But it also has negative consequences.

This practice tends to "condition" readers to look mostly at the top of a page because they assume that there is little of importance at the bottom. "Conditioned response" is a term used by behaviorist psychologists to mean that when a certain behavior is repeated often enough it tends to become a fixed habit. The evidence for such conditioning comes from a great deal of newspaper readership research which shows that the tops of pages received much larger percentages of readers than did the bottoms. The *Continuing Studies of Newspaper Readership,* made in the early 1950s, clearly showed the power of the tops of pages versus the bottoms.

The problem is that readers often don't have time to read the bottom, and thereby miss some stories. There also isn't enough space at the top for all important stories. Some will have to be placed lower on the page. It would be detrimental to readers for them to miss a story simply because it had been placed at or near the bottom.

The solution to the problem is to get into the habit of placing some important stories at different places on a page. How will readers recognize important stories when they are not placed at the top? Simply by their design treatment. Large or boldface headlines or boxed stories both help.

The Key Grid Lines: One of the most important artistic keys to contemporary design is the use of a column of white space to divide vertically a page into two uneven divisions such as two columns on the left and four on the right. The same idea can be used to divide a page horizontally through the use of bands of white space that cut across the page (see Figures 15-7 and 15-8).

What makes these spaces work is the fact that each clearly divides a page. The vertical division may run from the nameplate to bottom and the horizontal may run all the way across a page. These space divisions tend to simplify page structure.

In newspaper layout of a bygone age, the practice of dividing pages in this manner was frowned upon because it was feared that such divisions would cut a page into two distinct segments. But layout persons then did not realize how readers tend to perceive such page divisions. They didn't see them as two separate segments, but as one. That is because humans have a strong tendency to pull together mentally elements of objects that they see. Of course, in the days of an 8-column newspaper such a division may indeed have been too pronounced and affected page structure.

So these columns of space help implement the design. They not only simplify design, but they bring order to a page that tends to become complex because it contains many different shaped stories and photographs. Of course, pages can be designed without these spaces, but such pages usually are not as simple or orderly as those using key grid lines.

Other Contemporary Features

Other practices differentiate the traditional from the contemporary newspaper layout. Some practices are the result of major editorial policy and can be changed only by those in top authority, such as a publisher or an editor. Others, however, are within the province of the layout editor, who daily has the option of using traditional or contemporary treatments of editorial material.

Elimination of Column Rules

One of the distinguishing features of contemporary design is the elimination of column rules from the newspaper. The purpose is to bring more light (or white space) into the page and to bring about a cleaner looking page. When column rules are used, they simply add blackness to the page even though they separate the columns. But the additional white space not only separates the columns but makes the page more inviting to the reader because it is less black-appearing.

In eliminating column rules, editors did not simply replace a 6-point hairline rule with 6 points of white space. They added more white space so that the columns were more clearly separated. The minimum amount of white space between columns seems to be nine points, but more is preferred. The better-designed newspapers use no less than 12 points of white space and many use more.

Reduction in the Number of Columns to a Page

To gain more white space on a page, editors who use contemporary layout have reduced the number of columns to a page from eight to as few as four (see Figure 15-9), which releases more space to be used between columns than was formerly possible. In contemporary layout it is not unusual to find some pages with 14 to 18 points of space between columns.

Another benefit of reducing the number of columns to the page is that the body type is made more readable because the line widths are increased. From a standard 11-pica width, some newspapers have increased the column widths to more than 14 picas. SAU widths are now 12¼ picas.

On the inside pages, the reduction in number of columns has proved to be harder to work with because advertising often is sold on a basis of a narrower column width. Some newspapers use the wider column widths for news and narrower column widths for advertisements. The layout of such pages may be difficult because of the differences in measures.

Limited Use of Cutoff Rules

The cutoff rule is used sparingly in contemporary layout. Wherever white space can be substituted for a cutoff rule it should be used. When white space is substituted a bit more space is used so

Figure 15-9   A four column page with larger than usual column spaces.
[*Courtesy of the The Lerner Papers, Chicago*]

that the reader will clearly understand that two stories near each other are not related in any way. But there are certain times, especially when the page is crowded, that a cutoff rule is necessary. In such a case, the layout editor should not hesitate to use it. Some editors are using more cutoff rules more than they formerly did, for page clarification purposes.

Headline Styles in Contemporary Layout

The flush-left headline is used almost exclusively in contemporary makeup. Droplines, inverted pyramids, centered heads and hanging indentions are styles of the past. Flush left is preferred because it is free-form in appearance, a style that is distinctly modern and because it is so easy to set on the phototypesetting machines. On the other hand, each of the *other* three styles of headlines mentioned look old-fashioned and tend to call attention to themselves because of their unusual shapes.

Three other headline styles are sometimes considered contemporary. Each may serve a special purpose, so they are rarely used extensively. They are kickers, hammerheads and wickets.

A kicker is a line of type placed immediately above a main headline (see Figure 15-10). The purpose is to summarize quickly some outstanding feature of the story below, even as the main head underneath also provides additional summary. A principle of setting kickers is that they should be one-half the point size of the headline below. If the headline below is 48 point, the kicker should be about 24 point. Also, the kicker line should be at least half the width of the line below. If it is too short, it will create an ugly gap of white space at the right side of the headline. If it is too long, it will detract from the headline below.

2 buildings confiscated
West Side drug ring broken up

Figure 15-10 A kicker headline, underscored. Note that the kicker is set in roman, but the line underneath is in italic type.

A hammerhead is a one- or two-word kicker that is set in very large type to attract attention to the story (see Figure 15-12). Hammerheads stand out easily on a page. Hammerheads are sometimes called wickets. A wicket (sometimes called a reverse kicker) also is a kicker that is set larger than the line below it (see Figure 15-11).

In using a kicker, hammerhead or wicket, the disadvantages may outweigh the advantages. The danger is that these devices may call too much attention to themselves, primarily because they are attention-getting devices. If more than one of these are used on a page, the effect may be a series of white holes that tend to destroy the harmony of page unity. As an alternative to these headline treatments, makeup persons could use a boxed story or have headlines set to the right or in the center of a story. The latter are con-

'Miss' or ' Mrs.' preferred
Poll suggests majority of women want traditional designation, not 'Ms.'

Figure 15-11 A reverse kicker, sometimes called a wicket.

23-19

Bears amaze fans, 'Skins

by Terry Bannon
Herald sports writer

WASHINGTON — Finally there is something other than bad news from the Bears.

Making believers of doubting fans, the Bears eliminated the favored Washington Redskins from the National Football League playoffs with a dramatic 23-19 victory Sunday.

After falling behind 3-0, the Bears took the lead and then withstood three fourth-quarter drives in their territory. Now, the Super Bowl just one step away, Chicago is feeling playoff fever just as it did for the Cubs last October.

At the heart of the victory is coach Mike Ditka, the same hard-nosed man who was a tight end on that last championship Bears team back in 1963.

"WE REALLY felt that it was time for us to do something in Chicago," Ditka said. "We're proud to be Bears We're proud to be from the city. I just think it's time for the city of Chicago to take a bow."

The Bears get no rest in pursuit of football's top prize. They play for the National Conference championship Sunday against the 49ers in San Francisco.

San Francisco owns the league's best record, 16-1 after Saturday's playoff victory over the New York Giants. The 49ers, the 1982 Super Bowl champs, will be heavily favored.

In sports

- Offensive strategy pays off
- Gutsy defense excels again
- Big day for Bell
- McKinnon recovers from injury
- Skins ponder what happened
- Victory impresses 49ers

If the Bears can work their magic again, then it will be on to Super Bowl XIX in Palo Alto, Calif., Jan. 20. The opponent will be determined Sunday when Miami meets Pittsburgh in the American Conference title game in Miami.

THE ODDS were against the Bears Sunday, especially considering they started second-string quarterback Steve Fuller. Regular quarterback Jim McMahon was out with a kidney laceration.

Then, also, there was the deafening noise generated by a capacity crowd at RFK Stadium, where the Redskins were 7-0 in playoff games. Washington's last home playoff loss was by a 73-0 score to the Bears at Griffith Stadium in 1940.

The Bears took leads of up to 13 points, led by Fuller and running back Walter Payton. The Redskins crowd was stunned.

In the final quarter the Bears bent, but never broke. They even conceded

(Continued on Page 3)

Figure 15-12   The words "23-19" are a hammerhead. This may be the largest typeface on a page.

temporary treatments that accomplish the same task but do not call too much attention to themselves.

Use of Body Copy Set Flush Left, Ragged Right

One of the most dramatic design treatments is a column of body type set flush left, ragged right (Figure 15-13). Like the flush left headline, its free-form gives a page a contemporary appearance found in modern furniture, swimming pools and architecture. The use of one such column to a page also provides pleasant contrast to the remainder of the type, which is justified on both sides.

Figure 15-13   Flush left, ragged right.

Finally, such type allows more white space into the page than the flush left and flush right columns and this results in a cleaner looking page. In planning pages, care should be taken not to overdo the use of the flush-left, ragged-right style of column. When the entire page is set this way, the charm and elegance of the style may be lost because there is too much of it (Figure 15-14). Another suggestion for its use is that more leading may be required to make

Figure 15-14   A page set in all flush left, ragged right style. [*Courtesy of the* Marion *(Ind.)* Journal and Courier]

the lines easier to read. When they are set solid, they seem to be crowded. With the addition of even a 1-point lead per line, they appear to be easier to read.

Subheads in Layouts   In traditional forms of layout, long gray columns were often broken by the use of boldface paragraphs. Perhaps every fourth or fifth paragraph might be set boldface and indented one en on each side to minimize the effect of the boldness. It is true that pages never become masses of dull grayness through the use of intermittent boldface paragraphs. On the other hand, the page did become full of spots that distracted the reader somewhat and also made the page look too bold.

Subheads are usually three- or four-word summaries of an important fact in a paragraph immediately below it. The paragraphs selected should be about every fourth or fifth one after the lead. However, there is no rule requiring them to be at any precise places in a story. They should be placed wherever they look best in breaking up a long gray mass of reading matter.

The practice of using subheads, however, in place of boldface paragraphs is contemporary in style. The best way to use subheads is to set them flush left, keeping them consistent with the main headline styles. Then, too, they should be set in boldface italic, boldface sans serif, or any distinctly contrasting typeface. Because these lines will be so short and infrequent, they will not glare at the reader as the boldface does. In some newspapers, editors have tried subheads set flush right rather than flush left with apparent success. Centered subheads tend to look old-fashioned, however.

Another acceptable form of subhead is a boldface read-in of the first two or three words in selected paragraphs. This form of head looks fairly attractive, but not as much as a free-standing head that might require 2 points of space above and below it.

Some editors have tried using various-sized dots or bullets at the beginning of a paragraph as a means of breaking up large gray masses of type. Instead of allowing the usual 1-em paragraph indention, the dot is placed in the indented space. The effect, however, is to call attention to the dot. In fact, dots are sometimes used to help the reader find paragraphs that are more significant than others. So the makeup editor might place a dot before key paragraphs. But neither technique is as adequate as the use of subheads (Figure 15-15).

What To Do with Ears   In the discussion of nameplates, it was suggested earlier that the ears be eliminated by moving the nameplate either to the left or right side of the page and bringing a column of news up to the top. But when the newspaper's policy is to keep the nameplate in the

■ A 82-16 percent majority agrees that "in some of the mistakes he has made, his lack of experience is clear to see." Back in July 1979, a higher 88-10 percent majority agreed with that claim.

Square bullet breaks up monotony

With a stroke of the pen, the United States and a group of islands in the South Pacific are bringing an end to the last 11 trusteeships set up by the United Nations at the end of World War II. Tentative accord has been reached by negotiators for the

Boldface indention, with caps and lower case used to break up grayness

● Whole-life policies that do not pay dividends. The premiums on these policies are lower than those on dividend policies. This attracts people interested in making lower cash outlays.

Round bullet also used to break up long gray columns of type

BEFORE THE QUAKE hit, about a third of the town's population, including almost all the adult males who work, had moved to northern cities or to West Germany or Switzerland to find jobs and escape the south's severe poverty.

Boldface indention set in all caps

● **Graduate education**
● **Movement around and among organizations**
● **Commitment to long hours, including evenings and weekends**
● **A deferential spouse**
● **A family that can be uprooted and relocated**

Bullets used for emphasis

finish this week essentially unchanged," Golden adds.

Prime Boost Almost Certain
Last Friday, the Dow Jones average rose for the fifth straight day,

Boldface subhead

Figure 15-15   Methods of breaking up large masses of body copy.

center, then there is the likelihood that ears will be used to fill the gaps of white space on either side.

In contemporary design, ears have been eliminated because they have become distracting devices that call attention to themselves rather than to the news columns. Most often ears are set within a boxed rule of some kind, and no matter how light these rules, they set the ears off from everything else on the page. They not only distract from the news but they distract from the nameplate itself. Therefore, white space is preferable to ears. Only when the rules have been eliminated and the typeface used is unobtrusive (small and lightface types) should ears be used. In such cases the ears will not tend to distract.

Picture Size and Placement

In the scheme of contemporary layout, pictures are given dramatic treatment. They are sized larger, but that is not the main consideration. Now they are sized to be strongly vertical or strongly horizontal. The effect of such boldly shaped pictures is a dramatic change in page appearance, a change that makes a page look exciting. The reader can't help but look at the main picture nor can he help notice the difference in the entire page. Not every picture lends itself to such treatment, but when one is available and is significant, it should be handled in a contemporary manner. The editor must have the imagination to look at a smaller-sized picture and be able to visualize it in a larger size (Figures 15-16 and 15-17).

When such boldly shaped pictures are used, an increase in the amount of white space in the total page design should be made. Otherwise the picture alone may be too strong for all other material on the page and readers may have difficulty reading the news. White space should be increased between columns, headlines and stories as compensatory devices.

At times, questions arise about the use of pictures in outside columns and the directions in which individuals are facing. In the former situation, pictures may be used anywhere, even in outside columns if the page is designed with adequate white space between columns. When the page appearance is tight because of 2- or 3-

Figure 15-16 The strongly vertical photograph helps dramatize page design. [*Courtesy of the* Chicago Tribune]

Figure 15-17 Strongly horizontal and vertical photographs help drama-tize the page. [*Courtesy of the* St. Louis *(Mo.)* Post-Dispatch]

point column rules used throughout the paper, a picture in an out-side column may not look attractive. In the latter situation, it has been the traditional practice to have individuals looking into the paper rather than out of it. The assumption is that when a person shown in the picture is looking away from the page, the reader, too, will tend to look in the same direction and perhaps turn to some other page. Research is not available to prove the truth of this assumption and it is doubtful that it is true. But occasionally a reader may find it distracting and for that reason pictures ought to be faced inwardly. Most readers have been brought up on pages designed with pictures facing into a page.

Sometimes editors will flop a negative in order to have a person look in a different direction. In other words, by printing a negative on its reverse side the editor can bring about a change in direction. This may not look attractive, however, when a person's hair is parted on the wrong side due to the flopping of a negative.

Finally, there is a question about the traditional layout practice of not placing pictures on the folds. Contemporary layout ignores this practice because it started in the days when newspapers were sold folded, primarily from newsstands. Readers might make a decision to buy or not buy a newspaper on the basis of which newspaper looked best. Because only the top half of the paper was visible on the stand it was prepared in such a way as to make it attractive. Any picture printed across the fold could not be seen in its entirety. Perhaps a sale might have been lost if only half a picture were seen. Therefore, pictures were never positioned across the folds. Now the practice seems unreasonable. Although papers are still delivered folded, they are read unfolded and the entire picture is thereby visible. The only drawback is possible damage to a picture caused by printing on cheap newsprint. The picture may be unsightly because it is on the fold.

Another objection to placing pictures on the fold was that because the picture was a piece of art it should not be ruined by the fold. Here the reasoning is questionable. Readers ordinarily do not perceive pictures as art forms and are not upset because it appears on the fold. If the details of a picture should be obliterated because of a fold, then there might be some objection to the practice. But this rarely, if ever, happens. The main and only consideration about picture placement is to find the position where it best harmonizes with every other element on the page.

Elimination of Type Rules

Contemporary design is recognized easily because it is so simple. One of the ways that layout editors have used to simplify pages was to remove as many type rules from the page as possible. For that reason, column rules were the first to be eliminated, and the effect was attractive. Once these rules were elminated, more white space appeared on the page and it began to be easier to read than when rules had been used.

Next to go were jim dashes and finish dashes. Jim dashes were used to separate decks of a headline or to separate headlines from body type. But they were not needed. Finish or 30 dashes are still used in some newspapers but they too have been eliminated by many other editors.

The white space at the end of a story did not confuse the reader as it was feared. In fact, the white space made the page easy to read because it eliminated one more black line that cluttered the page.

Now two more rules should be eliminated if possible. The first is the cutoff rule, which should be used sparingly. White space, too, should be substituted wherever possible. Finally, the dateline rules at the top of Page One and inside pages should be removed. These also add to the clutter.

The End Product of Contemporary Layout

The preceding discussion concerned major elements of contemporary layout practices. If all were used, and with discretion, the results would be a newspaper that looked as follows:

It would be simply designed. It would be functional. It would be dramatic and exciting. It would be clean-looking. It would be slower-paced than traditionally designed papers. Older designs often looked hectic and bewildering. Newer designs would show the effect of planning and sophistication. Thus a modern newspaper would be inviting and easy to read.

Problems in Achieving Contemporary Design

The authors have examined, personally, hundreds of newspaper pages submitted to the Inland Daily Press Association Makeup and Design Contests over a period of 20 years and found the following significant problem areas in achieving contemporary layout.

1. *Cluttered pages.* Clutter means that the arrangement of stories on pages looks unplanned. Why would an editor deliberately make up a page without planning? The answer is that the editor probably did not intend for it to appear that way—but it did. Clutter is found when part of a page is overcrowded with stories and pictures and the other part is clean. Clutter also is found when an important story is buried among a group of unimportant stories. Finally clutter is found when a page has too many centers of interest so that a reader cannot easily focus his eyes on any one story because of the competition of other stories.

2. *Jig-saw puzzle design.* When stories are wrapped to nearby columns and are of varying column lengths, the page tends to look like a jig-saw puzzle. Not only is such a page difficult for a layout person to plan, but it is sometimes difficult for a reader to find the continuation of stories in adjacent columns. Such pages are confusing and unattractive to readers.

3. *Pages that are too dark in appearance.* Sometimes a page will appear dark and foreboding to the reader. This may happen because all the elements of a page are heavy in appearance. If a large, bold headline is used along with dark illustrations and headline typefaces that are too large for the body copy, the entire page may appear much too dark. Obviously such a page will be uninviting to some readers. No page should ever appear like that.

4. *Pages that are too gray.* Occasionally, the opposite occurs; a page is gray and consequently dull. Headline typefaces are medium to light. Pictures are small and not dark. There may not be much white space between columns or between stories. Such pages are also uninviting to many readers.

5. *A device calls too much attention to itself.* One of the most unattractive style of pages is that where a single element calls too much attention to itself. This element may be a nameplate that is too bold. Or it may be a cartoon, a four-color picture, a single story with too much emphasis on it or too much white space in only one section of the paper.

6. *Top-heavy pages.* Top-heavy pages tend to call too much attention to the upper stories, suggesting that those at the bottom are unimportant. (See Chapter 16 for a further discussion on this subject.)

7. *Pictures are too small.* Small pictures tend to look like spots on a page rather than important communication in visual form. They detract rather than enhance a page.

8. *Pictures are square rather than being horizontal or vertical.* Square pictures tend to be uninteresting, while a mixture of horizontal and vertical pictures tends to bring about pleasant space contrast.

9. *Two or more pictures are about the same size.* When two or more pictures are about the same size, they tend to look unattractive. One of these pictures should be dominating, while the others should be subordinating. Such contrast-sized pictures help make the entire page interesting.

10. *White space is unevenly distributed.* When one part of a page has much white space and other parts do not have such abundance of space, the imbalance not only calls attention to itself but the entire page looks unattractive.

If the principles of contemporary layout are practiced, as explained in this chapter, all of these just-named problems can be solved. The solutions are relatively simple to make. But they do require a sensitivity to the layout of the entire page. Practice in designing pages whose total layout is interesting and readable is an important goal for any editor.

16

Special Pages in Contemporary Design

Knowing the concepts of contemporary layout and design are important, but knowing how to implement them on special pages are equally important. The front page and the editorial, sports and lifestyle pages all have personalities because of the nature of the subject matter to be found there and partly because of the special efforts to harmonize the contents with the design.

The following materials, then, discuss the prevailing practices used by many newspapers in implementing design concepts.

Laying Out the Front Page

One carryover from the older layout textbooks still makes sense, namely that the front page ought to be a showcase of the newspaper. Because the front page does not carry advertising, its design is free from restrictions, so that it may reflect whatever the editor wishes it to reflect. Editors, however, although agreeing on the showcase concept, have not agreed on what should be displayed in the showcase. If one looks at the layout of most front pages in this country, one will not find anything particularly exciting unless it happens to be the news. If the news is not exciting, then the front page showcase may have little to show.

There is an urgent need for editors to use the front page showcase to reflect a more sincere interest in the legibility of the page. It is suggested, therefore, that of all possible alternatives that might be featured in the showcase the most significant one is that editors of the newspaper show that they care a great deal about individuals' reading problems. The front pages of many newspapers do not reflect this interest. Front pages are not always easy to read, especially when they are compared with other printed communication such as books or magazines. They are designed, instead, on the basis of a traditional format that represents the easiest and quickest way to get the newspaper on the street in order to meet its deadline.

Underlying the showcase concept, therefore, should be the following bases for front page layout:

1. The layout should reflect the editor's concern for the reader so that the page is not only easy to read but attractive and inviting. The front page should be easier to read than any other page in the newspaper. Any device that impedes reading should be eliminated or replaced, no matter how important it may be for editorial purposes. The use of freaks, refers, inserts and kickers have worthwhile editorial purposes, but they often mar the appearance of the page design.

2. The front page should also reflect the contemporary scene more than any other page in the newspaper. There is more opportunity on the front page than any other page to achieve this goal. It is not reasonable to place news in an old-fashioned setting, and the front page should not look like front pages of by-gone days.

3. The front page should be orderly. But the order need not be graded from the most important stories placed at the top of the page to less important stories at the bottom. Other kinds of order can accomplish the same goal.

4. In addition to reflecting contemporary design, the front page should be distinctive, with a personality of its own. Although it should serve to set the tone of the entire paper, the front page personality should be one that readers like and respect because the news on that page is the most significant in the paper.

5. Readers should be offered alternative designs rather than one that is used every day with little change. Although it is true that readers may learn to like a format with no differences from day to day, such formats are not reasonable because the news changes and designs should reflect these changes. The design itself, therefore, as well as the words, helps to communicate.

Structure of Front Page

One of the most important ways of achieving a well-designed front page is to use the principle of artistic dominance. Front pages are often busy and cluttered because there are too many stories competing for the readers' attention. As a result, readers often don't know where to look, directing their attention somewhere at the top because the largest and blackest headlines are located there. Even when a few strong headlines are located elsewhere on the page, readers can't focus their attention easily without some distraction from other headlines. In other words, the competition for attention is often too great. Another problem with front page structure is that the shape of the main story, aside from its headline, is often not dominant. A single- or double-column story, no matter how long, does not necessarily dominate a page. As a result, many front pages lack unity. Graphic designer Maitland Graves stated the problem as follows: "Equality of opposing forces produces incoherence. . . . Without dominance, a design disintegrates."[1]

To overcome the pull of competing headlines and stories lacking any visual power at all, the structure of the front page should employ the principle of dominance.

The layout person can employ this principle by first selecting one element to dominate the page. This element will undoubtedly be the story with the greatest news significance. Then, by careful placement, arrangement in columns, spacing and headline treatment, it is possible to achieve the goal of page dominance. The one element, however, need not be a story alone. It may consist of a story and a related picture, a number of related stories, or a picture story (Figure 16-1 and 16-2). A hairline box around the element, including generous amounts of white space, may help achieve dominance. But the traditional banner headline, with accompanying multiple-column deck, reading into a single-column story is not an example of page dominance.

When one element dominates a page, all other elements will clearly be subordinate. But this relationship is very subtle. An element may overdominate a page to such an extent that the reader has trouble reading shorter stories. On the other hand, the dominant element may not be dominating enough to keep it from competing with secondary elements. Here, the layout person simply has to develop a sense of good design. The situation demands a sensitivity that tells the editor when an element is either too strong or too weak, neither of which may be correct.

Furthermore, a major factor in creating a pleasing page structure involves shaping the main element so that it is pleasing as well as dominating. The layout person will have to use a sense of pleasing proportions to determine the shapes that add the most to page structure. Rectangular shapes are best. Odd shapes such as uneven wraps are poorest.

Finally, the placement of the dominating element is related to its size. When a story with a bold headline is crammed into a small corner of the page, the remainder of the page may be hard to lay out in a pleasing arrangement. The dominating element, therefore, should be relatively large and placed in position close to the optical center of the page. To have stories long enough to be a center of dominant interest, the editor may have to create a policy that makes longer stories possible. Many newspapers have no such pol-

1. Maitland Graves, *The Art of Color and Design* (New York: McGraw-Hill, 1941), p. 53, 54.

Figure 16-1 A number of different stories (including the News Summary) compete for attention. [*Courtesy of the* Jacksonville *(Fla.)* Journal]

icy, and as a result it is hard to create front page dominance with relatively short stories.

New Ordering on Front Page

The order of traditional layout on the front page was always to place the most important story in the upper-right corner. Other important stories may have been placed in the upper left, and less important stories were placed underneath. This is a logical way of ordering the placement of stories, but it isn't the only way. In fact, it isn't suited to contemporary design because it tends to produce

Figure 16-2 A dominant story (boxed) on the front page. [*Courtesy of the Beaumont (Tex.)* Enterprise]

top-heavy pages and pages that never seem to vary in appearance.

A new ordering is based on the rotation of reading from the largest story to the smallest one, where the largest story is the most dominant one. But now the most dominant story may be placed anywhere on the page, and because it is so dominant, it will be read first (assuming that the reader is interested in the news content). Readers easily see where the most dominant story is located and proceed from there to less dominant stories until they have finished reading the page. Because the dominant story may be moved from day to day, there should be no fixed pattern of front page layout that becomes prosaic. Each day should bring about an exciting design showing that the layout editor is attuned to placing the news of the day in a format unique for that day.

When reading a particular story, the reader's order is from the top down. When the story is continued to adjacent columns, however, the order is back up again to the top of the next column in which the story is continued. The best way to inform the reader where the story is continued is to wrap it at the top of the next column, underneath a headline. The squared-off design should immediately tell the reader the order of procedure without the loss of even a second.

Promotional Boxes on Front Page

In recent years, many large city newspapers have begun to use boxes at the top of the front page to promote news on the inside. These boxes fill the full six-column width and usually are printed in colors. The motivation for using these boxes has been to encourage reading of inside news stories and features. They are supposed to accomplish this by calling such articles to the readers' attention before they start reading the main news.

Whether these boxes do what they are supposed to has not been measured through any controlled research. Nevertheless, many editors use them because they feel that the boxes may work. However, many others use them because the competition does.

These boxes take many shapes and sizes. Listed on the next page are some of the alternatives that have been widely used (Also see Figure 16-3):

Figure 16-3 Various kinds of promotional boxes. [*Courtesy of* Chicago Tribune; Athens *(Ga.)* Banner-Herald; Mt. Prospect *(Ill.)* Herald; and the Milwaukee *(Wisc.)* Sentinel]

1. Use of bright colored tint backgrounds for boxes
2. Two boxes, each about one-inch deep, in different colors
3. Three boxes, each about one-inch deep, also in different colors
4. Shadow boxes in black and white or color
5. Boxes with colored borders and black printing inside
6. Boxes with colored line drawings and/or halftones

Since these boxes are an important part of front page design, the user should raise questions about their advantages and disadvantages. The following is a list of each:

Advantages of using promotional boxes.

1. They add color to a page. In many newspapers where layout budgets are tightly controlled, it is not easy to add more color. Yet papers with contemporary design are using more color than ever. It is expensive to add full-color halftones in order to brighten a page. But it is relatively inexpensive to add colorful boxes to meet a popular design trend.

2. They may do what they were created for: lead readers inside the newspaper. Advertisers, especially, will appreciate this because they increase the likelihood of their ads being seen.

3. They brighten the top half of a page. When newspapers are sold through street-vending machines, the colorful promotional boxes will stand out and, perhaps, sell the newspaper to potential readers.

Disadvantages of promotional boxes.

1. They make the front page top-heavy. They are often so bright and powerful that they pull readers' eyes away from stories below. Even when people are reading at the bottom of a page, their peripheral vision can see the bright colors at the top. If the story being read is strong enough, the reader will probably stay with it. But if the reader is only halfhearted in reading it, the boxes will be a distraction.

2. They do not easily blend in with the remainder of front page design. It is difficult to make such a powerful design element at the top fit in with the remainder of the page. There is assumed to be such a thing as "good design" in newspaper layouts. But these boxes make it difficult to achieve.

3. They add confusion to the front page. When the front page has many stories, the addition of brightly colored boxes only makes the page more complex. One of the features of contemporary design has been the trend towards simplicity, which in turn makes pages more inviting to the reader. Complexity tends to repell readers rather than invite them. The use of promotional boxes in their present form tends to make the front page design complex.

How to compensate for the power of promotional boxes. Since the decision to use promotional boxes is almost always a management decision, the layout personnel will have to compensate for them in some way. If it isn't done, these boxes will distract the reader's attention from more important news lower on the page. There are a number of methods for compensating as follows:

1. Use bolder, larger headlines throughout the front page. This provides some balance to the page.
2. Use some larger boxes with heavier rules on the page. Such boxes may help bring about centers of attention that could compete with the promotional boxes.
3. Use more colored tint blocks underneath black type. These colored tints counterbalance the color at the top.
4. Use larger and/or more photographs lower on the page.

Special Problems To Avoid in Front Page Layout

Listed below are some recurring problems contributing to poor design on the front page. If the reader's best interest serves as the underlying basis for design, these problems will not occur. But because they have occurred so often, they are mentioned here. See checklist on page 364.

1. Use of a daily banner headline. Readers either resent newspapers that use a large banner headline daily or they learn to discount the effect of large type used in such headlines. They assume that what is printed is not necessarily most important. In some newspaper offices, banners are used each day because it has become traditional since the days when newspapers were sold on newsstands. Editorial policy should be changed so that banners are used only when the news warrants them. If not, then the entire page structure is forced into a page where the readout almost always occurs at the top right, or, perhaps, somewhere at the top. It is difficult to create a contemporary design when a banner headline is used each day.
2. Breaking a page into two noticeable sections. When the layout editor attempts to use contemporary design through the use of page domination, there is the possibility he may divide the page into two equal parts. This has the effect of asking the reader to read either one or the other part but not both. One part may not naturally lead into the other. Therefore, attempts should be made to prevent such a dichotomy from occurring.

    Whenever a page is divided into two equal parts, it tends to be noticeable. For example, a six-column page divided into three columns on the left and three on the right is very noticeable. On the other hand, a page divided into four on the left and two on the right would attract no special attention. The same principle applies to page divisions horizontally. It is imperative to avoid page divisions of 50% each (Figure 16-4).
3. Alignment of elements. Layout editors sometimes have trouble noticing the effect of too many different alignments occurring

Figure 16-4   A page that is, for the most part, divided into three columns on the left and three on the right. [*Courtesy of* Muskegon *(Mich.)* Chronicle]

on a contemporary front page. Alignment means placing elements on a page so that they form an imaginary straight line. In traditional layout, alignment was easy because every story had to fit into a column structure, and columns were straight. In contemporary layout, stories and pictures may have different widths and be positioned differently. If they do not align, at least to some extent, the reader is faced with a ragged, unattractive appearance. Too many things seem to be vying for attention because there are too many different starting places. The goal, therefore, is to deliberately bring about more alignment without having all elements align. A little off-center placement adds a dash of interest and excitement to the page. A lot of the same thing becomes unattractive. Most alignment should take place on the left side so that the reader's eyes always return to the same position when reading. For example, it may not be as easy to read a column of type set flush left, ragged right as it is one set flush on both sides. The perfect alignment of the type set flush both sides brings about an orderly arrangement of lines, and readers know from experience where to find the next line. But flush left, ragged right is much easier to read than having both sides set ragged, as is sometimes done in advertisements. The design of type set with varying alignments presents an obstacle to reading. Lack of alignment on a page is something to be avoided.

4. Probably nothing affects a front page appearance more than pictures. When small pictures are used, the page tends to appear spotty and unattractive, no matter how important the news is. On the other hand, one or more large pictures tend to dramatize the appearance of the front page. If a large picture is sized to be strongly vertical or horizontal, then the page may appear even more dramatic and interesting. So one problem to avoid is the use of small pictures that add clutter to a page.

Along the same lines, it is important not to use two pictures of about the same size on the front page. One should be considerably larger than the other. This is a practice, therefore, of bringing contrast to a page. Good contrast usually means that the page will be interesting and appealing to the reader.

Finally, it is important to break the habit of creating front pages with pictures arranged in the same manner day after day. It is often difficult to dramatize story shapes or positioning because the news on any particular day may not lend itself to such techniques. But editors can get into a rut in using pictures the same way day in and day out. Pictures, however, can be used in so many different ways and in so many different placements that they offer the editor the most opportunity for transforming an ordinary looking page into something exciting. It does take some imagination to use pictures in an interesting manner. One example that offers readers a change of pace is that of using outline halftones occasionally, perhaps once a month. Such pictures can be overused, but once a month is hardly too much.

Inside Page Layout

Almost any page on which advertisements have been placed presents layout problems. The only space for news is whatever remains after the advertisements have been dummied. Often the person who dummies advertisements does not consider the problems of the news layout editor. Other times, the advertising person simply cannot find enough pages on which to place advertising without increasing the total number of pages in the newspaper. This person may cram the advertisements into most of the avail-

---

**CHECKLIST OF TEN WAYS
TO IMPROVE FRONT PAGE LAYOUT**

The following list is a summary of techniques discussed in this and previous chapters on making the front page more readable, and at the same time, more attractive and exciting. It is presented as a reminder of what can be done to improve front page design:

1. Create "open" as opposed to "tight" pages. This means adding more space between stories, pictures, and other page elements.

2. Use a large box on the page, with at least 12 points of white space between inside border and body type.

3. Use large vertical and/or horizontal pictures.

4. Mix direction of story shapes in uneven proportions: example: ⅓ vertical and ⅔ horizontal layout, or vice versa.

5. Use a news summary rather than many short stories on the page.

6. Make the bottom of the page as interesting as the top by use of large pictures, boxed stories or strong horizontal story shapes.

7. Avoid "holes" in the page caused by flush left headlines that are too short or kickers set in large type.

8. Have one story dominate the page, rather than two or three that are about the same length and/or size.

9. Divide the page into dramatic divisions such as 2:4, or nonprecise divisions.

10. Avoid too many boxes, rules, or other attention-getting devices that pull readers' eyes away from stories.

able space, leaving the news layout editor with design problems. Modern techniques of contemporary layout, therefore, are hard to apply on inside pages.

Some tabloid newspaper editors partially solve the problem by keeping the first few inside pages free of advertising. This practice gives the layout editor more opportunities to create attractive and readable inside pages. But larger-sized newspapers may not have the space to free such pages for news alone. To do so might result in other pages filled with so much advertising that neither the advertisements nor the news can be read easily. If the management, however, feels that it can spare the space, then a policy can be made that keeps advertising from the first few pages.

Picture Placement on Inside Pages

A previous discussion covered reasons why pictures should not be placed in corners of a page. To review: more important editorial material belongs in corners, and readers will find pictures no matter where they are placed on a page. A more reasonable approach, and one that will not affect page stability, is to place these pictures as low as possible on any given page. They will get high readership no matter where they are placed. Therefore, the most important positions (corners) should not be used for material that automatically receives high readership. Some kind of headline belongs in the corners: presumably, a headline and story of significance if possible. The objective is to get the story read. If the story is buried underneath the picture it may not be read because it is in a less attractive position. By giving a story an outstanding position, the editor may help the reader learn something significant. Meanwhile, the buried picture will brighten any position on the page (Figure 16-5). The bottoms of pages, particularly, where there is a combination of advertisements and editorial materials, need considerable brightening. Any effort to make this position more attractive not only benefits the reader, who finds the page better balanced, and the advertiser, because the reader will look at the bottom as well as the top of inside pages.

Advertising Placement

The layout editor has little control over the placement of advertisements. But it may be wise to consult with the advertising department about the possibility of placing advertisements in positions that enhance the design of inside pages for the benefit of both readers and advertisers. Traditionally, ads have been pyramided diagonally from the lower left of a page to the upper right. The left side of the newspaper, therefore, received most of the editorial material. This is a reasonable approach to advertising placement in relation to editorial matter because it always frees the left side of the page for news. Because reading took place from left to

Figure 16-5 Moving a photograph low on an inside page helps bring readers down the page. [*Courtesy of the* Mt. Prospect *(Ill.)* Herald]

right, it was assumed that all news material should align on the left as a means of making the page easy to read. Left- and right-hand pages were dummied in the same manner so that the pyramid faced the same direction on all pages (Figure 16-6).

It is just as reasonable, however, to believe that the present system of dummying advertisements is not always logical. Many readers do not see only one page at a time. Instead, they open the paper so that both the left- and right-hand sides of the paper are visible at once. Obviously readers cannot read two pages at one time but may see the total design of two facing pages in their

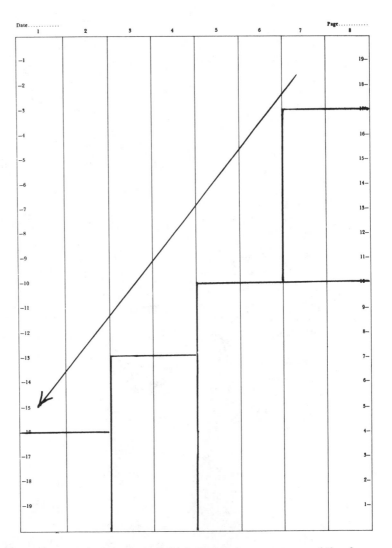

Figure 16-6   Typical method of placing advertisements: pyramiding from upper right to lower left.

peripheral vision (Figure 16-7). Therefore, the layout of a single page carrying advertisements should never be considered alone. The opposite page is also part of the total page design. Layout editors traditionally have not conceived of two facing pages as a single entity because they dummy only one page at a time. But it is reasonable to consider the combined effect of the two facing pages. In such a situation, the left side of the paper ought to be dummied so that the advertisements are placed in the position opposite of their placement on right-hand pages. This means that the advertisements on the left side of the page are dummied with the diagonal running from the top left to the lower right. The right-hand page is dummied oppositely. As a result of this makeup procedure, all

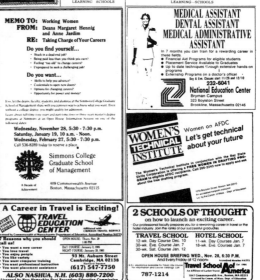

Figure 16-7a Two facing pages showing advertisements pryamided towards the center. This allows the news to be concentrated in the center. [*Courtesy of the* Boston *(Mass.)* Globe]

THE BOSTON GLOBE Tuesday, NOVEMBER 20, 1984 11

President Reagan gestures as he chats with others yesterday while participating in a program to discourage theft of farm equipment. Deputy sheriff (right) tagged some of the equipment on the President's Santa Barbara ranch as part of program. Other men are officials of the Santa Barbara and California Farm Bureaus. AP PHOTO

Group advocates US paramilitary moves

By Fred Hiatt
and Spencer Rich
Washington Post

WASHINGTON – The Reagan Administration in its second term should use "paramilitary assets" to weaken the governments of Vietnam, Cambodia, Libya and other unfriendly nations around the world, the Heritage Foundation said in a report submitted to the White House.

The operations are envisioned as part of a stronger US posture in the world, which the report said also rests on continuation of a military buildup, redoubled efforts to build missiles and a strong suspicion of the value of arms-control talks. Other countries where the United States should intensify or begin covert operations include Laos, Angola, Ethiopia, Afghanistan, Nicaragua and Iran, according to the report.

The recommendations on paramilitary action are contained in "Mandate for Leadership II," a compendium of more than 1300 proposals for President Ronald Reagan's second term put together by the conservative Heritage group.

The sections of the report on defense and arms control, which are scheduled to be released today, strongly support the Administration's efforts during the past four years to modernize the US military. The report said that the buildup must continue and that the Administration should buy more of some weapons, such as the B1 bomber, than now planned.

At the same time, the report sharply criticized Pentagon management during the first term and said the Secretary of Defense should take charge of efforts to improve the way weapons are purchased. The report said that the Administration's past "acquisition initiatives" have "not proved particularly effective."

The Heritage report strongly urged the Administration to abandon the Anti-Ballistic Missile Treaty, which the United States and the Soviet Union signed in 1972, and move swiftly to develop weapons that could defend MX missile sites against attacking missiles.

The report's disdain for the ABM treaty holds true for most other arms-control efforts.

Heritage representatives say the United States should not negotiate over antisatellite weapons or any form of strategic defense; should not seek a comprehensive test-ban treaty; should not ratify the Threshold Test Ban Treaty, which both superpowers observe, that limits underground testing to nuclear explosions of no more than 150 kilotons; should no longer abide by the guidelines of the unratified SALT 2 accord, which both the United States and Soviet Union have said they would respect; should not seek to negotiate a treaty banning chemical weapons, which would be "virtually impossible" to verify, and should not make new proposals in the stalled talks on strategic missiles, medium-range missiles or troop strengths in Europe.

Reagan budget advisers stymied on what to cut

■ BUDGET
Continued from Page 1

The official, expressing concern that the White House had backed itself into a corner, said it would be nearly impossible to achieve a $50 billion spending reduction by simply cutting such federal programs as Medicaid, Civil Service retirement, farm price supports and student aid.

He said that after ruling out all the untouchable areas in the budget – assuming that Reagan continues with his inclination not to cut military spending, raise taxes or touch Social Security – there remained only a total of $200 billion in spending that could be touched.

Those areas that Reagan has exempted, along with the interest on the debt, add up to two-thirds of total spending.

As a measure of the seriousness of the situation, the official said presidential counselor Edwin Meese was proposing again to eliminate the Departments of Education and Energy, transferring some of their functions to other Cabinet agencies that he said even such drastic moves would only result in relatively small savings. The entire Education Department budget is less than $18 billion.

The Administration official also said Meese gave out copies of a report by the conservative Heritage Foundation, recommending ways to cut the federal budget, at a Cabinet meeting last week. The document proposed allowing workers to withdraw gradually from the Social Security and Medicare systems and finance their benefits through Individual Retirement Accounts.

Deputy White House press secretary Marlin Fitzwater also acknowledged that the still unpublished report was distributed, but he said the document had no official standing and that the Administration has no intention of altering the Social Security system.

"The President's commitment not to change Social Security rules out any recommendations for change," Fitzwater said.

Some members of the budget group urge an across-the-board government spending freeze, while others contend there is no way to avoid cutting military spending.

As a result, the official said Reagan's option list would probably include three choices on military spending – a 7 percent increase, a 5 percent increase and no increase.

The official said some of the presidential aides involved in the budget process have been meeting in small groups to commiserate about the impossibility of their task and then to try to figure out a way to do it.

The group includes budget director David Stockman, White House chief of staff James A. Baker 3d, deputy chief of staff Michael K. Deaver, Treasury Secretary Donald Regan, Meese, presidential assistant Richard G. Darman, Craig L. Fuller, director of the Office of Cabinet Administration, and others.

Officially, White House aides have been tight-lipped about the budget process. Fitzwater said the Administration's goal was to balance the budget eventually, but no deadline was specified.

White House spokesman Larry Speakes said last week that Reagan had given his Cabinet secretaries "marching orders" to submit budget proposals that hold the line on government spending and require no tax increases.

Foreign policy team to stay as is, Reagan's aides say

United Press International

SANTA BARBARA, Calif. – White House officials, trying to squelch speculation of changes in the Administration's personnel roster, said yesterday that President Ronald Reagan will keep his foreign policy team intact into his second term.

The officials, worried that a flurry of rumors of a staff shakeup could undercut foreign policy in the coming months, said the principal members of Reagan's team will remain on board for the foreseeable future.

"Despite the talk, there's nothing going on in terms of changes in the national security apparatus," one senior Administration official said.

The official said Secretary of State George P. Shultz, Defense Secretary Caspar Weinberger, CIA Director William Casey and Robert McFarlane, the national security adviser, "have discussed it with the President and are planning to stay on" at Reagan's request.

While Shultz has announced through a spokesman that he has accepted Reagan's request to remain in office, questions continue about Weinberger, McFarlane and Casey.

The rumors fueling these questions have been attributed alternatively to State Department officials who view Weinberger and other hard-liners within the Administration as obstacles to arms control, and to conservatives hoping to install one of their own – such as Jeane Kirkpatrick, the US ambassador to the United Nations – in the job held by McFarlane.

In particular, one White House official cited a New York Times report last week suggesting, on the basis of statements by anonymous officials, that Weinberger might have to go if progress on arms control – a top Reagan priority – is to be realized.

The recurrence of such speculation about White House officials is taking pains to dismiss the notion of any change in the national security lineup and play down friction between the principals, including Shultz and Weinberger.

"They are going to stay," said one official, "and we are going to make progress."

The same official said there was no truth to reports McFarlane might be angling to become ambassador to Israel and insisted the national security adviser has no interest in leaving that post.

Confidence in government has increased, poll shows

Reuter

NEW YORK – Americans expressed greater confidence in government than they have in the last decade, in the first major public opinion poll since the election, but said they expect President Ronald Reagan to raise taxes despite his campaign pledges to the contrary.

The poll, conducted among 1798 voters between Nov. 8 and 14 – with a sampling error of plus or minus two points – showed that 57 percent expected Reagan to ask Congress for higher taxes.

Nevertheless, the New York Times/CBS News poll, published in yesterday's New York Times, showed 80 percent of the public believed the government was run for the benefit of the people.

The pollsters said this was the highest percentage since 1972, and compared it to the figure of four years ago that showed only 21 percent of the population had confidence in the government.

In addition, Americans were optimistic that in the next four years the Administration would assault any recession, would attempt to cut the federal budget deficit and would make a real effort to negotiate a good arms control agreement with the Soviet Union.

On recession, 58 percent of those polled felt Reagan would work to avoid it, and a similar number thought he would work to reduce the budget deficit, now running at $175.4 billion.

Asked whether they thought Reagan would "make a real effort to negotiate a good arms control agreement with the Soviet Union," 75 percent of those polled said yes.

Figure 16-7b **Two facing pages showing advertisements pyramided towards the center. This allows the news to be concentrated in the center.** [*Courtesy of the* Boston *(Mass.)* Globe]

the news is concentrated in the center between the two facing pages in a concave shape.

When pages are tightly dummied so that there is little room for news on the page, the arrangement just described will not work very well. In the latter situation, perhaps both pages should be dummied the traditional way; the layout editor will have to live with a situation where there is little that can be done to design an attractive page.

If there are at least two ¼ pages of space available on each of two facing pages, the editor should ask the advertising department whether the pyramid on the left-hand page can be reversed so that both left and right side pyramids decline toward the center fold. It is that simple. Where one page has about one-quarter of the space for news and the other has much more or less, the editor should ask that an advertisement be shifted to another page so that he can make up as many two facing page units as possible in an attractive design.

"Open" Inside Page Layout

There are times when it is impossible to change the pyramid direction of advertisements, either because of the advertising department's policy or because there is little time left. Yet there is another approach to improving inside page design provided space is available for news. Perhaps there may be as much as one-third or more of the space on a page for news. When that much space is available, the page may be considered to be "open." At that time a layout procedure may be used whereby the space immediately adjacent to advertisements is filled completely so that the top of the news aligns across the page with the top of the highest-positioned advertisement. What remains, then, is a rectangle of white space that is also available for news (Figure 16-8). A rectangular space is relatively easy to use for creating an attractive page design. If the page were filled in the traditional manner, then the odd-shaped space may or may not provide the means of creating an attractive page. The rectangular approach may be used only when the pyramid advertisements do not extend much above the fold.

"Tight" Inside Page Layout

Many times the layout editor is faced with so many advertisements on a page, or a few large advertisements, that there is little space for news. Either constitutes a *tight* page. In this situation, it is best to dummy a single long story in the remaining space than to use a number of short stories on the page (Figure 16-9). The long story may be wrapped from column to column until the space is filled. The reader should have no difficulty reading that story. On the other hand, where many short stories are dummied on a tight page, wraps are necessary and may be confusing to the reader because a headline may not cover each of them. There may not be enough time to reset a one-column headline in a two-column width, or there may not be enough multiple-column heads to cover all raw wraps. Furthermore, when many short stories are used on

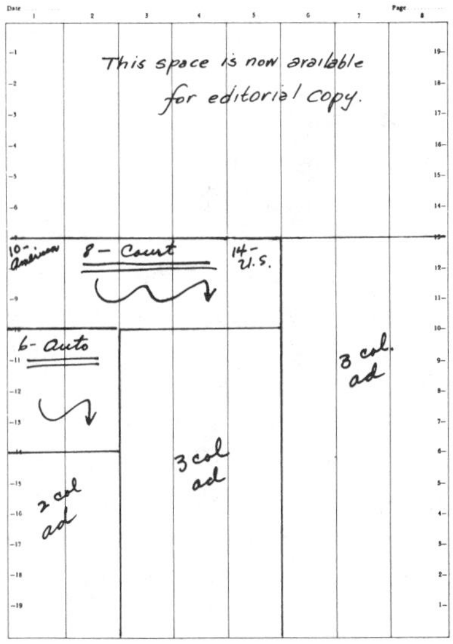

Figure 16-8 Rectangle of space that remains after stories are dummied so that the top one aligns with the top of a pyramided ad. The remaining space allows better inside page layout.

12-B—Sarasota Herald-Tribune Wed., Nov. 19, 1980

Rickles Tickles From New York To London To Vegas

Don Rickles

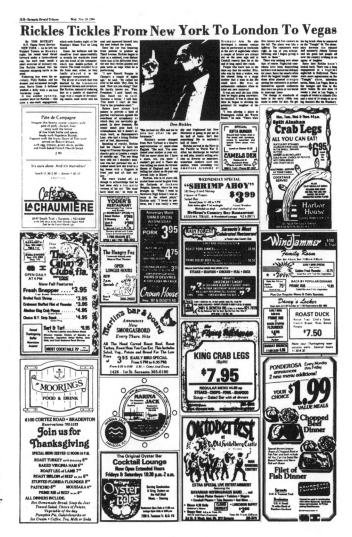

Figure 16-9 A single story wrapped from column to column is dummied into this advertisement-filled page. [*Courtesy of* Sarasota *(Fla.)* Herald-Tribune]

a tight page it may be difficult to avoid tombstones. If there are no long stories available and shorter ones must be used on tight pages, there is the possibility that more than one headline will be positioned across the top of the page, usually an unsightly layout procedure. If the placement of headlines in such positions cannot be avoided, then they should be alternated at the top to avoid tombstones. Perhaps a two-column headline can be alternated with a single-column head, or perhaps a headline set in a roman type can be alternated with one set in italics (Figure 16-10). Least effective from a layout point of view is the use of headlines positioned next to each other at the top where two-line heads are alternated with three-line heads, especially when both are set in the same size and typeface. Alternation should be more contrasting.

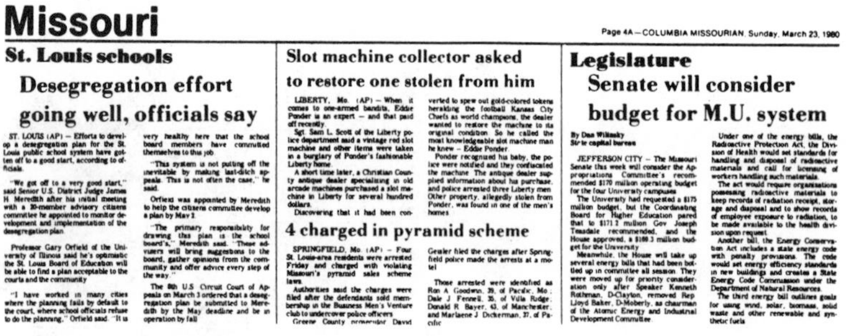

Missouri

Page 4A—COLUMBIA MISSOURIAN, Sunday, March 23, 1980

St. Louis schools

Desegregation effort going well, officials say

ST. LOUIS (AP) — Efforts to develop a desegregation plan for the St. Louis public school system have gotten off to a good start, according to officials.

"We got off to a very good start," said Senior U.S. District Judge James H. Meredith after his initial meeting with a 20-member advisory citizens committee he appointed to monitor development and implementation of the desegregation plan.

Professor Gary Orfield of the University of Illinois said he's optimistic the St. Louis Board of Education will be able to find a plan acceptable to the courts and the community.

"I have worked in many cities where the planning fails by default to the court, where school officials refuse to do the planning," Orfield said. "It is very healthy here that the school board members have committed themselves to this job.

"This system is not putting off the inevitable by making last-ditch appeals. This is not often the case," he said.

Orfield was appointed by Meredith to help the citizens committee develop a plan by May 1.

"The primary responsibility for drawing this plan is the school board's," Meredith said. "These advisers will bring suggestions to the board, gather opinions from the community and offer advice every step of the way."

The 8th U.S. Circuit Court of Appeals on March 3 ordered that a desegregation plan be submitted to Meredith by the May deadline and be in operation by fall.

Slot machine collector asked to restore one stolen from him

LIBERTY, Mo. (AP) — When it comes to one-armed bandits, Eddie Ponder is an expert — and that paid off recently.

Sgt. Sam L. Scott of the Liberty police department said a vintage red slot machine and other items were taken in a burglary of Ponder's fashionable Liberty home.

A short time later, a Christian County antique dealer specializing in old arcade machines purchased a slot machine in Liberty for several hundred dollars.

Discovering that it had been converted to spew out gold-colored tokens heralding the football Kansas City Chiefs as world champions, the dealer wanted to restore the machine to its original condition. So he called the most knowledgeable slot machine man he knew — Eddie Ponder.

Ponder recognized his baby, the police were notified and they confiscated the machine. The antique dealer supplied information about his purchase, and police arrested three Liberty men. Other property, allegedly stolen from Ponder, was found in one of the men's homes.

4 charged in pyramid scheme

SPRINGFIELD, Mo. (AP) — Four St. Louis-area residents were arrested Friday and charged with violating Missouri's pyramid sales scheme laws.

Authorities said the charges were filed after the defendants sold membership in the Business Men's Venture club to undercover police officers.

Greene County prosecutor David Gesler filed the charges after Springfield police made the arrests at a motel.

Those arrested were identified as Ron A. Goodwin, 29, of Pacific, Mo.; Dale J. Fennell, 35, of Villa Ridge; Donald R. Bayer, 43, of Manchester; and Marlaene J. Dickerman, 37, of Pacific.

Legislature

Senate will consider budget for M.U. system

By Dan Wilinsky
State capital bureau

JEFFERSON CITY — The Missouri Senate this week will consider the Appropriations Committee's recommended $170 million operating budget for the four University campuses.

The University had requested a $175 million budget, but the Coordinating Board for Higher Education pared that to $171.2 million. Gov. Joseph Teasdale recommended, and the House approved, a $169.3 million budget for the University.

Meanwhile, the House will take up several energy bills that had been bottled up in committee all session. They were moved up for priority consideration only after Speaker Kenneth Rothman, D-Clayton, removed Rep. Lloyd Baker, D-Moberly, as chairman of the Atomic Energy and Industrial Development Committee.

Under one of the energy bills, the Radioactive Protection Act, the Division of Health would set standards for handling and disposal of radioactive materials and call for licensing of workers handling such materials.

The act would require organizations possessing radioactive materials to keep records of radiation receipt, storage and disposal and to show records of employee exposure to radiation, to be made available to the health division upon request.

Another bill, the Energy Conservation Act, includes a state energy code with penalty provisions. The code would set energy efficiency standards in new buildings and creates a State Energy Code Commission under the Department of Natural Resources.

The third energy bill outlines goals for using wind, solar, biomass, solid waste and other renewable and synthetic fuels.

Figure 16-10 Alternated heads dummied to avoid tombstoning. [*Courtesy of the* Columbia *(Mo.)* Missourian]

Boxed Stories Brighten Inside Pages

Pictures invariably brighten inside pages, but they may not be available or they may be too large for the space. Another means of brightening inside pages is boxing one story on a page (Figure 16-11 and 16-12). Only those stories whose contents are significant should be boxed. Assuming that there usually will be at least one such story per page, it should be boxed with a 2-point rule. The size of the box should be at least two columns but preferably three columns wide. The reason is that only a box of sufficient size to be noticed can bring about dominant appearance. The effect of boxing a story is to enhance the appearance of the news portion of the page.

If there is any objection to the boxing process, it usually is that too much production time is taken. The type to be boxed may have to be reset to a narrower measure or a column of news may have to be eliminated to provide the space taken by the box, which is larger than regular-column width. When a column of news is eliminated as described previously, the remaining columns will have to be reset to odd-column measures, a procedure that usually is not appreciated because it takes so much time.

st.louis/wednesday

Wed., Nov. 26, 3A
ST. LOUIS POST-DISPATCH

New Program At Phillips Helping Elderly Keep PACE

By D.D. Obika
Of the Post-Dispatch Staff

Special District Board Seeks A New Image

By Howard S. Goller
Of the Post-Dispatch Staff

Martha G. Tucker, president of the Special
School District Board of Education, with her 18-

year-old daughter, Suzie, who is enrolled as a
student in the district.

Two Proposals Seek To Boost Funds For Roads

By Robert Goodrich
Post-Dispatch Jefferson City Bureau

Deaf Man Killed After Train Hits His Car In Kirkwood

Area Ready For Holiday And All The Fixings

By Marjorie Mandel
Of the Post-Dispatch Staff

Utility Aid Requests Received Monday

Lottery Number

CHICAGO (UPI) —

local

City Advances $9.8 Million For Bi-State

Construction Work To Close Ninth Street

City Delays Sale Of Mortgage Bonds

Figure 16-11 A large box brightens an inside page. [*Courtesy of the* St. Louis *(Mo.)* Post-Dispatch]

Yet the layout person will have to determine which is most important: improving the appearance of inside pages or keeping production costs down. If production cost is more important, then the editor simply forces news into vacant holes on inside pages regardless of the appearance. Many inside pages of newspapers are unsightly and difficult to read.

Figure 16-12 A tone border (top) helps brighten this page. Also a photograph at the bottom brings interest to the bottom. [*Courtesy of the* Findlay *(Ohio)* Courier]

A final problem relating to boxed stories and improving the appearance of inside pages concerns the practice of not dummying any more than a few large stories on such pages and allowing the makeup to be done by the printer. When this happens the page may show the lack of planning. The printer, plagued by the necessity of speeding up production, usually takes the most traditional route toward finishing the layout process. In fact, printers may be discouraged from even attempting new layout procedures. Therefore, the remainder of such layout is often less than the best. Even when the editor stands next to the printer and directs the filling of undummied inside pages, the result is apt to look poor. The best technique is to tightly dummy the remaining space in the editorial office and take enough time to make the pages as attractive as possible.

Figure 16-13 **Editorials set in larger type help make them easier to read.** [*Courtesy of the* St. Louis *(Mo.)* Post-Dispatch](see p. 376.)

Figure 16-14   A number of stories, boxed, helps make the editorial page interesting. [*Courtesy of the* **Carbondale** *(Ill.)* **Southern Illinoisan**]

Editorial Pages

The editorial page is sometimes better designed than any other page in a newspaper. The means for achieving a better design are as follows:

1. Setting editorials in a larger size type than ordinary body type used for news. If body type is 9-point, then editorials may be set either 11- or 12-point type (Figure 16-13).
2. Setting editorials in wider column widths. Although a paper may use a six-column format for news, the editorial page may be reduced to five columns, with each column wider than a typical news column.

Figure 16-15 Generous use of white space between editorials helps make the page inviting and more readable. [*Courtesy of the* Evansville *(Ind.)* Press]

3. Boxing editorials or stories. In order to make editorials (or stories) stand out from other materials on a page, they may be boxed in either a 2-point rule or perhaps a tone-border rule (Figure 16-14).

4. Bringing more white space into the page. Additional white space may be added to an editorial page by allowing twice as much space between editorials and stories than is used on news pages. For example, if the space between one story and another immediately underneath is normally two picas, then three and a half or four picas are used to separate stories on the editorial page (Figure 16-15).

5. Placement of cartoons on the editorial page has been changed from positions at the top to the center or lower part of the page. The cartoon will get attention no matter where it is placed on this page. Therefore, it should not occupy a position of major importance. Editorials should occupy this position.

6. The masthead, which formerly often occupied a position at the upper-left part of the page, has now been moved to the lower right where it does not compete for attention with editorials. There is no value in placing the masthead in such a dominating position as the upper left.

Figure 16-16   Horizontal layout at the bottom contrasts nicely with the vertical at the top. [*Courtesy of* Dallas *(Texas)* Times-Herald]

7. The use of photographs can enhance the appearance of editorial pages, but it is rarely done. The reason for limited use of photographs is probably more a matter of tradition than anything else. A few papers have started to use photographs on this page, and others are beginning to copy the practice.

8. Using more horizontal layout on the editorial page. Some editors have changed their designs to totally horizontal pages. Others have simply added more horizontal styling than before (Figure 16-15 and 16-16).

9. Using a strong stylistic device such as flush left, ragged right body copy on the editorial page may also provide a distinctive appearance (Figure 16-17).

Figure 16-17   Use of flush left and ragged right for editorials brings unique styling to a page. [*Courtesy of* Rapid City *(S. Dak.)* Journal]

**Editorial Page
Structure**

Despite all these techniques of improving editorial page appearance, some of them still are unattractive. There are a number of reasons why this is so. Probably the foremost reason is that the *page structure* is unattractive. White space may help a page, but that isn't all that is needed. A grid page is better than older styled layouts for editorial pages, because grid simplifies and organizes materials on a page. Editorial pages usually include much more than editorials, and there is a need to organize these diverse elements. Such pages contain various articles by columnists, letters to the editor, historical notes and other miscellaneous material. A grid design will usually help make editorial pages more readable.

Another structural problem concerns the sameness of page design that occurs over a long period of time. It tends to be boring. Some editors use an editorial page layout that never varies from day to day. The main advantage of a nonvarying design is that it provides the reader with a familiar page. But that page can often appear boring, especially if the editorials are not especially noteworthy. It is therefore reasonable to vary editorial page makeup. Perhaps three or four alternative designs should be prepared beforehand and alternated from time to time. On the other hand, too much variety would have no particular advantages.

But the concept of editorial page layout should be based on the desirability of utilizing full layout control, coupled with a desire to personalize the page better than any other page. Editors have complete control over the contents of the editorial page, something they may not have in the layout of front pages. Front page layout is often affected by the nature of the news, which results in designs that are a compromise between what is desired and what is most practical. But the editor does not have this problem on the editorial page. Furthermore, the nature of editorial material is personal. Editorials are personal messages from the editor to readers whereby opinions of the newspaper are expressed. Guest columnists tend to be personal in their approach to opinion or interpretation, and letters to the editor also reflect readers' personal opinions. The concept of editorial page layout, therefore, should be based on a more personalized design than used for any other page in the newspaper. A personalized style is warm, appealing and simple. The effect of such design is to make the page inviting. A complex and cold-looking page tends to make readers hesitate to read it. Because research has shown that readership traffic of editorial pages is often 50 percent less than on front pages, there is an urgent need to make the page more readable and increase traffic there. Presumably the editors have something to say and readers need help to read what has been written. Some newspapers have done remarkably well in executing this concept; many have not.

Other Layout Techniques for Editorial Pages

The masthead is often placed at the top of editorial columns, apparently to relate the name of the newspaper and its staff with the opinions shown below. Sometimes when the editorial page is placed within the first five pages of an issue, it serves as the source of necessary postal information for second-class matter. There is, however, a good reason for not placing the masthead at the top of editorial columns.

Editorials usually are found near the front of the newspaper, in the left-hand column of a left-hand page. The upper-left corner of the page, therefore, is assumed to be the most important position on the page, perhaps the most important position in the entire issue. It should be devoted to the most significant piece of information on the page, which is not the masthead. Editorials are much more significant and demand top position. There is little justification for wasting a key position. If the masthead is attractively designed, as many are, it will not matter where it is placed on the page. The best placement, therefore, is in the lower-right corner because in that position it can achieve readership without distracting from any other feature on the page.

Another editorial page feature that could well be buried is the editorial cartoon. As research has indicated, a cartoon will achieve readership no matter where it is located on a page. That being the case, why take one of the most crucial positions (top center) and place the cartoon there? If the position of the cartoon is fixed because of tradition, there is little that can be done. But attempts should be made to move it to the bottom, where it will still achieve readership and yet free the top position for more significant editorial material.

Although larger type, wider columns, more white space between the columns and a cleaner page are the result, the editorial page often lacks drama because there is too much type on the page and relatively few illustrations. Occasionally a small portrait of a columnist may appear somewhere on the page, but that plus the cartoon is the extent of decorative material. One key editorial or an important column may be boxed each day as a means of dominating the page. Sometimes editorials, although important, are not long enough to receive dramatic treatment. But often a columnist's material is. Even then, the same individual may not have an exciting column each day. But some other columnist may have material worthy of being boxed. The layout editor might select some story, editorial or column to be given a dramatic treatment each day.

Finally, large initial letters are sometimes used for the first letter of each editorial as a means of making the page look more attractive. Their use is debatable. On the one hand, they sometimes look attractive if not too many of them are placed on the page. They are decorative devices. But they pose problems for the composing room. They take careful preparation in typesetting and may look unattractive if poorly done. Perhaps the most significant factor in their use should be whether they enhance or detract from the editorials. When they are too bold or too large, they may detract. If there is not enough space around them, they may not look attractive. Therefore, the use of large initial letters as a desirable makeup device must be considered of indeterminate value.

Lifestyle Pages   The proper concept of lifestyle pages design generally has not been clear. The basic idea was to present news and features of interest to women in a distinctly feminine style. To implement that idea, a style of layout was devised that used lighter typefaces for headlines and body copy and perhaps a bit more space between the columns. Column rules were sometimes eliminated on these pages to help lighten the page. This concept, however, was really inadequate to fulfill the need for feminine design because the result was nothing more than lighter-appearing pages. The only change from the layout of other pages in the same issue was the lightness of the pages. But lightness is hardly the most significant dimension needed for communicating with women who are often sensitive to good design. Women's facial makeup, hair, clothes, homes and gardens all express sensitivity to some or large proportions of contemporary design. In other words, there is still a need to change lifestyle's page layout radically to be more in line with the contemporary frame of reference in which women tend to think. Of course many women object to the whole concept of writing pages devoted exclusively to women's interests, preferring a nonsexist approach.

The use of lightface types for headlines often can result in rather ugly pages. Simply because a typeface is lightface rather than boldface does not make it feminine. Furthermore, the widespread use of italic, script or cursive typefaces on lifestyle pages is intended to bring about a feminine appearance. But some of these typefaces are so grotesque they defeat the goal. For example, Lydian Cursive, Brush Script, Coronet or Mandate are types that, although different from roman faces, are not necessarily attractive on lifestyle pages. They are too ornate and are more suited for advertising. Ultra Bodoni Italic, Bodoni Book Italic, Cheltenham Light or Medium Italic and Century Italic also are not feminine. Garamond or Caslon Italic may be appropriate, but they lack charm in bolder versions and neither is a contemporary type style. Contemporary styles are noted for their extended appearance and their use of ultrafine serifs coupled with contrasting heavier elements.

Although headline types can help achieve a feminine styling, more than typeface selection is needed.

A number of newspapers, mostly the larger ones, have felt the need for change and have designed lifestyle pages that make them radically different from what they were before. They have adopted a newer concept, which is to make the page appear not feminine, but charming and dramatic (Figure 16-18). A page may appear feminine and yet may be in poor taste or lack charm. The newer concept has been implemented with bold and imaginative planning.

The most important means of implementing this new concept is to design, rather than make up, pages. In other words, pages are not dummied as pages have been traditionally—they are designed with the total page concept in mind. Because much of the material appearing on lifestyle pages is advance or time copy that can be set before the current news is set, there is usually time to design a page rather than build it piece by piece. But the task of designing is of such major importance that sometimes newspapers hire persons with strong commercial art backgrounds to create the lead lifestyle page. Unless the layout editor is capable of creating a dramatic, imaginative design, it should be left to experts. Young persons who are now becoming layout editors may have the kind of sensitivity and ability to design such pages.

Other than use of a total page design concept of dramatic appearance, some papers use four-color printing to further enhance the page. But color added to unimaginative design does not achieve the goal of the newer concept. In fact, it calls the inadequacy of design to the attention of readers.

It is important to note that lifestyle pages in smaller circulation newspapers have a somewhat different editorial concept that affects page design. In larger newspapers, such pages tend to be devoted to more feature articles dealing with homes, family and living. These articles are relatively long and are given adequate space on a page to make them look attractive. In smaller newspapers, a lifestyle page is more of an omnibus of news *and* features of interest mostly to women. In smaller newspapers, there tends to be more space devoted to engagements and wedding announcements, with appropriate photographs. Such pages pose problems to the layout person. Figure 16-19 shows how organization helps the page appear more attractive because it is more orderly.

Generally, the principles of good contemporary design apply to lifestyle pages as well as they do to any other page. This includes the use of large boxes, large photographs and modular design among others.

Figure 16-18 A family living page shows the effect of dramatic styling.
[*Courtesy of the* Mt. Prospect *(Ill.)* Herald]

Figure 16-19 Organized material on a lifestyle page makes it readable.
[*Courtesy of the* Salem *(Ore.)* Statesman-Journal]

Sports Pages

The most exciting pages in a newspaper ought to be the sports pages because almost all of the pictures show people in action. Unfortunately, such is not often the case. Sports page layout has frequently not shown much imagination or drama even though it is easier to bring about such results there than anywhere else in the newspaper.

Specifically, sports pages need good organization first. Nothing destroys the design of a page more than a number of interesting sports stories thrown about carelessly on a page. It is here that modular grid design is a simple solution to the problem, if properly used. An excellent example of a page that organizes sports stories into an exciting design is shown in Figure 16-20. Every story on that page has an opportunity to be read. Yet every story is drama-packed not only because of the headlines and pictures, but because of the page design.

Secondly, sports pages need powerful pictures and these are usually available. Some will need enlarging and others sharp cropping. But such pictures should not be small or cluttered on a page. Figure 16-21 is an example of a page that shows the power of large, dramatically sized pictures. The picture editor has to be aware of the opportunities afforded by such pictures, and the layout editor has to incorporate them into an interesting design on a sports page.

Finally, although large pictures help make a sports page exciting, they are not enough. The entire page needs to be considered. Often, only the top of such pages are interesting, while the bottom fades out. However, Figure 16-22 shows that both the top and bottom of a sports page can be interesting. A large boxed story placed at the bottom helps make the entire page interesting.

Conclusions on Special Page Layout

The principles of layout discussed apply to other special pages within the newspaper, even though there are some differences between these sections. The differences, for design purposes, however, are not that important. To a great extent the layout of these pages is affected by the dummying of advertisements. Rarely are they free of advertisements. The goal of editors should be to salvage a page whose design may have been distorted by the shape and positioning of the ads. Every attempt should be made to simplify these pages to the extent possible. It is virtually impossible to create the same kind of dramatic format required on the front, editorial and lifestyle pages.

Burying Standing Heads

The question is often raised about whether standing headlines such as **Sports, Financial,** or **Feature Section** should be buried somewhere in the middle of the page, thereby freeing top space for news. The answer: If such headlines can be buried, why use them at all? Will it not be obvious without a standing head that an indi-

Figure 16-20 A grid layout with dramatic use of photographs. [*Courtesy of the* Chicago Tribune]

vidual is reading the sports page or the financial page? It would take only a little while to learn from either the headlines or the pictures on a page. Therefore, the function of standing headlines is to keep readers from having to study other headlines or pictures to learn which section they are reading. Furthermore, if an index appears on the front page and it refers to a special page, then the standing headline serves as an advertisement to tell readers they have arrived at the correct section. Such labels, therefore, should not be buried.

Figure 16-21   **Strong horizontal and vertical photographs make this page exciting to look at.** [*Courtesy of* La Crosse (*Wis.*) Herald]

Bottoms of Special Pages Need Brightening

Because the bottoms of inside pages lack news space, the layout editor tends to allow that space to disintegrate. To whatever extent the bottoms of pages can be brightened, they should be. Pictures, horizontally made-up stories and boxes can help accomplish the job if the space is there. Even when the only editorial space available is a "well" between two ads, the editor can use a one-column picture at the bottom to help brighten the page.

Figure 16-22   A sports page where both the top and bottom are interesting. [*Courtesy of the* Lexington *(Ky.)* Herald-Leader]

Boxes or Pictures with Rounded Corners

Occasionally, to offer the reader a change of pace in design, the editor will round off the corners of pictures or boxes. The effect is novel and interesting, if not overdone. When used occasionally, it tends to brighten the page. When overused, it loses whatever novelty it has and may be ignored by readers.

Positioning of Columnists' Articles

Traditionally, columnists' articles are positioned in the same section of the newspaper every day so that readers will know where they may be found. But they need not be placed in or near major sections. If the columnist has a loyal following, chances are that readers will search for the column no matter where it appears. The main sports column is often placed in the most favorable position. It robs the more exciting sports stories because they must be placed in less conspicuous positions. The main columnist should be given a less favorable position to prevent this from happening. Readers will not avoid reading the column.

Datelines and Folios   The following suggestions discuss ways in which the layout person can improve the situation somewhat.

One way to help modernize inside pages is to eliminate datelines, folios and accompanying rules that traditionally have appeared at the tops of inside pages. They not only waste space, but they look old-fashioned. If the space occupied by the dateline (including the rule and some white space underneath) is 2 picas, as it often is, then multiplying that by 8 (for the eight-column page) equals 16 picas of space a page that is wasted. If that same issue has 84 pages in it, then it wastes 1344 picas (16×84) or 226 inches (almost a full page and a half each day.) Datelines cannot be eliminated entirely from pages where advertisements appear because they must be included in the tearsheets sent to the advertisers as proof of publication.

But datelines can be shortened into one- or two-column widths and condensed into not more than three lines. The top line may carry the page number; the second line, the newspaper's name; and the last line, the date. These three lines may be placed in the first column on left-hand pages and in the last column on right-hand pages. If there is no first or last column either because this is a full page advertisement or because an eight-column banner headline is used, then the three lines may be placed at the bottom of the page or run sideways, but both set in the margin. In some newspapers, the datelines are buried anywhere near the top of the newspaper in the most convenient place possible. After all, they can be circled when they appear on tearsheets. If the newspaper has an index, then the page number may be of considerable importance in helping readers find a page. In such cases, plans can be made to position the page numbers as close to the outside as possible.

Type Rules Used as   Laying out a page should consist of more than writing headlines
Stylistic Devices   or simply placing stories on a page. Even though the design that has been created through such practices may look attractive, it often could look more attractive if only some stylistic devices were added to the design.

One of the most frequently used stylistic devices in contemporary design is the use of type rules of various weights to add charm to a page. In Figure 16-23, two 12-point rules are used, one at the top and one at the bottom, in order to frame the page. The frame

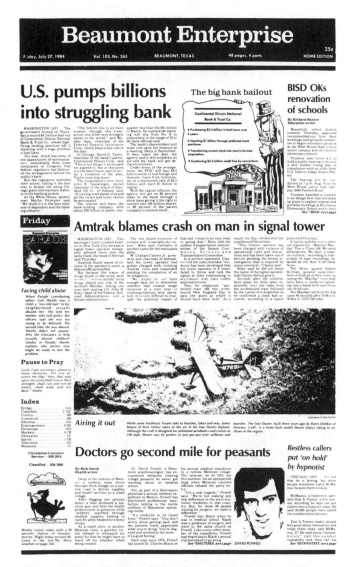

Figure 16-23 The use of 12-point rules at the top and bottom of this page frames the page. [*Courtesy of the* Beaumont *(Texas)* Enterprise]

seems to help hold the news inside, and helps readers perceive the entire page as a single entity instead of a collection of loosely arranged stories.

So popular have these type rules become that they are used in many different ways. Essentially all such rules separate stories on a page. But that is not all. They can add artistic charm to the layout. Whether they do or not depends on how well they are used. The following suggests some ways that they may be used:

1. A few rules on a page may be very attractive, but when many of them are used layout may be overdone. In other words, there is a point of diminishing return in using rules for style only.

2. Heavy rules, such as 12 or 14 points, can look attractive, but their saturation point (where they begin to make the page look unattractive) comes quickly. It takes fewer of them to make a page look bad than it does of four-, six- or eight-point rules (Figure 16-24).

3. When boxed rules are used, they should be relatively light, such as one-, two- or three-point weights. It should be obvious that

Figure 16-24 Heavy rules used to separate stories and provide styling. Sometimes these rules can be too heavy. [*Courtesy of the* Bellingham *(Wash.)* Herald]

many vertical and horizontal rules tend to become garish.

4. Rules may be used between stories; to underline headlines (both standing and regular heads); and between columns. When used between columns, they tend to add unnecessary weight to the page even when they are hairline widths (Figure 16-25).

5. Generous spacing around rules helps them to appear more attractive than when they are used on tightly spaced pages.

Figure 16-25   Use of vertical rules for styling. These rules appeared in a light blue color, and were not obtrusive. [*Courtesy of the* St. Louis *(Mo.)* Post-Dispatch]

6. They may be used around standing headlines such as found in compartmentalized news (local, regional, or national).

The objective of using these rules is for styling, primarily. Good taste in using them is a prerequisite for success.

Some Final Thoughts about Newspaper Design

Anyone who lays out a newspaper should be aware of some important ideas about newspaper design that fall outside the areas of concepts or techniques. The preceding chapters on design seem simple enough to implement. But in practice, it takes something beyond the text to execute. The following is a discussion of these extra dimensions.

There Is No Single Best American Newspaper Design

A study of a large sample of American newspapers will reveal that there are many kinds of designs being used and that there are as many differences as there are similarities. The implications of this fact is that there is no one newspaper that has the best design in the country. Instead there are many excellent designs in existence, even though they may differ considerably.

The implication of this fact is that designers should be able to have the freedom to innovate rather than have to copy someone else's design. This admonition does *not* mean that "anything goes" or that there is no discipline to design. But it does argue for a certain amount of tolerance by those in authority about what is possible in newspaper design.

After all, layout and design are not a science, but an art. They represent both feelings and logic. Therefore, there should be few absolutes in concepts or technique. Old-fashioned makeup had many absolute rules that could not be violated in creating a page design. Today, few of these old rules have survived. Almost any reasonable layout or design should be acceptable, if it fulfills a function *better than any alternative idea.* The problem is that not enough effort has gone into proving that one idea is better than another.

So today's newspaper layout and design personnel should be encouraged to be innovative as long as they are within the realm of reason. Some designers want no bounds on their creative efforts, but such an attitude is unreasonable.

Needed: Better Readability and More Attractiveness

It is likely that American newspaper design will change as time changes. In which direction should it change? The answer: In the direction of better readability and more attractiveness, and one should not supersede the other. However, one person's concept of attractiveness is not equal to another. We generally have to base our ideas on what most graphic designers would say looks attractive.

PART V

Editing for Other Media

17

Magazine Editing

The Sunday Special

For six days a week the staff of a metropolitan daily writes, edits, assembles and produces the daily paper. Then on Sunday emerges the giant, the marvel of American journalism. This mighty tome is crammed with news and news summaries, interpretives and features, sports, business and finance, real estate, comics, classified and display advertising, advertising supplements and magazines.

Advertising probably claims at least 60 percent of the Sunday paper's space. News and editorials, including interpretives and columns, may take roughly one-fourth of the remaining space and magazine supplements nearly one-half.

Unlike its daily counterpart, the Sunday edition has been days or weeks in the making. A closing deadline of four weeks before publication is not unusual for a four-color rotogravure magazine. Other supplements may have a closing deadline of about a week before publication.

Supplement sections have to be printed before the final run of the spot news, sports and markets. At one time some metropolitan dailies predated the Sunday edition. That is, they printed the entire Sunday paper in the middle of the week for delivery to outlying areas on Saturday or Sunday. Today, most run-of-press supplements have a one-week deadline. They are printed on the Friday before delivery.

Even with automation and high-speed presses, the production of the big Sunday edition is a week-long process involving the early closing of as many pages as possible.

Locally Edited Magazines

One of the gems of the Sunday paper is the locally edited magazine, especially those printed by rotogravure. These magazines differ from the oldtime Sunday supplement, started shortly after the Civil War, in that they no longer aim to startle and titillate or to concern themselves with the famous and the infamous. Instead, today's magazines seek to educate as well as to entertain and to portray real people close to the readers.

Although this weekly supplement is an integral part of the newspaper, it is distinctly a magazine. It is built like a magazine and printed like a magazine. It may be identified with its parent newspaper but it has a style and personality of its own.

The Sunday magazine is more carefully designed and edited than the hastily prepared news sections. And because readers tend to judge it as a magazine and not as just another section of the newspaper, the magazine editor is compelled to follow exacting standards of magazine presentation.

Although some newspaper magazines exhibit provincialism in both content and presentation, more are demonstrating that readers in all regions have common interests in topics such as medicine, science, psychiatry, economics, ecology and religion. Almost any topic may be associated in some manner with a particular area.

For example, why would the *Denver Post's Empire Magazine,* which bills itself as the voice of the Rocky Mountain Empire, feature a story on oil in Alaska? Because the oil rush there had some elements in common with the gold rush, a part of the heritage of the mountain states. Also, many of these states, especially Colorado, Wyoming and Utah with their oil shale deposits, are engaged in the exploration and production of oil. But this particular story happened by chance. A free-lance photographer had brought in striking photos he had taken on a trip to the frozen North Slope of Alaska. But without an accompanying story the editor could not use the pictures. Then a professional writer offered a story based on material he had collected in the same area. The result was a well-written and well-illustrated piece for *Empire* readers.

Writing that goes beyond the reach of the routine feature writer and pictures that surpass those shot by a harried news photographer have made the newspaper magazine a favorite with readers. One survey has shown that 59 percent of women and 48 percent of men read the average inside page of a local magazine section, even topping the readership for a nationally syndicated supplement distributed with the same papers.

Magazine Characteristics

A magazine format does not necessarily make a magazine. Some newspaper executives who have taken over the job of editing a Sunday magazine or an independent magazine fail to produce a good magazine because newspaper techniques differ from magazine techniques. Even display advertising may not be the same in newspapers as it is in magazines.

A magazine differs from a newspaper in many ways, including:

1. A better grade of paper, or stock. The cover paper may be heavier than the paper for inside pages. Different grades and weights of paper may be used for inside pages
2. Magazines use more color, not only in illustrations but in type and decoration as well.
3. Illustrations often are more dominant in a magazine than in a newspaper. The illustrations may run (or bleed) off the page or extend into the fold.
4. Magazines breathe; they use air or white space to emphasize text and illustrations much more often than newspapers.
5. Magazines vary typefaces to help depict the mood, tone or pace of the story (Figure 17-1). They use initial capital letters to help readers turn to the message or to break up columns of type (Figure 17-2). They wrap type around illustrations (Figure 17-3).
6. Magazines may use reverse plates (white on black) or use display type over the illustration (overprinting) for display heading or even text.
7. Magazines may vary the placement as well as the design of the headline (Figure 17-4).

"The first and singularly most difficult fact for many newspapermen to grasp about a Sunday newspaper magazine is that it is

Elegance

Set in French Script
with Clearcut initial.

DIGNITY

Set in Forum type.

Antiquity

Satanick

UNUSUALNESS

Newfangle

Fluency

Mandate

Distinctiveness

Civilite

CIRCUS

Playbill

Figure 17-1 Mood typefaces.

A WILD Alaskan wolf yawns broadly a
he lolls in the warm sun of the arcti
spring. Trumpeter swans dabble in a sma

There aren't any weekend beer par
pus. No pep rallies. No homecomin:
dormitories and no football team.

Figure 17-2 (Top) Two-line sunken initial cap. (Bottom) Upright initial cap.

The path of time that
will lead us from today
through the 21st cen-
tury will be lined with
many new mechanical
and electronic marvels,
better energy sources, and
new construction materials and
methods.

Figure 17-3 Wraparound type.

Figure 17-4 Headline designs.

not a newspaper," writes Henry Barker, special projects editor for the *Fort Myers* (Fla.) *News-Press.* He adds:

> A true Sunday magazine never will carry material that could have run practically anywhere in the paper but just happened to wind up in the magazine.
> A [cover story] should be able to pass three tests:
> 1. Does it feel big? Does it have relevance to the lives of many people, ask a question many people ask, deal with some area of common human experience?
> 2. Does it feel necessary? Can the reader be told why he should care about it right now? What's so important about it today?
> 3. Does it feel whole? Does it have a quality of compactness and unity; is it a single, solid thing, not a diffuse cloud?
> This third test is largely a problem of focus, the key element to every successful magazine story. Any story that lacks sharp focus on a theme, an individual or an event will never hold a reader.
> Each issue would carry . . . articles of 1,000 to 2,500 words—a cover story and secondary stories. With occasional exceptions the cover story would be the strongest, most important of the [stories]—a story with a loud ring of urgency about it for everyone in the state.
> Secondary story could be of less vital interest and contain more of a [regional] slant.

Subject matter could be anything clean enough to have lying around the family living room—profiles, perspectives on a big news story, surveys of what's new in a field, trend stories, narratives, first-person or as-told-to stories, humor, travel, fashion—so long as it passed those three tests, could be narrowed to a sharp focus and dealt with [area] people, places and things.[1]

The Editing Process

Unless an editor understands art, that editor cannot hope to produce a superior publication. Magazine editing is essentially a joint endeavor; the editor provides editorial excellence, and the artist creates the visual image.

Front pages of daily newspapers often look distressingly alike. But the magazine comes in a distinctive wrapper or cover that reflects the nature of the publication, stresses a seasonal activity or merely directs readers to the "goodies" inside the magazine.

News, as we have seen, may be presented in many styles, but the inverted pyramid usually prevails. In a magazine the space is likewise limited, but the writing style is more relaxed, more narrative and more personal. The pace of the magazine piece may be slower—but certainly not less dramatic—than that of the news story. Here is the beginning of a magazine feature:

In Chicago some middle-aged businessmen plan a skiing trip to Colorado. In Miami a middle-aged woman with high blood pressure seeks medical advice before leaving for Denver to visit her daughter. In Baltimore a family is cautioned against vacationing in Colorado because one of the children has a lung ailment.

All three of these examples involve a change from low to high altitude, and owing to air travel, making the change in a relatively short period.

Coupled with exertion, cold temperatures and high altitude, won't the businessmen who have been sedentary for months be risking heart attacks? Won't the visiting mother experience even higher blood pressure? And won't high altitude aggravate the child's illness?

Not until later in the story does the angle that normally would be in the lead of a news story appear:

Contrary to the popular belief that reduced oxygen pressure at high altitude has an adverse effect on the coronary artery system, research indicates high altitude may be beneficial and even afford a degree of protection against coronary artery disease.[2]

So rigid are the style requirements of some magazine editors that they lean heavily on staff writers, use staff writers to reshape freelance material or buy only from free-lancers who demonstrate they are acquainted with the magazine's requirements. Still, Sunday magazines may get more than half their material from free-lancers, a greater volume than is procured by the news sections.

1. "Magazine not just an extension," *Gannetteer,* March 1976 (p.1 of "Editorially Speaking" section).

2. Gerry Himes, "High altitude can be good," *Denver Post Empire,* March 28, 1976, p. 10.

Free-lance photographers likewise seek out the Sunday magazine market. One magazine editor remarked, "An exciting roto works like a magnet, drawing in talented free-lance contributors you never realized existed."

Article Headings

Typically, a newspaper uses illustrations to focus the readers' attention to a page. It relies on the headline to lure readers into the story. But in a magazine the whole page—headline, pictures, placement—is designed to stop the readers in their tracks. They may get part of the story from a big dramatic picture before they ever see the head. It is the combination of elements that must make readers say to themselves, "I wonder what this is all about."

The magazine editor is not confined to a few standarized typefaces for headings. Instead, the editor may select a face that will help depict the mood of the story. Nor is the editor required to put the heading over the story. It may be placed in the middle, at the bottom or on one side of the page.

The heading may occupy the whole page or only part of a page. It may be accented in a reverse plate or in some other manner. It may be overprinted on the illustration. More often it will be below the illustration rather than above it. Almost invariably it is short, not more than one line. Frequently it is a mere tag or teaser. A subtitle, then, gives the details:

Oil from the Heart Tree
    An exotic plant from Old China produces
    a cash crop for the South

I Can HEAR Again!
    This was the moment of joy, the rediscovering
    of sound: Whispers . . . rustle of a sheet . . .
    ticking of a clock

The Pleasure of Milking a Cow
    Coming to grips with the task at hand
    can be a rewarding experience,
    especially on cold mornings

Industry is finding
that it pays to rely on
    Models of Efficiency

Magazine Layouts

Type and illustrations, or gray and black blocks, are the dominant elements in newspaper page layout. In magazine layout a third block—white—is used more frequently. To the magazine art editor, white space is not wasted space but rather a means of emphasizing other elements.

The editor may use space generously around headings, between text and illustrations and around illustrations. The editor deliberately plans to get white space on the outside of the pages. To gain extra space, illustrations may bleed off the page.

Some stories are told effectively in text alone; others are told dramatically in pictures. The ideal is a combination of text and pictures, and the emphasis depends on the quality of the illustrations or the significance of the text. A picture's value, says one editor, is best exploited when it sweeps the reader rhythmically into the text. Too often, the story is adequate but good pictures are lacking, thus robbing the story of its dramatic appeal and producing a dull page of straight text.

A magazine page usually has these elements: (1) at least one dominant picture; (2) a title, preferably with a subtitle; and (3) a block of text, usually beginning with a typographical device that will compel the reader's attention to the opening of the story. The device may be a dingbat such as a black square followed by a few words in all-capital letters. Or it may be an initial capital letter, either an inset initial (its top lined up with the top of the indented small letter) or an upright or stick-up initial (the bottom of the initial lined up with the bottom of the other letters in the line) (see Figure 17-2).

Simplicity is the keynote in effective page layout. An easy, modular arrangement is more likely to attract readers than a tricky makeup with odd-shaped art and a variety of typefaces. Illustrations need not be in the same dimensions, but they should be in pleasing geometric proportions. Margins should be uniform or at least give the effect of being uniform. Usually the widest margin is at the bottom of the page, the next widest at the side, the third at the top and the narrowest at the inside or gutter. The content of the page is thus shoved slightly upward, emphasizing the eye level or optical center of a rectangle. The outside margin is larger than the gutter because the latter, in effect, is a double margin.

Kenneth B. Butler, author of a series of practical handbooks (published by Butler Typo-Design Research Center in Mendota, Ill.) treating the creative phases of magazine typography and layout, advises layout editors to touch each margin at least once, regardless of whether illustrations are used. He contends that the eye is so accustomed to the regular margin that even when the margin is touched only once, an imaginary margin is defined clearly in the reader's mind. If the illustration bleeds off the page, the margin on the bleed side may be widened to give more impact to the bleed device.

The art director must know the position of the page—whether left, right or double spread—and whether the page contains advertising. It also would help if the art director knew the content and appearance of the advertising on the page to avoid embarassing juxtaposition. If the art director is working on a one-page layout, he or she should know the content and appearance of the facing page.

The artist tries to visualize what the page is supposed to say. From experience the artist has developed a feel for the magazine page and knows how it will look on the finished page. The beginner may have to use trial and error to find an appropriate design. He or she may, for example, cut out pieces from construction paper to represent the black blocks, then juggle these blocks until a usable design is formed.

Layout is a means rather than an end in itself. If the reader becomes aware of the layout, the layout is probably bad.

One danger most art directors seek to avoid is cluttering. This occurs when too many illustrations are placed on the same page, when the pages are crowded because of lack of spacing or uneven spacing or when too many elements—dingbats, subtitles, boldface type—make the page appear busy. The primary goals of a layout are to catch and direct the reader's attention and to make the pages easy to read.

Copy Fitting

Widths of magazine columns may vary with the number, shape and size of the ads or the size and shape of the illustrations. It is not unusual for a magazine story to be strung over four pages in four different widths. The editor must be able to estimate whether the story will fit the space allocated. Video display terminals have simplified this process because they allow exact copy fitting even before the story is typeset. If VDTs are not available for copy fitting, the process is more difficult.

The most accurate manual method of determining copy length is by counting characters in the manuscript. These steps are used:

1. Count the number of typewritten characters, including spaces between words and for identations, in an average line of the manuscript. An average line can be determined visually or it can be measured by placing a ruler over most of the line endings and drawing a line down these endings.
2. Multiply the number of lines of copy by the number of characters to the average typewritten line. A line extending half the width of the line is counted as a full line.
3. Consult a type book to determine the CPP, characters per pica, for the body size and typeface. For example, 10-point Bodoni Book measures an average of 2.75 characters per pica. If the type line is to be 20 picas wide, then 55 typewritten characters will fill one line of type.
4. Divide the number of lines of type by the number of typeset lines per column inch. If the type is set in 10 point with 2-point spacing, the number of type lines per column inch is determined by dividing 72 (the number of points in an inch) by 12.

The result will be the number of column inches the manuscript will occupy.

The same figure can be obtained by multiplying the number of typeset lines by the point size (including leading space or spacing between lines) of the typeface, then dividing the total points by 72 to find column inches. To convert into pica depth, the point total is divided by 12 (points per pica) rather than by 72.

For fitting copy into a specified space, the method can be used in reverse. Suppose the space to be filled is 6 inches deep and 24 picas wide. The type is to be 12 point. The type chart shows 2.45 characters per pica or 59 characters to the 24-pica line. Twelve-point type set 6 inches deep requires 36 type lines. Multiplying 59 by 36 gives 2,124 characters. If the manuscript lines average 65 characters, then 32 lines of the manuscript will be needed.

A simpler method can be used. Set the typewriter stops at 59 characters and retype 36 lines of the manuscript. Some editors use ruled sheets so that for a given typeface, size and measure, the copy can be sent to the printer typed with the proper number of characters to the line. The typeset copy will correspond almost line for line with the copy.

Placement of Advertising

The usual newspaper practice is to pyramid the ads on the right of the page. In a magazine the ads generally go to the outside of the pages or may appear on both outside and inside, leaving the *well* for editorial copy. The ads need not restrict editorial display, especially if the well is on a double spread.

At magazines where the advertising manager determines ad placement, there is a give and take between ad manager and editor. The editor may want to start a story in a certain part of the magazine, but there is a two-column ad on the most likely page. The editor then asks the ad manager if the ad can be moved to another page. Unless the ad was sold with position guaranteed, the ad manager usually is able to comply.

Scheduling and Dummying

No story, heading or picture will leave the editor's desk until it has been properly slugged and scheduled. Sluglines relay information such as name of publication, the date the story is to be used, story identification and the number of the page on which the story is to appear. Other instructions placed on the copy may include the set (width of type line in picas), body type size and typographic indicators such as initial capitals or italics.

The headline copy likewise carries all the information needed for the desired style, size and set and a line to match the headline with the story.

Illustrations contain special instructions for the roto cameraman for effects such as cropping or mortising. Usually the photos are

FORM	PAGE	SLUG	TO ROTO	TIME
	1	COVER	7-3	
	2	POST TIME-LETTERS		
	3	FRITO PG 4/C		
	4	CAROUSEL	7-7	3⁰⁰
	5	MAY CO.		
	6	TOSHI	7-7	2⁰⁰
	7	"	7-7	2⁰⁰
	8	GHOST	7-8	9⁰⁰
	9		7-8	9⁰⁰
	10	MAGEE PG 4/C		
	11	MAGEE PG 4/C		
	12	GHOST	7-8	9⁰⁰
	13	SLEEP PG 4/C		
	14	LOMBARDI "	7-7	2⁰⁰
	15	HOMESTEAD PG 4/C		
32	16	DIGEST	7-7	3⁰⁰
33	17		7-7	3⁰⁰
34	18		7-7	3⁰⁰
35	19		7-7	3⁰⁰
36	20	DENVER DRY 20-32		
37	21			
38	22		7-8	8⁰⁰
39	23		7-8	8⁰⁰
40	24	HOUSE DOC	7-3	2³⁰
41	25	"	7-7	2⁰⁰
42	26	LIBRARY	7-7	2⁰⁰
43	27	"	7-7	2⁰⁰
44	28	FOOD	7-3	2⁰⁰
45	29	FOOD	7-3	2⁰⁰
46	30	JOHN	7-11	9⁰⁰
47	31			
48	32			
49	33	DIGEST	7-8	2⁰⁰
50	34	MOUSE	7-8	2⁰⁰
51	35	"	7-8	2⁰⁰
52	36	MAY CO PG 4/C		
53	37	MAY CO PG 4/C		
54	38	DANCERS	7-8	2⁰⁰
55	39	"	7-8	2⁰⁰
56	40			
57	41			
58	42			
59	43			
60	44			
61	45			
62	46			
63	47			
64	48			

Figure 17-5   A Sunday magazine schedule.

numbered consecutively through a story and carry the number of the page on which they are to appear.

The schedule is simply a record to remind the editor of the copy that has been edited and sent on for processing. An important item in the schedule is a line showing the date and time the material was delivered to roto (Figure 17-5).

As he or she starts to plan for an edition, the editor first obtains a schedule for the issue, showing the pages on which ads have been dummied and whether the ads are in monotone, duotone or full-color. This schedule then tells the editor how much space is available and the likely color positions.

Closing deadlines regulate the priority of editing. A story may start toward the end of a run of monotone but spill over to a four-color page. This means the story will have to make the earlier deadline of the four-color pages rather than the later deadline of the monotone pages (Figure 17-6).

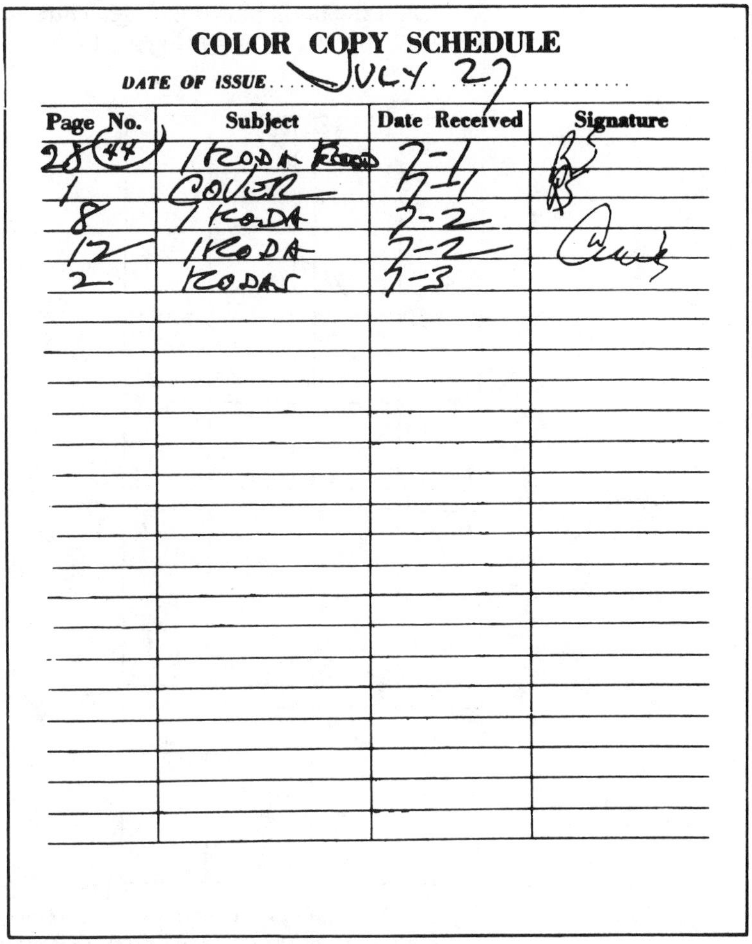
COLOR COPY SCHEDULE

DATE OF ISSUE JULY 27

Page No.	Subject	Date Received	Signature
28 (44)	1 KODAK Food	7-1	
1	COVER	7-1	
8	1 KODA	7-2	
12	1 KODA	7-2	
2	KODAK	7-3	

Figure 17-6 A color schedule for a Sunday magazine.

Imposition
This would suggest that the editor should know something about imposition, or the arrangement of pages for binding. Imposition refers to the way the pages are positioned on the reproduction proof and not the way they will appear on the printed sheet. The printer can give the editor the imposition pattern, or the editor can diagram the imposition if the editor knows whether pages in the form are upright or oblong.

For a 16-page form, upright and printed work and turn, the editor makes three right-angle folds and numbers the pages. This will show Page One opposite Page 8, 16 opposite 9, 13 opposite 12, 4 opposite 5. The remaining eight pages will be in this order—7 and 2, 10 and 15, 11 and 14, 6 and 3. For an oblong form, printed work and turn, the pattern is 1 and 16, 4 and 13, 5 and 12, 8 and 9, 15 and 2, 14 and 3, 11 and 6, 10 and 7. Again, the editor may determine the pattern by making three parallel or accordion folds and one right-angle fold. Or the editor may use the following formula: the size of the book plus one page. Thus, in a 32-page section, Page 4 is opposite 29 (33 − 4) (Figure 17-7).

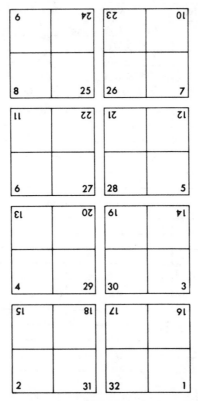

Figure 17-7 Imposition pattern for a 32-page section in 4-page forms. The pattern is obtained by gathering four quarter-sheets and making two right-angle folds. The facing pages total 33 (pages in the section plus one).

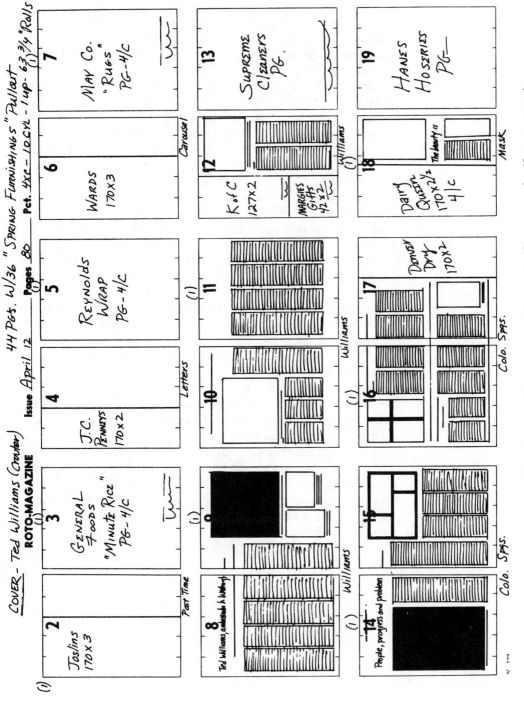

Figure 17-8   A sample of the Thumbnail Dummy roughing out the first pages of a 48-page magazine. (See pg. 410)

If the editor has a spread story, he or she tries to get the pages on the fewest forms possible to avoid tying up too many forms with one story. Understanding imposition also can serve as a guide in using color. If one page in a four-page form is in full color, four forms will be needed, one each for red, yellow, blue and black. The other three pages on the same form can accommodate color with little added expense.

Page layout usually starts with the preparation of a thumbnail or miniature dummy. The rough sketch shows pages blocked off in rectangles of facing pages (Figure 17-8).

The thumbnail dummy serves as the artist's working plan. It gives the first image of the total publication. Using the thumbnail as a guide, the artist is ready to sketch the layout on full-sized sheets (Figures 17-9a, 17-9b, 17-9c).

First the artist receives photocopy proofs for copy checking and correction. These are returned to the composing room for changes. Then the artist receives corrected proofs, which are used for the pasteup, on slick paper. All the elements in the pasteup are arranged precisely as they will appear in print. In a sense, the artist assumes the function of makeup editor, and in arranging the proofed material on the page makes sure that flaws in magazine makeup are avoided. Among such flaws are leaving a widow or lone word at the top of the column, placing subheads near the feet of the columns or in parallel positions in accent columns, or having the last line on the right-hand page of a continued story end with a period.

When the pasteup is completed it goes to the makeup department, where a negative of the page materials is stripped in. Generally the art director insists on inspecting page proofs to be sure the makeup pattern has been followed.

At some magazines the editors receive duplicate sets of corrected proofs. One set is used to check further for errors; the other is used in a pasteup. Galley proofs used for this pasteup bear numbers on each paragraph corresponding with the galley number. This helps the makeup worker in the printing department locate the proper galley.

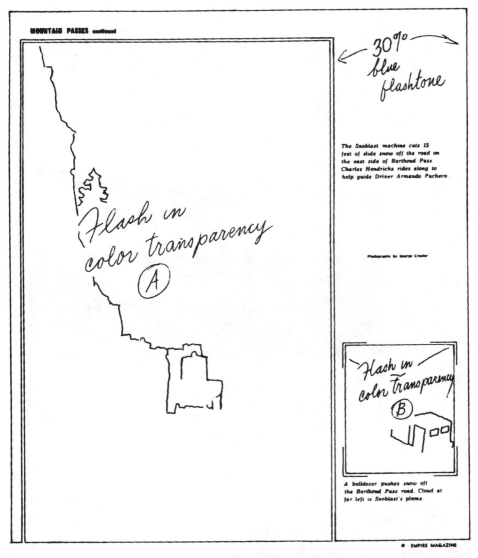

← 30% blue flashtone →

The Snoblast machine cuts 15 feet of slide snow off the road on the east side of Berthoud Pass. Charles Hendricks rides along to help guide Driver Armando Pacheco.

Photography by George Crouter

Flash in color transparency (A)

Flash in color transparency (B)

A bulldozer pushes snow off the Berthoud Pass road. Cloud at far left is Snoblast's plume.

© EMPIRE MAGAZINE

Figure 17-9a Completed paste up is ready for the roto cameraman. Note the instructions for flashing-in unattached photographs and for line and tone work, created for double-exposing the negative or positive.

SOLID

65%

50%

30%

20%

Figure 17-9b **FLASH TONES**

world

pleasure of it when I'm on the ground. And there is a cute little farm set, complete with the farmhouse, barn and outbuildings, a mirror for a pond and a nice assortment of animals. There's the farmer's truck and tractor, and look, he drives a school bus, too. He has plowed his fields, and the pasture land is starting to green up. The ground shows through in spots, like a carpet that is wearing out.

Here comes a train winding through the hills of a toy display in a department store. Will that little car on the road around the bend stop in time? Yes, the crossing gate is going down. At a little country airport a wee plane, like ours, is landing, and there's another one approaching in back of him—much too close. That second plane should have waited just a little longer, but it's all right now; they've both landed safely.

There's so much to oversee from up here. I just can't do everything at once. Now look at that factory belching reddish-brown smoke into the air. The sky ahead is completely filled with this ominous cloud. We'll have to do something about that. That has no place in this sparkling world of mine.

A lovely lake is nestled in the hills with some sailboats skimming over it, their wakes trailing through the water like knives cutting through the frosting on a cake. And back in that sheltered inlet is a fisherman, perhaps with a load of microscopic fish. Where have I seen that campground before, with the tents scattered through the woods where the little creek tumbles into the lake? Why, I know, that's the model Indian village we made for a display in grade school.

This miniature world of mine has everything you could possibly want. Wouldn't it be a delight to go down there and live? Back on earth again, the vantage point will be lower, but may I keep these pictures in my mind, and may I keep this joy in my heart.

There's really no place in my personal kingdom for an ominous cloud. But that'll change soon.

There's a cute little farm set, complete with farmhouse and barn, and a mirror for a pond.

Figure 17-9c   Full-sized page layout.

Magazine Production

A magazine editor relies on an artist to help achieve editorial excellence. By the same token the artist relies on a production expert, usually a printer, to help produce the best possible publication within the budget.

The editor is responsible for providing the printer with complete specifications of the magazine, not only the size of the publication, the number of pages and the press run but the use and placement of color, the number and size of the illustrations, the type area, size of type and any items that will require special handling.

The editor can save money, and make the printer happy, by giving clear and adequate instructions, presenting clean copy, editing the copy thoroughly rather than making changes in proofs, reading and returning promptly all proofs, meeting copy deadlines and giving the printer time to do top-quality work.

Stock

An editor should have some acquaintance with the elementary principles of production. In addition to imposition, there are two other key elements—stock and composition—with which the editor must be familiar.

Paper comes in various sizes, weights and textures. Use of the stock and its appearance determine the class of paper used. One grade may be used for the cover, another for inside pages. One grade may be preferred for color, another if the pages are in black and white. In offset printing the grade must be designed to accommodate moisture and other problems peculiar to offset printing. In roto printing the selection is determined by the paper's ability to absorb the large amount of ink required in that process.

The magazine editor is concerned with only three of the many classifications of stock—newsprint, book and cover. Newsprint does not necessarily mean cheap paper. A good grade of offset newsprint takes halftones with 100-line screens. Rotogravure, by comparison, frequently allows the use of 150-line screens.

The surface smoothness of book paper is determined by the degree of calendering or smoothing during the paper-making process. Antique or eggshell has a minimum of calendering, hence its resemblance to paper used in the early days of printing. More extensive calendering is used on machine finish, giving a smoother surface. English finish, next in the degree of calendering, was used primarily in letterpress. Super-calendered paper has the slickest surface of the uncoated book stocks.

Coating is a supplementary process giving the paper a surface suitable for fine-screened halftones. Coated finishes range from dull-coated, which is smooth but not glossy, to grades of glossy-coated, usually called enamel finish.

Paper weight is calculated on the basis[3] size of a ream (500 sheets) of a particular paper. For book paper the basis size is 25 × 38 inches. Fifty-pound book paper is the weight of a ream of book paper in a sheet size of 25 × 38 inches. Sheet stock can be ordered in many sizes other than 25 × 38 inches. For web presses, stock is ordered by the roll. However the paper is packaged, the basis weight prevails.

For example: a booklet is 6 × 9 inches, 48 pages of 40-pound paper and a run of 25,000 copies: $\frac{25 \times 38}{6 \times 9}$ = 16 × 2 both sides of sheet) = 32 × 500 = 16,000 pages in one ream. That makes 48 × 25,000 = $\frac{240,000}{16,000}$ = 75 reams; 75 × 40 = 3,000 pounds of paper.

The basis of size of newsprint is 24 × 36. Most newsprint is 28- or 30-pounds basis weight. Some magazines use the same weight of paper on the cover as used on inside pages. Heavier cover stock may call for a different basis size, usually 20 × 26 inches.

The different weights of basic sheet sizes may cause confusion. The basic sheet size for bond paper, for instance, is 17 × 22 inches. But 20-pound bond is not the equivalent of 20-pound book paper. Each sheet of 20-pound bond would be the equivalent of approximately 50-pound book because of the differences in the basic sheet sizes.

An editor who intends to bleed pages of a magazine may run into a higher paper cost because trimming is needed on pages with bleeds.

Composition

The editor need not know the cost basis of composition (the setting of type). The editor should realize, however, that straight matter can be composed more quickly and more economically than lines of small capitals, numbered lines, various indentations (see Figure 17-3) and initial capital letters. Complicated work takes more time and thus increases labor costs.

Other Cost Items

Press-run costs reflect the time required to print the job. Here the printing process can determine the speed of the press run. Rotogravure is the fastest, then offset and finally letterpress. But gravure printing is limited to plants with roto presses and generally is more expensive than the other processes. Letterpress and offset costs differ primarily according to the number of illustrations used. Offset is cheaper when the ratio of illustrations to type is high and when the press run is higher.

3. This term generally is used in describing paper sizes and weights. The word may be interchanged with *basic*.

The cost of ink depends on the amount needed and this varies with the grade of paper, the printing process and other factors. Tint blocks and zinc etchings, for example, require extra ink. The cost of using color includes, in addition to the ink itself, the cost of washing up rollers and fountains on the press. If color is applied by sizing or by metallic powders, printers may charge the equivalent of two extra colors.

Printing in color entails the separation of the colors as well as plates or negatives for each color and an additional expense in makeup and press work.

18

Broadcast News Editing

Most of the techniques suggested for the presentation of news in newspapers apply as well to news on radio and television. Those responsible for news copy for any medium must have good news judgment, a feeling for an audience and the ability to handle the language.

Broadcast news differs from other types of news in two major respects. Both radio and television news programs must aim at the majority audience and cannot, as newspapers can, serve the interests of the minority. And because the broadcast newscaster must pack enough items into the newscast to give listeners and viewers the feeling they are getting a summary of the big and significant news of the moment, condensation is required.

A newspaper often offers its readers a 1,000-word story, then lets the readers decide how much of the story, if any, they want to read. The broadcast audience has no such choice. If the newscaster gives too much time to items in which listeners and viewers have only a mild interest, they can turn the dial.

Here are wire service accounts of the same story, one intended for the newspaper members, the other for radio and television stations:

MASSENA, N.Y. (AP)—Unarmed Canadian police scuffled with some 100 Mohawk Indians today and broke an Indian blockade of the international bridge that goes through Mohawk territory in linking the United States and Canada.

The Indians put up the human and automobile blockade after Canadian government officials refused to stop levying customs duties on Indians—duties the Indians say are illegal under the Jay Treaty of 1794.

Figure 18-1 Newsroom of a network-affiliated television station. [*Courtesy of KMGH-TV, Denver.*]

The Indians had brought 25 automobiles into line at the center of the bridge linking the United States and Canada, and Indian women had thrown themselves in front of police tow trucks to hinder the clearing of the roadway.

There were no reports of serious injury. Forty-eight Indians were arrested—including most leaders of the protest—and taken into Canadian custody by police on Cornwall Island.

A spokesman for the Indians called for the other five nations of the Iroquois Confederacy to join the protest Thursday.

The Indians went on the blockade warpath after the Canadian government refused Tuesday to stop customs duties on Indians who live on the St. Regis Reservation, part of which is in the United States and part in Canada.

Scattered fighting and shoving broke out among the Mohawks and police when officers tried to move in to clear away the automobile blockade. One automobile and two school buses were allowed over the international span around noon.

A newspaper copy editor might trim as many as 50 words from that lengthy story to make it tighter and to eliminate repetition. The story was pared to about 70 words for the broadcast wire roundup item:

(MASSENA, NEW YORK)—UNARMED CANADIAN POLICE HAVE ARRESTED 48 MOHAWK INDIANS. THE INDIANS HAD FORMED A HUMAN WALL AND BLOCKED THE INTERNATIONAL BRIDGE LINKING CANADA AND THE UNITED STATES NEAR MASSENA, NEW YORK, TODAY.

THE MOHAWKS ARE UP IN ARMS ABOUT CANADA'S INSISTENCE ON COLLECTING CUSTOMS DUTIES FROM INDIANS TRAVELING TO AND FROM THEIR RESERVATION ON THE BRIDGE. THEY SAY IT'S A VIOLATION OF THE 1794 JAY TREATY.

As an item in the news summary, it was cut even more:

Figure 18-2 Assignment desk for a television news operation. The editor's telephone is a direct line to a radio station newsroom. Another telephone is used for emergency messages and a third connects with the station's mobile units. The panel in the background monitors police and fire calls. [*Courtesy of KMGH-TV, Denver.*]

FORTY-EIGHT INDIANS HAVE BEEN ARRESTED BY CANADIAN POLICE NEAR THE NEW YORK STATE BORDER. THE INDIANS BLOCKED THE BRIDGE, WHICH LINKS THE U-S AND CANADA. THEY CLAIM VIOLATION OF A 1794 TREATY. THE MOHAWKS SAY THEY PLAN NO BLOCKADE TOMORROW.

News is written and edited so that readers will have no trouble reading and understanding it. Broadcasters must write news that they can read fluently and that sounds right to the listeners. Broadcast news style must be so simple that listeners can grasp its meaning immediately. The language must be such that even casual listeners will feel compelled to give the story their full attention.

A reader's eyes may on occasion deceive but not to the extent that the listener's ears deceive. If the reader misses a point while reading, he or she can go over the material again. If the listener loses a point, he or she likely has lost it completely. All radio-television news manuals caution against the use of clauses, especially those at the beginning of a sentence and those that separate subject and predicate. *The AP Radio-Television News Stylebook* uses this example: "American Legion Commander John Smith, son of Senator Tom Smith, died today." Many listeners may be left with the incorrect impression that Sen. Tom Smith died.

The broadcast message is warm and intimate, never flippant or crude. The tone is more personal than that of the newspaper story. It suggests, "Here, Mr. Doe, is an item that should interest you."

The refreshing, conversational style of broadcast news writing has many virtues that all news writers might study. Broadcast writing emphasizes plain talk. The newspaper reporter may want to echo a speaker's words, even in an indirect quote: "The city manager said his plan will effect a cost reduction at the local government level." Broadcast style calls for simple words: "The city manager said his plan will save money for the city."

The newspaper headline is intended to capture the attention and interest of news readers. The lead on the broadcast news story has the same function. First, a capsule of the news item, then the details:

> THE F-B-I SAYS THERE WAS AN OVER-ALL 19 PERCENT CRIME RATE INCREASE THE FIRST MONTHS OF THIS YEAR. AND THE CRIME THAT INCREASED THE MOST WAS PURSE-SNATCHING—UP 42 PERCENT. . . .

> THE NEW YORK STOCK MARKET TOOK A SHARP LOSS AFTER BACKING AWAY FROM AN EARLY RISE. TRADING WAS ACTIVE. VOLUME WAS 15 (M) MILLION 950-THOUSAND SHARES COMPARED WITH 16 (M) MILLION 740-THOUSAND FRIDAY. . . .

The newscast is arranged so that the items fall into a unified pattern. This may be accomplished by placing related items together or by using transitions that help listeners shift gears. Such transitions are made with ideas and skillful organization of facts and not with crutch words or phrases. Said UPI, "Perhaps the most overworked words in broadcast copy are MEANWHILE, MEANTIME and INCIDENTALLY. Forget them, especially 'incidentally.' If something is only 'incidental' it has no place in a tight newscast."

Broadcast copy talks. It uses contractions and, often, fragmentary sentences. It is rhythmic because speech is rhythmic. The best broadcast copy teems with simple active verbs that produce images for the listener.

The present tense, when appropriate, or the present perfect tense create immediacy and freshness in good broadcast copy and help eliminate repetition of "today." An example:

> AN AWESOME WINTER STORM HAS BLANKETED THE ATLANTIC SEABOARD—FROM VIRGINIA TO MAINE—WITH UP TO 20 INCHES OF SNOW. GALE-FORCE WINDS HAVE PILED UP SIX-FOOT DRIFTS IN VIRGINIA, BRINGING TRAFFIC THERE AND IN WEST VIRGINIA TO A VIRTUAL HALT. THE STORM HAS CLOSED SCHOOLS IN SIX STATES.
>
> TRAINS AND BUSES ARE RUNNING HOURS LATE. PENNSYLVANIA AND MASSACHUSETTS HAVE CALLED OUT HUGE SNOW-CLEARING FORCES.

Copy Sources

Copy for the broadcast newsroom comes from the wires of news-gathering associations and from local reporters. The news agencies deliver the news package in these forms:

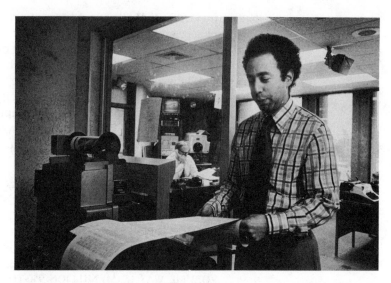

Figure 18-3 A television station news producer goes over a news service broadcast wire. [*Courtesy of KMGH-TV, Denver.*]

1. *Spot summary,* a one-sentence item:

> (DENVER)—F-B-I sharpshooters have shot and killed a gunman who killed two hostages aboard a private plane at Stapleton International Airport in Denver.

2. *Five-minute summary:*

> (DENVER)—F-B-I agents fatally shot a gunman early today as he boarded an airline jet in Denver which he thought was to fly him to Mexico. The F-B-I said the gunman had his two hostages with him at the time of the shooting. He had held them on a small private plane for seven hours. Before he left the first plane, the gunman had told authorities over the radio, "I'll tell you what. I'm still gonna have this gun right up the back of his (the hostage's) head, and it's gonna be cocked, and if anybody even budges me, it's gonna go off, you know that."—DASH—
>
> The chief of the Denver office of the F-B-I, Ted Rosack, said 31-year-old Roger Lyle Lentz was killed shortly after midnight, ending an episode that began in Grand Island, Nebraska, and included two separate flights over Colorado aboard the commandeered private plane. Neither hostage was injured.

3. *Takeout.* This is a detailed, datelined dispatch concerning one subject or event.
4. *Spotlights and vignettes.* Both are detailed accounts, the latter usually in the form of a feature.
5. *Flash.* This is seldom used and is restricted to news of the utmost urgency. A flash has no dateline or logotype and is limited to one or two lines. It is intended to alert the editor and is

not intended to be broadcast. The flash is followed immediately by a bulletin intended for airing.

6. *Bulletin.* Like the flash, it contains only one or two lines. A one-line bulletin is followed immediately by a standard bulletin giving details.

7. *Double-spacers.* This indicates a high-priority story not as urgent as a bulletin. The double-spacing makes the item stand out on the wire and calls the item to the attention of news editors:

> HOSTAGES (TOPS)
>
> (DENVER)—AN F-B-I SPOKESMAN SAYS A GUNMAN WAS SHOT TO DEATH AFTER HE SEIZED A PRIVATE PLANE IN NEBRASKA, ORDERED THE PILOT TO FLY TO DENVER AND HELD TWO HOSTAGES FOR SEVEN HOURS. F-B-I SPOKESMAN TED ROSACK SAYS THE GUNMAN, 30-YEAR-OLD ROGER LENTZ OF GRAND ISLAND, NEBRASKA, WAS SHOT AND KILLED IN AN EXCHANGE OF GUNFIRE WITH F-B-I AGENTS ABOARD A CON-VAIR 990 AT STAPLETON INTERNATIONAL AIRPORT.
>
> ROSACK SAYS THE HOSTAGES WERE NOT HURT.

8. *Special slugs.* These include AVAILABLE IMMEDIATELY (corresponds to the budget on the news wire), NEW TOP, WITH (or SIDEBAR), SPORTS, WOMEN, FARM, WEATHER, BUSINESS, CHANGE OF PACE, PRONUNCI-ATION GUIDE, EDITORS NOTE, ADVANCE, KILL, COR-RECTION, SUBS (OR SUBS PREVIOUS).

Some local stations broadcast the news in the form they receive it from the news agency. This may suggest that an announcer dashes into the newsroom, rips the latest summary off the machine and goes on the air with it. Although that may have been true in the early days and at the smaller stations, the practice is becoming increasingly rare because news has commercial as well as public service value. Furthermore, the many typographical errors in wire copy force the reporter to read it and edit for errors. Here is a fairly typical example:

> A U-S DEPARTMENT OF AGRICULTURE OFFICIAL SAYS IN DEN-VER HE FEELS INSPECTION REPORTS OF COLORADO MEAT-PLANTING PACKS HAVE BEEN ACCURATE.

How about "packing plants"?

Most broadcast news today is handled by trained reporters who know how to tailor the news for a specific audience. This is done by combining items from several roundups and double-spacers to create the desired format. Increasingly, almost all wire copy is rewritten before it is assembled for broadcast to give the listener some variety in items that may be repeated several times during the broadcast period.

Some radio and television stations subscribe to the national newswire of a wire service as well as to the broadcast newswire. That provides a greater number and variety of stories.

Preparation of Copy

All copy should be typed and triple-spaced. Copy should be easier to read in capital and lower case than in all caps but because reporters are used to reading all-cap wire copy, some prefer the all-cap script style. If a letter correction is to be made in a word, the word should be scratched out and the correct word substituted in printed letters. If word changes are made within sentences, the editor should read aloud the edited version to make sure the revised form sounds right. If the copy requires excessive editing it should be retyped before it is submitted to an anchorperson.

Most television news anchors read stories on the air using a script projection system called a TelePrompTer. The TelePrompTer works by beaming a picture of the script to a monitor mounted on the studio camera. The script image reflects in a two-way mirror mounted over the camera lens, so the newscaster actually can read the script while appearing conversational and pleasant. There is no need to refer to notes.

To accommodate the TelePrompTer system, script copy should be typed with dark ink and at a specified width. Such copy averages only four words a line, so that the newscaster's eyes do not have to travel noticeable distances back and forth across the page.

All editing of broadcast copy is done with the newscaster in mind. If a sentence breaks over from one page to another, the newscaster will stumble. No hyphens should be used to break words from one line to the next.

News editors prefer to put each story on a separate sheet. That enables them to rearrange the items or to delete an item entirely if time runs short. A few briefs tacked near the end of the newscast help fill the allotted time.

Properly edited broadcast copy also should include pronunciation aids, when necessary. The most common dilemma for newscasters concerns place names, many of which get different pronunciations in different regions. No newscaster should confuse the Palace of Versailles (vur-SIGH) in France with the town of Versailles (vur-SALES) in Missouri. The copy editor should add the phonetic spelling to the script, and the newscaster can underline the word on his copy as a reminder.

The wire services provide a pronunciation list of foreign words and names appearing in the day's report. The guide is given in phonetic spelling (Gabon—Gaboon') or by indicating the rhyme (Blough—rhymes with how; Likelike Highway—rhymes with leaky-leaky).

Broadcast Style

Phonetic Spelling System Used by Wire Services

A—like the "a" in cat	OW—like the "ow" in cow
AH—like the "a" in arm	U—like the "u" in put
AW—like the "a" in talk	UH—like the "u" in but
AY—like the "a" in ace	K—like the "c" in cat
EE—like the "ee" in feel	KH—gutteral
EH—like the "ai" in air	S—like the "c" in cease
EW—like the "ew" in few	Z—like the "s" in disease
IGH—like the "i" in tin	ZH—like the "g" in rouge
IH—like the "i" in time	J—like the "g" in George
OH—like the "o" in go	SH—like the "ch" in machine
OO—like the "oo" in pool	CH—like the "ch" in catch

Abbreviations

No abbreviations should be used in radio-television news copy with these exceptions:

1. Common Usage: Dr. Smith, Mrs. Jones, St. Paul.
2. Names or organizations widely known by their initials: U-N, F-B-I, G-O-P (but AFL-CIO).
3. Acronyms: NATO.
4. Time designations: A-M, P-M.
5. Academic degrees: P-H-D.

Punctuation

To indicate a pause where the newscaster can catch a breath, the dash or a series of dots is preferable to a comma: The House plans to give the 11-billion-500-million dollar measure a final vote Tuesday . . . and the Senate is expected to follow suit—possibly on the same day.

The hyphen is used instead of the period in initials: F-B-I. The period is retained in initials in a name: J. D. Smith. All combined words should have the hyphen: co-ed, semi-annual. (Spelling should also use the form easiest to pronounce: employee.)

Contractions are more widely used in broadcast copy than in other news copy to provide a conversational tone. Common contractions—isn't, doesn't, it's, they're—may be used in both direct and indirect quotes:

> MEMBERS OF THE TRANSPORT WORKERS UNION IN SAN FRANCISCO SAY IF THE MUNICIPAL STRIKE DOESN'T BEGIN LOOKING LIKE A GENERAL STRIKE BY THIS AFTERNOON, THEY'LL RE-CONSIDER THEIR SUPPORT OF THE WALK-OUT. THE REFUSAL BY DRIVERS TO CROSS PICKET LINES SET UP BY STRIKING CRAFT UNIONS HAS SHUT DOWN MOST TRANSPORTATION IN THE CITY.

Good broadcast writers avoid contractions when they want to

stress verbs, especially the negative: "I do not choose to run" instead of "I don't choose to run."

Even in broadcast copy, contractions should not be overworked. Nor should the awkwardly contrived ones be attempted. The result would be something like this:

> It's possible there's been a major air disaster in Europe.
>
> A British airliner with 83 persons aboard disappeared during the day and is considered certain to've crashed in the Austrian Alps.
>
> Apparently no search'll be launched tonight. There's no indication of where the aircraft might've gone down.

Quotation Marks

The listener cannot see quotation marks. If the reporter tries to read them into the script—"quote" and "end of quote"—the sentence sounds trite and stilted. It is easier and more natural to indicate the speaker's words by phrases such as "and these are his words," "what he called," "he put it in these words," "the speaker said." Direct quotes are used sparingly in the newscast. If quotes are necessary, they should be introduced casually and the source should precede the quotation:

> THE SOVIET NEWS AGENCY TASS SAID TODAY THAT SOVIET SCIENTISTS WERE AWARE OF AN IMPENDING EARTHQUAKE THIS MONTH IN CENTRAL ASIA FIVE DAYS BEFORE IT HAPPENED. . . .
>
> THE NEWS AGENCY SAID, IN THESE WORDS, "AT THAT TIME, A CONNECTION WAS FIRST NOTICED BETWEEN THE GAS-CHEMICAL COMPOSITION OF ABYSSAL (DEEP) WATERS AND UNDERGROUND TREMORS."

Quotation marks are placed around some names that would otherwise confuse the reporter:

> IN AN ANSWER TO AN S-O-S, THE U-S COAST GUARD CUTTER "COOS BAY" ALONG WITH OTHER VESSELS STEAMED TO THE AID OF THE STRICKEN FREIGHTER. THE NORWEGIAN VESSEL "FRUEN" PICKED UP NINE SEAMEN FROM THE "AMBASSADOR" IN A TRICKY TRANSFER OPERATION IN THE TEMPEST-TOSSED SEAS.

In this illustration the reporter is more likely to fumble "tempest-tossed seas" than the names of the vessels.

Figures

Numbers are tricky in broadcast copy. "A million" may sound like "eight million." No confusion results if "one million" is used.

In most copy, round numbers or approximations mean as much as specific figures. "Almost a mile" rather than "5,200 feet," "about half" rather than "48.2 percent," "just under two percent" rather than "1.9 percent."

An exception is vote results, especially where the margin is close. It should be "100-to-95 vote" rather than "100–95 vote." The writer or editor can help the listener follow statistics or vote tallies by inserting phrases such as "in the closest race" and "in a landslide victory."

Fractions and decimals should be spelled out: one and seven-eighths (not 1 7/8), five-tenths (not 0.5).

Numbers under 10 and over 999 are spelled out and hyphenated: one, two, two-thousand, 11-billion-500-million, 15-hundred (rather than one-thousand-500), one-and-a-half million dollars (never $1.5 million).

When two numbers occur together in a sentence the smaller number should be spelled out: twelve 20-ton trucks.

Any figure beginning a sentence should be spelled out.

Figures are used for time of day (4:30 this afternoon), in all market stories and in sports scores and statistics (65-to-59, 5-foot-5). If results of horse races or track meets appear in the body of the story, the winning times should be spelled out: two minutes, nine and three-tenths seconds (rather than 2:9.3).

In dates and addresses the *-st, -rd, -th* and *-nd* are included. June 22nd, West 83rd Street. Figures are used for years: 1910.

On approximate figures, writers sometimes say, "Police are looking for a man 50 to 60 years of age." This sounds like "52" to the listener. It should read, "Police are looking for a man between 50 and 60 years old."

Titles

The identification prepares the ear for the name. Therefore, the identification usually precedes the name: Secretary of State Brown. Some titles are impossible to place before the name: The vice president of the Society for the Preservation and Encouragement of Barbershop Quartet Singing, Joe Doe. Use "Vice president Joe Doe of the Society for the Preservation and Encouragement of Barbershop Quartet Singing." Use "Police Chief Don Vendel" rather than "Chief of Police Don Vendel."

Some radio and television newsrooms insist that the president should never be referred to by his last name alone. It would be President Reagan, the president or Mr. Reagan.

Broadcast copy seldom includes middle initials and ages of persons in the news. Of course, some initials are well-known parts of names and should be included: Richard M. Nixon.

Ages may be omitted unless the age is significant to the story: "A 12-year-old boy—Mitchell Smith—was crowned winner," and so on. Ages usually appear in local copy to aid in identification. Place the age close to the name. It should not say, "A 24-year-old university student died in a two-car collision today. He was John Doe." Use "A university student died. . . .He was 24-year-old John Doe."

Obscure names need not be used unless warranted by the story. In many cases the name of the office or title suffices: "Peoria's police chief said," and so on. The same applies to little-known place names or to obscure foreign place names. If the location is important it may be identified by placing it in relation to a well-known place—"approximately one hundred miles south of Chicago." In local copy, most names and places are important to listeners and viewers.

Where several proper names appear in the same story, it is better to repeat the name than to rely on pronouns unless the antecedent is obvious. Also, repeat the names rather than use *the former, the latter* or *respectively.*

Datelines

The site of the action should be included in broadcast copy. The dateline may be used as an introduction or a transition: "In Miami." Or the location may be noted elsewhere in the lead: "The Green Bay Packers and the Chicago Bears meet in Chicago tonight in the annual charity football game."

On the newspaper wire *here* refers to the place where the listener is. Because radio and television may cover a wide geographical area, such words as *here* or *local* should be avoided. Said a UPI radio news editor, "If the listener is sitting in a friendly poker game in Ludowici, Georgia, and hears a radio report of mass gambling raids 'here,' he may leap from the window before realizing the announcer is broadcasting from Picayune, Mississippi."

Time Angle

In the newspaper wire story nearly everything happens "today." Radio copy breaks up the day into its component parts: "this morning," "early tonight," "just a few hours ago," "at noon today." The technique gives the listener a feeling of urgency in the news. Specific time should be translated for the time zone of the station's location: "That will be 2:30 Mountain Time."

In television, especially, use of the present and present perfect tenses helps eliminate the time angle:

> SEARCHERS HAVE FOUND THE WRECKAGE OF A TWIN-ENGINE AIR FORCE PLANE IN PUERTO RICO AND CONTINUE TO LOOK FOR THE BODIES OF SIX OF THE AIRCRAFT'S EIGHT CREWMEN. AUTHORITIES CONFIRM THAT THE PLANE, MISSING SINCE SATURDAY, CRASHED ATOP A PEAK 23 MILES SOUTHEAST OF SAN JUAN.

Taste

Broadcast news editors should be aware of all members of their audience—the young and the aged, the sensitive and the hardened. Accident stories can be reported without the sordid details of gore and horror. Borderline words that may appear innocent to the reader carry their full impact when given over the more intimate instruments of radio and television. If spicy items of divorce and suicide are tolerated by the station, at least they can be saved until the late-hour news show when the young are in bed.

The wire services protect the editor by prefacing the morbid or "gutsy" items with discretionary slugs:

> (FOR USE AT YOUR DISCRETION)
>
> (RAPE)

MIAMI, FLORIDA—POLICE IN MIAMI REPORT THEY SUSPECT
JOHN DOE IN THE CRIMINAL ASSAULT (RAPE) OF AN 18-YEAR-
OLD GIRL. DOE—27 YEARS OLD—WAS ARRESTED IN THE CITY
MUSEUM AND CHARGED WITH STATUTORY ASSAULT (RAPE).

(END DISCRETIONARY MATTER)

References to physical handicaps or deformities are avoided
unless they are essential to the story. Never say "blind as a bat,"
"slow as a cripple" and the like. Similarly, unless they are essential, reference to color, creed or race should not be used.

Wire services handle items involving pertinent profanity by
bracketing the profanity:

"GODFREY SAID—IT HURTS (LIKE HELL)."

The practice of including a humorous item, usually near the end,
in a newscast has produced some unfunny stories such as the one
about a man breaking his neck by tripping over a book of safety
hints. But a truly humorous item lightens the heavy news report.
Invariably it needs no embellishment by the editor or reporter.

On many stations someone other than the news reporter gives
the commercials. One reason, among others, for this practice is to
disassociate the newsperson from the commerical plugger. Even
so, the director or reporter should know the content of commercials sandwiched in news. If a news story concerns a car crash in
which several are killed, the item would not be placed ahead of a
commercial of an automobile dealer. Airlines generally insist that
their commericals be canceled for 24 hours if the newscast contains a story of an airliner crash, a policy that is likewise applied
to many metropolitan newspapers.

The sponsor does not control or censor the news. The story of a
bank scandal should never be omitted from a news program sponsored by a bank. Nor should a sponsor ever expect sponsorship to
earn news stories publicizing the business.

Attributions

Attribution is an important aspect of all news writing. If an error
is discovered, the writer has an "out" if the item has official attribution. Example: "The state patrol said Smith was killed when his
car overturned in a ditch" rather than "Smith was killed when his
car overturned in a ditch." Attribution can also be vital in the
event of any court action over a story written and aired by the
news staff.

Should identification of accident victims be made before relatives have been notified? Some stations insist on getting the coroner's approval before releasing names of victims. If the release is
not available, the tag would be, "Police are withholding the name
of the victim until relatives have been notified."

In stories containing condition reports on persons in hospitals, the report should not carry over the same condition from one newscast to another without a check with the hospital to find out whether there has been a change.

Audio Tapes

All news copy for radio and television should show the date, the time block, the story slug, the writer's name or initials, the story source and whether the story has a companion tape cartridge or a video segment. If there is more than one tape accompanying a story, the slug would indicate the number of tapes. A tape cartridge is simply a tape recording or audio tape from a news source.

If a tape is used, a cue line is inserted for each tape. Many stations use a red ribbon to type the out-cues or place red quotation marks around the cue line. At the end of the tape, the radio newscaster should again identify the voice used on the tape.

If several tapes are used in one newscast, the tapes should be spaced so that the same voices, or series of voices, are not concentrated in one part. The control room needs time to get the tapes ready for broadcast.

The out-cues of the tape should be noted in the *exact* words of the person interviewed. That will ensure that the engineer will not cut off the tape until the message is concluded. The producer should provide the engineer or boardman with a list of news cartridges to be used and the order in which the producer intends to use them.

The same would hold true of telephone interviews, either taped or live.

The broadcast reporter also may have access to audio news services provided by networks, group-owned facilities and the wire services. These feeds, provided to the station on audio tapes, may be voiced reports or actuality situations. See Figure 18-4 for a wire service audio tape feed.

Listeners with news tips frequently call the station newsroom. Such tips often lead to scoops. Newsroom personnel receiving such calls should try to get as much information as possible, including the caller's name and telephone number. If a telephoned message is to be used on the air, the reporter should get the caller's permission to use his voiced interview.

If a tip sounds important, the reporter checks it out by telephone with the Police Department or sheriff's office before using it on the air. It is illegal to use information obtained from radio monitors. This prohibition, however, is flagrantly violated in times of emergency. During such times, police dispatchers are too busy to take calls from 15 or 20 broadcasting stations. A reporter would be derelict in not warning the listeners of an oncoming flood or tornado merely because he couldn't reach a dispatcher to confirm what he was hearing on the police radio.

Television News

Newspapers communicate with printed words, radio with spoken words and television with spoken words and moving pictures. Editing a television news or special event show involves all three levels. As described by Chet Huntley, one-time National Broadcasting Co. news commentator, television news editing is the marriage of words to pictures, words to sound, pictures to sound and ideas to ideas.

Reuven Frank, former president of NBC News, contended that the highest power of television is to produce an experience. Tele-

```
T

(SIXTH AUDIO ROUNDUP)
73 :12 A GREAT NECK, N.Y. (PATRICIA MEARNS, WIFE OF AIRMAN MISSING
    IN NORTH VIETNAM, WHO JUST RETURNED FROM PARIS TO PLEAD FOR NEWS
    OF HUSBAND) RESPONDS TO NORTH VIETNAMESE SUGGESTION THAT POW
    WIVES JOIN PEACE GROUPS TO WORK FOR END OF WAR (IN PEACE)
74 :26 A GREAT NECK (PAT MEARNS) DOESN'T BLAME U-S FOR HER PREDICA-
    MENT (SITUATION)
75 :40 A GREAT NECK (PAT MEARNS) REFLECTS ON REASONS FOR TRIP TO
    PARIS (LOTS OF US)
76 :42 V WASHINGTON (GENE GIBBONS, FOR VACATIONING UPI·FARM EDITOR
    BERNARD BRENNER) HOUSE INVESTIGATION OF MEAT PRICES OPENS WITH
    TESTIMONY FROM ANGRY HOUSEWIFE
77 :22 A SAN FRANCISCO (CHARLES O'BRIEN, CHIEF DEPT ATT GENERAL FOR
    (CALIF) SAYS CALIFORNIA CONSIDERING SUEING CAR MAKERS FOR SMOG
    DAMAGE (CALIFORNIA)
78 :42 A WASHINGTON (SEN ALAN CRANSTON, D-CALIF) CONDEMNS RISING
    UNEMPLOYMENT AND NIXON ADMINISTRATION INFLATION FIGHT
    (UNACEPTABLE)
79 :33 V UNITED NATIONS (MORRISON KRUS) AGREEMENTS NOT TO BE
    RENEWED FOR U-S BASES IN LIBYA
                            UPI/AUDIO/NEW YORK
                                BA953PED..
```

Figure 18-4 **A United Press International audio tape feed roundup. The roundup, called a billboard, shows the news editor the number of the cut or selection and the length of the taped message. The first figure represents the number of the selection; the second shows the length of the tape in seconds. The letter A following the time indicates an actuality or a taped voice of a news source such as a governor. The letter V indicates a voicer or the voice of a wire service correspondent. V/A would indicate both an actuality and the correspondent's voice—an interview type. The words in the message itself provide an introduction to the tape by the newsman. The words in parentheses at the end of the selection are the out-cue words, showing the conclusion of the voice on tape. Out-cue words are not needed on voicers because the correspondents follow a standard out-cue, such as "This is Morrison Krus reporting for United Press International." Normally, six audio roundups are delivered daily.**

vision cannot disseminate as much information as newspapers, magazines or even radio. But in many instances it causes viewers to undergo an experience similar to what would happen if they were at the scene. One can feel sympathy when reading about napalmed civilians or the drowning of a child at a swimming pool. But watching the same thing on a television newscast is a wrenching, personal experience that gets people worked up, even angry. Television is an instrument of power, not because of the facts it relates but because it conveys an experience to viewers.

Words speak for themselves to the newspaper reader. In radio, a newscaster voices the words for the listener. In television, the newscaster is there, talking directly to the viewer about the news. The newscaster is the key actor and many a station has fallen behind in ratings for its news shows, not because the station did not have good reporters and cameramen or lacked a well-paced news format, but because competing stations had better on-air talent.

In the early days of television, stations hired journalists to report and write the news, then handed over the polished manuscript to a good-looking announcer with mellifluous tones. Today more and more newscasters are men and women with journalistic backgrounds who may not sound like movie stars but who know what they are talking about (Figure 18-5).

Television news editing, the sorting or processing of the news for television, requires more time than for radio. Producers and

Figure 18-5 News, weather, sports. These have become the traditional pattern in television news. In this modern console the performers are able to view the show's progress. Behind every newscast is a team to support those behind the microphone. These include producer, director, assignment editor, reporters, photographers, camera operators, video editors and the like. [*Courtesy of KMGH-TV, Denver.*]

writers must spend hours reviewing, sifting and editing all the material available for a single half-hour newscast.

They use these criteria in selecting items: the significance of the item, whether it is interesting either factually or visually, how long it is and how well its content complements the rest of the program.

All local newsfilm or videotape must be examined before it is edited to determine which of it to use and how much to cut. Sometimes a film may have relatively little news value but is included because of its visual quality. A barn fire might not rate mention on a radio newscast but the video could be spectacular.

Network tapes also are examined. Late afternoon network news stories are reviewed to determine what can be lifted for the late-evening local news program. The networks provide their affiliates with an afternoon news feed for use as the affiliates see fit. This closed-circuit feed from New York consists of overset material not used on the network news. These feeds are recorded on videotape and usually include more than a dozen one- to two-minute video stories from the nation and the world. The producer has to monitor these feeds to decide which stories to use.

Chain-owned stations maintain a Washington or New York bureau that sends member stations daily video reports. These, too, must be reviewed.

In addition to editing these film and videotape reports, the producer must also go over the vast amount of wire service news and facsimile pictures, not to mention stories filed by station reporters. Having selected what to use, the producer's next job is to determine how and where it can be used within the few minutes allotted the news show.

Most American television stations today use portable electronic videotape equipment as well as the traditional 16mm film cameras in gathering the news. These tape minicams, known as ENG (for electronic news gathering), shoot 3/4-inch videotape, usually in 15-minute cassettes. The small recorder and battery pack give the ENG camera crew enough mobility to cover fast-paced news stories, and, although the minicam rig is heavier than a film camera, the ENG photographer can see immediately the pictures shot instead of having to wait, often hours, for film to be developed. That instant image-making, along with the high picture quality and increased editing advantages, make the ENG rig well worth the weight.

It is the 3/4-inch videotape editing systems that have transformed television news production procedures most in recent years. The tape editor plays back on one recording machine the pictures shot in the field, selects the shots he or she wants, their length and order, and assembles the edited story by transfer-dubbing those shots to a second tape cassette in another recorder.

The editor also may add reporter's narrative, natural sound recorded in the field, music and other audio components to the same edited cassette. In most situations, ENG editing is more precise, more versatile and quicker than film editing. Best of all, the editor finishes with a compact videocassette containing all the elements of the story. That simplifies production of the newscast.

In film editing, the editor looks over the images on the film and deletes (by cutting and splicing) the images he or she does not want to use. An audio tape is edited by running the tape through a playback machine, cutting out the sounds not wanted and rejoining the audio tape with adhesive.

One distinct advantage of videotape editing is that original video is not destroyed during the transfer dubbing. So, if an editor wants to lengthen a shot already transfer-dubbed, the editor simply repeats the edit and lets the recorder run longer. With film, the editor would have cut the film on the first edit and been unable to reattach those missing seconds without a visible splice.

Film remains reliable in its own way. It may be broadcast with sound (sound-on-film or SOF), with natural sound under (audible background noise) or as silent film (SiFilm or SIL). Many budget-conscious television news directors like film's lower cost and better maintenance record than videotape's. Fast-developing ENG equipment remains expensive and still somewhat fragile for slam-bang news gathering use.

In a typical newscast, the anchor newscasters, sitting in a brightly lighted studio set, read stories into studio cameras. The newscasters also introduce edited videotape and film stories, which beam onto the air when the newscast director instructs an engineer to start the playback machines. A studio camera also may shoot close-ups of still pictures in the studio to help illustrate stories.

The minicam's portability has added in recent years a new dimension to local television newscasts. Lightweight transmitters allow a reporter and engineer to beam live reports back from remote locations—even from an airborne helicopter—straight to the station and onto the air. Portable editing rigs mean the remote reports can include packaged pieces as well.

Copy Formats

There are almost as many copy formats and scripting styles as there are broadcast newsrooms. Terminology varies, as well. In one newsroom the script designation "voiceover" (or "VO") might refer to an anchorperson's reading over silent film or videotape; in another newsroom "voiceover" might refer to the reporter's recorded voice running with video.

Figures 18–6 and 18–7 are typical scripts from KOMU-TV in Columbia, Mo. They are from a 6 o'clock newscast devoted to local news.

The robbery arrest story (Fig. 18-6) calls for the anchor to read it all, but after a few lines the picture will change from the newscaster's face to videotape illustrating the story. The script instructions tell the director that the video source is ENG videotape, to begin as the anchor says "an eyewitness" and to last for 22 sec-

```
NewsCenter 8  Slug arrest
Newscast 6  Date 9/1  Writer mm                                    Length :28

  moc:                      Columbia police have

                            charged a Moberly

                            man with last week's

                            robbery of the Boone

  ENG :22                   County Bank.
- - - - - - - - - - - - - - - - - - - - - - - - - - - - - - - -
  ENG :00-:22               An eyewitness

  Cassette E-100            identified 23-year old

  Cut 1 Cued                Robert Wilson of

  VOICEOVER                 Moberly as the man

                            who took almost

                            10-thousand dollars

                            from the bank

  Key: File Tape            Friday afternoon.
       (:05-:10,)           Acting on a tip,

                            police took Wilson

                            into custody this

                            morning in downtown

                            Columbia.
                                      (more)


NewsCenter 8  Slug arrest ADD
Newscast 6  Date 9/1  Writer mm                                    Length --

  tape rolling for          Wilson denies
    VOICEOVER:
                            committing the robbery,

                            but remains in jail

                            under 50-thousand

                            dollar bond.

                            These bank photographs

                            show the robber

                            escaping with the

                            money bag under

                            his arm.
- - - - - - - - - - - - - - - - - - - - - - - - - - - - - - - -
  back to moc:              Police say they

                            also want to question

                            Wilson about a series

                            of burglaries in the

                            county over the past

                            year.
```

Figure 18-6 Television script indicating use of voiceover. The anchor continues to read the script while videotape illustrates the story. [*Courtesy of KOMU-TV, Columbia.*]

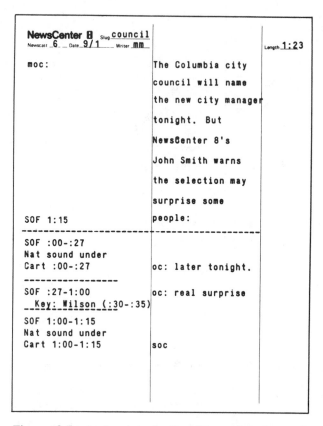

Figure 18-7 Anchor introduction. The anchor shares the reporting with another reporter whose story is on film. [*Courtesy of KOMU-TV, Columbia.*]

onds. Other designations show the number of the cassette, the location of the story of the cassette ("Cut 1 cued") and whatever written information ("key") will be superimposed on the screen and when.

Figure 18-7 shows the other common TV script, the anchor's introduction to a packaged report. In this story, the anchor shares the reading with the reporter. This example involves a filmed story, so the scripting differs from the previous example. The "soc" designation alerts the director that the reporter's narration ends with a standard outcue such as "John Smith, NewsCenter 8, Columbia."

A good television script should not compete with the pictures. It should prepare the viewer for what he or she is about to see or specify what may be difficult to see, but it should avoid repeating what the viewer can see or hear. If the mayor has criticized the city's water supply and his statement is on videotape, the script merely sets up the statement with a brief introduction. Good scripts also direct the viewer's attention to significant details in the video, but they should avoid phrases such as "we're now looking" or "this picture shows."

PART VI

A Look to the Future

19

Newspapers and the Future

Newspaper publishers of the 1970s were fond of talking about the technological "revolution" brought about by the introduction of video display terminals. Without a doubt, VDTs brought dramatic change to an industry long overdue for major technological innovation. The introduction of VDTs, high-speed phototypesetters and other computerized equipment permitted significant reductions in the work force of a labor-intensive industry. In retrospect, however, what occurred in the 1970s may have been merely the beginning. Technological change expected during the remainder of the 1980s and during the 1990s may make the developments of the past decade seem significant only in comparison to the relative inactivity of the previous 75 years.

Author and futurist Anthony Smith argues that "in this era of technological change, the term revolution is often applied with indecent haste to mere innovation."[1] Smith believes, however, that a third great transformation—computerization—is occurring in techniques for storing and manipulating information, the basis of human knowledge. He argues that this transformation is as significant as the transformations brought about by writing and printing. If that is true, this decade and the next will be particularly significant for the world's advanced nations and, perhaps, for developing nations as well. Indeed, change of this magnitude easily

1. Anthony Smith, *Goodbye Gutenberg: The Newspaper Revolution of the 1980s* (New York: Oxford University Press, 1980), p. 3.

could narrow the gap in knowledge between the nations of the industrialized world and those of the Third World.

Speculation about the impact of computerization on the world community is beyond the scope of this book and probably is better left to sociologists. But computerization's impact on the newspaper industry of the future, while far from clear, merits further examination. Presumably, those who read these pages have a stake in the industry's future, regardless of whether they plan newspaper careers or careers in competing media. The purpose of this chapter, then, is to examine the changes now taking place in the industry and to examine the impact of the changes promised by the futurists. Of necessity, some of this involves speculation on the part of the authors and others. It is offered with the realization that the only certain change is change itself.

Pagination

The newspaper industry emerged from the 1970s buoyed by the successes of major computerization, a slowdown in the loss of readers (see Chapter 2) and continued profitability. Technological innovation had helped to solve many of the industry's ills, and by 1980 it was clear that the era of technological change was far from finished. In that year Hastech Inc. placed on the market its PagePro, the first interactive page layout system capable of fulfilling all the required functions of full-scale pagination. Pagination allows the editor to compose a page on a video terminal, and when the page is finished, to send it to a typesetter for output. Because the page is complete as it emerges from the typesetter, the page makeup process in the composing room is eliminated and reductions in the work force are possible.

Understandably, publishers are receptive to any innovation that promises reductions in staffing and, as a result, payroll cost reductions. It still is far from clear, however, that major reductions in payrolls will be possible because of the introduction of pagination equipment. When VDTs were introduced, newspapers were able to eliminate redundant keyboarding in the composing room, and some large newspapers were able to trim more than 100 employees from their payrolls. Few newspapers have that many people involved in page makeup, so the savings will not be as great. In fact, newspapers that have converted to pagination have found it necessary to *add* layout editors on the copy desk because the exacting process of page design with a computer is more time-consuming than manual methods in which page dummies are used. If more editors are needed, pagination may be difficult to cost-justify, at least for the present.

Such a development, however, will merely slow the introduction of pagination, not prevent it. Pagination is a vital link in a grander scheme for newspaper automation that calls for the disappearance of the composing room as we know it. In order to grasp the significance of this concept, it is necessary to understand the difference in partial pagination and total pagination. Partial pagination, the form being introduced at U.S. newspapers, allows editors to create pages with all text matter in place but without drawings and photographs. Those must be processed separately and added to the page before it is photographed for platemaking.

Several companies, however, already are manufacturing devices that permit the digitalization of photographs, a step that is necessary in achieving total pagination. Such machines scan artwork or a photograph with a laser beam and produce line drawings or screened halftones in the size requested by the operator. As the laser beam scans the photograph, it creates a digitalized, or computer readable, version of what it sees. The machine's internal computer uses the digital signals to drive another laser beam, which in turn exposes the desired image on photosensitive paper. The paper is then processed in the same manner as phototypesetting paper. The digitalization of photographs requires massive amounts of computer storage space because the device must faithfully reproduce thousands of tiny pixels, or picture elements, that make up the finished screened photograph. Magnetic bubble memory and other advancements in computer storage make it possible to do this at a reasonable cost. As recently as 1975 the cost of that much storage space would have been prohibitive.

Total pagination, then, requires the linking of pagination systems, digitalization equipment and typesetters with the capability of producing both text and digitalized photos. Several companies are offering such equipment, but to date no newspaper has converted entirely to this system.

When total pagination systems are in place, most of the work done in the composing room, as we know it today, will be unnecessary. It is reasonable to assume that publishers will move quickly to reduce the size of a department that typically accounts for 25 percent of payroll costs. So, while partial pagination may not result in great savings, total pagination will.

Those developing total pagination systems geared early efforts to producing typeset pages. Ironically, their success may well render typesetting obsolete. If it is possible to develop a pagination system capable of producing a complete page with a laser-based phototypesetter, and it clearly is, the next logical step is to bypass the typesetter and to use the data generated by the pagination system to drive laser-based platemakers. This already is being done. When all the pieces are put together, the composing room as we know it will disappear.

The futurists suggest taking this concept one step farther by eliminating the printing plate and constructing computer-controlled presses. Ink-jet presses, already in use by commercial printers, offer limited promise in accomplishing this. As the paper passed through the press, the pagination computer would control the opening and closing of thousands of tiny ink-jet nozzles, which would spray the desired image onto the page. Implementation of computer-controlled presses appears to be unlikely in the immediate future.

Most of the technological innovations of the 1970s focused on ways to automate newsroom operations with the goal of eliminating redundant keyboarding in the composing room. The introduction of VDTs accomplished that, so most of the current research of engineers and computer programmers focuses on ways to cut costs even more in the composing room and in the pressroom as well. Clearly, though, elimination of work functions in those areas places additional production burdens on those in the newsroom.

Digital Cameras

Meanwhile, research continues on ways to improve newsroom functions. One development project, for example, involves the perfection of a digital camera. One early version already is being marketed by Sony. A photographer equipped with one could snap a picture at the scene of an accident, and a microcomputer in the photographer's pack would convert the image into digital language for transmission to the office computer by radio or telephone line. The layout editor would call the photo to the pagination screen, crop it, enlarge or reduce it and position it on the page. A newspaper equipped with digital camera, total pagination and computer-controlled printing theoretically could print a photograph within minutes after it was taken. Because there would be no need to replate to change the content of a newspaper using computer-controlled presses, it would be possible to produce a publication tailored to the individual. If someone wanted a paper with more sports coverage than a neighbor desired, but less business news, that would be possible. The editor would merely instruct the computer to create an individually tailored, addressed newspaper. That, of course, would create nightmarish problems for circulation departments, which would have to ensure that the right paper reached the right customer, but technically such a system is possible. The fact is that all the equipment to do these things, which sound like processes better-suited for a scientific laboratory than newspapers, already exist. The technical experts say that the biggest tasks remaining are to perfect the devices and to integrate them into a unified system. Much of this apparently will happen years from now, if at all. But it is most important to remember that in 1968 one prominent editor envisioned electronic editing "by the turn of the century." It arrived two years later.

Interim Solutions

Newspaper publishers are not waiting for futuristic solutions to their problems. In the interim they are doing much to ensure the long-term survival of their industry.

Many are creating new and inviting sections tailored to the needs of readers. Editors no longer publish newspapers and ask that readers accept what they are given. Increasingly, newspapers try to determine through surveys and other means what readers want. Then editors try to produce sections designed with readers in mind. This effort has produced easy-to-read sections on personal finance, entertainment, participant sports and similar fare. More of that can be expected in the future. In addition, editors have increased the production of zoned sections that go only to readers in certain parts of a city. Such sections contain news of small municipalities in the area that would never find its way into the metro sections.

Editors also are producing sections with more color to appeal to readers.

Finally, some newspapers are trying to find new ways to package the news. Quite a few newspapers are programming news for cable television channels, and many larger ones are providing stories for computer-accessed retrieval systems.

Threats to Newspapers	Despite the generally optimistic views of publishers on the future of the newspaper industry, it remains to be seen whether technological advancement can provide answers for all of the industry's problems. And it clearly has problems. The newspaper industry is still labor-intensive, ranking near the top in total employees with the mammoth automotive and steel industries.[2] Even more troublesome are dismal long-range prospects for solution of the distribution problem, one that is particularly acute for afternoon newspapers. Clogged city streets make it difficult to deliver the afternoon newspaper, and the government continues to drag its feet on establishment of rapid transit systems that could relieve that congestion.

Equally as disturbing is the question of whether newsprint production can keep pace with consumption, and, even if newsprint is available, whether newspapers can afford to buy it without radically altering their economic structure. Historically, publishers have preferred advertising rate increases to subscription price increases when it became necessary to offset the spiraling costs of newsprint. Advertisers, in turn, have shown increased reluctance to bear the entire cost. Consequently, publishers have been forced to raise subscription and single-copy rates. Experience shows that price increases often result in decreased circulation, which, in turn, makes newspapers less attractive as an advertising medium. So far, publishers have done a remarkable job of walking this tightrope, but one wonders when the balance will tilt so severely that no viable solution can be found.

2. *Facts About Newspapers* (Washington: American Newspaper Publishers Association, published annually).

Even in this area publishers have turned to technology for answers. Experiments sponsored by the American Newspaper Publishers Association Research Institute show that kenaf, a plant closely related to hemp, can be mixed with wood pulp to produce an acceptable grade of newsprint. Kenaf is a field crop that grows quickly, requires little care and can be grown in almost all areas of the United States. It could be a less costly substitute for slow-growing trees, which tie up land for 10 to 20 years during maturation. The Cuban government, meanwhile, is conducting experiments to determine whether bagasse, the residue of sugar cane stalks, can be used to produce newsprint and create an important new market for a byproduct of that island's most important cash crop.[3] Unfortunately, neither kenaf nor sugar cane is grown in quantity in the United States, and convincing farmers to produce those crops may prove difficult. Most publishers view with disdain the prospect of dependence on foreign imports, particularly those from such nations as Cuba.

So, while advancing technology offers hope that the newspaper industry's problems can be solved, there is no assurance that this will be the case.

Home Retrieval Systems

Ironically, technology closely related to that used in newsroom editing systems, coupled with technology long employed by an old nemesis, television, could threaten the very future of newspapers.

Home information retrieval systems, often referred to as videotex systems, may become an effective alternative to the printed newspaper. Such systems allow the consumer to select information from a centrally located computer data base on a home computer terminal or on a standard television set with an inexpensive attachment. The data base can be huge and contain far more information than can be put in the daily newspaper.

Two forms of videotex systems appear to be evolving. One, called viewdata, requires that the viewing device be linked to the computer by telephone line or cable television circuit. The user scans a series of indexes displayed on the screen, and with a keypad attached to the receiver, searches out the item desired. The amount of information that can be obtained through such systems is limited only by the capacity of the central computer. The second type of videotex system, teletext, requires no direct connection to the computer. The unused portion of a standard television signal carries data that can be captured and held for display on the screen by a small device attached to a standard television set. The amount of information that can be transmitted is somewhat limited because each screenful of information must be retransmitted every few seconds to prevent long delays in availability of the

3. *Presstime,* June 1980, p. 45.

material. Teletext systems would appear to have their greatest value in sparsely populated areas where cable television is not available and telephone links to remote computers would be too costly.

England took the early lead in developing videotex systems. The British Broadcasting Corp. introduced its Ceefax service in the mid 1970s and BBC's competitor, the Independent Broadcasting Authority, introduced Oracle soon thereafter. Both are teletext systems. The British Post Office operates Prestel, a viewdata system using telephone lines, which the post office controls. Similar systems have appeared in European countries and in Japan. In the United States, the *Miami Herald* has operated a viewdata system, called Viewtron; other newspapers have announced plans to do so; and at least two television stations have experimented with teletext. Several companies with no traditional media ties have established data bases that allow those with home computers to dial long-distance numbers to establish computer-to-computer links for information retrieval.

To understand the significance of such developments, it is necessary to appreciate fundamental differences in traditional media forms. Television has tremendous eye appeal because of its ability to use color, and it provides immediacy because, unlike newspapers, it relies upon no cumbersome distribution network. Television, however, never managed to displace newspapers as some predicted in the 1940s because newspapers, too, have some advantages. They are portable, and they permit the transmission of large volumes of information—such as classified and grocery ads—which television finds difficult to handle.

It is possible to attach a simple printout device, similar to those used in newspaper offices to provide paper copies of stories composed on a video display terminal, to a videotex receiver in the home. When this is done, the videotex consumer has a device with all the advantages of both television and newspapers. The information can have all the eye appeal of color television because it is displayed on a television screen; it is immediate because of the broadcast or direct-line link to the central computer; it is possible to make the information portable by requesting a printout; and the volume of information available far exceeds that found in newspapers.

Clearly, then, videotex could pose a threat to both newspapers and television. Nevertheless, it would be premature to suggest that the demise of newspapers is inevitable. It is not yet known whether consumers will be willing to read large volumes of information on a television screen or whether they will be inclined to make printouts of the information they want. As Anthony Smith writes, "The history of communication devices is littered with accounts of deluded hopes and predictions embarrassingly unfulfilled. The Victorians thought that the telephone would rapidly become an instrument of mass entertainment. Newspaper editors in the 1930s were confident that television could never become a medium of news. Computer experts in the 1950s believed that three or four computers would be the total number required to fulfill the needs of an entire society."

Of course, there have been successes, too, including the conversion of newspapers to VDTs. Smith concludes: "In outlining the scope of the new media in the next decade or two, one has therefore to use both a mental brake and a mental accelerator. . . . Past technologies *can* leap ahead much faster than can be foreseen if they come to satisfy a newly arisen social need. It is imagination rather than calculation that often makes the difference."[4]

**Government's
Role**

If the newspaper industry fails to solve its major problems of newsprint supply and distribution, the development of videotex inevitably will be speeded. It is even reasonable to ponder whether newspapers, as we know them today, will disappear. Such a development should not necessarily be viewed with alarm. Newspapers already store text in a form readily adaptable to videotex, so it is reasonable to assume that newspapers would play a major role in the new medium's development. Government, of course, could block that path by restricting cross-ownership of newspapers and videotex systems during the developmental period. If that happens, a plethora of new problems arises. Companies with no commitment to the ideals of good journalism could become owners of videotex systems. What, then, happens to the traditional doctrine of objectivity, news values, editorial freedom and standards of ethic?

Perhaps even worse, a reduction in the number of newspapers, and magazines as well, would mean that the impact of the last of the media free of government-imposed content rules and licensing would be diminished. Television and radio are subject to the Fairness Doctrine and equal time provisions and must have licenses— granted by the government—to operate. Cable television systems typically are regulated by local government, and the Federal Communications Commission in some cases restricts the services they can offer. Telephone service also is subject to government regulation and licensing. Newspapers and magazines, as all institutions, must comply with laws, but they are not licensed, and they are not subject to content regulation similar to the equal time provision. So, if newspapers and magazines are less prevalent, government has greater control of the media through its control of licensing and content. Richard Nixon, when president, tried to harass broadcasters by delaying FCC license renewals for stations that had reported unfavorably on his activities. The *Washington Post,*

---

4. Smith, *Goodbye Gutenberg,* p. 242.

which was subject to no such regulation, exposed Nixon's involvement in the Watergate affair. Is it possible that with most media subject to government regulation even more serious abuses of authority could occur in the future? We have no way of knowing, but it is an ominous prospect for those who believe in press freedom and who view the press as a watchdog over government.

| The Future of Journalists | If the impact of newspapers diminishes in the future, it is reasonable to ask where that leaves those now training for careers as journalists. No futurist has yet suggested seriously that computers can be trained to gather the news, to take photographs or to edit. It seems clear that, while the tools of the journalist may change, the function of the journalist will not. There will continue to be a demand for competent reporters, photographers and editors for the foreseeable future. |

Newspaper Style

The stylebooks of The Associated Press and United Press International are reference books as well as stylebooks, and much useful information can be found in them. This appendix is a condensation of the key rules of usage found in those stylebooks. *Webster's New World Dictionary* is the primary source for references not found in the stylebooks. The information herein is used with permission.

Capitalization

In general, avoid unnecessary capitals. Use a capital letter only if you can justify it by one of the principles listed here:

Proper Nouns

Capitalize nouns that constitute the unique identification for a specific person, place or thing: *John, Mary, America, Boston, England.*

Some words, such as the examples just given, are always proper nouns. Some common nouns receive proper noun status when they are used as the name of a particular entity: *General Electric, Gulf Oil.*

Proper Names

Capitalize common nouns such as *party, river, street* and *west* when they are an integral part of the full name for a person, place or thing: *Democratic Party, Mississippi River, Fleet Street, West Virginia.*

Lowercase these common nouns when they stand alone in subsequent references: *the party, the river, the street.*

Lowercase the common noun elements of names in all plural uses: *the Democratic and Republican parties, Main and State streets, lakes Erie and Ontario.*

Popular Names

Some places and events lack officially designated proper names but have popular names that are the effective equivalent: *the Combat Zone* (a section of downtown Boston), *the Main Line* (a group of Philadelphia suburbs), *the South Side* (of Chicago), *the Badlands* (of North Dakota), *the Street* (the financial community in the Wall Street area of New York).

The principle applies also to shortened versions of the proper names for one-of-a-kind events: *the Series* (for the World Series), *the Derby* (for the Kentucky Derby). This practice should not, however, be interpreted as a license to ignore the general practice of lowercasing the common noun elements of a name when they stand alone.

Derivatives

Capitalize words that are derived from a proper noun and still depend on it for their meaning: *American, Christian, Christianity, English, French, Marxism, Shakespearean.*

Lowercase words that are derived from a proper noun but no longer depend on it for their meaning: *french fries, herculean, manhattan cocktail, malapropism, pasteurize, quixotic, venetian blind.*

Other key points of capitalization:

academic departments Use lowercase except for words that are proper nouns or adjectives: *the department of history, the history department, the department of English, the English department.*

administration Lowercase: *the administration, the president's administration, the governor's administration, the Reagan administration.*

air force Capitalize when referring to U.S. forces: *the U.S. Air Force, the Air Force, Air Force regulations.*

Use lowercase for the forces of other nations: *the Israeli air force.*

animals Capitalize the name of a specific animal, and use Roman numerals to show sequence: *Bowser, Whirlaway II.*

For breed names, follow the spelling and capitalization in *Webster's New World Dictionary.* For breeds not listed in the dictionary, capitalize words derived from proper nouns, use lowercase elsewhere: *basset hound, Boston terrier.*

army Capitalize when referring to U.S. forces: *the U.S. Army, the Army, Army regulations.*

Use lowercase for the forces of other nations: *the French army.*

Bible   Capitalize, without quotation marks, when referring to the Scriptures of the Old Testament or the New Testament. Capitalize also related terms such as *the Gospels, Gospel of St. Mark, the Scriptures, the Holy Scriptures.*

Lowercase *biblical* in all uses.

Lowercase *bible* as a nonreligious term: *My dictionary is my bible.*

brand names   When they are used, capitalize them.

Brand names normally should be used only if they are essential to a story.

Sometimes, however, the use of a brand name may not be essential but is acceptable because it lends an air of reality to a story: *He fished a Camel from his shirt pocket* may be preferable to the less specific *cigarette.*

building   Capitalize the proper names of buildings, including the word building if it is an integral part of the proper name: *the Empire State Building.*

bureau   Capitalize when part of the formal name for an organization or agency: *the Bureau of Labor Statistics, the Newspaper Advertising Bureau.*

Lowercase when used alone or to designate a corporate subdivision: *the Washington bureau of The Associated Press.*

cabinet   Capitalize references to a specific body of advisers heading executive departments for a president, king, governor, etc.: *The president-elect said he has not made his Cabinet selections.*

The capital letter distinguishes the word from the common noun meaning "cupboard," which is lowercase.

Cabinet titles   Capitalize the full title when used before a name, lowercase in other uses: *Secretary of State Alexander Haig,* but *Malcolm Baldridge, secretary of commerce.*

century   Lowercase, spelling out numbers less than 10: *the first century, the 20th century.*

For proper names, follow the organization's practice: *20th Century-Fox, Twentieth Century Fund, Twentieth Century Limited.*

chairman, chairwoman   Capitalize as a formal title before a name: *company Chairman Henry Ford, committee Chairwoman Margaret Chase Smith.*

Do not capitalize as a casual, temporary position: *meeting chairman Robert Jones.*

Do not use *chairperson* unless it is an organization's formal title for an office.

chief Capitalize as a formal title before a name: *He spoke to Police Chief Michael Codd. He spoke to Chief Michael Codd of the New York police.*

Lowercase when it is not a formal title: *union chief Walter Reuther.*

church Capitalize as part of the formal name of a building, a congregation or a denomination; lowercase in other uses: *St. Mary's Church, the Roman Catholic Church, the Catholic and Episcopal churches, a Roman Catholic church, a church.*

Lowercase in phrases where the church is used in an institutional sense: *He believes in separation of church and state. The pope said the church opposes abortion.*

city council Capitalize when part of a proper noun: *the Boston City Council.*

Retain capitalization if the reference is to a specific council but the context does not require the city name: *BOSTON (AP)—The City Council . . .*

Lowercase in other uses: *the council, the Boston and New York city councils, a city council.*

committee Capitalize when part of a formal name: *the House Appropriations Committee.*

Do not capitalize committee in shortened versions of long committee names: *the Special Senate Select Committee to Investigate Improper Labor-Management Practices,* for example, became the *rackets committee.*

congress Capitalize *U.S. Congress* and *Congress* when referring to the U.S. Senate and House of Representatives. Although Congress sometimes is used as a substitute for the House, it properly is reserved for reference to both the Senate and House.

constitution Capitalize references to the U.S. Constitution, with or without the *U.S.* modifier: *The president said he supports the Constitution.*

When referring to constitutions of other nations or of states, capitalize only with the name of a nation or a state: *the French Constitution, the Massachusetts Constitution, the nation's constitution, the state constitution, the constitution.*

Lowercase in other uses: *the organization's constitution.*
Lowercase *constitutional* in all uses.

courthouse Capitalize with the name of a jurisdiction: *the Cook County Courthouse, the U.S. Courthouse.* Lowercase in other uses: *the county courthouse, the courthouse, the federal courthouse.*

Court House   (two words) is used in the proper names of some communities: *Appomattox Court House, Va.*

court names   Capitalize the full proper names of courts at all levels.

Retain capitalization if U.S. or a state name is dropped: *the U.S. Supreme Court, the Supreme Court; the Massachusetts Superior Court, the state Superior Court, the Superior Court, Superior Court.*

For courts identified by a numeral: *3rd District Court, 8th U.S. Circuit Court of Appeals.*

directions and regions   In general, lowercase *north, south, northeast, northern,* etc., when they indicate compass direction; capitalize these words when they designate regions.

federal   Use a capital letter for the architectural style and for corporate or governmental bodies that use the word as part of their formal names: *Federal Express, the Federal Trade Commission.* (See separate entries for governmental agencies.)

Lowercase when used as an adjective to distinguish something from state, county, city, town or private entities: *federal assistance, federal court, the federal government, a federal judge.*

Also: *federal District Court* (but *U.S. District Court* is preferred) and *federal Judge John Sirica* (but *U.S. District Judge John Sirica* is preferred).

federal court   Always lowercase. The preferred form for first reference is to use the proper name of the court.

Do not create nonexistent entities such as *Manhattan Federal Court.* Instead, use *a federal court in Manhattan.*

food   Most food names are lowercase: *apples, cheese, peanut butter.*

Capitalize brand names and trademarks: *Roquefort cheese, Tabasco sauce, Smithfield ham.*

Most proper nouns or adjectives are capitalized when they occur in a food name: *Boston brown bread, Russian dressing, Swiss cheese, Waldorf salad.*

Lowercase is used, however, when the food does not depend on the proper noun or adjective for its meaning: *french fries, graham crackers, manhattan cocktail.*

former   Always lowercase. But retain capitalization for a formal title used immediately before a name: *former President Nixon.*

geographic names   Capitalize common nouns when they form an integral part of a proper name, but lowercase them when they stand alone: *Pennsylvania Avenue, the avenue; the Philippine Islands, the islands; the Mississippi River, the river.*

Lowercase common nouns that are not part of a specific proper name: *the Pacific islands, the Swiss mountains, Chekiang province.*

government   Always lowercase: *the federal government, the state government, the U.S. government.*

governmental bodies   Follow these guidelines:

FULL NAME: Capitalize the full proper names of governmental agencies, departments and offices: *the U.S. Department of State, the Georgia Department of Human Resources, the Boston City Council, the Chicago Fire Department.*

WITHOUT JURISDICTION: Retain capitalization in referring to a specific body if the dateline or context makes the name of the nation, state, county, city, etc., unnecessary: *the Department of State* (in a story from Washington), *the Department of Human Resources* or *the state Department of Human Resources* (in a story from Georgia), *the City Council* (in a story from Boston), *the Fire Department* or *the city Fire Department* (in a story from Chicago).

Lowercase further condensations of the name: *the department, the council,* etc.

FLIP-FLOPPED NAMES: Retain capital letters for the name of a governmental body if its formal name is flopped to delete the word *of: the State Department, the Human Resources Department.*

GENERIC EQUIVALENTS: If a generic term has become the equivalent of a proper name in popular use, treat it as a proper name: *Walpole State Prison,* for example, even though the proper name is *the Massachusetts Correctional Institution-Walpole.*

PLURALS, NONSPECIFIC REFERENCES: All words that are capitalized when part of a proper name should be lowercased when they are used in the plural or do not refer to a specific existing body. Some examples:

All states except Nebraska have a state senate. The town does not have a fire department. The bill requires city councils to provide matching funds. The president will address the lower houses of the New York and New Jersey legislatures.

heavenly bodies   Capitalize the proper names of planets, stars, constellations, etc.: *Mars, Arcturus, the Big Dipper, Aries.*

For comets, capitalize only the proper noun element of the name: *Halley's comet.*

Lowercase *sun* and *moon,* but if their Greek names are used, capitalize them: *Helios* and *Luna.*

historical periods and events   Capitalize the names of widely recognized epochs in anthropology, archaeology, geology and history: *the Bronze Age, the Dark Ages, the Middle Ages, the Pliocene Epoch.*

Capitalize also widely recognized popular names for periods and events: *the Atomic Age, the Boston Tea Party, the Civil War, the Exodus* (of the Israelites from Egypt), *the Great Depression, Prohibition.*

Lowercase *century: the 18th century.*

Capitalize only the proper nouns or adjectives in general descriptions of a period: *ancient Greece, classical Rome, the Victorian era, the fall of Rome.*

holidays and holy days   Capitalize them: *New Year's Eve, New Year's Day, Groundhog Day, Easter, Hanukkah,* etc.

house of representatives   Capitalize when referring to a specific governmental body: *the U.S. House of Representatives, the Massachusetts House of Representatives.*

Capitalize shortened references that delete the words *of Representatives: the U.S. House, the Massachusetts House.*

Retain capitalization if *U.S.* or the name of a state is dropped but the reference is to a specific body:

BOSTON (AP)—The House has adjourned for the year.

Lowercase plural uses: *the Massachusetts and Rhode Island houses.*

Apply the same principles to similar legislative bodies such as *the Virginia House of Delegates.*

judge   Capitalize before a name when it is the formal title for an individual who presides in a court of law. Do not continue to use the title in second reference.

Do not use *court* as part of the title unless confusion would result without it:

No *court* in the title: *U.S. District Judge John Sirica, District Judge John Sirica, federal Judge John Sirica, Judge John Sirica, U.S. Circuit Judge Homer Thornberry, appellate Judge John Blair.*

Court needed in the title: *Juvenile Court Judge Angela Jones, Criminal Court Judge John Jones, Superior Court Judge Robert Harrison, state Supreme Court Judge William Cushing.*

When the formal title *chief judge* is relevant, put the court name after the judge's name: *Chief Judge John Sirica of the U.S. District Court in Washington, D.C.; Chief Judge Clem-*

ent F. Haynsworth Jr. of the 4th U.S. Circuit Court of Appeals.

Do not pile up long court names before the name of a judge. Make it *Judge John Smith of Allegheny County Common Pleas Court.* Not: *Allegheny County Common Pleas Court Judge John Smith.*

Lowercase *judge* as an occupational designation in phrases such as *beauty contest judge Bert Parks.*

legislature Capitalize when preceded by the name of a state: *the Kansas Legislature.*

Retain capitalization when the state name is dropped but the reference is specifically to that state's legislature:

TOPEKA, Kan (AP)—Both houses of the Legislature adjourned today.

Capitalize *legislature* in subsequent specific references and in such constructions as: *the 100th Legislature, the state Legislature.*

Lowercase *legislature* when used generically: *No legislature has approved the amendment.*

Use *legislature* in lowercase for all plural references: *The Arkansas and Colorado legislatures are considering the amendment.*

magazine names Capitalize the name but do not place it in quotes. Lowercase *magazine* unless it is part of the publication's formal title: *Harper's Magazine, Newsweek magazine, Time magazine.*

Check the masthead if in doubt.

monuments Capitalize the popular names of monuments and similar public attractions: *Lincoln Memorial, Statue of Liberty, Washington Monument, Leaning Tower of Pisa,* etc.

mountains Capitalize as part of a proper name: *Appalachian Mountains, Ozark Mountains, Rocky Mountains.*

Or simply: *the Appalachians, the Ozarks, the Rockies.*

nationalities and races Capitalize the proper names of nationalities, peoples, races, tribes, etc.: *Arab, Arabic, African, Afro-American, American, Caucasian, Cherokee, Chinese* (both singular and plural), *Eskimo* (plural *Eskimos*), *French Canadian, Gypsy (Gypsies), Japanese* (singular and plural), *Jew, Jewish, Latin, Negro (Negroes), Nordic, Oriental, Sioux, Swede,* etc.

Lowercase *black* (noun or adjective), *white, red, mulatto,* etc.

Lowercase derogatory terms such as *honky* and *nigger.* Use them only in direct quotes when essential to the story.

navy   Capitalize when referring to U.S. forces: *the U.S. Navy, the Navy, Navy policy.*

Lowercase when referring to the naval forces of other nations: *the British navy.*

newspaper names   Capitalize *the* in a newspaper's name if that is the way the publication prefers to be known.

Lowercase *the* before newspaper names if a story mentions several papers, some of which use *the* as part of the name and some of which do not.

organizations and institutions   Capitalize the full names of organizations and institutions: *the American Medical Association; First Presbyterian Church; General Motors Corp.; Harvard University; Harvard University Medical School; the Procrastinators Club; the Society of Professional Journalists, Sigma Delta Chi.*

Retain capitalization if *Co., Corp.* or a similar word is deleted from the full proper name: *General Motors.*

FLIP-FLOPPED NAMES: Retain capital letters when commonly accepted practice flops a name to delete the word *of: College of the Holy Cross, Holy Cross College; Harvard School of Dental Medicine, Harvard Dental School.*

Do not, however, flop formal names that are known to the public with the word *of: Massachusetts Institute of Technology,* for example, not *Massachusetts Technology Institute.*

planets   Capitalize the proper names of planets: *Jupiter, Mars, Mercury, Neptune, Pluto, Saturn, Uranus, Venus.*

Capitalize *earth* when used as the proper name of our planet: *The astronauts returned to Earth.*

Lowercase nouns and adjectives derived from the proper names of planets and other heavenly bodies: *martian, jovian, lunar, solar, venusian.*

plants   In general, lowercase the names of plants, but capitalize proper nouns or adjectives that occur in a name.

Some examples: *tree, fir, white fir, Douglas fir, Dutch elm, Scotch pine, clover, white clover, white Dutch clover.*

police department   In communities where this is the formal name, capitalize *police department* with or without the name of the community: *the Los Angeles Police Department, the Police Department.*

If a police agency has some other formal name such as *Division of Police,* use that name if it is the way the department is known to the public. If the story uses *police depart-*

ment as a generic term for such an agency, put *police department* in lowercase.

If a police agency with an unusual formal name is known to the public as a police department, treat *police department* as the name, capitalizing it with or without the name of the community. Use the formal name only if there is a special reason in the story.

If the proper name cannot be determined for some reason, such as the need to write about a police agency from a distance, treat *police department* as the proper name, capitalizing it with or without the name of the community.

Lowercase police department in plural uses: *the Los Angeles and San Francisco police departments.*

Lowercase *the department* whenever it stands alone.

political parties and philosophies   Capitalize both the name of the party and the word *party* if it is customarily used as part of the organization's proper name: *the Democratic Party, the Republican Party.*

Capitalize *Communist, Conservative, Democrat, Liberal, Republican, Socialist,* etc., when they refer to the activities of a specific party or to individuals who are members of it. Lowercase these words when they refer to political philosophy.

Lowercase the name of a philosophy in noun and adjective forms unless it is the derivative of a proper name: *communism, communist; fascism, fascist.* But: *Marxism, Marxist; Nazism, Nazi.*

pontiff   Not a formal title. Always lowercase.

pope   Capitalize when used as a formal title before a name; lowercase in all other uses: *Pope John Paul II spoke to the crowd. At the close of his address, the pope gave his blessing.*

presidency   Always lowercase.

president   Capitalize *president* only as a formal title before one or more names: *President Reagan, Presidents Carter and Reagan.*

Lowercase in all other uses: *The president said today. He is running for president. Lincoln was president during the Civil War.*

religious references   The basic guidelines:

DEITIES: Capitalize the proper names of monotheistic deities: *God, Allah, the Father, the Son, Jesus Christ, the Son of God, the Redeemer, the Holy Spirit,* etc.

Lowercase pronouns referring to the deity: *he, him, his, thee, thou, who, whose, thy,* etc.

Lowercase *gods* in referring to the deities of polytheistic religions.

Capitalize the proper names of pagan and mythological gods and goddesses: *Neptune, Thor, Venus,* etc.

Lowercase such words as *god-awful, goddamn, godlike, godliness, godsend.*

LIFE OF CHRIST: Capitalize the names of major events in the life of Jesus Christ in references that do not use his name: *The doctrines of the Last Supper, the Crucifixion, the Resurrection* and *the Ascension* are central to Christian belief.

But use lowercase when the words are used with his name: *The ascension of Jesus into heaven took place 40 days after his resurrection from the dead.*

Apply the principle also to events in the life of his mother: *He cited the doctrine of the Immaculate Conception and the Assumption.* But: *She referred to the assumption of Mary into heaven.*

RITES: Capitalize proper names for rites that commemorate the Last Supper or signify a belief in Christ's presence: *the Lord's Supper, Holy Communion, Holy Eucharist.*

Lowercase the names of other sacraments.

Capitalize *Benediction* and the *Mass.* But: *a high Mass, a low Mass, a requiem Mass.*

OTHER WORDS: Lowercase *heaven, hell, devil, angel, cherub, an apostle, a priest,* etc.

Capitalize *Hades* and *Satan.*

seasons   Lowercase *spring, summer, fall, winter* and derivatives such as *springtime* unless part of a formal name: *Dartmouth Winter Carnival, Winter Olympics, Summer Olympics.*

senate   Capitalize all specific references to governmental legislative bodies, regardless of whether the name of the nation or state is used: *the U.S. Senate, the Senate; the Virginia Senate, the state Senate, the Senate.*

Lowercase plural uses: *the Virginia and North Carolina senates.*

The same principles apply to foreign bodies.

Lowercase references to nongovernmental bodies: *The student senate at Yale.*

sentences   Capitalize the first word of every sentence, including quoted statements and direction questions:
Patrick Henry said, "I know not what course others may take, but as for me, give me liberty or give me death."

Capitalize the first word of a quoted statement if it constitutes a sentence, even if it was part of a larger sentence in the original: *Patrick Henry said, "Give me liberty or give me death."*

In direct questions, even without quotation marks: *The story answers the question, Where does true happiness really lie?*

Social Security　Capitalize all references to the U.S. system.

Lowercase generic uses such as: *Is there a social security program in Sweden?*

state　Lowercase in all *state of* constructions: *the state of Maine, the states of Maine and Vermont.*

Do not capitalize *state* when used simply as an adjective to specify a level of jurisdiction: *state Rep. William Smith, the state Transportation Department, state funds.*

Apply the same principle to phrases such as *the city of Chicago, the town of Auburn,* etc.

statehouse　Capitalize all references to a specific statehouse, with or without the name of the state: *The Massachusetts Statehouse is in Boston. The governor will visit the Statehouse today.*

Lowercase plural uses: *the Massachusetts and Rhode Island statehouses.*

subcommittee　Lowercase when used with the name of a legislative body's full committee: *a Ways and Means subcommittee.*

Capitalize when a subcommittee has a proper name of its own: *the Senate Permanent Subcommittee on Investigations.*

titles　In general, confine capitalization to formal titles used directly before an individual's name. Lowercase and spell out titles when they are not used with an individual's name: *The president issued a statement. The pope gave his blessing.*

Lowercase and spell out titles in constructions that set them off from a name by commas: *The vice president, Walter Mondale, declined to run again. John Paul II, the current pope, does not plan to retire.*

ABBREVIATED TITLES:　The following formal titles are capitalized and abbreviated as shown when used before a name outside quotations: *Dr., Gov., Lt., Gov., Rep., Sen.* and certain military ranks. Spell out all except *Dr.* when they are used in quotations.

All other formal titles are spelled out in all uses.

ACADEMIC TITLES:　Capitalize and spell out formal titles such as *professor, dean, president, chancellor, chairman,* etc., when they precede a name. Lowercase elsewhere.

Lowercase modifiers such as *history* in *history Professor Oscar Handlin* or *department* in *department Chairman Jerome Wiesner.*

FORMAL TITLES: Capitalize formal titles when they are used immediately before one or more names: *Pope John Paul II, President Washington, Vice Presidents John Jones and William Smith.*

LEGISLATIVE TITLES: Use *Rep., Reps., Sen.* and *Sens.* as formal titles before one or more names in regular text. Spell out and capitalize these titles before one or more names in a direct quotation. Spell out and lowercase *representative* and *senator* in other uses.

Spell out other legislative titles in all uses. Capitalize formal titles such as *assemblyman, assemblywoman, city councilor, delegate,* etc., when they are used before a name. Lowercase in other uses.

Add *U.S.* or *state* before a title only if necessary to avoid confusion: *U.S. Sen. Herman Talmadge spoke with state Sen. Hugh Carter.*

First Reference Practice. The use of a title such as *Rep.* or *Sen.* in first reference is normal in most stories. It is not mandatory, however, provided an individual's title is given later in the story.

Deletion of the title on first reference is frequently appropriate, for example, when an individual has become well known: *Barry Goldwater endorsed President Reagan's budget plan today. The Arizona senator said he believes the budget is sound.*

Second Reference. Do not use a legislative title before a name on second reference unless part of a direct quotation.

Congressman, Congresswoman. Rep. and *U.S. Rep.* are the preferred first-reference forms when a formal title is used before the name of a U.S. House member. The words *congressman* or *congresswoman,* in lowercase, may be used in subsequent references that do not use an individual's name, just as *senator* is used in references to members of the Senate.

Congressman and Congresswoman should appear as capitalized formal titles before a name only in direct quotation.

Organizational Titles. Capitalize titles for formal, organizational offices within a legislative body when they are used before a name: *Majority Leader James C. Wright, Chairman Les Aspin of the House Armed Services Committee.*

MILITARY TITLES: Capitalize a military rank when used as a formal title before an individual's name.

Spell out and lowercase a title when it is substituted for a name: *Gen. John J. Pershing arrived today. An aide said the general would review the troops.*

ROYAL TITLES: Capitalize *king, queen,* etc., when used directly before a name.

trademark A trademark is a brand, symbol, word, etc., used by a manufacturer or dealer and protected by law to prevent a competitor from using it: *Astroturf,* for a type of artificial grass, for example.

In general, use a generic equivalent unless the trademark name is essential to the story.

When a trademark is used, capitalize it.

union names The formal names of unions may be condensed to conventionally accepted short forms that capitalize characteristic words from the full name followed by *union* in lowercase.

Abbreviations and Acronyms

A few universally recognized abbreviations are required in some circumstances. Some others are acceptable depending on the context. But in general, avoid alphabet soup.

The same principle applies to acronyms—pronounceable words formed from the initial letters in a series of words: *ALCOA, NATO, radar, scuba,* etc.

Guidance on how to use a particular abbreviation or acronym is provided in entries alphabetized according to the sequence of letters in the word or phrase.

Some general principles:

Before a Name

Abbreviate the following titles when used before a full name outside direct quotations: *Dr., Gov., Lt. Gov., Mr., Mrs., Ms., Rep., the Rev., Sen.* and certain military designations. Spell out all except *Dr., Mr., Mrs.* and *Ms.* when they are used before a name in direct quotations.

After a Name

Abbreviate *junior* or *senior* after an individual's name. Abbreviate *company, corporation, incorporated* and *limited* when used after the name of a corporate entity.

In some cases, an academic degree may be abbreviated after an individual's name.

With Dates or Numerals

Use the abbreviations *A.D., B.C., a.m., p.m., No.,* and abbreviate certain months when used with the day of the month.

In Numbered Addresses

Abbreviate *avenue, boulevard* and *street* in numbered addresses: *He lives on Pennsylvania Avenue. He lives at 1600 Pennsylvania Ave.*

States and Nations The names of certain states, the United States and the Union of Soviet Socialist Republics (but not of other nations) are abbreviated with periods in some circumstances.

Acceptable But Not Required Some organizations and government agencies are widely recognized by their initials: *CIA, FBI, GOP.*

If the entry for such an organization notes that an abbreviation is acceptable in all references or on second reference, that does not mean that its use should be automatic. Let the context determine, for example, whether to use *Federal Bureau of Investigation* or *FBI.*

Avoid Awkward Constructions Do not follow an organization's full name with an abbreviation or acronym in parentheses or set off by dashes. If an abbreviation or acronym would not be clear on second reference without this arrangement, do not use it.

Names not commonly before the public should not be reduced to acronyms solely to save a few words.

An alphabetical listing of other key points involving abbreviations and acronyms:

academic degrees If mention of degrees is necessary to establish someone's credentials, the preferred form is to avoid an abbreviation and use instead a phrase such as: *Alma Jones, who has a doctorate in psychology.*

Use an apostrophe in *bachelor's degree, a master's,* etc.

Use such abbreviations as *B.A., M.A., LL.D.* and *Ph.D.* only when the need to identify many individuals by degree on first reference would make the preferred form cumbersome. Use these abbreviations only after a full name, never after just a last name.

When used after a name, an academic abbreviation is set off by commas: *Daniel Moynihan, Ph.D., spoke.*

Do not precede a name with a courtesy title for an academic degree and follow it with the abbreviation for the degree in the same reference.

addresses Use the abbreviations *Ave., Blvd.* and *St.* only with a numbered address: *1600 Pennsylvania Ave.* Spell them out and capitalize when part of a formal street name without a number: *Pennsylvania Avenue.* Lowercase and spell out when used alone or with more than one street name: *Massachusetts and Pennsylvania avenues.*

All similar words (*alley, drive, road, terrace,* etc.) always are spelled out. Capitalize them when part of a formal name without a number; lowercase when used alone or with two or more names.

Always use figures for an address number: *9 Morningside Circle.*

Spell out and capitalize *First* through *Ninth* when used as street names; use figures with two letters for *10th* and above: *7 Fifth Ave., 100 21st St.*

aircraft names Use a hyphen when changing from letters to figures; no hyphen when adding a letter after figures.

AM Acceptable in all references for the amplitude modulation system of radio transmission.

a.m., p.m. Lowercase, with periods. Avoid the redundant *10 a.m. this morning.*

armed services Do not use the abbreviations *U.S.A., USAF* and *USN.*

assistant Do not abbreviate. Capitalize only when part of a formal title before a name: *Assistant Secretary of State George Ball.* Wherever practical, however, an appositional construction should be used: *George Ball, assistant secretary of state.*

association Do not abbreviate. Capitalize as part of a proper name: *American Medical Association.*

attorney general, attorneys general Never abbreviate. Capitalize only when used as a title before a name: *Attorney General William French Smith.*

Bible Do not abbreviate individual books of the Bible.

Citations listing the number of chapter(s) and verse(s) use this form: *Matthew 3:16, Luke 21:1–13, 1 Peter 2:1.*

brothers Abbreviate as *Bros.* in formal company names: *Warner Bros.*

For possessives: *Warner Bros.' profits.*

Christmas Never abbreviate *Christmas* to *Xmas* or any other form.

CIA Acceptable in all references for *Central Intelligence Agency.*

c.o.d. Acceptable in all references for *cash on delivery* or *collect on delivery.* (The use of lowercase is an exception to the first listing in *Webster's New World*).

company, companies Use *Co.* or *Cos.* when a business uses either word at the end of its proper name: *Ford Motor Co., American Broadcasting Cos.* But: *Aluminum Company of America.*

If *company* or *companies* appears alone in second reference, spell the word out.

The forms for possessives: *Ford Motor Co.'s profits, American Broadcasting Cos.' profits.*

corporation   Abbreviate as *Corp.* when a company or government agency uses the word at the end of its name: *Gulf Oil Corp., the Federal Deposit Insurance Corp.*

Spell out *corporation* when it occurs elsewhere in a name: *the Corporation for Public Broadcasting.*

Spell out and lowercase *corporation* whenever it stands alone.

The form for possessives: *Gulf Oil Corp.'s profits.*

detective   Do not abbreviate.

district attorney   Do not abbreviate.

doctor   Use *Dr.* in first reference as a formal title before the name of an individual who holds a doctor of medicine degree: *Dr. Jonas Salk.*

The form *Dr.,* or *Drs.* in a plural construction, applies to all first-reference uses before a name, including direct quotations.

If appropriate in the context, *Dr.* also may be used on first reference before the names of individuals who hold other types of doctoral degrees. However, because the public frequently identifies *Dr.* only with physicians, care should be taken to assure that the individual's specialty is stated in first or second reference. The only exception would be a story in which the context left no doubt that the person was a dentist, psychologist, chemist, historian, etc.

In some instances it also is necessary to specify that an individual identified as *Dr.* is a physician. One frequent case is a story reporting on joint research by physicians, biologists, etc.

Do not use *Dr.* before the names of individuals who hold only honorary doctorates.

Do not continue the use of *Dr.* in subsequent references.

ERA   Acceptable in all references to baseball's *earned run average.* Acceptable on second reference for *Equal Rights Amendment.*

FBI   Acceptable in all references for *Federal Bureau of Investigation.*

FM   Acceptable in all references for the frequency modulation system of radio transmission.

ICBM, ICBMs   Acceptable on first reference for intercontinental ballistic missile(s), but the term should be defined in the body of a story.

Avoid the redundant *ICBM missiles.*

incorporated Abbreviate and capitalize as *Inc.* when used as part of a corporate name. It usually is not needed, but when it is used, do not set off with commas: *J.C. Penney Co. Inc. announced . . .*

IQ Acceptable in all references for *intelligence quotient.*

junior, senior Abbreviate as *Jr.* and *Sr.* only with full names of persons or animals. Do not precede by a comma: *Joseph P. Kennedy Jr.*

The notation *II* or *2nd* may be used if it is the individual's preference. Note, however, that *II* or *2nd* are not necessarily the equivalent of junior—they often are used by a grandson or nephew.

If necessary to distinguish between father and son in second reference, use *the elder Smith* or *the younger Smith.*

mount Spell out in all uses, including the names of communities and of mountains: *Mount Clemens, Mich.; Mount Everest.*

mph Acceptable in all references for *miles per hour* or *miles an hour.*

No. Use as the abbreviation for *number* in conjunction with a figure to indicate position or rank: *No. 1 man, No. 3 choice.*

Do not use in street addresses, with this exception: *No. 10 Downing St.,* the residence of Britain's prime minister.

Do not use in the names of schools: *Public School 19.*

point Do not abbreviate. Capitalize as part of a proper name: *Point Pleasant.*

saint Abbreviate as *St.* in the names of saints, cities and other places: *St. Jude; St. Paul, Minn.; St. John's, Newfoundland; St. Lawrence Seaway.*

state names Follow these guidelines:

STANDING ALONE: Spell out the names of the 50 U.S. states when they stand alone in textual material. Any state name may be condensed, however, to fit typographical requirements for tabular material.

EIGHT NOT ABBREVIATED: The names of eight states are never abbreviated in datelines or text: *Alaska, Hawaii, Idaho, Iowa, Maine, Ohio, Texas* and *Utah.*

ABBREVIATIONS REQUIRED: Use the state abbreviations listed at the end of this section:

In conjunction with the name of a city, town, village or military base in most datelines.

In conjunction with the name of a city, county, town, village or military base in text. See examples in punctuation section below.

In short-form listings of party affiliation: D-Ala., R-Mont.

The abbreviations are:

Ala.	Kan.	Nev.	R.I.
Ariz.	Ky.	N.H.	S.C.
Ark.	La.	N.J.	S.D.
Calif.	Md.	N.M.	Tenn.
Colo.	Mass.	N.Y.	Vt.
Conn.	Mich.	N.C.	Va.
Del.	Minn.	N.D.	Wash.
Fla.	Miss.	Okla.	W.Va.
Ga.	Mo.	Ore.	Wis.
Ill.	Mont.	Pa.	Wyo.
Ind.	Neb.		

TV Acceptable as an adjective or in such constructions as *cable TV*. But do not normally use as a noun unless part of a quotation.

UFO, UFOs Acceptable in all references for *unidentified flying object(s)*.

U.N. Used as an adjective, but not as a noun, for *United Nations*.

U.S. Used as an adjective, but not as a noun, for *United States*.

Punctuation and Hyphenation

Think of punctuation and hyphenation as a courtesy to your readers, designed to help them understand a story.

Inevitably, a mandate of this scope involves gray areas. For this reason, the punctuation entries in the stylebooks refer to guidelines rather than rules. Guidelines should not be treated casually, however.

ampersand (&) Use the ampersand when it is part of a company's formal name: *Baltimore & Ohio Railroad, Newport News Shipbuilding & Dry Dock Co.*

The ampersand should not otherwise be used in place of *and*.

all- Use a hyphen.

all-around (not all-round) all-out
all-clear   all-star

anti- Hyphenate all except the following words, which have specific meanings of their own:

antibiotic	antiknock	antiphony
antibody	antimatter	antiseptic
anticlimax	antimony	antiserum
antidote	antiparticle*	antithesis

antifreeze	antipasto	antitrust
antigen	antiperspirant	antitoxin
antihistamine	antiphon	antitussive

*And similar terms in physics such as antiproton.

This approach has been adopted in the interests of readability and easily remembered consistency.

apostrophe (')   Follow these guidelines:

POSSESSIVES: See the possessives entry.

OMITTED LETTERS: *I've, it's, don't, rock 'n' roll. 'Tis the season to be jolly. He is a ne'er-do-well.*

OMITTED FIGURES: *The class of '62. The Spirit of '76. The '20s.*

PLURALS OF A SINGLE LETTER: *Mind your p's and q's. He learned the three R's and brought home a report card with four A's and two B's. The Oakland A's won the pennant.*

DO NOT USE: For plurals of numerals or multiple-letter combinations.

by   In general, no hyphen. Some examples:

| byline | byproduct |
| bypass | bystreet |

By-election is an exception.

co-   Retain the hyphen when forming nouns, adjectives and verbs that indicate occupation or status:

co-author	co-owner	co-signer
co-chairman	co-partner	co-star
co-defendant	co-pilot	co-worker
co-host	co-respondent (in a divorce suit)	

(Several are exceptions to *Webster's New World* in the interests of consistency.)

Use no hyphen in other combinations:

coed	coexist	cooperative
coeducation	coexistence	coordinate
coequal	cooperate	coordination

Cooperate, coordinate and related words are exceptions to the rule that a hyphen is used if a prefix ends in a vowel and the word that follows begins with the same vowel.

colon The most frequent use of a colon is at the end of a sentence to introduce lists, tabulations, texts, etc.

Capitalize the first word after a colon only if it is a proper noun or the start of a complete sentence: *He promised this: The company will make good all the losses.* But: *There were three considerations: expense, time and feasibility.*

INTRODUCING QUOTATIONS: Use a comma to introduce a direct quotation of one sentence that remains within a paragraph. Use a colon to introduce longer quotations within a paragraph and to end all paragraphs that introduce a paragraph of quoted material.

PLACEMENT WITH QUOTATION MARKS: Colons go outside quotation marks unless they are part of the quotation itself.

comma The following guidelines treat some of the most frequent questions about the use of commas. Additional guidelines on specialized uses are provided in separate entries.

For more detailed guidance, consult "The Comma" and "Misused and Unnecessary Commas" in the Guide to Punctuation section in the back of *Webster's New World Dictionary.*

IN A SERIES: Use commas to separate elements in a series, but do not put a comma before the conjunction in a simple series: *The flag is red, white and blue. She would nominate Tom, Dick or Jane.*

Put a comma before the concluding conjunction in a series, however, if an integral element of the series requires a conjunction: *I had orange juice, toast, and ham and eggs for breakfast.*

Use a comma also before the concluding conjunction in a complex series of phrases: *The main points to consider are whether the athletes are skillful enough to compete, whether they have the stamina to endure the training, and whether they have the proper mental attitude.*

WITH EQUAL ADJECTIVES: Use commas to separate a series of adjectives equal in rank. If the commas could be replaced by the word *and* without changing the sense, the adjectives are equal: *a thoughtful, precise manner; a dark, dangerous street.*

Use no comma when the last adjective before a noun outranks its predecessors because it is an integral element of a noun phrase, which is the equivalent of a single noun: *a cheap fur coat* (the noun phrase is fur coat); *the old oaken bucket; a new, blue spring bonnet.*

WITH INTRODUCTORY CLAUSES AND PHRASES:
A comma normally is used to separate an introductory clause or phrase from a main clause: *When he had tired of the mad pace of New York, he moved to Dubuque.*

The comma may be omitted after short introductory phrases if no ambiguity would result: *During the night he heard many noises.*

But use the comma if its omission would slow comprehension: *On the street below, the curious gathered.*

WITH CONJUNCTIONS: When a conjunction such as *and, but* or *for* links two clauses that could stand alone as separate sentences, use a comma before the conjunction in most cases: *She was glad she had looked, for a man was approaching the house.*

As a rule of thumb, use a comma if the subject of each clause is expressly stated: *We are visiting Washington, and we also plan a side trip to Williamsburg. We visited Washington, and our senator greeted us personally.* But no comma when the subject of the two clauses is the same and is not repeated in the second: *We are visiting Washington and plan to see the White House.*

The comma may be dropped if two clauses with expressly stated subjects are short. In general, however, favor use of a comma unless a particular literary effect is desired or it would distort the sense of a sentence.

INTRODUCING DIRECT QUOTES: Use a comma to introduce a complete, one-sentence quotation within a paragraph: *Wallace said, "She spent six months in Argentina and came back speaking English with a Spanish accent."* But use a colon to introduce quotations of more than one sentence.

Do not use a comma at the start of an indirect or partial quotation: *He said his victory put him "firmly on the road to a first-ballot nomination."*

BEFORE ATTRIBUTION: Use a comma instead of a period at the end of a quote that is followed by attribution: *"Rub my shoulder," Miss Cawley suggested.*

Do not use a comma, however, if the quoted statement ends with a question mark or exclamation point: *"Why should I?" he asked.*

WITH HOMETOWNS AND AGES: Use a comma to set off an individual's hometown when it is placed in apposition to a name: *Mary Richards, Minneapolis, and Maude Findlay, Tuckahoe, N.Y., were there.*

However, the use of the word *of* without a comma between the individual's name and the city name generally is preferable: *Mary Richards of Minneapolis and Maude Findlay of Tuckahoe, N.Y., were there.*

If an individual's age is used, set it off by commas: *Maude Findlay, 48, Tuckahoe, N.Y., was present.* The use of the word *of* eliminates the need for a comma after the hometown if a state name is not needed: *Mary Richards, 36, of Minneapolis and Maude Findlay, 48, of Tuckahoe, N.Y., attended the party.*

IN LARGE FIGURES: Use a comma for most figures higher than 999. The major exceptions are: street addresses *(1234 Main St.),* broadcast frequencies *(1460 kilohertz),* room numbers, serial numbers, telephone numbers, and years *(1976).*

PLACEMENT WITH QUOTES: Commas always go inside quotation marks.

dash   Follow these guidelines:

ABRUPT CHANGE: Use dashes to denote an abrupt change in thought in a sentence or an emphatic pause: *We will fly to Paris in June —if I get a raise. Smith offered a plan—it was unprecedented—to raise revenues.*

SERIES WITHIN A PHRASE: When a phrase that otherwise would be set off by commas contains a series of words that must be separated by commas, use dashes to set off the full phrase: *He listed the qualities—intelligence, charm, beauty, independence—that he liked in women.*

ATTRIBUTION: Use a dash before an author's or composer's name at the end of a quotation: *"Who steals my purse steals trash."—Shakespeare.*

IN DATELINES:
 NEW YORK (AP)—The city is broke.

IN LISTS: Dashes should be used to introduce individual sections of a list. Capitalize the first word following the dash. Use periods, not semicolons, at the end of each section. Example:
 Jones gave the following reasons:
 —He never ordered the package.
 —If he did, it didn't come.
 —If it did, he sent it back.

WITH SPACES: Put a space on both sides of a dash in all uses except the start of a paragraph and sports agate summaries.

ellipsis (...)   In general, treat an ellipsis as a three-letter word, constructed with three periods and two spaces, as shown here.

Use an ellipsis to indicate the deletion of one or more words in condensing quotes, texts and documents. Be especially careful to avoid deletions that would distort the meaning.

ex-   Use no hyphen for words that use *ex-* in the sense of *out of:*

excommunicate   expropriate

Hyphenate when using *ex* in the sense of *former:*
ex-convict   ex-president

Do not capitalize *ex-* when attached to a formal title before a name: *ex-President Carter.* The prefix modifies the entire term: *ex-New York Gov. Nelson Rockefeller;* not *New York ex-Gov. Nelson Rockefeller.*
Usually *former* is better.

exclamation point (!)   Follow these guidelines:
EMPHATIC EXPRESSIONS: Use the mark to express a high degree of surprise, incredulity or other strong emotion.
AVOID OVERUSE: Use a comma after mild interjections. End mildly exclamatory sentences with a period.
PLACEMENT WITH QUOTES: Place the mark inside quotation marks when it is part of the quoted material: *"How wonderful!" he exclaimed. "Never!" she shouted.*
Place the mark outside quotation marks when it is not part of the quoted material: *I hated reading Spenser's "Faerie Queene"!*

extra-   Do not use a hyphen when *extra-* means *outside of* unless the prefix is followed by a word beginning with *a* or a capitalized word:

extralegal   extraterrestrial
extramarital   extraterritorial

But:

extra-alimentary   extra-Britannic

Follow *extra-* with a hyphen when it is part of a compound

modifier describing a condition beyond the usual size, extent or degree:

extra-base hit	extra-large book
extra-dry drink	extra-mild taste

fore- In general, no hyphen. Some examples:

forebrain	foregoing
forefather	foretooth

There are three nautical exceptions, based on long-standing practice:

fore-topgallant	fore-topsail
fore-topmast	

full- Hyphenate when used to form compound modifiers:

full-dress	full-page
full-fledged	full-scale
full-length	

great- Hyphenate *great-grandfather, great-great-grandmother,* etc.
   Use *great grandfather* only if the intended meaning is that the grandfather was a great man.

hyphen Hypens are joiners. Use them to avoid ambiguity or to form a single idea from two or more words.
   Some guidelines:
   AVOID AMBIGUITY: Use a hyphen whenever ambiguity would result if it were omitted: *The president will speak to small-business men.* (*Businessmen* normally is one word. But *The president will speak to small businessmen* is unclear.)
   COMPOUND MODIFIERS: When a compound modifier—two or more words that express a single concept—precedes a noun, use hyphens to link all the words in the compound except the adverb *very* and all adverbs that end in *ly: a first-quarter touchdown, a bluish-green dress, a full-time job, a well-known man, a better-qualified woman, a know-it-all attitude, a very good time, an easily remembered rule.*
   Many combinations that are hyphenated before a noun are not hyphenated when they occur after a noun: *The team scored in the first quarter. The dress, a bluish green, was attractive on her. She works full time. His attitude suggested that he knew it all.*

But when a modifier that would be hyphenated before a noun occurs instead after a form of the verb *to be,* the hyphen usually must be retained to avoid confusion: *The man is well-known. The woman is quick-witted. The children are soft-spoken. The play is second-rate.*

The principle of using a hyphen to avoid confusion explains why no hyphen is required with *very* and *ly* words. Readers can expect them to modify the word that follows. But if a combination such as *little-known man* were not hyphenated, the reader could logically be expecting *little* to be followed by a noun, as in *little man.* Instead, the reader encountering *little known* would have to back up mentally and make the compound connection on his own.

TWO-THOUGHT COMPOUNDS: *serio-comic, socio-economic.*

COMPOUND PROPER NOUNS AND ADJECTIVES: Use a hyphen to designate dual heritage: *Italian-American, Mexican-American.*

No hyphen, however, for *French Canadian* or *Latin American.*

AVOID DUPLICATED VOWELS, TRIPLED CONSONANTS: Examples:

anti-intellectual   shell-like
pre-empt

WITH NUMERALS: Use a hyphen to separate figures in odds, ratios, scores, some fractions and some vote tabulations. See examples in entries under these headings.

When large numbers must be spelled out, use a hyphen to connect a word ending in *y* to another word: *twenty-one, fifty-five,* etc.

SUSPENSIVE HYPHENATION: The form: *He received a 10- to 20-year sentence in prison.*

in- No hyphen when it means "not"

inaccurate   insufferable

Often solid in other cases:

inbound   infighting
indoor   inpatient (n., adj.)
infield

A few combinations take a hyphen, however:

in-depth   in-house
in-group   in-law

Follow *Webster's New World* when in doubt.

-in   Precede with a hyphen:

break-in   walk-in
cave-in   write-in

parentheses   In general, use parentheses around logos, as shown in the datelines entry, but otherwise be sparing with them.

Parentheses are jarring to the reader. Because they do not appear on many news service printers there is also the danger that material inside them may be misinterpreted.

The temptation to use parentheses is a clue that a sentence is becoming contorted. Try to write it another way. If a sentence must contain incidental material, then commas or two dashes are frequently more effective. Use these alternatives whenever possible.

There are occasions, however, when parentheses are the only effective means of inserting necessary background or reference information.

periods   Follow these guidelines:

END OF DECLARATIVE SENTENCE: *The stylebook is finished.*

END OF A MILDLY IMPERATIVE SENTENCE: *Shut the door.*

Use an exclamation point if greater emphasis is desired: *Be careful!*

END OF SOME RHETORICAL QUESTIONS: A period is preferable if a statement is more a suggestion than a question: *Why don't we go.*

END OF AN INDIRECT QUESTION: *He asked what the score was.*

INITIALS: *John F. Kennedy, T.S. Eliot.* (No space between T. and S., to prevent them from being placed on two lines in typesetting.)

Abbreviations using only the initials of a name do not take periods: *JFK, LBJ.*

ENUMERATIONS: After numbers or letters in enumerating elements of a summary: *1. Wash the car. 2. Clean the basement.* Or: *A. Punctuate properly. B. Write simply.*

possessives   Follow these guidelines:

PLURAL NOUNS NOT ENDING IN S: Add *'s*: *the alumni's contributions, women's rights.*

PLURAL NOUNS ENDING IN S: Add only an apostrophe: *the churches' needs, the girls' toys, the horses' food, the ships' wake, states' rights, the VIPs' entrance.*

NOUNS PLURAL IN FORM, SINGULAR IN MEANING: Add only an apostrophe: *mathematics' rules, measles' effects.* (But see INANIMATE OBJECTS below.)

Apply the same principle when a plural word occurs in the formal name of a singular entity: *General Motors' profits, the United States' wealth.*

NOUNS THE SAME IN SINGULAR AND PLURAL: Treat them the same as plurals, even if the meaning is singular: *one corps' location, the two deer's tracks, the lone moose's antlers.*

SINGULAR NOUNS NOT ENDING IN S: Add *'s*: *the church's needs, the girl's toys, the horse's food, the ship's route, the VIP's seat.*

Some style guides say that singular nouns ending in *s* sounds such as *ce, x,* and *z* may take either the apostrophe alone or *'s.* See SPECIAL EXPRESSIONS below, but otherwise, for consistency and ease in remembering a rule, always use *'s* if the word does not end in the letter *s*: *Butz's policies, the fox's den, the justice's verdict, Marx's theories, the prince's life, Xerox's profits.*

SINGULAR COMMON NOUNS ENDING IN S: Add *'s* unless the next word begins with *s*: *the hostess's invitation, the hostess' seat; the witness's answer, the witness' story.*

SINGULAR PROPER NAMES ENDING IN S: Use only an apostrophe: *Achilles' heel, Agnes' book, Ceres' rites, Descartes' theories, Dickens' novels, Euripides' dramas, Hercules' labors, Jesus' life, Jules' seat, Kansas' schools, Moses' law, Socrates' life, Tennessee Williams' plays, Xerxes' armies.*

SPECIAL EXPRESSIONS: The following exceptions to the general rule for words not ending in *s* apply to words that end in an *s* sound and are followed by a word that begins with *s*: *for appearance' cost, my conscience' voice.*

PRONOUNS: Personal, interrogative and relative pronouns have separate forms for the possessive. None involves an apostrophe: *mine, ours, yours, his, hers, its, theirs, whose.*

Caution: If you are using an apostrophe with a pronoun, always double-check to be sure that the meaning calls for a contraction: *you're, it's, there's, who's.*

Follow the rules listed above in forming the possessives of other pronouns: *another's idea, other's plans, someone's guess.*

COMPOUND WORDS: Applying the rules above, add an apostrophe or *'s* to the word closest to the object possessed: *the major general's decision, the major generals' decisions, the attorney general's request, the attorneys generals' request.* See the plurals entry for guidelines on forming the plurals of these words.

Also: *anyone else's attitude, John Adams Jr.'s father, Benjamin Franklin of Pennsylvania's motion.* Whenever practical, however, recast the phrase to avoid ambiguity: *the motion by Benjamin Franklin of Pennsylvania.*

JOINT POSSESSION, INDIVIDUAL POSSESSION: Use a possessive form after only the last word if ownership is joint: *Fred and Sylvia's apartment, Fred and Sylvia's stocks.*

Use a possessive form after both words if the objects are individually owned: *Fred's and Sylvia's books.*

DESCRIPTIVE PHRASES: Do not add an apostrophe to a word ending in *s* when it is used primarily in a descriptive sense: *citizens band radio, a Cincinnati Reds infielder, a teachers college, a Teamsters request, a writers guide.*

Memory Aid: The apostrophe usually is not used if *for* or *by* rather than *of* would be appropriate in the longer form: *a radio band for citizens, a college for teachers, a guide for writers, a request by the Teamsters.*

An *'s* is required, however, when a term involves a plural word that does not end in *s: a children's hospital, a people's republic, the Young Women's Christian Association.*

DESCRIPTIVE NAMES: Some governmental, corporate and institutional organizations with a descriptive word in their names use an apostrophe; some do not. Follow the user's practice: *Actors Equity, Diners Club, the Ladies' Home Journal, the National Governors' Conference, the Veterans Administration.* See separate entries for these and similar names frequently in the news.

QUASI POSSESSIVES: Follow the rules above in composing the possessive form of words that occur in such phrases as *a day's pay, two weeks' vacation, three days' work, your money's worth.*

Frequently, however, a hyphenated form is clearer: *a two-week vacation, a three-day job.*

DOUBLE POSSESSIVE: Two conditions must apply for a double possessive—a phrase such as *a friend of John's*—to occur: 1. The word after *of* must refer to an animate object, and 2. The word before *of* must involve only a portion of the animate object's possessions.

Otherwise, do not use the possessive form on the word after *of: The friends of John Adams mourned his death.* (All the friends were involved.) *He is a friend of the college.* (Not *college's,* because *college* is inanimate).

Memory Aid: This construction occurs most often, and quite naturally, with the possessive forms of personal pronouns: *She is a friend of mine.*

INANIMATE OBJECTS: There is no blanket rule against creating a possessive form for an inanimate object, particularly if the object is treated in a personified sense. See some of the earlier examples, and note these: *death's call, the wind's murmur.*

In general, however, avoid excessive personalization of inanimate objects, and give preference to an *of* construction when it fits the makeup of the sentence. For example, the earlier references to mathematics' rules and measles' effects would better be phrased: *the rules of mathematics, the effects of measles.*

post- Follow *Webster's New World.* Hyphenate if not listed there. Some words without a hyphen:

postdate	postgraduate	postscript
postdoctoral	postnuptial	postwar
postelection	postoperative	

Some words that use a hyphen:

post-bellum   post-mortem

prefixes See separate listings for commonly used prefixes.

Three rules are constant, although they yield some exceptions to first-listed spellings in *Webster's New World Dictionary:*

Except for *cooperate* and *coordinate,* use a hyphen if the prefix ends in a vowel.

Use a hyphen if the word that follows is capitalized.

Use a hyphen to join doubled prefixes: *sub-subparagraph.*

pro- Use a hyphen when coining words that denote support for something. Some examples:

pro-business	pro-life
pro-labor	pro-war

No hyphen when *pro* is used in other senses:

produce	pronoun
profile	

question mark Follow these guidelines:
   END OF A DIRECT QUESTION: *Who started the riot?*
      Did she ask who started the riot? (The sentence as a whole is a direct question despite the indirect question at the end.)
      You started the riot? (A question in the form of a declarative statement.)
   INTERPOLATED QUESTION: *You told me—Did I hear you correctly?—that you started the riot.*
   MULTIPLE QUESTIONS: Use a single question mark at the end of the full sentence:
      Did you hear him say, "What right have you to ask about the riot?"
      Did he plan the riot, employ assistants, and give the signal to begin?
      Or, to cause full stops and throw emphasis on each element, break into separate sentences: *Did he plan the riot? Employ assistants? Give the signal to begin?*
   CAUTION: Do not use question marks to indicate the end of an indirect question:
      She asked who started the riot. To ask why the riot started is unnecessary. I want to know what the cause of the riot was. How foolish it is to ask what caused the riot.
   QUESTION AND ANSWER FORMAT: Do not use quotation marks. Paragraph each speaker's words:
      Q. Where did you keep it?
      A. In a little tin box.
   PLACEMENT WITH QUOTATION MARKS: Inside or outside, depending on the meaning:
      Who wrote "Gone With the Wind"?
      He asked, "How long will it take?"
   MISCELLANEOUS: The question mark supersedes the comma that normally is used when supplying attribution for a quotation: *"Who is there?" she asked.*
quotation marks The basic guidelines for open-quote marks (") and close-quote marks ("):

FOR DIRECT QUOTATIONS: To surround the exact words of a speaker or writer when reported in a story:

"I have no intention of staying," she replied.

"I do not object," he said, "to the tenor of the report."

Franklin said, "A penny saved is a penny earned."

A speaker said the practice is "too conservative for inflationary times."

RUNNING QUOTATIONS: If a full paragraph of quoted material is followed by a paragraph that continues the quotation, do not put close-quote marks at the end of the first paragraph. Do, however, put open-quote marks at the start of the second paragraph. Continue in this fashion for any succeeding paragraphs, using close-quote marks only at the end of the quoted material.

If a paragraph does not start with quotation marks but ends with a quotation that is continued in the next paragraph, do not use close-quote marks at the end of the introductory paragraph if the quoted material constitutes a full sentence. Use close-quote marks, however, if the quoted material does not constitute a full sentence.

DIALOGUE OR CONVERSATION: Each person's words, no matter how brief, are placed in a separate paragraph, with quotation marks at the beginning and the end of each person's speech:

"Will you go?"

"Yes."

"When?"

"Thursday."

NOT IN Q/A: Quotation marks are not required in formats that identify questions and answers by Q. and A.

NOT IN TEXTS: Quotation marks are not required in full texts, condensed texts or textual excerpts.

IRONY: Put quotation marks around a word or words used in an ironic sense: *The "debate" turned into a free-for-all.*

UNFAMILIAR TERMS: A word or words being introduced to readers may be placed in quotation marks on first reference:

Broadcast frequencies are measured in "kilohertz."

Do not put subsequent references to kilohertz in quotation marks.

AVOID UNNECESSARY FRAGMENTS: Do not use quotation marks to report a few ordinary words that a speaker or writer has used:

Wrong: *The senator said he would "go home to Michigan" if he lost the election.*

Right: *The senator said he would go home to Michigan if he lost the election.*

PARTIAL QUOTES: When a partial quote is used, do not put quotation marks around words that the speaker could not have used.

Suppose the individual said, "I am horrified at your slovenly manners."

Wrong: *She said she "was horrified at their slovenly manners."*

Right: *She said she was horrified at their "slovenly manners."*

Better when practical: Use the full quote.

QUOTES WITHIN QUOTES: Alternate between double quotation marks *("or")* and single marks *('or')*:

She said, "I quote from his letter, 'I agree with Kipling that "the female of the species is more deadly than the male," but the phenomenon is not an unchangeable law of nature,' a remark he did not explain."

Use three marks together if two quoted elements end at the same time: *She said, "He told me, 'I love you.'"*

PLACEMENT   WITH   OTHER   PUNCTUATION: Follow these long established printers' rules:

The period and the comma always go within the quotation marks.

The dash, the semicolon, the question mark and the exclamation point go within the quotation marks when they apply to the quoted matter only. They go outside when they apply to the whole sentence.

re-   The rules in prefixes apply. The following examples of exceptions to first-listed spellings in *Webster's New World* are based on the general rule that a hyphen is used if a prefix ends in a vowel and the word that follows begins with the same vowel:

re-elect	re-enact	re-entry
re-election	re-engage	re-equip
re-emerge	re-enlist	re-establish
re-employ	re-enter	re-examine

For many other words, the sense is the governing factor:

| recover (regain) | resign (quit) | reform (improve) |
| re-cover (cover again) | re-sign (sign again) | re-form (form again) |

Otherwise, follow *Webster's New World.* Use a hyphen for words not listed there unless the hyphen would distort the sense.

semicolon   In general, use the semicolon to indicate a greater separation of thought and information than a comma can convey but less than the separation that a period implies.

suffixes   See separate listings for commonly used suffixes.
Follow *Webster's New World Dictionary* for words not in this book.
If a word combination is not listed in *Webster's New World,* use two words for the verb form; hyphenate any noun or adjective forms.

suspensive hyphenation   The form: The 5- and 6-year-olds attend morning classes.

Numerals

A numeral is a figure, letter, word or group of words expressing a number.

Roman numerals use the letters *I, V, X, L, C, D* and *M.* Use Roman numerals for wars and to show personal sequence for animals and people: *World War II, Native Dancer II, King George VI, Pope John Paul II.*

Arabic numerals use the figures *1, 2, 3, 4, 5, 6, 7, 8, 9* and *0.* Use Arabic forms unless Roman numerals are specifically required.

The figures *1, 2, 10, 101,* etc., and the corresponding words— *one, two, ten, one hundred one,* etc.—are called cardinal numbers. The term ordinal number applies to *1st, 3rd, 10th, 101st, first, second, tenth, one hundred first,* etc.

Follow these guidelines in using numerals:

Large Numbers

When large numbers must be spelled out, use a hyphen to connect a word ending in *y* to another word; do not use commas between other separate words that are part of one number: *twenty; thirty; twenty-one; thirty-one; one hundred forty-three; one thousand one hundred fifty-five; one million two hundred seventy-six thousand five hundred eighty-seven.*

Sentence Start

Spell out a numeral at the beginning of a sentence. If necessary, recast the sentence. There is one exception—a numeral that identifies a calendar year.

Wrong: *993 freshman entered the college last year.*

Right: *Last year 993 freshmen entered the college.*
Right: *1976 was a very good year.*

Casual uses   Spell out casual expressions:
A thousand times no! Thanks a million. He walked a quarter of a mile.

Proper Names   Use words or numerals according to an organization's practice: *20th Century-Fox, Twentieth Century Fund, Big Ten.*

Figures or Words   For ordinals:
Spell out first through ninth when they indicate sequence in time or location—*first base, the First Amendment, he was first in line.* Starting with *10th,* use figures.
Use *1st, 2nd, 3rd, 4th,* etc., when the sequence has been assigned in forming names. The principal examples are geographic, military and political designations such as *1st Ward, 7th Fleet* and *1st Sgt.*

Other Uses   For uses not covered by these listings: Spell out whole numbers below 10, use figures for 10 and above. Typical examples: *The woman has three sons and two daughters. She has a fleet of 10 station wagons and two buses.*

In a Series   Apply the appropriate guidelines: *They had 10 dogs, six cats and 97 hamsters. They had four four-room houses, 10 three-room houses and 12 10-room houses.*
What follows is an alphabetical listing of other key points of using numerals.

addresses Always use figures for an address number: *9 Morningside Circle.*
Spell out and capitalize *First* through *Ninth* when used as street names; use figures with two letters for *10th* and above: *7 Fifth Ave., 100 21st St.*

ages Always use figures. When the context does not require years or years old, the figure is presumed to be years.

aircraft names Use a hyphen when changing from letters to figures; no hyphen when adding a letter after figures.
Some examples for aircraft often in the news: *B-1, BAC-111, C-5A, DC-10, FH-227, F-14, Phantom II, F-86 Sabre, L-1011, Mig-21, Tu-144, 727-100c, 747, 747B, VC-10.*

amendments to the Constitution Use *First Amendment, 10th Amendment,* etc.
Colloquial references to the Fifth Amendment's protection against self-incrimination are best avoided, but where appropriate: *He took the Fifth seven times.*

Arabic numerals The numerical figures *1, 2, 3, 4, 5, 6, 7, 8, 9, 10.*
In general, use Arabic forms unless denoting the sequence

of wars or establishing a personal sequence for people and animals.

betting odds   Use figures and a hyphen: *The odds were 5–4. He won despite 3–2 odds against him.*

　　The word *to* seldom is necessary, but when it appears it should be hyphenated in all constructions: *3-to-2 odds, odds of 3-to-2, the odds were 3-to-2.*

Celsius   Use this term rather than centigrade for the temperature scale that is part of the metric system.

　　When giving a Celsius temperature, use these forms: *40 degrees Celsius* or *40 C* (Note the space and no period after the capital C) if degrees and Celsius are clear from the context.

cents   Spell out the word *cents* and lowercase, using numerals for amounts less than a dollar: *5 cents, 12 cents.* Use the *$* sign and decimal system for larger amounts: *$1.01, $2.50.*

　　Numerals alone, with or without a decimal point as appropriate, may be used in tabular matter.

congressional districts   Use figures and capitalize *district* when joined with a figure: *the 1st Congressional District, the 1st District.*

　　Lowercase *district* whenever it stands alone.

court decisions   Use figures and a hyphen: *The Supreme Court ruled 5–4, a 5–4 decision.* The word *to* is not needed, but use hyphens if it appears in quoted matter: *"the court ruled 5-to-4, the 5-to-4 decision."*

court names   For courts identified by a numeral: *2nd District Court, 8th U.S. Circuit Court of Appeals.*

dates   Always use Arabic figures, without *st, nd, rd* or *th.*

decades   Use Arabic figures to indicate decades of history. Use an apostrophe to indicate numerals that are left out; show plural by adding the letter *s: the 1890s, the '90s, the Gay '90s, the 1920s, the mid-1930s.*

decimal units   Use a period and numerals to indicate decimal amounts. Decimalization should not exceed two places in textual material unless there are special circumstances.

dimensions   Use figures and spell out inches, feet, yards, etc., to indicate depth, height, length and width. Hyphenate adjectival forms before nouns.

　　Use an apostrophe to indicate feet and quote marks to indicate inches *(5'6")* only in very technical contexts.

distances   Use figures for 10 and above, spell out one through nine: *He walked four miles.*

district Use a figure and capitalize district when forming a proper name: *the 2nd District.*

dollars Use figures and the $ sign in all except casual references or amounts without a figure: *The book cost $4. Dad, please give me a dollar. Dollars are flowing overseas.*

For specified amounts, the word takes a singular verb: *He said $500,000 is what they want.*

For amounts of more than $1 million, use the $ and numerals up to two decimal places. Do not link the numerals and the word by a hyphen: *She is worth $4.35 million. She is worth exactly $4,351,242. He proposed a $300 billion budget.*

The form for amounts less then $1 million: *$4, $25, $500, $1,000, $650,000.*

election returns Use figures, with commas every three digits starting at the right and counting left. Use the word *to* (not a hyphen) in separating different totals listed together: *Jimmy Carter defeated Gerald Ford 40,827,292 to 39,146,157 in 1976* (this is the actual final figure).

Use the word *votes* if there is any possibility that the figures could be confused with a ratio: *Nixon defeated McGovern 16 votes to 3 votes in Dixville Notch.*

Do not attempt to create adjectival forms such as *the 40,827,292-39,146,157 vote.*

fractions Spell out amounts less than *1* in stories, using hyphens between the words: *two-thirds, four-fifths, seven-sixteenths,* etc.

Use figures for precise amounts larger than *1,* converting to decimals whenever practical.

Fractions are preferred, however, in stories about stocks.

When using fractional characters, remember that most newspaper type fonts can set only ⅛, ¼, ⅜, ½, ⅝, ¾ and ⅞ as one unit; use 1½, 2⅝, etc. with no space between the figure and the fraction. Other fractions require a hyphen and individual figures, with a space between the whole number and the fraction: *1 3-16, 2 1-3, 5 9-10.*

highway designations Use these forms, as appropriate in the context, for highways identified by number: *U.S. Highway 1, U.S. Route 1, U.S. 1, Route Q, Illinois 34, Illinois Route 34, state Route 34, Route 34, Interstate Highway 495.* On second reference only for Interstate: *I-495.*

mile Use figures for amounts under 10 in dimensions, formulas and speeds: *The farm measures 5 miles by 4 miles. The car slowed to 7 mph. The new model gets 4 miles more per gallon.*

Spell out below 10 in distances: *He drove four miles.*

millions, billions Use figures with million or billion in all except casual uses: *I'd like to make a billion dollars.* But: *The nation has 1 million citizens. I need $7 billion.*

Do not go beyond two decimals: *7.51 million persons, $2.56 billion, 7,542,500 persons, $2,565,750,000.* Decimals are preferred where practical: *1.5 million.* Not: *1½ million.*

Do not mix millions and billions in the same figure: *2.6 billion.* Not *2 billion, 600 million.*

Do not drop the word million or billion in the first figure of a range: *He is worth from $2 million to $4 million.* Not: *$2 to $4 million,* unless you really mean $2.

Note that a hyphen is not used to join the figures and the word million or billion, even in this type of phrase: *The president submitted a $300 billion budget.*

minus sign Use a hyphen, not a dash, but use the word minus if there is any danger of confusion.

Use a word, not a minus sign, to indicate temperatures below zero: minus 10 or 5 below zero.

No. Use as the abbreviation for number in conjunction with a figure to indicate position or rank: *No. 1 person, No. 3 choice.*

Do not use in street addresses, with this exception: *No. 10 Downing St.,* the residence of Britain's prime minister.

Do not use in the names of schools: *Public School 19.*

page numbers Use figures and capitalize *page* when used with a figure. When a letter is appended to the figure, capitalize it but do not use a hyphen: *Page 2, Page 10, Page 20A.*

One exception: *It's a Page One story.*

percentages Use figures: *1 percent, 2.5 percent* (use decimals, not fractions), *10 percent.*

For amounts less than 1 percent, precede the decimal with a zero: *The cost of living rose 0.6 percent.*

Repeat percent with each individual figure: *He said 10 percent to 30 percent of the electorate may not vote.*

political divisions Use Arabic figures and capitalize the accompanying word when used with the figure: *1st Ward, 10th Ward, 3rd Precinct, 22nd Precinct, the ward, the precinct.*

proportions Always use figures: *2 parts powder to 6 parts water.*

ratios Use figures and a hyphen: *the ratio was 2-to-1, a ratio of 2-to-1, a 2-1 ratio.* As illustrated, the word *to* should be omitted when the numbers precede the word *ratio.*

Always use the word *ratio* or a phrase such as *a 2-1 majority* to avoid confusion with actual figures.

scores Use figures exclusively, placing a hyphen between the totals of the winning and losing teams: *The Reds defeated the Red Sox 4-3, the Giants scored a 12-6 football victory over the Cardinals, the golfer had a 5 on the first hole but finished with a 2-under-par score.*

Use a comma in this format: *Boston 6, Baltimore 5.*

sizes Use figures: *a size 9 dress, size 40 long, 10½ B shoes, a 34½ sleeve.*

speeds Use figures. *The car slowed to 7 mph, winds of 5 to 10 mph, winds of 7 to 9 knots, 10-knot winds.*

Avoid extensively hyphenated constructions such as *5-mile-per-hour winds.*

telephone numbers Use figures. The forms: *(212) 262–4000, 262–4000, (212) MU2–0400.* If extension numbers are given: *Ext. 2, Ext. 364, Ext. 4071.*

temperatures Use figures for all except zero. Use a word, not a minus sign, to indicate temperatures below zero.

times Use figures except for noon and midnight. Use a colon to separate hours from minutes: *11 a.m., 1 p.m., 3:30 p.m.*

Avoid such redundancies as *10 a.m. this morning, 10 p.m. tonight* or *10 p.m. Monday night.* Use *10 a.m. today, 10 p.m. Monday,* etc., as required by the norms in time element.

The construction *4 o'clock* is acceptable, but time listings with *a.m.* or *p.m.* are preferred.

weights Use figures: *The baby weighed 9 pounds, 7 ounces. She had a 9-pound , 7-ounce boy.*

years Use figures, without commas: *1985.* Use an *s* without an apostrophe to indicate spans of decades or centuries: *the 1890s, the 1800s.*

Years are the lone exception to the general rule in numerals that a figure is not used to start a sentence: *1984 was a very good year.*

Grammar, Spelling and Word Usage

This section lists common problems of grammatical usage, word selection and spelling.

a, an Use the article *a* before consonant sounds: *a historic event, a one-year term* (sounds as if it begins with the letter *w*), *a united stand* (sounds like *you.*).

Use the article *an* before vowel sounds: *an energy crisis, an honorable man* (the *h* is silent), *an MBA record* (sounds as if it begins with the letter *e*), *an 1890s celebration.*

accept, except   *Accept* means to receive.
Except means to exclude.

adverse, averse   *Adverse* means unfavorable: *She predicted adverse weather.*
Averse means reluctant, opposed: *He is averse to change.*

affect, effect   *Affect,* as a verb, means to influence: *The game will affect the standings.*
Affect, as a noun, is best avoided. It occasionally is used in psychology to describe an emotion, but there is no need for it in everyday language.
Effect, as a verb, means to cause: *He will effect many changes in the company.*
Effect, as a noun, means result: *The effect was overwhelming. She miscalculated the effect of her actions. It was a law of little effect.*

aid, aide   Aid is assistance.
An *aide* is a person who serves as an assistant.

ain't   A dialectical or substandard contraction. Use it only in quoted matter or special contexts.

allude, refer   To *allude* to something is to speak of it without specifically mentioning it.
To *refer* is to mention it directly.

allusion, illusion   *Allusion* means an indirect reference: *The allusion was to his opponent's record.*
Illusion means an unreal or false impression: *The scenic director created the illusion of choppy seas.*

among, between   The maxim that *between* introduces two items and *among* introduces more than two covers most questions about how to use these words: *The funds were divided among Susan, Robert and William.*
However, *between* is the correct word when expressing the relationships of three or more items considered one pair at a time: *Negotiations on a debate format are under way between the network and the Jackson, Kennedy and Mondale committees.*
As with all prepositions, any pronouns that follow these words must be in the objective case: *among us, between him and her, between you and me.*

anticipate, expect   *Anticipate* means to expect and prepare for something; *expect* does not include the notion of preparation:
They expect a record crowd. They have anticipated it by adding more seats to the auditorium.

anybody, any body, anyone, any one   One word for an indefinite reference: *Anyone can do that.*

Two words when the emphasis is on singling out one element of a group: *Any one of them may speak up.*

apposition   A decision on whether to put commas around a word, phrase or clause used in apposition depends on whether it is essential to the meaning of the sentence (no commas) or not essential (use commas).

because, since   Use *because* to denote a specific cause-effect relationship: *He went because he was told.*

Since is acceptable in causal sense when the first event in a sequence led logically to the second but was not its direct cause: *He went to the game, since he had been given the tickets.*

blond, blonde   Use *blond* as a noun for males and as the adjective for all applications: *She has blond hair.*

Use *blonde* as a noun for females.

boy   Applicable until 18th birthday is reached. Use *man* or *young man* afterward.

brunet, brunette   Use *brunet* as a noun for males, and as the adjective for both sexes.

Use *brunette* as a noun for females.

burglary, larceny, robbery, theft   Legal definitions of burglary vary, but in general a *burglary* involves entering a building (not necessarily by breaking in) and remaining unlawfully with the intention of committing a crime.

Larceny is the legal term for the wrongful taking of property. Its nonlegal equivalents are stealing or theft.

Robbery in the legal sense involves the use of violence or threat in committing larceny. In a wider sense it means to plunder or rifle, and may thus be used even if a person was not present: *Her house was robbed while she was away.*

Theft describes a larceny that did not involve threat, violence or plundering.

USAGE NOTE: You rob a person, bank, house, etc., but you steal the money or the jewels.

collective nouns   Nouns that denote a unit take singular verbs and pronouns: *class, committee, crowd, family group, herd, jury, orchestra, team.*

Some usage examples: *The committee is meeting to set its agenda. The jury reached its verdict. A herd of cattle was sold.*

PLURAL IN FORM: Some words that are plural in form become collective nouns and take singular verbs when the group or quantity is regarded as a unit.

Right: *A thousand bushels is a good yield.* (A unit.)

Right: *A thousand bushels were created.* (Individual items.)

Right: *The data is sound.* (A unit.)

Right: *The data have been carefully collected.* (Individual items.)

compose, comprise, constitute *Compose* means to create or put together. It commonly is used in both the active and passive voices: *She composed a song. The United States is composed of 50 states. The zoo is composed of many animals.*

Comprise means to contain, to include all or embrace. It is best used only in the active voice, followed by a direct object: *The United States comprises 50 states. The jury comprises five men and seven women. The zoo comprises many animals.*

Constitute, in the sense of form or make up, may be the best word if neither *compose* nor *comprise* seems to fit: *Fifty states constitute the United States. Five men and seven women constitute the jury. A collection of animals can constitute a zoo.*

Use *include* when what follows is only part of the total: *The price includes breakfast. The zoo includes lions and tigers.*

contractions Contractions reflect informal speech and writing. *Webster's New World Dictionary* includes many entries for contractions: *aren't* for *are not,* for example.

Avoid excessive use of contractions. Contractions listed in the dictionary are acceptable, however, in informal contexts or circumstances where they reflect the way a phrase commonly appears in speech or writing.

contrasted to, contrasted with Use *contrasted to* when the intent is to assert, without the need for elaboration, that two items have opposite characteristics: *He contrasted the appearance of the house today to its ramshackle look last year.*

Use *contrasted with* when juxtaposing two or more items to illustrate similarities and/or differences: *He contrasted the Republican platform with the Democratic platform.*

dangling modifiers Avoid modifiers that do not refer clearly and logically to some word in the sentence.

Dangling: *Taking our seats, the game started.* (Taking does not refer to the subject, game, nor to any other word in the sentence.)

Correct: *Taking our seats, we watched the opening of the game.* (Taking refers to we, the subject of the sentence.)

either Use it to mean *or the other,* not *both.*

Right: *She said to use either door.*

Wrong: *There were lions on either side of the door.*

Right: *There were lions on each side of the door. There were lions on both sides of the door.*

either ... or, neither ... nor The nouns that follow these words do not constitute a compound subject; they are alternate subjects and require a verb that agrees with the nearer subject: *Neither they nor he is going. Neither he nor they are going.*

essential clauses, nonessential clauses These terms are used instead of restrictive clause and nonrestrictive clause to convey the distinction between the two in a more easily remembered manner.

Both types of clauses provide additional information about a word or phrase in the sentence.

The difference between them is that the essential clause cannot be eliminated without changing the meaning of the sentence—it so "restricts" the meaning of the word or phrase that its absence would lead to a substantially different interpretation of what the author meant.

The nonessential clause, however, can be eliminated without altering the basic meaning of the sentence—it does not "restrict" the meaning so significantly that its absence would radically alter the author's thought.

PUNCTUATION: An essential clause must not be set off from the rest of a sentence by commas. A nonessential clause must be set off by commas.

The presence or absence of commas provides the reader with critical information about the writer's intended meaning. Note the following examples:

Reporters who do not read the stylebook should not criticize their editors. (The writer is saying that only one class of reporters, those who do not read the stylebook, should not criticize their editors. If the *who ... stylebook* phrase were deleted, the meaning of the sentence would be changed substantially.)

Reporters, who do not read the stylebook, should not criticize their editors. (The writer is saying that all reporters should not criticize their editors. If the *who ... stylebook* phrase were deleted, this meaning would not be changed.)

USE OF WHO, THAT, WHICH: When an essential or nonessential clause refers to a human being or an animal with a name, it should be introduced by *who* or *whom.* (See the *Who, Whom* entry.) Do not use commas if the clause is essential to the meaning; use them if it is not.

That is the preferred pronoun to introduce essential clauses that refer to an inanimate object or an animal without a name. *Which* is the only acceptable pronoun to introduce a nonessential clause that refers to an inanimate object or an animal without a name.

The pronoun *which* occasionally may be substituted for *that* in the introduction of an essential clause that refers to an inanimate object or an animal without a name. In general, this use of *which* should appear only when *that* is used as a conjunction to introduce another clause in the same sentence: *He said Monday that the part of the army which suffered severe casualties needs reinforcement.*

essential phrases, nonessential phrases   These terms are used instead of restrictive phrase and nonrestrictive phrase to convey the distinction between the two in a more easily remembered manner.

The underlying concept is the one that also applies to clauses:

An *essential phrase* is a word or group of words critical to the reader's understanding of what the author had in mind.

A *nonessential phrase* provides more information about something. Although the information may be helpful to the reader's comprehension, the reader would not be misled if the information were not there.

PUNCTUATION: Do not set off an essential phrase from the rest of a sentence by commas:

We saw the award-winning movie "One Flew Over the Cuckoo's Nest." (No comma, because many movies have won awards, and without the name of the movie the reader would not know which movie was meant.)

They ate dinner with their daughter Julie. (Because they have more than one daughter, the inclusion of Julie's name is critical if the reader is to know which daughter is meant.)

Set off nonessential phrases by commas:

We saw the 1976 winner in the Academy Award competition for best movie, "One Flew Over the Cuckoo's Nest." (Only one movie won the award. The name is informative, but even without the name no other movie could be meant.)

They ate dinner with their daughter Julie and her husband, David. (Julie has only one husband. If the phrase read *and her husband David,* it would suggest that she had more than one husband.)

The company chairman, Henry Ford II, spoke. (In the context, only one person could be meant.)

Indian corn, or maize, was harvested. (*Maize* provides the reader with the name of the corn, but its absence would not change the meaning of the sentence.)

DESCRIPTIVE WORDS: Do not confuse punctuation rules for nonessential clauses with the correct punctuation when a nonessential word is used as a descriptive adjective. The distinguishing clue often is the lack of an article or pronoun:

Right: *Julie and husband David went shopping. Julie and her husband, David, went shopping.*

Right: *Company Chairman Henry Ford II made the announcement. The company chairman, Henry Ford II, made the announcement.*

every one, everyone Two words when it means each individual item: *Every one of the clues was worthless.*

One word when used as a pronoun meaning all persons: *Everyone wants his life to be happy.* (Note that *everyone* takes singular verbs and pronouns.)

farther, further *Farther* refers to physical distance: *He walked farther into the woods.*

Further refers to an extension of time or degree: *She will look further into the mystery.*

fewer, less In general, use *fewer* for individual items, *less* for bulk or quantity.

flaunt, flout To *flaunt* is to make an ostentatious or defiant display: *She flaunted her beauty.*

To *flout* is to show contempt for: *She flouts the law.*

flier, flyer *Flier* is the preferred term for an aviator or a handbill.

Flyer is the proper name of some trains and buses: *The Western Flyer.*

good, well *Good* is an adjective that means something is as it should be or is better than average.

When used as an adjective, *well* means suitable, proper, healthy. When used as an adverb, *well* means in a satisfactory manner or skillfully.

Good should not be used as an adverb. It does not lose its status as an adjective in a sentence such as *I feel good.* Such a statement is the idiomatic equivalent of *I am in good health.* An alternative, *I feel well,* could be interpreted as meaning that your sense of touch was good.

hopefully It means in a hopeful manner. Do not use it to mean *it is hoped, let us hope* or *we hope.*

Right: *It is hoped that we will complete our work in June.*

Right: *We hope that we will complete our work in June.*

Wrong as a saying to express the thought in the previous two sentences: *Hopefully, we will complete our work in June.*

imply, infer Writers or speakers *imply* in the words they use. A listener or reader *infers* something from the words.

in, into *In* indicates location: *He was in the room.* *Into* indicates motion: *She walked into the room.*

lay, lie The action word is *lay.* It takes a direct object. *Laid* is the form for its past tense and its past participle. Its present participle is *laying.*

Lie indicates a state of reclining along a horizontal plane. It does not take a direct object. Its past tense is *lay.* Its past participle is *lain.* Its present participle is *lying.*

When *lie* means to make an untrue statement, the verb forms are *lie, lied, lying.*

like, as Use *like* as a preposition to compare nouns and pronouns. It requires an object: *Jim blocks like a pro.*

The conjunction *as* is the correct word to introduce clauses: *Jim blocks the linebacker as he should.*

majority, plurality *Majority* means more than half of an amount. *Plurality* means more than the next highest number.

marshal, marshaled, marshaling, Marshall *Marshal* is the spelling for both the verb and the noun: *Marilyn will marshal her forces. Erwin Rommel was a field marshal.*

Marshall is used in proper names: *George C. Marshall, John Marshall, the Marshall Islands.*

obscenities, profanities, vulgarities Do not use them in stories unless they are part of direct quotations and there is a compelling reason for them.

Confine the offending language, in quotation marks, to a separate paragraph that can be deleted easily.

In reporting profanity that normally would use the words *damn* or *god,* lowercase *god* and use the following forms: *damn, damn it, goddamn it.* Do not, however, change the offending words to euphemisms. Do not, for example, change *damn it* to *darn it.*

If a full quote that contains profanity, obscenity or vulgarity cannot be dropped but there is no compelling reason for the offensive language, replace letters of an offensive word with a hyphen. The word *damn,* for example, would become
d--- or ----.

off of The *of* is unnecessary: *He fell off the bed.* Not: *He fell off of the bed.*

on Do not use *on* before a date or day of the week when its absence would not lead to confusion: *The meeting will be held Monday. He will be inaugurated Jan. 20.*

Use *on* to avoid an awkward juxtaposition of a date and a proper name: *John met Mary on Monday. He told Reagan on Thursday that the bill was doomed.*

Use *on* also to avoid any suggestion that a date is the object of a transitive verb: *The House killed on Tuesday a bid to raise taxes. The Senate postponed on Wednesday its consideration of a bill to reduce import duties.*

over It is interchangeable with *more than.*

Usually, however, *over* refers to spatial relationships: *The plane flew over the city. More than* is used with figures: *More than 40,000 fans were in the stadium.*

people, persons Use *people* when speaking of a large or uncounted number of individuals: *Thousands of people attended the fair. Some rich people pay few taxes. What will people say?* Do not use *persons* in this sense.

Persons usually is used when speaking of a relatively small number of people who can be counted, but people also may be used:

Right: *There were 20 persons in the room.*
Right: *There were 20 people in the room.*

People is also a collective noun that takes a plural verb and is used to refer to a single race or nation: *The American people are united.* In this sense, the plural is *peoples: The peoples of Africa speak many languages.*

principal, principle *Principal* is a noun and adjective meaning someone or something first in rank, authority, importance or degree: *She is the school principal. He was the principal player in the trade. Money is the principal problem.*

Principle is a noun that means a fundamental truth, law, doctrine or motivating force: *They fought for the principle of self-determination.*

prior to *Before* is less stilted for most uses. *Prior to* is appropriate, however, when a notion of requirement is involved: *The fee must be paid prior to the examination.*

reign, rein The leather strap for a horse is a *rein,* hence figuratively: *seize the reins, give free rein to, put a check rein on.*

Reign is the period a ruler is on the throne: *The king began his reign.*

should, would Use *should* to express an obligation: *We should help the needy.*

Use *would* to express a customary action: *In the summer we would spend hours by the seashore.*

Use *would* also in constructing a conditional past tense, but be careful:

Wrong: *If Soderholm would not have had an injured foot, Thompson would not have been in the lineup.*

Right: *If Soderholm had not had an injured foot, Thompson would not have been in the lineup.*

spelling   The basic rule when in doubt is to consult the stylebooks followed by, if necessary, a dictionary.

Memory Aid: Noah Webster developed the following rule of thumb for the frequently vexing question of whether to double a final consonant in forming the present participle and past tense of a verb:

If the stress in pronunciation is on the first syllable, do not double the consonant: *cancel, canceling, canceled.*

If the stress in pronunciation is on the second syllable, double the consonant: *control, controlling, controlled; refer, referring, referred.*

If the word is only one syllable, double a consonant unless confusion would result: *jut, jutted, jutting.* An exception, to avoid confusion with *buss,* is *bus, bused, busing.*

Here is a list of commonly misspelled words:

accommodate	council	likable
adviser	counsel	machine gun
Asian flu	drought	percent
ax	drunken	percentage
baby-sit	embarrass	restaurant
baby sitter	employee	restaurateur
baby-sitting	eyewitness	rock 'n' roll
cannot	firefighter	skillful
cave in (v.)	fulfill	subpoena
cave-in (n., adj.)	goodbye	teen-age (adj.)
chauffeur	hanged	teen-ager (n.)
cigarette	harass	under way
clue	hitchhiker	vacuum
commitment	homemade	weird
consensus	imposter	whiskey
consul	judgment	X-ray (n.,
copter	kidnapping	v. and adj.)

subjunctive mood   Use the subjunctive mood of a verb for contrary-to-fact conditions, and expressions of doubts, wishes or regrets:

If I were a rich man, I wouldn't have to work hard.
I doubt that more money would be the answer.
I wish it were possible to take back my words.

Sentences that express a contingency or hypothesis may use either the subjunctive or the indicative mood depending on the context. In general, use the subjunctive if there is little likelihood that a contingency might come true:

If I were to marry a millionaire, I wouldn't have to worry about money.

If the bill should overcome the opposition against it, it would provide extensive tax relief.

But:

If I marry a millionaire, I won't have to worry about money.

If the bill passes as expected, it will provide an immediate tax cut.

that (conjunction) Use the conjunction *that* to introduce a dependent clause if the sentence sounds or looks awkward without it. There are no hard-and-fast rules, but in general:

That usually may be omitted when a dependent clause immediately follows a form of the verb to say: *The president said he had signed the bill.*

That should be used when a time element intervenes between the verb and the dependent clause: *The president said Monday that he had signed the bill.*

That usually is necessary after some verbs. They include: *advocate, assert, contend, declare, estimate, make clear, point out, propose* and *state.*

That is required before subordinate clauses beginning with conjunctions such as *after, although, because, before, in addition to, until* and *while: Haldeman said that after he learned of Nixon's intention to resign, he sought pardons for all connected with Watergate.*

When in doubt, include *that.* Omission can hurt. Inclusion never does.

that, which, who, whom (pronouns) Use *who* and *whom* in referring to persons and to animals with a name: *John Jones is the man who helped me.* See the Who, Whom entry.

Use *that* and *which* in referring to inanimate objects and to animals without a name.

See the Essential clauses, Nonessential clauses entry for guidelines on using *that* and *which* to introduce phrases and clauses.

under way Two words in virtually all uses: *The project is under way. The naval maneuvers are under way.*

One word only when used as adjective before a noun in a nautical sense: *an underway flotilla.*

verbs In general, avoid awkward constructions that split infinitive forms of a verb *(to leave, to help,* etc.) or compound forms *(had left, are found out,* etc.).

Awkward: *She was ordered to immediately leave on an assignment.*

Preferred: *She was ordered to leave immediately on an assignment.*

Awkward: *There stood the wagon that we had early last autumn left by the barn.*

Preferred: *There stood the wagon that we had left by the barn early last autumn.*

Occasionally, however, a split is not awkward and is necessary to convey the meaning:

He wanted to really help his mother.
Those who lie are often found out.
How has your health been?
The budget was tentatively approved.

who, whom   Use *who* and *whom* for references to human beings and to animals with a name. Use *that* and *which* for inanimate objects and animals without a name.

Who is the word when someone is the subject of a sentence, clause or phrase: *The woman who rented the room left the window open. Whom do you wish to see?*

See the Essential clauses, Nonessential clauses entry for guidelines on how to punctuate clauses introduced by *who, whom, that* and *which.*

who's, whose   *Who's* is a contraction for *who is,* not a possessive: *Who's there?*

Whose is the possessive: *I do not know whose coat it is.*

widow, widower   In obituaries: A man is survived by his wife, or leaves his wife. A woman is survived by her husband, or leaves her husband.

Guard against the redundant *widow of the late.* Use *wife of the late* or *widow of.*

Proofreading

Proofs have several uses other than that of indicating typographical errors.

Copy editors, as we have seen in Chapter 9, use a galley proof or a photocopy proof as a marker to show where insertions and new leads go.

Copy editors also may be assigned the task of updating overset matter and stories that made the later editions but not the earlier ones. Before the pages are torn up at the end of the press run, an editor goes over the paper, circling items that should be retained for future use. Proofs of the circled stories go to the desk for updating. Proofs of overset material likewise go to the desk for updating.

At larger papers a dozen or so proofs may be made from each strip of type. A set goes to each department head, including the desk chief, and perhaps to the wire service of which the paper is a member or client.

Duplicate sets of revised proofs go to the layout editor on offset papers and to editors of out-of-office publications for paste-up dummies. When the dummies are returned, type is assembled in pages and page proofs go to the respective editors.

When the page has been assembled, a layout editor or some other executive should scan the page to note:

- Whether the date, the issue number and the page number in the folio are correct.
- Whether the headlines have been placed over the right stories.

• Whether the pictures are right side up.
• Whether the sluglines have been removed.
• Whether the jump-line information is accurate.
• Whether a layout change is properly noted in the index.

The Proofreader   Thorough editing should be done on the paper copy or VDT before the story ever reaches the composing room. A proof is no place to make editing judgments. Misspelled words and names, factual errors, grammatical errors and libelous statements have to be changed even though the errors should have been caught in the editing. But minor or nit-picking errors usually are allowed to remain. The reason is a matter of cost. One change in a line of type may result in the resetting of a paragraph of type. Sometimes, where a word replacement is desired, a word of similar character length can be used, thus averting the resetting of more than one line.

One of the irritating flaws, and one that may or may not be corrected on proofs, is improper division of words at the end of the type line. Here are a few taken at random from several columns of type: "reci-pient" for *recip-ient,* "opera-te" for *oper-ate,* "pal-aver" for *pa-laver,* "ne-bula" for *neb-ula,* "reven-ue" for *reve-nue,* "obes-ity" for *obesi-ty,* "implac-able" for *implaca-ble,* "child-ren" for *chil-dren.*

Even in computerized typesetting, in which rules, rule exceptions and tables can be applied, word division accuracy can never be reliable because of ambiguities, dual meanings, different hyphenations for identically spelled words and different hyphenations in different usages.

In newspaper composition one hyphenation occurs in every seven lines of text, depending on the type size and line length. Roughly 10 percent of these hyphenations will be in error. Some newspapers manually reset the incorrect lines after the type has been set. Some do not, as already indicated in the examples given of words incorrectly divided.

If VDTs are used the editor has complete control of the typesetting. But if compositors must retype the copy, all that changes. Compositors are expected to follow copy. Some hew to this rule so closely that they faithfully reproduce misspelled words. Others take it upon themselves to make corrections. If the copy editor suspects that a compositor will try to second-guess, the editor indicates that the spelling as written is correct no matter what the compositor thinks. If the name is Billi, the copy editor or reporter marks *cq* or *ok* above the spelling so that it will not'come out as Billie.

Compositors, like other humans, look at one word but see another. Errors that spell a word are harder to catch than a misspelling. So, costumer comes out as customer, miliary as military, eclectic as electric, exorcise as exercise, diary as dairy, collage as college, calvary as cavalry, model as motel, farce as force, defective as detective, morality as mortality, bottle as battle, conservation as conversation, winch as wench.

Proofreading Methods

Two methods are used in marking proofs. One is the formal or book method in which two marks are used—one within the line, to indicate the offender, and the other in the margin, to indicate the correction. If only one error appears in the line, the correction is noted in the left margin. If more than one error occurs, the corrections are in the right margin, each correction being separated by a slash mark (Figure II-1).

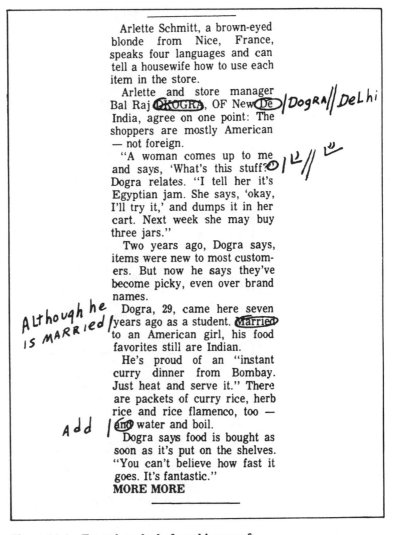

Figure 11-1 Formal method of marking proofs.

The second method is the guideline system, probably used by the majority of newspapers. Here a line is drawn from the error within a line to the nearest margin. If several errors appear within the same type line, the guidelines may be drawn to both margins. Care is taken not to obliterate the place in the type line where the error occurs (Figure II-2).

In neither system is the correction made inside the type line or between lines of type.

If more than one error appears in the same word, the word

Figure 11-2   Informal or newspaper method of marking proofs.

should be circled and the correct word printed in the margin. Also, it is usually safer to rewrite a figure in the margin than to indicate changes in the figure by proof symbols.

**Using Proof
Symbols**

If several lines have to be inserted, it is better to type the lines and show on the proof where they are to be inserted rather than to attempt to write the lines in longhand on the margin of the proof.

Proof symbols are used to indicate editorial changes (Figure II-3) and typographical changes (Figure II-4).

Editorial Changes

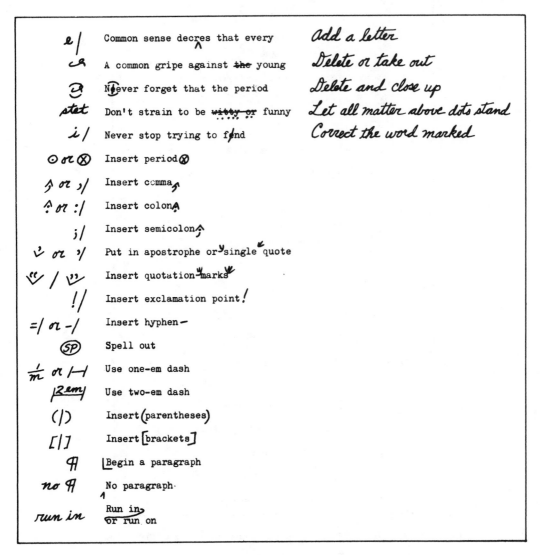

Figure 11-3 Standard proofreading symbols.

Typographical
Changes

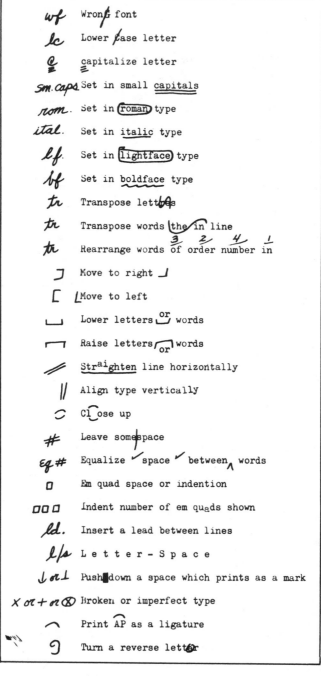

wf   Wrong font

lc   Lower case letter

C̲   capitalize letter

sm.caps Set in small capitals

rom.   Set in roman type

ital.   Set in italic type

lf.   Set in lightface type

bf   Set in boldface type

tr   Transpose letters

tr   Transpose words the in line

tr   Rearrange words of order number in

⌐   Move to right ⌐

[Move to left

⊔   Lower letters or words

⊓   Raise letters or words

⫽   Straighten line horizontally

‖   Align type vertically

⊂   Close up

Leave some space

Eq #   Equalize space between words

▢   Em quad space or indention

▢▢▢   Indent number of em quads shown

ld.   Insert a lead between lines

l/s   L e t t e r - S p a c e

↓ or ⊥ Push down a space which prints as a mark

✗ or + or ⊗ Broken or imperfect type

⌢   Print AP as a ligature

ꀹ   Turn a reverse letter

Figure 11-4 **Standard proofreading symbols and how they are applied.**

Data Base Searches

Each day thousands of news stories and magazine articles are written, and many of them contain material that can be invaluable to reporters researching stories. Those articles also can be invaluable for copy editors who need to check facts.

Until recently, it was impractical for copy editors to consult such resources if they were not located in the newspaper library. Going to the public library to check a fact was out of the question because of the time involved. Now, however, many newspapers have installed computer terminals that provide access to literally thousands of data bases with material on almost every conceivable subject.

Among the most useful data bases to journalists are the comprehensive files of Dialog, a Palo Alto, Calif., company that has files on everything from national statistics (American Statistics Index) to magazine article listings (Magazine Index). Unfortunately, many of Dialog's services still require the researcher to go to the original document for the complete text. Only a synopsis of the article is provided.

Of greater value to the fast-paced world of daily journalism may be services such as that provided by Dow Jones News Retrieval. These full-text services allow the user to read a story exactly as it was published in *The Wall Street Journal.* Let's say you are searching for an offbeat story you remember reading in the *Journal* about a haunted house in Louisiana. You go to your computer terminal and sign on to the Dow Jones News Retrieval free-text search service. The service asks you to describe key words that might help locate the article. You enter *Louisiana* and find that the service has 441 listings, or articles, containing that word. That won't do. It would take far too long to search all those articles for the one in question, and you are being charged for each minute connected to the service. You must narrow the search, so you decide to ask the computer for the number of stories that contain the words *Louisiana* and *ghosts.* There are two stories that fit the description. You give the computer a simple command to display the first of the two stories on the screen. The result is shown in Figure III-1.

```
             DOCUMENT=     1 OF        2    PAGE =    1 OF    16
AN           841031-0161.
HL           As Spooky Places Go,
             An Inn in the Bayous
             Goes a Bit Too Far

             ---

             'Most Haunted House' Teems
             With Spirits, Legend Says;
             How Our Man Faces Them
             ---

             By Bryan Burrough
                                            - MORE -
```

```
             DOCUMENT=     1 OF        2    PAGE =    2 OF    16
             Staff Reporter of The Wall Street Journal
DD           10/31/84
SO           WALL STREET JOURNAL (J)
TX               ST. FRANCISVILLE, La. -- They never extinguish all the
             lights at the Myrtles, a 188-year-old mansion outside this
             sleepy bayou town. Total darkness, legend says, brings out
             ghoulish things that go bump in the night.
                 At first glance, the house doesn't look haunted. Huge oaks
             dripping Spanish moss cover the plantation, and out back a
             gazebo sits on an island in a tiny pond. The white two-story
                                            - MORE -
```

```
             DOCUMENT=     1 OF        2    PAGE =    3 OF    16
             mansion is attractively encircled by a veranda lined with
             colonial-blue wrought iron.
                 But those who know about the Myrtles whisper stories of
             phantoms and voodoo curses, of two long-dead girls who peer
             into the mansion's windows at night, of picture frames that
             fly from the wall and of a ghostly one-eared slave woman who
             glides by the canopied beds at night, chilling the bones of
             those she encounters.
                 Unexplained sights and sounds have been observed by
             everyone from psychics to local officials, and since the
                                            - MORE -
```

```
             DOCUMENT=     1 OF        2    PAGE =    4 OF    16
             Myrtles was converted into a six-bedroom inn four years ago,
             the owner says, many tourists have been so spooked in the
             night that they have vowed never to return. As for me, in the
             words of the "Ghostbusters" movie theme song, "I ain't 'fraid
             of no ghosts." I agree to spend a weekend there, in the
             building that the book "Houses of Horror" by Richard Winer
             calls America's most haunted house. . . .
```

Figure III-1

That's it. The search has turned up the story you remembered. But the search words you used were unique, and the computer indicated there were two stories that matched the description. Is it possible there was a followup you missed? To determine that, you decide to look at the other story (see Figure III-2).

```
         DOCUMENT=      2 OF     2    PAGE =    1 OF    16
AN       840614-0143.
HL         LEISURE & ARTS:
         Mississippi Mermaids: World's Fair Takes a Dive
         ---
         By Manuela Hoelterhoff
DD       06/14/84
SO       WALL STREET JOURNAL (J)
TX         New Orleans -- The last time the Crescent City had a huge
         exposition was 100 years ago, and the event is not happily
         remembered. The director absconded with part of the state
                                  - MORE -
```

```
         DOCUMENT=      2 OF     2    PAGE =    2 OF    16
         treasury, attendance was lower than projected and reviews
         were mixed, despite such unusual exhibitions as 200,000
         insect species from Maryland and a reception hosted by
         costumed pigs.
           Maybe a combo of smart porkers playing jazz would help out
         the current World's Fair, which opened on May 12 for a
         six-month run. Despite a decade of planning and a cost of
         $350 million, America, never mind the world, hasn't been
         rushing down to this 84-acre extravaganza deposited along the
         Mississippi River. Attendance figures have been well below
                                  - MORE -
```

Figure III-2

It's obvious why our search revealed *Louisiana* for this story, but it isn't about a haunted house. The last paragraph, however, reveals why our search gave us two choices (see Figure III-3).

```
         DOCUMENT=      2 OF     2    PAGE =   15 OF    16
           After Nov. 11, this show will be returning to Paris via a
         stop in Washington, and the expo site will be redeveloped
         into yet another waterside shrine of gentrification via Rouse
         Co. and a second investment group. Mr. Gehry's striking
         theater will come down, and at most a small chunk of
         Wonderwall will be preserved. I cannot think of a city less
         in need of additional ethnic harbor-view food shops than New
         Orleans, which overflows with gumbo and already has a market
         by the river. Still, I guess even this dull prospect will be
         better than what happened to the fairgrounds in Knoxville --
                                  - MORE -
```

```
         DOCUMENT=      2 OF     2    PAGE =   16 OF    16
         decrepit and abandoned, frequented only by joggers and
         ghosts.
```

Figure III-3

The writer merely happened to write a story from Louisiana that included the word *ghosts*. The two stories found in this search indicate not only how useful such data bases can be but also the limitations of search techniques. On one hand, you found the article you sought, but you wasted time looking at one that produced nothing of use.

Such limitations apply to card catalog searches of libraries, too. While data base search techniques may not be perfect, the results give the copy editor far more flexibility in checking facts than ever was possible before. Thus, the ability of the editor to check facts is vastly expanded. Widespread use of data base searches at newspapers and broadcast stations should make the news reports of the future more accurate than ever.

Here are some of the major data bases of interest to journalists. There are thousands, and this is merely a sample:

BRS/After Dark
1200 Route 7
Latham, N.Y. 12110
(518) 783-1161

CompuServe
P.O. Box 20212
5000 Arlington Centre Blvd.
Columbus, Ohio 43220
(800) 848-8199

Dialog
3460 Hillview Ave., Dept. 79
Palo Alto, Calif. 94304
(800) 227-1927

Dow Jones News Retrieval
P.O. Box 300
Princeton, N.J. 08540
(800) 345-8500

The Source
P.O. Box 1305
McLean, Va. 22101
(703) 734-7523

Glossary

Accordion fold parallel folds on sheet of paper to determine an imposition pattern.

Acetate transparent sheet placed over art in mechanical color separation.

Ad short for advertisement.

Ad alley section in mechanical department where ads are assembled.

Add material to be added to news story, usually with a number and slug: add 1 fire.

Add end addendum to a story after it has been apparently closed.

Ad lib unscripted comment made before a microphone.

Ad-side advertising department as distinguished from editorial department.

ADV abbreviation for advance. A story intended for later use.

Advance story sent out in advance of the scheduled publication date.

Agate name of a type size, e.g., agate type, or type that is 5½ points high. Advertising is also sold on the basis of agate lines, or 14 agate lines to an inch.

Air white space.

Align to place adjacent to an even base line on a horizontal plane.

Alley portion in composing room devoted to special sections, such as ad alley.

All up all copy has been set into type.

Alphanumeric   pertaining to a character set that contains letters, numerals and usually other characters.

A.M.   morning edition.

Analog   data in the form of varying physical characteristics such as voltage, pressure, speed, etc. A computer term.

Angle   special aspect of a story; a slant.

Antique   rough-surfaced paper resembling old handmade papers.

AP   short for The Associated Press, a major news agency.

Art   newspaper or magazine illustrations.

Astonisher   same as exclamation point.

Attribution   source of the material in a story.

Audio tape   tape on which sound has been transcribed.

Autofunctions   copy symbols or commands placed on copy. Used to instruct the computer on type sizes, column widths, etc.

Auxiliary storage   any peripheral devices (tape, disk, etc.) upon which computer data may be stored.

A wire   usually the main slow-speed wire of a wire service.

Back timing   timing of a script so that it ends at the proper time.

Back up   printing the reverse side of a sheet.

Bad break   bad phrasing of a headline; bad wrapping of headline type; bad arrangement of type in columns that gives the reader the impression a paragraph ending is the end of the story.

Bagasse   residue of sugar cane stalks used experimentally as a substitute for wood pulp in making newsprint.

Bank   the lower portion of a headline (deck).

Banner   usually a headline stretching across all columns of a newspaper.

Barker   reversed kicker in which the kicker is in larger type than the lines below it. Also called a hammer.

Bastard type   type that varies from the standard column width.

Baud   speed rate of transmission. News personnel speak in terms of 66 or 1,200 words a minute. Computer personnel talk of 1,200 bits (or 150 characters) a second.

Binary   a base 2 numbering system using the digits 0 and 1. Widely used in computer systems whose binary code may represent numbers, letters, and punctuation marks. Performs "in" and "out" or "on" and "off" function.

Binder   inside page streamer; head that binds together two or more related stories.

Bit   one eighth of a byte in computer terminology. Combinations of eight basic bits yield up to 256 characters.

Black and white '   reproduction in one color (black).

Black Letter   text or Old English style of type.

Blanket head   headline over several columns of type or over type and illustration.

Bleed   running an illustration off the page.

Blooper   any embarrassing error in print or broadcast.

Body   main story or text; body type is the size of type used for the contents.

Boil   to trim or reduce wordage of a story.

Boiler plate   syndicated material.

Boldface   type that is blacker than normal typeface; also black face. Abbreviated bf.

Book   sheet of paper on which a story is written. A basic category of printing paper.

Book number   number assigned to each item in a wire service report.

Box   unit of type enclosed by a border.

Brace   type of makeup, usually with a banner headline and the story in the right-hand column. A bracket.

Break   point at which a story turns from one column to another. An exclusive story.

Break over   story that jumps from one page to another.

Brightener   short, amusing item.

Broadside   large sheet printed only on one side.

Broken box   splitting the lines of a box to accommodate words or pictures. Also split box.

Broken heads   headlines with lines of different widths.

Budget (or BJT, called "News Digest" by AP)   listing of the major stories expected to be delivered by the wire service.

Bug   type ornament; a logotype; a star or other element that designates makeovers.

Bulldog   an early edition of a newspaper.

Bulletin   last-minute story of significance; a wire service designation of a story of major importance, usually followed by bulletin matter. Abbreviated bun.

Bullets   large periods used for decoration, usually at the beginning of paragraphs.

Bumper   two elements placed side by side or one immediately beneath the other. A bumped headline is also called a tombstone.

Bureau code letters   each wire service uses its own code letters to designate a bureau. UPI uses WA for Washington, the AP uses WX.

Byline   credit given to the author.

Byte   in computer terms, one alphanumeric character.

Canned copy   copy released by press agents or syndicates.

Canopy head   streamer headline from which two or more readout heads drop.

Caps   short for capital letters or upper-case letters.

Caption   display line over a picture or over the cutline. Also used as a synonym for a cutline. Also called an overline.

Cartridge   holder for audio tapes. Also a staccato lead.

Cathode ray tube (CRT)   an electronic vacuum tube with a screen on which information may be stored or displayed by means of a multigrid modulated beam of electrons. The display tube in a VDT. Also used as a character generator in some high-speed phototypesetters.

Centered   type placed in the middle of a line.

Center spread   two facing pages made up as one in the center of a newspaper section; also called double truck.

Character   an alphanumeric or special symbol.

Character generator   a cathode ray tube or similar device used to display characters in high-speed phototypesetters.

Chase   metal frame in which forms are locked before printing or stereotyping.

Chaser   fast, urgent replate.

Cheesecake   slang for photographs emphasizing women's legs. Good newspapers don't use such pictures.

Circuits   refers to wire services used. The A wire is the main trunk news circuit. Regional news trunk systems carry letter designations such as B, G and E wires and the D wire, the nationwide business news circuit. The S wire usually refers to a state trunk circuit or the sports circuit. High-speed circuits have replaced many of these.

Circumlocution   wordy, roundabout expressions. Also redundancy.

Circus makeup   flamboyant makeup featuring a variety of typefaces and sizes.

City room   main newsroom of a newspaper. The city editor presides over the city desk.

Clean copy   copy with a minimum of typographical or editing corrections. Clean proof is proof that requires few corrections.

Clips   short for clippings of newspaper stories.

Closeup   photo showing head or head and shoulders or an object seen at close range.

Closing   time at which pages are closed. Also ending.

Cloze   method of testing readability. Respondents are asked to fill in words in blank spaces.

Col.   abbreviation for column.

Cold type   reproduction of characters composed photographically.

Color page   page on which color is used.

Column inch   unit of space measurement; one column wide and one inch deep.

Column rule   printing units that create vertical lines of separation on a page.

Combination cut   engraving that includes both halftone and line work.

Combo   short for combination, pictures of the same subject used as a single unit.

Compose   type is set or composed in a composing room by a compositor.

Composition   all typesetting.

Computer   a device capable of accepting information, applying prescribed processes to the information, and supplying the results of these processes; a computer system usually consists of input and output devices, storage, arithmetic and logical units and a control unit. Various types of computers are calculators, digital computers and analog computers.

Computer program   a set of stored instructions that controls all hardware.

Constant   element used regularly without change. Also called standing or stet material.

Copy   words typewritten by reporters or editors from which type is set. Printers set copy.

Copy cutter   composing room worker who distributes copy among compositors.

Copy fitting   editing copy to fit a required space.

Copyholder   person who reads manuscript while another person marks the proof.

Copyreader   antiquated term for copy editor, one who edits copy and writes headlines.

Core   the main memory of a computer in which data may be stored. Also called "Core Memory."

CPU   an abbreviation for Central Processing Unit. That portion of the computer that handles input, output and memory.

CQ   abbreviation for correct.

CQN   abbreviation for correction.

Credit line   line indicating source of a story.

Crop   to eliminate unwanted portions of a photograph. Marks used to show the elimination are called crop marks.

Crossline   headline composed of a single line.

Cue   signal given to announcer; a line in a script indicating a change.

Cursor   a mobile block of light the size of a single character on the VDT screen indicating the position at which an editing change is to be made.

Cut   illustration or engraving. Or, a direction to trim or shorten a story.

Cut-in   may refer to an initial letter beginning a paragraph or to a side head that is set into the opening lines of a paragraph.

Cutline   explanatory material, usually placed beneath a picture. Also called underline, legend and caption.

Cutoff   hairline that marks the point where the story moves from one column to another or to separate boxes and cuts from text material or to separate a headline from other elements.

Cx short for correction. Indicates that corrections are to be made in type. Also called fix.

Cycle complete news report for either morning or afternoon newspapers.

Cycle time the length of time used by a computer for one operation, usually measured in microseconds (millionths) or nanoseconds (billionths).

Dangler short for dangling participle or similar grammatical error.

Dash short line separating parts of headlines or headline and story.

Data any kind of information that can be processed by a computer.

Dateline opening phrase of story showing origin, source and sometimes date of story.

Dead newspaper copy or type that is no longer usable.

Deadline the shutoff time for copy for an edition.

Debug eliminating problems in a new or revised computer program or system.

Deck section of a headline.

Delete take out. The proofreader uses a symbol for a delete mark.

Desk standing alone, usually the copy desk. Also city desk, sports desk, etc.

Digit in computers, a character used to represent one of the non-negative integers smaller than the radix, e.g., in decimal notation, one of the characters 0 to 9.

Digital in computers, pertaining to data in the form of digits, in contrast with analog.

Dingbat typographic decoration.

Disk drive a unit somewhat like a record turntable that contains a computer storage disk pack and rotates it at high speed.

Disk pack a set of magnetic disks used by computers for storing data or text. Also called disk cartridge.

Disk storage a means of storing data on a magnetic disk, a technique similar to magnetic tape or record, so that data can be read into the computer, changed by the computer or erased.

Display term given to a type of advertising that distinguishes it from classified advertising. Display lines are those set in larger sizes than regular body type.

Dissolve in broadcasting, a smooth transition from one image to another.

DL wire service abbreviation for day lead (afternoon papers).

Dog watch late shift of an afternoon paper or early shift of a morning paper. Also lobster trick.

Double spacer term used on broadcast news wire to designate a story of unusual significance. Extra space is used between copy lines to alert the editor to the story.

Double truck two pages at the center of a section made up as a single unit.

Down style headline style using a minimum of capital letters.

Dropout a subsidiary headline. Also called deck.

Dub transfer of film or tape.

Dummy diagram outlining the makeup scheme. A rough dummy has little detail; a paste-up dummy is created by pasting page elements on a sheet of paper the actual size of the page.

Dump a routine that causes the computer to dump data from storage to another unit.

Dupe short for duplicate or carbon copy.

Dutch wrap breaking body type from one column to another not covered by the display line. Also called dutch turn or raw wrap.

Ears small box on one or both sides of the nameplate carrying brief announcements of weather, circulation, edition and the like.

EBCDIC Extended Binary Coded Decimal Interchange Code. An eight-bit computer code that can represent 256 characters.

Edition one of several press runs such as city edition and late home edition.

Em measurement of type that is as wide as it is high. A pica em is 12 points wide. Some printers still refer to all picas as ems.

En one-half em. Mostly used to express space. If the type is in 10 points, an indentation of an en would equal 5 points.

Endmark symbol (such as # or 30) to indicate the close of the story. An end dash (sometimes called a 30 dash) is used at the end of the story in type.

Etching process of removing nonprinting areas from a relief plate by acid.

Extra now rare, a special edition published to carry an important news break.

Eyebrow another name for a kicker head.

Face style or cut of type; the printing surface of type or of a plate.

Family as applied to type, all the type in any one design. Usually designated by a trade name.

Fat head headline too large for the space allowed for it.

FAX short for facsimile or transmission by wire of a picture.

Feature to give special prominence to a story or illustration. A story that stresses the human-interest angle.

Feed story or program electronically transmitted to other stations or broadcast to the public.

Filler   short items, usually set in type in advance and used to fill out space in a column of type. Also called briefs or shorts.

Fingernails   parentheses.

Fix   to correct or a correction.

Flag   title of paper appearing on Page One. Also nameplate.

Flash   brief announcement by a wire service of urgent news. Usually followed by a bulletin.

Float   ruled sidebar that may go anywhere in a story. To center an element in space that is not large enough to fill.

Floorman   printer.

Flop   illustration reversed in engraving.

Flush   even with the column margin. Type aligned on one side. Alignment may be either on left or right side.

Folio   lines showing the newspaper name, date and page number.

Follow   related matter that follows main story. Abbreviated folo.

Follow copy   set the story as sent; disregard seeming errors. Abbreviated fc.

Followup   second-day story.

Format   physical form of a publication. Also, a series of alphas and/or numerics that cause a computer to function in certain special ways.

Frame makeup   vertical makeup.

Freaks   devices that depart from normal indented body and headline type, etc.

Futures file   record kept by the city desk of future events.

FYI   for your information.

Gain   sound level.

Galley   metal tray used to hold hot type.

Galley proof   print of the assembled type, used in proofreading.

Gatekeeper   one who decides whether to pass a news story along. The account of an event goes through many gatekeepers before it reaches the reader.

Glossy   photograph with a hard, shiny finish.

Gobbledygook   editor's slang for material characterized by jargon and circumlocution. Also spelled goddledegook.

Gothic   sans serif type. Also called block letter.

Graf   short for paragraph.

Gravure   process of photomechanical printing. Also rotogravure or intaglio (printing ink is transferred to paper from areas sunk below the surface) printing.

Grease pencil   type of pencil used to make crop marks on pictures.

Guideline   instructions on copy to direct a printer. Usually includes slug, edition, section, etc.

Gutter   vertical space that separates one page from another on two facing pages. Also, long unbroken space between two columns of type.

Hairline finest line available in printing. Often used for rules between columns.

Halftone photoengraving. A dot pattern gives the illusion of tones.

Hammer see Barker.

Handout release story from a public relations firm.

Hanger headline that descends from a banner. Also called readout.

Hanging indent headline style in which the top line is set full measure and succeeding lines are indented from the left.

Hard copy original copy, distinguishing it from monitor copy or carbon copy. Also a glossy photographic print as contrasted to facsimile.

Hard news spot news or news or record as contrasted to features and background material.

Hardware the physical equipment that is part of the overall production system. (Computers, phototypesetting machines, etc.)

Hard-wired electronically connected, as in the case of one or more pieces of hardware connected to others.

Head count number of letters and spaces available for a headline.

Headlinese overworked short words in a headline, such as *cop, nab, hit, set.*

Head shot photo of person's head or head and shoulders. Also called face shots and mug shots.

HFR hold for release.

Highlight white or light portions of a photograph. Also the high point of a story.

Hold for release copy that is not to be used until a specified time.

Holdout portion held out of a story and placed in the overset.

Hood border over the top and both sides of a headline.

Hot metal linecaster slugs as opposed to cold type or type set photographically.

HTK headline to come. Also HTC.

Hugger mugger newspaper lead crammed with details.

Hyphenless justification a system of justifying lines by interword and interletter spaces, without breaking any words at the end of lines. Usually accomplished by computers.

Imposition process of placing type and illustrations in pages.

Impression any printing of ink on paper. Also appearance of the printed page. Also the number of times a press has completed a printing cycle.

Index newspaper's table of contents, usually found on Page One.

Initial (Initial cap) first letter in a paragraph set in type larger than the body type.

Input bringing data or text from external sources (typewriters, paper tape, through interfaces, etc.) into computer storage.

Insert   addition to a story placed within the story.

Interface   a device through which one piece of computer hardware or equipment "speaks" to another. The translation of output to input.

Intro   short for introduction. Opening copy to film or tape. Also, wire service term for lead of story.

Inverted pyramid   news story structure in which the parts are placed in a descending order of their importance. Also a headline in inverted pyramid shape.

Issue   all copies produced by a newspaper in a day.

Italics   slanted letter form. Shortened form is itals.

Jargon   language of a profession, trade or group. Newspaper jargon.

Jump   to continue a story from one page to another.

Jump head   headline over the continued portion of a story.

Jump lines   continuation lines: continued on Page X.

Justify   spacing out a line of type to fill the column; spacing elements in a form so form can be locked up.

K   thousands of units of core or computer storage referring to storage for bytes, usually in multiples of 4.

Kenaf   field crop used experimentally as a substitute for wood pulp in making newsprint.

Kicker   overline over a headline. Also eyebrow.

Kill   to discard copy, type, mats and so on.

Label head   dull, lifeless headline. Sometimes a standing head such as **News of the World.**

Layout   pattern of typographic arrangement. Similar to dummy.

Lead   beginning of a story or the most important story of the day (pronounced "leed").

Lead   piece of metal or spacing increment varying from ½ to 3 points placed between lines of type for spacing purposes (pronounced "led").

Leaders   line of dots.

Leading   process of placing leads between lines of type.

Lead out   to justify a line of type.

Legend   information under an illustration. Also cutline.

Letterpress   technique of printing from raised letters. Ink is applied to the letters, paper is placed over the type and impression implied to the paper, resulting in printing on paper.

Library   newspaper's collection of books, files and so on. Also called morgue.

Ligature   two or more letters run together for superior typesetting—fi, ffi.

Linecaster   any keyboarded machine that casts lines of type.

Line cut   engraving without tones. Used for maps, charts and so on.

Line gauge   pica rule or a ruler marked off in pica segments.

Logotype   single matrix of type containing two or more letters commonly used together: AP, UPI. Also a combination of the nameplate and other matter to identify a section. Also an advertising signature. Commonly abbreviated logo.

Lower case   small letter as distinguished from a capital letter. Abbreviated lc.

Machine language   a language used directly by a computer; a set of instructions a computer can recognize and execute.

Macro instruction   a single instruction that is expanded to a predetermined sequence of instructions during the assembly of a computer program.

Magnetic storage   any device using magnetic materials as a medium for computer storage of data: magnetic disk, film, tape, drum, core, etc.

Makeover   to change page content or layout.

Makeready   process of aligning elements on the page to assure a uniform impression.

Makeup   design of a newspaper page. Assembling elements in a page.

Marker   proof or tearsheet used to show where inserts are to go after story has been sent to the composing room or other instructions for guidance of printers and makeup editors.

Masthead   informational material about a newspaper, usually placed on the editorial page.

Mat   short for matrix or mold for making a stereotype plate in letterpress printing. The mat of a page is made of papier-mâché. In typesetting machines, the matrix is made of brass.

Measure   length of a line of type.

Modem   a piece of hardware that facilitates interfacing between two other pieces of hardware in a system.

Monitor copy   tearsheet copy or copy produced electronically. A monitor is also a television or radio receiver. To monitor is to watch or time a radio or television program.

Montage   succession of pictures assembled to create an overall effect. Usually a single photograph using several negatives.

Morgue   newspaper reference library or repository for clippings.

Mortise   cutaway section of an engraving into which type is inserted.

Mug shot   same as photo closeup or face shot.

Multiplexor (MUX)   a device that allows the computer to handle input or output simultaneously from several different devices connected to it.

Must   matter that someone in authority has ordered published.

Nameplate name of newspaper displayed on Page One. Also called flag, title or line.

News hole space left for news and editorial matter after ads have been placed on pages.

Newsprint low-quality paper used to print newspapers.

NL slug on copy and notation on a marker indicating new lead. Also, wire service designation for night lead.

Obit abbreviation for obituary.

OCR optical character reader, or "scanner," which converts typewritten material to electronic impulses for processing within a computer system. The process itself also is known as OCR, optical character recognition. Employs technology now considered outdated.

Offset method of printing differing from letterpress. A photograph is taken after the page has been assembled. The negatives are placed over a light-sensitive printing plate and light is exposed through the open spaces of the negative. The result is that the letters are hardened and the nonprinting surface is washed away. This method of printing involves inking the printed plate with water and then with ink. The water resides only on the nonprinting surface, whereas the ink resides on the printing surface. The inked letters are then printed on a rubber blanket, which in turn prints (or offsets) on paper.

On-line a unit "on-line" is interfaced in the computer system as opposed to units operating independently of the system.

Op. ed. page opposite the editorial page.

Optional matter that may be used without regard to the time element. Also called time copy, grape and AOT (any old time).

Outcue cue telling a news director or engineer that a film or tape is near the end.

Outlined cut halftone with background cut out. Also silhouette.

Output data coming from the computer system, either in printed, typeset or paper tape form.

Overset type in excess of amount needed.

Pad to make a story longer with excess words.

Page proof proof of an entire page.

Pagination makeup of a newspaper page on a computer terminal to allow output of the composed page. Also, the organization of pages within the newspaper.

Parameter symbol in computer programming indicating a constant such as a figure.

Parens short for parentheses.

Photocomposition type composed photographically.

Photolithography printing process such as offset where the impression is transferred from a plate to a rubber roller and to paper.

Pica   linear measure in 12 points. A pica em is a standard measure but only 12-point type can be a pica em.

Pickup   material in type that is to be used with new material such as a new lead.

Pix   short for pictures. The singular may be pic or pix.

Pixel   small picture element to denote gray or color values for computer storage.

Plate   stereotyped or lithographic page ready for the press.

Play   prominence given a story, its display. Also the principal story.

Point   unit of printing measurement, approximately $\frac{1}{72}$ inch. Actually .01384 inches. Also any punctuation mark.

Pos.   positive film image.

Precede   material such as a bulletin or an editor's note appearing at the top of a story.

Predate   edition delivered before its announced date. Usually a Sunday edition delivered to outlying areas.

Printer   machine that produces copy by telegraphic impulses. A Teletype machine. Also a person who prepares composition for imprinting operations.

Printout   visual copy produced by a computer, usually for proofreading. Same as master copy or tear sheet.

Process color   method of printing that duplicates a full-color original copy.

Proof   print of type used for proofreading purposes.

Proofreader   one who corrects proofs.

Prop   an object used during a newscast to give credence to an item.

Pullout   a special section within a paper but designed to be removed from the main portion.

Purge   a method by which data or text is removed from computer storage by erasure from the disk.

Put to bed   to lock up forms for an edition.

Pyramid   arrangement of ads in half-pyramid form from top right to lower left.

Quad   short for quadrant, a blank printing unit for spacing.

Quadrant   layout pattern in which the page is divided into fourths.

Query   brief message outlining a story. Also a question put to a news source.

Queue   directing a story file to another operation, such as a line printer or photocomposition machine. The electronic equivalent of an in-basket or holding area.

Quotes   short for quotation marks.

Race   classification of type, such as roman, text, script.

Rack   cabinet in which composition is kept.

Railroad   to rush copy to the printer before it is edited; to rush type to press without proofreading. Also a term for a headline type.

Read in   secondary head leading in to the main head.

Readout   secondary head accompanying a main head.

Rear projection   projection of a film, photo, map or graph placed on a screen behind the newscaster.

Regional split   interruption in the wire to permit the transmission of regional news.

Register   alignment of plates to get true color reproduction.

Release copy   copy to be held until a specified release time. Same as advance copy.

Repeat   a rerun of a story for a wire service member or client.

Reperforator   machine that produces tape for automatic typesetting.

Replate   to make a page over after an edition has gone to press.

Retouch   to alter a photograph by painting or airbrushing.

Reverse plate   reversing the color values so that white letters are on a black background.

Revised proof   second proof after corrections have been made.

Ribbon   another name for a banner or streamer headline.

Rim   outer edge of a copy desk. Copy editors once were known as rimmen.

Rip and read   derogatory expression applied to radio newspersons who simply read the latest summary from the radio wire without careful editing.

Rising initial   initial capital letter that aligns with the body type at the base line.

Rivers   streaks of white space within typeset columns caused by excessive word spacing or letterspacing.

ROP   run of the paper. Stories or art that do not demand upfront position. Ads that may appear anywhere in the paper. Color printed in a newspaper without the use of special presses.

Rotogravure   means of printing from recessed letters. One of the major printing techniques (along with letterpress and offset). Used mostly in catalogs, magazines and fine color work.

Rough   may be applied to a dummy that gives little or no detail or to an uncorrected, unjustified proof.

Roundup   compilation of stories.

Rules   any line that is printed. Lines are cast in type metal form. Hairline rules are often used in newspaper work. The underscore of the preceding is a type rule.

Run   reporter's beat.

Runaround   method of setting type around a picture.

Run-in   to incorporate sentences or lists into one paragraph.

Running story   story handled in takes or small segments. Each take is sent to the composing room as soon as it is edited.

Runover   portion of a story that continues from one page to the next. Also a jump story.

Sans serif   typeface without serifs.

Sc   proofreader's mark meaning "see copy."

Schedule   list of available stories and pictures; desk's record of stories edited.

Scoop   to get an exclusive story. Also a beat.

Screen   to view film or videotape.

Script   in broadcast news, the arrangement of news, together with an opening and closing and leads to commercials.

Scroll   a means of moving story text forward or backward so it can be displayed on a VDT screen.

Second front page   first page of the second section. Also called a split page.

Section page   first page of a pullout section.

Serifs   the fine cross strokes at the top and bottom of most styles of letters.

Set solid   lines of type without extra spacing between lines.

Shirt tail   slang for follow story.

Short   brief item of filler.

Sidebar   brief story with a special angle that goes with the main story.

Signature   group of pages on one sheet. Also an advertiser's name displayed in an ad.

Silhouette   form of halftone with the background removed. Same as outline cut.

Skyline   headline across top of page over nameplate. Also called over-the-roof head.

Slant   angle of a story. A story written a certain way.

Slug   label identifying a story. Same as guideline or catchline. Also a piece of metal used for spacing. Also used to designate linecaster slugs.

Software   the programs that make computer hardware work.

Sound-on-film   film carrying its own sound track. Abbreviated SOF.

Sound under   audio level where background sounds may be heard.

Space out   direction to the printer to add space between lines until the story fills the space allotted for it.

Split   term used to designate a break in a wire service circuit to permit the filing of other material, such as regional news.

Split page   first page of the second section of a newspaper.

Split run   making a change in part of a press run of the same edition.

Spot news   news obtained firsthand; fresh news.

Spread   story prominently displayed, often over several columns and with art.

Squib   short news item or filler.

Standalone   a picture without an accompanying story.

Standing box   type box kept on hand for repeated use. Likewise with standing head.

Standing type   similar to standing boxes and head; type kept standing for future use.

Standupper   television report at the scene with the camera on the reporter.

Step lines   headline with top line flush left, second line centered and third line flush right.

Stereotype   process of casting a plate from a papier-mâché mold.

Stet   let it stand. Disregard correction.

Stinger   another term for kicker or eyebrow.

Stock   paper used for any printing job.

Straight matter   copy set in one size of type for the main reading matter of a page. Also called body type.

Streamer   another name for a banner or a ribbon headline.

String   clippings of stories, usually from a correspondent.

Stringer   correspondent paid on space rate. In television news, a freelance cameraman.

Strip-in   to insert one illustrative element into another.

Sub   short for substitute. *Sub bomber* means a new story for a story slugged bomber.

Subhead   one- or two-line head used within the body of a story in type. Also called column break.

Summary   may be a news index or a news roundup. A summary lead gives the gist of the facts in the story.

Super card   in television, white lettering on a black card.

Supplemental service   syndicated service in addition to major wire service.

System   a combination of computer programs and hardware designed to perform specific tasks.

TAB   indicates tabular matter in wire service copy.

Tabloid   newspaper format, usually four or five columns wide and approximately 14 inches deep.

Take   small part of a running story. Also the part of a story given to a compositor.

Tear sheet   sheet or part of a sheet used for corrections. Also copy produced by a computerized copy follower.

Tease   news announcement before the station break with details to follow the break.

Telephoto   UPI system of transmitting pictures by wire.

Teletext   home information retrieval system using television signal for transmission of data.

Teletype   automatic printer used to send and receive wire copy.

Teletypesetter device attached to a linecaster so that the typesetting is controlled by perforated tape. Abbreviated TTS—copy (and tape) for papers with Teletypesetters.

Terminal a point in a system or communication network at which data can either enter or leave.

Thirty dash end mark.

Thumbnail half-column portrait. Also a rough sketch or dummy.

Tie-back part of a story providing background material.

Tight paper paper containing so much advertising there is limited space for news.

Time copy copy that may be used anytime. Also called grape, plug copy and so on.

Toenails quotation mark or apostrophe. Also parentheses.

Tombstone to place headlines of the same type side by side. Such adjacent heads are called bumped heads.

Turn story same as jump story (continues from last column on one page to first column on the next page).

Typo short for typographical error.

Undated story without a dateline (but usually a credit line) summarizing related events from different origins.

Underline same as cutline.

Update to bring a story up to date or to give it a timely angle.

UPI short for United Press International, a major news agency.

Up style headline style in which each word is capitalized.

VDT an acronym for video display terminal, a device that looks like a typewriter with a small television set attached. Stories may be composed or corrected on these units.

Videotape tape that projects pictures.

Videotex home information retrieval systems using television-type displays.

Viewdata home information retrieval system using direct link to computer through telephone or cable television lines.

Vignette halftone with a fading background. Also a feature story or sketch.

Visible tape perforations arranged so that they spell words or symbols.

VTR short for videotape recording.

wf short for wrong font or type of a different size or style from that used in text.

Wicket kicker-like element placed to one side of a headline.

Widow one or two words appearing at the end of a paragraph and on the last line. It is unsightly because of the excessive white space appearing after the widow, particularly at the top of a column.

Wirephoto AP system of transmitting pictures by wire.

Wooden head   one that is dull and lifeless.

Wrap around   ending the top line of a headline with a preposition, conjunction or the like, or splitting words that are properly a unit. Also, setting type to wrap around a picture.

Wrapup   complete story. Wire services use a wrapup to contain in one story all elements of the same story sent previously.

Index